Lecture Notes in Computer Science   8192

Commenced Publication in 1973
Founding and Former Series Editors:
Gerhard Goos, Juris Hartmanis, and Jan van Leeuwen

Jacques Blanc-Talon   Andrzej Kasinski
Wilfried Philips   Dan Popescu
Paul Scheunders (Eds.)

Advanced Concepts for Intelligent Vision Systems

15th International Conference, ACIVS 2013
Poznań, Poland, October 28-31, 2013
Proceedings

 Springer

Volume Editors

Jacques Blanc-Talon
DGA, Bagneux, France
E-mail: confs.blanctalon@free.fr

Andrzej Kasinski
Poznań University of Technology, Poznań, Poland
E-mail: akas@ar-kari.put.poznan.pl

Wilfried Philips
Ghent University, Ghent, Belgium
E-mail: wilfried.philips@telin.ugent.be

Dan Popescu
CSIRO ICT Centre, Sydney, NSW, Australia
E-mail: dan.popescu@csiro.au

Paul Scheunders
University of Antwerp, Belgium
E-mail: paul.scheunders@ua.ac.be

ISSN 0302-9743　　　　　　　　　　e-ISSN 1611-3349
ISBN 978-3-319-02894-1　　　　　　e-ISBN 978-3-319-02895-8
DOI 10.1007/978-3-319-02895-8
Springer Cham Heidelberg New York Dordrecht London

Library of Congress Control Number: 2013950933

CR Subject Classification (1998): I.4, I.5, C.2, I.2, I.2.10, H.3-4

LNCS Sublibrary: SL 6 – Image Processing, Computer Vision, Pattern Recognition,
and Graphics

Typesetting: Camera-ready by author, data conversion by Scientific Publishing Services, Chennai, India

Printed on acid-free paper

Springer is part of Springer Science+Business Media (www.springer.com)

Preface

This volume collects the papers accepted for presentation at the 15th International Conference on "Advanced Concepts for Intelligent Vision Systems" (ACIVS 2013), which took place in City Park Hotel, Poznan, Poland. Following the first meeting in Baden-Baden (Germany) in 1999, which was part of a large multiconference, the ACIVS conference has since then developed into an independent scientific event and has maintained the tradition of being a single-track conference. ACIVS 2013 attracted scientists from 23 different countries, mostly from Europe, but also from Algeria, China, Japan, South Korea, the United Arab Emirates, and the USA.

Although ACIVS is a conference on all areas of image and video processing, submissions tend to gather within some major fields of interest. This year, video analytics and biometry proved popular topics. As in the past, many papers on image analysis, segmentation, and classification were presented as well.

A conference like ACIVS would not be feasible without the concerted effort of many people and the support of various institutions. The paper submission and review procedure was carried out electronically and a minimum of three reviewers were assigned to each paper. From 111 submissions, 63 papers were selected for presentation, either orally or as posters. A large and energetic Program Committee, helped by additional referees – listed on the following pages – completed the long and demanding reviewing process. We would like to thank all of them for their timely and high-quality reviews.

Last but not least, we would like to thank all the participants who trusted in our ability to organize this conference for the 15th time. We hope they attended a stimulating scientific event and enjoyed the atmosphere of the ACIVS social events in the city of Poznan.

July 2013

Jacques Blanc-Talon
Andrzej Kasinski
Dan Popescu
Wilfried Philips
Paul Scheunders

Organization

Acivs 2013 was organized by Poznan University of Technology, located in Poland.

Steering Committee

Jacques Blanc-Talon	DGA, France
Wilfried Philips	Ghent University/iMinds, Belgium
Dan Popescu	CSIRO, Australia
Paul Scheunders	University of Antwerp, Belgium

Organizing Committee

Zuzanna Domagaa	Poznan University of Technology, Poland
Michal Fularz	Poznan University of Technology, Poland
Marek Kraft	Poznan University of Technology, Poland
Adam Schmidt	Poznan University of Technology, Poland
Krzysztof Walas	Poznan University of Technology, Poland

Program Committee

Alin Achim	University of Bristol, UK
Hamid Aghajan	Stanford University, USA
Marc Antonini	Universit de Nice-Sophia Antipolis, France
Marie Babel	Inria-IRISA, France
Philippe Bolon	University of Savoie, France
Don Bone	Cannon Information Systems Research, Australia
Salah Bourennane	Ecole Centrale de Marseille, France
Dan Dumitru Burdescu	University of Craiova, Romania
Jocelyn Chanussot	Grenoble Institute of Technology, France
Jennifer Davidson	Iowa State University, USA
Arturo de la Escalera Hueso	Universidad Carlos III de Madrid, Spain
Eric Debreuve	University of Nice-Sophia Antipolis, France
Zuzanna Domagaa	Poznan University of Technology, Poland
Frdric Dufaux	ENST, France
Michal Fularz	Poznan University of Technology, Poland
Jrme Gilles	UCLA, USA
Georgy Gimel'farb	The University of Auckland, New Zealand
Markku Hauta-Kasari	University of Eastern Finland, Finland

Dimitris Iakovidis	Technological Educational Institute of Lamia, Greece
Arto Kaarna	Lappeenranta University of Technology, Finland
Zoltan Kato	University of Szeged, Hungary
Ron Kimmel	Technion, Israel
Marek Kraft	Poznan University of Technology, Poland
Hamid Krim	North Carolina State University, USA
Kenneth Lam	The Hong Kong Polytechnic University, SAR China
Patrick Le Callet	Polytech Nantes/Universit de Nantes, France
Alessandro Ledda	Artesis University College Antwerp, Belgium
Gonzalo Pajares Martinsanz	Universidad Complutense, Spain
Javier Mateos	University of Granada, Spain
Fabrice Mriaudeau	Universit de Bourgogne, France
Jean Meunier	Universit de Montral, Canada
Adrian Munteanu	Vrije Universiteit Brussel, Belgium
Fernando Pereira	Instituto Superior Tcnico, Portugal
Stuart Perry	Canon Information Systems Research Australia, Australia
Wojciech Pieczynski	TELECOM SudParis, France
Marc Pierrot-Deseilligny	IGN, France
Aleksandra Pizurica	Ghent University/iMinds, Belgium
William Puech	LIRMM, France
Gianni Ramponi	Trieste University, Italy
Paolo Remagnino	Kingston University, UK
Patrice Rondao Alface	Alcatel-Lucent Bell Labs, Belgium
Adam Schmidt	Poznan University of Technology, Poland
Mubarak Shah	University of Central Florida, USA
Andrzej Sluzek	Khalifa University, United Arab Emirates
Hugues Talbot	ESIEE, France
Marc Van Droogenbroeck	University of Lige, Belgium
Peter Veelaert	Ghent University/iMinds, Belgium
Nicole Vincent	Universit Paris Descartes, France
Krzysztof Walas	Poznan University of Technology, Poland
Gerald Zauner	Fachhochschule Oberösterreich, Austria
Pavel Zemcik	Brno University of Technology, Czech Republic
Djemel Ziou	Sherbrooke University, Canada

Reviewers

Alin Achim	University of Bristol, UK
Hamid Aghajan	Stanford University, USA
Marie Babel	Inria-IRISA, France
Jacques Blanc-Talon	DGA, France
Nyan Bo Bo	Gent University/iMinds, Belgium

Philippe Bolon	University of Savoie, France
Don Bone	Cannon Information Systems Research, Australia
Salah Bourennane	Ecole Centrale de Marseille, France
Dan Dumitru Burdescu	University of Craiova, Romania
Jocelyn Chanussot	Grenoble Institute of Technology, France
Thierry Chateau	Institut Pascal, France
Gabriela Csurka	Xerox Research Centre Europe, France
Boguslaw Cyganek	AGH University of Science and Technology, Poland
Emmanuel D'Angelo	Advanced Silicon S.A., Switzerland
Arturo de la Escalera Hueso	Universidad Carlos III de Madrid, Spain
Eric Debreuve	University of Nice-Sophia Antipolis, France
Ivana Despotovic	Ghent University/iMinds, Belgium
Severine Dubuisson	Laboratoire d'Informatique de Paris 6, France
Frdric Dufaux	ENST, France
Jrme Gilles	UCLA, USA
Georgy Gimel'farb	The University of Auckland, New Zealand
Bart Goossens	Ghent University/iMinds, Belgium
Sebastian Gruenwedel	Ghent University, Belgium
Markku Hauta-Kasari	University of Eastern Finland, Finland
Dimitris Iakovidis	Technological Educational Institute of Lamia, Greece
Arto Kaarna	Lappeenranta University of Technology, Finland
Richard Kleihorst	Xetal and Ghent University, Belgium
Marek Kraft	Poznan University of Technology, Poland
Kenneth Lam	The Hong Kong Polytechnic University, SAR China
Patrick Le Callet	Polytech Nantes/Universit de Nantes, France
Alessandro Ledda	Artesis University College Antwerp, Belgium
Dominique Luzeaux	DGA, France
Henri Maitre	Telecom ParisTech, France
Antoine Manzanera	ENSTA ParisTech, France
Gonzalo Pajares Martinsanz	Universidad Complutense, Spain
Javier Mateos	University of Granada, Spain
Jean Meunier	Universit de Montral, Canada
Adrian Munteanu	Vrije Universiteit Brussel, Belgium
Sergio Orjuela Vargas	Ghent University, Belgium
Fernando Pereira	Instituto Superior Tcnico, Portugal
Stuart Perry	Canon Information Systems Research Australia, Australia
Wilfried Philips	Ghent University/iMinds, Belgium
Aleksandra Pizurica	Ghent University/iMinds, Belgium
Dan Popescu	CSIRO, Australia

Table of Contents

Acquisition, Pre-processing and Coding

Efficient Low Complexity SVC Video Transrater with Spatial
Scalability 1
    Christophe Deknudt, François-Xavier Coudoux, Patrick Corlay,
    Marc Gazalet, and Mohamed Gharbi

Visual Data Encryption for Privacy Enhancement in Surveillance
Systems 13
    Janusz Cichowski, Andrzej Czyżewski, and Bożena Kostek

Distance Estimation with a Two or Three Aperture SLR Digital
Camera 25
    Seungwon Lee, Joonki Paik, and Monson H. Hayes

Acquisition of Agronomic Images with Sufficient Quality by Automatic
Exposure Time Control and Histogram Matching 37
    Martín Montalvo, José M. Guerrero, Juan Romeo, María Guijarro,
    Jesús M. de la Cruz, and Gonzalo Pajares

An Enhanced Weighted Median Filter for Noise Reduction in SAR
Interferograms 49
    Wajih Ben Abdallah and Riadh Abdelfattah

High Precision Restoration Method for Non-uniformly Warped
Images 60
    Kalyan Kumar Halder, Murat Tahtali, and Sreenatha G. Anavatti

Noise Robustness Analysis of Point Cloud Descriptors 68
    Yasir Salih, Aamir Saeed Malik, Nicolas Walter, Désiré Sidibé,
    Naufal Saad, and Fabrice Meriaudeau

Restoration of Blurred Binary Images Using Discrete Tomography 80
    Jozsef Nemeth and Peter Balazs

Minimum Memory Vectorisation of Wavelet Lifting 91
    David Barina and Pavel Zemcik

Magnitude Type Preserving Similarity Measure for Complex Wavelet
Based Image Registration 102
    Florina-Cristina Calnegru

Biometry

Real-Time Face Pose Estimation in Challenging Environments   114
    Mliki Hazar, Hammami Mohamed, and Ben-Abdallah Hanêne

Human Motion Capture Using Data Fusion of Multiple Skeleton
Data   126
    *Jean-Thomas Masse, Frédéric Lerasle, Michel Devy, André Monin,
    Olivier Lefebvre, and Stéphane Mas*

Recognizing Conversational Interaction Based on 3D Human Pose   138
    *Jingjing Deng, Xianghua Xie, Ben Daubney, Hui Fang, and
    Phil W. Grant*

Upper-Body Pose Estimation Using Geodesic Distances
and Skin-Color   150
    Sebastian Handrich and Ayoub Al-Hamadi

A New Approach for Hand Augmentation Based on Patch Modelling . . .   162
    Omer Rashid Ahmad and Ayoub Al-Hamadi

Hidden Markov Models for Modeling Occurrence Order of Facial
Temporal Dynamics   172
    Khadoudja Ghanem

Adaptive Two Phase Sparse Representation Classifier for Face
Recognition   182
    Fadi Dornaika, Youssof El Traboulsi, and Ammar Assoum

Automatic User-Specific Avatar Parametrisation and Emotion
Mapping   192
    *Stephanie Behrens, Ayoub Al-Hamadi, Robert Niese, and
    Eicke Redweik*

Classification and Recognition

Optimizing Contextual-Based Optimum-Forest Classification
through Swarm Intelligence   203
    *Daniel Osaku, Rodrigo Nakamura, João Papa, Alexandre Levada,
    Fábio Cappabianco, and Alexandre Falcão*

A Mobile Imaging System for Medical Diagnostics   215
    Sami Varjo and Jari Hannuksela

Fast Road Network Extraction from Remotely Sensed Images   227
    Vladimir A. Krylov and James D.B. Nelson

Partial Near-Duplicate Detection in Random Images by a Combination
of Detectors   238
    Andrzej Śluzek

Object Recognition and Modeling Using SIFT Features   250
   Alessandro Bruno, Luca Greco, and Marco La Cascia

Painting Scene Recognition Using Homogenous Shapes   262
   Razvan George Condorovici, Corneliu Florea, and Constantin Vertan

A Novel Graph Based Clustering Technique for Hybrid Segmentation
of Multi-spectral Remotely Sensed Images   274
   *Biplab Banerjee, Pradeep Kumar Mishra, Surender Varma, and
Buddhiraju Krishna Mohan*

Depth, 3D and Tracking

Planar Segmentation by Time-of-Flight Cameras   286
   Rudi Penne, Luc Mertens, and Bart Ribbens

An Efficient Normal-Error Iterative Algorithm for Line Triangulation . . .   298
   Qiang Zhang, Yan Wu, Ming Liu, and Licheng Jiao

Moving Object Detection System in Aerial Video Surveillance   310
   Ahlem Walha, Ali Wali, and Adel M. Alimi

An Indoor RGB-D Dataset for the Evaluation of Robot Navigation
Algorithms   321
   *Adam Schmidt, Michał Fularz, Marek Kraft, Andrzej Kasiński, and
Michał Nowicki*

Real-Time Depth Map Based People Counting   330
   František Galčík and Radoslav Gargalík

Tracking of a Handheld Ultrasonic Sensor for Corrosion Control
on Pipe Segment Surfaces   342
   *Christian Bendicks, Erik Lilienblum, Christian Freye, and
Ayoub Al-Hamadi*

Extended GrabCut for 3D and RGB-D Point Clouds   354
   Nizar K. Sallem and Michel Devy

Efficient Implementations and Frameworks

A Resource Allocation Framework for Adaptive Selection of Point
Matching Strategies   366
   Quentin De Neyer and Christophe De Vleeschouwer

VTApi: An Efficient Framework for Computer Vision Data Management
and Analytics   378
   *Petr Chmelar, Martin Pesek, Tomas Volf, Jaroslav Zendulka, and
Vojtech Froml*

Computational Methods for Selective Acquisition of Depth
Measurements: An Experimental Evaluation   389
    Pierre Payeur, Phillip Curtis, and Ana-Maria Cretu

A New Color Image Database TID2013: Innovations and Results   402
    Nikolay Ponomarenko, Oleg Ieremeiev, Vladimir Lukin, Lina Jin,
    Karen Egiazarian, Jaakko Astola, Benoit Vozel, Kacem Chehdi,
    Marco Carli, Federica Battisti, and C.-C. Jay Kuo

Performance Evaluation of Video Analytics for Surveillance On-Board
Trains   414
    Valentina Casola, Mariana Esposito, Francesco Flammini,
    Nicola Mazzocca, and Concetta Pragliola

GPU-Accelerated Human Motion Tracking Using Particle Filter
Combined with PSO   426
    Boguslaw Rymut, Bogdan Kwolek, and Tomasz Krzeszowski

Low Level Image Analysis and Segmentation

Modelling Line and Edge Features Using Higher-Order Riesz
Transforms   438
    Ross Marchant and Paul Jackway

Semantic Approach in Image Change Detection   450
    Adrien Gressin, Nicole Vincent, Clément Mallet, and
    Nicolas Paparoditis

Small Target Detection Improvement in Hyperspectral Image   460
    Tao Lin, Julien Marot, and Salah Bourennane

The Objective Evaluation of Image Object Segmentation Quality   470
    Ran Shi, King Ngi Ngan, and Songnan Li

A Modification of Diffusion Distance for Clustering and Image
Segmentation   480
    Eduard Sojka and Jan Gaura

Flexible Multi-modal Graph-Based Segmentation   492
    Willem P. Sanberg, Luat Do, and Peter H.N. de With

The Divide and Segment Method for Parallel Image Segmentation   504
    Thales Sehn Körting, Emiliano Ferreira Castejon, and
    Leila Maria Garcia Fonseca

Unsupervised Segmentation for Transmission Imaging of Carbon
Black   516
    Lydie Luengo, Hélène Laurent, Sylvie Treuillet, Isabelle Jolivet, and
    Emmanuel Gomez

Tree Symbols Detection for Green Space Estimation   526
    Adrian Sroka and Marcin Luckner

Hierarchical Layered Mean Shift Methods   538
    Milan Šurkala, Karel Mozdřeň, Radovan Fusek, and Eduard Sojka

Globally Segmentation Using Active Contours and Belief Function   546
    Foued Derraz, Miloud Boussahla, and Laurent Peyrodie

Video Analytics

Automatic Monitoring of Pig Activity Using Image Analysis   555
    Mohammad Amin Kashiha, Claudia Bahr, Sanne Ott,
    Christel P.H. Moons, Theo A. Niewold, Frank Tuyttens, and
    Daniel Berckmans

IMM-Based Tracking and Latency Control with Off-the-Shelf IP PTZ
Camera   564
    Pierrick Paillet, Romaric Audigier, Frederic Lerasle, and
    Quoc-Cuong Pham

Evaluation of Traffic Sign Recognition Methods Trained
on Synthetically Generated Data   576
    Boris Moiseev, Artem Konev, Alexander Chigorin, and
    Anton Konushin

Robust Multi-camera People Tracking Using Maximum Likelihood
Estimation   584
    Nyan Bo Bo, Peter Van Hese, Sebastian Gruenwedel,
    Junzhi Guan, Jorge Niño-Castañeda, Dirk Van Haerenborgh,
    Dimitri Van Cauwelaert, Peter Veelaert, and Wilfried Philips

A Perception-Based Interpretation of the Kernel-Based Object
Tracking   596
    Vittoria Bruni and Domenico Vitulano

Efficient Detection and Tracking of Road Signs Based on Vehicle
Motion and Stereo Vision   608
    Chang-Won Choi, Sung-In Choi, and Soon-Yong Park

Incremental Principal Component Analysis-Based Sparse
Representation for Face Pose Classification   620
    Yuyao Zhang, Y. Benhamza, Khalid Idrissi, and Christophe Garcia

Person Detection with a Computation Time Weighted AdaBoost   632
    Alhayat Ali Mekonnen, Frédéric Lerasle, and Ariane Herbulot

Perspective Multiscale Detection of Vehicles for Real-Time Forward
Collision Avoidance Systems   645
    Juan Diego Ortega, Marcos Nieto, Andoni Cortes, and Julian Florez

Learning and Propagation of Dominant Colors for Fast Video
Segmentation..   657
    Cédric Verleysen and Christophe De Vleeschouwer

A Key-Pose Similarity Algorithm for Motion Data Retrieval   669
    Jan Sedmidubsky, Jakub Valcik, and Pavel Zezula

Training with Corrupted Labels to Reinforce a Probably Correct
Teamsport Player Detector   682
    Pascaline Parisot, Berk Sevilmiş, and Christophe De Vleeschouwer

Spherical Center-Surround for Video Saliency Detection Using Sparse
Sampling   695
    Hamed Rezazadegan Tavakoli, Esa Rahtu, and Janne Heikkilä

Semantic Concept Detection Using Dense Codeword Motion   705
    Claudiu Tănase and Bernard Mérialdo

Author Index   715

Efficient Low Complexity SVC Video Transrater with Spatial Scalability

Christophe Deknudt, François-Xavier Coudoux, Patrick Corlay, Marc Gazalet, and Mohamed Gharbi

I.E.M.N., OAE Department, UMR 8520, University of Valenciennes
Le Mont Houy 59313 Valenciennes Cedex 9, France
`christophe.deknudt@gmail.com`
`{francois-xavier.coudoux,patrick.corlay,`
`marc.gazalet,mohamed.gharbi}@univ-valenciennes.fr`
`http://www.univ-valenciennes.fr/DOAE/index-doae`

Abstract. In this paper we propose a new H.264 SVC transrating architecture for spatially scalable SVC compressed video streams. The algorithm is low complexity based, it applies to spatially scalable pre-encoded video streams and allows fine bit rate granularity while keeping highest spatial resolution. Simulation results demonstrate that transcoded bit streams produce satisfying picture quality even at bit rate reduction up to 66%. The comparison with MGS compressed video streams shows that the proposed transrating aslgorithm offers satisfying performances compared to MGS when bit rate reduction remains limited. Moreover quality scalability is obtained thanks to our algorithm even if the SVC compressed video bitstream has not been processed using MGS scalability right from the start[1].

Keywords: Video compression, H.264, SVC, Spatial Scalability, Transcoding, Medium Grain Scalability (MGS).

1   Introduction

Several multimedia services such as video on demand (VoD) and video streaming are based on the wide use of pre-encoded video streams [1]. Scalable Video Coding (SVC) constitutes an attractive solution in order to pre-encode video contents with the possibility to further access to a variety of formats, temporal resolution and/or quality levels [2]-[3]. Consequently, the number of available scalable video contents is expected to widely increase in the next few years given that state_of_the_art H.264/AVC compression standard integrates currently a

---

[1] This work was supported in part by the French National Research Agency through the TOSCANE project.
C. Deknudt is with Softthinks, Villeneuve dAscq, France.
F.-X. Coudoux, P. Corlay M. Gazalet and M. Gharbi are with Institut dElectronique, de Microlectronique et de Nanotechnologie.

J. Blanc-Talon et al. (Eds.): ACIVS 2013, LNCS 8192, pp. 1–12, 2013.
© Springer International Publishing Switzerland 2013

scalable extension while a scalable version of the new emerging HEVC standard is under development. The so-called spatial, temporal, and so-called SNR scalabilities can theoretically be combined together in order to account for the wide variety of new digital image formats, frame rates and delivery networks. In this case, however, the SVC encoding process becomes very complex and can lead to a significant loss in coding efficiency compared to single-layer coding. When pre-encoded streams are transmitted, it can become necessary to reduce the initial bit rate of the compressed bit stream according to the available bandwidth or user demand. In this case, bit rate conversion also called transrating may be required as an alternative solution to the inherent scalability offered by SVC [4]. There has been a lot of recent scientific work on H.264/AVC and SVC transrating also called dynamic shaping [5]-[6]-[7]. In particular, Van de Walle et al. have been very active in this research field and have proposed several original contributions. In [8], they proposed a low complexity SNR transcoding for H.264/AVC compressed streams which is based on requantization. In [9], they present an efficient architecture for H.264/AVC to SNR scalable SVC fast transcoding. It should be noticed that the present authors have also proposed in a previous work a low complexity transrating architecture based on frequency selectivity for H.264/AVC video bit streams without drift for intra-coded frames [10].

In this paper the previous transrating architecture is extended to the case of SVC pre-encoded video streams with spatial scalability only, i.e. SNR scalability has not been considered at first during the encoding stage. In this case, the so-called base layer corresponds to the lowest spatial resolution, and then each supplementary enhancement layer allows increasing the spatial resolution. Basically, bit rate reduction of spatially scalable encoded video streams is made possible by removing one spatial enhancement layer at a time from the compressed bit stream. Unfortunately, such rate adaptation leads to very coarse granularity hence poor flexibility and efficiency. Moreover, spatial resolution decreases each time the bit rate is reduced.

We propose a new approach for efficient SVC transrating of spatially scalable compressed video streams. Our solution permit to obtain a finer bitrate granularity. To our knowledge, this paper presents the first solution for transrating of SVC compressed video streams supporting spatial scalability only. In what follows, we only describe the proposed algorithm based on simple dyadic spatial scalability with two layers. However, the solution can be extended to arbitrary resolution factors and multiple enhancement layers. The proposed algorithm consists in removing selectively residual transform coefficients from the enhancement layer of highest spatial resolution. In order to guarantee real time processing, it should be of low computational complexity compared to a traditional full decode-full recode approach. Hence, the transrating solution is based on open-loop architecture. Two solutions are proposed based on a thorough analysis of macroblock encoding modes: first, the selection of transform coefficients is applied to all macroblocks of the highest enhancement layer given that the encoding process is modified such that intra-layer intra-prediction is forbidden. Then, the second algorithm is limited to macroblocks encoded by means of inter-frame prediction with no restriction of the coding process. Simulation results show that both algorithms offer fine rate granularity, with very satisfying visual quality of the transrated video sequence free of severe drift error distortion while preserving highest spatial resolution.

The paper is organized as follows. In Section 2, we give a brief overview of SVC spatial scalability and the corresponding encoding tools. Then, the transrating solutions based on frequency selectivity are presented in detail. Simulation results are given in Section 4. A comparison with a combined hybrid Medium Granularity Scalability (MGS)/spatial scalability approach is proposed. We show that the proposed solution provides good results for moderate bit rate reductions. Moreover, the hybrid MGS/spatial scalability solution introduces a bit rate increase and, above all, this solution must be initially planned at the encoding stage while the proposed transrating scheme allows bit rate/quality adaptation of a SVC bit stream even if this stream only supports spatial scalability. Finally, Section 5 gives the conclusions.

2   Overview of SVC Spatial Scalability

Fig. 1 illustrates the concept of spatial scalability with two spatial layers. In this case, the SVC coding structure is organized in two dependency layers: a base layer noted here Layer 0, and an enhancement layer corresponding to residual data of higher spatial resolution noted here Layer 1.

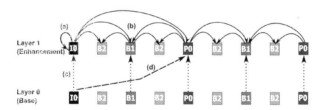

Fig. 1. Illustration of SVC spatial scalability with two layers: the different encoding modes are noted (a) to (d)

For each dependency layer, the basic concepts of motion-compensated prediction and intra-prediction (solid arrows) are used as in single-layer coding. Classically, the intra, predicted, and bidirectional pictures are noted I, P, and B, respectively. Additionally, the so called inter-layer prediction (dotted and dashed arrows) is introduced in SVC to exploit redundancy between dependency layers and hence increase coding efficiency [11]. If we consider one macroblock belonging to the enhancement layer, different encoding modes can be encountered which are noted (a) to (d) in Fig. 1:

(a) *Intra-layer intra-prediction*: intra-prediction is applied on neighbouring blocks from the enhancement layer;

(b) *Motion-compensated intra-layer prediction*: in this case, previous and/or future frames used for motion estimation belong to the enhancement layer;
(c) *Inter-layer intra-prediction*: in this case, known as INTRA_BL prediction mode, the corresponding block in the base layer is up-sampled prior to be used as prediction signal;
(d) *Motion-compensated inter-layer prediction*: previous and/or future frames used for motion estimation belong to the base layer.

In [12], it was been shown that the transrating process is strongly dependent of the macroblock type. In order to provide a statistical analysis of the macroblock modes used in SVC compressed streams, the well-known *City*, *Crew*, *Mobcal*, *Harbour* and *Soccer* sequences have been encoded using the JSVM 9.15 reference software algorithm with spatial scalability. Here the base layer consists in the CIF-resolution sequence, while the enhancement layer consists in the 4CIF-resolution version. Different quantization parameters are used, namely QP=18, 24, 30 and 36, and the IBBBPBBBPBBBI hierarchical GoP structure is considered. The same QP value is used for both base and enhancement layer.

Table 1 gives statistics of the macroblock types in the enhancement layer slices as a function of the frame type, namely I, P or B, for all sequences.

Table 1. Distribution (in %) of macroblock types in enhancement layer slices

	All Slices Types	Intra Slices	Predicted Slices	Bidirect. Slices
Skipped	21	-	16	25
Base layer mode	26	-	25	21
Intra 16×16	6	29	22	0
Predicted	6	-	37	-
Bidirectional	41	-	-	54
Intra Base layer Mode	-	71	-	-

We verify logically that bidirectional macroblocks are the most encountered since B slices are predominantly present in the considered hierarchical GoP structure. The base layer mode macroblocks are encoded using inter-layer prediction whatever the intra-frame or inter-frame coding type. The macroblocks encoded using intra-frame are either of type INTRA_16×16 (6%, intra-layer prediction) or INTRA_BL type (included in the 26% base layer mode, inter-layer prediction). We note that with this JSVM encoder revision, the macroblocks using intra-layer intra-frame prediction (intra prediction used in H.264/AVC) are only of INTRA_16×16 type. We verify that INTRA_16×16 macroblocks using intra-frame intra-layer prediction correspond to 29% in I slices, 22% in P slices, and 0% in B slices, respectively.

In the next Section, we will first propose to restrict the intra-frame prediction only to the INTRA_BL macroblock type in order to avoid drift error. We discuss the impact of this limitation on both bit rate and video quality.

3   Description of the Two Proposed Algorithms

Fig. 2 gives the general block diagram of the proposed transrating architecture in the specific case of three layers: one base layer, and two spatial enhancement layers.

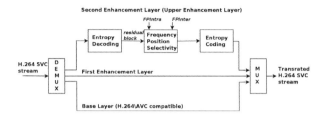

Fig. 2. Block diagram of the proposed SVC transrating architecture with spatial scalability

Obviously, the proposed architecture can be applied to a SVC compressed bit stream with spatial scalability and any number of enhancement layers.

The proposed solution is based on frequency selectivity: in the present case, it consists in selectively removing residual transform coefficients from macroblocks of the highest enhancement layer, the other layers being left untouched. Hence, low frequency coefficients that have significant visual influence are left unchanged and kept in a zigzag order until a given frequency position (FP) which varies from 1 (only the DC coefficient remains) to 16 (all coefficients are preserved). Practically, the FP parameter used to transrate intra-coded blocks (noted hereafter FP_{intra}) can be chosen independent of the one used to transrate inter-coded blocks (noted hereafter FP_{inter}) in order to increase the transrater flexibility.

Unfortunately, due to the wide use of predictive coding by SVC, such coefficient removal leads to so-called drift error in the reconstructed video sequence. Considering spatial scalable SVC, drift error may appear into a single frame, a group of pictures, or a layer. It has been shown in [13] that drift error remains perceptually negligible in the case of inter-prediction. It is true for a wide variety of video contents sequences with a moderate motion.

Also, we verify on the basis of subjective evaluation of reconstructed sequences that drift error is acceptable when dealing with INTRA_BL macroblocks, as the base layer which serves as reference is left untouched. However, a problem arises when considering intra-layer intra-prediction. In this case, the removal of transform coefficients leads to drift error which severely degrades the reconstructed video sequence.

Hence, it is necessary to specifically adapt the transrating process to this macroblock type. Two solutions have been proposed:

1. The first solution needs to slightly modify the spatial scalable SVC encoder, but the resulting spatial scalable SVC bit stream remains fully compatible

with any spatial scalable SVC decoder. Such modification is possible when considering that the video streams are pre-encoded, like in VOD or streaming: in this case, video service providers has a perfect command of the encoder and can therefore restrict the proprietary spatial scalable SVC encoder to a limited number of authorized macroblock types if necessary. Consequently, we propose to make the intra-layer intra-prediction macroblock type unauthorized during the spatial scalable SVC encoding process. We verify that this restriction leads to a negligible average rate overhead of about 1.5%. Such overhead is clearly acceptable as in return, the transrating process is simplified by indistinctly applying frequency selectivity to any macroblock type in the highest enhancement layer.

2. Because drift error is mainly visually annoying in the case of intra-prediction, we propose in the second solution to apply frequency selection only to macroblocks encoded by means of inter-prediction. This limitation slightly reduces the performance of the transrating algorithm but offers the great advantage that the transrating algorithm is of lower computational complexity and is compatible with any spatial scalable SVC-compressed video stream.

In the following Section, we demonstrate the performances of the two solutions in terms of bit rate reduction as well as reconstructed video quality.

4   Simulation Results

Extensive simulations were performed in order to evaluate the two transrating architectures. The well-known *City*, *Crew*, *Harbour*, *Soccer* and *Mobcal* sequences have been encoded using the JSVM 9.15 reference software algorithm with spatial scalability. These sequences have been chosen because they offer a wide range of spatial and temporal complexity characteristics. As mentioned previously, the base layer consists in the CIF-resolution sequence, while the enhancement layer consists in the 4CIF-resolution version. Different quantization parameters were used, namely QP=18, 24, 30 and 36, and a IBBBPBBBBPBBBI hierarchical GoP structure was considered. Targeted bit rate values are achieved by modifying QP settings.

In a first approach, the FP_{intra} and FP_{inter} transrating parameters are chosen equal, i.e $FP_{intra} = FP_{inter} = FP$. However, it should be noted that FP_{intra} and FP_{inter} can be chosen different leading theoretically to 256 possible intermediate bit rates, even if some of the (FP_{intra}, FP_{inter}) combinations might result in the same bit rate. We use the well-known peak signal-to-noise ratio (PSNR) in order to evaluate the video quality because it remains nowadays the most widely used objective metric in the video community. Results are given here for the luminance component; similar results were obtained for the chrominance components.

First, we consider the transrating solution for which intra-prediction is limited to the INTRA_BL mode only in the highest enhancement layer. Remember that this solution requires the modification of the spatial scalable SVC encoding process. Fig. 3 gives the rate-distortion performances of the first spatial scalable

SVC transrating architecture with spatial scalability for the *City* sequence. Similar results were obtained with other sequences. Only the results obtained for FP varying from 1 to 10 are given for clarity of the figure. For each QP value, two anchors are also given for comparison:

- One high anchor located on the right corresponding to the PSNR and corresponding bit rate values when both base and enhancement layers are available (this could be considered as the special case: FP=16, full quality);
- One low anchor located on bottom-left which corresponds to the case when only the CIF base layer is available and up-scaled to 4CIF spatial resolution using the up-sampling filter described in [14].

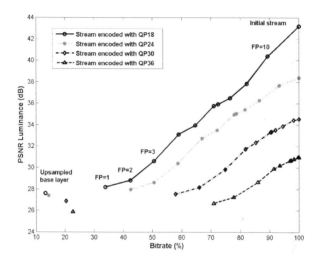

Fig. 3. SVC transrating of the upper spatial enhancement layer: PSNR as a function of bit rate - *City* sequence

Initially, only these two versions, i.e. only these two bit rates/quality levels, are available thanks to spatial scalability. We can note that maximal bit rate reduction value is logically reduced when the quantization parameter increases. Indeed, the stronger the quantization, the less the number of remaining residual coefficients. However, the maximal bit rate reduction is very significant and varies up to 66% (*City* sequence, QP=18 and FP=1). It should be noted that each FP parameter value leads to an intermediate bit rate thus offers great flexibility while keeping highest spatial resolution.

In terms of video quality, we compute the PSNR values for all intermediate bit rates resulting from spatial scalable SVC transrating. We note that:

- The PSNR difference between the two anchors FP=16 (no transrating) and FP=1 (DC coefficient only) is maximal for QP=18 and is equal to about 15 dB. This PSNR difference is about 4 dB for QP=36.

– The PSNR corresponding to the up-sampled base layer is logically always lower than the PSNR obtained when the enhancement layer is available, even with FP=1. In this later case, the PSNR difference tends to increase when the compression ratio becomes higher.

As suggested in Section 2, we now restrict frequency selectivity to the macro-blocks encoded by means of motion-compensated prediction. Fig. 4 shows for the *City* sequence and different quantization parameters values, a comparison between the two following cases:

– Macro-blocks using intra- as well as inter-image prediction are both transrated ($FP_{intra} = FP_{inter}$ varying from 1 to 16, dashed curve);
– Only macro-blocks using inter-image prediction are transrated ($FP_{intra} = 16$ and FP_{inter} varying from 1 to 16, plain curve).

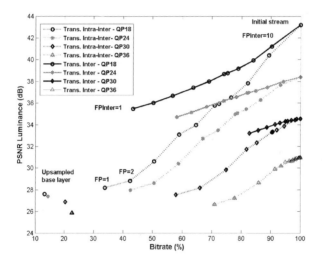

Fig. 4. SVC transrating of the upper spatial enhancement layer (Inter macroblocks): PSNR as a function of bit rate - *City* sequence

Once again, simulation results are similar for the other sequences. The results for the other sequences are available in [15]. We verify for all sequences and all quantization parameter values that the PSNR is better when the transrating operation is restricted to inter-image prediction. The PSNR difference with the up-sampled base layer case is more important. However, the maximum bit rate reduction is reduced. This difference tends to increase when higher quantization parameters are used. Visually speaking, it should also be noticed that no spurious discontinuities appear at the boundaries between inter-coded and intra-coded blocks after transrating.

Fig. 5 gives an illustrative visual example of the performances obtained with the proposed spatial scalable SVC transrater.

Fig. 5a) and Fig. 5d) correspond respectively to:

- The CIF version reconstructed from the base layer and upsampled to the highest resolution. The corresponding visual quality is poor as the reconstructed picture suffers from a severe loss of details. The PSNR is equal to 27 dB;
- The full 4-CIF version reconstructed from both base and enhancement layers. It corresponds to the best visual quality, with a PSNR equals to 43.13 dB.

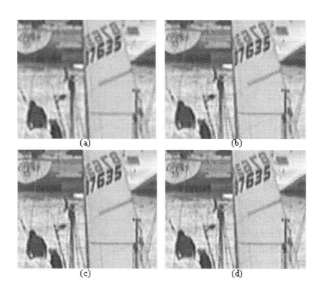

Fig. 5. Illustrative example of the performances of the proposed SVC transrating solution, Harbour sequence (image #000, QP=18, intra-coded), from top to bottom: (a) up sampled base layer (PSNR-Y=27 dB); (b) FP=3 (PSNR-Y=31,84 dB); (c) FP=6 (PSNR-Y=38,09 dB); (d) full-quality not transcoded version with FP=16 (PSNR-Y=43,13 dB).

Thanks to the proposed spatial scalability-based SVC transrating algorithm, it is possible to adapt the bit rate and to have access to intermediate visual quality levels. This is illustrated in Fig. 5b) and Fig. 5c), which correspond to transrated versions with highest spatial resolution and FP=3 and FP=6, respectively. The corresponding pictures are characterized by highest spatial resolution and clearly exhibit a better visual quality with enhanced textures and details (for example, see rigging as well as numbers on the sail and characters on the hull), with increased PSNR values of 31.84dB and 38.09dB, respectively.

These results are encouraging and it is possible to propose an architecture for transcoding H.264 spatial scalable SVC as the inter mode to limit the complexity of the transcoder. Thus, this architecture does not require forcing macroblocks from the intra-layer intra-image mode to the inter-layer intra-image one (IN-TRA_BL). The advantage of this solution is not negligible since it is possible to transcode any spatial scalable SVC compressed video stream. Recall that in this case, however, it is necessary to implement the two types of entropy coding: the CAVLC (chosen in this work) and CABAC.

To conclude, the approach proposed in our transrating scheme leads to progressive bit rate reduction as provided by quality scalability (also called SNR scalability) using Medium Granularity Scalability (MGS). Thanks to MGS, video throughput can be dynamically adapted by discarding any enhancement layer NAL unit from a SNR scalable bit stream. In addition, SVC provides the possibility to distribute the enhancement layer transform coefficients among several slices quality refinement layers with each of them containing refinement coefficients for particular transform basis functions only. Hence, it is interesting to compare the performances of the proposed transrating architecture to the ones obtained thanks to this specific MGS feature. Experiments have been performed on different video test sequences and lead to similar results. In practice, there are many different ways to configure SVC layers to meet specific requirements. In what follows, a comparison is made for the Mobcal sequence between the proposed solution (case 1) and a case of SVC using MGS (case 2):

- Case 1: we apply the proposed transrating algorithm on a spatial scalable SVC compressed video bitstream with the following characteristics:
  - base layer: 720x576, 25fps, QP=28
  - enhancement layer: 1280x720, 50fps, QP=28
  - seven frequency positions are selected : FP1 (DC only), FP3, FP4, FP5, FP6, FP7 and FP16.
- Case 2 : we consider a SVC compressed video bitstream with combined spatial and SNR (MGS) scalabilities:
  - base layer (BL): 720x576, 25fps, QP=28
  - enhancement layer 1 (EL1): 1280x720, 50fps, QP=32
  - enhancement layer 2 (EL2): 1280x720, 50fps, QP=28 (using MGS). Seven points are selected with respect to FP values; they correspond to the following EL2 transform coefficient repartition in the MGS original slice: DC, DC:AC2, DC:AC3, DC:AC4, DC:AC5, DC:AC6, and DC:AC15.

Results for the *Mobcal* sequence are given in Fig. 6 below.

We note here that the proposed transrating scheme offers better results compared to MGS, for bit rates higher than 8 Mb/s. For lower bit rates, the results are in favour of the MGS scheme. In particular, the PSNR corresponding to the enhancement layer 1 with MGS (QP=32) is significantly higher. It should be noted however that the performances obtained with our transrating solution should be improved by considering QP values higher than 32. Anyway, our transrating solution remains very attractive in the case when only spatial scalability has been originally used at the SVC encoding stage.

Practically, SVC suffers from high computational complexity; moreover, it is not easy to optimize coding parameters when different types of scalability are applied together. Consequently, video contents are often encoded by means of

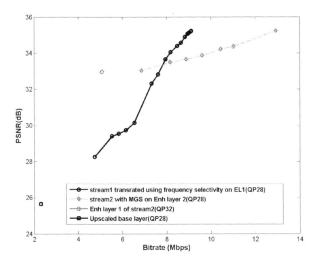

Fig. 6. Comparison between SVC transrating using spatial scalability and MGS - *Mobcal* sequence

SVC using one scalability at a time. In the case of spatial scalable SVC bit streams, only two quality scalability levels are available: BL combined with EL (full high-definition version) or BL only (standard definition version eventually up sampled). Conversely, our transrating architecture authorizes to refine progressively video quality of spatially scalable bit streams while keeping highest spatial resolution level. Clearly this constitutes a great advantage for this original transrating method.

5   Conclusion

In this paper, we presented an original solution for transrating of SVC compressed video bitstreams supporting spatial scalability only. The proposed architecture is open-loop and low complexity, to ensure real time processing of the enhancement layer. Transrating by frequency selection is applied to macroblocks of the enhancement layer and leads to intermediate bit rates with graceful video degradation between the quality of the up sampled base layer and the quality corresponding to the addition of the full enhancement layer. Depending on the quantization parameter used for spatial scalable SVC encoding, we demonstrated that the output bit rate after transrating can be reduced up to 66%, while preserving highest spatial resolution. Among the two developed transrating solutions, the second one restricts the transrating process only to macroblocks using inter-picture prediction (inter mode). This limitation allows reducing the computational complexity of the solution while avoiding drift error. Moreover, this second transcoding architecture has the great advantage to be compatible with any spatial scalable SVC compressed video stream. Further work will concern

first a mechanism to dynamically control the FP parameter based on the desired
bit rate reduction, as well as the effects of varying FP values according to the
picture/slice/macroblock types. The authors will also consider the extension of
the present work to the new HEVC compression standard.

References

1. Simpson, W.: Video over IP, 2nd edn. Focal Press (2008)
2. Develder, C., Lambert, P., Van Lancker, W., Moens, S., Van de Walle, R., Nelis, J.,
   Verslype, D., Latr, S., Staelens, N., Vercammen, N., Vermeulen, B., Masschelein,
   B., Van Leeuwen, T., Macq, J.-F., Struyve, K., De Turck, F., Dhoedt, B.: Delivering
   scalable video with QoS to the home. Telecommunication Systems 49, 129–148
   (2012)
3. Van Wallendael, G., Van Lancker, W., De Cock, J., Lambert, P., Macq, J.-F., Van
   de Walle, R.: Fast channel switching based on SVC in IPTV environments. IEEE
   Transactions on Broadcasting 58, 57–65 (2012)
4. Vetro, A., et al.: Video transcoding architectures and techniques: an overview.
   IEEE Signal Proc. Magazine 20, 18–29 (2003)
5. De Cock, J., Notebaert, S., Lambert, P., Van de Walle, R.: Motion-refined rewriting
   of H.264/AVC-coded video to SVC streams. Journal of Visual Communication and
   Image Representation 22(5), 391–400 (2011)
6. Hait, N., Malah, D.: Model-Based Transrating of H.264 Coded Video. IEEE Trans.
   on Circuits and Systems for Video Technology 19(8), 1129–1142 (2009)
7. Wu, Z., Yu, H., Tang, B., Chen, C.W.: Adaptive Initial Quantization Parameter Determination for H.264/AVC Video Transcoding. IEEE Trans. on Broadcasting 58(2), 277–284 (2012)
8. De Cock, J., Notebaert, S., Lambert, P., De Wolf, K., Van de Walle, R.: Low-
   Complexity SNR Transcoding for H.264/AVC. In: International Conference on
   Communication, Internet and Information Technology, pp. 728–731. ACTA Press,
   St-Thomas (2006)
9. De Cock, J., Notebaert, S., Lambert, P., Van de Walle, R.: Architectures for Fast
   Transcoding of H.264/AVC to Quality-Scalable SVC Stream. IEEE Transactions
   on Multimedia 11, 7 (2009)
10. Deknudt, C., Corlay, P., Bacquet, A.S., Zwingelstein-Colin, M., Coudoux, F.-X.:
    Reduced Complexity H.264/AVC Transrating based on Frequency Selectivity for
    High-Definition Streams. IEEE Trans. on Consumer Electronics 56(4), 2430–2437
    (2010)
11. Richardson, I.: The H.264 Advanced Video Compression Standard, 2nd edn. Wiley
    & Sons (2010)
12. Lefol, D., Bull, D., Canagarajah, N., Redmill, D.: An Efficient Complexity Scalable
    Video Transcoder with Mode Refinement. Signal Processing: Image Communica-
    tion 22(4), 421–433 (2007)
13. Lefol, D., Bull, D., Canagarajah, N.: Performance Evaluation of Transcoding Al-
    gorithms for H.264. IEEE Trans. on Consumer Electronics 52(1), 215–222 (2006)
14. ITU-T and ISO/IEC JTC1, JVT-T201r2, Joint Draft 7 of SVC Amendment, Re-
    vision 2 (2006)
15. Deknudt, C.: Mise en œuvre d'architectures de transcodage vido H.264/AVC et
    SVC: application à la transmission optimisée de la vidéo Haute Définition. PhD
    dissertation, University of Valenciennes (2011)

Visual Data Encryption for Privacy Enhancement in Surveillance Systems

Janusz Cichowski[1], Andrzej Czyżewski[1], and Bożena Kostek[2]

[1] Multimedia Systems Department, Gdansk University of Technology,
[2] Audio Acoustics Laboratory, Gdansk University of Technology,
Narutowicza 11/12, 80-233, Gdansk, Poland
{jay,andcz}@sound.eti.pg.gda.pl, bokostek@audioacoustics.org

Abstract. In this paper a methodology for employing reversible visual encryption of data is proposed. The developed algorithms are focused on privacy enhancement in distributed surveillance architectures. First, motivation of the study performed and a short review of preexisting methods of privacy enhancement are presented. The algorithmic background, system architecture along with a solution for anonymization of sensitive regions of interest are described. An analysis of efficiency of the developed encryption approach with respect to visual stream resolution and the number of protected objects is performed. Experimental procedures related to stream processing on a single core, single node and multiple nodes of the supercomputer platform are also provided. The obtained results are presented and discussed. Moreover, possible future improvements of the methodology are suggested.

Keywords: privacy protection, data security, information security, cryptography, multicore processing.

1 Introduction

Increasing popularity of cloud computing architectures allows engineers to overcome the problem of limited performance of single core computation. If optimization of the algorithms executed in a single thread is not sufficient, parallelization is the only way to improve the performance and reduce the computation time. In specific scientific areas such as intelligent surveillance, parallel computations are particularly useful.

Monitoring of wide urban spaces, e.g. large urbanized areas, is based on a large number of multimedia data streams. Moreover, these multimedia streams have to be transmitted via wide-band communication channels because of high video resolution requirements and the presence of additional data streams such as audio and metadata. The multimedia streams from sources connected to the distributed infrastructure are collected in the supercomputing cluster, where real-time processing is applied for object detection [1], object tracking [2], object classification and re-identification in different cameras [3], face detection [4], license plate detection [5], dangerous events detection and crowd behavior prediction [6], [7], [8].

J. Blanc-Talon et al. (Eds.): ACIVS 2013, LNCS 8192, pp. 13–24, 2013.
© Springer International Publishing Switzerland 2013

The supercomputer named GALERA, listed as one of the TOP500 most powerful computers in the world, is the crucial part of the experiments presented. For the appropriate management of multimedia data streams, a special software framework for the supercomputer was required. That's why the KASKADA framework [9] was developed as an operating system for the supercomputing cluster, which enables obtaining, storing, managing and erasing multimedia streams, tasks and services within the whole cluster, without the user's supervision. The algorithmic background of the framework was realized employing a multilayer architecture. In the first layer algorithms are installed, being integrated in the second layer as simple services, subsequently, several simple services are connected in the workflow named as the complex service. The framework distributes automatically simple tasks across available nodes to realize the complex service. The distributed and parallel approach for computation allows processing multimedia streams in real time without a significant delay.

An extensive amount of data is transmitted via a large number of visual streams, part of which may be treated as sensitive personal data, posing a threat for social privacy. The right and needs for privacy cannot prevent sending sensitive data, and be a cover for crime, fraud or vandalism, thereby, a specific privacy protection and enhancement approach to data processing has to be realized. Implementation of reversible anonymization is an adequate solution for privacy issues. The proposed solution enables protecting each sensitive object detected in the processed stream. In some critical situations, there is a possibility to extract visual content without any perceptual degradation, employing visual encryption algorithms. Algorithmic basis and the key knowledge of encryption are required for protected data extraction. An unprivileged user watching the anonymized stream is able to see only noise-like rectangular areas instead of sensitive objects. Nowadays, simple anonymization algorithms are used for the privacy protection in media and surveillance systems. Several of them were implemented in the developed framework, i.e.: cutting out, blurring, mosaicing and bit shifting algorithms. However, each of them employs the non-reversible data protection. They destroy the visual content permanently.

There are also more advanced methods available based on face de-identification [10] or automatic face swapping described in the referenced literature [11]. The approach proposed by Bitouk [11] uses a face swapping technique which protected the identity of a face image by automatically substituting it with replacements taken from a large library of public face images. However, due to aggressive de-identification, the original face image can be lost. There exists also a very sophisticated approach based on human skin segmentation [12], but it is dedicated to human face protection only. The scheme proposed by Rodriguez allows the decryption of a specific region of the image and results in a significant reduction in encrypting and decrypting processing time. The existing methods appear to be suitable for the offline (non-real time) processing of single images, also they are successfully employed in biometrics. However, the ultimate goal is to preserve the anonymity of visual streams in real time. Furthermore, usually there is not any support to recover the protected data. People causing potential security threats are protected as much as bystanders. Therefore, in order to balance the security and privacy issues, a reversible encryption in the visual domain was engineered and practically realized.

2 Privacy Preserving with Visual Encryption

Visual encryption enables encoding the original video stream (frame by frame) in a way that the output stream look like random colored noise. The encrypted stream may be decoded on the receiver side, whereas the extraction of the original content requires an encryption key validation and the reversible processing. The principles of visual encryption are suitable for privacy enhancement immune to safety hazards. There are several methods described in the literature [14], based on cryptography and allowing for protection of the personal data. The existing methods are generally based on the symmetrical encryption approach, which requires the hashing key transmitted via a secure channel. Unfortunately, in practice it is difficult to provide another secure communication stream for transmitting the data. Encrypted data transmitted through the public channel are safe and not able to be watched by a casual viewer. In this type of system, the sensitive key transmission poses the biggest security threat. Otherwise, the processing time in case of the cryptographic approach is usually longer than in case of non-reversible methods. One solutions is the application of low-level processing employing the DSP-based hardware, [15]. Unfortunately, it might practically be impossible to apply adequate hardware extensions to the existing surveillance architecture in this case. Consequently, software-based approach is more easily feasible with regard to the developed framework.

Development of a smart surveillance technology causes an increase of interest in privacy and anonymity issues. The public fear related to lack of privacy motivates researchers to evaluate the visual encryption algorithms based on random pixels permutation [16]. The idea of encryption employing permutations of pixels requires a generation of the permutation matrix with a specific pseudorandom seed. The pixels located in the sensitive ROI (rectangular) are spatially shifted according to the generated permutation matrix content. The decryption is possible only if the permutation matrix is recovered on the recipient's side. The data set including information about ROI dimensions and the seed for the pseudorandom number generator are required to recover the permutation matrix. The encryption procedure may be enhanced by multiple permutations, requiring a generation of several permutation matrices. Moreover, each matrix has to comprise a different generator seed which influences the complexity of the encryption key. The sensitive content is embedded into the transmitted frame. No other data sources are required for the protected data recovering. Knowledge of permutation seeds, ROI dimensions are necessary to recover data. The complexity of the algorithm based on pseudorandom permutations motivates researchers to simplify the encryption procedure in order to omit the negative influence on data safety. The idea of pixel relocation is based on a relocation scheme instead of the permutation matrix. A specific relocation scheme for pixel shifting is used. Examples of relocation schemes are presented in Fig. 1.

Fig. 1. Example relocation schemes

Sample relocation schemes provide a demonstrative case only, presenting the pixel shuffling sequence inside an area of size of 3×3 pixels. The relocation schemes which are practically employed in the developed framework should not be presented publicly due to security issues. The use of at least three non-contradictory relocation patterns are required. A pair of contradictory patterns applied on any region may cause a security leak. Image regions with large dimensions (depending on the visual stream resolution) and not-square shape are usually processed. The deployed schemes should allow for shifting as high number of pixels as possible, and they should be independent from the ROI (Region of Interest) shape. The larger ROI dimensions are, the greater relocation matrix is.

The relocations are executed for each pixel inside the ROI, pixels are then moved to new locations in the two-dimensional space. Typically, the color images/frames are processed. Depending on the used color space (RGB, YUV, YCbCr, etc.), values of the color components for each pixel are invariant. The relocation may be applied to gray-scale images as well as to color images. The processing is realized in the spatial domain instead of the transformation domain because of the ease of encryption and decryption. A low computational complexity is achieved at the expense of incomplete resistance against lossy visual compression. Artifacts may be encountered with regard to the compression ratio. The higher the compression rate, the more degradation in the decrypted frame is observed. The lossless compression does not entail any quality degradation in the decrypted regions. The impact of lossy compression on image and video quality was more extensively described in the conference paper by the authors [17].

The main advantage of the relocation approach is the possibility of data encryption employing only a few relocation schemes. In practice, three schemes are sufficient. The encryption is realized using adopted schemes with an unrestricted sequence order, additionally, different directions of relocation are allowed. In case of a rectangular shape, there are four possible directions: $0°$, $90°$, $180°$, $270°$. Changes of direction require rotation of the scheme by the specified angle. The rotated scheme allows shifting the pixels in another way than before the rotation. The relocation schemes have to be organized in a cascade, so that several iterations of processing are needed. The order of relocation schemes in the cascade may be identical for each color component, or a different order of schemes may be applied for each color layer separately in order to enhance data protection. An example of the relocation cascade processing is presented in Fig. 2.

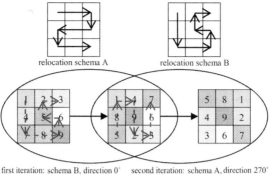

relocation schema A   relocation schema B

first iteration: schema B, direction 0°   second iteration: schema A, direction 270°

Fig. 2. Simple processing of the relocation cascade

The presented workflow includes two iterations operating on different schemes and directions. The input matrix of size 3×3 on the left is different to the output matrix on the right. The length (the number of schemes) of the relocation cascade influences the processing time and the complexity of the encryption key. It is crucial to establish unified nomenclature for encoder and decoder, because identical interpretation of the key word on the transmitter and receiver sides is needed. Independently of the nomenclature the relocation patterns have to comply with the paradigm of the symmetrical encryption. Practically used encryption keys are much longer and they allow executing an unlimited number of iterations, thereby, the processing time will increase. With a simple assumption that three relocation schemes were involved, each one is able to relocate pixels in four directions and since there are up to three color components, the simple encryption key may be written using a sequence of six bits, as shown in Fig. 3.

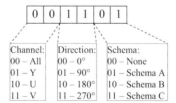

| 0 | 0 | 1 | 1 | 0 | 1 |

Channel:	Direction:	Schema:
00 – All	00 – 0°	00 – None
01 – Y	01 – 90°	01 – Schema A
10 – U	10 – 180°	10 – Schema B
11 – V	11 – 270°	11 – Schema C

Fig. 3. Simple encryption key representation

The application of the proposed methodology to a real image is shown in Fig. 4. The same cascade of relocations as presented in Fig. 1 was applied sequentially for each pixel component, the result of which is given in Fig. 4b. The same relocations were employed separately for each color component and the results are presented in Fig. 4c for the RGB color model, and in Fig. 4d for the YUV color model.

a)   b)   c)   d)

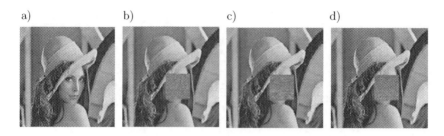

Fig. 4. Face encryption based on pixel relocation algorithm: a) original frame, b), c) and d) encrypted images utilizing different relocation cascades

The image after the encryption does not contain any visible sensitive information. The data protection is realized properly provided the sensitive regions of interests are precisely detected. Sensitive regions were detected employing pre-existing algorithms for moving objects [2] and face detection [4]. Using both of them, it was feasible to speed up the Haar-like feature detection due to limiting the number and sizes of the areas of interests employing Gaussian Mixture Models for background subtraction. The rectangular areas extracted by the detection module are treated by the anonymization module as the sensitive data.

The proposed encryption approach was developed as a part of the privacy enhancement module for real-time video stream anonymization in the existing framework. The anonymization procedure was applied to the last stage of processing, both simple and the reversible anonymization algorithms were implemented. The reversible anonymization was implemented in order to enable recovering protected content in case of some critical emergency. The results of data recovering from the encrypted images are presented in Fig. 5, together with the perceptual quality degradation inside the recovered ROIs after JPEG compression using the highest quality setting.

Figs. 5b, c, d shows the results of decryption of the images presented in Figs. 4b, c, d. The decrypted ROIs were compared using MSE (Mean Square Error) with the original image, values over figures express the differences between the images. In Fig. 5b, the same relocation schemes were applied for each color component, in Fig. 5c different relocation cascade was used for each separated color channel in RGB color model, in Fig. 5d the separated color components in YUV model were shuffled employing independent schemes. The obtained results shown in Fig. 5b and Fig. 5d are similar, application of the relocations using the YUV color model as well as relocation of pixels without separation of the color channels yield significantly better results than applying relocations employed to separate channels in the RGB color model. In Figs. 5b, d, perceptual quality of the images obtained allows the viewer to recognize the deanonymized person easily. In Fig. 5c, quality of the decrypted area is much worse, recognition of a person's identity is possible, but a higher compression rate may cause obscuring important parts of the image. The weak robustness of the data encrypted using the decomposed RGB channels is a result of the JPEG algorithm, where the YC_bC_r color space is used. The YC_bC_r and YUV separate the luminance (Y)

a) MSE = 0.0   b) MSE = 36.63   c) MSE = 67.03   d) MSE = 38.92

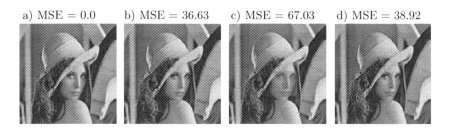

Fig. 5. Content decryption after JPEG compression: a) original image, b), c) and d) decrypted images after different encryptions.

and chrominance (C_b, C_r or U, V) components, those color models are similar. Moreover, data degradation was significantly higher for relocations employing RGB channels than YUV components.

Features of the transmitting channel and the presence of the lossy video compression caused that the comprehensive research on the influence the visual lossy compression of the encrypted data was very useful. The results obtained in earlier experiments showed that the developed encryption algorithm is sufficiently robust to be applied together with the visual compression. However, an analysis of the channel requirements and the type of potential compression algorithm are necessary. Quality degradation may be encountered in the decrypted frames because of the video compression applied.

3   Implementation and Experiments

In this Section cluster-based performance evaluation focused on privacy preserving is presented. The practical application of the presented privacy enhancement methodology was implemented as complex service in the KASKADA framework [9]. A sensitive object detection was realized using the above mentioned algorithms. Users of the developed service are able to define an object type for anonymization employing a graphical interface implemented in the KASKADA framework. There are several object classes including faces, plates, moving objects, silhouettes and cars, nevertheless users can define manually fixed ROIs to anonymize static objects or to avoid unwanted product advertisements, e.g. by anonymizing commercial logos. Sample anonymized frames are shown in Fig. 6. The most common object classes related to surveillance systems are faces (Fig. 6a), license plates (Fig. 6b) and whole silhouettes (Fig. 6c). The decrypted frames after anonymization should not be published due to privacy-preserving issues.

The main disadvantage of the presented algorithm, apart from dependence on the type of color space, is processing time. There are three factors affecting processing time and its cost. A variety of presets were simulated and measured

Fig. 6. Privacy enhancement with pixel relocation algorithm: a) faces, b) license plates, c) human silhouettes

according to different key word length, various sizes of ROI and different number of areas. The experiments were performed on a desktop computer, on a single node of a supercomputer and on the node group of a computer cluster. In order to unify the simulations for all tested cases, a Full HD (1920 × 1080) video stream was processed. Video acquired from the RTSP (Real Time Stream Protocol)-based IP camera was compressed using H.264 standard. The output file was 1 hour long with a frame rate of 15 fps. Experiments conducted are described and the obtained results are provided in the following Subsections.

3.1 Simulations Focused on Encryption Key Complexity

Firstly, influence of the encryption key complexity on the processing time was measured. In order to simplify the encryption procedure, the relocation schemes were applied to all pixels without channels decomposition. The encryption keys were designed to realize 1, 2, 4, 8, 16, 32, 48, 64, 96, 128, 192, 256, 384, 512 and 640 iterations. The processed ROI size was heuristically defined as 100 × 100, (common encountered size of the detected faces in high resolution surveillance streams). Processing time for various key complexity and different test environments is plotted in Fig. 7.

The obtained results were as expected, the single object was always processed faster on a desktop computer than on a single node of a supercomputer. The desktop test bed was based on the Intel Core i5-650 CPU (2 cores, 4 threads, 3.2 GHz) supported by 8 GB random access memory. Cluster nodes were based on the Intel Xenon Core E5345 CPUs (8 cores, 16 threads, 2.33 GHz), together with at least 16 GB RAM. The task of a single object encryption has to be realized completely by the single thread, it was not susceptible to be parallelized. Processing time for a single node (solid line) was equal to the one for the cluster (dot line). On the other hand, processing time on a desktop PC (dashed line) was lower than on two other systems. The node/cluster computations were prepared for parallel processing, thus tasks were organized into separated threads, after algorithm execution the thread supervising mechanism is taken place [9]. The management thread generates a computational overhead, so processing time is likely to increase.

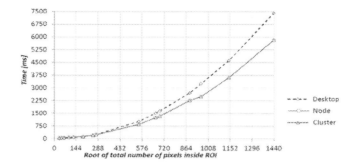

Fig. 7. Time of processing according to encryption key complexity

3.2   Simulations Focused on a ROI Size

The following part of the experiment concerns the influence of the encrypted area dimensions on the processing time. Employing the results obtained in the first simulation, it was possible to design an adequate encryption key realizing 48 relocation procedures. The main objective of this part of experiment is to simulate the occurrence of the sensitive objects with different dimensions in the processed visual stream. The test set contained manually defined objects of the following dimensions: 32×32, 48×48, 64×64, 96×96, 128×128, 192×192, 256×256, 320×240 (QVGA), 640×480 (VGA), 768×576 (PAL), 800×600 (SVGA), 1024×768 (XGA), 1280×720 (HD720), 1280×1024 (SXGA), 1920×1080 (HD1080). The encryption of the objects greater than 256×256 allows simulating the encryption of a full frame using a specific video resolution standard. For each of the defined objects, the same encryption sequence was used. The square root of the total number of pixels inside a specific area of interests is given along the axis X in order to plot the results presented in Fig. 8.

Similarly to what was discussed in the previous Subsection, processing of a single object cannot be parallelized using a greater number of nodes of the supercomputer cluster. Initially, processing time on a desktop unit (dashed line) was lower than on the node/cluster (solid/dot line), the computational overhead

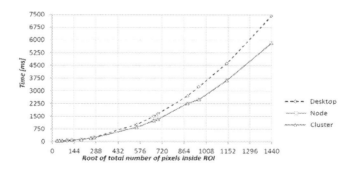

Fig. 8. Time of processing according to object dimensions

for thread management was greater than for the case of the algorithm execution. Processing time of an object with dimensions 192×192 pixels was the same for each test environment. The color lines cross and the cross point time value equals to 120 ms. Processing of objects greater than 192×192 pixels was faster on the node/cluster than on the computer. In the border conditions, the difference of processing time between the desktop and the node/cluster equals to 1400 ms. Encryption of large objects requires a large amount of memory, because the ROI pixels are temporarily stored inside RAM during processing.

Processing time increases in proportion to the key complexity and objects dimensions. Both factors do not allow for execute parallel computation of algorithms. Inclusion of a new object or employing a more sophisticated encryption key scheme caused a small reduction of the processing frame rate.

3.3   Simulations Focused on the Number of Objects

Finally, the occurrence of a large number of objects was simulated employing existing supercomputing environment [9]. The test sets contained different number of manually defined objects in the visual stream consisting of: 1, 2, 4, 8, 12, 16, 24, 32, 48, 64, 96, 128 or 160 non-overlapped objects. The objects size was fixed to 96×96 pixels, the encryption key was set to perform 48 relocation cycles, whereas test constraints were appointed using the previously obtained results. Each cluster node is able to compute the results employing up to 16 parallel threads. The results of experiments are plotted in Fig. 9.

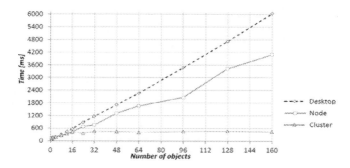

Fig. 9. Time of processing according to the number of objects

Processing up to four objects was faster on a desktop PC than on each other setup. If more than four objects were encountered in the processed frame, then computation on a node/cluster is faster than on the desktop computer. Processing time on a PC increases linearly. Processing on a node consumes the same amount of time as on the whole cluster up to the moment when 16 objects appeared in the video frame. For the number of objects greater than 16, processing was distributed among an adequate number of nodes. The node processing time increases nonlinearly together with the increasing number of objects. The differences between processing time on a PC and on the node equals to 2000 ms for the maximum number of objects. Processing time for the cluster computation achieves saturation if more than 16 objects are simultaneously processed. The increased number of objects did not influence processing time, it remained constant for more than 16 objects. The single node processes 16 objects simultaneously, for each 16 objects detected in a frame the separated single node is employed. Parallel processing on the cluster was thereby realized, whereas for a single node and for more nodes, processing time equals 440 ms. Consequently, it turned out that processing of the video stream with the 160 objects requires to involve 10 nodes of the supercomputer cluster.

Performance of the solution proposed depends on available nodes, i.e. for experiments only 10 nodes were engaged, in practice up to 336 nodes may be used. In this case up to 5367 objects may be processed online, though this number of objects is not achievable using even high resolution CCTV cameras. Processing time is given by Eq. 1:

$$t_{n<c} = t_{\max(n(w,h))} \cdot n$$
$$t_{n\geq c} = t_{\max(n(w,h))} \cdot c \tag{1}$$

where: n – number of detected objects, c – number of available threads, $t_{\max(n(w,h))}$ – processing time for the largest object detected, $t_{n<c}$ – processing time for the number of objects smaller than number of available thread, $t_{n\geq c}$ – processing time for the number of objects equal or greater than number of available threads.

4   Conclusions

The proposed approach is an alternative for classic pseudo-code ciphers, in which the encryption key is given as specific sequence of relocations instead of pseudo-number generator seeds.

The results obtained in a sequence of experiments confirmed the usefulness of a supercomputer cluster usage for the high resolution video stream processing and encryption. The supercomputing processing becomes profitable when more than 16 objects are detected in a video stream. Typically encountered objects for high resolution streams are smaller than 100×100 pixels. The number of objects occurring practically in a single frame of visual surveillance stream is close to 20. The anonymization procedure allows for enhancing the privacy level in the distributed surveillance system. The reversible anonymization preserves privacy without any significant degradation of safety. The pixel relocation method is dependent on the processed color model, whereas the analysis of the color space inside the transmission channel is necessary to protect the sensitive content. The future work will focus on a formal analysis of the encryption algorithm security level employing the visual privacy model, and formal security tools.

Acknowledgments. Research is partially subsidized from the budget of the project ADDPRIV ("Automatic Data relevancy Discrimination for a PRIVacy-sensitive video surveillance") No. 261653, being a part of the European Seventh Framework Program.

References

1. Kim, K., Davis, L.S.: Object detection and tracking for intelligent video surveillance. In: Lin, W., Tao, D., Kacprzyk, J., Li, Z., Izquierdo, E., Wang, H. (eds.) Multimedia Analysis, Processing and Communications. SCI, vol. 346, pp. 265–288. Springer, Heidelberg (2011)
2. Czyżewski, A., Dalka, P.: Moving Object Detection and Tracking for the Purpose of Multimodal Surveillance System in Urban Areas. In: Tsihrintzis, G.A., Virvou, M., Howlett, R.J., Jain, L.C. (eds.) New Direct. in Intel. Interac. Multimedia, SCI, vol. 142, pp. 75–84. Springer, Heidelberg (2008)
3. Ellwart, D., Czyżewski, A.: Viewpoint independent shape-based object classification for video surveillance. In: International Workshop on Image Analysis for Multimedia Interactive Services, Delft, Netherlands (2011)
4. Viola, P., Jones, M.: Robust Real-Time Face Detection. International Journal of Computer Vision 57(2), 137–154 (2004)
5. Sheng, H., Wen, C., Li, Q., Xiong, Z.: Real-Time Anti-Interference Location of Vehicle License Plates Using High-Definition Video. IEEE Intelligent Transportation Systems Society 1(4), 17–23 (2009)
6. Szczodrak, M., Kotus, J., Kopaczewski, K., Opatka, K., Czyżewski, A., Krawczyk, H.: Behavior Analysis and Dynamic Crowd Management in Video Surveillance System. In: International Workshop on Database and Expert Systems Applications, pp. 371–375 (2011)
7. Szwoch, G., Dalka, P., Czyżewski, A.: Objects classification based on their physical sizes for detection of events in camera images. In: Signal Processing: Algorithms, Architectures, Arrangements, and Applications. New Trends in Audio and Video, pp. 15–20 (2008)
8. Andrade, E.L., Blunsden, S., Fisher, R.B.: Hidden Markov models for optical flow analysis in crowds. In: International Conference on Pattern Recognition, pp. 460–463 (2006)
9. Krawczyk, H., Knopa, R., Proficz, J.: Basic management strategies on KASKADA platform. In: International Conference on Computer as a Tool, pp. 1–4 (2011)
10. Newton, E., Sweeney, L., Malin, B.: Preserving Privacy by De-identifying Facial Images. IEEE Transactions on Knowledge and Data Engineering 17(2), 232–243 (2005)
11. Bitouk, D., Kumar, N., Dhillon, S., Belhumeur, P.N., Nayar, S.K.: Face Swapping: Automatically Replacing Faces in Photographs. ACM Transactions on Graphics, Proceedings of SIGGRAPH (2008)
12. Rodrigues, J.M., Puech, W., Bors, A.G.: Selective Encryption of Human Skin in JPEG Images. In: IEEE International Conference on Image Processing, pp. 1981–1984 (October 2006)
13. Korus, P., Szmuc, W., Dziech, A.: A scheme for censorship of sensitive image content with high-quality reconstruction ability. In: IEEE International Conference on Multimedia and Expo, pp. 1073–1078 (July 2010)
14. Bloom, J.A., Cox, I.J., Fridrich, J., Kalker, T., Miller, M.L.: Digital Watermarking and Steganography, Boston (2008)
15. Chattopadhyay, A., Boult, T.: PrivacyCam: A Privacy Preserving Camera Using uCLinux on the Blackfin DSP. In: IEEE Workshop on Embedded Vision Systems (2007)
16. Carrillo, P., Kalva, H., Magliveras, S.: Compression Independent Reversible Encryption in Video Surveillance. Journal on Information Security (December 2009)
17. Cichowski, J., Czyżewski, A.: Reversible Video Stream Anonymization for Video Surveillance Systems Based on Pixels Relocation and Watermarking. IEEE International Conference on Computer Vision, Workshop on Visual Surveillance, 1971–1977 (November 2011)

Distance Estimation with a Two or Three Aperture SLR Digital Camera

Seungwon Lee, Joonki Paik, and Monson H. Hayes

Graduate School of Advanced Imaging Science, Multimedia, and Film
Chung-Ang University
Seoul, Korea
mhh3@gatech.edu

Abstract. When a camera is modified by placing two or more displaced apertures with color filters within the imaging system, it is possible to estimate the distances of objects from the camera and to create 3-d images. In this paper, we develop the key equations necessary to estimate the distance of an object and discuss the feasibility of such a system for distance estimation in applications such as robot vision, human computer interfaces, intelligent visual surveillance, 3-d image acquisition, and intelligent driver assistance systems. In particular, we discuss how accurately these distances may be estimated and describe how distance estimation may be performed in real-time using an appropriately modified video camera.

1 Introduction

In many applications, such as robot vision, human computer interfaces, intelligent visual surveillance, 3-d image acquisition, and intelligent driver assistance systems, it is important to be able to estimate the distance of objects within the field of view of a camera or the relative distance between two or more objects. Depending on the system that is used, there are many different approaches for distance estimation, such as estimating the disparity of objects in stereo image pairs or using a time-of-flight camera.

In this paper, we consider the capture of stereo information and the estimation of the distances of objects using a standard SLR camera that has been modified by inserting two or three off-axis apertures into the camera lens. While such cameras have been used for autofocusing [1], multifocusing [2], and distance estimation [3], [4], here the focus is on the relationship between the location of objects in the image plane as a function of the location of the apertures, the resolution of the distance estimates that are produced with such a camera, the calibration of such a system, and their use in real-time estimation of the distance of objects from a video sequence.

2 Color Filter Aperture Cameras

In order to capture stereo image data in a manner that mimics the human visual system, one needs a pair of lenses that are separated some distance from each

J. Blanc-Talon et al. (Eds.): ACIVS 2013, LNCS 8192, pp. 25–36, 2013.

Fig. 1. An SLR camera with three off-axis apertures that are covered by red, green, and blue filters

other and that capture an image of the same scene at the same time. Dual lens or dual camera capturing systems have been around since the late nineteenth century, and today there is a variety of systems of varying complexity that capture stereo imagery. These range from cameras for the hobbyist, such as the Fujifilm *FinePix 3D* Digital Camera or lenses that turn a digital SLR cameras into a 3-d camera, such as the Loreo *3D Lens in a Cap* or the Panasonic Lumix lens, to high end systems for applications such as movie production.

A simple modification to the optics of a camera, however, will also allow for the capture of 3-D images and provide the ability to estimate the distance of objects within the scene of a camera. One such system is the multiple color filter aperture camera shown configured in Fig. 1 with three displaced apertures [2]. If the apertures are covered with different colored filters, such as red and cyan in a dual-aperture camera or red, green, and blue in a three-aperture camera, then each aperture will generate a separate image in one or more color planes of the camera. Since the apertures are displaced from each other with respect to the optical axis of the lens, a point on an object will be shifted by different amounts through the apertures where the amount of shift is a function of its distance from the camera. As shown in the following sections, this provides the means for estimating the distances of objects within the field of view of the camera.

2.1   Off-Axis Imaging

For an imaging system represented by a single lens with a focal length f and an aperture that is centered on the optical axis of the lens, Gauss' thin lens equation is

$$\frac{1}{v_0} + \frac{1}{z_0} = \frac{1}{f}$$

where v_0 is the distance of the image plane from the vertex of the lens and z_0 is the location of plane of focus of the lens [5]. However, if the aperture of the lens is not centered on the optical axis as illustrated in Fig. 2, then objects within the field of view of the camera will be shifted in the image plane, and the amount of

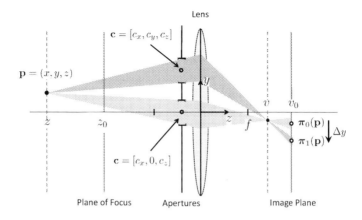

Fig. 2. Off-Axis Imaging: The effect of an off-axis aperture on the projection of a point onto the image plane

the shift will be a function of the distance of the object from the camera. More specifically, suppose that the center of the aperture is located at $\mathbf{c} = (c_x, c_y, c_z)$. If $\mathbf{p} = (x, y, z)$ is a point to the left of the lens and $\boldsymbol{\pi}(\mathbf{p}) = (\pi_x(v_0), \pi_y(v_0))$ is the projection of this point onto the image plane at v_0, then [6], [7].

$$\pi_x(v_0) = -v\frac{x}{z} + \left(1 - \frac{v_0}{v}\right)\frac{c_x z - c_z x}{z - c_z} \tag{1}$$

$$\pi_y(v_0) = -v\frac{y}{z} + \left(1 - \frac{v_0}{v}\right)\frac{c_y z - c_z y}{z - c_z} \tag{2}$$

Note that when $\mathbf{p}$ is in the plane of focus at z_0, then $v = v_0$ and, independent of the location of the aperture, the projection will be at

$$\boldsymbol{\pi}(\mathbf{p}) = -\frac{v}{z}(x, y)$$

which is the same as the perspective projection of $\mathbf{p}$ for a pinhole camera. However, when $\mathbf{p}$ is not in the plane of focus, then the projection will depend on the location of the aperture and the distance of the point $\mathbf{p}$ from the lens. In addition, the point $\mathbf{p}$ will generate a blur disk around the projected point $\boldsymbol{\pi}(\mathbf{p})$ with a diameter b that is approximately [8]

$$b \approx d\,\frac{|z - z_0|}{z_0}\,\frac{f}{|z - f|} \tag{3}$$

where d is the diameter of the aperture.

2.2   Image Shifting Due to Aperture Displacements

When a camera is configured with two or more apertures, then each aperture will, in general, project points in the object plane to different points in the image plane. More specifically, suppose that one aperture is at $\mathbf{c}_1 = (c_x, c_y, c_z)$ and another is displaced a distance Δy along the y-axis to $\mathbf{c}_2 = (c_x, c_y + \Delta c_y, c_z)$. From Eq. (2) it follows that the projections of the point $\mathbf{p} = (x, y, z)$ shown in Fig. 2 will be a distance Δy away from each other along the y-axis in the image plane, where

$$\Delta y = \left(1 - \frac{v_0}{v}\right) \frac{z}{z - c_z} \Delta c_y \tag{4}$$

Note that if $\mathbf{p}$ is in the plane of focus, then $v = v_0$ and the projected points will will be the same. However, when $z > z_0$ (the point $\mathbf{p}$ is at a distance greater than the plane of focus), then $v < v_0$ and $\Delta y < 0$. On the other hand, when $z < z_0$ (the point $\mathbf{p}$ is closer to the lens than the plane of focus), then $v > v_0$ and $\Delta y > 0$. Since

$$1 - \frac{v_0}{v} = 1 - \frac{z_0}{z} \frac{z - f}{z_0 - f} = \frac{f}{z} \frac{z_0 - z}{z_0 - f} \tag{5}$$

then substituting this relationship into Eq. (4) gives

$$\Delta y = f \frac{z_0 - z}{(z_0 - f)(z - c_z)} \Delta c_y \tag{6}$$

If $z \gg c_z$ and $z \gg f$, then

$$\Delta y \approx f \left(\frac{1}{z} - \frac{1}{z_0}\right) \Delta c_y \tag{7}$$

By symmetry, if the apertures are separated by a distance Δc_x along the x-axis, then there will be an equivalent relationship for the distance Δx between the two projected points along the x-axis.

2.3   Converting Image Shifts from Millimeters to Pixels

If c_y, z, and z_0 are expressed in meters in Eq. (6), then the change in the location of the projection, Δy, will also be in meters. To express Δy in pixels, it is necessary to know what type of sensor is used in the camera. For a camera with an $N_1 \times N_2$ array of pixels and an image sensor that is $W \times H$ mm in size, then the distance between two pixels (in mm) will be

$$\alpha = \sqrt{\frac{W \cdot H}{N_1 \cdot N_2}} \quad \text{mm} \tag{8}$$

and the expression for Δy, measured in pixels, becomes

$$\Delta y = \frac{f}{\alpha} \frac{z_0 - z}{(z_0 - f)(z - c_z)} \Delta c_y \tag{9}$$

A plot of Δy versus z using Eq. (9) is shown in Figure 3 for a 10 megapixel camera (3872×2592) with an APS-C sensor of size 25.2×16.7 mm, a 150 mm lens, a plane of focus that is set to 100 meters, and an aperture shift of 28 mm. Note that the amount that a point moves in the image plane for each meter it moves in the object plane increases significantly as the object gets closer to the camera, a relationship that is well-known in stereo imaging.

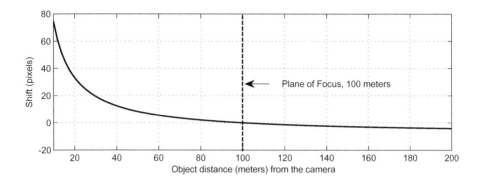

Fig. 3. The amount of shift that occurs in the image plane of a 10 megapixel camera as a function of the distance of an object from the camera for an aperture displacement of 28 mm with a plane of focus set at 100 meters.

3   Distance Estimation

Equations (1) and (2) show how a point $\mathbf{p} = (x, y, z)$ in the object plane will be projected onto the image plane with an off-axis aperture. Equation (9) shows how much a projected point will move along the y-axis when the aperture is moved a distance Δc_y along the y-axis. In the following subsections, we describe how Eq. (9) may be used to estimate the distance of an object using a multi-aperture camera, discuss the camera calibration that is required, and examine the resolution of the distance estimates that are produced using such a camera.

3.1   Color Channels and Aperture Geometry

In most digital color cameras, a color filter array is placed over the pixel sensors to capture color information. The most common is the Bayer array consisting of red, green, and blue filters that generate three channels of color data. Therefore, if each color channel is imaged through a different off-axis aperture with a color filter that is matched to the color of the pixel sensor filter, then objects in the red, green, and blue channels will be shifted with respect to each other and the amount of the shift will be a function of the distance the object is from the camera. Thus, by finding these color shifts, the distances of objects from the camera may be estimated. Consider, for example, the three-aperture geometry shown in Fig. 4(a) where the red, green, and blue filtered apertures are moved radially a distance r away from the optical axis [2].

The three apertures form an equilateral triangle, and the distance between each aperture is $r\sqrt{3}$. If an object at a distance z is captured by this camera, since the blue and red apertures are shifted along the y-axis, then the object in the blue channel will be shifted with respect to the object in the red channel along the y-axis by an amount given in Eq. (9). Therefore, if the correspondence between points in the blue and red images can be found for a point $\mathbf{p}$ on the

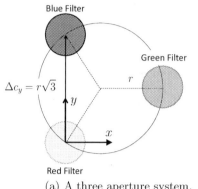

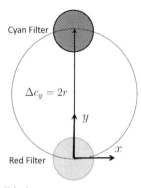

(a) A three aperture system.   (b) A two aperture system.

Fig. 4. Placement of color filter apertures using (a) three apertures with red, green, and blue filters and (b) two apertures with red and cyan filters

object, then the difference in the locations of the projected points, Δy, provides information that is sufficient to estimate the distance of the point $\mathbf{p}$ from the camera. Specifically, solving Eq. (9) for z we have

$$z = \frac{z_0 f \Delta c_y + c_z \alpha \Delta y (z_0 - f)}{f \Delta c_y + \alpha \Delta y (z_0 - f)} \qquad (10)$$

Note that the distance may also be estimated by finding the relative displacements of an object between the red and green channels or between the blue and green channels. Although these apertures are displaced by the same distance with respect to each other, the shifting in the image plane will be along different lines. In order to increase the accuracy of the estimate, the distance estimates produced from each pair of color channels may be averaged,

$$z = \frac{1}{3} \sum_{k=1}^{3} \frac{z_0 f \Delta c_y + c_z \alpha \Delta y_k (z_0 - f)}{f \Delta c_y + \alpha \Delta y_k (z_0 - f)} \qquad (11)$$

A dual aperture geometry is shown in Fig. 4(b). In this case, one aperture is covered with a red filter and the other with a cyan (green plus blue) filter, and the distance between the apertures is $\Delta c_y = 2r$. Since both green and blue are passed through the cyan filter, object distances may be estimated by either finding the relative displacements of an object between the red and green color channels or between the red and blue channels, or between both pairs and averaging the two displacements.

3.2   Calibration

Before Eq. (10) may be used to estimate the distance of an object, it is necessary to determine the camera parameters f, α, Δc_y, and c_z. For a fixed focal length camera, f will be given in the lens specification. If a zoom lens is used, an additional step of calibration would be required. The value of α that converts shifts in millimeters to shifts in pixels may be determined from the image sensor specifications as discussed in Sect. 2.3.

It is assumed that c_z, the location of the apertures along the z-axis, is the same for all apertures. In this case, the value of c_z may be found using a simple calibration procedure as follows. First, the camera is focused on an object at a known distance z_0 from the camera, thereby setting the plane of focus to a given value. (Note that the object will be in focus when the images in the three color channels are perfectly aligned.) Then, with two additional objects at different but known distances, z_1 and z_2, the shifts between two color channels of each object are found. Assume, for example, that the shifts between the blue and red channels are Δy_1 and Δy_2 for the first and second object, respectively. From Eq. (9), it follows that the ratio of these shifts is

$$\frac{\Delta y_1}{\Delta y_2} = \frac{(z_0 - z_1)(z_2 - c_z)}{(z_0 - z_2)(z_1 - c_z)}$$

Therefore, solving for c_z we have

$$c_z = \frac{\dfrac{z_0 - z_1}{z_0 - z_2} z_2 - \dfrac{\Delta y_1}{\Delta y_2} z_1}{\dfrac{z_0 - z_1}{z_0 - z_2} - \dfrac{\Delta y_1}{\Delta y_2}}$$

Once c_z is known, then Eq. (9) may be used to solve for Δc_y, the displacement between the red and blue apertures in the three-aperture system or between the red and cyan apertures in the dual-aperture camera. More specifically, using the object at distance z_1 with shift Δy_1, and solving Eq. (9) for Δc_y gives

$$\Delta c_y = \frac{\Delta y_1}{f} \frac{(z_0 - f)(z_1 - c_z)}{z_0 - z_1}$$

To increase the accuracy of the estimate of c_z, multiple objects at distances $z_1, z_2, \ldots, z_n$ with displacements $\Delta y_1, \Delta y_2, \ldots, \Delta y_n$ may be used, pairwise, to form estimates $c_z(1), c_z(2), \ldots, c_z(m)$ and these estimates may then be averaged,

$$c_z = \frac{1}{m} \sum_{k=1}^{m} c_z(k)$$

to produce the final value of c_z. Similarly, multiple objects may be used to form estimates of Δc_y, and an average of these estimates used for Δc_y.

For the three-aperture camera, the distance between the blue and green apertures and between the red and green apertures should be the same as the distance between the blue and red apertures. However, if necessary, these distances may be found using the same calibration procedure described above. The only thing that will change is that the shifts in the image plane will be in different directions.

3.3   Finding the Plane of Focus and Estimating the Color Shifts

Once the camera has been calibrated, Eq. (10) may be used to find the distance of an object from its displacement Δy in two color channels, provided that the plane of focus, z_0, is known.[1] Since z_0 is generally unknown and may change from one image to the next, it is necessary to find the plane of focus, and there are several ways that this may be done. One approach would be to set the plane of focus on an object that is a known distance, z_0, from the camera. Another approach would be to find the shift between the color channels of an object that is a known distance, z^*, from the camera, and solve Eq. (9) for z_0,

$$z_0 = f \frac{\alpha \Delta y(z^* - c_z) - z^* \Delta c_y}{\alpha \Delta y(z^* - c_z) - f \Delta c_y} \tag{12}$$

Once the plane of focus has been determined, the last step is to find the distance Δy between the projections of a point on an object whose distance is to be determined. This is equivalent to the stereo correspondence problem, and there are many approaches that may be used. Perhaps the simplest is to define a block of pixels around a projected point or an object of interest in one channel, and find the corresponding block in the other channel that maximizes the correlation between the two blocks. This approach is efficient for two reasons. First, only blocks along a given direction need to be searched since the shift is known to be in a direction that is defined by the geometry of the apertures. The shift between the red and blue channels in the three-aperture system, for example, is known to be along the y-axis. Secondly, if the distances of objects are known to lie within a given range, $z_{min} \leq z \leq z_{max}$, then this will place a limit the range of possible shifts, $(\Delta y)_{min} \leq \Delta y \leq (\Delta y)_{max}$. However, unlike typical stereo matching problems, the correspondence problem here is a bit more difficult because of the fact that when a block of pixels is separated into two color channels, and one channel is displaced with respect to the other, it is not always possible to find the correct disparity. Consider, for example, a block of 16×16 pixels with the upper half of the block being green and the lower half being red. When this block of pixels is separated into red and green color channels as illustrated in Fig. 5, there is an *apparent* shift $\Delta y = 8$ pixels even before one channel is shifted with respect to the other. The basic problem is that the three color channels of an image will generally have different intensities and, therefore, the brightness constancy property that is assumed in many disparity estimation approaches does not apply. Therefore, it is important to consider an approach that does not assume the constant brightness property, such as the elastic registration method proposed by Periaswamy [10]. Another approach that may be used is to identify key feature points of an object in the two channels and find the shift that does the best job of aligning the points [9]. Since the estimation of relative shifts of projected points in the image plane is not the focus of this paper, the reader is referred to the references for more details.

---

[1] For apertures not displaced along the y-axis, the shift will be estimated along the appropriate direction.

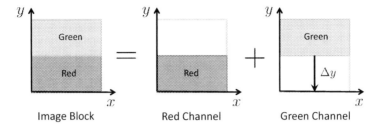

Fig. 5. Illustration of the difficulty in the correspondence problem when an image is separated into different color channels

3.4 Distance Resolution

To determine the accuracy of a distance estimate using a multiple aperture camera, we may differentiate Eq. (9) with respect to z as follows,

$$\frac{d}{dz}\Delta y = \frac{f}{\alpha}\frac{c_z - z_0}{(z - c_z)^2(z_0 - f)}\Delta c_y$$

which gives the number of pixels that the projection of an object in the image plane will move for each meter that the object moves along the z-axis. The *resolution* of a distance estimate may then be defined to be the magnitude of the inverse of this derivative,

$$\text{Res}(z, \Delta c_y) = \left|\frac{d}{dz}\Delta y\right|^{-1} = \frac{\alpha}{f}\frac{(c_z - z)^2|z_0 - f|}{|c_z - z_0||\Delta c_y|} \quad \text{meters/pixel}$$

which is the distance in meters that an object must move to produce a shift of one pixel in the image plane. Assuming that $z \gg f$ and $z \gg c_y$, the resolution is approximately

$$\text{Res}(z, \Delta c_y) \approx \frac{\alpha}{f}\frac{z^2}{|\Delta c_y|} \quad \text{meters/pixel}$$

Note that the resolution is inversely proportional to Δc_y, a relationship that is well-known in stereo imaging. Specifically, with a pair of cameras, as the distance between the camera lenses increases, the disparity increases, which implies that a more precise distance measurement may be found. A plot of the resolution as a function of z is shown in Figure 6 for a 10 megapixel camera with an APS-C sensor of size 25.2×16.7 mm, and a 150 mm lens, when the plane of focus is set to 100 meters and the apertures are separated by a distance of 28 mm. Note that an object at 100 meters must move fifteen meters to produce a shift of one pixel, whereas an object at 20 meters must move only 0.604 meter.

4 Two Aperture versus Three Aperture Cameras

In Section 3, two different multiple aperture geometries were presented. The first consists of three color filtered apertures (red, green, and blue) that are moved

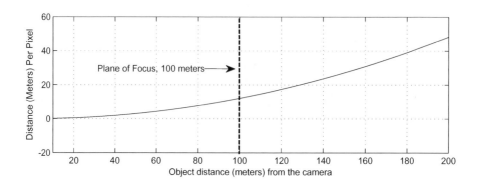

Fig. 6. Distance resolution. The number of meters an object must move as a function of z to produce a change of one pixel in Δy for an aperture displacement of 28 mm.

radially a distance r from the optical axis at angles of 120° with respect to each other. The second has two color filtered apertures (red and cyan) that are moved in opposite directions a distance r away from the optical axis. Both geometries may be used to estimate the distances of objects from the camera, but each one has its own advantages and disadvantages. For example, a three aperture camera produces lower resolution distance estimates than a dual-aperture camera due to the fact that the distance between each pair of apertures in a three-aperture camera is smaller than the equivalent dual-aperture camera. For example, if the maximum distance between two apertures in a dual-aperture camera is $2r$, then the maximum distance will be $r\sqrt{3}$ in a three aperture camera. However, with a three-aperture system, three independent distance estimates may be found from each pair of apertures (red and green, red and blue, and blue and green), whereas for the dual-aperture camera. only two independent estimates may be found - one from the shift between the red and blue color channels, and one from the red and green color channels (recall that the cyan filter passes both blue and green). Another advantage of the three-aperture geometry is that disparities along two orthogonal axes may be estimated, whereas for the dual-aperture camera the disparity along only one axis may be found. This has implications for objects that are aligned with the axis of the dual-aperture camera such as an extended wall or fence. Finally, an interesting feature of the dual-aperture camera is that it may be used to create a 3-D image that may be viewed using a pair of anaglyphic glasses [7].

5   Examples

Shown in Fig. 7 are two frames from video sequences that were captured using a three-aperture camera and used to estimate the distance of an object (person) from the camera. Although this is an example of some preliminary results, our current and future work is focused on real-time distance estimation, methods

 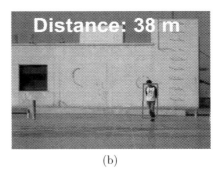

(a)   (b)

Fig. 7. Frames from a video sequence used to estimate the distance of objects from the camera using a three aperture system

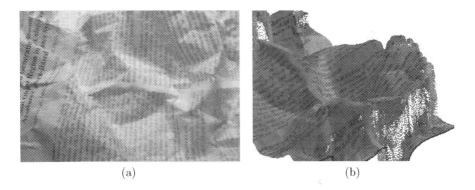

(a)   (b)

Fig. 8. (a) The image of a crumpled piece of paper using a dual color filter array camera, (b) the estimated 3-D depth map

for evaluating and improving the accuracy of the distance estimates, and incorporating a Kalman filter to help in the distance estimation. Another example is shown in Fig. 8(a) where a dual-aperture camera with red and cyan colored filters is used to form an image of a crumpled piece of paper. Using a pair of anaglyphic glasses, a 3-D image of the crumpled piece of paper may be viewed (it is best to expand the image to a larger size for best viewing). An estimate of the shifting that occurs in the image plane is illustrated in Fig. 8(b) and the reconstruction of a depth map of the image is shown in Fig. 8(c) [4].

6   Conclusions

In this paper, we have considered the modification of an SLR camera by adding a two or three color filter aperture into the lens of a camera that create displacements of objects in the image plane that are a function of the distance of the object from the camera. The focus was on the relationship between the distance of an object and the amount of shift that occurs in the image plane, and a discussion of the resolution that is possible for a given aperture separation. Two examples were given to demonstrate that such a camera might provide a simple and effective way to either create a 3-D image or to estimate the distances of objects within the field of view of the camera.

References

1. Koh, K., Kuk, J.G., Jin, B., Choi, W., Cho, N.: Autofocus Method Using Dual Aperture and Color Filters. Journal of Electronic Imaging 20(3) (July 2011)
2. Kim, S., Lee, E., Hayes, M., Paik, J.: Multifocusing and Depth Estimation Using a Color Shift Model-Based Computational Camera. IEEE Trans. on Image Processing 21(9), 4152–4166 (2012)
3. Amari, Y., Adelson, E.H.: Single-Eye range Estimation by Using Displaced Apertures with Color Filters. In: Proc. 1992 Int. Conf. on Industrial Electronics, Control, Instrumentation, and Automation, vol. 3, pp. 1588–1592 (November 1992)
4. Lee, S., Kim, N., Jung, K., Hayes, M., Paik, J.: Single Image-Based Depth Estimation Using Dual Off-Axis Color Filtered Aperture Camera. In: Proc. 2013 Int. Conf. on Acoustics, Speech, and Sig. Processing, Vancouver, Canada (May 2013)
5. Hecht, E.: Optics. Addison-Wesley (2001)
6. Dou, Q., Favaro, P.: Off-axis aperture camera: 3D shape reconstruction and image restoration. In: IEEE Conf. on Computer Vision and Pattern Recognition, pp. 1–7 (2008)
7. Lee, S., Paik, J., Hayes, M.: Stereo Image Capture and Distance Estimation with an SLR Digital Camera. In: Proc. 15th IASTED International Conference on Signal and Image Processing, Banff, Canada (July 2013)
8. Bae, S., Durand, F.: Defocus Magnification. Eurographics 2007 26(3) (2007)
9. Maik, V., Cho, D., Shin, J., Har, D., Paik, J.: Color shift Model-Based Segmentation and Fusion for Digital Auto-focusing. J. Imaging Science Tech. 51, 368–379 (2007)
10. Periaswamy, S., Farid, H.: Elastic Registration in the Presence of Intensity Variations. IEEE Trans. on Medical Imaging 32(7), 865–874 (2003)

Acquisition of Agronomic Images with Sufficient Quality by Automatic Exposure Time Control and Histogram Matching

Martín Montalvo[1], José M. Guerrero[2], Juan Romeo[2], María Guijarro[2],
Jesús M. de la Cruz[1], and Gonzalo Pajares[2]

[1] Dpt. Computer Architecture and Automatic, Facultad de Informática,
Universidad Complutense of Madrid, 28040 Madrid, Spain
[2] Dpt. Software Engineering and Artificial Intelligence, Facultad de Informática,
University Complutense of Madrid, 28040 Madrid, Spain
{mmontalvo,jmguerre,mguijarro,jmcruz,pajares}@ucm.es,
jromeo99@hotmail.com

Abstract. Agronomic images in Precision Agriculture are most times used for crop lines detection and weeds identification; both are a key issue because specific treatments or guidance require high accuracy. Agricultural images are captured in outdoor scenarios, always under uncontrolled illumination. CCD-based cameras, acquiring these images, need a specific control to acquire images of sufficient quality for greenness identification from which the crop lines and weeds are to be extracted. This paper proposes a procedure to achieve images with sufficient quality by controlling the exposure time based on image histogram analysis, completed with histogram matching. The performance of the proposed procedure is verified against testing images.

Keywords: Uncontrolled illumination, Automatic Exposure Time, Histogram analysis, Histogram matching, Machine Vision, Precision Agriculture.

1 Introduction

Nowadays, the use of robotic systems, equipped with vision-based sensors, for site specific treatments in agronomic tasks, including Precision Agriculture (PA) is in continuous growth. Crop row detection and weeds identification are two common tasks in PA. Crop row detection allows to identify the main lines with respect to which the weeds are located [1-10]. Additionally, crop lines are commonly used for guidance of the robot [11-13]. Detection and identification should be done with the highest possible accuracy [14].

It is well-known, in the computer vision community that the digital signal generated by a CCD-based sensor camera varies according to four factors which can be conveniently combined: exposure time, iris aperture, automatic white balance and amplification of gains [15]. The goal is to achieve the highest image quality as possible to achieve also the highest accuracy. From the point of view of the automatic control they are based on the image histogram analysis. However, when the gains are

J. Blanc-Talon et al. (Eds.): ACIVS 2013, LNCS 8192, pp. 37–48, 2013.

changed continuously in order to achieve the desired quality, unwanted effects occur with unstable signals and high oscillations in the image [16]. The auto-iris requires the use of a motorized optical lens for such purpose, which is not appropriate in machine vision systems on-board tractors. Auto image white balance [17] needs the identification of grey colour points from a white or with a relevant brightness that are not common in the specific region in the field under treatment.

This paper is focused on the automatic control of the exposure time, improving the procedure in [14], where the exposure time is also empirically adjusted. The objective of maximum accuracy is closer under a good exposure time control. Indeed, when low exposure time is applied the digital image is most times acquired with low contrast. On the contrary, for a large exposure time, the image becomes saturated. Because our vision system is on-board a tractor with the engine running and moving with working speeds between 4-6 km/h in rough terrains, the camera is submitted to vibrations and undesired movements. Because of the above, the textures in the field move across the image plane in the CCD; thus, if the exposure time is high, they appear blurred.

Our application achieves a trade-off with the best exposure time and minimum blur effect, i.e. with sufficient image quality to distinguish the green parts among other parts in the agricultural field. With such purpose we design an automatic procedure to control the exposure time based on the image histogram analysis. Different approaches have been designed to control the exposure time are based on empirical adjustments based on the histogram analysis and also based on luminance measures [18]. We apply statistical histogram properties to control the exposure time.

Once the exposure time is adjusted, it is still possible an additional improvement based on histogram matching between the current histogram and a histogram used as reference. The involved histograms correspond with the three RGB spectral channels of the Region Of Interest (ROI) which is to be treated. Automatic exposure time control and histogram matching make the two main contributions of this paper.

The paper is organized as follows. Section 2 describes the materials used designs the proposed approach, which contains several modules to improve the image quality. Section 3, provides the results obtained under different testing conditions. Finally, Section 4 provides the main relevant conclusions.

2   Materials and Methods

2.1   Materials

The camera-based sensor consists of three essential physical parts: a) CCD-based device embedded in a housing with its electronic equipment and interfaces for power supply and to the computer; b) optical lens and c) ultraviolet and infrared cut filter. Figure 1 displays these parts assembled as a whole.

The CCD is a Kodak KAI 04050M/C sensor with a Bayer colour filter with GR pattern; resolution of 2,336×1,752 pixels and 5.5×5.5 μm pixel-size. This device is designed under the SVS4050CFLGEA model [19] which is robust enough and very suitable for agricultural applications. This device offers several possibilities that can be externally controlled: a) exposure time, which determines the time taken to capture the image; b) Red, Green and Blue gains, where a value can be set for each channel, including auto-calculation of the gains, based on white balance; c) information about the operating temperature. This Gigabit Ethernet device is connected to a cRIO-9082 with dual-core controller, 1.33 GHz and LX150 FPGA running under LabView 2011 from National Instruments [20] which is robust enough and specifically designed for real-time processing; both features are very suitable for our agricultural application. Because the application occurs in harsh environments (containing dust, drops of liquid from sprayers and other undesired elements) it is encapsulated inside its housing with IP65 protection and internally equipped with an automatic fan which is triggered if the temperature overpasses 50°C, figure 1.

The optical system consists in a Schneider Cinegon 1.9/10-0901 lens [21], with manual iris aperture (f-stop) ranging from 1.9 to 16 and manual lockable focus. It is valid for sensor format up to a diagonal value of 1", i.e. maximum image circle of 16 mm, and equipped with F-mount which can be adapted to C-mount. The focal length is fixed to 10 mm with a field of view above 50° with object image distance from infinity to 7.5 mm, which allows the mapping of a width of 3 m required for our application. Its spectral range varies from 400 to 1000 nm, i.e. visible and Near-Infrared (NIR). The images are captured with perspective projection.

The natural illumination contains a high infra-red component. The sensor is high sensitive to the NIR radiation and to a lesser extent to the Ultra-Violet (UV) radiation. The NIR heavily contaminates the three spectral channels (Red, Green and Blue) producing images with hot colours. This makes crop lines and weeds identification unfeasible because their greenness. To avoid this undesired effect, the system is equipped with a Schneider UV/IR 486 cut filter [22] where wavelengths below 370 nm and above 760 nm are blocked, i.e. both UV and NIR radiation.

Fig. 1. Tractor with the camera-based sensor on-board the tractor

We have acquired 1358 images at the CSIC-CAR facilities in Arganda del Rey (Madrid) March 2013 in a cereal field, with the tractor stopped and also walking around the field. No maize crops are available in this season of the year. Because our application is specifically designed for maize crops, crop lines preserve their separation of 75 cm from each other like in real maize crops. This has been achieved by sowing barley with the expressed separation between the crop lines. Existing weeds in the field have been allowed to grow freely without any control. We have also acquired 60 additional images for setting the parameters involved in the proposed procedure. The ROI, used for reference in front of the tractor, is located on the ground to three meters away from the point of intersection of the imaginary vertical line passing through the centre of the CCD and the ground. It covers three meters wide and three meters long.

2.2   Method

The proposed automatic method is sketched in figure 2; it consists of three main modules, namely: (*a*) Decision making; (*b*) Exposure Time (ET) modification; (*c*) Image quality improvement; (*b*) Greenness identification.

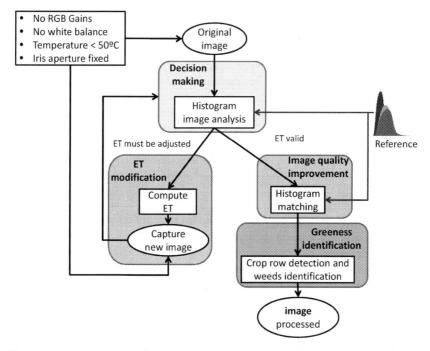

Fig. 2. Automatic procedure for controlling the exposure time for greenness identification

The box in the upper left part assumes the following system requirements, which are to be applied during the proposed procedure:

Gains: specify that the images are captured with fixed gains values, set to the unity value, i.e. no gains are applied to specific RGB spectral channels. As mentioned before in [16] when gains change continuously the signals generating the images could become unstable producing oscillations and errors, affecting the image quality.

Iris aperture: the iris aperture is fixed to an intermediate value, i.e. with f-stop set to 8. This guarantees that sufficient illumination is received in the CCD without excess and without default. It should be possible to use auto-iris systems that are able to adjust the aperture according to the degree of illumination based on a motorized system. In agricultural applications it is a common practice to try to simplify or eliminate physical systems due to adverse working conditions and sometimes extreme in the outdoor environments where tractors work. Automatic control of these systems is also based on properties of the image histogram.

White balance: unlike what happens normally in commercial cameras, no white balance is applied, because our ROI could no contain the required reference white patch; moreover we are not interested in a good image quality from the point of view of human visualization; on the contrary, our interest is focused on image quality from the point of view of machine vision.

Temperature: the illumination variability is controlled with the proposed automatic approach. The temperature is always below 50°C. This guarantees the CCD chip works properly, as specified by the manufacturer.

2.3   Decision Making Process and ET Modification

This process is intended to make a decision about if the ET must be modified or it is valid, without requiring any change. With such purpose we compute the histogram of the ROI for the three RGB spectral channels, which the source of information for the proposed decision making process. Figure 3(*a*) displays an original image with the ROI outlined on the field under perspective projection and with the system geometry known [14]. Figure 3(*b*) displays the corresponding histogram obtained from the ROI.

Depending on the ET value, the image quality varies considerably; this is reflected on the histogram. Indeed, Figures 4 and 5 display two images with low quality due to two very different reasons; the image in figure 4 is underexposed because of its low contrast and brightness values; the image in figure 5 is overexposed due to two opposite reasons. The corresponding histograms display large tails oriented towards high/low brightness values with high concentration of values in the part of low/high brightness values respectively.

How can we identify these two undesired situations? The analysis of the histogram provides sufficient information to do that. The histogram is defined by its corresponding discrete function $h(g) = n_g$, where g represents the grey level and n_g is the number of pixels with grey level g. Because our images are 8-bit per each RGB channel, g ranges in $[0, 255]$. Dividing $h(g)$ by the total number of pixels in the image, we can compute the probability $p(g) = h(g)/(M \times N)$, where M and N are the two dimensional sizes of the image. The histogram provides useful image statistics that are exploited for determining the image quality. Let g be a random variable denoting grey levels, where the *nth* moment of g about the mean is defined as:

$$\mu_n(g) = \sum_g (g-m)^n p(g) \text{ with } m = \sum_g g \cdot p(g) \tag{1}$$

According to [23] the most important statistical parameters to assess the image quality are: mean, m; variance, $v = \mu_2(g)$; skewness, $\gamma = \mu_3(g)\mu_2^{-3/2}(g)$ and kurtosis, $\kappa = \mu_4(g)\mu_2^{-2}(g)$. The mean determines the average level of brightness, where low, high and medium values indicate the degree of light that impacts the CCD-device. The variance provides information about the distribution of values around the mean. The skewness measures the asymmetry in the distribution. A right skewness is presented when the histogram displays a large tail oriented towards low brightness values and high concentration in the part of high brightness values (negative skewness). In the opposite case the skewness is positive. The kurtosis provides information about the peakedness in the distribution; low kurtosis indicates flat top parts in the histogram around the mean but high values are indicative of peaks around the mean with high slopes and large tails. In [10] has been verified that only mean and skewness are of relevance but not kurtosis nor variance. Moreover in our specific application where our ROI contains only Red and Green as the dominant spectral channels, only it is required the analysis of these two channels but not the Blue one. Thus, based on those considerations we have designed the following decision rule, where the new exposure time (ET) is computed based on the current one (ET$_{curr}$). A histogram is used as reference; it provides the following two reference values m_{Rref} and m_{Gref} that are the corresponding mean values of this histogram for the R and G spectral channels. These values are empirically selected as described in section 3.

$$while \ \left(m_i \geq m_{ui} \ and \ \gamma_i \geq |\gamma_{ui}| \right) \ or \ \left(m_i \leq m_{li} \ and \ \gamma_i \geq \gamma_{li} \right)$$

$$ET = \left(\frac{m_{Rref} + m_{Gref}}{m_R + m_G} \right) ET_{curr} \tag{2}$$

$$otherwise \ ET = ET_{curr}$$

where i represents the red channel so as on the green and m_i and γ_i are the corresponding mean (m_R and m_G) and skewness (γ_R and γ_G) values for the histogram under analyis; the subindices u and l means upper and lower values limiting the corresponding statistical parameters; the absolute value $|\gamma_{ui}|$ is considered because in this case the skewness is negative with relative high values. Section 3 describes the setting of these parameters.

When the ET is updated because the conditions in equation (2) are met, a new image is captured and it is again submitted to the decision making module for histogram analysis. Otherwise, ET is considered valid, but still the image quality can be improved based on a histogram matching procedure as described below.

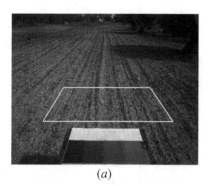
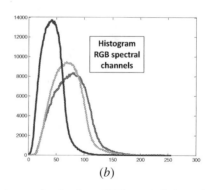

(a) (b)

Fig. 3. (a) Original image with the ROI; (b) histogram for the three RGB spectral channels in the ROI

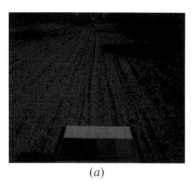 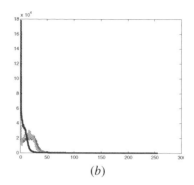

(a)   (b)

Fig. 4. (a) Original image with low contrast; (b) histogram for the three RGB spectral channels in the ROI

 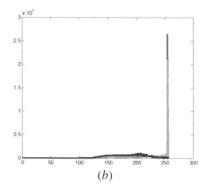

(a)   (b)

Fig. 5. (a) Original image with high contrast; (b) histogram for the three RGB spectral channels in the ROI

2.4   Image Quality Improvement and Greenness Identification

Based on histogram matching the image quality is improved as follows. We have the reference histogram (h_r), which is selected according to the procedure described below in section 3.1 and the histogram obtained from the incoming image under processing (h_c). For each histogram we compute the cumulative probabilities,

$$P\left(g_r\right)=\sum_{i=0}^{g_r} p\left(g_i\right) \text{ and } P\left(g_c\right)=\sum_{i=0}^{g_c} p\left(g_c\right) \tag{3}$$

The procedure for histogram matching is as follows: for each $P(g_c)$ associated to the grey level value, g_c, we search for the closest $P(g_r)$ value with its g_r grey level value and change g_c by g_r.

After histogram matching, we apply the procedure described in [2] for greenness identification.

3   Results

3.1   Selection of Parameters and the Reference Histogram

As mentioned before, we have acquired 1358 images which have been processed on-line with the tractor in movement at 4 Km/h approximately. The processing has been carried out under the cRIO-9082 and stored in the hard disk.

Previous to this processing, we have adjusted the parameters involved in equation (2). This was carried out in a simulated field during January 2013, where 60 images were acquired under different exposure times with the goal to achieve underexposed, normal and overexposed images. The images were also acquired under different illumination conditions due to the existence of abundant clouds, alternating with intense light and shade spaces. A first set (A) of 30 images were captured with exposure times between 0.5 and 2.5×10^4 µs obtaining underexposed images, figure 6(a) displays a representative image of this set; a second set (B) of 30 images captured with exposure times between 2.6 and 4.5×10^4 µs, obtaining normal images, figure 6(b) displays a representative image of this set; finally, a third set (C) of 30 images captured with exposure times between 4.6 and 6.5×10^4 µs obtaining overexposed images, figure 6(c) displays a representative image of this set. The averaged values obtained from the three sets are displayed in table 1.

(a) (b) (c)

Fig. 6. Images captured with different exposure times for adjusting parameters: (a) underexposed (0.5-2.5 µs); (b) normal (2.6-4.5 µs); c) overexposed (4.6-6.5 µs)

The reference histogram, used for histogram analysis and matching, which is required in the proposed approach and sketched in figure 2, is determined at the beginning of the experiments as follows. We capture different original images until to achieve a high degree of satisfaction with any of them. When this is achieved, the histogram from the ROI is the one used as reference. The degree of satisfaction is established and verified against the expert human criterion according to two major verifications, namely: a) the detected crop lines follow the real crop lines in the image and b) the patches from weeds match with the ones that really exist. The computed crop lines appear overlapped over what is considered as real crop lines. Weeds are also identified considering that they appear in the inter-crop lines with a width of 60 pixels, on average, based on the crop lines. Figure 7 displays a processed image with the crop lines and weed patches detected inside the ROI, the histogram of this ROI is the one displayed in figure 3(b), which is characterized by the following relevant statistical measures: $m_R = 75.1$, $m_G = 69.0$, $\gamma_R = 0.77$ and $\gamma_G = 0.96$. As we can see, the mean values are closer to the mean reference values m_{Rref} and m_{Gref} than from the other mean values. The absolute values for skewness are smaller than those obtained from sets A and C.

Table 1. Averaged values of parameters used in equation (2)

Sets	m_{lR}	γ_{lR}	m_{lG}	γ_{lG}	m_{Rref}	m_{Gref}	m_{uR}	γ_{uR}	m_{uG}	γ_{uG}
A	26.7	9.4	24.6	10.7	–	–	–	–	–	–
B	–	–	–	–	82.2	75.4	–	–	–	–
C	–	–	–	–	–	–	229,2	-4.7	225,4	-4.5

Fig. 7. Identification of crop lines and weed patches in the ROI

3.2   Design of a Test Strategy

In order to assess the validity of our proposed method we have designed the following test strategy.

The tractor is positioned at ten different locations in the field. At each position we apply the method proposed, obtaining five images. This is intended to capture images under different illumination conditions, caused by the variability due to the high density of clouds. Also, for each position we force the ET with different values to capture ten underexposed and overexposed images, five in each case. The values of ET are fixed according to the ranges defined in section 3.1.

At each position we test for correctness in both, weeds detection and crop lines localization.

A ground-truth image of the ROI is built at each location from the obtained binary image after greenness identification. This binary image is manually touched up, so that isolated or groups of pixels are relabeled as white or black pixels, according to a human expert criterion. Thus, at each position we compare the weed detection against the corresponding ground-truth by computing the Correct Classification Percentage (PCC) index [24],

$$PCC = \frac{TW + TB}{TW + TB + FW + FB} \qquad (4)$$

where TW (true whites) and TB (true blacks) are the number of white/black pixels respectively in the image that are also white/black in the ground-truth; FW (false whites) and FB (false blacks) are the number of white/black pixels respectively in the image that are also black/white in the ground-truth.

With respect crop lines detection, we verify the correct layout of the lines on the rows. A line is considered correct when it appears traced along the middle of the row where it is located. On the contrary, if some line is missing, i.e. not identified, or it does not fit to the crop line concerned because a significant deviation, it is considered an error.

Table 2 displays the averaged PCC values over the images analyzed for weed detection and the percentage of success for crop lines detection. The values for normal images are obtained with and without histogram matching.

Table 2. PCC values for weed detection and percentage of success for crop lines detection for underexposed, normal (with and without histogram matching) and overexposed images

	under exposed	normal + histogram matching		over exposed
		No	Yes	
PCC (weeds)	63.2	87.2	**91.1**	42.9
% (crop lines)	57.1	89.9	**95.6**	9.2

The proposed strategy has been also tested with the tractor walking in the field, capturing an image every second. The original image and the processed are both stored for posterior analysis. Here, we verify the correct crop lines detection according to the testing procedure above. With the 1358 tested, the percentage of success achieved is 97%. We have also verified qualitatively the performance of the proposed approach with respect weed detection; to do that we have randomly selected the 2% of the available images, i.e. 28, and we have built the corresponding ground-truth for the ROIs under processing. The averaged PCC achieved is 90.2 i.e. with the same order of magnitude as that previously obtained.

According to the results above, we have verified the performance of the proposed approach. Indeed, when the images are incorrectly acquired, either under or over exposition, the results are worse than the ones acquired with exposure times that produce normal images. Also the performance is improved by histogram matching.

From results in table 2 we can see that the worst situation is the one with over exposition, this is because when this occurs the sensor is impacted with not possibility of recovery. With under exposure still is possible to achieve some results. Both situations must be avoided, but specially the over exposure.

4   Conclusions

We have proposed an effective approach for controlling the exposure time during the acquisition of agronomic images in outdoor environments under uncontrolled illumination and also with a tractor walking in the field during agronomic tasks. Histogram matching is also applied for image quality improvement.

Both processes represent an important contribution to deal with this kind of images oriented toward precision agriculture tasks.

Acknowledgements. The research leading to these results has been funded by the European Union's Seventh Framework Programme [FP7/2007-2013] under Grant Agreement No. 245986 in the Theme NMP-2009-3.4-1 (Automation and robotics for sustainable crop and forestry management). The authors wish also to acknowledge to the project AGL2011-30442-C02-02, supported by the Ministerio de Economía y Competitividad of Spain within the Plan Nacional de I+D+i. We would like to express our sincere gratitude to Pablo Gonzalez-de-Santos, Luis Emmi, Mariano González, César Fernández-Quintanilla, José Dorado, Angela Ribeiro and co-workers for their great support and help provided during the field arrangement.

References

1. López-Granados, F.: Weed detection for site-specific weed management: mapping and real-time approaches, Weed Research 51, 1–11 (2011).
2. Romeo, J., Pajares, G., Montalvo, M., Guerrero, J. M., Guijarro, M., Ribeiro, A. Crop Row Detection in Maize Fields Inspired on the Human Visual Perception. The ScientificWorld Journal, vol. 2012, Article ID 484390, 10 pages, doi:10.1100/2012/484390 (2012).
3. Søgaard, H.T., Olsen, H.J. Determination of crop rows by image analysis without segmentation. Computers and Electronics in Agriculture. 38(2), 141–158 (2003).
4. Hague, T., Tillett, N., Wheeler, H. Automated crop and weed monitoring in widely spaced cereals. Precision Agriculture, 1(1), 95–113, (2006).
5. Slaughter, D. C., Giles, D. K., Downey, D. Autonomous robotic weed control systems: a review. Computers and Electronics in Agriculture, 61(1), 63–78 (2008).
6. Montalvo, M., Pajares, G., Guerrero, J.M., Romeo, J., Guijarro, M., Ribeiro, A., Ruz, J.J., Cruz, J.M.. Automatic detection of crop rows in maize fields with high weeds pressure. Expert Systems Applic., 39, 11889–11897 (2012).
7. Guerrero, J.M., Pajares, G., Montalvo, M., Romeo, J., Guijarro, M. Support Vector Machines for crop/weeds identification in maize fields. Expert Systems Applic., 39, 11149–11155 (2012).
8. Montalvo, M., Guerrero, J.M., Romeo, J., Emmi, L., Guijarro, M., Pajares, G. Automatic expert system for weeds/crops identification in images from maize fields. Expert Systems Applic., 40, 75–82 (2013).
9. Guerrero, J.M., Guijarro, M., Montalvo, M., Romeo, J., Emmi, L., Ribeiro, A., Pajares, G. Automatic expert system based on images for accuracy crop row detection in maize fields. Expert Systems Applic., 40, 656–664 (2013).
10. Romeo, J., Pajares, G., Montalvo, M., Guerrero, J.M., Guijarro, M., Cruz, J.M. A new Expert System for greenness identification in agricultural images. Expert Systems Applic., 40, 2275–2286 (2013).
11. Fontaine, V., Crowe, T.G. Development of line-detection algorithms for local positioning in densely seeded crops. Canadian Biosystems Engineering, 48, 7.19–7.29 (2006).
12. Astrand, B., Baerveldt, A. J. A vision based row-following system for agricultural field machinery. Mechatronics, 15, 251–269, (2005).
13. Leemans, V., Destain, M. F. Application of the Hough transform for seed row location using machine vision. Biosystems Engineering, 94(3), 325–336, (2006).
14. Romeo, J., Guerrero, J.M., Montalvo, M., Emmi, L., Guijarro, M., Gonzalez-de-Santos, P., Pajares, G. Camera Sensor Arrangement for Crop/Weed Detection Accuracy in Agronomic Images. Sensors, 13, 4348-4366, (2013).

15. Kremens, R., Sampat,, N., Venkataraman, S., Yeh, T. System implications of implementing auto-exposure on consumer digital cameras. SPIE Electronic Imaging'99 Conference, Vol. 3650, January (1999).
16. Jiang T., Kuhnert, K.D., Nguyen, D., Kuhnert, L. Multiple templates auto exposure control based on luminance histogram for onboard camera. In Proc. IEEE Int. Conf. on Computer Science and Automation Engineering (CSAE), vol. 3, 237-241, June 10-12, Shanghai, China (2011).
17. Vuong, Q.K., Yun, S.H., Kim, S. A New Auto Exposure and Auto White-Balance Algorithm to Detect High Dynamic Range Conditions Using CMOS Technology. In Proc. of the World Congress on Engineering and Computer Science (WCECS) 2008, October 22-24, San Francisco, USA (2008).
18. Nourani-Vatani, N., Roberts, J. Automatic Camera Exposure Control. In Proc. of the Australian Conf. Robotics and Automation, 1-6, December, Brisbane, Australia (2007).
19. SVS-VISTEK. The Focal Point of Machine Vision, 2013. Available online: http://www.svsvistek.com/ (accessed on 1 May 2013).
20. National Instruments. Available online: http://spain.ni.com/ (accessed on 1 May 2013).
21. Scheneider Kreuznach. C-Mount Lenses compact series 1″. Available online: http://www.
22. schneiderkreuznach.com/en/industrial-solutions/lenses-and-accessories/products/, (accessed on 1 May 2013).
23. Scheneider Kreuznach. Tips and Tricks 2013. Available online: http://www.schneiderkreuznach.com/en/photo-imaging/ product-field/b-w-fotofilter/products/filtertypes/ special-filters/486-uvir-cut/(accessed on 1 May 2013).
24. Holub, O., Ferreira, S. T. Quantitative histogram analysis of images. Computer Physics Communications, 175, 620–623, (2006).
25. Rosin, P.L., Ioannidis, E. Evaluation of global image thresholding for change detection. Pattern Recognit. Lett., 24, 2345–2356 (2003).

An Enhanced Weighted Median Filter for Noise Reduction in SAR Interferograms

Wajih Ben Abdallah[1] and Riadh Abdelfattah[1,2]

[1] COSIM Lab, University of Carthage, Higher School of Communications of Tunis
Route de Raoued KM 3.5, Cite El Ghazala Ariana 2083
benabdallah.wajih@supcom.rnu.tn
[2] Département ITI, Telecom Bretagne, Institut de Telecom
Technopôle Brest-Iroise CS 83818
29238 Brest Cedex 3 - France
riadh.abdelfattah@supcom.rnu.tn

Abstract. In this paper, we describe a new filtering method based on the weighted median filter and the Lopez and Fabregas noise reduction algorithm operating in the wavelet domain. It is developed for the reduction of the impulse phase noise in synthetic aperture radar interferograms (InSAR). Our contribution to the classic weighted median filter consists of using the InSAR coherence map to generate the weights. While the developed approach prioritizes the high-coherence areas to compute the median filter outputs, the computation of the weights depends on the coherence values within the used window. The developed algorithm is then tested on a simulated data set as well as a set of Radarsat-2 raw data and ERS-2 SLC images acquired over the region of Mahdia and Ben Guerden respectively in Tunisia. The results validation is considered through computing the unwrapped phase of the filtered interferogram by using the SNAPHU algorithm.

1 Introduction

The Synthetic Aperture Radar interferometry (InSAR) exploits the phase difference (interferogram), directly related to the distance between the sensor and the imaged target, from two single look complex images [1]. It has mainly two direct applications: the first is to compute the digital elevation model (DEM) and the second is to provide informations about the terrain changes caused by geological phenomena such as the earthquakes, landslides, subsidence, etc...[2],[3].

The InSAR process suffers from the presence of speckle noise within the processed raw data [4]. This will generate an additive noise in the interferometric phase that will make very difficult the exploitation of such information. Thus, the filtering is necessary before any use of the interferogram data. Many approaches have been proposed to filter the SAR interferogram such as the Gaussian filter [5], the median filters [6] and filters based on the minimisation of the mean square error [7]. In other context, the minimization of the total variation was extensively used in order to limit the oscillations in any regularized image while

J. Blanc-Talon et al. (Eds.): ACIVS 2013, LNCS 8192, pp. 49–59, 2013.

preserving the edges of the fringe pattern in this case [8]. Also, the unscented Kalman filter [9] is used to filter the noise and unwrap the phase simultaneously.

There are many works that used the multilook processing [10] to reduce the noise in the interferogram. This technique is based on the compute of the average of neighbours pixels. For example, Lee *et al.* [11] consider that the multilook phase noise has an hypergeometric probability distribution and compute its standard deviation as a function of the coherence and the number of looks. But this approach is used only in the spatial domain.

In another way, many approaches operating in the wavelet domain were proposed. The one published by López and Fàbregas [12] gives a new technique to filter the SAR interferogram by applying the Discrete Packet Wavelet Transform (DPWT). The major advantage of this method is to extract the useful signal presented in the interferogram by amplifying it and filters the noisy phases. This amplification in the wavelet domain gives better results than the Lee and multilook filters [12]. But the filtered interferogram still having a noise which look like an impulse noise (Fig. 1-(b) and (e)). For this reason, we propose, in this paper, a new process to compensate this problem by applying the Weighted Median Filter (WMF) [13], mainly used to eliminate the impulse noise, to filter the noisy areas remained in the Lopez filtered interferogram. The choice of the WMF is based on its capability to remove the noise with preserving the fringe pattern of the interferogram. But to adapt the classic WMF to the SAR interferogram, we proposed an enhanced weighted median filter (EWMF) where the coherence map of the corresponding interferogram is taken into account to compute the weights. To validate our approach, we compute the unwrapped filtered phase image using a Quality-Guided unwrapping method presented in [22]. The quality guided algorithm are an efficient technique to reproduce the original unwrapped phase value from the interferograms. There are many different methods which use the quality guided algorithm in the literature, and it applied in 2D phase image [14], [15] as well as in the 3D profilometry [16].

This paper is organized as follows: Section 2 reviews the WInP filter, proposed in [12], and section 3 describes the proposed approach with the Enhanced Weighted Median Filter. The effectiveness of the filter is demonstrated in Section 4, using simulated data set as well as Radarsat-2 SLC data from the region of Mahdia (Tunisia). The results are compared with the adaptive filter proposed by Lee *et al.* [17], the WInP filetr [12] and the classic weighted median filter [13]. Section 5 gives the conclusion.

2   Review on The WInP Filter

The Synthetic Aperture Radar systems produce for each acquisition a complex values image [20]. Then for two acquisitions the correlation coefficient γ between the two complex images is computed. The corresponding phase $\theta = \arg[\gamma]$ is the interferometric phase. As any measure process, the interferometric phase is

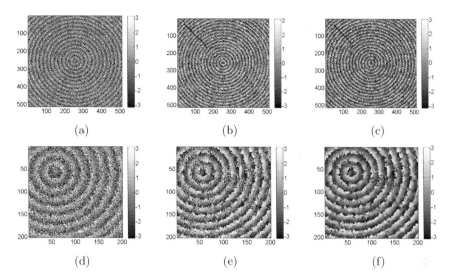

Fig. 1. First row: Filtering results of simulated interferogram ($|\rho| = 0.4$) representing a cone: (a) the original noisy image, (b) filtered with WInP filter, (c) and filtered with the proposed approach EWMF. Second row: Filtering results of a selected area (marked by a black square in (a)) (d) the original image (e) filtered with WInP filter and with (f) the proposed approach EWMF.

affected by a phase noise n. Lee *et al.* [17] proved that it can be represented as an additive noise in the real domain:

$$\phi = \varphi + n \qquad (1)$$

where ϕ and φ are the observed and original phase respectively and n is zero mean noise which depends on the number of looks k and the coherence value $|\gamma|$. The original phase and the noise are supposed to be independent from each other [17]. The noise model given at (1) is expressed in the complex domain to avoid the phase jumps in real domain which prevent the correct unwrapping of the interferometric phase [21]. The observed phase is rewritten in the complex domain as follows:

$$e^{j\phi} = \cos(\varphi + n) + j\sin(\varphi + n) \qquad (2)$$

To detect the noise pixels in the SAR interferogram, López and Fàbregas [12] propose to apply the three scales wavelet transform and the Discrete Packet Wavelet Transform (DPWT) at the third decomposition level to create an equivalent model. Then the pixel that represents a signal coefficient in those 16 sub bands is located by using a generated mask defined based on two parameters [12]. The output phase image of the DPWT algorithm is infected by an impulse noise. An example of filtering result on a simulated interferogram representing a cone using this approach is illustrated in (Fig. 1). This inherent noise to the InSAR fringes have to be reduced before the unwrapping step. For this reason we aim to apply the Weighted Median Filter to the output of the DPWT filter. The

WMF will smooth the noise presented in the filtered interferogram with preserving the fringe pattern which is indispensable before the unwrapping process. So we propose to take advantage of the dependencies between the two complex SAR images to compute the weights of the filter using the coherence map produced by those two complex data.

3   Enhanced Weighted Median Filter

The general Weighted Median Filter proposed in [13] is a variation of the median filter by weighting the values of the entry. If we consider an observation window $X^{i,j} = (X_1^{i,j}, ..., X_N^{i,j})$ with size N, where i, j are the locations of a given pixel respectively in row and column, and a given signed integer weight values $(W_1, ..., W_N)$, then the output of the weighted median filter is defined by:

$$Y^{i,j} = Median(|W_1| \diamond sgn(W_1)X_1^{i,j}, ..., |W_N| \diamond sgn(W_N)X_N^{i,j}) \quad (3)$$

Where $\diamond$ is the replication operator defined as $W_n \diamond X_n = (X_n^{i,j}, ..., X_n^{i,j}) \ W_n$ times. The advantage of using signed weights is to minimise more the cost

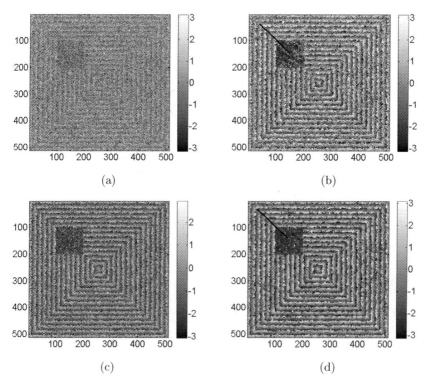

(a)   (b)

(c)   (d)

Fig. 2. Filtering result of simulated interferogram ($|\rho| = 0.4$) representing a truncated pyramid: (a) with Lee filter,(b) with WInP filter, (c) with classic weighted median filter and (d) with the proposed approach EWMF.

function associated to the WM filter and give better Mean Absolute Filter Error (MAE) than using the positive wights filter [13].

In [18], Vijay *et al.* proposed a more generalized expression to compute the weight values as positif floats as follows [18]:

$$Weight(i,j) = \exp\{-\alpha|original(i,j) - reference(i,j)|\} \qquad (4)$$

where $\alpha > 0$, *orginal* is the original noisy image and *reference* is the filtered image by median filter.

In the case of SAR interferogram, we propose to compute the weight values using the InSAR coherence image, that measure the degree of correlation between the two SLC image coefficients, as well as the interferometric phase image filtered by WInPF filter [12]. In this paper, we propose a modification of (4) by choosing the *reference* image as the WInPF filter output image and the parameter α as a variation of the InSAR coherence as follows:

$$weight = e^{-(1-|\gamma|)|IM-REF|} \qquad (5)$$

This mean that in the case of a coherent target ($|\gamma(i,j)| = 1$), which corresponds to a signal pixels, the weight of the corresponding pixel is 1. However, this weight becomes $e^{-|IM(i,j)-REF(i,j)|}$ in case of non coherent target ($|\gamma(i,j)| = 0$), which may be associated with the noisy pixels.

In order to benefit of both advantages of the weighted median filter [13] (signed **integer** weights) and recursive weighted median filter [18] (unsigned **float** weights), we propose to get the weight values as signed floats. To do so, we compute the sign of the weights by assuming that the pixels whose coherence values are smaller than a given threshold S_h, are marked as negative weights. Then the general expression of the weights is given as follows:

$$weight = sign(|\gamma| - S_h)e^{(|\gamma|-1)|IM-REF|} \qquad (6)$$

After obtaining the weights of the filter, the last step is to compute the median value of the filter by applying the following algorithm to the interferometric phase image filtered by WInPF [13]. This algorithm was adapted with the new weight estimation approach for the SAR interferogram.

Algorithm:
Step 1: we compute the threshold $T_0 = 1/2 \sum_{i=1}^{N} |W_i|$
Step 2: we multiply the observation samples X_i with their weight signs.
Step 3: the observation samples are sorted from smaller to bigger.
Step 4: we calculate the corresponding absolute values of the sorted observation samples.
Step 5: by summing the absolute weights, beginning with the maximum samples, the output is signed sample whose absolute weight causes the sum to become $\geq T_0$.

Note that the phase values of the observation image (REF) must be positives (between 0 and 2π) in order to homogenous weighted data in step 2 and 3. The experimental results are given in the next section.

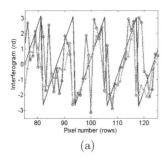
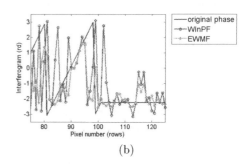

(a)   (b)

Fig. 3. Spatial resolution result of a part from : (a) the black line shown in Fig. 1-(b) and (b) the black line shown in Fig. 2-(b). The solid line represents the original phase without noise, the line with circle (o) for the filtered phase with WInPF and the line with asterisk (*) for the EWMF result.

Table 1. PSNR of the five approaches with 512×512 size phase image and different correlation values

	$|\rho|$	Lee Filter	Kuan Filter	WINPF	WMF	EWMF
	0.4	41.480	42.1608	42.418	43.684	**44.110**
Cone	0.7	42.780	45.920	46.581	45.867	**47.214**
	0.9	44.922	48.120	48.970	47.898	**49.131**
	0.4	41.420	42.096	42.073	43.728	**44.056**
Truncated	0.7	42.810	45.909	46.692	45.978	**47.363**
pyramid	0.9	44.990	48.087	49.435	47.997	**49.649**

4   Experimental Results

We used in this paper two kind of interferogram: the first one is simulated phase images produced by Matlab representing a cone and a truncated pyramid with a size of 512×512 pixels and maximum height 60π and 30π respectively. The second one is two given pairs of single look complex (SLC) data acquired with the Radarsat-2 and ERS-2 satellites over Mahdia and Ben Guerden respectively in Tunisia. The baseline between each acquisition of the two satellites are 206.23m and 425.72m respectively. The corresponding interferograms and the coherence maps for these two pairs were generated using NEST software [24].

For the simulated images, the two interferograms are generated with one look noise phase. In this paper, we compared the proposed approach with the Lee filter [17], Kuan filter [23], WInP filter [12] and the classic weighted median filter [13]. Note that the threshold S_h is computed as 10% of the maximum value in the coherence map. For the visual comparison, the filtering results of the simulated interferograms are shown in Fig. 1 and Fig. 2. To illustrate more clearly the

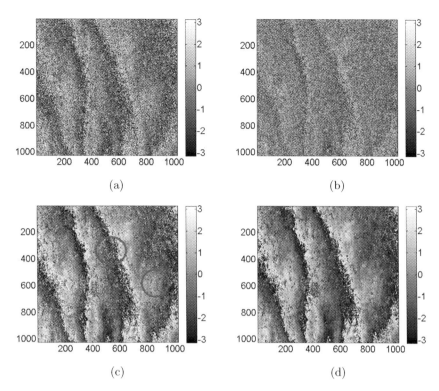

Fig. 4. Filtering result of the real interferogram data acquired over the region of Mahdia in Tunisia (a) the original noisy phase image (b) filtered with Lee filter (c) filtered result with WInPF filter (d) and with proposed approach.

difference between the WInPF and EWMF approaches, a selected area of the cone image is zoomed as shown in Fig. 1. We notice that the proposed approach preserve the edges of the fringes more better than WInP filter as shown with the spatial resolution in Fig. 4. For the quantitative comparison, we compute the Peak Signal to Noise Ratio PSNR between the filtered and the original interferometric phase without noise. In TABLE 1 it is shown the comparison results between the five filtering approaches with a correlation value $|\rho|$ varying from 0.4 to 0.9. We notice that the proposed approach EWMF gives the best PSNR with all correlation values with an improvement reaching 4**dB** for the truncated pyramid.

In the case of real interferograms, the Fig. 3 shows the filtering results comparaison between Lee filter [17], WInPF [12] and our proposed approach for the Mahdia interferogram. In Fig. 5, we maked a comparaison between Kuan filter [23], WInPF and the proposed method filtering results. For the two tested real interferograms we notice that there are many noisy areas that hasn't been

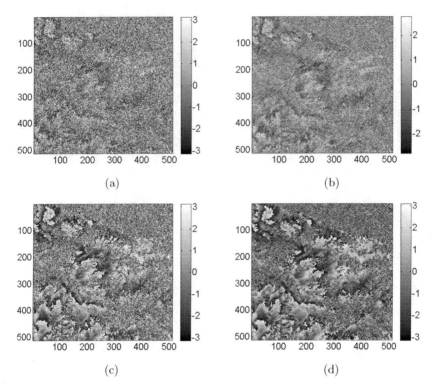

Fig. 5. Filtering result of the real interferogram data acquired over the region of Ben Guerden in Tunisia (a) the original noisy phase image (b) filtered with Kuan filter (c) filtered result with WInPF filter (d) and with proposed approach

filtered by WInPF method (marked in the WInPF output phase image Fig. 4-(c) and Fig. 5-(c) with red circles) but it has been detected and filtered by the proposed approach (Fig. 4-(d) and Fig. 5-(d)). After the filtering process of the real SAR interferograms, we validated our approach by computing the unwrapped filtered phase images and their corresponding Digital Elevation Models (DEM) and compare them with the DEM of the same acquired region provided by ASTER Global DEM and available in the Land Processes Distributed Active Archive Center website (http://gdex.cr.usgs.gov)al interferogram. In this paper we used the Statistical-Cost Network-Flow Algorithm for Phase Unwrapping (SNAPHU) to calculate the unwrapping phase images [25]. The histograms of the absolute errors between the real DEMs, given from ASTER, and the obtained DEMs after unwrapping of the filtering phase with WInPF and EWMF filters are shown in Fig. 6. A simple visual comparaison between the four histograms shows that in the both cases our proposed filter give lowest error rate.

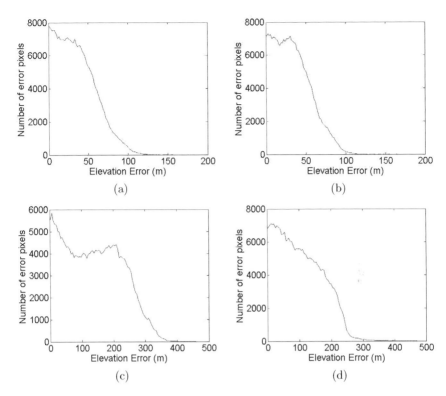

Fig. 6. The distribution histogram of the elevation error between the DEM from ASTER satellite and the DEMs computed from the unwrapped filtered interferogram of RadarSAT-2 (a) filtered by WInPF (b) filtered by EWMF and of ERS-2 (c) filtered with WInPF and (d) with EWMF

5   Conclusion

In this paper, we presented a new approach to reduce the impulse noise in the filtered SAR interferometric phase image produced by the WInPF filter. This approach is based on the weighted median filter by using the coherence information to compute the weight values of the filter. The proposed method is tested with simulated and real interferograms and the result is compared with four other filters. The quantitative and visual comparisons show that our approach gives best results with respect to the Signal to Noise Ratio and preserves more the edges of the fringes. Also, the developed approach is validated by computing the number of height error pixels between the DEM of the filtered unwrapped images and the DEM provided by ASTER satellite.

Acknowledgment. The authors would like to thank the Canadian Space Agency for offering us the Radarsat-2 data within the context of the SOAR-E 5088 project.

References

1. Abdelfattah, R., Nicolas, J.M.: Topographic SAR Interferometry Formulation for High-Precision DEM Generation. In: IEEE Trans. Geosci and Remote Sensing. LNCS, vol. 40(11), pp. 2415–2426
2. Bamler, R., Hartl, P.: Synthetic Aperture Radar Interferometry. Inverse Problems 14 (1998)
3. Massonnet, D., Feigl, K.L.: Radar interferometry and its application to changes in the earth's surface. Reviews of Geophysics 36(4), 441–500 (1998)
4. Zebker, H.A., Villasenor, J.: Decorrelation in interferometric radar echoes. IEEE Trans. Geosci. Remote Sens. 30(5), 950–959 (1992)
5. Geudtner, D., Schwabisch, M., Winter, R.: SAR-interferometry with ERS-1 data. In: Proc., PIERS 1994 (1994)
6. Candeias, A., Mura, J., Dutra, L., Moreira, J., Santos, P.: Interferogram phase noise reduction using morphological and modified median filters. In: Proc. IEEE (IGARSS 1995), vol. 1, pp. 166–168 (1995)
7. Fornaro, G., Guarnieri, A.M.: Minimum mean square error space-varying filtering of interferometric sar data. IEEE Trans. Geosci. Remote Sens. 40(1), 11–21 (2002)
8. Osher, S., Burger, M., Goldfarb, D., Xu, J., Yin, W.: An Iterative Regularization Method for Total Variation Based Image Restoration. SIAM Journal 4, 460–489 (2005)
9. Xie, X., Pi, Y.: Phase noise filtering and phase unwrapping method based on unscented Kalman filter. Journal of Systems Engineering and Electronics 22(3), 365–372 (2011)
10. Huang, Y., Van Genderen, J.L.: Comparison of several multi-look processing procedures in INSAR processing for ERS-1,2 tandem mode. In: Proc. of the Fringe, ESA Workshop (1996)
11. Lee, J.S., Hoppel, K.W., Mango, S.A.: Intensity and phase statistics of multilook polarimetric and interferometric SAR imagery. IEEE Trans. Geosci. Remote Sensing 32(5), 1017–1027 (1994)
12. Martinez, C.L., Fàbregas, X.: Modeling and Reduction of SAR Interferometric Phase Noise in the Wavelet Domain. IEEE Trans. Geosci Remote Sensing 40(12), 2553–2566 (2002)
13. Arce, G.R.: A general weighted median filter structure admitting negative weights. IEEE Trans. on Signal Processing 46(12), 3195–3205 (1998)
14. Kemao, Q., Gao, W., Wang, H.: Windowed Fourier-filtered and quality-guided phase-unwrapping algorithm. Applied Optics 49(7), 1075–1079 (2010)
15. Ma, L., Li, Y., Wang, H., Jin, H.: Fast algorithm for reliability-guided phase unwrapping in digital holographic microscopy. Applied Optics 51(36), 8800–8807 (2012)
16. Chen, K., Xi, J., Yu, Y.: Fast quality-guided phase unwrapping algorithm for 3D profilometry based on object image edge detection. In: Computer Vision and Pattern Recognition Workshops (CVPRW), pp. 64–69 (2012)
17. Lee, J., Papathanassiou, K., Ainsworth, T., Grunes, M., Reigber, A.: A new technique for noise filtering of SAR interferometric phase images. IEEE Trans. Geosci. Remote Sensing 36, 1456–1465 (1998)
18. Vijay Kumar, V.R., Manikandan, S., Vanathi, P.T., Kanagasabapathy, P., Ebenezer, D.: Adaptive Window Length Recursive Weighted Median Filter for Removing Impulse Noise in Images with Details Preservation. ECTI Trans. on Elect. Eng., Electronics and Com. 6(1), 73–80 (2008)

19. Abdelfattah, R., Nicolas, J.M.: Interferometric SAR coherence magnitude estimation using second kind statistics. IEEE Trans. Geosci. Remote Sensing 44, 1942–1953 (2006)
20. Goldstein, R., Zebker, H., Werner, C.: Satellite radar interferometry: Two-dimensional phase unwrapping. Radio Science 23(4), 713–720 (1988)
21. Hess-Nielsen, N., Wickerhauser, M.: Wavelets and time frequency analysis. Proc. IEEE, Digital Object Identifier 84 (1996)
22. Zhong, H., Tang, J., Zhang, S., Chen, M.: An Improved Quality-Guided Phase-Unwrapping Algorithm Based on Priority Queue. IEEE Geosci. Remote Sensing Letters 8(2), 364–368 (2011)
23. Kuan, D., Sawchuk, A., Strand, T., Chavel, P.: Adaptive restoration of images with speckle. IEEE Trans. Acoustics, Speech and Signal Processing 35(3), 373–383 (1987)
24. Next ESA, All rights reserved (2013), http://nest.array.ca/
25. Chen, C.W., Zebker, H.A.: Phase Unwrapping for Large SAR Interferograms: Statistical Segmentation and Generalized Network Models. IEEE Trans. Geosci. Remote Sensing 40(8), 1709–1719 (2002)

High Precision Restoration Method for Non-uniformly Warped Images

Kalyan Kumar Halder, Murat Tahtali, and Sreenatha G. Anavatti

School of Engineering and Information Technology
The University of New South Wales
Canberra, ACT 2600, Australia
k.halder@student.unsw.edu.au,
{m.tahtali,a.sreenatha}@adfa.edu.au

Abstract. This paper proposes a high accuracy image restoration technique to restore a quality image from the atmospheric turbulence degraded video sequence of a static scenery. This approach contains two major steps. In the first step, we employ a coarse-to-fine optical flow estimation technique to register all the frames of the video to a reference frame and determine the shift maps. In the second step, we use an iterative First Register Then Average And Subtract (iFRTAAS) method to correct the geometric distortions of the reference frame. We present a performance comparison between our proposed method and existing statistical method in terms of restoration accuracy. Simulation experiments show that our proposed method provides higher accuracy with substantial gain in processing time.

Keywords: Atmospheric turbulence, image registration, image restoration, and optical flow.

1 Introduction

For long-range imaging systems, the prevailing effects of atmospheric turbulence comprise random geometric distortions as well as non-uniform image blurring [1–3]. The image degradation effects arise from random inhomogeneities in the temperature distribution of the atmosphere, causing variations of refractive index along the optical transmission path which are more prominent near to the ground [3–5]. These cause significant effects in the fields of surveillance and astronomy where the original image is extremely important [6, 7]. Over the last few decades, numerous image processing techniques have been proposed for the image deconvolution and the compensation of blurring effects. A few methods have also been proposed to correct the geometric distortions.

Huebner and Greco [3] present a performance comparison of four blind deconvolution algorithms that they applied to the restoration of turbulence degraded images. The methods are: linear Inverse Wiener Filter (IWF), non-linear Lucy-Richardson Deconvolution (LRD), Iterative Blind Deconvolution (IBD), and deconvolution using Principal Component Analysis (PCA). Among these methods,

J. Blanc-Talon et al. (Eds.): ACIVS 2013, LNCS 8192, pp. 60–67, 2013.

PCA based blind deconvolution provides better results, especially shorter processing time and more robustness to noise [4]. In [6], the authors propose a blur identification and image restoration method by minimizing the Second-Order Central Moment (SOCM) of images. A lucky imaging system is proposed in [7] to restore turbulence degraded astronomical images. In [8], an iterative maximum-likelihood-estimation algorithm is proposed for reconstruction of superresolved images. Further modification is needed for the above methods in order to improve compensation for geometric distortions.

Image registration is an important part of image restoration, which estimates the geometric distortions using the distorted frames. Real-time implementation of restoration techniques needs a faster and accurate image registration technique. There are many image registration algorithms such as differential elastic image registration, B-spline based non-rigid image registration, gradient based optical flow and cross-correlation. The FRTAAS method in [1, 2] is proposed for the restoration of non-uniformly warped images based on differential elastic registration. FRTAAS provides somewhat accurate and stable results, although it is computationally very intensive, in the order of hours to process the shift maps. It also has the limitation of assuming the average wander of each pixel of a static scenery over a long enough period of time to be zero. The non-rigid image registration based image restoration also provides good results, but it still needs several minutes for a single registration [5] compared to elastic registration on the same machine. Mao and Gilles [9] propose a novel approach for image restoration based on a variational model solved by Bregman Iterations and operator splitting method. A gradient technique for optical flow estimation is described in [10]. In [11], a statistical algorithm is proposed for geometric corrections of atmospheric turbulence degraded sequences. A variant of FRTAAS (FRTAASv) image restoration method based on Minimum Sum of Squared Differences (MSSD) image registration is implemented in [12], but the limitation of using MSSD algorithm is the loss of sub-pixel accuracy in pixel registration. A high accuracy coarse-to-fine optical flow estimation technique is proposed in [13]. This technique is further modified by Liu in [14]. The author uses Iterative Reweighted Least Square (IRLS) instead of Euler-Lagrange method to make the method simpler and easier to understand.

In this paper, we propose a modified FRTAAS method namely iFRTAAS to restore a geometrically accurate image from videos distorted by atmospheric turbulence. We use the coarse-to-fine flow estimation algorithm for image registration to take advantage of it's speed and robustness. The performance of the proposed method is compared against an earlier statistical method by applying them to synthetically warped video sequences.

2   Proposed Image Restoration Method

The wander of a given pixel of a static scenery with respect to it's true position over a certain period of time is shown in Fig. 1. The FRTAAS method assumes that the average wander of each pixel is zero and the average wander of a pixel

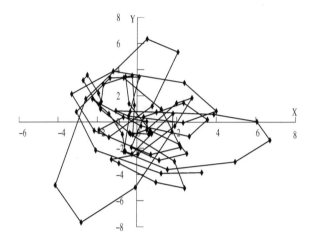

Fig. 1. Wander of a given pixel with respect to it's true position

with respect to any fixed point yields the true position. This assumption is true for a set of points in Euclidean space but not exactly applicable for a set of turbulence degraded images. Most importantly, the determination of the centroid of each pixel depends on the choice of a good reference point. In the case of a sequence of images, one can choose one of them at random as the reference image. The reference image may lack certain features of the original image due to the effects of turbulence, which will also be present in it's restored version [15, 16]. The iFRTAAS method is introduced for the two reasons: (i) update the centroid of each pixel iteratively to take it more closer to the true value, and (ii) partially compensate for lack of features in the restored frame since the reference frame is changed in each iteration.

Let an atmospheric turbulence degraded video consists of N warped frames. We consider the first frame as the initial reference frame. The complete procedure is described in steps below:

Step 1: Employ a pixel registration technique [14] to determine the pixel shift maps $x_s(x, y, t)$ and $y_s(x, y, t)$ of all the frames with respect to the reference frame (Fig. 2).

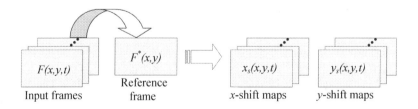

Fig. 2. Image registration against the reference frame

Step 2: Calculate the centroid shift maps C_x and C_y by

$$C_x(x, y) = \frac{1}{N} \sum_{t=1}^{N} x_s(x, y, t)$$

$$C_y(x, y) = \frac{1}{N} \sum_{t=1}^{N} y_s(x, y, t)$$

(1)

Step 3: Calculate the inverse of the centroid shift maps as

$$C_x^{-1}(x, y) = -C_x\big(x - C_x(x, y, t), y - C_y(x, y, t)\big)$$
$$C_y^{-1}(x, y) = -C_y\big(x - C_x(x, y, t), y - C_y(x, y, t)\big)$$

(2)

Step 4: Dewarp the reference frame using (3).

$$F^*(x, y) = F\big(x + C_x^{-1}(x, y), y + C_y^{-1}(x, y)\big)$$

(3)

Step 5: Select the dewarped frame $F^*(x, y)$ as reference frame for next iteration and repeat steps 1-4 until convergence is achieved.

3 Simulation Experiments

The proposed method is implemented in MATLAB along with the heavy processing in C/C++ MEX code and tested on an Intel Core i7-2600 CPU 3.40GHz machine with 8GB RAM. In order to evaluate the performance of the two methods, two different video sequences of 80 warped frames are generated using the Lena (512×512 pixels) and Theophilus (512×512 pixels) test frames. The simulated warp is generated by creating a 13×13 mesh of control points over the test frames. The control points are given a temporally smooth random walk around their unwarped location on the grid, with zero mean. Each control point's random walk is generated by low-pass filtering a random sequence at 5Hz with maximum amplitude of 5 pixels at 25fps.

The simulation results of the proposed method are compared with those of the statistical method proposed in [11]. It takes about 0.96s for our proposed method for the pixel registration and dewarping of a pair of 512×512 frames. It requires only 3-4 iterations to achieve convergence. The time required for the statistical method to process a single frame is about 1.58s, 1.65 times higher than our proposed method. Fig. 3(a) and (b) show the original Lena frame and the first warped frame, respectively. The restored versions of the Lena frame using the statistical and proposed methods are shown in Fig. 3(c) and (d), respectively. Fig. 3(e) and (f) show the difference between original and restored frames for the two methods. In a similar way, Fig. 4(a) and (b) show the original Theophilus frame and the first warped frame, respectively. The restored Theophilus frames using the statistical method and proposed method are shown in Fig. 4(c) and (d). Difference images for the two methods are also shown in Fig. 4(e) and (f). The loss of detail and "watercolor effect" in the restored images by the statistical

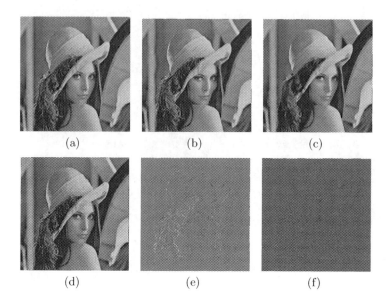

Fig. 3. (a) original Lena frame, (b) first warped frame, (c) restored frame using statistical method, (d) restored frame using proposed method, (e) intensity difference between (a) and (c), (f) intensity difference between (a) and (d)

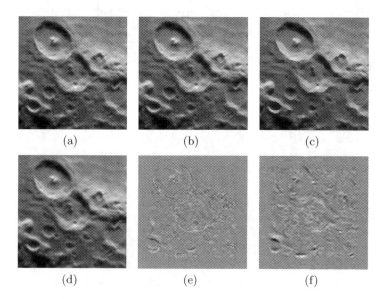

Fig. 4. (a) original Theophilus frame, (b) first warped frame, (c) restored frame using statistical method, (d) restored frame using proposed method, (e) intensity difference between (a) and (c), (f) intensity difference between (a) and (d)

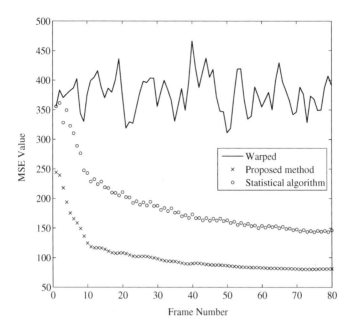

Fig. 5. MSE plot of warped and restored frames using statistical and proposed methods with respect to the original Lena image

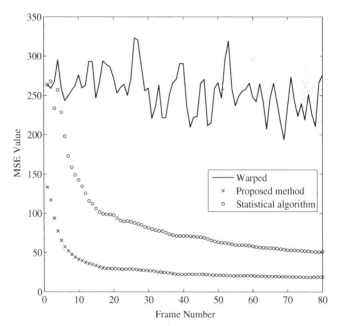

Fig. 6. MSE plot of warped and restored frames using statistical and proposed methods with respect to the original Theophilus image

method is evident from simple visual comparison. The difference images for the proposed method are also darker than those using statistical method, indicating lower residuals.

The intensity Mean Squared Error (MSE) of the warped frames and the reference frames restored again after each new frame are calculated with respect to the original images. Fig. 5 shows a frame by frame MSE comparison for the Lena video sequence. The plots get better as the centroids settle down. The MSE values of the restored frames are 146.41 and 81.01 for the statistical method and the proposed method, respectively. Fig. 6 shows a similar comparison for the Theophilus video sequence and the MSE values are 51.14 and 18.80, respectively. From a purely MSE perspective, the proposed method provides about 40-60% improvement on the residuals of the restored frames.

4   Conclusion

We successfully implemented our proposed iFRTAAS image restoration method using a coarse-to-fine optical flow estimation technique to be able to compensate for geometric distortions. We also compared the results to another algorithm proposed to correct non-uniformly warped sequences. It was demonstrated that using our proposed iFRTAAS method, high accuracy restoration of the reference frame is possible with considerable computational time reductions. Further work will involve the consideration of other atmospheric effects such as blurring and the implementation of the method on GPUs (Graphical Processing Units) for near real-time operation.

References

[1] Tahtali, M., Fraser, D., Lambert, A.J.: Restoration of non-uniformly warped images using a typical frame as prototype. In: Proc. TENCON, pp. 1–6 (2005)
[2] Tahtali, M., Lambert, A.J., Fraser, D.: Restoration of nonuniformly warped images using accurate frame by frame shiftmap accumulation. In: Proc. SPIE, vol. 6316 (2006)
[3] Huebner, C.S., Greco, M.: Blind deconvolution algorithms for the restoration of atmospherically degraded imagery: a comparative analysis. In: Proc. SPIE, vol. 7108 (2008)
[4] Li, D., Mersereau, R.M., Simske, S.: Atmospheric turbulence-degraded image restoration using principal components analysis. IEEE Geoscience and Remote Sensing Letters 4(3), 340–344 (2007)
[5] Zhu, X., Milanfar, P.: Image reconstruction from videos distorted by atmospheric turbulence. In: Proc. SPIE, vol. 7543 (2010)
[6] Yan, L., Jin, M., Fang, H., Liu, H., Zhang, T.: Atmospheric-turbulence-degraded astronomical image restoration by minimizing second-order central moment. IEEE Geoscience and Remote Sensing Letters 9(4), 672–676 (2012)
[7] Zhang, S., Wu, Y., Zhao, J., Wang, J.: Astronomical image restoration through atmosphere turbulence by lucky imaging. In: Proc. SPIE, vol. 8009 (2011)
[8] Gerwe, D.R., Plonus, M.A.: Superresolved image reconstruction of images taken through the turbulent atmosphere. J. Opt. Soc. Am. A. 15(10), 2620–2628 (1998)

[9] Mao, Y., Gilles, J.: Non rigid geometric distortions correction-application to atmospheric turbulence stabilization. Inverse Problems and Imaging 6(3), 531–546 (2012)

[10] Clyde, D., Scott-Fleming, I., Fraser, D., Lambert, A.: Application of optical flow techniques in the restoration of non-uniformly warped images. In: Proc. DICTA, pp. 195–200 (2002)

[11] Abdoola, R., Wyk, B., Monacelli, E.: A simple statistical algorithm for the correction of atmospheric turbulence degraded sequences. In: Proc. Annual Symposium of the Pattern Recognition Association of South Africa (2010)

[12] Tahtali, M., Lambert, A.J., Fraser, D.: Graphics processing unit restoration of non-uniformly warped images using a typical frame as prototype. In: Proc. SPIE, vol. 7800 (2010)

[13] Brox, T., Bruhn, A., Papenberg, N., Weickert, J.: High accuracy optical flow estimation based on a theory for warping. In: Pajdla, T., Matas, J(G.) (eds.) ECCV 2004. LNCS, vol. 3024, pp. 25–36. Springer, Heidelberg (2004)

[14] Liu, C.: Beyond pixels: exploring new representations and applications for motion analysis. Massachusetts Institute of Technology (2009)

[15] Pennec, X.: Probabilities and statistics on riemannian manifolds: a geometric approach. Research Report 5093, INRIA (2004)

[16] Micheli, M., Lou, Y., Soatto, S., Bertozzi, A.L.: A linear systems approach to imaging through turbulence. Journal of Mathematical Imaging and Vision, 1–17 (2013)

Noise Robustness Analysis of Point Cloud Descriptors

Yasir Salih[1,2], Aamir Saeed Malik[1], Nicolas Walter[1], Désiré Sidibé[2],
Naufal Saad[1], and Fabrice Meriaudeau[2]

[1] Centre for Intelligent Signal & Imaging Research,
UniversitiTeknologi PETRONAS, 31750 Tronoh, Malaysia
[2] Université de Bourgogne - Le2i UMR CNRS 6306, 71200 Le Creusot, France

Abstract. In this paper, we investigate the effect of noise on 3D point cloud descriptors. Various types of point cloud descriptors have been introduced in the recent years due to advances in computing power, which makes processing point cloud data more feasible. Most of these descriptors describe the orientation difference between pairs of 3D points in the object and represent these differences in a histogram. Earlier studies dealt with the performances of different point cloud descriptors; however, no study has ever discussed the effect of noise on the descriptors performances. This paper presents a comparison of performance for nine different local and global descriptors amidst 10 varying levels of Gaussian and impulse noises added to the point cloud data. The study showed that 3D descriptors are more sensitive to Gaussian noise compared to impulse noise. Surface normal based descriptors are sensitive to Gaussian noise but robust to impulse noise. While descriptors which are based on point's accumulation in a spherical grid are more robust to Gaussian noise but sensitive to impulse noise. Among global descriptors, view point features histogram (VFH) descriptor gives good compromise between accuracy, stability and computational complexity against both Gaussian and impulse noises. SHOT (signature of histogram of orientations) descriptor is the best among the local descriptors and it has good performance for both Gaussian and impulse noises.

Keywords: 3D descriptors, features histogram, noise robustness, point cloud library.

1   Introduction

Advances in 3D generation devices are resulting in the popularity of 3D images and many fields have ventured the use of 3D sensors. Computer vision applications such as object recognition, detection and content based retrieval are already established topics for 2D images processing. However, due to the huge amount of information in 3D data, 3D computer vision applications have only been explored in the recent years. This is mostly due to the advances in computing power and storage devices [1]. Furthermore, providing a unique description to the point cloud data is an important step for many 3D applications. 3D description algorithm tends to focus more on the

J. Blanc-Talon et al. (Eds.): ACIVS 2013, LNCS 8192, pp. 68–79, 2013.

structure and the shape of the point cloud unlike the 2D descriptor which only describes the appearance and texture of the points [2].

Different 3D surface detection and description algorithms have been proposed in the literature. 3D keypoints detection methods focus on extracting distinct points on the surface that can be uniquely identified. The point cloud library (PCL) includes many types of 3D descriptors among others point cloud data processing and presentation tools [2]. For recognition and matching applications, surface descriptors provide a very useful and unique signature for a given 3D point cloud. Surface detector and descriptors are always coupled together so that the detectors identify the salient regions (points) within the point cloud while the descriptors assign a unique signature to it. In the recent years, various types of 3D descriptors have been presented to the community, thanks to the availability of required computing power which was not viable in the past [2].

This paper presents a new study for evaluating the robustness of famous surface descriptors in the presence of noise. It is widely known that 3D sensors suffer from noise which is very challenging and hard to remove specially in the depth direction. Despite the studies conducted on the performances of 3D descriptors, no study was presented on evaluating their robustness to various noise conditions. As noise is a common problem in real applications, it was difficult to judge which method will produce the best results. Indeed, previous comparisons have focused on repeatability and accuracy of detected keypoints in the 3D data [2] regardless of the noise or degradation that the image is subjected to. Therefore, the performance results are quite misleading since some good descriptors may fail dramatically in the presence of noise.

Thus, an extensive evaluation of noise robustness of 3D descriptors is presented in this paper. The remaining of the paper is organized as follows: Section 2 briefly presents nine 3D descriptors commonly used in the literature and available in the PCL library. Section 3 explains the evaluation methodology for these descriptors as well as the type of data and noise being used in the studies. Section 4 summarizes the evaluation results and discusses the robustness of the operators to varying level of noise. Finally, Section 5 concludes this paper with main findings about the performances of surface descriptors in the presence of noise and gives recommendations to achieve good performances with the discussed descriptors.

2   Related Works

This section covers previous research on 3D descriptors analysis presented in the literature with focus on the evaluation metrics used in each study. In addition, this section also covers studies about noise modeling for 3D sensors with emphasis on the Kinect sensor because it is commonly used in many vision applications.

2.1   Evaluation of 3D Descriptors

Tombari et al. [3] presented some performance comparison when they introduced SHOT descriptor including noise robustness. However, they only compared SHOT against what was widely available at that time which was spin images (SI), 3D shape context (3DSC) and expectation maximization descriptors. Sukno et al. [4] presented a comparative study of different 3D descriptors for recognizing craniofacial landmarks. The objective of their study was to investigate the accuracy and the usable range of these descriptors on per-landmark bases. They had investigated 26 landmarks using 6 descriptors (SHOT, SI, 3DSC, USC, PFH, and FPFH). They found that the average accuracy among all experiments can give misleading results as it was heavily influenced by the extrema values. For example, they found that 3DSC has the best average accuracy but it is only best for 5 out of 26 landmarks while SHOT and SI provide better results for more than 8 landmarks. Aldoma et al. [2] presented an extensive evaluation of different local and global 3D descriptors available in the PCL library. However their evaluation focused mainly on the implementation of these descriptors in PCL library and they showed a complete implementation pipeline for both local and global descriptors. These descriptors were compared in terms of accuracy and descriptor size without considering the effect of noise.

2.2   3D Sensor Noise Modeling

3D data can suffer from various types of noise depending on the type of sensor used. General laser rangefinders have better accuracy compared to ultrasound as they suffer less attenuation (and scattering) from the transmission medium [5]. Although both sensors show high errors when scanning a reflective or transparent object such as a glass wall [6].This paper focuses on Kinect sensor because it is widely used in robotics and computer vision applications. In addition it is handy, easy to use and comes at low price compared to other type of 3D sensors [7]. Khoshelham and Elberink [8] conducted noise analysis for Kinect sensor and recommended its use for short distances (up to 3m) as the quality of measurement degrades at larger distances due to noise. Cai et al. [9] presented a detailed modeling of Kinect sensor noise and they concluded that the sensor's SNR ratio decreases quadratically with the depth. Similar findings have been reported by Zhang and Zhang [10] in their study for calibrating depth and RGB sensors.

Sun et al. [5] worked on characterizing noise of 3D scanner (Konica Minolta Vivid 910), they concluded that the noise present in this scanner is neither Gaussian nor have independent distribution. In addition, they managed to synthesize the noise in this scanner using Gaussian like distribution based on Fourier spectrum of the 3D data. Camplani and Salagado [11] have shown that noise present in Kinect data have Gaussian distribution and can be considered as white noise. Nguyen et al. [12] modeled the lateral and axial noise distribution of Kinect sensor using Gaussian probability function. They have found that lateral noise increases linearly with distance while the axial noise increases quadratically.

3   Point Cloud Descriptors

This section briefly reviews some of the well-known 3D descriptors used in the computer vision/graphics societies. These descriptors can be categorized into two

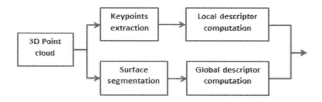

Fig. 1. Global vs. local point cloud descriptors

main groups; global descriptors and local descriptors. Global descriptors describe the global geometry of all points in the point cloud. This is achieved by firstly segmenting the image into coherent regions and then giving a unique descriptor to each segment. On the other hand, local descriptors describe the local neighborhood of selected points in the point cloud known as keypoints.

Fig. 1 illustrates the differences between local and global descriptors [4]. The common aspect among all these descriptors is that they are based on histograms of deviations. Table 1 shows a quick summary about the properties of four global descriptors used in this study.

3.1   Global 3D Descriptors

Global descriptors describe the geometry of subsets of 3D points in the cloud. Global descriptors are more complex than local descriptors and they are used for object recognition and shape retrieval applications. Table 1 summarizes the properties of the following four global point cloud descriptors:

1. Point Feature Histograms (PFH): This descriptor captures the orientation difference between the query point and each of its neighbors [13].
2. Viewpoint Feature Histogram (VFH): This is a modified version of the PFH descriptor that includes the global view direction of the point cloud [2].
3. Clustered View-point Feature Histogram (CVFH): Firstly the object is segmented into smaller regions then computing the VFH descriptor for each segment [14].
4. Ensemble Shape Functions (ESF): It is a collection of 10 shape functions that describe the structure of the point cloud [15].

Table 1. Proproties of Globlal Descriptors

Descriptor	VFH	PFH	CVFH	ESF
Descriptor size	308	125	308/segment	640
Using normal	Yes	Yes	Yes	Yes
Processing time	Moderate	High	Very high	Moderate

3.2   Local 3D Descriptors

Local descriptors describe the local neighborhood around a point in a 3D point cloud. These descriptors are mostly used for surface registration application. Table 2 summarizes the properties of the five local point cloud descriptors that follow:

1. Fast Point Feature Histograms (FPFH): This is a modified version of the PFH by reducing the number of neighbors used for computing orientation differences [2].
2. 3D Shape Context (3DSC): This descriptor considers a sphere superimposed on the query point and divides it into smaller segments. At each segment, the number of points in it is computed and weighted inversely by the segment density [3].
3. Unique Shape Context (USC): USC is a modified version of 3DSC that uses only one unique reference frame for the spherical grid [3].
4. Signature of Histogram of Orientations (SHOT): This is similar to 3DSC but instead of counting the number of points in each segment it computes the relative orientation angle between each point and the query point [2].
5. Spin images (SI): This descriptor encodes the distance between pair of points and the distance between the second point projected on the normal of the query point using a 153 bin histogram [2].
6. Point Feature Histogram (PFH): PFH can be used as local descriptor as well where the search radius is defined to cover the neighborhood of the keypoint only.

Table 2. Proproties of LocalDescriptors

Descriptor	FPFH	SHOT	SI	3DSC	USC	PFH
Descriptor size	33	352	153	125	125	125
Using surface normal	Yes	Yes	Yes	No	No	Yes
Computational complexity	Low	Moderate	Low	Very high	High	High

4   Evaluation Methodology

Noise analysis is highly important for selecting good 3D descriptors for noise sensitive applications. This section discusses and justifies the choice of noise type, followed by a discussion on the data collection process and how the experiments have been conducted. Finally, experimental results are presented for both local and global descriptors and an overall evaluation is presented.

4.1   Noise Modeling

3D sensors like any other electronic device can suffer from two types of noise; thermal noise and shot (impulse noise). Shot noise appears as random spikes in the point due to sensor defects and it is much easier to remove with smoothing methods [8]. In the case of Kinect device, shot noise is less dominant and it could be removed within the device itself. Thermal noise is due to electronics carrier and it is characterized by a Gaussian distribution of zero means and suitable standard deviation [11-12]. It is important to note that errors in the Kinect (triangulation based sensor) depend on the distance between the sensor and the object as well as noise. Thus, in order to focus the attention on the Kinect noise, all datasets used in this study are taken from the same distance from the sensor in order to normalize the distance effect.

Fig. 2 shows point cloud data corrupted with Gaussian noise at two different variances and one sample of impulse noise. It is clear that Gaussian noise degrade the point cloud integrity more than the impulse noise because it affects the whole point cloud. Impulse noise appears at random location but with large magnitude (noisy points appear to have extreme depth values).

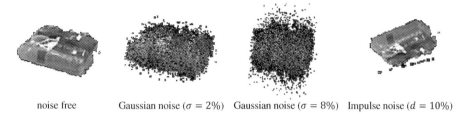

noise free   Gaussian noise ($\sigma = 2\%$)   Gaussian noise ($\sigma = 8\%$)   Impulse noise ($d = 10\%$)

Fig. 2. Samples of point cloud data corrupted with Gaussian and impulse noise

Table 3 illustrates examples of histograms for three descriptors (FPFH, SHOT and VFH) before and after adding the noise to point cloud. Two types of noise have been considered; Gaussian with variance of 10% and impulse noise with density of 10%. Since the Gaussian noise affects the whole image, most descriptors are expected to perform poorly. In contrast impulse noise affects parts of the image only and this makes descriptors more robust to this type of noise and it could be eliminated by a simple smoothing operation. FPFH exhibits significant change with Gaussian noise but remain stable for impulse noise. SHOT descriptor exhibits large change due to Gaussian noise and the locations of the peaks changes while it is stable for the impulse noise. VFH descriptor exhibits small changes due to Gaussian noise and no noticeable change for the impulse noise.

Table 3. Sample for 3D Descriptors with and without Noise

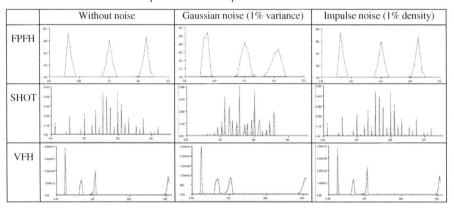

4.2   Data Collection

For comprehensive evaluation of 3D descriptors in the presence of noise we use two dataset. The first one is public dataset (RGB-D dataset) from the Washington

| Our RGB-D dataset | RGB-D dataset |

Fig. 3. Sample of Kinect acquired object used in the experiment with object acquired at our laboratory and object from Washington University (RGB-D dataset) available on internet [16]

University [16]. This contains around 300 different objects at variable view angles. All the data have been acquired at a distance of 1m from the sensor. The second dataset has been collected at our laboratory which contains 50 objects scanned using Kinect sensor at a distance of 1m from the sensor as well.

4.3   Evaluating Local Descriptors

The procedure for assessing the local descriptors (SHOT, 3DSC, USC, FPFH, PFH and SI) starts by extracting keypoints from the noise free data. Since local descriptors describe the neighborhood of a point, the same points should be maintained in the query and training dataset. In this experiment, 14000 3D SIFT keypoints have been extracted only for the data without noise and then the descriptor of this point is computed in the training and query datasets. The training descriptor is the descriptor computed for all samples in the dataset before adding noise. In the query stage, 10 levels of Gaussian and impulse noises were added to the point cloud data. For each noise type and level, the local descriptor is computed for each of the previously extracted keypoints. The noise variance or density for Gaussian and impulse noise respectively has been varied from 0% (no noise) to 10%. Each query descriptor is matched against all the training dataset using L1-norm and the matching score is computed using Equation (1). This matching score was introduced because it gives a rating of how far is the best match from the ground truth. The constant epsilon has been added to avoid undefined numbers in the case of perfect match. For fairness to all descriptors, the support size of computing surface normal was fixed at 3cm and the support size for computing the descriptor was fixed at 5cm.

$$F = \frac{bestMatchDistance + \epsilon}{trueMatchDistance + \epsilon} \tag{1}$$

Fig. 4 shows Gaussian noise response graph (average and standard deviation) for six local descriptors computed for RGB-D dataset (300 objects). Based on average matching rate, USC and 3DSC descriptor scored the best performance as they maintained more than 80% matching rate even with the maximum Gaussian noise level and their standard deviation is less than the one recorded for other descriptors.

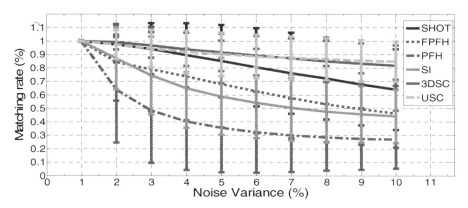

Fig. 4. Performance of local descriptors with Gaussian noise

SHOT descriptor followed next in performance where it scores above 70% matching at the highest noise level. However, it is standard deviation is very large 20%. This is due to the fact that SHOT unlike USC encodes the orientations of the points instead of their numbers in each spherical grid. 3D point orientation is more susceptible to Gaussian noise because it is derived from surface normal. FPFH and SI have poor matching rate as both rely on surface normal for their computations. In addition, both FPFH and SI have very high standard deviation due to noise. This indicates that they are not stable under Gaussian noise effect. PFH descriptor shows very poor performance because it is computed in a local sense as this descriptor is usually used as global descriptor with a larger neighborhood.

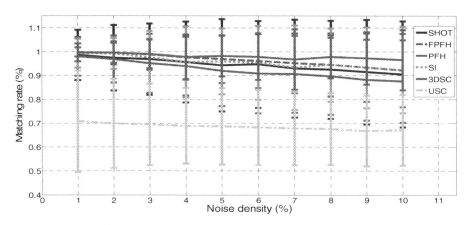

Fig. 5. Performance of local descriptors with impulse noise

Fig. 5 shows local descriptors response to impulse noise. 3DSC descriptor showed excellent performance with 95% matching rate at the maximum noise level however the result's standard deviation increases with noise. This excellent performance could be because 3DSC uses multiple orientations of the principal direction over the spherical grid. USC showed very poor results because it uses only one unique

principal direction over the grid. USC scored only 70% accuracy for the minimum
noise level and it has standard deviation more than 20%. This indicates USC does not
only give poor results with impulse noise but it is also not stable under this noise
condition. Normal based descriptors (SI, PFH, FPFH and SHOT) showed good
matching rate which is around 90% at the maximum noise level and their standard
deviation increase with noise density to up to 20% in the case of SHOT descriptor
whereas the standard deviation of other descriptors remain below this value.

4.4   Evaluating Global Descriptors

In global point cloud descriptors, the whole object was treated as one segment for
computing the descriptor. Initially, a database of descriptors has been created for all
point cloud objects used (training dataset). In the query stage, each of the point cloud
objects was corrupted with noise similar to the method for local descriptors. Four
global descriptors have been investigated (VFH, PFH, CVFH and ESF). Fig. 6 shows
matching rate of global descriptors when Gaussian noise was introduced. The figure
displays both the average matching rate for 300 objects (RGB-D dataset) and the
standard deviation of the results as a measure for matching stability. Generally,
CVFH and VFH have better performance than PFH and ESF. However the results
exhibit large variations between different samples. At low noise levels VFH has better
matching rate than CVFH but when the noise level is increased CVFH is better. This
is because CVFH was computed for small segments while VFH was computed for the
whole object thus it includes more noise. PFH descriptor has low performance than
VFH and CVFH and at 10% noise variance it goes down to 50% matching rate. In
addition, the standard deviation recorded for PFH is much higher the VFH and
CVFH. ESF has similar performance as PFH. However ESF reflects fewer changes
due to noise compared to PFH. Poor performance of ESF is because this descriptor
has much lower accuracy than other global descriptors even without introducing
noise [2]. In addition to that the shape functions that build this descriptor are sensitive
to noise.

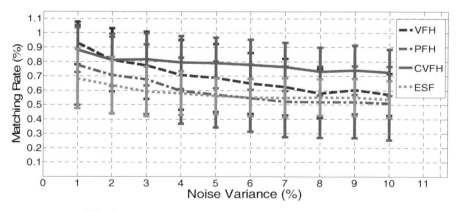

Fig. 6. Performance of global descriptors with Gaussian noise

Fig. 7 shows global descriptors response to impulse noise. Unlike the Gaussian noise normal based descriptors show better response both in average matching rate and the results consistency. PFH leads the global descriptors with overall performance above 90% matching rate even at the maximum noise level and the standard deviation is around 10%. VFH comes next with matching rate above 80% at the maximum noise level and constant standard deviation which is more than 10%. CVFH showed acceptable matching rate for impulse noise which goes down to 70% at the maximum noise level and the standard deviation is slightly increasing with noise. VFH and CVFH have opposite response to both Gaussian and impulse noises because the effect of Gaussian noise is much larger on VFH than CVFH whereas for impulse noise VFH performs better than CVFH. Gaussian noise affects the normal estimation step of both descriptors and since VFH is computed for the whole object it is degraded more than CVFH. Whereas the impulse noise affects the segmentation step of the CVFH descriptor which results different segments at different noise levels which reduces the matching rate. ESF showed poor behavior when impulse noise was introduced with almost a constant matching rate of about 70% for all noise levels and the results standard deviation is below 10% for all levels. This is because ESF does not use normal in it computations and thus impulse ripples are not smoothed and they directly affect the shape functions that build this descriptor.

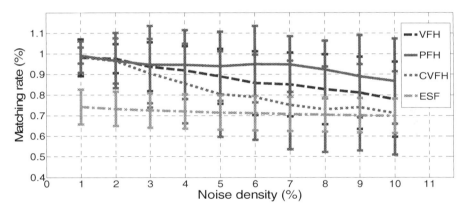

Fig. 7. Performance of global descriptors with impulse noise

4.5   Results Analysis

All the results shown were conducted for the RGB-D dataset because it is larger in size (300 objects). Nevertheless, these results are same as the one obtained from our local dataset (50 objects) except that for our local dataset a background removal step is applied on the point cloud data before computing the descriptors. The previous set of experiments proved that 3D descriptors (both local and global) have very different responses for Gaussian and impulse noises. In general, most of 3D descriptors are more robust to impulse noise than Gaussian noise. This is because impulse noise affects only parts of the object while the Gaussian noise affects the whole object. Although the noise levels tested are very high, some descriptors showed good matching accuracy and consistent behavior for the tested objects.

Descriptors who are based on surface normal (PFH, FPFH, VFH, CVFH, SI and SHOT) are highly affected by Gaussian noise because the surface changes due to noise and the normal component for each point will change as well which lead to a different descriptor been computed. On the other hand the same types of descriptors are very robust to impulse noise because the normal computation step smooth the impulse noise ripples from the surface. 3D descriptors which are based on points count in a spherical grid around the query point (3DSC, USC and to some extent SHOT) are more robust to Gaussian noise. This is because the Gaussian noise is additive and normally with lower magnitude than the point itself. Thus the point will not move from its spherical grid and it will contribute to the same bin in the descriptor despite the noise. While in the case of impulse noise the magnitude of change due to noise is high and the point will be moved from its spherical grid. As a result, the descriptor changes and it produces poor matching results. SHOT descriptor showed a mixed behavior between normal based descriptors and points count based descriptors because it divides the point cloud in spherical grids but instead of encoding the number of points it encodes their orientation differences similar to normal based descriptors. 3DSC descriptor showed excellent results for both impulse and Gaussian noises because it computes the same descriptor for multiple reference orientations which creates multiple descriptors for the same keypoint at different rotations and translations from the query point. This makes the descriptor always able to find the best match. However this comes at a huge computational burden.

5   Conclusion

This paper evaluated the robustness of point cloud descriptors for Gaussian and impulse noises. The study measured the average matching rate and the results standard deviation for six local descriptors and four global descriptors at various noise levels. Both local and global descriptors behave differently to Gaussian and impulse noises. For Gaussian noise, normal based descriptors have reduced performance. This is because the Gaussian noise affects the normal of the 3D points which leads to a different descriptor being computed and thus low matching rate. The same descriptors are very robust to impulse noise because the normal computation step removes impulse ripples from the point cloud. 3DSC descriptor showed excellent robustness for both impulse and Gaussian noises because it creates multiple copies of the same descriptor at different orientations and translations. USC descriptor is similar to 3DSC but rather computed for one orientation showed good matching rate for Gaussian noise. However, it has very poor results for impulse noise. ESF descriptor has poor performance for both Gaussian and impulse noises. In term of results stability most descriptors showed small increase in standard deviation with noise. PFH and SI are not stable with Gaussian noise while USC is not stable with impulse noise.

As a conclusion, 3DSC descriptor showed the best performance among the local descriptors but it has very high computational complexity. SHOT descriptor has good matching rate for both Gaussian and impulse noises and it has moderate computational complexity. Among the global descriptors, VFH descriptor showed acceptable performance for both Gaussian and impulse noises and it has moderate computational complexity compared to PFH and CVFH.

References

1. Lakehal, A., El Beqqali, O.: 3D shape retrieval using characteristics level images. In: Proceedings of International Conference on Multimedia Computing and Systems, pp. 302–306 (May 2012)
2. Aldoma, A., Marton, Z.-C., Tombari, F., Wohlkinger, W., Potthast, C., Zeisl, B., Rusu, R.B., Gedikli, S., Vincze, M.: Point cloud library: three-dimensional object recognition and 6 DoF pose estimation. IEEE Robotics & Automation Magazine, 80–91 (September 2012)
3. Tombari, F., Salti, S., Di Stefano, L.: Unique Signatures of Histograms for Local Surface Description. In: Daniilidis, K., Maragos, P., Paragios, N. (eds.) ECCV 2010, Part III. LNCS, vol. 6313, pp. 356–369. Springer, Heidelberg (2010)
4. Sukno, F.M., Waddington, J.L., Whelan, P.F.: Comparing 3D Descriptors for Local Search of Craniofacial Landmarks. In: Bebis, G., et al. (eds.) ISVC 2012, Part II. LNCS, vol. 7432, pp. 92–103. Springer, Heidelberg (2012)
5. Sun, X., Rosin, P.L., Martin, R.R., Langbein, F.C.: Noise in 3D laser range scanner data. In: Proceedings of IEEE International Conference on Shape Modeling and Applications, pp. 37–45 (2008)
6. Mériaudeau, F., Rantoson, R., Fofi, D., Stolz, C.: Review and comparison of Non-Conventional Imaging Systems for 3D Digitization of transparent objects. Journal of Electronic Imaging 21(2), 021105 (2012)
7. Khoshelham, K.: Accuracy analysis of kinect depth data. In: Proceedings of ISPRS Workshop Laser Scanning, pp. 1–6 (2011)
8. Khoshelham, K., Elberink, S.O.: Accuracy and resolution of Kinect depth data for indoor mapping applications. Sensors 12(2), 1437–1454 (2012)
9. Cai, Q., Gallup, D., Zhang, C., Zhang, Z.: 3D deformable face tracking with a commodity depth camera. In: Daniilidis, K., Maragos, P., Paragios, N. (eds.) ECCV 2010, Part III. LNCS, vol. 6313, pp. 229–242. Springer, Heidelberg (2010)
10. Zhang, C., Zhang, Z.: Calibration between depth and color sensors for commodity depth cameras. In: Proceedings of IEEE International Conference on Multimedia and Expo, pp. 1–6 (2011)
11. Camplani, M., Salgado, L., Polit, U.: Efficient spatio-temporal hole filling strategy for kinect depth maps. In: Proceedings of SPIE - The International Society for Optical Engineering, vol. 8290, pp. 1–10 (2012)
12. Nguyen, C.V., Izadi, S., Lovell, D.: Modeling Kinect Sensor Noise for Improved 3D Reconstruction and Tracking. In: Proceedings of 2nd International Conference on 3D Imaging, Modeling, Processing, Visualization & Transmission, pp. 524–530 (2012)
13. Rusu, R.B.: Semantic 3D Object Maps for Everyday Manipulation in Human Living Environments. PhD thesis, University of Munich (2010)
14. Aldoma, A., Tombari, F., Rusu, R.B., Vincze, M.: OUR-CVFH – Oriented, Unique and Repeatable Clustered Viewpoint Feature Histogram for Object Recognition and 6DOF Pose Estimation. In: Pinz, A., Pock, T., Bischof, H., Leberl, F. (eds.) DAGM/OAGM 2012. LNCS, vol. 7476, pp. 113–122. Springer, Heidelberg (2012)
15. Wohlkinger, W., Vincze, M.: Ensemble of shape functions for 3D object classification. In: Proceedings of IEEE International Conference on Robotics and Biomimetic, pp. 2987–2992 (2011)
16. Lai, K., Bo, L., Ren, X., Fox, D.: A large-scale hierarchical multi-view RGB-D object dataset. In: Proceedings of IEEE International Conference on Robotic and Automation, Shanghai, China, pp. 1–8 (May 2011)

Restoration of Blurred Binary Images Using Discrete Tomography

Jozsef Nemeth[1] and Peter Balazs[2]

[1] Department of Computer Algorithms and Artificial Intelligence,
University of Szeged, H-6701 Szeged, P.O. Box 652., Hungary
[2] Department of Image Processing and Computer Graphics,
University of Szeged, H-6701 Szeged, P.O. Box 652., Hungary
{nemjozs,pbalazs}@inf.u-szeged.hu

Abstract. Enhancement of degraded images of binary shapes is an important task in many image processing applications, *e.g.* to provide appropriate image quality for optical character recognition. Although many image restoration methods can be found in the literature, most of them are developed for grayscale images. In this paper we propose a novel binary image restoration algorithm. As a first step, it restores the projections of the shape using 1-dimensional deconvolution, then reconstructs the image from these projections using a discrete tomography technique. The method does not require any parameter setting or prior knowledge like an estimation of the signal-to-noise ratio. Numerical experiments on a synthetic dataset show that the proposed algorithm is robust to the level of the noise. The efficiency of the method has also been demonstrated on real out-of-focus alphanumeric images.

1 Introduction

Restoration of distorted images is a key step in many applications. Degradations usually come in many forms such as motion blur, camera misfocus and noise. Misfocus and motion blur can be described by so called blurring functions (filters) while noise usually follows a specific distribution as a good approximation.

There are many methods in the literature for digital image enhancement including simple ones and more sophisticated algorithms. Unsharp masking [12] is one of the widely used tools to enhance image contrast. This basically photographic technique is used since the first half of the 20th century to increase the sharpness of images. Its digital version is used in many image processing softwares. Inverse filtering (or deconvolution) of images is another technique for recovering an image that is blurred by a known low-pass filter. It tries approximately inverting the process that caused an image to be blurred. Researchers have been studying deconvolution methods for several decades, and have approached the problem from different directions.

Basically, deconvolution is very sensitive to noise. This problem can be handled using the Wiener filter [16] which can be used when the point-spread-function (PSF, the filter which was used to blur the image) and the signal-to-noise ratio are known. Blind deconvolution [6] is a technique for recovering an image that was blurred using an unknown PSF. This iterative approach improves the estimation of the PSF and the

J. Blanc-Talon et al. (Eds.): ACIVS 2013, LNCS 8192, pp. 80–90, 2013.

scene in each iteration, thus the convergence depends on how accurate is the initial estimation of the PSF.

The restoration of bi-level images like document images has been addressed by several researchers (see [4], [5], [7] and [14]). Most of these methods trace back the problem to the solution of a system of equations which then solved by iterative optimization. Although these techniques are intensely studied, they are still time-consuming and require good parameter settings which makes the usage of them difficult in practice. The size of the point spread function is usually also limited.

In [13] Sharif *et al.* proposed a discrete tomography based binary deconvolution method. The size of the PSF was restricted to 3×3 and the restoration of the projections was handled as a simple linear inverse problem. Moreover, the method applied the Ryser's algorithm [11] requiring a further time-consuming process to resolve the switching component ambiguities.

In this paper we propose an efficient Tikhonov-regularization [15] based method to reconstruct the projections of the original binary shapes. The main advantage of this approach is that the best value of the regularization parameter can be automatically set using the L-curve method [3]. In the second step the binary shapes are reconstructed using efficient network-flow discrete tomography algorithm [1]. The efficiency of the method has been examined on synthetic as well as on real images. The performance of the proposed method has also been compared to a well-known, widely-used method.

This paper is organized as follows. Section 2 describes the proposed method. In Section 2.1 the deconvolution of the projections is discussed, while in Section 2.2 the discrete tomography reconstruction method is described. Section 3 presents the experimental results.

2   The Method

The goal of image restoration is to reconstruct an original image $f \in \mathbb{R}^{u \times v}$ from its degraded observation $g \in \mathbb{R}^{u \times v}$ which is blurred and noisy. The degradation process (as usually) modelled as the convolution of the original image with the PSF and the addition of some noise:

$$g = h ** f + n, \tag{1}$$

where $h \in \mathbb{R}^{p \times q}$ is the point spread function, $**$ denotes the 2-dimensional convolution operator and $n \in \mathbb{R}^{u \times v}$ is the additive noise. In this paper we assume that the PSF is known. Our goal is to restore binary images, such as $b \in \{0,1\}^{u \times v}$. However, in the case of real images the scaling of the intensity values can be arbitrary. Therefore we introduce the unknown scale factor $s \in \mathbb{R}$ and

$$f = sb \tag{2}$$

in the degradation model Eq. (1).

Let denote by $\breve{f}^{\theta}$ the projection vector of any image f along any directional angle θ, *i.e.* $\breve{f}^{\theta}$ is the discrete approximation of the well-known Radon transform [2] in direction θ (we simply write $\breve{f}$ when the actual direction is not important). Here we take advantage of the following property of the Radon transform: the result of the Radon transform

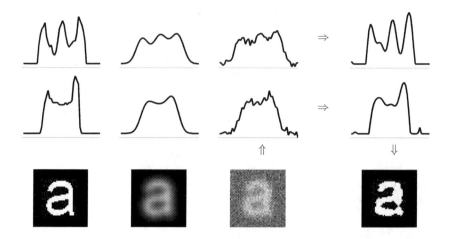

Fig. 1. The degradation model and the basic idea of the proposed method. **First three columns:** the original binary image, the blurred image and the blurry and noisy image and their horizontal (top) and vertical (middle) projections. **Fourth column:** the method restores the projections of the binary image from the projections of the degraded image then reconstructs the binary shape.

of a two dimensional convolution is the same as the one dimensional convolution of the Radon transformed functions, *i.e.* if $g = h * *f$ then $\check{g} = \check{h} * \check{f}$, where $*$ denotes the 1-dimensional convolution operator. A similar relation is true for the addition. Thus the relationship between the projections of the original and the degraded images can be expressed as

$$\check{g} = \check{h} * \check{f} + \check{n}. \tag{3}$$

For a direction set $\Omega = \{\theta_i | i = 1, \ldots, k\}$ the proposed method first estimates each projection $\check{f}^{\theta_i}$ of the unknown original image from the projections $\check{g}^{\theta_i}$ of the degraded image and then as a second step reconstructs f from its estimated projections (see Figure 1).

2.1 Deconvolution of the Projections

In this section we introduce a Tikhonov-regularization [15] based method for the deconvolution of the projections. Convolution is a linear operation, thus Eq. (3) can be written as

$$\check{g} = H\check{f} + \check{n}, \tag{4}$$

where the H matrix represents the convolution operation with the filter $\check{h}$. Since $\check{n}$ is unknown, this system of linear equations is ill-posed and it requires regularization which penalizes solutions of large norm. The standard version of the Tikhonov regularization takes the form

$$\check{f}_\lambda = \arg\min_{\check{f}} \|H\check{f} - \check{g}\|_2^2 + \lambda^2 \|\check{f}\|_2^2, \tag{5}$$

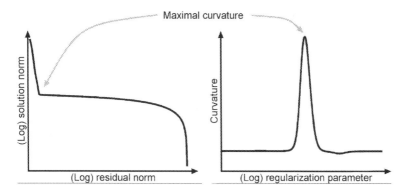

Fig. 2. A typical L-curve and its curvature. The best trade-off between the norm of the residual and the norm of the solution is assigned by the maximal curvature value.

where λ is a positive constant, the regularization parameter, that controls the smoothness of the solution. As λ increases the norm of the residual $\|H\breve{f}_\lambda - \breve{g}\|_2^2$ also increases (*i.e.* $\breve{f}_\lambda$ becomes less accurate), while the norm of the solution $\|\breve{f}_\lambda\|_2^2$ decreases (*i.e.* $\breve{f}_\lambda$ becomes smoother). An explicit solution for a given value of λ is given by

$$\breve{f}_\lambda = (H^T H + \lambda^2 I)^{-1} H^T \breve{g}, \tag{6}$$

where I denotes the identity matrix. To determine a suitable value of the regularization parameter λ we used the so-called L-curve method [3]. The L-curve is a log-log plot of the norm of the residual and the norm of the solution for different regularization parameters:

$$\mathcal{L} = \{(\log_2 \|H\breve{f}_\lambda - \breve{g}\|_2^2, \log_2 \|\breve{f}_\lambda\|_2^2), \lambda \geq 0\}. \tag{7}$$

To obtain an optimal trade-off between the two values, the L-curve method proposes to choose λ^* which maximizes the curvature κ_λ of the curve $\mathcal{L}$ (see Figure 2). Although the L-curve method requires for a large set of different λ values to evaluate Eq. (6), it is still computationally efficient approach.

Since the elements of the projection vectors are non-negative we are interested in a solution of Eq. (4) such that $\breve{f} \geq 0$. Unfortunately there is no simple explicit solution for this problem, but a typical iterative approach can be applied. For that purpose, we denoted by $\breve{f}^+$ the version of the vector $\breve{f}$ in which all negative values were set to 0. Let $\breve{f}_0 = \breve{f}_{\lambda^*}$ the initial estimation. In each iteration step the method estimates $\breve{f}_i$ that approximates $\breve{f}_{i-1}^+$ (see Figure 3). This can be formulated by the following minimization problem:

$$\breve{f}_i = \arg\min_{\breve{f}} \|H\breve{f} - \breve{g}\|_2^2 + \lambda^{*2}\|\breve{f}\|_2^2 + \|\breve{f} - \breve{f}_{i-1}^+\|_2^2 \tag{8}$$

which introduces an additional term to Eq. (5) that prefers similarity to the non-negative version of the previous estimation. This form of the *generalized* Tikhonov regularization has an explicit solution:

$$\breve{f}_i = (H^T H + (1 + \lambda^{*2})I)^{-1}(H^T \breve{g} + \breve{f}_{i-1}^+). \tag{9}$$

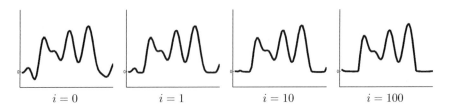

$$i = 0 \qquad i = 1 \qquad i = 10 \qquad i = 100$$

Fig. 3. The evolution of the estimation of the projection vector during the iteration

The iteration ends if $\|\check{f}_i - \check{f}_{i-1}\|_2^2 < \epsilon \|\check{f}_{i-1}\|_2^2$ for an appropriately small $\epsilon > 0$. The resulting vector $\check{f} = \check{f}_i^+$ will be the estimation of the projection vector. The pseudo code of this algorithm can be found in Algorithm 1. Furthermore the residual $\|H\check{f} - \check{g}\|_2^2$ approximates $\check{n}$ and thus the variance σ_n^2 of the additive noise n can be easily estimated.

Algorithm 1. Restoration of a projection vector

    Input   : The $\check{g}$ projection of the degraded image and the PSF
    Output: The reconstructed vector $\check{f}$
1 Find λ^* and $\check{f}_{\lambda^*}$ using the L-curve method and standard Tikhonov method (Eq. (6))
2 Let $\check{f}_0 = \check{f}_{\lambda^*}$
3 **repeat**
4   Update the estimation using generalized Tikhonov method (Eq. (9))
5 **until** $\|\check{f}_i^+ - \check{f}_{i-1}^+\|_2^2 < \epsilon \|\check{f}_{i-1}^+\|_2^2$
6 Return with $\check{f} = \check{f}_i^+$.

2.2 Binary Image Reconstruction

In this section we propose a method to reconstruct the binary image from the vectors $\check{f}^{\theta_i}$ using a standard discrete tomography technique. The reconstruction requires the $\check{b}^{\theta_i} = \check{f}^{\theta_i}/s$ binary projections. Unfortunately the scale factor s can not be determined explicitly but the upper and lower bounds of its possible values can be easily estimated. For that purpose, consider the maximal scaled projection value $M = \max_{\theta_i}\{\max\{\check{f}^{\theta_i}\}\}$

and let D be the length of the segment of the image that the projection ray corresponding to M intersects. It can be assumed that $1 \leq M/s \leq D$ so we can define a set of the possible values of the scale factor s as follows:

$$S = \{k/M, k = 1, \ldots, \lfloor D \rfloor\}. \tag{10}$$

For each $s \in S$ we obtain the vectors $\check{b}^{\theta_i} = \lceil \check{f}^{\theta_i}/s \rceil$ as estimations of the projections of the unknown binary image b.

In this paper we consider the reconstruction from the vertical and horizontal projection vectors $\check{b}^0$ and $\check{b}^{\pi/2}$. The discrete tomography technique described in in this section

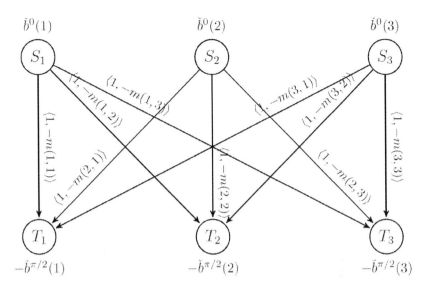

Fig. 4. Associated network for a 3×3 case. The supply and demand values for the source nodes S_i and the sink nodes T_j are given by the vectors $\check{b}^0$ and $\check{b}^{\pi/2}$ respectively. Each of the edges has a flow capacity equal to 1 while the flow costs are given by the model image $m \in \mathbb{R}^{3 \times 3}$.

requires that these two vectors have equal sum. However, in practice this is not guaranteed since these vectors are obtained by rounding. To equalize the two vectors we uniformly decreased the elements of the vector of the largest sum. We decreased by 1 the highest elements of the same number as the difference between the two vectors.

It is well known, that usually two projections are not enough to reconstruct binary images, *i.e.* , there can be many binary images that have the same projections while in some other cases there is no binary image that satisfies the projections. We define the tomographic equivalence class:

$$U = U(\check{b}^0, \check{b}^{\pi/2}) = \{z \in \{0,1\}^{u \times v} : z^0 = \check{b}^0, z^{\pi/2} = \check{b}^{\pi/2}\}. \tag{11}$$

Although in general case $|U| > 1$, we are interested in a solution which is the most similar to the input image g. Fortunately finding such a solution is quite straightforward. For that purpose a model image m has been created from the input image g by removing noise of variance σ_n^2 (which has been estimated after the estimation of the projections, see Section 2.1). The expectation that the solution z_s should be similar to the model image means that on those (x, y) positions where $z(x, y) = 1$ it is most likely that the model image has high grayscale values. This can be formulated by the following minimization problem:

$$z_s = \arg\min_{z \in U} \left(-\sum_{x,y} z(x,y) m(x,y) \right). \tag{12}$$

This way the reconstruction problem can be traced back to the *minimum cost maximal flow* (MCMF) problem [1]. In this network the *supply* and *demand* nodes are

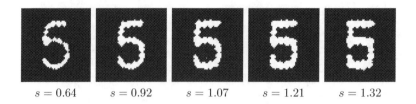

$s = 0.64$ $s = 0.92$ $s = 1.07$ $s = 1.21$ $s = 1.32$

Fig. 5. Reconstruction results for different $s \in S$ scale values

representing the projection vectors while the edges are representing the image pixels (see Figure 4). The edge $S_x \to T_y$ corresponding to the (x, y) pixel has a flow capacity equal to 1 and a flow cost equal to $-m(x, y)$. The minimum cost maximal flow can be found in polynomial time [8] and it determines the solution z_s of the discrete tomography problem. The pixel $z_s(x, y)$ gets a value of 1, if and only if the flow passes through the edge $S_x \to T_y$. As it has been noted previously in some cases the projections can not be satisfied, *i.e.* , U is empty. In such cases we simply discard the current scale factor and the corresponding projections. We also note that the original input image g could also be used as model image, however the results would be somewhat more noisy.

For different scale factors $s \in S$ the method finds different binary solutions z_s (see Figure 5). To choose an optimal solution z, the method compares each z_s to the input image g in least-squares sense

$$z = \arg \min_{z_s} \|s(h * *z_s) - g\|^2. \tag{13}$$

It should be noted that theoretically it is not impossible that $|U| = 0$ for each scale factor $s \in S$. In this case the proposed method could not provide any solution. However in practice we found that U containes at least one solution for most of $s \in S$.

The pseudo code of the algorithm can be found in Algorithm 2. As for the time complexity of the overall algorithm, the reconstruction of the projections require a matrix inversion in each iteration step which has a polynomial time consumption while the reconstruction of the binary shapes for each scale factor $s \in S$ using the MCMF approach has also polynomial time complexity. Hence the overall method is computationally efficient.

Algorithm 2. Pseudo code of the proposed algorithm

    Input : The degraded grayscale image g and the PSF h
    Output: The reconstructed binary image z
1 Estimate the projections $\check{f}^0$ and $\check{f}^{\pi/2}$ using the method described in Section 2.1
2 **foreach** $s \in S$ **do**
3   Reconstruct the binary image z_s from the vectors $\check{b}^0 = \left[\check{f}^0/s\right]$ and $\check{b}^{\pi/2} = \left[\check{f}^{\pi/2}/s\right]$
       using the method described in Section 2.2
4 **end**
5 Return with $z = z_s$ according to Eq. (13)

Table 1. Test results on the synthetic dataset of the Richardson-Lucy method and the proposed method. The average δ measures on 62 alphanumeric characters for different levels of blur and SNR are shown. The cases when the proposed method provided better results are depicted in bold.

Richardson-Lucy method						Proposed method				
σ	5dB	2.5dB	0dB	-2.5dB	-5dB	σ	5dB	2.5dB	0dB	-2.5dB	-5dB
1.0	9.93	12.66	15.94	21.78	30.58	1.0	10.83	**12.31**	**14.44**	**18.88**	**24.15**
2.0	12.01	14.57	17.80	23.99	31.21	2.0	14.67	15.69	**17.19**	**20.80**	**22.61**
3.0	10.30	13.06	16.85	21.96	29.98	3.0	17.41	18.34	19.94	**21.66**	**24.58**
4.0	14.47	16.98	20.30	26.44	35.26	4.0	21.53	23.38	25.17	27.53	**29.44**
5.0	21.28	24.04	27.07	32.87	41.44	5.0	26.47	28.43	30.90	**32.50**	**35.75**

3 Experiments and Comparison

To examine the performance of the method we created a synthetic dataset of images of 62 alphanumeric characters (of size 59×59 pixels) and their 1550 degraded versions. Each image was blurred by Gaussian filters with standard deviations $\sigma = 0, 1, \ldots, 5$. White noises of different levels was added to each blurred image to implement signal-to-noise ratios covering values of 5, 2.5, 0, -2.5, -5 dB. The reconstruction results were evaluated using the following normalized symmetric difference

$$\delta = \frac{|B \triangle Z|}{|B| + |Z|} \cdot 100\%, \qquad (14)$$

where B and Z denote the set of the foreground pixels of the original image b and the reconstructed image z respectively.

For comparison we have chosen the Richardson–Lucy algorithm [10] because this method also assumes that the PSF is known and does not require an estimation of the strength of the noise. On the other hand this method is developed for grayscale images thus thresholding is required. The Otsu [9] method has been found as the best choice for this task. To improve the results of both methods, small isolated pixel groups has been removed from the images by the following way. First, a morphological closing has been applied to connect regions and isolated pixels that are close to each other. Then 8-connected pixel groups containing at most a certain number of pixels has been removed. Finally, a *logical AND* operation with the original shape has been applied to undo the morphological closing. It has to be noted that the Richardson-Lucy method produced much more of such artifacts. The summary of the test results is shown in Table 1. It can be seen that the proposed method provided better results in low SNR cases. This is due to the L-curve based estimation of the regularization parameter which implicitly gives a robust estimation of the level of the noise. On the other hand, in higher SNR cases the 2-dimensional deconvolution methods (like the Richardson–Lucy algorithm) can provide more accurate restorations.

The Richardson–Lucy algorithm requires a couple of Fourier transforms in each iteration step, thus for fixed number of iterations, its time complexity is $\mathcal{O}\left(uv \log\left(uv\right)\right)$.

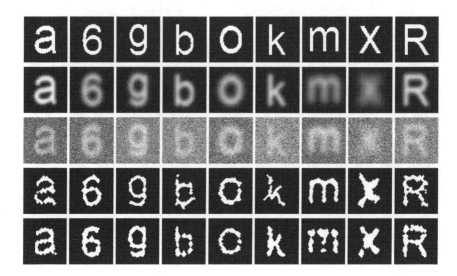

Fig. 6. Example reconstruction results on synthetic images. **First three rows:** The original binary shapes, the blurred images, and the blurred and noisy version (from top to middle). **Fourth and fifth rows:** The results of the Richardson-Lucy method and the proposed method respectively.

As we discussed in the previous section, the proposed method has a polynomial time complexity. We implemented our method in `Matlab`, but the network-flow algorithm was written in `C`. This inefficient mixed solution resulted longer running times (an average of ≈ 5 sec.), while the Richardson–Lucy algorithm was very fast (below 0.1 sec.). However a more efficient implementation of our method is feasible.

3.1   Real Images Taken with Fixed-Focus Cameras

Nowadays optical character recognition (OCR) is one of the most important functionalities of mobile devices. Nevertheless many modern devices are equipped with fixed-focus or full-focus (Extended Depth of Field - EDoF) lens. While these cameras in many cases provide better image quality than many auto-focus cameras, they usually can not be used for OCR because the images of A4 pages or business cards taken from a distance about 20 cm are out-of-focus. Therefore the enhancement of such images is an interesting task. We extracted a set of letters from images of A4 papers taken with an EDoF camera. Gaussian filters has been used as PSFs and their variances has been determined empirically. The results of the Richardson-Lucy method and the proposed method are shown in Figure 7. It can be observed that the proposed method provided in same cases better results, thus it can be regarded as a promising alternative. We note that it is not clear that Gaussian filter approximates the best the out-of-focus effect. Disk shaped low-pass filters has also been tested but while the proposed method performed similarly, the Richardson-Lucy method provided much weaker results.

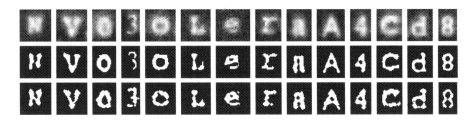

Fig. 7. Example results on letters extracted from out-of-focus document images taken with EDoF camera. The original images are shown in the first row. The reconstruction results of the Richardson-Lucy method can be found in the second row and the results of the proposed method are in the third row.

4 Conclusion

A novel binary image reconstruction approach has been proposed. The method first restores the projections of the shape using 1-dimensional deconvolution then reconstructs the binary image using efficient discrete tomography technique. The main advantage of the method is that it does not require parameter setting or prior knowledge like an estimation of the signal-to-noise ratio. The optimal trade-off between the residual and the accuracy is determined automatically. Numerical experiments on synthetic images showed that the method is robust to the level of the noise and can outperform a widely-used method in low SNR cases. The efficiency of the method has also been demonstrated on real alphanumeric images taken with fixed-focus camera.

Acknowledgements. This research was supported by the OTKA PD100950 project of the National Scientific Research Fund and by the European Union and the State of Hungary, co-financed by the European Social Fund in the framework of TÁMOP 4.2.4. A/2-11-1-2012-0001 'National Excellence Program'.

References

1. Batenburg, K.J.: Network flow algorithms for discrete tomography. In: Herman, G., Kuba, A. (eds.) Advances in Discrete Tomography and Its Applications, pp. 175–205. Applied and Numerical Harmonic Analysis, Birkhäuser Boston (2007)
2. Deans, S.R.: The Radon transform and some of its applications. A Wiley-Interscience publication, Wiley (1983)
3. Hansen, P.C., O'Leary, D.P.: The use of the L-curve in the regularization of discrete ill-posed problems. SIAM Journal on Scientific Computing 14, 1487–1503 (1993)
4. Kim, J., Jang, S.: High order statistics based blind deconvolution of bi-level images with unknown intensity values. Optics Express 18(12), 12872–12889 (2010)
5. Lam, E.Y.: Blind bi-level image restoration with iterated quadratic programming. IEEE Transactions on Circuits and Systems Part 2: Express Briefs 54(1), 52–56 (2007)
6. Lam, E.Y., Goodman, J.W.: Iterative statistical approach to blind image deconvolution. Journal of the Optical Society of America A 17(7), 1177–1184 (2000)

7. Li, T.H., Lii, K.S.: Deblurring two-tone images by a joint estimation approach using higher-order statistics. In: Proc. of IEEE SP Workshop on Higher-Order Statistics, pp. 108–111 (1997)

8. Orlin, J.B.: A polynomial time primal network simplex algorithm for minimum cost flows. In: Proc. of the Seventh Annual ACM-SIAM Symposium on Discrete Algorithms, SODA 1996, pp. 474–481. SIAM, Philadelphia (1996)

9. Otsu, N.: A threshold selection method from gray-level histograms. IEEE Transactions on Systems, Man and Cybernetics 9(1), 62–66 (1979)

10. Richardson, W.H.: Bayesian-based iterative method of image restoration. J. Opt. Soc. Am. 62(1), 55–59 (1972)

11. Ryser, H.: Combinatorial properties of matrices of zeros and ones. In: Classic Papers in Combinatorics, pp. 269–275. Modern Birkhäuser Classics, Birkhäuser Boston (1987)

12. Schalkoff, R.J.: Digital Image Processing and Computer Vision. John Wiley & Sons, New York (1989)

13. Sharif, B., Sharif, B.: Discrete tomography in discrete deconvolution: Deconvolution of binary images using ryser's algorithm. Electronic Notes in Discrete Mathematics 20, 555–571 (2005)

14. Shen, Y., Lam, E.Y., Wong, N.: Binary image restoration by positive semidefinite programming. Optics Letters 32(2), 121–123 (2007)

15. Tikhonov, A., Arsenin, V.: Solutions of ill-posed problems. Scripta series in mathematics, Winston (1977)

16. Wiener, N.: Extrapolation, Interpolation, and Smoothing of Stationary Time Series with Engineering Applications. John Wiley & Sons, New York (1949)

Minimum Memory Vectorisation
of Wavelet Lifting

David Barina and Pavel Zemcik

Faculty of Information Technology, Brno University of Technology
Bozetechova 1/2, 612 66 Brno, Czech Republic
{ibarina,zemcik}@fit.vutbr.cz

Abstract. With the start of the widespread use of discrete wavelet
transform the need for its effective implementation is becoming increasingly more important. This work presents a novel approach to discrete
wavelet transform through a new computational scheme of wavelet lifting. The presented approach is compared with two other. The results
are obtained on a general purpose processor with 4-fold SIMD instruction set (such as Intel x86-64 processors). Using the frequently exploited
CDF 9/7 wavelet, the achieved speedup is about 3× compared to naive
implementation.

Keywords: discrete wavelet transform, lifting scheme, parallelization,
vectorisation, SIMD.

1 Introduction

The discrete wavelet transform (DWT) is mathematical tool which is able to decompose discrete signal into lowpass and highpass frequency components. Such
a decomposition can be performed at several scales. DWT is often used as the
basis of sophisticated compression algorithms. This is the case of JPEG 2000
and Dirac compression standards in which CDF 9/7 wavelet [4] is employed for
lossy compression. Responses of this wavelet can be computed by a convolution
with two FIR filters, one with 7 and the other with 9 coefficients. For the DWT
computation, the well known Mallat's [8] filtering scheme can be used. Alternatively, one can use usually faster scheme called lifting which was presented by I.
Daubechies and W. Sweldens in [5]. Lifting data flow graph consists of regular
grid computational scheme suitable for SIMD vectorisation. Both of the algorithms can be performed over some approximation of real numbers. This paper
focuses on single-precision floating-point format.

In contemporary personal computers (PCs), the general purpose microproces-
sor with SIMD instruction set is often found. In case of the x86-64 architecture,
the appropriate instruction set used here is SSE (Streaming SIMD Extensions).
This 4-fold SIMD set fits exactly the CDF 9/7 lifting data flow graph.

In this work, we discuss vectorisation (parallelization) of 1-D discrete wavelet
transform on processors with SIMD extensions. Two of the discussed methods

J. Blanc-Talon et al. (Eds.): ACIVS 2013, LNCS 8192, pp. 91–101, 2013.
© Springer International Publishing Switzerland 2013

can be used in memory limited systems. Specifically, we focus on the PC and similar platforms.

The rest of the paper is organized as follows. More traditional approaches to DWT computation are reviewed in Section 2. Section 3 describes opportunities for lifting scheme parallelizations and presents the proposed approach. The vectorisation methods are compared in Section 4. Finally, Section 5 concludes the paper.

2   Related Work

In 2000, the problem of minimum memory implementations of lifting scheme was addressed in [3] by Ch. Chrysafis and A. Ortega. This approach is very general and it is not focused on parallel processing. Anyway, this is essentially the same method as the on-line or pipelined computation mentioned in other papers (although not necessarily using lifting scheme nor 1-D transform). Especially, its variation was presented six year later in [6] which is specifically focused on CDF 9/7 wavelet transform. The work was also later extended to [2] where same authors addressed a problem of minimum memory implementation of 2-D transform.

In [7] R. Kutil *et al.* presented SIMD parallelizations of several frequently used wavelet filters. This vectorisation is applicable only on those filters discussed in their paper. Specifically, vectorisation of CDF 9/7 wavelet computed using lifting scheme is vectorised here by a group of four successive pairs of coefficients. Unlike a general approach proposed in our paper, their 1-D transform vectorisation handles coefficients in blocks. Our vectorisation process pairs of coefficients one by one immediately when available (without packing into groups).

According to the number of arithmetic operations, the lifting scheme [5] is today's most efficient scheme for computing discrete wavelet transforms. Any discrete wavelet transform with finite filters can be factored into a finite sequence of N pairs of predict and update convolution operators P_n and U_n. Each predict operator P_n corresponds to a filter $p_i^{(n)}$ and each update operator U_n to a filter $u_i^{(n)}$. Block diagram of such a system is depicted in Figure 1.

$$P_n(z) = \sum_{i=-l_n}^{g_n} p_i^{(n)} z^{-i} \tag{1}$$

$$U_n(z) = \sum_{i=-m_n}^{f_n} u_i^{(n)} z^{-i} \tag{2}$$

This factorisation is not unique. For symmetric filters, this non-uniqueness can be exploited to maintain symmetry of lifting steps.

Consider the decomposition of the signal of length of L samples. Without loss of generality one can assume only signals with even length L. Possible remaining coefficient can treated separately in the prolog or epilog phases together with border extension. Thus, the transform contains $S = L/2$ pairs of resulting

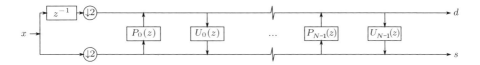

Fig. 1. Block diagram of lifting scheme. The system consists of $2N$ lifting steps. For simplicity, the scaling of the resulting coefficients was ommited.

wavelet coefficients (s, d). The s coefficients represent a smoothed signal. On the contrary, the d coefficients form a difference or detail signal.

In their paper [5], Daubechies and Sweldens demonstrated an example of CDF 9/7 transform factorisation which resulted into four lifting steps ($N = 2$) plus scaling of coefficients. In this example, the individual lifting steps use 2-tap symmetric filters for the prediction as well as the update. This can be graphically described as shown in Figure 2. Here, outer arrows represents 2-tap symmetric filter and inner arrow represents predicted (resp. updated) coefficient. In all figures shown in this paper, the coefficients of these four 2-tap symmetric filter are denoted α, β, γ and δ respectively.

Fig. 2. Elementary lifting operation (P_n or U_n) of the CDF 9/7 wavelet. The flow in the middle is just added into result at the bottom. Side flows are multiplied by a constant first.

When coefficient scaling is omitted, the calculation of a pair of the DWT coefficients at the position l (s_l and d_l) is performed by four such a lifting steps. Intermediate results ($s_l^{(n)}$ and $d_l^{(n)}$) can be appropriately shared between neighbouring pairs of coefficients (s_l and d_l). Finally, the calculation of the complete CDF 9/7 DWT is depicted in Figure 3. This is an in-place implementation, which means the DWT can be calculated without allocating auxiliary memory. Resulting coefficients (s_l and d_l) are interleaved in place of the input signal.

3 Vectorisation

The calculation scheme described in the previous section can be realized in a number of different ways. In this work, three of such ways are described. The main difference between them is in the order of lifting steps evaluation. Alternatively, the data flow graph in Figure 3 can be split into areas that are evaluated sequentially according to their data dependencies.

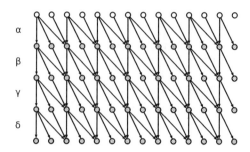

Fig. 3. Complete data flow graph of CDF 9/7 wavelet transform. The input signal is on top, output at the bottom. The graph borders must be treated in a special way using prolog and epilog phases.

3.1 Naive Approach

The naive approach of data flow graph evaluation directly follows the lifting steps (n). Thus, all intermediate $s^{(1)}$ and $d^{(1)}$ coefficients are evaluated in the first step. Then, all $s^{(2)}$ and $d^{(2)}$ are evaluated in second step, etc. For a better understanding see the block diagram in Figure 4. Unfortunately, this algorithm requires several reads and writes of the intermediate results $s_l^{(n)}$ and $d_l^{(n)}$. For long signals, these intermediate results will be several times evicted from the CPU cache in favor of other intermediate results. Consequently, many cache misses during such a computation will occur.

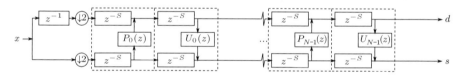

Fig. 4. Block diagram of the horizontal lifting scheme vectorisation. The parts bounded with a dashed line correspond to the areas of parallel computation.

In this paper, this method is called the horizontal vectorisation. This name reflects the fact that the data flow graph is split in horizontal areas as in Figure 5. In each area, elementary calculations are independent and can be computed in parallel. For simplicity, the scaling of coefficients and the prolog and epilog phases were omitted in the referenced figure. An entire signal of $2S$ samples must be loaded into the memory which is not suitable for memory limited systems.

3.2 Vertical Vectorisation

Another way of lifting data flow graph evaluation is the double-loop approach [6]. This approach is referred to as the vertical vectorisation. Earlier, it was described in [3] focusing on low memory systems but without vectorisation.

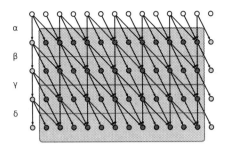

Fig. 5. The horizontal vectorisation of the CDF 9/7 data flow graph. The scaling of co-efficients was omitted. The computation within the highlighted areas can be processed in parallel.

The P_n and U_n filters need not be causal. In general, non-causal systems requires storing the whole input signal into memory (as can be seen from Figure 5). This is not suitable for fast or memory limited signal processing as well as for a vectorisation. Therefore, it would be appropriate to convert non-causal lifting steps (P_n and U_n) to causal systems. The key to force these filtering steps to be causal is the introduction of appropriate delays.

$$\mathcal{P}_n(z) = z^{-l_n} P_n(z) = \sum_{i=0}^{g_n+l_n} p_{i-l_n}^{(n)} z^{-i} \tag{3}$$

$$\mathcal{U}_n(z) = z^{-m_n} U_n(z) = \sum_{i=0}^{f_n+m_n} u_{i-m_n}^{(n)} z^{-i} \tag{4}$$

The transition from non-causal to causal system introduce a delay z^{-l_n} on both inputs of the prediction filtering step P_n. In the bottom input s, the delay can be distributed into both branches. This leads to a causal system $\mathcal{P}_n$ as in (3). Analogously, a delay of m_n samples is introduced on both inputs of update step U_n. Again, this delay can distributed into branches of upper input d. The resulting equation is shown in (4). For simplicity, the adjacent delays can combined into single one. Finally in (5), delays of η_n, μ_n and ν_n samples appear around each pair of filtering steps P_n and U_n. The resulting block diagram is shown in Figure 6.

$$\eta_n = l_n \tag{5a}$$

$$\mu_n = l_n + m_n \tag{5b}$$

$$\nu_n = m_n \tag{5c}$$

In this method, the lifting computation is transformed into one loop instead of multiple loops over all the coefficients. Therefore, one pair of lifting coefficients s_l and d_l is computed in each iteration of such a single loop. However, the computations within each of these areas cannot be directly parallelized due to data

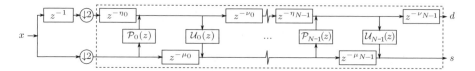

Fig. 6. Block diagram of vertical lifting scheme vectorisation. The part bounded with dashed line correspond to the area of parallel computation.

dependencies. Even so, this procedure is advantageous because the coefficients are read and written only once. Consequently, this prevents unnecessary cache misses. In our 1-D case, the SIMD vectorisation of this method lies in processing of four adjacent areas in parallel like in [7]. The data flow graph is split in vertical areas of width of two coefficients as in Figure 7. Furthermore, this approach is particularly useful for multidimensional (e.g. 2-D) transform on PC platform where several data rows are processed in single loop at once using n-fold SIMD instructions.

Fig. 7. Vertical vectorisation of the CDF 9/7 data flow graph. The computation within the highlighted areas cannot be processed in parallel due to data dependencies.

3.3 Proposed Method

The main contribution of this paper is the following approach. This method is referred to as the diagonal vectorisation here. It is especially useful on limited memory systems because it can start iteration of vectorised loop immediately when a new pair of coefficients is available. Another area of application can be the Intel x86-64 or similar architecture equipped with small CPU cache and SIMD instruction set.

The subsequent lifting operations $\mathcal{P}_n$ and $\mathcal{U}_n$ inside the area of vectorisation above cannot be computed in parallel due to data dependencies. To eliminate these dependencies another delay of one sample is introduced on both lines s and d, see Figure 8.

Similarly to the case of vertical vectorisation, multiple loops of naive approach are transformed into the single loop over all the coefficients. One pair of resulting coefficients s and d is produced in each iteration. Unlike the vertical approach,

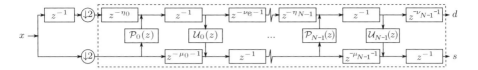

Fig. 8. Block diagram of diagonal lifting scheme vectorisation. In contrast to the vertical vectorisation, a delay of 1 sample is introduced on both lines s and d. This removes immediate data dependencies between subsequent lifting operators $\mathcal{P}_n$ and $\mathcal{U}_n$. Consequently, these lifting operators can be evaluated in parallel.

the elementary lifting operations evaluated in single loop iterations are shifted with respect to each other. This shift removes the data dependency within these loop iteration. Therefore, the elementary operations can be now computed in parallel. This is advantageous especially on the PC platform for processing with SIMD instructions. This approach in called diagonal vectorisation here. Corresponding slices of the data flow graph are depicted in Figure 9.

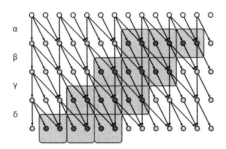

Fig. 9. Diagonal vectorisation of the CDF 9/7 data flow graph. The computation within the highlighted areas can be processed in parallel.

In contrast to the vertical vectorisation, the proposed method does not require buffering of the input samples into groups of width corresponding to the used SIMD instruction set. A pair of resulting coefficients is available immediately after processing a pair of input samples. On the other hand, it is necessary to choose a wavelet with one such lifting factorisation which has the same number of lifting steps (i.e. $2N$) like components of the SIMD set. Depending on the instruction set being used, more shuffling instruction may be needed to implement the proposed diagonal vectorisation (which is the case of Intel's SSE).

Considering the CDF 9/7 wavelet with $N = 2$ pairs of lifting steps, the diagonal vectorisation can be accelerated e.g. using Intel's MMX instruction set with 16-bit integer or fixed-point numbers, SSE set with single-precision floating-point numbers, SSE2 set with 16-bit integer or fixed-point numbers or AVX set with double-precision floating-point numbers.

4   Evaluation

The implementations of the approaches described in the previous section was evaluated on two x86-64 computers. This comparison was performed on 1-D forward DWT using CDF 9/7 wavelet. All the implementations work over a sequence of single-precision floating point numbers. According to platform performance, a length of the sequence was progressively extended from vector of 32 samples with geometrical step of 1.28 up to 55 millions of samples. The transform was computed including a final coefficient scaling and correct border extensions. The resulting coefficients remain interlaced at their original positions.

The first platform used in this paper is a classical PC with x86-64 CPU. All the results are obtained on Intel Core2 Duo CPU E7600 at 3.06 GHz with 32 kB of Level 1 data cache and 3 MB of Level 2 cache. The Level 1 data cache is 8-way set associative with cache lines of 64 bytes. The processor is equipped with 4-fold SSE instruction set. Thus, the SSE instructions are able to perform simple operation on four 32-bit single-precision floating point numbers in parallel. The evaluated programs ran under 64-bit Linux system and had been compiled by GCC 4.6.3 with -O2 option. All programs were executed on a lightly loaded system. In addition, the K-best measurement system have been used.

Measurement results were verified on a second PC with x86-64 CPU. In this case, the results are obtained on AMD Athlon 64 X2 4000+ at 2.1 GHz with 64 kB L1 data cache and 512 kB of L2 cache. The L1 data cache is 2-way set associative cache with cache lines of 64 bytes. As well as Intel Core2, the Athlon is equipped with SSE set. Programs ran under 64-bit Linux and had been compiled by GCC 4.7.2 with -O2 option. Although running at lower frequency compared to Intel, the AMD is in general faster in this task.

The evaluation is shown in Figure 10 and Figure 11. The horizontal vectorisation fails with samples exceeding the CPU cache size due to extensive cache misses. In contrast, the vertical and diagonal vectorisation show stability with increasing input length. In case of the proposed method, the achieved speedup is up to 3.1× on Intel and 3.1× on AMD.

The created implementation of all three algorithms used in this paper can be downloaded from the Internet.[1] The vertical and diagonal vectorisation methods were implemented using SSE intrinsics and inline assembly (no auto-vectorisation of GCC was used). In both cases, aligned memory access instructions was used to access the coefficients. This required merging of several loop iterations (the areas in Figure 7 and Figure 9) into the single one.

Table 1 shows the comparison of the different algorithms in terms of memory consumption. Each of the method require t samples to start iteration of the vectorised loop and b memory cells to store intermediate results. The horizontal vectorisation needs whole signal of $2S$ samples (S pairs of coefficients) to be loaded into memory. On this signal, up to S independent operations can evaluated in parallel. In contrast, the vertical vectorisation needs only $2T$ samples to start iteration of the vectorised loop in that T lifting operators can be evaluated

---

[1] http://www.fit.vutbr.cz/research/view_product.php?id=211

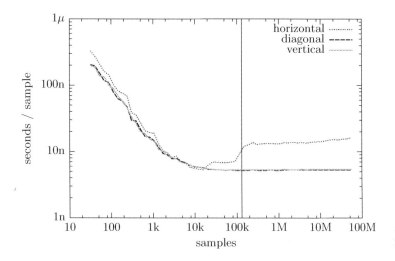

Fig. 10. Comparison of all three vectorisation approaches on the AMD x86-64 platform. The vertical line represents the size of the L2 CPU cache.

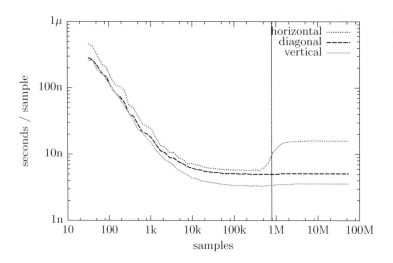

Fig. 11. Comparison performed on the Intel x86-64 platform. The vertical line shows the size of the L2 CPU cache.

Table 1. Memory consumption of vectorisation methods. Each method needs t samples to start iteration and b memory words to pass intermediate results between them. In each iteration, up to q operations can be evaluated in parallel. The numbers in parentheses are related to SSE implementations of the CDF 9/7 transform.

vectorisation	t samples	b coefficients	q operations
horizontal	$2S$	$2S$	S
vertical	$2T$ (8)	$2N$ (4)	T (4)
diagonal	2 (2)	$6N - 2$ (10)	$2N$ (4)

in parallel. In the case of 3-tap P and U operators, this vectorisation needs only $2N$ memory words to store intermediate results between such subsequent iterations. Finally, the diagonal vectorisation requires only 2 new samples for each iteration which evaluate $2N$ lifting operators in parallel.

Table 2 shows execution times of the algorithms measured up to 55 millions of samples. The vertical and diagonal vectorisation were implemented using mostly SSE intrinsics and in specific cases inline assembly (to have more control over the register allocation). Theoretical speedup in both cases is 4× due to using of the SSE instructions. Note, that the speedup in Table 2 is shown relatively to the implementation of the horizontal vectorisation (first row) which is significantly slowed down due to extensive cache misses. This is the reason why there is a value higher than the theoretical speedup 4×. Figure 11 and Figure 10 shows that the vertical and diagonal vectorisation exhibit similar properties. In these two cases, the actual speedup approaching the theoretical one. This is specifically apparent for lengths of an input vector bigger than the CPU cache size.

Table 2. Execution times per sample measured for 55 millions of samples. All times are related to SSE implementations of the CDF 9/7 transform.

vectorisation	Intel		AMD	
	ns/sample	speedup	ns/sample	speedup
horizontal	15.8	1.0	16.4	1.0
vertical	**3.6**	**4.4**	5.4	3.0
diagonal	5.1	3.1	**5.3**	**3.1**

5 Conclusion

This paper presented a novel method of minimum memory discrete wavelet transform utilizing SIMD instructions. The proposed method was compared to two other approaches – the naive implementation and similar vectorisation introduced in [7]. The achieved speedup goes asymptotically to 3.1× on the Intel Core2 Duo CPU and 3.1× on the AMD Athlon 64 X2 CPU. This speedup was achieved for CDF 9/7 wavelet using SSE instruction set. The data flow graph of this transform consists of 4 elementary lifting operations which exactly fits into 4-fold SSE registers in the proposed diagonal vectorisation. Moreover, the proposed method requires only two new samples to start iteration of SIMD vectorised loop.

Our next research will focus to an adaptation of the proposed approach to the 2-D wavelet transform. Specifically, we will use the diagonal vectorisation in the single-loop approach proposed by R. Kutil in [6]. The other direction may be an adaptation to other architectures, e.g. ARM processors or FPGA-based systems. It would also be interesting to compare the single-precision floating-point implementation with fixed-point implementations or implementations of reversible integer-to-integer (ITI) wavelet transform [1].

Acknowledgements. This work has been supported by the EU FP7-ARTEMIS project IMPART (grant no. 316564) and the national Technology Agency of the Czech Republic project RODOS (no. TE01020155).

References

1. Adams, M.D.: Reversible integer-to-integer wavelet transforms for image coding. Ph.D. thesis, Department of Electrical and Computer Engineering, University of British Columbia, Vancouver, BC, Canada (September 2002)
2. Chrysafis, C., Ortega, A.: Line-based, reduced memory, wavelet image compression. IEEE Transactions on Image Processing 9(3), 378–389 (2000)
3. Chrysafis, C., Ortega, A.: Minimum memory implementations of the lifting scheme. In: Proceedings of SPIE, Wavelet Applications in Signal and Image Processing VIII. SPIE, vol. 4119, pp. 313–324 (2000)
4. Cohen, A., Daubechies, I., Feauveau, J.C.: Biorthogonal bases of compactly supported wavelets. Communications on Pure and Applied Mathematics 45(5), 485–560 (1992)
5. Daubechies, I., Sweldens, W.: Factoring wavelet transforms into lifting steps. Journal of Fourier Analysis and Applications 4(3), 247–269 (1998)
6. Kutil, R.: A single-loop approach to SIMD parallelization of 2-D wavelet lifting. In: Proceedings of the 14th Euromicro International Conference on Parallel, Distributed, and Network-Based Processing (PDP), pp. 413–420 (2006)
7. Kutil, R., Eder, P., Watzl, M.: SIMD parallelization of common wavelet filters. In: Parallel Numerics 2005, pp. 141–149 (2005)
8. Mallat, S.: A Wavelet Tour of Signal Processing: The Sparse Way. With contributions from Gabriel Peyré, 3rd edn. Academic Press (2009)

Magnitude Type Preserving Similarity Measure for Complex Wavelet Based Image Registration

Florina-Cristina Calnegru

University of Pitesti, Department of Computer Science, str.
Targul din Vale, nr.1, Pitesti, Romania
`calnegru_florina@yahoo.com`

Abstract. Most of the similarity measures, currently used for image registration, aim to model the relation between the intensities of correspondent pixels. This is true even for some of the similarity measures that are not directly defined on the intensities of the images to be registered, but on some transformed version of those images. A potential problem with this approach is that it relies on the values of intensities, for which in most of the times it is too difficult to predict their pattern of variation. A way to circumvent this problem is to define a similarity measure on the domain of the magnitudes of complex wavelet coefficients, as the magnitudes are less affected by noise than the intensities. This property of robustness to noise allows to predict a certain behavior of the corresponding magnitudes, namely that they will preserve their type. This means that large (small) magnitudes from the complex wavelet transform of one image will correspond to large (small) magnitudes in the complex wavelet transform of the other image. Starting from this constancy in the behavior of complex wavelet magnitudes, we propose a new similarity measure that has sub pixel accuracy, robustness to noise and is faster than the most related known similarity measure.

1 Introduction

Image registration is the process of overlaying two images of the same scene, taken at different moments in time, or from different viewpoints, or by different sensors[1]. The two images involved in the process of image registration are named target image and reference image. An important general technique for image registration is optimal image registration. Its core idea is to define a (dis)similarity measure between the reference image and the target image, and then to look for the transformation that will optimize this (dis)similarity. A (dis)similarity measure is a function that quantifies the (in)dependency between two measurements[2]. For the (dis)similarity measures used in the context of image registration the two measurements are the images to be registered.

A (dis)similarity measure can be defined on the domain of the intensities of the images or it can be defined on a transformed version of the images. Examples of (dis)similarity measures defined on the raw images are the correlation coefficient, with its improvements [3], [4], the sum of squared differences [5], deterministic sign change [6], etc. Most of these (dis)similarity measures are sensitive to intensity changes between correspondent pixels of the two images.

J. Blanc-Talon et al. (Eds.): ACIVS 2013, LNCS 8192, pp. 102–113, 2013.

Similarity measures, can also be defined on the results of some processing performed on the initial images. Rank based (dis)similarity measures and the (dis)similarities based on the computation of joint probabilities of corresponding intensities can be included in this category. Examples of rank based (dis)similarity measures are Spearman's Rho [7], rank distance [2], etc. In general these kind of measures are based on the idea that the intensities of corresponding points have related ranks in the two images. Since this is usually false in the case of multimodal images, the use of rank based (dis)similarity measures is confined to single modality registration. Example of (dis)similarities based on the computation of joint probabilities of corresponding intensities are energy of joint probability distribution [8], material similarity [2], Shannon mutual information [9], [10], Rényi mutual information [11], joint entropy [12], etc. The underlying assumption of some of these latter (dis)similarities is that, for registered images, to an intensity in the reference image corresponds a single intensity in the target image [2], assumption which is not always true.

Another type of (dis)similarity measures defined on transformed versions of the images are the ones computed between corresponding layers of magnitudes of complex wavelets coefficients [13], [14]. Instead of assuming a certain type of relation between intensities, these dissimilarities try to model the relation between the magnitudes of correspondent complex wavelet coefficients. [13] proposed a similarity measure, named wavelet layers correlation, which is equivalent to considering, for two aligned images, that the relation between the magnitudes, of correspondent layers of complex wavelet coefficients, is linear. The value of their similarity measure, is equal to the multiplication of the correlation coefficients of all the pairs of correspondent layers of magnitudes. A potential problem with this approach is that sometimes, small local perturbations in the linear dependency can appear. [14] circumvented this problem by proposing that the overlapping between two images should be controlled not by the values of the magnitudes of wavelet coefficients, which can be altered by many factors, but by the nature (i.e small or large) of those magnitudes, that they model with the help of hidden state variables. They propose an algorithm that has two stages. In the first stage they model, for every image, the distributions of small and large magnitudes, from every layer, with the help of an iterative algorithm. In the second stage they use those distributions to count the number of magnitudes of the same type (i.e large or small) that every two correspondent layers have in common. They obtain thus, for each pair of correspondent layers, the frequency of having in both layers small magnitudes and the frequency of having in both layers large magnitudes. For a pair of correspondent layers, they add those frequencies, obtaining the frequency of similar types of magnitudes. Their similarity measure is the product of the frequencies of similar types, associated to all the pairs of correspondent layers. Since they use an iterative algorithm to compute the mean and variance of the distributions of large and small magnitudes, for every layer of the two images, their algorithm can be time costly. In plus, the way they model the distributions can be sensitive to the values of the magnitudes. This entails that their classification into large and small magnitudes might be dependent on the actual magnitudes of every layer, and thus not robust in relation to variations of those magnitudes. Since their similarity measure is constructed on the classification of the magnitudes into large and small, their similarity can be influenced by the values of the magnitudes.

Starting from the idea that the values of the magnitudes of wavelet coefficients are influenced by associated hidden state variables, which can take the values *large* or *small*, we propose a new dissimilarity measure that can be employed for image registration. The differences between our dissimilarity measure and the dissimilarity from [14] are that we employ a different technique for inferring the parameters of the distributions and that we define our dissimilarity measure in a totally different way. More specifically, we use supervised learning to obtain for every type of images (like for example retina images, brain images, etc.) the parameters of the distributions. Once we have computed, for a type, T, of images, those parameters, we use them every time we want to determine the dissimilarity between two images of type T. The first advantage is that in this way our algorithm is less computational expensive than the algorithm from [14]. The second advantage is that for every two layers of correspondent magnitudes we employ the same parameters, independently of the particular images that we currently register, which makes our algorithm less sensitive to the current magnitude values. Unlike the dissimilarity from [14], our dissimilarity measure is based on the Kullback - Leibler divergence [15] between the probabilities that correspondent layers have their magnitudes in a certain configuration of states. This makes again our dissimilarity more robust to variations in the magnitude values, since we assume no crisp classification into large or small magnitudes.

This article is structured as follows. In section 2, we present the construction of our dissimilarity measure, namely the type divergence. In section 3, we expose some details necessary for the implementation of type divergence. In section 4, we disclose the results of our tests . In section 5, we present our conclusions.

2   Type Divergence

In this section we present the construction of our dissimilarity measure together with the intuition behind it. We named our dissimilarity measure, type divergence. Its value, for two images, is computed by using the complex wavelet magnitudes of the two images, that are its arguments. We employed the complex wavelet transform [16], for our dissimilarity measure, because it has a great directional selectivity and it is almost shift and rotational invariant, and thus more appropriate for registration than, for example, the discrete wavelet transform. More specifically, we availed ourselves of the dual tree complex wavelet transform [16], which uses 6 mother wavelets, that distinguish spectral features oriented at $\{-75°, -45°, -15°, 75°, 45°, 15°\}$.

We chose to define our dissimilarity on the domain of the magnitudes of complex wavelet coefficients, rather than on the domain of the intensities, because the complex wavelet transform has two important properties [16]. The first is that the magnitudes of the complex wavelet coefficients are always large for wavelets that overlap singularities and small on smooth regions. The second is that complex wavelet coefficients are robust to noise, which means that is to be expected that a large magnitude is indicative of the existence of a physical singularity, and it is not the response to some noise from the image. This means that for two registered images , the magnitudes of corresponding complex wavelet coefficients (i.e. associated to the same mother wavelet, scaled with the same factor and translated at the same position) should be of the same type, i.e. either both small or both large.

In order to integrate this intuition into the definition of a dissimilarity measure we need a way to define large and small magnitudes. A crisp classification of the magnitudes into large and small might pose some problems especially for magnitudes that are naturally (i.e. because of the physical region that their associated wavelets overlap) near the decision boundary of the used classifier. The classification of correspondent magnitudes might differ in the two images, as the wavelet coefficients are subjected to variations, and this, in turn, would lead to the violation of the rule which asserts that, for two registered images, on their common region, large magnitude correspond to large magnitude, and small magnitudes to small magnitudes. One way to circumvent this problem, while still following the basic rule of type preservation for corresponding magnitudes, is to work in a probabilistic framework. In this way magnitudes, that are otherwise near the boundary of a crisp classifier, will receive a probability of being small and a probability of being large, not dismissing from the start their true type.

Before presenting our algorithm we need to introduce the definition of a layer of magnitudes. A layer of magnitude of wavelet coefficients is the set of all the magnitudes of the coefficients associated to the same mother wavelet, scaled with the same factor.

In order to construct our dissimilarity measure, we consider that every magnitude, from a layer, is the instantiation of a random variable, whose behavior is determined by an associated hidden variable, that can have two values: *small* and *large*. When the hidden variable is small, the values, that the random variable, associated to a magnitude, can take are described by a certain probability distribution and when the hidden variable is large, these values are described by another probability distribution. Hence we need to express the rule of type preservation in a probabilistic framework. In order to do that, we first define this rule for the magnitudes from correspondent layers, and then, we integrate these definitions, such that we have a description of this rule, that can be applied to the complex wavelet transforms of the two registering images. For two correspondent magnitude layers, we consider that the rule of type preservation is respected, if the probability that the hidden variables from a layer are in a certain state, is approximately equal to the probability that the hidden variables from the other layer are in the same state. How exactly we quantify this 'approximately equal', we will see later. For two complex wavelet transforms, we consider that the rule of type preservation is respected, if this rule is respected for all the correspondent layers of magnitude. We present bellow the mathematical formulation of this idea .

We consider that to each layer, correspond two random fields whose variables are denoted by W_i, and S_i respectively, where i stands for a particular location in the layer. The values of the variable W_i, belonging to the first random field of a layer, correspond to the possible magnitude values associated to the location i, from that layer. S_i is a hidden binary random variable whose values can be: *small* or *large*, and that conditions the values of W_i. Let us denote by $f_{W_i \mid S_i}$ the conditional probability distribution of W_i, given S_i. In order to generate a realization of W_i, we first generate a realization, say s of S_i , and then draw an observation w according to $f_{W_i \mid S_i}$ (w $|S_i = s$). As it was already pointed out in [14], the conditional probability distributions $f_{W_i \mid S_i}$ (w $|S_i$ = s) can be modelled as log-normal distributions, that is for $s \in \{small, large\}$ we have:

$$f_{W_i \mid S_i}(w \mid S_i = s) = \left(1/\left(w \cdot \sigma_s \sqrt{2\pi}\right)\right) \cdot e^{-(\ln w - \mu_s)^2/2\sigma_s^2} \tag{1}$$

Moreover we assume that for every layer, all the variables W_i, corresponding to the first random field of the same layer are identically distributed, given their hidden variables. We further assume that all the variables W_i from a level of decomposition (i.e. corresponding to the 6 mother wavelets for the same scale factor) are identically distributed, given their hidden variables. This means that for all the variables from a level of decomposition, that are in the same state, we only need a single mean and a single variance to characterize their conditional distributions. In order to estimate the means and variances for all the levels of decomposition we manually divide, for a number of training image of the same type, as the images that we intend to register, the magnitudes of every layer into small and large, and use the results to estimate, with the help of maximum likelihood, the means and variances. The maximum likelihood estimates of mean and variance for the k- th level of decomposition are:

$$\mu_{k, large} = \sum_{w \in L_{large}^k} \ln w \; \Big/ N_{large}^k \tag{2}$$

$$\sigma_{k, large} = \sqrt{\sum_{w \in L_{large}^k} \left(\ln w - \mu_{k,large}\right)^2 \Big/ N_{large}^k} \tag{3}$$

where $N_{large}^k = \left|L_{large}^k\right|$, $|\,.\,|$ represents the cardinal of a set, L_{large}^k is the training set with large magnitudes from the k-th level of decomposition. $\mu_{k,small}$ and $\sigma_{k,small}$ are computed with the same formulas as above in which we replace *large* with *small*.

Let $W = (W_1,...,W_n)$ be the random variables associated to the magnitudes of the layer j from the k-th level of decomposition, of the wavelet transform for the reference image. Let $S = (S_1,...,S_n)$ be the hidden variables of this layer. Let us denote $P(s_1,...,s_n) = P(S_1 = s_1,...,S_n = s_n)$; $P(s_1,...,s_n \mid w_1,...,w_n) = P(S_1 = s_1,...,S_n = s_n \mid W_1 = w_1,...,W_n = w_n)$ $P(w_i \mid s_i) = P(W_i = w_i \mid S_i = s_i) \; \forall i = \overline{1,n}$. Then according to Bayes' rule:

$$P(s_1,...,s_n \mid w_1,...,w_n) \simeq P(w_1,...,w_n \mid s_1,...,s_n) P(s_1,...,s_n) \tag{4}$$

where $\simeq$ signifies 'approximately equal'. We also assume that any W_i, is independent with respect to other $W_r, r \neq i$ (from its layer or any other layer) and to other hidden variables (i.e. different from its own hidden variable), given its own hidden variable. Then according to the chain rule of probability we can write:

$$P(s_1,...,s_n \mid w_1,...,w_n) \simeq P(s_1,...,s_n) \prod_{i=1}^{n} P(w_i \mid s_i) \tag{5}$$

If we denote $M_1 = \{i \in \{1,...,n\} \mid S_i = small\}$, $M_2 = \{i \in \{1,...,n\} \mid S_i = large\}$, $N_1 = |M_1|$, $N_2 = |M_2|$ then (5) is equivalent with (6)

$$P(s_1,...,s_n \mid w_1,...,w_n) \simeq \frac{1}{\left(\sqrt{2\pi}\sigma_{k,small}\right)^{N_1} \left(\sqrt{2\pi}\sigma_{k,\,large}\right)^{N_2} \displaystyle\prod_{i \in M_1} w_i \prod_{j \in M_2} w_j} P(s_1,...,s_n) \cdot$$
$$\cdot e^{-\sum\limits_{i \in M_1} \frac{\left(\ln w_i - \mu_{k,small}\right)^2}{2\sigma_{k,small}^2}} e^{-\sum\limits_{j \in M_2} \frac{\left(\ln w_j - \mu_{k,\,large}\right)^2}{2\sigma_{k,large}^2}} \tag{6}$$

Analogously if $V = (V_1,...,V_n)$ represent the random variables, associated to the magnitudes of the layer j from the k-th level of decomposition, of the wavelet transform for the target image, then we can write:

$$P(s_1,...,s_n \mid v_1,...,v_n) \simeq \frac{1}{\left(\sqrt{2\pi}\sigma_{k,small}\right)^{N_1} \left(\sqrt{2\pi}\sigma_{k,large}\right)^{N_2} \displaystyle\prod_{i \in M_1} v_i \prod_{j \in M_2} v_j} \cdot P(s_1,...,s_n) \cdot$$
$$\cdot e^{-\sum\limits_{i \in M_1} \frac{\left(\ln v_i - \mu_{k,small}\right)^2}{2\sigma_{k,small}^2}} e^{-\sum\limits_{j \in M_2} \frac{\left(\ln v_j - \mu_{k,large}\right)^2}{2\sigma_{k,large}^2}} \tag{7}$$

For the layers j, from the k-th level of decomposition of the target image and the reference image, in order to quantify the 'approximately equal' that appears in the intuition of the rule of type preservation, as it is presented above, we use the Kullback - Leibler divergence from $P(S_1,...,S_n \mid w_1,...,w_n)$ to $P(S_1,...,S_n \mid v_1,...,v_n)$

$$D_{KL}^{jk}\left(P(S_1,...,S_n \mid w_1,...,w_n) \| P(S_1,...,S_n \mid v_1,...,v_n)\right) =$$
$$= \sum_{(s_1,...,s_n)} \left(P(s_1,...,s_n) \cdot lr(M_1,M_2) \cdot rv(M_1,M_2) \cdot rc(M_1,M_2) \cdot ex(M_1,M_2)\right) \tag{8}$$

$$lr(M_1,M_2) = -\sum_{i \in M_1} \left(\ln w_i - \mu_{k,small}\right)^2 \Big/ 2\sigma_{k,small}^2 + \sum_{i \in M_1} \left(\ln v_i - \mu_{k,small}\right)^2 \Big/ 2\sigma_{k,small}^2 -$$
$$\sum_{l \in M_2} \left(\ln w_l - \mu_{k,large}\right)^2 \Big/ 2\sigma_{k,large}^2 + \sum_{l \in M_2} \left(\ln v_l - \mu_{k,large}\right)^2 \Big/ 2\sigma_{k,large}^2 \tag{9}$$

$$rv(M_1,M_2) = 1 \Big/ \left(\sqrt{2\pi}\sigma_{k,small}\right)^{N_1} \left(\sqrt{2\pi}\sigma_{k,large}\right)^{N_2} \tag{10}$$

$$rc(M_1,M_2) = 1 \Big/ \left(\prod_{i \in M_1} w_i \prod_{l \in M_2} w_l\right) \tag{11}$$

$$ex(M_1,M_2) = e^{-\sum\limits_{i \in M_1} \left(\ln w_i - \mu_{k,small}\right)^2 \Big/ 2\sigma_{k,small}^2} e^{-\sum\limits_{l \in M_2} \left(\ln w_l - \mu_{k,large}\right)^2 \Big/ 2\sigma_{k,large}^2} \tag{12}$$

We consider that the two wavelet transform associated to the target image and the reference image respect the rule of type preservation if the following value is minimum:

$$\prod_k \prod_j Div_{KL}^{jk} \tag{13}$$

$$Div_{KL}^{jk} = \max\Big(D_{KL}^{jk}\big(P(S_1,...,S_n \mid w_1,...,w_n) \parallel P(S_1,...,S_n \mid v_1,...,v_n)\big),$$
$$D_{KL}^{jk}\big(P(S_1,...,S_n \mid v_1,...,v_n) \parallel P(S_1,...,S_n \mid w_1,...,w_n)\big)\Big) \tag{14}$$

3   Implementation

The problem with (14) is that its complexity is $O(2^n \cdot J \cdot K)$, where n is the number of magnitudes of the largest layer, K is the number of decomposition levels and J is the number of layers for each level. This means that most of the times, the problem is not tractable. Hence we need an approximation of (14) that is less computational expensive, and that is still indicative of the measure in which the rule of type preservation is respected. A way to do that is to start from the obvious fact that, usually, in an image there are relatively few areas with singularities and much more smooth areas. This means that usually, in any layer, the number of large magnitudes is much smaller than the number of small magnitudes. So, one idea to decrease the complexity of (14) is to detect, for every layer from the reference image, the regions that most plausible contain large magnitudes, and evaluate (14) only on those regions. This means that we are interested in preserving the state of the hidden variables only on those regions and not on every entire layer. The method will be indicative of the measure in which the rule of type preservation is respected on the most quintessential and discriminative regions of the reference image , which means that we do not introduce a significant loss of accuracy by this approximation. We have further decreased the complexity of the algorithm by limiting the configurations, of the hidden state variables, over which we compute the Kullback - Leibler divergence. In this way we verify for every pair of correspondent layers how close their considered posterior probabilities are, when we compare them only on some key configurations. In the following we formalize the ideas presented above and we arrive at the final expression for the type divergence.

We denote the layer j of the k-th level of decomposition of the reference image by L_j^k For every L_j^k we determine the region R_j^k that most probable contains large magnitude as:

$$R_j^k = \Big\{ i \in \{1,...,\mid L_j^k \mid\} \mid w_i \in L_j^k, \ln w_i > \mu_{k,\text{large}} \Big\} \tag{15}$$

Let $q_j^k = \mid R_j^k \mid$. We denote by C_j^k the key configurations of the hidden state variables, associated to the magnitudes, whose indices are in R_j^k, for which we choose to verify how close their posterior probabilities are, in the two images. We have constructed C_j^k as follows. The first configuration of C_j^k is the one in which all but two of the hidden state variables are large. The others are small. In order to obtain the next configuration, we have changed the state of two randomly chosen hidden variable from large to small, while also modifying into large, the states of the variables that were small in the previous configuration. We have performed the same modifications to obtain any future configuration from a current configuration and we obtained all the configurations of c_j^k. We consider that all the configurations for the hidden variables are equally probable and we denote $M_1^a = \{i \in R_j^k \mid S_i = \text{small}\}$, $M_2^a = \{i \in R_j^k \mid S_i = \text{large}\}$. We define for the correspondent layers j, of the k-th level of decomposition, the approximation of the Kullback - Leibler divergence from (8) as :

$$AD_{KL}^{jk}\left(P(S_1,...,S_n \mid w_1,...,w_n) \parallel P(S_1,...,S_n \mid v_1,...,v_n)\right) =$$
$$= \sum_{\left(s_{i_1},...,s_{i_{q_j^k}}\right) \in C_j^k, \left(i_1,...,i_{q_j^k}\right) \in R_j^k} \left(lr(M_1^a,M_2^a) \cdot rv(M_1^a,M_2^a) \cdot rc(M_1^a,M_2^a) \cdot ex(M_1^a,M_2^a)\right) \tag{16}$$

We define the type divergence as

$$\text{TD} = \sum_j \sum_k \ln\left(ADiv_{KL}^{jk}\right) \tag{17}$$

$$ADiv_{KL}^{jk} = \max\left(AD_{KL}^{jk}\left(P(S_1,...,S_n \mid w_1,...,w_n) \parallel P(S_1,...,S_n \mid v_1,...,v_n)\right),\right.$$
$$\left. AD_{KL}^{jk}\left(P(S_1,...,S_n \mid v_1,...,v_n) \parallel P(S_1,...,S_n \mid w_1,...,w_n)\right)\right) \tag{18}$$

In the expression of type divergence we use the natural logarithm, because without it the values of TD would be very small, which can sometimes be a problem, like for example when we try to normalize them to the interval [0, 1]. The normalization to the interval [0, 1] can be useful when we try to compare TD with other (dis)similarity measures , by applying, for instance, the protocol of evaluation of similarity measures from [17]. In (18) when both AD_{KL}^{jk} are 0 we replace $\ln\left(ADiv_{KL}^{jk}\right)$ with the natural logarithm of 1 / realmax, where realmax is the largest real number that can be represented in the memory of a computer.

4   Experimental Results

4.1   Synthetic Data

In order to evaluate TD on synthetic data, we have transformed it into a similarity measure, by multiplying it by (- 1). We computed the resulted accuracy according to the computation strategy proposed in [17], as a part of the protocol to evaluate the performance of similarity measures, for rigid image registration purposes. Briefly, this computation strategy can be described as follows. First of all, the point x_0 in the parameter space, representing the parameters corresponding to the transformation that registers the images, is assumed to be known. Second, the similarity measure is assumed to be normalized to the interval [0, 1]. The computation scheme determines N lines in the parameters space, all centered in x_0. Each of the N line is defined by a randomly selected starting position, at a distance R from x_0, and its mirror point. Along each line, besides x_0, M evenly spaced points, X_{nm}, $n = \overline{1, N}$; $m = \overline{-M/2, M/2}$, are considered. The evaluation of the accuracy, proposed in [17] is :

$$ACC = \sqrt{\frac{1}{N}\sum_{n=1}^{N}\left\|X_{n,\max} - X_0\right\|^2} \tag{19}$$

In our case, $X_{n,\max}$, $\max \in \{-M/2,...,M/2\}$ is the position of the global maximum of the type divergence along the line n, and $\|.\|$ is the Euclidean distance.

In order to compare the accuracy of our similarity measure to the accuracy of other similarity measures we took the reference image, presented in Fig. 1 (a), and transformed it in a number of controlled ways. The first transformation that we performed on the reference image, such that we obtain the first target image, presented in Fig. 1 (b), is contrast stretch. The second target image, presented in Fig 1(c), is obtained from the reference through adding a Gaussian noise with uniform variance equal to 0.01 and mean 0. The third target image, depicted in Fig 1(d) is the reference image to which we added Gaussian white noise of local variance. The fourth target image, from Fig. 1 (e), is the reference image, perturbed with Poisson noise. The fifth target image, from Fig. 1(f) is obtained from the reference image by adding salt and pepper noise. The sixth target image, depicted in Fig. 1(g) is the reference image perturbed with speckle noise. The seventh target image from Fig. 1(h) is a blurred version of the reference image obtained by filtering it with a Gaussian rotationally symmetric filter of size 10 x 10 and variance 10. The eighth target image from Fig. 1(i) is a blurred version of the reference image obtained by applying to it a Gaussian rotationally symmetric filter of size 5 x 5 and variance 5. The ninth target image from Fig 1 (j) is the reference image that we transformed, as shown in [2], in order to artificially obtain the effect of shadows. The transformation consist of dividing the reference image into four quadrants and adding the values -30, -10, 10, 30 to the intensities of each of the four quadrants. The tenth image, depicted in Figure 1 (k) is the reference image transformed, such that we simulate the effect of smoothly varying radiometric changes. More specifically, assuming that the reference image has n_r rows and n_c columns, and that the intensity in the reference image at (x, y) is I, we replace this intensity in the target image with the intensity O computed as $O = I + 50 \cdot \sin(4\pi y / n_r) \cdot \cos(4\pi x / n_c)$ [2]. The eleventh target image, depicted in Fig. 1 (l) is obtained by changing the intensities of the reference image by a sinusoidal function, such that we have the effect that the target image seems to be acquired by a different modality from the modality through which the reference image is captured. More exactly if we denote by I the intensity at a pixel in the reference image, then the intensity O at the same pixel in target image is $O = I \cdot (1 + \cos(\pi \cdot I / 255))$ as indicated in [2].

For the pairs formed from the reference image and each of the eleven target images, we compute the accuracy of our similarity measure versus the accuracy of the following similarity measures: correlation coefficient, correlation ratio [18], mutual information and wavelet layers correlation. We took for each pair of target image and reference image, 30 lines in the parameter space (i.e $N = 30$), and for each line, we selected 30 evenly spaced points (i.e. $M = 30$), besides x_0. This means that for every pair of images we evaluate TD, by using approximately 900 transformations. Since we have 11 pairs of images, this means that overall we evaluate TD for approximately 10000 transformations. We summarize the results in Table 1.

Table 1. Comparative accuracy

Perturbation type	Accuracy Correlation coefficient	Accuracy Correlation ratio	Accuracy Mutual Information	Accuracy Wavelet layers correlation	Accuracy Type divergence
Contrast stretch (Fig. 1 (b))	0.0	0.0	0.0	0.0	0.0
Gaussian noise - uniform variance (Fig. 1 (c))	0.1232	0.1232	0.1485	0.0742	0.0
Gaussian noise local variance (Fig. 1(d))	0.1232	0.1232	0.1339	0.0742	0.0
Poisson noise (Fig. 1 (e))	0.0742	0.0371	0.0742	0.0371	0.0
Salt and pepper noise (Fig. 1 (f))	0.1231	0.0	0.0	0.0742	0.0
Speckle Noise (Fig. 1 (g))	0.1174	0.1114	0.0742	0.0371	0.0
Blurred with Gaussian filter of size 10 x10 and std = 10 (Fig. 1 (h))	0.0371	0.0371	0.0	0.0525	0.0525
Blurred with Gaussian filter of size 5x5 and std = 5 (Fig. 1 (i))	0.0	0.0	0.0	0.0	0.0
Shadows (Fig. 1(j))	0.0	0.0	0.0	0.0	0.0
Smoothly varying radiometric changes (Fig. 1(k))	0.0	0.0	0.0	0.0	0.0
Different modality (Fig. 1(l))	1.0372	0.0	0.0	0.0	0.1893

4.2   Real Data

In order to further assess the suitability of TD for image registration, we have used it to register 60 pairs of real unimodal retina images, that differ by an affine transformation. More specifically we have optimized, with the help of simulated annealing, the type divergence between the reference image and the target image of each pair. We considered that the parameters that register the two images are the parameters that represent the optimum (in our case the minimum) of TD ,as returned by simulated annealing. If we denote, for a pair of images, (I_1, I_2), by $T\theta_t$ the real transform (the transform that is used to obtain I_2 from I_1. and that is inferred from groundtruth) and by $T\theta_a$ the transform outputted by the algorithm, then the accuracy for that pair is computed as:

$$\sum_{i=1}^{P} \frac{\|T\theta_t(x_i, y_i) - T\theta_a(x_i, y_i)\|}{P}, \; (x_i, y_i)_{i=\overline{1,P}} \text{ are groundtruth points in } I_1 \qquad (20)$$

We summarized in table 2 the results obtained in this way for TD versus the results obtained for wavelet layers correlation. We took 5 as the threshold for the accuracy, because we measured the accuracy against the ground truth, which is man made and thus not totally accurate.

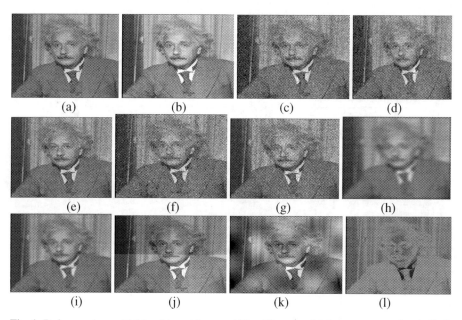

(a)   (b)   (c)   (d)

(e)   (f)   (g)   (h)

(i)   (j)   (k)   (l)

Fig. 1. Reference image((a))and target images ((b) - (l)), over which we compute the similarity measures from Table 1

Table 2. Test results on real data

Image cathegory	Percent of image pairs registered by *wavelet layers correlation* with an accuracy < 5 pixels	Percent of image pairs registered by *type divergence* with an accuracy < 5 pixels
Retina	98.3%	100%

5   Conclusions

In this paper we have proposed a new dissimilarity measure that can be used for rigid image registration, namely the type divergence. This measure is not defined on the intensities of the images but on the magnitudes of their complex wavelet coefficients. By requiring only that the type of the magnitudes be preserved, type divergence can better cope with a wider range of local variations (as demonstrated in Table 1), being more robust to all the studied cases of noise (practically unaffected by noise as suggested by the results from Table 1), than any of the similarity measures to which we compared it. This measure is, in general, the most accurate of the measures that we studied (as proved in Table 1 and Table2) and is faster than the closest existent dissimilarity measure introduced in [14] (as shown in section 1).

References

1. Zitova, B., Flusser, J.: Image registration methods: a survey. Image and Vision Computing 21(11), 977–1000 (2003)
2. Goshtasby, A.: Image Registration. Principles, Tools and Methods. Springer, London (2012)
3. Berthilsson, R.: Affine Correlation in International Conference on Pattern Recognition, Brisbane, Qld, pp. 1458–1461 (1998)
4. Kaneko, S., Satoh, Y., Igarashi, S.: Using selective correlation coefficient for robust image registration. Pattern Recognition 36, 1165–1173 (2003)
5. Brown, L.G.: A survey of image registration techniques. ACM Computing Surveys 24(4), 325–376 (1992)
6. Venot, A., Devaux, J.Y., Herbin, M., Lebruchec, J.F., Dubertret, L., Raulo, Y., Roucayrol, J.C.: An automated system for the registration and comparison of photographic images in medicine. IEEE Trans. Med. Imaging 7(4), 298–303 (1988)
7. Conners, R.W., Harlow, C.A.: A theoretical comparison of texture algorithms. IEEE Trans. Pattern Anal. Mach. Intell. 2(3), 204–222 (1980)
8. Shapiro, L.G., Stockman, G.C.: Computer Vision. Prentice Hall, Upper Saddle River (2001)
9. Viola, P.A.: Alignment by Maximization of Mutual Information. Ph.D. thesis, Massachusetts Institute of Technology (1995)
10. Collignon, A., Vandermeulen, A., Suetens, P., Marchal, G.: 3D multi-modality medical image registration based on information theory. Computational Imaging and Vision 3, 263–274 (1995)
11. Wachowiak, M.P., Smolikova, R., Tourassi, G.D., Elmaghraby, A.S.: Similarity metrics based on nonadditive entropies for 2D-3D multimodal biomedical image registration. In: Medical Imaging Conf., Proc. SPIE, San Diego, CA, vol. 5032, pp. 1090–1100 (2003)
12. Shannon, C.E.: The mathematical theory of communication. In: Shannon, C.E., Weaver, W. (eds.) The Mathematical Theory of Communication, pp. 29–125. University of Illinois Press, Urbana (1949); reprint 1998
13. Calnegru, F.-C.: A Probabilistic Framework for Complex Wavelet Based Image Registration. In: Maino, G., Foresti, G.L. (eds.) ICIAP 2011, Part I. LNCS, vol. 6978, pp. 9–18. Springer, Heidelberg (2011)
14. Calnegru, F.: Hidden State Probabilistic Modeling for Complex Wavelet Based Image Registration. In: International Conference on Computer Vision and Image Processing, pp. 1226–1232 (2011)
15. Kullback, S.: Information theory and statistics. John Wiley and Sons, New York (1959)
16. Selesnick, I.W., Barniuk, R.G., Kingsbury, N.G.: The Dual-Tree Complex Wavelet Transform. IEEE Signal Processing Magazine 22(6), 123–151 (2005)
17. Skerl, D., Likar, B., Pernus, P.: A Protocol for Evaluation of Similarity Measures for Rigid Registration. IEEE Transactions on Medical Imaging 25(6), 779–791 (2006)
18. Matthäus, L., Trillenberg, P., Fadini, T., Finke, M., Schweikard, A.: Brain mapping with transcranial magnetic stimulation using a refined correlation ratio and Kendall's τ. Stat. Med. 27, 5252–5270 (2008)

Real-Time Face Pose Estimation
in Challenging Environments

Mliki Hazar[1], Hammami Mohamed[2], and Ben-Abdallah Hanêne[1]

[1] MIRACL-FSEG, University of Sfax, 3018 Sfax, Tunisia
mliki.hazar@gmail.com
hanene.benabdallah@fsegs.rnu.tn
[2] MIRACL-FS, University of Sfax, 3018 Sfax, Tunisia
mohamed.hammami@fss.rnu.tn

Abstract. A novel low-computation discriminative feature representation is introduced for face pose estimation in video context. The contributions of this work lie in the proposition of new approach which supports automatic face pose estimation with no need to manual initialization, able to handle different challenging problems without affecting the computational complexity (~58 milliseconds per frame). We have applied Local Binary Patterns Histogram Sequence (LBPHS) on Gaussian and Gabor feature pictures to encode salient micro-patterns of multi-view face pose. Relying on LBPHS face representation, an SVM classifier was used to estimate face pose. Two series of experiments were performed to prove that our proposed approach, being simple and highly automated, can accurately and effectively estimate face pose. Additionally, experiments on face images with diverse resolutions prove that LBPHS features are efficient to low-resolution images, which is critical challenge in real-world applications where only low-resolution frames are available.

Keywords: Face pose estimation, LBPH, SVM.

1   Introduction

In the context of computer vision, face pose estimation is defined as the ability to deduce the person's face orientations regarding its three degree of freedom: Yaw, Pitch and Roll. Actually, knowing face pose provides an important cue in many computer vision applications like: driver assisted system, virtual reality, intelligent monitoring, human-computer interaction, etc. As part of biometric applications, face pose estimation is a key step in face-based biometric systems as it is important to find out the face pose apart from the identity of the person.

The broad variation in face appearance due to dissimilarity in skin-color, facial features, and shape complicates the design of an accurate face pose estimation system. In our work and so as to develop a universal face pose estimation system, we strove for an approach which is able to overcome the most challenging problems occurring while estimating face pose in video context. The main contributions of this paper are:

J. Blanc-Talon et al. (Eds.): ACIVS 2013, LNCS 8192, pp. 114–125, 2013.
© Springer International Publishing Switzerland 2013

- Introducing full autonomous approach where there is no manual intervention and no prospect of manual initialization or detection.
- Handling near and far field images with both high and low resolution independently to lighting disparity. Moreover, estimating face pose of multiple people in one frame without affecting the computational complexity of the system.
- Presenting an autonomous user approach which does not depend on user identity, providing then a higher degree of subject independence. Hence the system is closed, in the sense that it must not be retrained for a new user.

The objective of the proposed approach is to contribute to pattern recognition in biometrics by suggesting a new approach for face pose estimation which estimate face pose in pitch and yaw with sufficient range of allowed motion independently from the identity of the person. This paper addresses this issue by introducing a new discriminative feature representation for face pose estimation. Our approach uses five filters, one Gaussian and four Gabor filters with different scales and orientations to extract relevant local facial features. Then multi-view face representation is computed using Local Binary Patterns (LBP). Actually, LBP is an operator which encodes the local facial features in multi-resolution spatial histogram and combines local intensity distribution with the spatial information. Such properties make LBP robust to noise and local image transformations due to illumination variations and occlusion. In fact, the idea behind the use of LBP is that the face can be perceived as a combination of micro-patterns which are invariant to grey scale transformation. Once we combine these micro-patterns, a global description of the face pose is obtained. This global description is modeled as a histogram sequence by concatenating the histograms of these micro-patterns of all the local Gabor and Gaussian pattern maps. This histogram provides a compact feature representation that is robust to minor deviations. In fact, such histogram describes the face pose on three different levels of locality: the labels for the histogram involve information about the patterns on a pixel-level, the labels are summed over a small micro-pattern to produce information on a regional level and the regional histograms are concatenated to build a global description of the face pose. Regarding classification step, we have used Support Vector Machine (SVM) to train facial feature and then estimate face pose. Experiment study reveals a significant improvement in face estimation accuracy while using LBPHS feature extraction.

The following section is dedicated to a brief study of related work. The outlines of our proposed approach are presented in details in section 3. The experimental findings and results will be detailed in section 4. The last section will wrap up the discussion by providing a conclusion and some reflections on our future research studies.

2   Related Work

Many previous studies were devoted to the topic of face pose estimation. The existing methods can be classified in two main approaches: appearance-based approach and facial features-based approach.

2.1   Appearance-Based Approach

Appearance-based approach uses the entire face region to estimate face pose. It perceives face pose estimation issue as a multi-class classification problem. The goal is to find the relationship between the face region features and a previous face pose model. This broad category of approach encompasses three minor sub-categories of methods: Template matching methods, Non-linear regression methods and Detector array methods.

Template Matching Method. The detected face is compared to a set of face Template exemplars (models) labeled with discrete pose in order to find the most similar face pose view. To perform face pose view matching, some comparison metrics are used like the normalized cross-correlation at multiple image resolutions [1] or the mean squared error (MSE) over a sliding window [2]. Template matching methods are appealing because only positive examples are required; however face pose estimation could be affected by a single noisy measurement.

Non-linear Regression Methods. These methods aim to build a face pose model from a set of labeled training data, such model will provide discrete or continuous pose estimation for any new face pose sample. Support vector regressors [3] and neural networks [6] were mainly used to directly project an image into face pose space. To model the continuous variation of the face pose, dimensionality reduction techniques were often used to build new low-dimensional manifold able to recover successfully the face pose. Principal component analysis (PCA) [4] and its nonlinear kernel version KPCA [5] were used as dimensionality reduction techniques.

Detector Array Methods. The face pose is estimated by training multiple face pose detectors, each detector for different discrete pose. The image is then evaluated by a detector trained on many images with a supervised learning algorithm. Some of detector array are mainly Support Vector Machine [7] and FloatBoost classifiers [8]. These systems afford excellent invariance to identity, but due to the complexity of training many detectors, they have been limited to fewer discrete poses.

2.2   Feature-Based Approach

Feature-based approach assumes that there is a casual relationship between the 3D face pose and some facial properties. It estimates face pose from a set of facial features such as eyes, nose and mouth. Three sub-categories were perceived to describe the conceptual methods that have been used to estimate face pose: Flexible models methods, Geometric methods and Tracking methods.

Flexible Models Methods. They make comparisons at the feature level in order to fit a flexible model to the facial structure already mapped. Flexible models require local facial feature detection step like eyes corners, nose or mouth corners. Elastic Graph Matching (EGM) [9] and Active Shape Model (ASM) [10] are mainly used to find the minimum distance between these features and the flexible model. Actually, flexible models are limited to head pose orientations from which some facial feature (the outer corners of both eyes) are visible. Moreover, it depends on facial images resolution.

Geometric Methods. These methods use facial feature points' arrangement and configuration to estimate the face pose. In [11], the deviation of nose angle and the movement of a bilateral symmetry face axis are used as human perception cues to estimate the face pose. A different set of five points (inner and outer of eyes and nose tip points) was also used [12] to determine the face pose from the normal to the plane. Even though many of these features are simple, the difficulty lies in detecting these features with high accuracy and handling outlying or missing feature.

Tracking Methods. Temporal continuity and smooth motion information were used as cues features to provide permanent face pose estimation over time. Tracking methods follow local facial feature points within face region from frame to frame. Then, feature matching process is performed using SIFT descriptors [13] or RANSAC techniques [14] to compute face pose under full perspective projection. These methods require initialization face pose step in order to produce a new model or fit a previous one.

Actually, resolution is a subtle problem as it makes it tricky to detect precisely facial feature. Accordingly, we have avoided to process with feature-based approach as it depends on the accurate detection of facial feature points and is typically more sensitive to occlusion than appearance-based methods which use information from the entire face region. In point of fact, appearance based methods inspect the appearance change of the face including wrinkles, bulges and furrows and can encode micro patterns which is important for face pose estimation task. Taking all this into account, we introduce a new appearance-based approach to estimate face pose in real-world applications where most of faces are in low resolution.

3   Proposed Approach

In our procedure, we aim to develop an appearance-based approach for face pose estimation using Local Binary Pattern Histogram Sequences (LBPHS). The overall of our proposed approach is described in Figure 1.

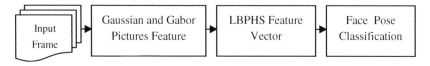

Fig. 1. Our proposed approach for face pose estimation

Actually, our proposed approach is based on psychophysical studies in saccadic eye movements [24] which show that local appearance information is essential for classification step. In fact, people can recognize objects when they try to find regions where discriminating information is detected. Our approach uses this finding to estimate face pose, by dividing face images into sub-regions and comparing the similarities between these sub-patterns. Accordingly, we apply two filters: Gaussian and Gabor filters to obtain five different Gaussian and Gabor pictures. Each Gaussian and Gabor picture is converted to Local Binary Pattern map which is further divided into non-overlapping rectangle regions (micro-patterns). For each micro-pattern a histogram is computed. Then, we have concatenated the Local Binary Pattern Histogram of all these micro-patterns to build the final histogram sequence which model the face pose. Finally, Support Vector Machine (SVM) was applied to estimate the face pose. The following sub-sections will describe this procedure in detail.

3.1   Gaussian and Gabor Pictures Feature

Before applying Gaussian and Gabor filters, we have normalized the input face image. Hence the face is converted to grayscale image level, resized to 64 ×64 pixels resolution and then preprocessed by histogram equalization to reduce lighting conditions effects.

Since we have opted for appearance based approach which uses the general appearance of the face, we have used Gaussian filter as it typically helps to reduce image noise and reduce face feature tricky details.

Indeed, the idea behind the choice of Gabor filter is motivated by the fact that Gabor filter process in similar way to the receptive field profiles of the mammalian cortical cells [25]. This property makes this filter well adequate for vision processing since it displays efficient characteristics of spatial locality and orientation selectivity. Moreover, Gabor filter can handles face shape and orientation in multi-view face images which are very important features for face pose estimation problem. Actually, we have exploited the multi-resolution and multi-orientation of Gabor filters to describe the local information of the face pose with prominent features. The Gabor representation of face image is derived by convolving the image with the Gabor filters which is defined as follow:

$$\psi_{\mu,\upsilon}(z) = \frac{||k_{\mu,\upsilon}||^2}{\sigma^2}\, e^{\left(\frac{-||k_{\mu,\upsilon}||^2\,||z||^2}{2\sigma^2}\right)}\left[e^{i\,k_{\mu,\upsilon}\,z} - e^{\frac{-\sigma^2}{2}}\right] \tag{1}$$

$$k_{\mu,\upsilon} = k_\upsilon e^{i\phi_\mu},\ k_\upsilon = 2^{-\frac{\upsilon+2}{2}},\ \phi_\mu = \mu\frac{\pi}{8} \tag{2}$$

Where: μ and υ define the orientation and scale of the Gabor filter; σ is the sigma of the Gaussian envelope. We have employed a discrete set of two different scales with ($\upsilon = 0,\ 2$) and two orientations with ($\mu = 0,\frac{\pi}{2}$), then four feature pictures were computed. Overall, we have five feature face pose pictures, where the dimension of each one is 4096 (64×64).

3.2   Local Binary Pattern Sequence Histogram (LBPHS)

To provide robust description of each facial pose picture, we have applied LBPHS which is not only robust to face variations but also describes face pose pictures with much discriminating power. So as to enhance the information in each facial feature pose picture, we encode the intensity of Gaussian picture feature and the magnitude values of Gaussian pictures using LBP operator. The LBP operator was first introduced by Ojala et al. [27]. This operator labels the pixels of an image by thresholding the 3x3 neighborhood of each pixel with the center value and considering the result as a binary number. An example of the LBP operator is shown in Figure 2.

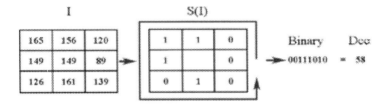

Fig. 2. The basic LBP operator

Then the histogram of the labels can be used as a texture descriptor. The histogram H of an image $f(x, y)$ with gray levels in the range $[0, k-1]$ is defined as follow:

$$H_i = \sum_{x,y} I\{f(x,y) = i\}, i = 0, 1, \dots k - 1 \tag{3}$$

Where i is the ith gray level, H is the number of pixels in the image with gray level i and

$$I\{A\} = \begin{cases} 1, & A \text{ is True} \\ 0, & A \text{ is False} \end{cases} \tag{4}$$

This histogram encloses information about the distribution of the local regions such as edges, spots and flat areas. However, face pose variations appear typically more on some specific regions in face picture. Therefore, we exploit local feature histogram to summarize the region property and maintain also spatial information. For this purpose, the image is divided into multiple non-overlapping regions called micro-patterns (R_0, R_1 ... R_{m-1}) from which a histogram was extracted. Then, every histogram estimated from the micro-patterns are concatenated into a single histogram sequence to represent the given face pose image. This spatially enhanced histogram is defined as:

$$H_{i,j} = \sum_{x,y} I\{f_l(x,y) = i\} I\{(x,y) \in R_j\} \tag{5}$$

Where: $i = 0,\dots n-1$ and $j = 0,\dots m-1$.

In our experiment, for a 64×64 feature face pose picture, the region (micro-pattern) is set to 16×16. The number of bins in the histogram $H_{i,j}$ is 256, hence the dimension of $H_{i,j}$ is 20480 (5×16×256). Figure 3 shows the process of computing LBPHS face pose feature vector.

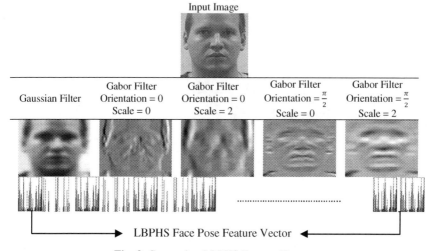

Fig. 3. Computing LBPHS Feature Vector

3.3   Face Pose Classification

In our work, we are mainly interested to five different face pose classes: Up, Down, Frontal, Left and Right. To train face pose classes, we have used Pointing'04 data set [15] which is composed of 15 sets of images for 15 persons wearing glasses or not with various skin colors. Each set contains 2 series of 93 images of the same person with different pitch and yaw angles (Figure 4).

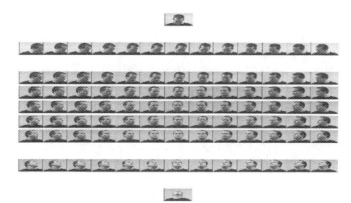

Fig. 4. Yaw/Pitch angles examples from POINTING'04 dataset

To build our face pose estimation system, we have proceeded with SVM classifier thanks to its performance in statistical learning theory and robustness for face pose estimation task [16]. Actually, Support Vector Machine is an efficient technique for classification [26] which carries out an implicit mapping of data into a higher dimensional feature space.

Given a training set of labeled examples A = $\{(x_i, y_i), i = 1...n\}$ where $x_i \in R^n$ and $y_i \in \{1, -1\}$. A new test data x is classified using the decision function f(x) defined as follow:

$$f(x) = sgn(\sum_{i=1}^{n} \alpha_i y_i K(x_i, x) + b) \qquad (6)$$

Where α_i are the Lagrange multipliers of a dual optimization problem, and $K(x_i, x)$ is a kernel function. Given a nonlinear mapping ϕ that embeds input data into feature space, kernels have the form of $K(x_i, x_j) = (\phi(x_i) \cdot \phi(x_j))$. SVM finds a linear separating hyper plane with the maximal margin to separate the training data in feature space. b is the parameter of the optimal hyper plane.

Since SVM classifier makes binary decisions, multi-class classification here is accomplished by a cascade of binary classifiers together with a voting scenario. Thereby, we have represented each sample of the Pointing'04 data set by an LBPHS features vector. Then, an SVM classifier is applied to find out the separating plane that has maximum distance to the closest points (support vector) in the training set. Actually, we have used two SVM, one trained for pitch face pose and one for yaw face pose. Table 1 shows the way we have divided the dataset into five main face pose classes.

Table 1. POINTING'04 dataset division into five face pose classes

Rotation degree	Yaw Pose			Pitch Pose		
	[- 30°, 30°]	[45°, 90°]	[- 45°, - 90°]	- 90°	90°	[- 30, 30]
Face Pose Classes	Frontal	Left Profile	Right Profile	Down	Up	Frontal

4   Experiments

To evaluate the performance of our proposed approach for face pose estimation, we have carried out two series of experiments: the first one aims to compare our approach with the existing works and the second one seeks to appraise the performance of our trained face pose models on another different image and video dataset.

4.1   First Series of Experiments

To evaluate the accuracy of our proposed approach, we have compared its performance with the most known works for face pose estimation. In order to make works comparable, we have proceeded in the same way as these previous methods when training and testing face pose. This comparison study is described in table 2 in term of mean absolute error and classification rate.

Using Pointing'04 dataset, our proposed approach proves more effectiveness than the four previous methods. Actually, we record the least mean absolute rate and the highest classification rate in yaw and pitch. These results prove that using LBPHS processing on face image provides more discriminating feature to deal with face pose classification task than using classic pixel intensity information.

Table 2. Comparative study

Dataset	Methods	Mean Absolute Error		Classification Rate	
		Yaw	Pitch	Yaw	Pitch
Pointing'04	Associative Memories [22]	10.1°	15.9°	50.0%	43.9%
	High-Order SVD [23]	12.9°	17.97°	49.25%	54.84%
	PCA [23]	14.11°	14.98°	55.20%	57.99%
	LEA [23]	15.88°	17.44°	45.16%	50.61%
	Our Method	5.96°	9.54°	65.12%	58.88%
CAS PEAL	B. Ma [19]	-	-	97.14%	-
	Our Method	0.73°	-	95.30%	-

Regarding CAS-PEAL dataset [17] which is a yaw face pose dataset, our approach achieves good results comparing to B.Ma approach [19] as we use a vector feature of length 20480 however the length of the feature vector in B.Ma approach is 163840 which is 8 time more longer than our proposed feature vector. Although our feature vector is shorter, it succeeds to describe efficiently face pose and reaches good classification accuracy with minimum error rate.

4.2   Second Series of Experiments

This series of experiments aims to evaluate the accuracy of our five face pose models (Frontal, Profile Left, Profile Right, Up, Down) which were built using Pointng'04 dataset. To achieve such evaluation, we have studied the performance of these face pose models on two dataset: FacePix Image Dataset [18] and our recorded video dataset which deal with different face pose constraints. This evaluation study is described in table 3 in term of classification rate and time per frame.

Actually, permanent face detection and tracking in video was performed using our previous proposed methods for face detection [20] and tracking [21].

This experiment study reveals the robustness of our face pose models to handle different challenging problems. In fact, our approach succeeds to overcome both of illumination and resolution variation constraints, and can also deal with partial occlusion problem. Some examples from our recorded video dataset are presented in table 4.

Table 3. Experimental study of our proposed face pose models

Data Set	Description		Classification Rate		Time (ms)
			Yaw	Pitch	
FacePix	450 Samples		91.55 %	-	-
Our Video Recorded Data set	One face	Seq.1	93.4 %	90.7 %	57
		Seq.2	90.5 %	63.6 %	55
	Multiple faces	Seq.1	91.6 %	100 %	120
		Seq.2	90.4 %	86.1 %	124
	Different face resolution	Seq.1	92.3 %	100 %	58
		Seq.2	94.2 %	94.9 %	57
	Illumination variation	Seq.1	89.2 %	95 %	58
		Seq.2	87.6 %	82 %	58
	Partial face occlusion (Glasses)	Seq.1	94.4 %	95.4 %	62
	Resolution and illumination variation	Seq.1	85.5 %	89 %	60

Table 4. Examples from our recorded dataset

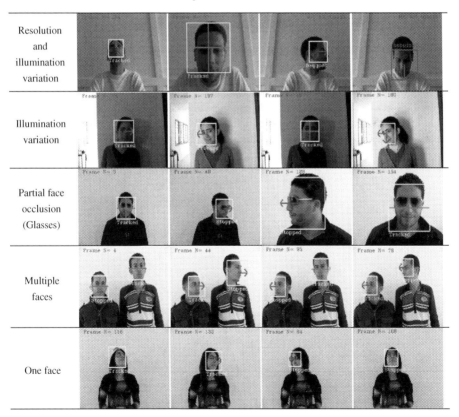

Besides, our proposed approach estimates the face pose either for one face or multiple faces in one frame without affecting the computational complexity of the system (~ 58 ms/frame for one face and ~122 ms/frame for multiple faces). Furthermore, our face pose models provide high degree of subject independency as they estimate yaw and pitch face pose regardless of user identity.

Therefore, we can conclude that our proposed face pose models using LBPHS operator is efficient to deal with many face pose problems either in image or video context.

5   Conclusion

We described in this paper a new face pose estimation approach based on LBPHS operator. The novelty of the approach lies in the ability to deal with different challenging problems in video context. Actually, our proposed approach is invariant to identity, have sufficient range of allowed motion and require no manual intervention. Applying LBPHS operator on Gaussian and Gabor feature pictures, we have encoded multi-view face pose using feature histogram. Then these face feature histogram were used as an input for an SVM classifier to estimate pose. The effectiveness of our proposed approach was proved using two different series of experiments.

In our future works, we seek to use the output of face pose estimation module to choose which biometric modality is more reliable for person identification. In fact, if we perceive profile pose it's more suitable to use ear modality; otherwise, in frontal view, it's more reliable to use face modality.

References

1. Beymer, D.: Face Recognition Under Varying Pose. In: Proc. IEEE Conf. Computer Vision and Pattern Recognition, pp. 756–761 (1994)
2. Niyogi, S., Freeman, W.: Example-Based Head Tracking. In: Proc. IEEE Int'l Conf. Automatic Face and Gesture Recognition, pp. 374–378 (1996)
3. Cascia, M.L., Sclaroff, S., Athitsos, V.: Fast, Reliable Head Tracking Under Varying Illumination: An Approach Based on Registration of Texture-Mapped 3D Models. IEEE Trans. Pattern Analysis and Machine Intelligence 22(4), 322–336 (2000)
4. Sherrah, J., Gong, S., Ong, E.-J.: Face Distributions in Similarity Space under Varying Head Pose. Image and Vision Computing 19(12), 807–819 (2001)
5. Wu, J., Trivedi, M.: A Two-Stage Head Pose Estimation Framework and Evaluation. Pattern Recognition 41(3), 1138–1158 (2008)
6. Voit, M., Nickel, K., Stiefelhagen, R.: Multi-view Head Pose Estimation using Neural Networks. Face Processing in Video (2005)
7. Huang, J., Shao, X., Wechsler, H.: Face Pose Discrimination Using Support Vector Machines (SVM). In: Proc. 14th Int'l Conf. Pattern Recognition, pp. 154–156 (1998)

8. Zhang, Z., Hu, Y., Liu, M., Huang, T.: Head Pose Estimation in Seminar Room Using Multi View Face Detectors. In: Multimodal Technologies for Perception of Humans: Proc. First Int'l Workshop Classification of Events, Activities and Relationships, pp. 299–304 (2007)
9. Cootes, T., Edwards, G., Taylor, C.: Active Appearance Models. IEEE Trans. Pattern Analysis and Machine Intelligence 23(6), 681–685 (2001)
10. Cootes, T., Taylor, C., Cooper, D., Graham, J.: Active Shape Models—Their Training and Application. Computer Vision and Image Understanding 61(1), 38–59 (1995)
11. Wilson, H., Wilkinson, F., Lin, L., Castillo, M.: Perception of Head Orientation. Vision Research 40(5), 459–472 (2000)
12. Gee, A., Cipolla, R.: Determining the Gaze of Faces in Images. Image and Vision Computing 12(10), 639–647 (1994)
13. Lowe, D.: Distinctive Image Features from Scale-Invariant Keypoints. Int'l J. Computer Vision 60(2), 91–110 (2004)
14. Zhao, G., Chen, L., Song, J., Chen, G.: Large Head Movement Tracking Using SIFT-Based Registration. In: Proc. ACM Int'l Conf. Multimedia, pp. 807–810 (2007)
15. Gourier, N., Letessier, J.: The Pointing 04 Data Sets, Pointing 2004, ICPR, Visual Observation of Deictic Gestures (2004)
16. Kwong, J.N.S., Gong, S.: Learning Support Vector Machines for A Multi-View Face Model. In: Proc. of the British Machine Vision Conference (1999)
17. Gao, W., Chen, X.: The CAS-PEAL Large-Scale Chinese Face Database and Baseline Evaluations. IEEE Transaction on Systems, man, and Cybernetics – Part A: Systems and Humans 38(1) (2008)
18. Little, G., Krishna, S., Black, J., Panchanathan, S.: A methodology for evaluating robustness of face recognition algorithms with respect to changes in pose and illumination angle. In: ICASSP (2005)
19. Ma, B., Zhang, W., Shan, S., Chen, X., Gao, W.: Robust Head Pose Estimation Using LGBP. In: The 18th International Conference on Pattern Recognition (2006)
20. Mliki, H., Hammami, M., Ben-Abdallah, H.: Real time face detection based on motion and skin color information. In: ISPA 2012, pp. 799–806 (2012)
21. Mliki, H., Hammami, M., Ben-Abdallah, H.: Multi-constraints Face Detect-Track System. In: Cortesi, A., Chaki, N., Saeed, K., Wierzchoń, S. (eds.) CISIM 2012. LNCS, vol. 7564, pp. 224–235. Springer, Heidelberg (2012)
22. Gourier, N., Maisonnasse, J., Hall, D., Crowley, J.: Head Pose Estimation on Low Resolution Images", Multimodal Technologies for Perception of Humans. In: Proc. First Int'l Workshop Classification of Events, Activities and Relationships, pp. 270–280 (2007)
23. Tu, J., Fu, Y., Hu, Y., Huang, T.: Evaluation of Head Pose Estimation for Studio Data. In: Multimodal Technologies for Perception of Humans: Proc. First Int'l Workshop Classification of Events, pp. 281–290 (2007)
24. Minut, S., Mahadevan, S., Henderson, J.M., Dyer, F.C.: Face recognition using foveal vision. In: IEEE International Workshop on Biologically Motivated Computer Vision, pp. 424–433 (2000)
25. Liu, C., Wechsler, H.: Gabor Feature Based Classiffication Using the Enhanced Fisher Linear Discriminant Model for Face Recognition. IEEE Trans. Image Processing 11(4) (2002)
26. Vapnik, V.N.: Statistical Learning Theory. Wiley, New York (1998)
27. Ojala, T., Pietikainen, M., Harwood, D.: A comparative study of texture measures with classification based on feature distributions. Pattern Recognition 29, 51–59 (1996)

Human Motion Capture Using Data Fusion of Multiple Skeleton Data

Jean-Thomas Masse[1,2], Frédéric Lerasle[1,3], Michel Devy[1],
André Monin[1], Olivier Lefebvre[2], and Stéphane Mas[2]

[1] CNRS, Laboratoire d'Analyse et d'Architecture des Systèmes
7 avenue du colonel Roche, F-31400 Toulouse, France
{jean-thomas.masse,frederic.lerasle,michel.devy,
andre.monin}@laas.fr
[2] Magellium SAS,
F-31520 Ramonville Saint-Agne, France
{olivier.lefebvre,stephane.mas}@magellium.fr
[3] Université de Toulouse, UPS, LAAS
F-31400 Toulouse, France

Abstract. Joint advent of affordable color and depth sensors and super-realtime skeleton detection, has produced a surge of research on Human Motion Capture. They provide a very important key to communication between Man and Machine. But the design was willing and closed-loop interaction, which allowed approximations and mandates a particular sensor setup. In this paper, we present a multiple sensor-based approach, designed to augment the robustness and precision of human joint positioning, based on delayed logic and filtering, of skeleton detected on each sensor.

Keywords: Human Posture Reconstruction, Motion Capture, Data Fusion, Delayed Logic, Kalman Filter, Kinect.

1 Introduction

Interest in Human Motion Capture (HMC for short, MoCap in general) is rising. Each video game entertainment systems companies introduced devices to provide this input. One of them, Microsoft Kinect, proved a commercial success [1], and introduced a reliable budget alternative to expansive time-of-flight cameras and texture-dependent stereo benches. The device is powered by PrimeSense's patented technology of structured light sensing [2]. The chip also powers the equivalent device Asus Xtion Pro Live [3] used in this paper.

While HMC is interesting for User Interaction in software design, it is also of paramount importance for robotics and surveillance, where it allows communication and interpretation of intents. In other fields there is also a surge of papers using the Kinect, for instance in education, sociology, and health.

Multiple SDKs exist, such as the Kinect-exclusive Microsoft Kinect SDK and the open-framework OpenNI [4]. PrimeSense developed the OpenNI Middleware NiTE [5] for OpenNI. It is what produces the user segmentation and skeleton. The algorithms

J. Blanc-Talon et al. (Eds.): ACIVS 2013, LNCS 8192, pp. 126–137, 2013.
© Springer International Publishing Switzerland 2013

exploit machine learning on foreground-segmented depth maps to detect the body parts. Since it only needs a depth map generator, we could have used any such maps from any sensor, such as a Kinect, or even a time-of-flight or stereo camera. That is why, in this paper, we will call *sensors* the Xtions we used to acquire our data.

However, this approach is mono-sensor, and prone to occlusion and perspective deformation. Literature focuses mainly on investigating the precision of the sensor's depth sensing [6] [7], or HMC from low-level data fusion [8]. But few, if any, tackle the problem of Motion Capture and skeleton precision, by fusing skeletons and comparing with a commercial MoCap system. That is why our goal is two-fold: (1) implement a high-level framework working atop monocular techniques and leveraging the multiple points of view; and (2) use a commercial Motion Capture system to get access to the ground truth necessary to measure our improvement over monocular.

The structure of the paper is as follows: first, we position ourselves against related works. Section 3 formalizes our approach. Before the results section, we describe the ground truth acquisition. The last section contains our conclusions and perspectives.

2   Related Work

NiTE/OpenNI, if similar to Microsoft Research Team's solution [9], [10], relies on the learning algorithm of Random Forests. It is very fast, and relatively accurate. Although it tries to cope up with self-occlusion, it is bound by monocular limitations. Also, filtering is very basic. It is only to smooth, and not predict.

Literature on Motion Capture by classical camera and computer vision techniques is very rich, as the survey from Moeslund et al. shows [11]. Better self-occultation resistance is beginning at three or four cameras [12]. These kinds of setup do require additional care to maintain data spatial and temporal coherence. Relying on color cues and silhouette [13], video MoCap is successful. However, it can not work in some circumstances such as absence of texture, where active sensors prevail [14].

HMC is the sensing of the physical quantity of the Human body joints position. As such, temporal reasoning is natural. There is a great amount of works in the video-based HMC literature [15]. In pedestrian tracking, tracking-by-detection approaches are more often combined with Delayed Logic [16], [17], [18]. To our best knowledge, such delayed logic principle has never been extended to depth sensor based HMC, where purely track-by-detection approaches [19] are privileged for the moment. Also, while multi depth sensor-based MoCap research exists [8], it focuses on low level sensor data fusion instead of high level skeleton reconstruction. Therefore, it constitutes natural and interesting to try to extend and rely on the OpenNI framework.

At any rate, ground truth is the base on which to measure results. Some work, such as HumanEva [20], described their eponym public multi-view video datasets for human motion estimation with ground truth. Few have investigated this since a large-scale, public RGB-D database with ground truth is yet to be found published.

Based on our own ground truth, our multi-sensor strategy leverages both: temporal information is exploited using Filtering techniques, and is fed at the same level than the skeleton measurements to a delayed-logic type of trajectory smoother that ensures the trajectory is consistent with observations and physical constraints.

3   Description of Our Approach

In this section, we will first describe the formalism of our approach and then detail each step. An overview of the formalism-derived framework is located mid-way in subsection 3.3.

3.1   Formalism

As in much of current HMC software, the goal is to estimate $X = [X^j]_{j \in J}$, the Euclidian positions of a restricted but representative set J of joints from the human skeleton. They are: the hands, elbow, shoulders, feet, knees, hips, torso, neck and head. At each time step t, each sensor $k \in K$ produces a foreground segmentation bitmap S_t^k over the depth bitmap, and detect a skeleton measurement $Y_t^k = [Y_t^{j,k}]_{j \in J}$. We additionally choose not to limit ourselves to the measurements produced by NiTE so we consider instead $L \supset K$ the superset of hypotheses. For sets like J, K and L, we may use K instead of $|K|$ or $card(K)$ for ease of notations where applicable.

Each measurement is of the form $Y_t^l = X_t + V_t^l, \forall l \in L$, where V_t^l is the error of the skeleton reconstruction. This error is certainly neither white nor Gaussian.

Due to speed constraints, we chose to limit the search to those hypotheses, looking for the reconstruction with the smallest error. For increased stability, we also optimize over a time lapse of $M \in \mathbb{N}$ consecutive frames.

For ease of notation, we simply write Y_t^l the event $\hat{X}_t = Y_t^l$. The goal is then to find:

$$Y_{t-M:t}^* = \underset{\{Y_s^{l_s}\}_{s=t-M:t}}{\text{argmax}} \ \mathbb{P}\left(\{Y_s^{l_s}\}_{s=t-M:t} \middle| \{S_{t-M:t}^k\}_{k \in K}\right) \tag{1}$$

This type of problem, called delayed logic, or Modal Trajectory Estimation, has already been solved by dynamic programming. Its formalism is described in the following subsection.

3.2   Delayed-Logic

According to [21], the final position of the optimized trajectory can be found as:

$$Y_t^* = \underset{Y_t^{l_t}}{\text{argmax}} \ \mathcal{J}_t^*\left(Y_t^{l_t}, \{S_{t-M:t}^k\}_{k \in K}\right) \tag{2}$$

where $\mathcal{J}_t^*$ is the marginal Bayesian likelihood:

$$\mathcal{J}_t^*\left(Y_t^{l_t}, \{S_{t-M:t}^k\}_{k \in K}\right) \triangleq \underset{Y_{t-M:t-1}}{\max} \ \mathbb{P}\left(\{S_{t-M:t}^k\}_{k \in K} \middle| \{Y_s^{l_s}\}_{s=t-M:t}\right) \mathbb{P}\left(\{Y_s^{l_s}\}_{s=t-M:t}\right) \tag{3}$$

Beginning with the knowledge of its initial value $\mathcal{J}_{t-M}^*\left(Y_{t-M}^{l_{t-M}}, \{S_{t-M}^k\}_{k \in K}\right) = \mathbb{P}\left(\{S_{t-M}^k\}_{k \in K} \middle| Y_{t-M}^{l_{t-M}}\right) \times \mathbb{P}\left(Y_{t-M}^{l_{t-M}}\right)$, it can be recursively computed by

$$
\mathcal{J}_t^*\left(Y_t^{l_t}, \{S_{t-M:t}^k\}_{k\in K}\right)
$$
$$
= \max_{Y_{t-1}^{l_{t-1}}} \left(\mathbb{P}\left(\{S_t^k\}_{k\in K} \middle| Y_t^{l_t}\right) \times \mathbb{P}\left(Y_t^{l_t} \middle| Y_{t-1}^{l_{t-1}}\right) \times \mathcal{J}_{t-1}^*\left(Y_{t-}^{l_t}, \{S_{t-M:t-1}^k\}_{k\in K}\right) \right) \qquad (4)
$$

where $\mathbb{P}\left(\{S_t^k\}_{k\in K} \middle| Y_t^{l_t}\right)$ can be considered as an observation probability for which we have to find an observation model, and $\mathbb{P}\left(Y_t^{l_t} \middle| Y_{t-1}^{l_{t-1}}\right)$ a transition probability for which we have to find a dynamic model.

Finally, one implementation exploiting this finding is the Viterbi [22] algorithm.

Before detailing the rest of those, let us summarize the whole framework as it stands.

3.3 Overview

An overview of the process is given by Fig. 1. The framework receives from each sensor $k \in K$, the user segmentations S_t^k and derived skeleton Y_t^k. We consider the segmentation to be reliable so we use it as an observation to measure the probability of a skeleton $\mathbb{P}\left(\{S_t^k\}_{k\in K} \middle| Y_t^{l_t}\right)$. The measured skeletons are fed to a Kalman Filter to introduce prediction in the process. All the skeletons $Y_t^l, l \in L \supset K$ are introduced at the end of the trellis of possible trajectories of length M. Transition probabilities $\mathbb{P}\left(Y_t^{l_t} \middle| Y_{t-1}^{l_{t-1}}\right)$, based on dynamics are combined to observation probability computed earlier. Finally, a Viterbi-like algorithm computes the most likely trajectory

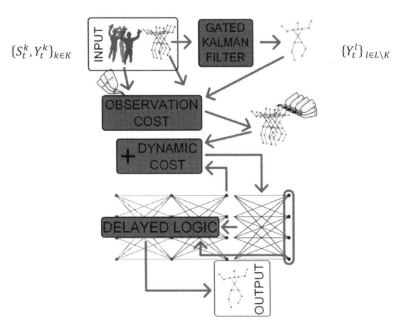

Fig. 1. Block-diagram of our approach

$$\{\hat{X}_{t-M}, ..., \hat{X}_t\} = \underset{Y_{t-M}^{l_{t-M}}, ..., Y_t^{l_t}}{\operatorname{argmax}} \ p\left(Y_{t-M}^{l_{t-M}}, ..., Y_t^{l_t} \middle| S_{t-M}^K, ..., S_t^K\right)$$

through the trellis. The whole process' estimation of the joints positions is $\hat{X}_t$.

We first wanted to complement the K skeleton hypothesis with dynamics-based randomly generated hypothesis, in a fashion similar to Markovian approaches. For instance, Particle Filters have already been applied successfully in similar situations [23], but was first discarded in favor of trying a dynamic programming approach, and second, out of concern for the heavy computation cost of the observation. Using a Kalman Filter to produce a supplementary skeleton hypothesis appeared to be an intermediate, cheaper and more sophisticated alternative.

In the following subsections, we describe the formalism and implementation of each step in more detail: the Observation and Dynamics Models, and the Gated Kalman Filter.

3.4   Observation Model

In order to assess likelihood of a skeleton estimate, the readily available data we could compare against was the foreground segmentation produced in the detection of the skeletons by NiTE, as illustrated in Fig. 2. As far as we could figure, the middleware seems to use a background substraction, as it is lost if the sensor is moved. New

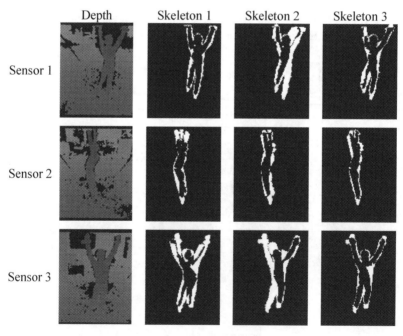

Fig. 2. Example of "exclusive or" of two segmentation images, taken from our dataset acquired with a system of 3 sensors fully presented in Section 4. A white pixel means only one segmentation encompassed this pixel. One can see that reprojected in another viewpoint, the seemingly correct skeleton (in diagonal frames, where the skeleton is generated from the same image) can produce varying results. Images are horizontally truncated here for presentation purposes.

objects entering the field of view are labeled and kept independent afterward, and depth sensing is insensible to texture and color traps contrary to video segmentation.

As the user segmentation $S_t^k(i,j)$ is the foreground segmentation over i,j of the user seen from the sensor k, it can be compared to an artificial segmentation $\mathbb{S}_t^l(i,j)$ based on projecting a skeleton Y_t^l made of white cylinders on the image.

To compute a distance between foreground segmentation maps, we simply count the number of pixels exclusively in one or the other image, that is, the exclusive or, or sum of the absolute difference in each pixel $d_t(k,l) = \sum_{i,j} \left| S_t^k(i,j) - \mathbb{S}_t^l(i,j) \right|$.

As-is, d_t varies with the total coverage of the body on the image, that is, the distance of the user to the sensor. Therefore, we have to normalize. We do it over the total area of the body in the sensor image, giving a mostly distance-insensitive measure, if we ignore sampling effects of working with bitmaps. The result is:

$$\mathrm{D}_t(k,l) = \frac{d_t(k,l)}{\sum_{i,j} S_t^k(i,j)} \tag{5}$$

We then model the probability density $\mathbb{P}\left(\{S_t^k\}_{k\in K} \middle| Y_t^{l_t}\right)$ of having a correct observation, as the normal distribution around a D_t of an average $\mu = 0.1$ due to noise and approximating the limbs to cylinders and of standard deviation $\sigma = 0.1$, meaning

$$\mathbb{P}\left(\{S_t^k\}_{k\in K} \middle| Y_t^{l_t}\right) \triangleq \prod_{k\in K} \frac{1}{\sqrt{2\cdot\pi\cdot\sigma^2}} e^{-\frac{(\mathrm{D}_t(k,l)-\mu)^2}{2\cdot\sigma^2}} \tag{6}$$

It can be noted that the full size of 640×480 pixels has not been used in implementation. We use a smaller resolution of 160×120 to speed up calculation and remain super-realtime. Also, instead of maximizing the probability, the Viterbi algorithm is applied as-is, minimizing $\sum_{k\in K} \frac{(\mathrm{D}_t(k,l)-\mu)^2}{\sigma^2}$ instead for the same result, but faster computation, and no floating-point underflow. Indeed, with 45 degrees of freedom, the (especially dynamics) probability density sometimes valued below $2.22507e - 308$, rounding to 0. We employed the same conversion for the Dynamics model, as it also uses a Gaussian probability model.

3.5   Dynamics Model

Considering the Cartesian nature of our joint model, a correct dynamic model is difficult to obtain. We believe that using an articulatory model would make more sense but would be too long to compute, incompatible with our current speed objective.

For now, the Dynamics model goal is to remove jitter and promote temporal continuity. It is useful, for instance, if the skeleton suddenly flips left and right, as this is not possible for a human.

Therefore, we use a centered Gaussian density for each joint, with standard deviation attuned for each joint based on ground truth standard deviation at capture rate.

$$\mathbb{P}\left(Y_t^{l_t} \middle| Y_{t-1}^{l_{t-1}}\right) \triangleq \prod_{j\in J} \frac{1}{\sqrt{2\cdot\pi\cdot\sigma_j^2}} e^{-\frac{\left(Y_t^{j,l_t} - Y_{t-1}^{j,l_{t-1}}\right)^2}{2\cdot\sigma_j^2}} \tag{7}$$

3.6   Measurement-Gated Kalman Filter

The Kalman Filter we employed uses a very simple skeleton model to maintain speed. Each j joint's state X^j is tracked separately as follows (units in mm, timestep is $20^{-1}s$):

$$X^j = (x \quad y \quad z \quad \dot{x} \quad \dot{y} \quad \dot{z})^T \quad (S)$$
$$X_t^j = A \cdot X_{t-1}^j + W_{t-1} \quad (E), \quad Z_t^j = H \cdot X_{t-1}^j + V_{t-1} \quad (O)$$
$$W \sim \mathcal{N}(0,Q) \quad and \quad V \sim \mathcal{N}(0,R) \quad (N)$$
$$H = (I_3 \quad 0_3) \quad (O_M), \quad A = \begin{pmatrix} I_3 & I_3 \\ 0_3 & 0.8 \cdot I_3 \end{pmatrix} \quad (E_M)$$
$$Q = \begin{pmatrix} 100^2 \cdot I_3 & 0 \\ 0 & 100^2 \cdot I_3 \end{pmatrix} \quad (N_{M1}), \quad R = 200^2 \cdot I_3 \quad (N_{M2})$$

For ease of discourse and establishing variable names, we remind the main equations of processing a Kalman Filter:

$$\hat{X}_{t+1}^{j-} = A \cdot \hat{X}_t^j \tag{8.1}$$

$$S_{t+1} = H \cdot P_{t+1}^{j-} \cdot H^T + R$$
$$r_{t+1}^j = Y_{t+1}^j - H \cdot \hat{X}_{t+1}^{j-} \tag{8.2}$$

$$K_{t+1} = P_{t+1}^{j-} \cdot H^T \cdot S_{t+1}^{-1}$$
$$\hat{X}_{t+1}^j = \hat{X}_{t+1}^{j-} + K_{t+1} \cdot r_{t+1}^j$$
$$P_{t+1}^j = P_{t+1}^{j-} - K_{t+1} \cdot H \cdot P_{t+1}^{j-} \tag{8.3}$$

$$\left(\hat{X}_{t+1}^{j-}, P_{t+1}^{j-}\right) = \left(\hat{X}_{t+1}^j, P_{t+1}^j\right) \tag{8.1'}$$

Step (8.1) gets done once at every time step. (8.2) is used to test the Measurement Gate explained below. If the measurement passes the gate (i.e. it is to be processed) then step (8.3) is done. For each additional measurement, step (8.1') is done before resuming at step (8.2). If no measurement is fitting through the gate, then the reverse assignation from (8.1') is made (the estimate is only the prediction).

This model has but one drawback, non-compliance to an articulated body. But in practice, since the measurements are from an articulatory-body compliant system, the results are approximately so. However, no conversion is needed from input format and parameters are straightforward.

Unfortunately, all the joints do not follow such a model even remotely. For instance, if the user is sideways, both the feet may be measured at the same place. To prevent such measure from being integrated (which heavily degrades the performance), a measurement gate (or residual monitoring) is implemented.

This technique first published in [24] consists in rejecting Y_t^j from processing if $(r_t^j)^T \cdot S_t^{-1} \cdot r_t^j > g_t^2$, where r_t^j is the innovation, S_t the residual covariance matrix, and g_t is the gating threshold. g_t is generally set between 1 and 3, expressing "innovation's L2-norm is beyond g_t residual sigmas." This generally indicates a faulty sensor; as such phenomenon has 32%, 5% or 0.2% probability of happening for $g_t=1$, 2 or 3. Since we have redundancy in measurements, a single correct measurement is sufficient. If no measurements are taken into account, the Error variance P_t^j eventually gets big enough to allow the measurement through the gate (as S_t depends on P_t^j, and also repeatedly gets incremented by R).

4   Our Multi-sensor Platform Setup and Data Acquisition

Our objective is to appreciate the precision in the one-sensor and our multi-sensor system's estimation of the human body joints' positions. Therefore, we decided to use the Motion Capture system from Motion Analysis [25].

This acquisition was meant to serve three purposes:
- First, evaluate the performance of NiTE from several angles: frontal (as it was designed), and also sideways and behind;
- Second, create a dataset to exploit in a learning algorithm;
- Third, create a dataset to test fusion and other learning algorithms on.

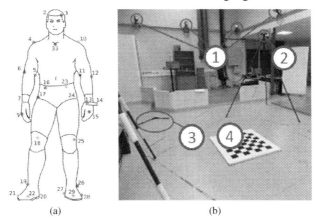

(a)   (b)

Fig. 3. Precision measurement experiment. (a) Motion Capture markers setup [25], and (b) Motion Capture (① are 4 of the 10 IR or NIR cameras) and Xtion (②) setup, with MoCap reference frame (③) and 1 m² camera calibration chessboard (④) also present.

We placed and oriented the MoCap reference frame on the RGB calibration chessboard, respectively ③ and ④ in Fig. 3(b), in order to localize all the sensors in MoCap reference frame. Localizing the device's RGB sensor was sufficient because the Depth-to-RGB registration is factory-determined and readily available in and done by OpenNI. Works show that significant improvement can be made, but only in the close range of the sensor [26].

Time synchronization was subsequently achieved by MoCap marker projection (Fig. 3(a)) in RGB frames. On such a frame, a fast marker would leave a blurry trail. Since the MoCap frames were 10 times as numerous, we fine-tuned the time synchronization so as to project the marker on the middle of the blur. Then, all the depth streams were synchronized to MoCap since the frames of each were all time-stamped.

We also considered sequences short enough (90 seconds on average) for time drift to be insignificant compared to the end result precision.

Acquired data consist of two sets, labeled IRSS35, with a full set of MoCap markers (35), allowing for skeleton building; and NS-CAP13, with a reduced set of markers (13), for quick testing. Both feature several sequences covering exercise and sport moves, and regular moves and poses from regular life, and extremely varying random poses for completion. IRSS35 has nine sequences, sometimes rerecorded, totaling 16 minutes or upward of 21569 workable depth frames.

It must be noted that each sequence is not a simple movement, but a mix and match of actions such as weight lifting, running, squats, as well as more mundane movement such as dancing, broom handling (broom not detected), and moving furniture.

5   Evaluation and Results

The presented results of our approach are achieved real-time at 20Hz with a monothread CPU application on an Intel Core i7 2760QM (2.40 Ghz). As it was offline filtering, the PNG decompression of the user images occupied 80% of the computations. This means NiTE may run its 3 own threads on the same CPU core and the framework will still perform the same online.

Fig. 4 shows the proportion of skeleton frames whose joints were closer than a distance from ground truth (50, 100, 150 and 200 mm. Those are cumulative). Each skeleton proposed by the OpenNI single-sensor detector has an entry (*Sensor 1* to *Sensor 3*) for comparison. Additionally, we made the Oracle *Sensor Best5* pseudo-result whose output is the skeleton of the *Sensor* which had at that time the lowest cumulated distance to the reference positions of the joints.

The three tested setups were:

- *Our approach*, based on Viterbi algorithm fed with the three skeletons and first-order gated Kalman filter:
- A single, 0-order (no speed in state) ungated *Kalman*, for reference;
- The described implementation with no additional skeleton provided other than the single sensors'. It is the *"Delayed Logic Only"* entry.

The figures allow us to come to three conclusions.

First, a Viterbi-type implementation, without any additional skeleton, then acting as a sensor selector, can closely match the expected result of being precise based on joints.

Second and third, adding additional skeletons choices brings two advantages: slightly increased reliability, as fewer frames are outside the outstanding distance of 200 mm from ground truth; and much increased precision, as the amount of positions lower than the 50 mm mark increases.

Besides, *Sensor 3* was primarily faced during the experiment (except during rotation movements). The statistics indicate that while this Kinect will be the most reliable over all joints, it is not necessarily the most precise everywhere. Indeed, the other two sensors have better statistics over one side of the body.

Effect differs on the type of joint: from the always-visible such as the head, the increase in precision is higher, while the increase in reliability is better seen at occluded joints, such as the feet. Hands exhibit both since they are alternatively occluded or visible during manipulations.

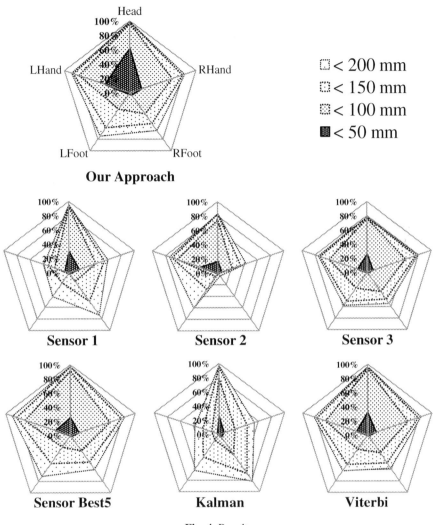

Fig. 4. Results

6   Conclusion and Perspectives

In this paper, we described a complex framework applying concepts from Dynamic Programming, Filtering and Vision. The result was positively compared to other classic and "perfect" algorithms using ground truth acquired from a commercial Motion Capture System. The framework original contribution runs in super-realtime fashion, that is, achieving real-time speed with a budget of a fraction of a CPU core. The result is a single, more accurate skeleton from the results of separate monocular skeleton reconstructions.

The results were attained using only simple techniques and making numerous sim-
plifications, such as working only in Cartesian space, using only a single prediction
model, and using 2D reprojection. We would like to improve upon these results by
going over these assumptions, trying several models in parallel, adaptive models,
going into articulatory space, or using a voxel-based observation. Also, we consider
leveraging the power of GPU for the latter part.

Acknowledgements. The research leading to these results has received funding from
the European Community's Seventh Framework Programme FP7/2007-2013
FoF.NMP.2011-2 - under grant agreement No 285380 - PRACE.

References

1. Alfonso, D.: Microsoft Investor Relations - Press Release, http://www.microsoft.
   com/investor/EarningsAndFinancials/Earnings/PressReleaseAndW
   ebcast/fy11/q2/default.aspx (accessed January 27, 2011)
2. Freedman, B., Shpunt, A., Arieli, Y.: Distance-Varying Illumination and Imaging Techniques for Depth Mapping. United States Patent US 20100290698 A1 (November 18,
   2010)
3. ASUS: ASUS Xtion PRO LIVE,
   http://www.asus.com/Multimedia/Xtion_PRO_LIVE/
4. WordPress: OpenNI I The standard framework for 3D sensing,
   http://www.openni.org/
5. PrimeSense: NiTE Middleware - PrimeSense,
   http://www.primesense.com/solutions/nite-middleware/
6. Binney, D., Boehm, J.: Performance Evaluation of the PrimeSense IR Projected Pattern
   Depth Sensor, University College London, London, United Kingdom (2011)
7. Andersen, M., Jensen, T., Lisouski, P., Mortensen, A., Hansen, M., Gregsersen, T.,
   Ahrendt, P.: Kinect Depth Sensor Evaluation for Computer Vision Applications, Aarhus
   (2012)
8. Zhang, L., Sturm, J., Cremers, D., Lee, D.: Real-Time Human Motion Tracking using Multiple Depth Cameras. In: Proc. of the International Conference on Intelligent Robot Systems, IROS (2012)
9. Shotton, J., Fitzgibbon, A., Cook, M., Sharp, T., Finocchio, M., Moore, R., Kipman, A.,
   Blake, A.: Real-time human pose recognition in parts from single depth images. In: 2011
   IEEE Conference on Computer Vision and Pattern Recognition (CVPR), pp. 1297–1304
   (2011)
10. Taylor, J., Shotton, J., Sharp, T., Fitzgibbon, A.: The Vitruvian manifold: Inferring dense
    correspondences for one-shot human pose estimation. In: IEEE Conference on Computer
    Vision and Pattern Recognition (CVPR), pp. 103–110 (2012)
11. Moeslund, T., Hilton, A., Krüger, V.: A survey of advances in vision-based human motion
    capture and analysis. Computer Vision and Image Understanding 104(2-3), 90–126 (2006)
12. Deutscher, J., Reid, I.: Articulated Body Motion Capture by Stochastic Search. Interna-
    tional Journal of Computer Vision 61(2), 185–205 (2005)
13. Hofmann, M., Gavrila, D.: Multi-view 3D Human Pose Estimation combining Single-
    frame Recovery, Temporal Integration and Model Adaptation. In: IEEE Conference on
    Computer Vision and Pattern Recognition, CVPR 2009, pp. 2214–2221 (2009)

14. Abramov, A., Pauwels, K., Papon, J., Worgotter, F., Dellen, B.: Depth-supported real-time video segmentation with the Kinect. In: IEEE Workshop on Applications of Computer Vision (WACV), pp. 457–464 (2012)
15. Forsyth, D., Arikan, O., Ikemoto, L., O'Brien, J., Ramanan, D.: Computational Studies of Human Motion: Part 1, Tracking and Motion Synthesis. In: Foundations and Trends in Computer Graphics and Vision (2006)
16. Wojek, C., Walk, S., Schiele, B.: Multi-cue onboard pedestrian detection. In: IEEE Conference on Computer Vision and Pattern Recognition, CVPR 2009, Miami, FL, pp. 794–801 (2009)
17. Benfold, B., Reid, I.: Stable Multi-Target Tracking in Real-Time Surveillance Video. In: CVPR, pp. 3457–3464 (2011)
18. Berclaz, J., Fleuret, F., Fua, P.: Robust People Tracking with Global Trajectory Optimization. In: Society, I. (ed.) Proceedings of the 2006 IEEE Computer Society Conference on Computer Vision and Pattern Recognition, vol. 1, pp. 744–750 (2006)
19. Andriluka, M., Roth, S., Schiele, B.: People-Tracking-by-Detection and People-Detection-by-Tracking. In: IEEE Conference on Computer Vision and Pattern Recognition, CVPR 2008, Anchorage (2008)
20. Sigal, L., Balan, A., Black, M.: HumanEva: Synchronized Video and Motion Capture Dataset for Evaluation of Articulated Human Motion. International Journal of Computer Vision 87(1-2), 4–27 (2010)
21. Larson, R.E., Peschon, J.: A dynamic programming approach to trajectory estimation. IEEE Transactions on Automatic Control 11(3), 537–540 (1966)
22. Viterbi, A.J.: A personal history of the Viterbi algorithm. IEEE Signal Processing Magazine 23(4), 120–142 (2006)
23. Mekonnen, A.A., Lerasle, F., Herbulot, A.: Cooperative passers-by tracking with a mobile robot and external cameras. Computer Vision and Image Understanding (2012)
24. Maybeck, P.: Stochastic models, estimation, and control. Academic Press (1979)
25. Maloney, R.: Movement Analysis Products, http://www.motionanalysis.com/html/movement/products.html (accessed January 4, 2013)
26. Herrera, C., Kannala, D., Heikkila, J., Joint Depth, J.: Color Camera Calibration with Distortion Correction. IEEE Transactions on Pattern Analysis and Machine Intelligence 34(10) (2012)

Recognizing Conversational Interaction Based on 3D Human Pose

Jingjing Deng, Xianghua Xie*, Ben Daubney, Hui Fang, and Phil W. Grant

Department of Computer Science, Swansea University,
Singleton Park, Swansea SA2 8PP, United Kingdom
x.xie@swansea.ac.uk
http://csvision.swan.ac.uk

Abstract. In this paper, we take a bag of visual words approach to investigate whether it is possible to distinguish conversational scenarios from observing human motion alone, in particular gestures in 3D. The conversational interactions concerned in this work have rather subtle differences among them. Unlike typical action or event recognition, each interaction in our case contain many instances of primitive motions and actions, many of which are shared among different conversation scenarios. Hence, extracting and learning temporal dynamics are essential. We adopt Kinect sensors to extract low level temporal features. These features are then generalized to form a visual vocabulary that can be further generalized to a set of topics from temporal distributions of visual vocabulary. A subject-specific supervised learning approach based on both generative and discriminative classifiers is employed to classify the testing sequences to seven different conversational scenarios. We believe this is among one of the first work that is devoted to conversational interaction classification using 3D pose features and to show this task is indeed possible.

Keywords: 3D human pose, conversational interaction classification, interaction analysis, Kinect sensor.

1 Introduction

Human action and activity recognition has proved to be viable in video surveillance applications throughout the years [11,1,18], though it still remains an open and challenging problem. There is however already a body of work interested in the detection and recognition of social interaction between multiple people [5,7], which is particularly difficult since the actions of multiple subjects must be inferred and understood.

From the feature selection perspective, both low-level appearance features, such as color, dense optical flow, spatio-temporal interest point, and high-level human pose features have been investigated. However, initially, the dependence on low-level features has meant that the class of social interactions examined

---

* Corresponding author.

J. Blanc-Talon et al. (Eds.): ACIVS 2013, LNCS 8192, pp. 138–149, 2013.

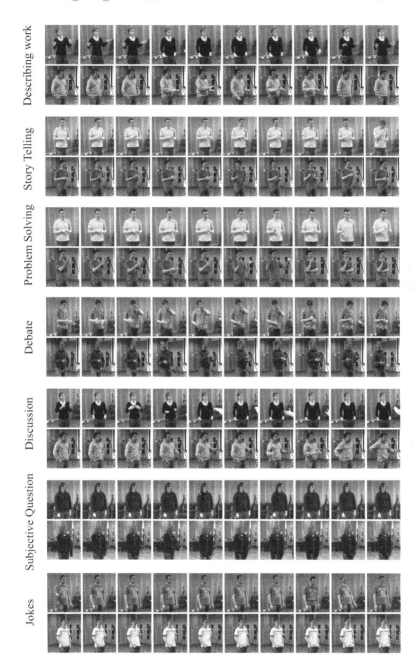

Fig. 1. Examples of observations made for each pair during different conversational interactions. The time difference between each consecutive frame shown is two seconds. For better visualization, only upper body is shown.

thus far typically have been limited to those that can be readily identified and most easily described by a particular set of motions or poses, e.g. handshake or high-five. Alternatively, observation is made at a coarse level to recognize interactions, which are only dependent on high-level tracking of entire individuals, e.g. in a surveillance setting. Furthermore, Yao *et al.* [2] have shown that pose-based features outperform low-level appearance features to some extent in the short-time action recognition task. However, the estimation of human pose, particularly in 3D that is considered as a strong cue to action and activity recognition, is problematic and inaccurate, which directly leads to little attention to the pose-based action and activity recognition methods in last decades.

In this work, we propose to leverage recent advances in technology in extracting 3D pose using a consumer sensor (Microsoft Kinect) to examine the feasibility of detecting much more high-level behavioral interactions between two people. Rather than recognizing just key social events, we attempt to analyze and detect different conversational interactions. We investigate whether just by observing the 3D pose of two interacting people we can recognize the type of conversation they are conducting. This work is in part motivated by recent work that showed features derived from 3D human pose are much more discriminative than their low-level image based counterparts e.g. [2]. Therefore, we believe that having access to these features provides the capacity of detecting and classifying much more subtle interactions than currently possible. Often the differences between the interactions examined in this work are not themselves intuitive. Moreover, there are large variations among individuals when performing the same task. Hence, our emphasis in this work is to classify, in a *subject-specific* supervised fashion, short clips of conversational interactions into seven different categories that are defined based on individual tasks, such as debate a topic and problem solving, rather than primitive interactions, such as monologue and exchange. Each clip in our case may contain multiple primitive interaction types. We examine the extent of the visual cues provided by humans in recognizing conversational interactions. We thus employ discriminative methods to carry out the classification. In addition, we apply a generative method based on Hidden Markov Model (HMM), which is a popular choice for recognizing sequential action and activity through modeling the dynamics with varying temporal duration, e.g. [15,14,9,16,17]. A coupled version of HMM is also used to explicitly model the interactions. We recognize that generalizing conversational scenarios across subjects is far more challenging than discriminating them. However, this work is useful in understanding the role of bodily movement in conversational interaction and is a necessary step towards generic, non-subject specific modeling. We believe this to be the first work devoted to conversational interactions where we are interested in identifying the content of a conversation using pose features.

2   Data Set Acquisition

Data was collected using a two-Kinect set-up, each person was recorded using a Kinect Sensor, which captured pose at 30fps. Each of the cameras was slightly

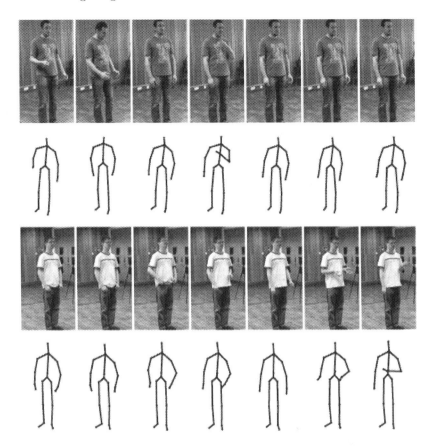

Fig. 2. Example 3D poses from a pair during "Describing Work". Note that the RGB images were captured by separately synchronized cameras at different viewing angles to Kinect - hence the discrepancy in pose. The RGB data is not used in this study.

offset from a direct frontal view so that the participants did not occlude one another. The participants were given seven tasks to complete. The first task was to discuss an area of their current work. The second task was to prepare an interesting story to tell their partner, such as a holiday experience. The third task was to jointly find the answer to a problem. The fourth task was a debate, where the participants were asked to prepare arguments for a particular point of view on an issue we gave to them. In the fifth task they were asked to discuss between them the issues surrounding a statement and come to agreement whether they believe the statement is true or not. The sixth task was to answer a subjective question, and the seventh task was to take it in turn telling jokes to one another. A full description of the different tasks are provided in Table 1.

Each set of seven tasks took about 50 minutes. They were told roughly how long each task to take as a guide, however, they were not being timed or interrupted. Before each task, there were given the opportunity to reread any

Table 1. Description of each of the tasks given to the participants to perform

#	Task Name	Description
1	Describing Work	Each participant was asked to describe to their partner their current work or a project they have involved with. Following this each participant then repeated it back so as to confirm they had understood.
2	Story Telling	Each participant was asked to think of an interesting story they could tell their partner, such as a holiday experience or an experience of a friend.
3	Problem Solving	The participants were given a problem they were asked to think of the solution of together. The problem was "Do candles burn in space and if so what shape and direction?".
4	Debate	The participants were asked to prepare arguments for a given point of view on the topic "Should University education be free?" and then debate this between them.
5	Discussion	The participants were asked to jointly discuss the issues surrounding a statement and come to agreement whether they believe the statement is true or not. The statement was "Social Networks have made the world a better place?"
6	Subjective Question	The participants were asked to discuss a subjective question which was "If you could be any animal, what animal and why?"
7	Telling jokes	The participants were asked to take it turn telling jokes to one another, each participant was provided with three different jokes to learn before attending.

associated material with the task that they may have forgotten. At the end of the session, participants were generally surprised by how much time had passed. A sample of the data collected for each conversational interaction is presented in Fig 2, and the whole dataset is available for download from the following link[1].

3   Proposed Method

As there is no well-defined primitive action or activity categories for conversational interaction, and the gestures vary with different subjects, it is unrealistic to manually annotate the data set. Inspired by the works [13,8,2], the unlabeled low-level features are generalized as a bag of visual words, based on which high-level conversational interaction classification is carried out. The low-level 3D pose features are extracted directly from kinematic human model. Gaussian Mixture Models (GMMs) are fitted to the low-level feature space, and the Gaussian components constitute the vocabulary of visual words. A further generalization of visual words to higher level topics is also investigated. Both discriminative and generative models are trained and applied to recognize the class of unknown sequences for each pair of subjects. The flowchart shown in Fig. 3 illustrates the

---

[1] http://csvision.swan.ac.uk/converse.html

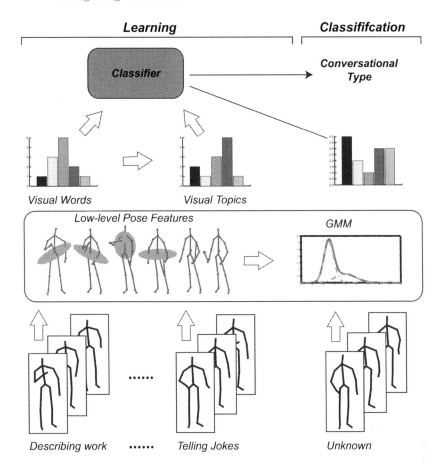

Fig. 3. Flowchart of the proposed method

steps from pose feature extraction, to unsupervised clustering and generalization, and to supervised classification.

3.1 Low-Level Pose Feature

3D pose features have been shown to be useful in motion capture data retrieval and action recognition. Motivated by existed work, such as [2,10,12], we extract three types of features to depict the pose and motion of the upper body. These geometry features extracted from a kinematic chain are simple but powerful for representing human gesture and motion over time. The first set of feature measure the distance between a joint and a reference plane defined using different parts of the body (see Fig. 4(b,c,d,e)). The second set of feature we use measure the distance between two joints at different time intervals and is depicted in Fig. 4(d). The third set of feature measure the velocity of individual joints (see Fig. 4(g)).

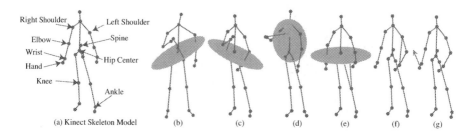

Fig. 4. Visualization of the pose-based features. (a) illustrates the Kinect skeleton model. (b), (c) (d), & (e) shows four reference planes. (f) illustrates the distance between two joints. (g) illustrates a velocity feature at the right hand joint.

There are four reference planes used to quantify the movement of certain joints in the kinematic chain. The first two reference planes are used to measure the distance and velocity of joints on the lower arms, i.e. hands, wrists and elbows. Both planes are located at the same spine point. One of the two planes is defined by the vector connecting the spine and left shoulder (Fig. 4(b)), and the other is defined by the vector connecting the spine and right shoulder (Fig. 4(c)). The former is used to measure the lower arm joints on the left side and the latter is for right side. The two vectors connecting hip center from two shoulders define the third reference plan (Fig. 4(d)), which is used to measure movements of lower arm joints from both arms. The fourth plan is perpendicular to the third plan and crossing the same spine point (Fig. 4(e)). This reference plan is used to measure movement of knees and ankles (ankle points are more stable than feet in Kinect estimation). The overlapping in measurement is to make sure that the 3D motion of those joints are captured among those 2D measurement combinations. Next, we provide the definition for each measurement of joint movement.

The 3D location of a joint at time slice t is denoted as $\omega_{i,t} \in R^3$ and the vector defined by two joints by $\pi_{ij,t} \in R^3$, where i and j indicates the identity of the joints. We define two types of plane $\phi_{ijk,t}$ which is spanned by the joints $\omega_{i,t}, \omega_{j,t}, \omega_{k,t}$, and the plane $\psi_{ijk,t}$ passing through $\omega_{k,t}$ and whose normal vector is aligned with $\pi_{ij,t}$. The normal vector of the plane $\phi_{ijk,t}$ can also be represented by $\pi_{ijk,t}$.

The feature F_d representing the Euclidean distance between joints over Δt is defined as: $F_d = D\{(\omega_{i,t}), (\omega_{j,t+\Delta t})\}$. If $i = j$, then the feature measures the distance of movement of the joint over time Δt, otherwise, it measures the distance between two different joints separated by time.

The features F_{pd1} and F_{pd2} measure the shortest distance from joint $\omega_{n,t}$ to the plane $\phi_{ijk,t+\Delta t}$ and the plane $\psi_{ijk,t+\Delta t}$, respectively, which are defined as: $F_{pd1} = D\{(\omega_{n,t}), (\phi_{ijk,t+\Delta t})\}$ and $F_{pd2} = D\{(\omega_{n,t}), (\psi_{ijk,t+\Delta t})\}$

We also extract F_{jv}, F_{pv}, the component of the joints' velocity along the direction of the vector $\pi_{ij,t+\Delta t}$ and vector $\pi_{ijk,t+\Delta t}$, respectively, which are defined as: $F_{jv} = V\{(\omega_{n,t}), (\pi_{ij,t+\Delta t})\}$ and $F_{pv} = V\{(\omega_{n,t}), (\pi_{ijk,t+\Delta t})\}$. Furthermore, we estimate head orientation from RGB camera output based on the face localization method [4] and parametric head pose estimation technique [6]. Thus, 49 different low-level pose features are extracted from the Kinect data, with $\Delta t = 1.0s$.

3.2   Middle-Level Visual Words and Topics

The extracted low-level pose features are direct measurements of relative motion at a short time window. Although similar features have been found powerful in classifying primitive actions with short time span [2], what kind of feature is appropriate choice for conversational scenario classification is still an undetermined question, as we cannot decide the conversational scenarios two people conducting just based on the short-term motions. In this work, we adopt the bag of words approach to derive mid-level features that are suitable for classification of conversational interactions, each of which may contain various amount of primitive actions. Different from video analysis where for instance the spatial-temporal interesting points are detected from sequential images using space-time corner detectors or separable linear filters, in our case, the raw data is the locations of joints in the kinematic model. Consequentially, we are concerned with the distributions of those geometrical features across time. We hence using unsupervised clustering to generate visual words across the whole sequence and across all subjects to create a visual vocabulary. A further generalization to visual topics is then performed based on the distribution of visual words in an extended time span that is often larger than typical primitive action.

In information retrieval and natural language processing, the Latent Dirichlet Allocation (LDA) model has been widely used to discover abstract "topics" from a collection of words or low level features. Niebles *et. al.* [13] applied the LDA model to extract action categories from low-level spatial-temporal words in an unsupervised fashion. Inspired this work, we extract the visual words and topics from the low-level pose features. Firstly, a visual vocabulary was constructed by fitting GMMs to each dimension of the low-level pose feature space. We consider each Gaussian component as a visual word. Then, we further assume that those visual words are generated by a mixture of visual topics. To learn those visual topics, we split the sequences into 600 frames sections each of which is considered as a visual document that contains multiple visual topics. The LDA model [3] with a fixed number of latent topics is then applied to all documents, and assigns each visual word in the documents to a potential topic. Next, we use the distributions of those visual words and topics to classify different conversational scenarios.

3.3   Classifiers

Both discriminative classifier and generative classifier are employed in this work, namely Support Vector Machine (SVM), Random Forest (RF) and HMMs. SVM and RF are popular discriminative models for supervised classification. The main reason of choosing them is that they are effective tool to evaluate the discriminative power of our features. Meanwhile, the generative model, HMM could provide us another perspective in understanding the process of conversational interactions, as it is suitable for modeling the dynamics in the sequential data.

Based on two different middle-level descriptors, visual words and topics, two set of classifiers were trained independently. To train and test the classifiers, each recorded sequence is split into 500 frames sections. Each section is labeled as the task from which it is extracted and used as a single example, both for training and testing. For the discriminative models, the histogram of visual words or topics is computed, and used as feature vector for each section. We learn a random forest with 100 decision trees by randomly sampling with replacement from the complete training set. An SVM with $k(x_i, x_j) = \exp(-\gamma\|x_i - x_j\|^2)$ as its kernel function is trained on the same training set. For the HMM, the feature vector of each frame in the section corresponds to an observation node expanded across time. We learn separate HMMs for each of the seven conversational classes. Whilst HMMs are well suited to classifying sequences of different lengths, training a HMM on the section with 150 observation nodes is computationally expensive. Whereas we do not want to inadvertently introduce any bias into the results as because of differing temporal lengths. We down-sample each section by the factor of 12, so that each 150 frames sequence was composed of observations from 13 time instances. As the same as the way we train the discriminative model, two sets of HMM models are learned based on two different middle-level descriptors, i.e. visual words and visual topics. However, a better approach to encode interaction between two subjects using HMM is to use separate HMMs to represent each person and then adding an edge between the two persons across time to build a Coupled HMM (CHMM) [15]. Hence, compared to feature concatenation, CHMM more explicitly model interactions between two subjects.

4   Experimental Result

The approach described in Section 2 was used to collect the data set used in the presented experiments. In total all tasks were completed by 5 different pairs of people, which resulted in more than 500,000 frames. Each class is not obviously distinct from the others, and although there are some representative poses of each class it would be extremely difficult to determine the class using only pose from a single frame. Another major challenge of the data set is the sheer variation in the types of motion and gestures performed by each participant during the task. Even the neutral pose of each participant as they are listening is very different. These make it very difficult for generative methods to classify. The whole dataset is available for download from the following link[2].

To carry out the classification, 10-fold *subject-specific* cross validation is adopted, that is all the sequences were sequentially chopped into 10 segments so that neighboring samples are not distributed across training set and testing set. All the classifier were trained on the same training set independently.

---

[2] http://csvision.swan.ac.uk/converse.html

Table 2. Average subject-specific classification results using the features from only one participant

	Original features	Visual words			Visual topics		
	HMM	HMM	SVM	RF	HMM	SVM	RF
Describing Work	0.79	0.79	0.73	0.84	0.83	0.77	0.80
Story Telling	0.61	0.55	0.49	0.49	0.39	0.65	0.66
Problem Solving	0.50	0.24	0.34	0.27	0.11	0.79	0.79
Debate	0.55	0.33	0.43	0.82	0.12	0.63	0.60
Discussion	0.60	0.48	0.49	0.52	0.36	0.57	0.58
Subjective Question	0.34	0.11	0.25	0.08	0.03	0.67	0.71
Jokes	0.52	0.25	0.34	0.19	0.04	0.57	0.62
Average	0.56	0.39	0.44	0.39	0.27	0.66	0.68

We first test the pose features from only a single person, that is to understand how much information can be extracted by observing one participant in order to determine the topic of their conversation. Table 2 shows the average performance for each method in classifying the seven scenarios using visual words and visual topics as the discriminative feature. When using visual words, an average of 44% and 39% were achieved by SVM and RF classifiers, respectively. When using visual topics, which produces significantly shorter feature vectors (25 vs 340), their performances were increased to 66% and 68%, respectively (see Table 2). This was a significant performance increase for SVM and RF classifiers when using visual topics. It is however notable that HMM performed poor with both features, 36% and 27% compared to a random chance of 14% and 56% accuracy when using original pose features. A reasonable explanation to this is that there are lots of similarities among different scenarios which leads to similarities in low-level features and mid-level descriptors. While generalizing the individual conversation scenario, at current setting HMM emphasized the commonality in the data and hence compromised its discriminative power. This implies that detecting rare events and actions may help the generalization as they are likely more discriminative. It also shows the subtlety in the data set and perhaps large individual variation as well.

For the next experiment we combine features from two participants by concatenating their features before feeding into the classifiers. The results are shown in Table 3. There were broad improvements reported by all three classifiers. For the HMM method, we built a coupled model so that each subject corresponds to a single HMM and both were linked together. The visual words performance improved from 39% to 43%, and from mere 27% to 34% for visual topics. The SVM and RF reported somewhat greater increase in performance, with best result of 76% achieved by RF using visual topics. This clearly highlights the benefit of having multiple streams of information when observing people during an interaction as they can be used to better discriminate the task being performed.

The results we have achieved suggested that it is possible to classify conversational interactions just based on human poses alone for individual pair of

Table 3. Average subject-specific classification results using the features pair two participant

	Original features	Visual words			Visual topics		
	CHMM	CHMM	SVM	RF	CHMM	SVM	RF
Describing Work	0.85	0.85	0.78	0.90	0.92	0.86	0.87
Story Telling	0.78	0.60	0.66	0.52	0.49	0.71	0.77
Problem Solving	0.56	0.19	0.52	0.32	0.16	0.81	0.86
Debate	0.56	0.40	0.59	0.46	0.19	0.65	0.67
Discussion	0.77	0.64	0.63	0.63	0.54	0.63	0.69
Subjective Question	0.31	0.15	0.38	0.17	0	0.75	0.80
Jokes	0.44	0.19	0.51	0.23	0.06	0.64	0.67
Average	0.61	0.43	0.58	0.46	0.34	0.72	0.76

subjects. The generalization of pose interactions, as expected, is a harder problem than discriminating among each others. Whilst the Kinect sensor permits direct estimation of 3D pose that is currently more robust and accurate than RGB camera methods, the data collected still contains some noise, as does the features extracted. However, despite this we have shown that recognition of conversational interactions with subtle differences can still be achieved with high accuracy. More participant data is necessary to analyze the effectiveness of generalized features, and this is leading to a new type of interaction analysis.

5   Conclusion

We presented a comprehensive study on gesture cues in understanding human conversational activity. The difference among the seven scenarios are rather subtle, and the primitive actions and interactions are commonly exhibited across different scenarios. Middle level motion descriptor were generalized from low level pose features obtained from Kinect output. Both discriminative model and generative model were investigated in order to classify subject-specific different types of conversational interactions. It is evident that good classification accuracy can be achieve using discriminative methods. The results also suggests that it is possible to distinguish conversational topic based on the pose movement from a single person. It is however more challenging to generalize different scenarios across subjects. An even larger data set and perhaps more sophisticated HMM models would improve the performance. However, we believe this work offer a somewhat different perspective to action and interaction analysis.

References

1. Aggarwal, J.K., Ryoo, M.S.: Human activity analysis: A review. ACM Comput. Surv. 43(3), 16 (2011)
2. Yao, A., Gall, J., Fanelli, G., Gool, L.V.: Does human action recognition benefit from pose estimation? In: Proceedings of the British Machine Vision Conference, pp. 67.1–67.11. BMVA Press (2011)

3. Blei, D., Ng, A., Jordan, M.: Latent dirichlet allocation. The Journal of Machine Learning Research 3, 993–1022 (2003)
4. Fang, H., Deng, J., Xie, X., Grant, P.W.: From clamped local shape models to global shape model. In: Proceedings of the 2013 International Conference on Image Processing, ICIP (2013)
5. Fathi, A.: Social interactions: A first-person perspective. In: Proceedings of the 2012 IEEE Conference on Computer Vision and Pattern Recognition (CVPR), CVPR 2012, pp. 1226–1233. IEEE Computer Society, Washington, DC (2012), http://dl.acm.org/citation.cfm?id=2354409.2354936
6. Gee, A.H., Cipolla, R.: Determining the gaze of faces in images. Image and Vision Computing 12, 639–647 (1994)
7. Holte, M.B., Tran, C., Trivedi, M.M., Moeslund, T.B.: Human pose estimation and activity recognition from multi-view videos: Comparative explorations of recent developments. IEEE Journal of Selected Topics in Signal Processing 6(5), 538–552 (2012)
8. Hospedales, T., Gong, S., Xiang, T.: Video behaviour mining using a dynamic topic model. International Journal of Computer Vision, 1–21 (2012)
9. Ivanov, Y.A., Bobick, A.F.: Recognition of visual activities and interactions by stochastic parsing. IEEE Trans. Pattern Anal. Mach. Intell. 22(8), 852–872 (2000)
10. Kovar, L., Gleicher, M.: Automated extraction and parameterization of motions in large data sets. ACM Trans. Graph. 23(3), 559–568 (2004)
11. Moeslund, T.B., Hilton, A., Krüger, V.: A survey of advances in vision-based human motion capture and analysis. Computer Vision and Image Understanding 104(2-3), 90–126 (2006)
12. Müller, M., Röder, T., Clausen, M.: Efficient content-based retrieval of motion capture data. ACM Trans. Graph. 24(3), 677–685 (2005)
13. Niebles, J., Wang, H., Fei-Fei, L.: Unsupervised learning of human action categories using spatial-temporal words. International Journal of Computer Vision 79(3), 299–318 (2008)
14. Oliver, N., Garg, A., Horvitz, E.: Layered representations for learning and inferring office activity from multiple sensory channels. Comput. Vis. Image Underst. 96(2), 163–180 (2004), http://dx.doi.org/10.1016/j.cviu.2004.02.004
15. Oliver, N., Rosario, B., Pentland, A.: A bayesian computer vision system for modeling human interactions. IEEE Trans. Pattern Anal. Mach. Intell. 22(8), 831–843 (2000)
16. Ryoo, M.S., Aggarwal, J.K.: Semantic representation and recognition of continued and recursive human activities. Int. J. Comput. Vision 82(1), 1–24 (2009)
17. Ryoo, M.S., Aggarwal, J.K.: Stochastic representation and recognition of high-level group activities. Int. J. Comput. Vision 93(2), 183–200 (2011)
18. Turaga, P.K., Chellappa, R., Subrahmanian, V.S., Udrea, O.: Machine recognition of human activities: A survey. IEEE Trans. Circuits Syst. Video Techn. 18(11), 1473–1488 (2008)

Upper-Body Pose Estimation
Using Geodesic Distances and Skin-Color

Sebastian Handrich and Ayoub Al-Hamadi

Institute of Information Technology and Communications,
Otto-von-Guericke-University Magdeburg, Germany
{sebastian.handrich,ayoub.al-hamadi}@ovgu.de

Abstract. We propose a real-time capable method for human pose estimation from depth and color images that does not need any pre-trained pose classifiers. The pose estimation focuses on the upper body, as it is the relevant part for a subsequent gesture and posture recognition and therefore the basis for a real human-machine-interaction. Using a graph-based representation of the 3D point cloud, we compute geodesic distances between body parts. The geodesic distances are independent of pose and allow the robust determination of anatomical landmarks which serve as input to a skeleton fitting process using inverse kinematics. In case of degenerated graphs, landmarks are tracked locally with a mean-shift algorithm based on skin color probability.

1 Introduction

Gesture recognition plays an important role in real human computer interaction (HCI) environments since it is very intuitive and close to natural human-human interaction. The analysis of gestures in HCI systems requires a robust and real-time capable estimation of the human pose. In the literature pose estimation techniques can be categorized by several criteria: (1) Whether the approach is a learning based method or not, (2) Whether the pose estimation is based on single frames or frame sequences, (3) dimensionality of the input data, i.e. the approach is image based or 3D, (4) use of markers or marker-less. Learning based approaches [1] [2] try to match several observed features with a set of previously trained poses. For this, typical machine learning methods like neural networks or support vector machines are used. An advantage of these methods is that they require a less accurate feature extraction compared to learning free approaches but are restricted to previously trained poses. Methods without any prior knowledge, e.g. [3], require an exact feature extraction but can estimate general poses. Much research has been done on image-based pose estimation techniques which are usually based on features like skin color [4], contours [5] and silhouettes [6] but often lack the ability to resolve ambiguities, e.g. self-occlusions. One possibility to resolve the ambiguities is the use of markers [7]. Typical applications for such an approach are the generation of ground truth data or motion-capture systems. In a real HCI environment, however, the need of wearing markers, is too awkward and not suitable. Another possibility to

J. Blanc-Talon et al. (Eds.): ACIVS 2013, LNCS 8192, pp. 150–161, 2013.

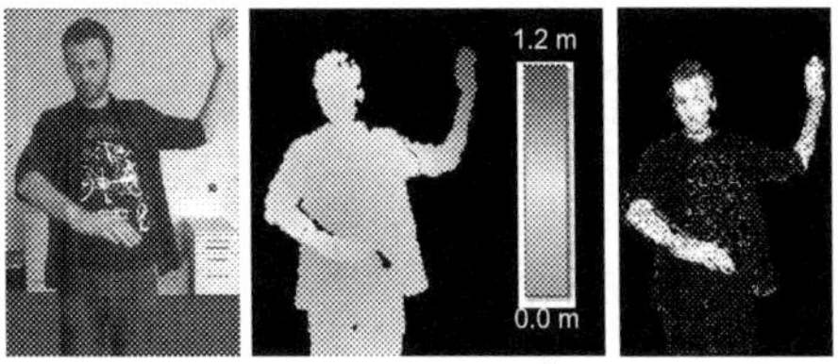

Fig. 1. *Left*: RGB color image of the scene with a user performing a pose. *Middle and Right*: Main features used for pose estimation are: Geodesic distances along the surface of the users body (*middle*) and skin color probability (*right*).

overcome the limits of the image-based pose estimation is the use of 3D data. The recent development in the field of 3D sensors – primarily time-of-flight (ToF) and structured infrared light (IR) based sensors – allows the generation and processing of dense depth maps in real time. Several authors have used 3D sensors for pose estimation [8] [9] [2].

In this work, we propose a method that tracks the upper body pose from depth data. Using a graph-based representation of the 3D information, we compute geodesic distances, i.e. distances along the surface of the human body, and extract anatomical landmarks which are used as input to a preliminary pose estimation. In the case of a degenerated graph, landmarks are determined locally by skin color tracking. A similar method was provided in [10], where the authors used geodesic distances and optical flow.

1. We provide a framework that robustly estimates and tracks human upper body poses in real time.
2. The method does not require any offline training or learning and estimates arbitrary poses, which is important for different HCI scenarios.
3. Due to the robust measurements of the anatomical landmarks based on geodesic distances, our method quickly recovers from tracking failures.
4. Typical parameters such as, the length of the forearm and upper arm, are not a priori required, but determined online.

2   Upper Body Pose Estimation

An overview of our proposed method is shown in figure 2. At each time instant the depth image D_t and color image I_t is captured from the Microsoft Kinect sensor. This capturing is performed in a separate thread, that triple buffers the sensor data. Thus, the reading thread, in which we perform the pose estimation, does not have to wait for the writing process to be completed, which results in a higher processing rate. The segmentation of the observed person is beyond the scope of this paper. We assume that D contains only depth image pixels that belong to an already segmented person.

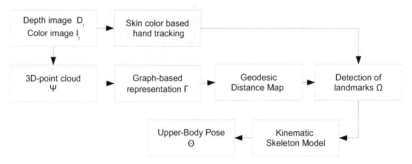

Fig. 2. Overview of the suggested method for upper-body pose estimation

Using the intrinsic camera parameters (principal point and focus length) and D_t, we then compute the 3D point cloud data Ψ. It is an organized point cloud, i.e. each 3D point (vertex) has only one corresponding depth image pixel in D_t. This is in terms of required computation time of great advantage in the next two steps, the computation of the graph based representation Γ of Ψ and the measurement of the geodesic distances (section 2.1).

Especially, when the user touches itself, the graph can, however, contain cycles and thus landmark positions for the elbows and hands are not determinable. To overcome this problem, we additionally use a local mean-shift tracker based on skin color probability to track the hand position in subsequent frames (Section 2.3).

Our goal is to detect 3D feature points (landmarks) Ω for the head, both shoulder, elbows and hands (section 2.2). Given these landmarks Ω, we then use methods of inverse kinematics to find an estimate of the upper-body pose Θ, i.e. to compute the joint rotations θ of a kinematic skeleton model (section 2.4).

2.1 Graph-Based Representation

Given the point cloud data Ψ, we compute a graph-based representation of it. The graph $\Gamma = (n, e)$ consists of nodes n and edges e. The graph creation and measurement of geodesic distances is performed in one single step. Each node n_i is described by three parameters

$$n_i = (\psi, d_g, n_p)_i, \tag{1}$$

where $\psi \in \Psi$ is the corresponding 3D point of the point cloud data, d_g is the total geodesic distance to the root node n_0 of the graph, and node n_p is its parent, i.e. predecessor, node. For the computation of Γ we make use of the fact that each node has a corresponding 2D projection $n_i' = (x, y)_i$ in the depth image. Instead of comparing each 3D point with each other, the graph creation can therefore be done very efficiently in the image domain.

A node n_i is connected to another node n_j by edge e if they fulfill one of two edge criteria, c_Γ^1 (eq. 3) or c_Γ^2 (eq. 4) . The set of edges is thus defined as:

$$e = \{(n_i, n_j) \in n \times n \mid c_\Gamma^1(i,j) \vee c_\Gamma^2(i,j)\}, \tag{2}$$

with the edge criteria:

$$c_\Gamma^1(i,j) = ||n_i(\psi) - n_j(\psi)||_2 \leq \epsilon_\Gamma \wedge d(n_i', n_j') \leq 1 \tag{3}$$

$$\begin{aligned} c_\Gamma^2(i,j) = &||D(n_i') - D(n_j')||_2 \leq \epsilon_\Gamma^D \wedge \\ &D(n_i') > \bar{D}_{ij} + \epsilon_\Gamma \wedge d(n_i', n_j') > 1, \end{aligned} \tag{4}$$

and $d(n_i', n_j') = ||(x,y)_i - (x,y)_j||_2$ is the 2D distance between the projections of node n_i and n_j to the depth image and $D(n_i')$ the depth value at location n_i'.

The first criterion (eq. 3) connects two nodes, whose Euclidean distance is below a threshold ϵ_Γ and whose 2D projections are adjacent points. This threshold depends on the resolution and density of the depth image. We used $\epsilon_\Gamma = 0.02m$. The criterion alone, however, is not sufficient. If two nodes, which should be connected by an edge, are separated by another occluding body part, in particular a limb, then the creation of the graph would be incorrect or, at worst, only performed for a subset of all nodes.

Thus, edge criterion c_Γ^2 (eq. 4) connects nodes with non adjacent projections $d(n_i', n_j') > 1$, if they have similar depth values $||D(n_i) - D(n_j)||_2 \leq \epsilon_\Gamma^D$ and are separated by 3D points that have a less mean depth value $\bar{D}_{ij}$. This is an extension to the method described in [10] as we do not require the projections of two nodes (n_i, n_j) to be adjacent points and can therefore create complete graphs also in the case of partial occlusions.

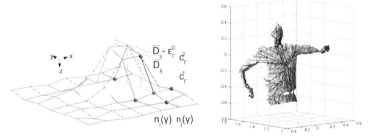

Fig. 3. *Left:* Schematic representation of the graph creation: 3D point cloud data is depicted as a mesh (gray lines). The current node (red sphere) is connected to the first node in each 2D direction that fulfills either edge criterion c_Γ^1 or c_Γ^2. *Right:* Results of the graph creation. Blue points show the 3D-point cloud data of the segmented user. A selection of the created graphs is depicted as black lines. The two graphs with maximum geodesic distance are shown as red and green lines.

We denote the Euclidean distance between two nodes connected by an edge as the weight of the edge $w(e_{i,j}) = ||n_i(\psi) - n_j(\psi)||_2$. The geodesic distance d_g of each node is then the cumulated weights of the sequence of edges that belong to the shortest path P back to the root node n_0: $d_g = \sum_{e \in P} w(e)$.

The shortest path P is found using the Dijkstra algorithm. In each iteration step, we search for the node with the smallest total geodesic distance d_g and set it as the current node. We implemented the list of all nodes as a priority queue, because it speeds up the search for current node significantly. Starting at the projected 2D point of the current node we determine for all four 2D-directions (up, down, left, right) the first valid 3D-point that fulfills an edge criterion. This is shown in figure 2.1. When graph creation is completed, we store the total geodesic distance d_g of each node in a 2D map Γ^M.

The choice of an appropriate root node n_0 is important. A good initialization is simply the centroid $\bar{\Psi}$ of the point cloud Ψ. The projection of this point may, however, be occluded by a limb in front of the torso. The graph creation would then begin in the limb and result in incorrect geodesic distances. To overcome this, we define a search window R_Γ centered around the projection of $\bar{\Psi}$ and search for the point with maximum depth D_0 . All nodes in R_Γ that have a similar depth value are then marked as candidates for the root node: $L_0 = \{n_i|\ ||D(n_i') - D_0||_2 \leq \epsilon_{D_0}\}_{n_i' \in R_\Gamma}$. As a root node, we then take the node, which is closest to $\bar{\Psi}$ and element of L_0:

$$n_0 = \arg\min_{n_i \in L_0} ||n_i(\psi) - \bar{\Psi}||_2. \tag{5}$$

2.2   Landmark Detection

In total we use eight landmark positions $\Omega_t = \{\omega_c, \omega_h, \omega_{sl}, \omega_{sr}, \omega_{el}, \omega_{er}, \omega_{wl}, \omega_{wr}\}$ that specify the 3D-position of the body center ω_c, head ω_h, left and right shoulder $\omega_s = (\omega_{sl}, \omega_{sr})$, elbow $\omega_e = (\omega_{el}, \omega_{er})$ and both hands $\omega_w = (\omega_{wl}, \omega_{wr})$.

The center position is identical with the root node of the graph, $\omega_c = n_0(\psi)$. The head appears in D as an elliptical region. We find such regions by a 2D template matching (sum of squared differences) between D and an template image T_H, which contains an ellipse, whose rotation and size depends on the last known head position. The head landmark ω_h is then the centroid of all 3D points that correspond to the resulting template location.

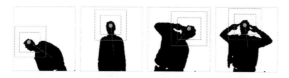

Fig. 4. Results of the head detection based on SSD template matching for various poses. The green points depicts the position of head. The inner rectangle defines the size of the template and the outer rectangle depicts the search region.

To find the hand landmark positions, we threshold the geodesic distance map $\Gamma_t^M > \tau$. We set τ to $\tau = 1m$. For each segmented region R_j, we find the node with maximum geodesic distance d_g^j and compute the mean 3D position x_j:

$$x_j = \sum_{n_i \mid n_i' \in R_j} \gamma(n_i) \mid d_g(n_i) > d_g^j - \Delta_d^w \tag{6}$$

with Δ_d^w the mean estimated geodesic extent of a hand ($\Delta_d^w = 0.2m$). The set $\{x_j\}$ may also contain 3D locations of the feet or even the head. We reject these locations by considering the Euclidean distance to the detected head landmark $||x_j - \omega_h||_2$ (not further described). The next step is to decide whether the remaining locations in $\{x_j\}$ refer to the left or right hand. For this, the Euclidean distances between nodes of the corresponding paths and the shoulder landmarks are used (Fig.5 left): Tracing back the paths (P_0, P_1) we search for the points (ψ_0^S, ψ_1^S) with minimum Euclidean distance to one of the shoulders and set the hand landmarks according to:

$$(\omega_{sl}, \omega_{sr}) = \begin{cases} (x_0, x_1), & \text{if } ||\psi_0^S - \omega_{sl}||_2 \leq ||\psi_1^S - \omega_{sr}||_2 \\ (x_1, x_0), & \text{otherwise} \end{cases} \tag{7}$$

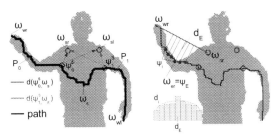

Fig. 5. *Left*: Discrimination between left and right hand based on the minimal Euclidean distances between shoulder landmarks and geodesic paths. *Right*: Detection of the elbow landmarks based on curvature analysis of the corresponding geodesic path.

For the elbow landmarks, we first detect, whether the arm of the person is bent. Here for, the Euclidean distances between the nodes of the hand paths and the 3D line $\omega_w \omega_s$ are determined (Fig.5 right). If the maximum distance exceeds a threshold the arm is considered to be bent and we set the elbow landmark ω_e to the corresponding graph node. Otherwise, we set the elbow landmark to the first node of the graph whose geodesic distance to the respective hand landmark is above a threshold. The threshold is initially set to $0.3m$ and updated each time the arm is bent.

2.3   Skin Color-Based Tracking

In cases where landmarks can not be detected by geodesic distances, we determine the hand landmark positions by tracking skin colored regions that are close to the last known position of the hand. At first, a skin color probability map I_s (Fig. 6b) is computed from the intensity image I_t (Fig. 6a). For each pixel its skin color probability is taken from a pre-computed look-up table (LUT). For this purpose, we have trained a naive Bayes classifier [11]:

$$p(skin|x) = \frac{p(x|skin) \cdot p(skin)}{p(x)} \qquad (8)$$

with $x = [cr, cb]^T$ the color components of the pixel in the YCrCb color space, where Y represents the luminance and C_r, C_b the chrominance values. The Bayes classifier was trained in an Histogram-based approach using a set of images containing skin and non-skin colored pixels:

$$p(x|skin) = \frac{n_s}{N_s}; \qquad p(skin) = \frac{N_s}{N_s + N_{\tilde{s}}} \qquad \text{and} \quad p(x) = \frac{n_s + n_{\tilde{s}}}{N_s + N_{\tilde{s}}}$$

where n_s, $n_{\tilde{s}}$ are the skin- and non skin histogram counts for each color $[cr, cb]_i$ and N_s, $N_{\tilde{s}}$ are the total sample sizes of skin and non skin colored pixels, respectively.

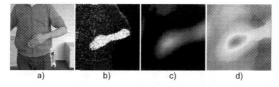

a)   b)   c)   d)

Fig. 6. Skin-color based hand tracking: (a) RGB intensity image. (b) Skin color probability map. (c) Detection of skin colored elliptical regions by means of normalized cross correlation between (b) and a template image. (d) Final probability map for hand position.

The hand appears as an elliptical skin colored region. In a template based step we find such regions in I_s. The template T_h contains a 2D-ellipse, whose size and rotation depend on the camera distance of the last known hand position and the relative position to the last known elbow location. The template match I_m is determined by means of normalized cross-correlation function (Fig. 6c). We assume that the hand position in the current frame is close to that in the prior frame and compute for each valid 3D-point $\in \bar{\Psi}$:

$$I_p = e^{-0.5(\bar{\Psi} - x_w)^2 / \sigma_w} \qquad (9)$$

with x_w the last known corresponding hand position. The two probability maps I_p and I_m are combined to a probability map I_h using equation 10 (Lukasiewicz t-norm):

$$I_h = max(I_p + I_m - 1, 0) \qquad (10)$$

Thus, I_h has a maximum in elliptical skin-colored regions, that match the size and rotation of the hand and are close to the last known hand position

(Fig. 6d). Its maximum position is found in a mean-shift step. To obtain the hand landmark position ω_w, we then average all 3D points that lie in a search window centered at the maximum location.

2.4   Kinematic Skeleton Model

The skeleton model (Figure 7) is defined by $\Theta = \{\mathbf{x}, q_{r0}, q_{r1}, q_{l0}, q_{l1}\}$. Here $\mathbf{x} = [x_c, x_h, x_{sl}, x_{sr}, x_{el}, x_{er}, x_{wl}, x_{wr}]^T \in \mathbb{R}^3$ denotes the position of the body center, the head, both shoulders, elbows and hands in world coordinates and $q \in \mathbb{H}$ the relative limb rotations of the left and right fore- and upper arm, respectively. The indices for left and right version of the skeleton joints are omitted.

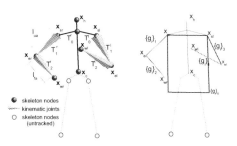

Fig. 7. *Left*: Kinematic skeleton model used in the CCD based fitting step. *Right*: Assignment of 3D points to individual body parts is based on the minimum Euclidean distance to each line in $\{g\}$.

The positions of the center, head, and shoulders are set to the corresponding landmark positions $[x_c, x_h, x_s]^T = [\omega_c, \omega_h, \omega_s]^T$. Thus, we only model the arms as kinematic chains: Let $T(q, t)$ denote a transformation with translation t and q. The joint positions are then given by:

$$x_e = T_0 T_1 [0\ 0\ 0\ 1]^T \qquad x_w = T_0 T_1 T_2 [0\ 0\ 0\ 1]^T$$

with transformation matrices:

$$T_0 = T(0, \omega_s) \qquad T_1 = T(q_0, [\pm l_u\ 0\ 0]^T) \qquad T_2 = T(q_1, [\pm l_f\ 0\ 0]^T)$$

and $l_u = ||\omega_e - \omega_s||_2$ and $l_f = ||\omega_w - \omega_e||_2$ the length of the upper- and forearm. The joint rotations (q_0, q_1) are computed by minimizing either

$$e_1 = [\omega_w - x_w, \omega_e - x_e]^T \text{ or} \tag{11}$$

$$e_2 = [\omega_w - x_w]^T \tag{12}$$

depending on whether the hand landmark was found using geodesic distances and we therefore detected an elbow landmark as target position (eq.11) or via skin color tracking (eq.12). We used the Cyclic Coordinate Descent method (CCD) because it is numerically stable, computationally inexpensive, and provides reasonable results for kinematic chains with only a few elements [12].

3   Experimental Results

We have created a set of test sequences to evaluate our proposed method. The sequences were recorded with a Microsoft Kinect for Windows sensor. The resolution was 640 by 480 and 320 by 240 for the color and depth image, respectively. Sampling frequency was 25 frames per second. We assume that no object is between the user and the sensor and that the user is facing the camera. This is a reasonable assumption in a gesture recognition environment. The test database contains both simple and complex poses. Here, simple means that body parts do not overlap. In particular, it means that the created graph is not circular and landmark positions of the hands and elbows can be detected by thresholding geodesic distances. In the complex test sequences, occlusions of body parts and self-contacts occurs. Overall, we have recorded eight test sequences with a length of 70 seconds each. The Microsoft SDK used to control the Kinect Sensor also provides a skeleton. This gives us the possibility to compare our pose estimation method to that of the Kinect. The proposed method is implemented in C++. On a standard dual core computer (2.66 GHz) we can process the sensor data and estimate complete upper-body poses with 22 frames per second. The processing speed differs from sampling frequency because in our implementation capturing and processing are implemented as two separated threads.

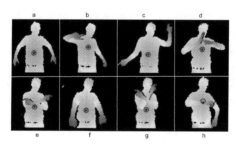

Fig. 8. Robust determination of geodesic distances for various poses. The color denotes the geodesic distance from the root node (blue circle).

We first investigated the measurement of geodesic distances. In Figure 8 the results of the geodesic distance measurement for various poses of the test sequences are shown. The color of each pixel of the depth map represents its geodesic distance to the root node (center of the blue unfilled circle). Green represents a distance of 0 meters and red pixels a distance of 1.2 meters. One can see that we can robustly measure the geodesic distances. In each of the shown examples the depth image pixels that represent the hands have the highest geodesic distances to the root node. We can therefore robustly detect the hands by thresholding the geodesic distances. This also true for complex poses, where both hands are connected (Fig.8d) or the user crosses the arms (Fig. 8e and 8g). As already mentioned the choice of an appropriate root node is important for a correct geodesic distance measurement. The authors in [10] have used the centroid of the point cloud (blue filled circle in Fig. 8). However, this is not sufficient if a limb is in front of the torso, because the projection of this point to the depth image could be located in an area that belongs to the limbs (e.g. Fig.8h). The geodesic distance measurement would then start in the limb instead of the torso. In fact, in [10] only poses are shown in which the torso is not occluded by a limb. Due to our described correction of of the root node (unfilled blue circles) we are able to compute geodesic distance even if limbs are in front of the torso as long as they are not too close to it.

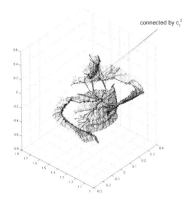

Fig. 9. Graph creation. We do not only connect nodes that are adjacent points in the depth image but also nodes that are separated by foreground objects (edge criterion c_Γ^2). The two paths with the largest geodesic distances (red and green) are also shown.

A further extension to the graph creation described in [10] is that we do not only connect nodes that are adjacent points in the depth image but also nodes that are separated by fore ground nodes (edge criterion c_Γ^2). If there were only graph edges between adjacent points in the depth image (edge criterion c_Γ^1), all 3D points in Fig.8h that are below the right fore arm in the depth image would not have been connected to the graph as they do not fulfill an edge criterion. This is also illustrated in Figure 9 which depicts a perspective view of the 3D point cloud and a subset of the detected geodesic pathes (black lines).

Figure 10 shows results of the landmark detection and skeleton fitting for a subset of poses of the test sequences. In the first row the raw point cloud data (blue dots) and the detected landmark positions are depicted. The second row shows the kinematic skeleton model that was fitted to the landmark positions. For a comparison to the Kinect skeleton, we projected the skeleton of our method (yellow) and that of the Kinect Sensor (magenta) back to depth data (third row). As it can be seen, in all cases the proposed method can determine the pose very well and the projected joint positions match the depth data. Our skeleton matches also very well that of the Kinect Sensor, but does not need any prior training. Tracking problems mainly occurs, if the hands are fully occluded. In this case the hand can neither be detected by thresholding the geodesic distance nor by skin color. However, the tracker can recover from tracking failures as soon as landmarks are determinable by geodesic distances again.

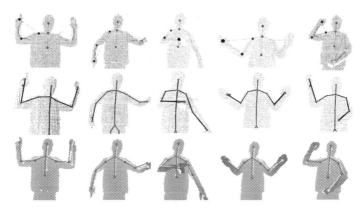

Fig. 10. Evaluation of the proposed method. Each image (a-f) shows the depth data and the projected skeleton of our approach (yellow) and the skeleton of the Microsoft Kinect SDK (magenta). Right next to each depth image a 3D-view of the skeleton is depicted. The thin orange lines show the Microsoft skeleton.

For an qualitative assessment, we manually labeled the positions $\{\hat{x}_i\}$ of the hand, shoulders and elbows in 3D and computed the mean Euclidean distances at each time instant to the joint positions $x_i \in \Theta$ obtained by our method.

$$e_{geo} = \frac{1}{N} \sum_i ||x_i - \hat{x}_i||_2. \tag{13}$$

A similar error was computed between the ground truth positions and the joint positions of the Kinect skeleton. In all 8 test sequences the error of our method was between $40mm - 120mm$ and $60mm - 140mm$ for the Kinect skeleton. The reason for this difference is the following: The landmark positions of the hands and elbows are located on the paths that were found by the Dijkstra algorithm. It computed for each node of the graph the shortest path to the root node. If the user bents his arm this path, however, does not run throught the center of the limb but is shifted towards its inner side. This is also shown in Fig. 9.

4   Conclusion and Discussion

In this work, we proposed a method for estimating and tracking the human upper-body pose from sequences of depth and color images. The method is a learning-free approach and does not need any pretrained pose classifiers. We can therefore track arbitrary poses as long as the user is not turned away from the camera and there is no object between the user and the camera.

At first, we segment the user based on the depth image and determine a graph based representation of the 3D-data. Using this graph, we measure the geodesic distances along the surface of the users body. By thresholding the geodesic distances, landmarks for hand and elbow locations can be obtained. The distinction between right and left arm are done by backtracking the corresponding geodesic pathes. In the cases where geodesic distances could not be measured (degenerated graph), hand landmarks are determined by tracking skin colored regions by means of a mean-shift algorithm. The presented experimental evaluation showed that we can robustly and exactly estimate arbitrary poses, which builds the basis for a subsequent gesture recognition process. The proposed method is real-time capable and can track rapid limb movements. Problems can occure, when multiple skin-colored regions exists, e.g. skin colored clothes. This is due to the simplicity of the used skin color tracker. In [13] we presented a multi hypotheses based approach tracker which we will integrate into the proposed approach.

References

1. Jaeggli, T., Koller-Meier, E., Gool, L.: Learning generative models for multi-activity body pose estimation. IJCV 83(2), 121–134 (2009)
2. Le Ly, D., Saxena, A., Lipson, H.: Pose estimation from a single depth image for arbitrary kinematic skeletons. CoRR, vol. abs/1106.5341 (2011)
3. Pons-Moll, G., Baak, A., Helten, T., Muller, M., Seidel, H.-P., Rosenhahn, B.: Multisensor-fusion for 3d full-body human motion capture. In: CVPR, pp. 663–670 (2010)
4. Srinivasan, K., Porkumaran, K., Sainarayanan, G.: Skin colour segmentation based 2d and 3d human pose modelling using discrete wavelet transform. Pattern Recognit. Image Anal. 21(4), 740–753 (2011)
5. Liang, Q., Miao, Z.: Markerless human pose estimation using image features and extremal contour. In: ISPACS, pp. 1–4 (2010)
6. Chen, D.C.Y., Fookes, C.B.: Labelled silhouettes for human pose estimation. In: Int. C. on Inform. Science, Signal Proc. a their App. (2010)
7. Wang, Y., Qian, G.: Robust human pose recognition using unlabelled markers. Appl. of Comp. Vision, 1–7 (2008)
8. Soutschek, S., Penne, J., Hornegger, J., Kornhuber, J.: 3-d gesture-based scene navigation in medical imaging applications using time-of-flight cameras. In: CVPR Workshops, pp. 1–6 (2008)
9. Hu, R.Z.-L., Hartfiel, A., Tung, J., Fakih, A., Hoey, J., Poupart, P.: 3d pose tracking of walker users' lower limb with a structured-light camera on a moving platform. In: CVPRW, pp. 29–36 (2011)
10. Schwarz, L.A., Mkhitaryan, A., Mateus, D., Navab, N.: Estimating human 3d pose from time-of-flight images based on geodesic distances and optical flow. In: IEEE Automatic Face Gesture Recog. a. WS, pp. 700–706 (2011)
11. Jones, M.J., Rehg, J.M.: Statistical color models with application to skin detection. Int. J. Comput. Vision 46(1), 81–96 (2002)
12. Wang, L.-C.T., Chen, C.C.: A combined optimization method for solving the inverse kinematics problems of mechanical manipulators. Robotics and Automation 7(4), 489–499 (1991)
13. Handrich, S., Al-Hamadi, A.: Multi hypotheses based object tracking in hci environments. In: ICIP, Orlando, USA, pp. 1981–1984 (2012)

A New Approach for Hand Augmentation Based on Patch Modelling

Omer Rashid Ahmad and Ayoub Al-Hamadi

Institute for Information Technology and Communications
Otto-von-Guericke University Magdeburg, Germany
{omer.ahmad,ayoub.al-hamadi}@ovgu.de
www.iikt.ovgu.de/nit.html

Abstract. In this paper, a novel patch-based modelling approach is proposed to augment the 3D models over the non-planar structure of hand. We present a robust real-time framework which first segment the hand using skin color information. To offer the subjects flexible interface (i.e., no restriction of covered arm), segmented skin-region is refined through distance descriptor which gives the hand's palm. Next, we measure the geometrical components from the hand's structure and compute the hand's curvature to detect the fingertips. The palm centroid and detected fingertips contribute to the patch-based modelling for which optimal path is derived for every detected fingertip. Further, we compute the patches using the path points for every two neighbor detected fingers and then the camera poses are estimated for these patches. These different camera poses are finally combined to generate a single camera pose, and then 3D models are augmented on non-planar hand geometry. The experimental results show that our proposed approach is capable to detect hand, palm centroid and fingertips, as well as integrate the generated patches for augmented reality application in real situations which proves its applicability and usability in the domain of Human Computer Interaction.

Keywords: Augmented Reality, Hand and Fingertip Detection, Pose Estimation.

1 Introduction and Related Work

Augmented Reality (AR) aims to combine the reality (real-world environment) and virtuality as realistic as possible. In the literature, the contents such as visual, graphics, avatars, etc. are augmented mainly in two main ways: marker-based AR and marker-less AR [6]. In the marker-based AR system, the visual contents are displayed on the fixed geometrical patterns (i.e., fiducials) whereas in the marker-less AR system, these contents are overlaid on the detected objects in the corresponding environment. The markers-less AR systems also comprehend the natural interaction mediums such as face, hands, torso, arms and fingers and provide an intuitive interface for interaction. In the Marker-less AR systems, the main challenge is to determine the consistent geometry from deformable

J. Blanc-Talon et al. (Eds.): ACIVS 2013, LNCS 8192, pp. 162–171, 2013.

Fig. 1. Presents the proposed patch-based modelling framework for Augmented Reality (AR) application

structures (i.e., hand) during free movements which is the main motivation of this paper.

In the literature, a wide range of research is reported on AR systems [1] both for marker and marker-less AR but in this paper, the focus is inclined towards the marker-less AR systems [13]. In the domain of marker-less AR systems, many researchers [3], [10], [11] aimed to provide natural and intuitive ways for the augmentation of contents over the detected objects. One of the interaction mediums is vision-based interaction in which hand, face, and fingers are detected and tracked to provide a natural and flexible way to interact with visual objects in AR systems.

An augmented reality system is proposed by [5], [8] to manipulate the super-imposed visual objects on the bare hand with a single camera. In their approach, the left hand is used as a virtual marker and the right hand is used as an interaction interface. Moreover, vision-based 2D interaction interface is developed with the AR object by utilizing the tracked fingertips and controlling it using the hand commands. In the same context, Lee et al. [10] introduces a system that track the user's hand with feature-based tracking system. In their approach, 3D model is mapped over the hand for the application of moving and placing objects. Similarly, in the work [14], Kinect camera is used to track and recognize the hand gestures on which the 3D models are augmented for virtual assembly in AR applications.

Another work is presented by Lee and Hoellerer [9] where the hand features (i.e., finger tips) are detected. In their approach, the pose of hand model is computed through calibration of fingertip coordinates by utilizing the ground-truth data. However, the augmentation works only when the hand is outstretched with all the fingers being distinctively detected. With similar assumption of outstretched hand, a marker-less AR system is presented in [12]. In this approach, the stereo camera system with depth information and features of the segmented hand are detected and through pose estimation, augmentation is performed on the palm. However, based on our analysis of literature, we have digged out the main finding as: first, the above approaches violated the main claims of naturalness because the user is enforced to keep its hand in a specific hand posture (e.g., out stretched hand). Second, the alternate approaches based on the hand modelling do not fit perfectly in this domain due to their training and testing process time (i.e., fitting the model on the hand). So, in this work, we are motivated to augment the visual contents in real-time with flexible hand postures.

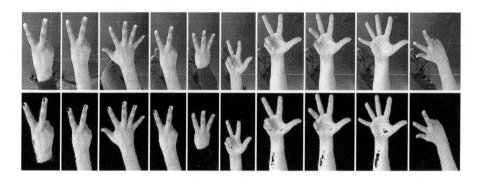

Fig. 2. Presents the original images and the corresponding skin color segmentation on the long and short sleeves images

In this paper, the main contributions are highlighted as follows: first, extraction of hand palm by applying distance transformation descriptor to prune the arm region associated with the hand; second, the fingertips are detected by performing the curvature analysis on contours points and are then thresholded to extract accurate fingertips; third, optimal joining paths from fingertips to palm is measured with inverse transformation method; fourth, camera pose estimation is performed on the computed planar structure (i.e., named as patches) on the hand; finally, this extracted estimated pose is augmented on our hand based AR system with 3D models which mimics the same geometry as performed by hand.

The contents of this paper are described as follows: the proposed approach is presented in Section 2 which is followed by the experimental results in Section 3 whereas the concluding remarks are sketched in Section 4.

2   Proposed Approach

In this section, the proposed hand-based Augmented Reality system is presented as follows:

2.1   Image Acquisition and Skin Color Segmentation

The images are acquired with the head mounted web camera which captures the 2D image streams. The captured images are transformed into YC_bC_r color space because skin color lies in a small region of chrominance components whereas the effect of brightness variation is reduced by ignoring the luminance (Y) channel. The skin segments are then detected from skin color distribution and are modelled by normal Gaussian distribution characterized by its mean and variance parameter. Normal Gaussian distribution probability for an observation $\mathbf{x}$ is calculated as:

$$\mathcal{P}\left(\mathbf{x}\right) = \frac{1}{2\pi\sqrt{|\Sigma|}}e^{-0.5\left((\mathbf{x}-\mu)^T\Sigma^{-1}(\mathbf{x}-\mu)\right)} \tag{1}$$

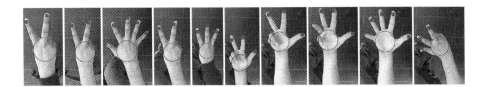

Fig. 3. Presents the palm (i.e., marked with red circle) and fingertip detections (i.e., marked with red filled rectangles) on the long and short sleeves image sequences. It shows that the palm center point is un-effected by using the distance scores on the long or short sleeves.

where μ and Σ represents mean vector and covariance matrix respectively of training data. The computed probability $\mathcal{P}(\mathbf{x})$ derived from above model categorize the pixels into *skin* and *non-skin* pixels. Later, the contours are extracted by applying the chain code representation on the detected skin color regions which eventually results in the hand segmentation. Fig. 2 presents the original images and computed results of the skin color segmentation. However, it is noted that the arm region is also categorized as skin and therefore, it is important to eliminate this region to get the accurate hand. In the next section, we describe the extraction process in detail.

2.2 Distance Transformation Descriptor

In the literature [4], the gesture recognition problems are addressed with the assumption that the subject must wear the long sleeves. But in the real scenarios, this assumption is violated especially in our research scenario. So, we first address this problem in the hand refinement process by measuring the parameters of distance transformation [2] as a descriptor. This descriptor helps in determining the hand and palm center, and therefore, eliminates the arm-region thus relaxing the assumption of subject dress code (shirt with short sleeves). In the proposed technique of [2], the standard distance transformation computes the distance of every image pixel to the closest zero image pixel named as its distance score *score*. But, we adapt this concept on the detected skin region and compute the Euclidean distance to get the transformed distance map using 3×3 window size. By using this descriptor, every skin pixel finds its shortest path to the nearest zero pixel. As the palm's center point is normally the farthest pixel in the image from the zero pixel, so we label this point as the hand's center point. Fig. 3 presents the bare hand of the subject with and without long sleeves and we can see that the distance scores help in computing the hand center point accurately.

2.3 Fingertip Detection

Finger defines the structure and semantics of the hand (e.g. in ASL, posture signs). So, we emphasize on the detection of the finger which is challenging due to the similar attributes of all the fingers (i.e., same visual characteristics). Based on this fact, we exploit the geometrical characteristics (i.e., contour) of the hand to extract the hand's fingers. So, the contour segment C_s of the detected hand in each image I is defined as: $I : \mathbf{C}_s = \{\mathbf{P}_i\}, i = 1, 2, \cdots, N$. P_i are the contour points in the segment s with the spatial location (x_i, y_i). Next, curvature is estimated by considering the neighbour contour points to detect the fingertip. Mathematically, from curvature values, we determine the ratio of length (i.e., sum of distances that a curve has), displacement measures the distance from the first to last point if curve covers a straight line. For each contour point P_i, we compute the curvature centered at i and each pixel-wise distance vector $\mathbf{d}_i$ is defined as: $\mathbf{d}_i = \{d_{(i-M/2)}, d_{(i-(M/2-1))}, \cdots, d_i, d_{i+1}, \cdots, d_{i+(M/2)-2}, d_{i+(M/2)-1}\}$ in which $d_i = \sqrt{(x_i - x_{(i+1)})^2 + (y_i - y_{(i+1)})^2}$. M is the window size or the number of selected contour points for curvature estimation. Moreover, this window size is adaptively determined according to the palm size. If the palm size is bigger, we consider more contour points in this window and vice versa. As each contour point is centered at i, so half of the window points are selected before this point and half of them after this point. The computed distances $\mathbf{d}_i$ are then summed up to get the final distance s_i for the window and is defined as:

$$s_i = \sum_{(i-M/2)}^{(i+M/2-1)} ||d_i|| \qquad (2)$$

The displacement for each contour point P_i is defined as the distance of the first and the last contour points inside the window:

$$r_i = ||P_{i-M/2} - P_{i+M/2}|| \qquad (3)$$

Curvature κ_i is computed from the following equation:

$$\kappa_i = s_i/r_i \qquad (4)$$

where i is the contour point of the hand at which curvature κ_i is estimated.

The main idea of finding the high curvature values from contour pixels results in the detection of fingertips. In the physical structure of the hand, the fingertips are always present at the high peak points, so we consider only those contour points which lie in these peak regions for detecting the fingertips. Moreover, we compute an empirical threshold of $\sqrt{2}$ in our experiments and remove all the points whose curvature is less than this threshold. After pruning these curvature points, we are left with o candidate points defined as: $\mathcal{L} = \{L_1, L_2, \cdots, L_o\}$. The next step is to find the corresponding candidate regions from the candidate points $\mathcal{L}$. Therefore, we apply the clustering operation to categorize these candidate points to build the candidate regions. A candidate region is the region where the candidate points are spatially clustered together $\mathcal{Q} = \{Q_1, Q_2, \cdots, Q_u\}$ where u is the total number of candidate points in a candidate region $\mathcal{R}$. Consequently, the number of candidate regions $\mathcal{R} = \{R_1, R_2, \cdots, R_v\}$ where v is the total number of candidate regions which represent the number of fingers (i.e., fingertips

Table 1. Confusion Matrix: Fingertip Detection

Sign	0	1	2	3	4	5
0	98.8	1.2	0.0	0.0	0.0	0.0
1	0.8	99.2	1.0	0.0	0.0	0.0
2	0.0	0.6	98.7	0.7	0.0	0.0
3	0.6	0.0	1.0	98.3	0.7	0.0
4	0.0	0.0	0.0	0.6	99.0	0.4
5	0.0	0.0	0.0	0.6	1.7	97.7

of the hand). Finally, the mean of each candidate region points are taken which gives us the reference *fingertips candidate points* $\mathcal{F} = \mathbf{f}_v, v = 1, 2, \cdots, V$ for a *candidate region* R as shown in Fig. 3. It is defined as:

$$f_v = \frac{1}{u} \sum_{j=1}^{u} Q_j \qquad (5)$$

In this way, we compute the fingertips using the curvature analysis. Table. 1 presents the confusion matrix of the detected fingertips on our dataset with the recognition rate of 98.6%.

2.4   Path Derivation

In previous sections, we have detected the fingertips f and the palm as separate components of but no concrete inferences can be made from these isolated components. However, for any meaningful expressions (i.e., gestures, posture, pose), it is pertinent to build the spatial relationship between the palm and fingertips f. In the proposed approach, this relationship is built by integrating the distance scores (*score*) and skin segmented pixels *skin* within a window which results in the path generation from the fingertips to the palm's center. So, practically given the fingertip point, we begin by traversing the fingertip pixel and take the search window of 3×3 for the path derivation process. In this window, we select the skin pixel values with the maximum distance score which is marked as the next representative pixel. The same process continues until the representative point finds the optimal route to the palm's center point. In this way, we obtain a list of representative points from *finger-to-palm* defining the path $Path_{(f_v \to palm)}$ from fingertips to palm. We repeat the same procedure for each finger f which results in a structural representation like the actual hand physics.

2.5   Patch Detection

Due to the deformable structure of the hand, it is important either to model the whole hand with some mathematical model to infer the poses or to consider some features (i.e., extracted from optical flow, or interest point detectors) and track them over time for the pose estimation. But, the main disadvantage of the hand modelling is the huge amount of training data required whereas for the tracking, it is very hard to get the consistent features in the homogeneous skin region of the hand which results in ambiguous poses. So, in the proposed approach, we have defined the idea of patches ζ which are derived from the correspondence of two neighbour fingers points (i.e., finger-to-palm points). To achieve this, we split our finger-to-palm path as active region AC and passive region PA. Active regions $(AC \subset Path_{(f_v \to palm)})$ correspond to the representative points which belongs to the fingers or are detected on the fingers. We term the passive region $(PA \subset Path_{(f_v \to palm)})$ as the representative points which are detected on the hand's palm (i.e., outside the finger region). So, we take the mean of these detected representative points and mark the points on the detected fingers as its active region. After that, the first and the last representative points are selected in the active region for every detected finger to establish the patches. A patch consists of four points derived from two detected neighbour fingers by concatenating their detected representative points in the active region $\zeta_{(i,i+1)} = \{AC_{(f_i^{start})}, AC_{(f_i^{end})}, AC_{(f_{i+1}^{start})}, AC_{(f_{i+1}^{end})}\}$ in which i and $i+1$ are the finger indexes to make the patch, *start* and *end* are the first and last points in active region AC. Finally, the patch is now attached to a pair of detected fingers of hand. As the hand has a non-planar structure and it is difficult to model any consistent geometry on it, so we represent them in the form of patches. Once we define our patches, it is necessary to compute the camera parameters (i.e., intrinsics and extrinsics) of this patch which can be interpreted and integrated with other patches for the final camera pose estimation.

2.6   Pose Estimation

The pose is defined with its translation and rotation matrix which we estimate here for every detected patch. To find the translation and rotation matrix of each patch, the calibration of the camera is a necessary step which gives the intrinsics parameters. The intrinsic parameters gives us the camera parameters (principal focal and center points) and distortion parameters. Using these parameters and the patch representative points, we get the translation and rotation matrix of the patch through 3D-2D point correspondences from solvePnP algorithm [7]. The individual translation and rotation matrices of each patch are then combined to get the final translation and rotation matrices of the pose. Fig. 4 presents the individual patches information along with the final pose estimation. In addition, as the proposed approach present an application for Augmented Reality system, so we have transformed the computed translation and rotation parameters for different 3D models by augmenting them on the hand as shown in Fig. 4.

3   Experimental Results

The experimental setup involves the tasks of data acquisition by head mounted web camera, palm and fingertip detection, path derivation, pose estimation based on the patch detection and the augmentation of the 3D models on the detected

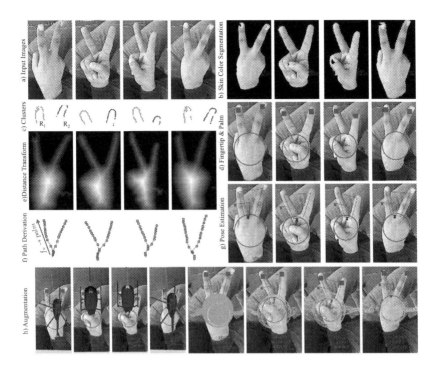

Fig. 4. presents the results of the proposed approach. a) Original images b) Skin color based hand segmentation c) Candidate regions and clusters derived for fingertip detection d) Detected palm and fingers e) Distance transformation with the brighter values indicating the higher scores and vice versa. f) Derived path from the fingertips to the palm. g) Patch detection and camera pose estimation for the detected patches. h) Augmentation of 3D objects (i.e., helicopter and kettle) on the hand region.

hand. We have demonstrated the applicability of our proposed patch-based augmented reality system on real-situations and 3D models of different objects (i.e., aeroplanes, helicopters, kettles etc.) are augmented on the fly over flexible subject's hand postures. In the experiments, we have selected low-cost web camera with 480*640 pixels image resolution. The experiments are conducted on 50 video observations of four subjects performing various hand postures (i.e., with varying fingers) having short-to-long sleeves. Also, it is to be noted that our algorithm doesn't require any prior training for the patch based detection and pose estimation process for the augmentation. The proposed framework runs with real-time processing at 25 fps on Intel processor 2.83 GHz with 4 cores hardware configuration.

Fig. 4 presents the image sequence performed by a subject. Fig. 4(a-b) presents the original frame and the skin segmented region respectively. Fig. 4(c) presents the distance transformation with the brighter values indicating the higher scores and vice versa. These scores help us to find the palm of the hand and by doing so, we are able to prune the arm region. The next step is to perform the fingertip detection for which the clustering operation is applied on the higher curvature values to define the candidate regions. These candidate regions are presented in Fig. 4(d) from which the mean is computed to detect the fingertips as shown in Fig. 4(e). Further, the path derivation process is shown in Fig. 4(f) which draws the path from the fingertips to the palm. The representative points in this path are splitted into active and passive region. Furthermore, the patches are made from the active points and pose estimated as shown in Fig. 4(g). Fig. 4(h) presents the augmentation of 3D object on the hand region.

4   Conclusion

In this paper, we have suggested a patch-based Augmented Reality system in which different components of the hand are detected. These detected components (i.e., fingers and palm) are then used to generate a patch based description for the hand on which the poses are estimated. The estimated poses determine the translation and rotation matrices which are used to augment different 3D models on the hand. We have achieved the successful augmentation of different 3D models over the dynamic moving hand postures. Moreover, we have presented the results of the fingertip detection process in the form of confusion matrix for our dataset however as we haven't found any similar dataset specific to the augmented reality, therefore the comparison with other datasets are missing. In the future work, we will consider the self-occluded poses (i.e., where the fingers intercept each other while moving) of the hand for the augmentation.

Acknowledgment. This work is supported by Transregional Collaborative Research Center SFB / TRR 62 "Companion-Technology for Cognitive Technical Systems" funded by German Foundation.

References

1. Azuma, R.T.: A survey of augmented reality. Presence: Teleoperators and Virtual Environments 6(4), 355–385 (1997)
2. Borgefors, G.: Distance transformations in digital images. Computer Vision, Graphics, and Image Processing 34(3), 344–371 (1986)
3. Buchmann, V., Violich, S., Billinghurst, M., Cockburn, A.: Fingartips: Gesture based direct manipulation in augmented reality. In: 2nd International Conference on Computer Graphics and Interactive Techniques in Australasia and South East Asia (GRAPHITE 2004), pp. 212–221 (2004)
4. Chu, S., Tanaka, J.: Hand gesture for taking self portrait. In: Jacko, J.A. (ed.) Human-Computer Interaction, Part II, HCII 2011. LNCS, vol. 6762, pp. 238–247. Springer, Heidelberg (2011)
5. Chun, J.C., Lee, B.S.: Dynamic manipulation of a virtual object in marker-less ar system based on both human hands. Transactions on Internet and Information Systems 4(4), 618–632 (2010)

6. Erol, A., Bebis, G., Nicolescu, M., Boyle, R.D., Twombly, X.: Vision-based hand pose estimation: A review. Computer Vision and Image Understanding 108(1-2), 52–73 (2007)
7. Hartley, R., Zisserman, A.: Multiple View Geometry in Computer Vision, 2nd edn. Cambridge University Press, New York (2003)
8. Lee, B.S., Chun, J.C.: Interactive manipulation of augmented objects in markerless ar using vision-based hand mouse. In: International Conference on Information Technology (ITNG), pp. 398–403 (2010)
9. Lee, T., Hoellerer, T.: Handy ar: Markerless inspection of augmented reality objects using fingertip tracking. In: ISWC 2007, pp. 83–90 (2007)
10. Lee, T., Hoellerer, T.: Hybrid feature tracking and user interaction for markerless augmented reality. In: IEEE Virtual Reality, pp. 145–152 (2008)
11. Malassiotis, S., Strintzis, M.: Real-time hand posture recognition using range data. Image and Vision Computing 26(7), 1027–1037 (2008)
12. Ng, K.P., Tan, G.Y., Wong, Y.P.: Vision-based hand detection for registration of virtual objects in augmented reality. International Journal of Future Computer and Communication 2(5), 423–427 (2013)
13. Noell, T., Pagani, A., Stricker, D.: Markerless camera pose estimation - an overview. In: Visualization of Large and Unstructured Data Sets - Applications in Geospatial Planning, Modeling and Engineering. 4, vol. 19, pp. 45–54 (2011)
14. Radkowski, R., Stritzke, C.: Interactive hand gesture-based assembly for augmented reality applications. In: Proceedings of the 2012 International Conference on Advances in Computer-Human Interactions, pp. 303–308. IEEE (2012)

Hidden Markov Models for Modeling Occurrence Order of Facial Temporal Dynamics

Khadoudja Ghanem

MISC Laboratory, University CONSTANTINE2, Constantine, Algeria
gkhadoudja@yahoo.fr

Abstract. The analysis of facial expression temporal dynamics is of great importance for many real-world applications. Furthermore, due to the variability among individuals and different contexts, the dynamic relationships among facial features are stochastic. Systematically capturing such temporal dependencies among facial features and incorporating them into the facial expression recognition process is especially important for interpretation and understanding of facial behaviors. The base system in this paper uses Hidden Markov Models (HMMs) and a new set of derived features from geometrical distances obtained from detected and automatically tracked facial points. We propose here to transform numerical representation which is in the form of multi time series to a symbolic representation in order to reduce dimensionality, extract the most pertinent information and give a meaningful representation to human. Experiments show that new and interesting results have been obtained from the proposed approach.

Keywords: Facial expression, HMM, Occurrence order, time series.

1   Introduction

Analyzing the dynamic of facial features and (or) the changes in the appearance of facial features (eye, eyebrows and mouth) is a very important step in facial expression understanding and interpretation. Many researchers attempt to study the dynamic behavior. Timing, duration, speed and occurrence order in which the temporal segment of the different face/body actions occur are crucial parameters related to dynamic behavior [1]. Timing, duration and speed have been analyzed in several studies [2,3,4,5]. Little attention has been given to occurrence order [3,5].

In this paper we propose to explicitly analyze one aspect of facial dynamics by detecting the occurrence order in which facial features movement occurs. For example, expressions typically associated with happiness contain AU6 and AU12, the fact is that is not known in which order each AU occur, this is what we want to discover.

As it is known, a facial expression recognition system consists generally of three steps: pre-processing, feature extraction and classification. In this paper we are not interested by the first step which relates to face localization, and registration to remove the variability due to changes in head pose and illumination.

J. Blanc-Talon et al. (Eds.): ACIVS 2013, LNCS 8192, pp. 172–181, 2013.

In the proposed approach, 18 facial characteristic points are manually localized on the first frame then tracked automatically for the rest of the sequence. Five facial distances are calculated for each frame from each video leading to a multivariate facial time series. These time series are then preprocessed to clean from noisy and to extract descriptive features. In this step, obtained time series are segmented by the detection of transition points, a label which define if the time series increases or decreases is assigned to each one and the rank of these points are saved. All time series associated to each video are then sorted to detect the order of changed time series. An annotation process is applied for each video to produce observation sequences. These observation sequences are used as input to a HMM to learn the best structure of each studied facial expression.

The main contributions of this paper are summarized as follows:

- Acquired data is in the form of multi time series. A pattern which repeats at regular intervals every time unit is sometimes associated to time series, it is called seasonality. In our case this pattern exists in eyelids time series (blinking), in this paper we propose to eliminate this component (section 3.2.1).
- Acquired data has high dimension (multi time series), interesting information is not directly accessible from the raw data this is why, a common prerequisite tasks is changing data representation, both for dimensionality reduction and information extraction. In order to have meaningful representations, we propose to build symbolic representations of time series by incorporating "the occurrence order parameter". The new constructed information elements which are in a higher level, are more comprehensible for human (sections 3.2.2 and 3.2.3).
- There are two categories in pattern recognition methods, structural and statistic methods. To benefit from the advantages of both categories, we propose to combine these two categories in the representation level. Consequently, we use the new proposed symbolic representation, then, we evaluate the derived features with HMM, a well known and suitable method for analyzing temporal behaviors from facial image sequences.
- New temporal rules in terms of interdependency between the different facial features are discovered. These rules aim to describe facial expressions.

The outline of the paper is as follows: section 2 gives an overview on some related work, section 3 explain the followed steps to analyze the considered dynamic parameter. Experiments and discussions are given in section 4 and finally section 5 concludes the paper.

2   Related Work

Several efforts have been recently reported on automatic analysis of facial expressions data [6, 7].

In [8], the proposed AUs recognition system used temporal rules. The algorithm performs recognition of temporal segments (i.e., onset, apex, offset) of each AU.

However, the method cannot recognize the full range of facial behavior, it detects only 27AUs. In another hand, it is not easy to segment action units in three classes "onset, apex and offset" because, generally, transitions are very fast, and with spontaneous emotions, expressions are not exaggerated so that the apex is not always reached.

In [9], a dynamic Bayesian network (DBN) is used to model the dependencies among different AUs. The main problem of this method is when AU is at its low-intensity level, so how to deduce relationships with other AU.

The work in [3] clearly shows that spontaneous brow actions (AU1, AU2 and AU4) have different morphological and temporal characteristics (intensity, duration, and occurrence order) than posed brow actions.

Similarly, it has been shown in [14] that the differences between spontaneous and deliberately displayed smiles are in the order of dynamics of shown behavior (e.g., the movement order of head and body) rather than in the configuration of the displayed expression.

In [10] and [11] Valstar and al proposed a geometric based approach, they were the first authors who addressed the problem of AU temporal segments recognition. They used motion history for facial action detection. And In [12] Koelestra et al proposed an appearance-based approach to facial expression recognition, they were the second group who propose a dynamic texture based method to detect all AUs and their temporal segments. But their method had some difficulties with some Aus. According to the authors, possibly, geometric approaches are better equipped to handle these Aus (e.g., AU5 and AU7).

For this reason and to reduce the number of detected facial features needed in a recognition process, we use facial Euclidian distances instead of action units, each distance characterizes a specific facial region. Furthermore, each distance replaces a set of action units in its activation. For instance the distances D2 and D6 control brow action units which are: AU1, AU4 when D2 increases respectively decreases and AU2 when D6 decreases. We note that most of the rest of upper action units can be replaced by distance D1. In the same way the distances D3, D4 control mouth movements (AU12, AU17, AU23, AU24, AU25, and AU27) and the distance D5 which is used to bind upper deformations with lower ones controls some combinations between upper Aus and lower ones. These distances can be sufficient to control the shape variations of facial components when studying a small set of facial expressions like the universal ones.

Because we want to explicitly study the dynamic behavior both HMM and DBN can be used. In this paper we choose to evaluate Hidden Markov Models.

3   System Overview

The diagram of the proposed system is shown in Fig.1:

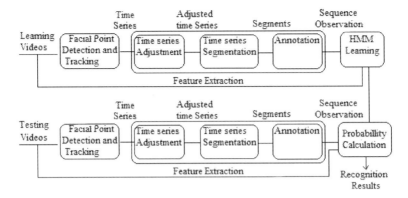

Fig. 1. Diagram of different steps to recognize facial expressions

3.1   Characteristic Facial Points Detection and Tracking

To extract facial features, and capture facial expression dynamics, 18 facial points for each participant's video were manually pointed, then automatically tracked for the rest of the sequence. The tracked points are: (as illustrated in Fig. 2) outer and inner eyebrow, eye corners and eyelids, centers of irises, mouth corners and lips.

Lucas_Kanade algorithm [13] is used to track these points. The main limitation inherent in this tracker is that the tracking became wrong as the number of sequence frames increases because of the accumulation of tracking errors over time. As we are interested only by the first frames, where a facial distance transit from the neutral state to the onset one, errors are negligible.

After tracking, each frame of the video data was represented as a vector of the 18 facial points' 2D coordinates.

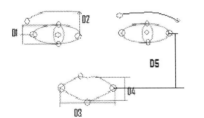

D1: Distance between upper and lower eyelids (Eye opening)
D2: Distance between the interior corner of eye and the interior corner of eyebrow
D3: Distance between left and right mouth corners (Mouth opening width)
D4: Distance between upper and lower lips (Mouth opening height)
D5: Distance between Eye and mouth corners.

Fig. 2. Characteristic distances

3.2   Feature Extraction

For each frame, geometric features D1 – D5 were calculated based on the positions of facial points (see Fig.2). Therefore, each frame of the captured video was represented as a 5-dimensional vector so each video segment containing n frames is represented as a 5Xn-dimensional vector. This leads to multivariate (5) time series.

A pattern which repeats at regular intervals every time unit is sometimes associated to time series, it is called seasonality. The study of the seasonality is a preliminary step in time series processing. Indeed, when the seasonality component exists, it is important to insulate it in order to be able to analyze its other characteristics. In our case this pattern exists in eyelids time series (blinking). Indeed, eye blinking is a natural reaction; its average speed is 300 to 400 Milliseconds. Generally, the eyelid automatically closes 10 to 30 times per minute. The adjusted seasonality for the time series associated to eyelids movement reflects real eyelids movements without blinking. In order to eliminate the blinking problem, we proceed to adjustment seasonality of D1 time series.

3.2.1   Adjustment of Time Series Seasonality

Seasonal adjustment is the process of identifying and removing the seasonal component from a time series. In search for measures that are independent of seasonal variations, several methods have been developed. One of the first mathematical methods developed for seasonal factor estimates has been the observational arithmetic mean method: the Moving Averages [14].

We propose a very simple algorithm to remove seasonality:

Algorithm 1.

```
1- Model time series as additional or multiplicative
model;
2- Check the presence of seasonality in eye time series :
by using Buys ballot plots   [15]
3- Estimate the Trend by moving averages method [32]
4- Estimate Seasonality:
     Compute data without trend (detrend) in our case it
is equal to : Yt/Ct
     Compute seasonal indices Sj (Subtract the mean
value from the detrended data to obtain what are often
referred to as raw seasonal).
     Correct seasonal indices by computing the mean of
these indices (S). If the mean is <>1 then S'j=Sj/S.
5- Compute new values of time series without seasonality.
```

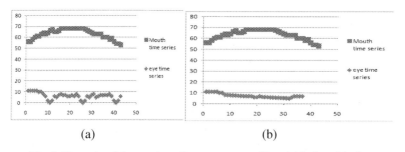

Fig. 3. Example of time series adjustment seasonality : (a) before (b) after

Another problem with obtained time series concerns mouth time series which can be disturbed by speaking. Blinking and speaking are usually manipulators and can disturb time series values. The solution for this problem is not discussed in this paper, however to test the proposed method we choose to remove the speech sections from studied sequences.

Interesting information is not directly accessible from the raw data this is why, a common prerequisite tasks is changing data representation, both for information extraction and dimensionality reduction.

What characterizes a temporal nature is the existence of an order (temporal) on the data. This criterion would greatly benefit our analysis of facial expression dynamics. Indeed, in order to have meaningful representations, we propose to build symbolic representations of time series by incorporating "the occurrence order parameter". The new constructed information elements which are in a higher level are more comprehensible for human.

Each video is characterized by 5 Time series and each time series counts more than 200 value(each value is for a particular frame of the video). To reduce time series dimensionality we proceed to time series segmentation. Time series segmentation can be seen as detection of transition points. Transition point correspond to the frame where the distance increases or decreases in correspondence to the first frame.

3.2.2   Time Series Segmentation and Detection of Transition Points

Many segmentation time series methods were developed [16, 17, 18], most of these methods are based on dynamic programming in order to reduce the number of obtained segments. However, in our situation, we are interested only by the detection of the first and the second segments (just to know if the time series increases or decreases). For this purpose we proceed to detect the first transition points from each time series. A transition point which corresponds to the start of emotion indicates the transition from neutral state to an onset one.

To detect transition points, a very simple algorithm based on a mobile mean is used, a label which define if the time series increases or decreases is assigned to each time series and the rank of these points are saved.

The proposed algorithm is as follows:

Algorithm 2.

```
For all time series
Changed_mean=mean(f(1),f(2))
t=3
 while t<=n & True;    Nouv_mean= mean(f(t),f(t-1))
  If  nouv_mean<changed_mean;
      rank_changed_frame=t;        Label_sens="-"
      Exit
  Else
     If nouv_mean>changed_mean
      rank_changed_frame=t;        Label_sens="+"
      Exit
     Endif
 Endif
endwhile(transition point detected OR no more frames for
a video)
End For (no more time series)
```

3.2.3   Annotation Process and Observations Definition

After segmentation, all time series associated to each video are sorted to detect the order of changed time series according to saved ranks. Then the annotation process is performed, each time series (distance) has two discrete states which represent the "decrease/increase" states of the distance.

It leads to a set of 2X5 features to describe each video.(2=the label assigned to each time series and its rank, 5=facial distance time series). These new features represent all possible observations which can be emitted from each HMM state.

In our experiments, each video sequence must begin in the neutral state and from each state the possible observations correspond to any of the 5 changed distances (which can increase or decrease).

To study the four (4) facial expressions which are Joy, Sadness, Anger and Disgust, we associate one left-right HMM to each facial expression.

4   Experiments and Results Evaluation

4.1   Facial Expression Data Sets

Cohn–Kanade posed database [19] consists of 100 university students. For our experiments, we selected 231 image sequences from the database. The sequences come from 96 subjects, with 1–4 posed expressions per subject (Joy, Anger, Sad and Disgust). MMI Posed database [20] is a resource for Action unit (AU) and basic emotion recognition from face video. The second set of data recorded was posed displays of the six basic facial expressions. For our experiments, we selected 100 image sequences from the database. Each video is composed by more than 100 frames. In our experiments we were interested by all frames displaying the expression from the neutral state, the beginning of the expression (onset) until the apex. We have used 20 frames from each video so about 2000 images. The two datasets contain recordings of subjects displaying posed facial expressions in frontal or near-frontal head poses and under controlled lighting conditions.

Semaine spontaneous dataset [21] contain displays of spontaneous expressions recorded in a natural environment. For our experiments, we selected 80 image sequences. The sequences come from 10 subjects. After removing the speech sections from each image sequences, we extract at least three sub sequences from each image sequence leading to more than 240 image sequences. Most of these sequences display joy expression (smile displaying).

4.2   Our Experiments

In order to evaluate the real performance of our approach , we have conducted different experiments. First we split each studied datasets into three parts, two parts were used as training sets and the last one as a test set. In the second experiment, we used a cross validation process. Obtained results are presented in table (1).In the third experiment and in order to test the ability to generalize to novel conditions, we have used one dataset in training and another in the test (cross datasets). In order to collect a set of examples that is as sparse as possible which spans the problem space completely, we added a last experiment were we use the two thirds of two datasets in the training step and the last third of the two datasets in the test step. All our experiments are Subject-Independent.

4.3   Evaluation

It is possible to draw many conclusions from the obtained results:

-Generally, the average result is lower than the results for training and testing on the same dataset. It is the case for CK dataset. But for the MMI dataset, the average result is higher than the results for training and testing on different datasets. This can be explained by the difference between the CK and MMI actors. Most actors in CK dataset display posed expressions in the same way, and MMI actors display expressions in different ways, this leads to a set of examples as sparse as possible producing by that more different observation sequences. As a result, when the training is done on a sparse set of examples (MMI dataset or MMI+CK) and the test is done on a less sparse set (CK Dataset or Semaine) which is included in the sparse one, obtained rates are higher than ones obtained in the opposite case.

-The structure of each left-right HMM is composed by three states, when considering the learned transition probability matrix, we can observe that sometimes there is no more transitions from one state, this can be explained by the fact that the studied facial expression has a slight intensity which means only one facial distance change. As a result the obtained observation sequence is composed by one or two facial changed distances. HMMs can learn from observation sequences with different length.

-When considering the learned observation matrix, we can observe, that different temporal rules can be deduced from this matrix with a consideration of certain constraints. For instance, deduced rules for Joy expression (with constraint: only D1,D3,D4 can change) are: The first facial changed distance with Joy expression is the distance between mouth corners (increases); The second facial changed distance can be the distance between mouth and eye corners (decreases), or the distance between lips (increases) or the distance between eyelids (decreases);The third facial changed distance can be the one which has not be changed in the second order.

Table 1. Cross Database Testing

Training Dataset	Test Dataset	Joy	Anger	Sadness	Disgust	Expressions
CK	CK	100%	100%	100%	81,81%	95.45%
CK	MMI	76.47%	47.06%	30.43%	58.62%	53.15%
CK	SEMAINE	91.89%	33.33%	90%	100%	78.81%
MMI	MMI	100%	80%	81.82%	70.59%	83.10%
MMI	CK	100%	56.58%	92.59%	91.35%	85.13%
MMI	SEMAINE	94.60%	75%	80%	100%	87.4%
CK+MMI	SEMAINE	94.60%	91.67%	100%	100%	**96.57%**

In the same way we can deduce temporal rules for Anger, Disgust and sadness.

-We can see that only 'first order' (one rule) is not sufficient to recognize expressions because many facial expressions can start in the same way when speaking about facial features deformations order. This is why the second and third order (when present) are considered to recognize facial expressions.

-When considering learned observation matrixes, we can see that Joy has low confusion with any other class. In another hand, high confusion can be observed between Anger and disgust and sometimes between Anger and Sad or Disgust and Sad. Confusion Matrixes confirm these findings.

-Posed Joy is generally recognized with a rate equal to 100%. It is the unique facial expression which is easily recognized. But when the expression is spontaneous, rate recognition do not reach the 100%. When analyzing joy observation sequences, we can observe that two sequences display mixed expressions (Joy with surprise), but when considering posed expressions, actors are asked to display just one expression: Joy, Sadness, Anger..... This is why, we have to train and test HMMs on spontaneous expressions. In this study as we have little examples of observation sequences in the spontaneous dataset, we cannot train HMMs on such set.

5   Conclusion and Future Work

In this paper, we have explicitly analyzed one aspect of facial features dynamics which is occurrence order of facial features deformations. Therefore, we propose a facial expression model based on HMMs to systematically discover and learn relationships between facial feature deformations. For expression classification, we have proved that it is not always required to model the full video sequence. Consequently few temporal rules are sufficient to recognize facial expressions. This study is very important for facial expression analysis and understanding. The experiments show that it is important to learn the model on a set of examples as sparse as possible to span the problem space completely. In the future we hope to learn and test the model on spontaneous datasets to deduce new temporal rules to distinguish between posed and spontaneous expressions.

References

1. Ekman, P., Rosenberg, E.L.: What the Face Reveals: Basic and Applied Studies of Spontaneous Expression Using the Facial Action Coding System, 2nd edn. Oxford University Press (2005)
2. Cohn, J.F., Schmidt, K.L.: The timing of facial motion in posed and spontaneous smiles. J. Wavelets, Multi-resolution and Information Processing 2(2), 121–132 (2004)
3. Valstar, M.F., Pantic, M., Ambadar, Z., Cohn, J.F.: Spontaneous versus Posed Facial Behavior: Automatic Analysis of Brow Actions. In: Proc. ACM Int'l Conf. Multimodal Interfaces, pp. 162–170 (2006)
4. Bartlett, M.S., Littlewort, G., Frank, M., Lainscsek, C., Fasel, I., Movellan, J.: Recognizing Facial Expression: Machine Learning and Application to Spontaneous Behavior. In: Proc. IEEE Int'l Conf. Computer Vision and Pattern Recognition, pp. 568–573 (2005)

5. Valstar, M.F., Gunes, H., Pantic, M.: How to Distinguish Posed from Spontaneous Smiles Using Geometric Features. In: Proc. ACM Int'l Conf. Multimodal Interfaces, pp. 38–45 (2007)
6. Zeng, Z., Pantic, M., Glenn, I., Roisman, T., Huang, S.: A survey of affect recognition Methods: Audio,Visual, and Spontaneous Expressions. IEEE Transactions on Pattern Analysis and Machine Intelligence 31(1) (2009)
7. Gunes, H., Schuller, B., Pantic, M., Cowie, R.: Emotion Representation, Analysis and Synthesis in Continuous Space: A Survey. In: Proc. of the 1st International Workshop on Emotion Synthesis, Representation, and Analysis in Continuous Space, IEEE FG, pp. 827–834. IEEE Press, Santa Barbara (2011)
8. Pantic, M., Patras, I.: Dynamics of facial expression: recognition of facial actions and their temporal segments form face profile image sequences. IEEE Trans. Systems, Man and Cybernetics – Part B 36(2), 433–449 (2006)
9. Tong, Y., Liao, W., Ji, Q.: Facial action unit recognition by exploiting their dynamics and semantic relationships. IEEE Trans. Pattern Analysis and Machine Intelligence 29(10), 1683–1699 (2007)
10. Valstar, M., Pantic, M.: Fully Automatic Facial Action Unit Detection and Temporal Analysis. In: Proc. IEEE Conf. Computer Vision and Pattern Recognition, vol. 3(149) (2006)
11. Valstar, M., Pantic, M., Patras, I.: Motion History for Facial Action Detection from Face Video. In: Proc. IEEE Conf. Systems, Man, and Cybernetics, pp. 635–640 (2004)
12. Koelstra, S., Pantic, M., Patras, I.: A Dynamic Texture-Based Approach to Recognition of Facial Actions and Their Temporal Models. IEEE Transactions on Pattern Analysis and Machine Intelligence 32 (2010)
13. Lucas, B.D., Kanade, T.: An Iterative Image Registration Technique with an Application to Stereo Vision. In: Proceedings of Imaging Understanding Workshop, pp. 121–130 (1981)
14. Makridakis, S., Wheelwright, S.C., Hyndman, R.J.: Forecasting: methods and applications, 3rd edn. John Wiley & Sons, New York (1998)
15. Klein, J.L.: Statistical Visions in Time. Cambridge University Press (1997)
16. Arlot, S., Celisse, A.: Segmentation of the mean of heteroscedastic data via cross-validation. Statistics and Computing, 1–20 (2010)
17. Guédon, Y.: Exploring the segmentation space for the assessment of multiple change-point models. Institut National de Recherche en Informatique et en Automatique, Cahier de recherche 6619 (2008)
18. Lavielle, M.: Detection of Changes using a Penalized Contrast (the DCPC algorithm) (2009), http://www.math.upsud.fr/_lavielleprogrammeslavielle.html
19. Kanade, J., Cohn, F., Tian, Y.: Comprehensive database for facial expression analysis. In: IEEE International Conference on Automatic Face and Gesture Recognition, pp. 46–53 (2000)
20. Pantic, M., Valstar, M.F., Rademaker, R., Maat, L.: Web-based Database for Facial Expression Analysis. In: Proc. IEEE Int'l Conf. Multmedia and Expo (ICME 2005), Amsterdam, The Netherlands (2005)
21. McKeown, G., Valstar, M., Cowie, R., Pantic, M., Schroder, M.: The SEMAINE database: Annotated multimodal records of emotionally colored conversations between a person and a limited agent. IEEE Transactions on Affective Computing 3, 5–17 (2012)

Adaptive Two Phase Sparse Representation Classifier for Face Recognition

Fadi Dornaika[1,2], Youssof El Traboulsi[1], and Ammar Assoum[3]

[1] University of the Basque Country UPV/EHU, San Sebastian, Spain
[2] IKERBASQUE, Basque Foundation for Science, Bilbao, Spain
[3] The Lebanese University, Tripoli, Lebanon

Abstract. Sparse Representation Classifier proved to be a powerful classifier that is more and more used by computer vision and signal processing communities. On the other hand, it is very computationally expensive since it is based on an L_1 minimization. Thus, it is not useful for scenarios demanding a rapid decision or classification. For this reason, researchers have addressed other coding schemes that can make the whole classifier very efficient without scarifying the accuracy of the original proposed SRC. Recently, two-phase coding schemes based on classic Regularized Least Square were proposed. These two-phase strategies can use different schemes for selecting the examples that should be handed over to the next coding phase. However, all of them use a fixed and predefined number for these selected examples making the performance of the final classifier very dependent on this ad-hoc choice. This paper introduces three strategies for adaptive size selection associated with Two Phase Test Sample Sparse Representation classifier. Experiments conducted on three face datasets show that the introduced schemes can outperform the classic two-phase strategies. Although the experiments were conducted on face datasets, the proposed schemes can be useful for a broad spectrum of pattern recognition problems.

1 Introduction

Sparse Representation Classifiers (SRC) are more and more used by computer vision and signal processing communities [1,2,3] due to their good performance. The original SRC is based on combining two ideas: collaborative representation of a test sample [4], and (ii) sparse coding [1,5]. Recently, it has been shown that the performance of Sparse Representation Classifier can be enhanced by simply exploiting locality. For instance, [6] demonstrated that if the sparse coding uses only the nearest neighbor instead of the whole data set, the computational complexity of the original SRC [1] can be reduced without scarifying the accuracy. The original SRC is very computationally expensive since it is based on an L_1 minimization. Its computational load will increase as the number of training samples increases.

Thus, SRC is not very useful for scenarios demanding a rapid decision or classification. For this reason, researchers have addressed other coding schemes

J. Blanc-Talon et al. (Eds.): ACIVS 2013, LNCS 8192, pp. 182–191, 2013.
© Springer International Publishing Switzerland 2013

that will make the whole classifier very efficient without scarifying the accuracy of the original proposed SRC. Several strategies adopt a two-phase coding scheme that uses a classic Regularized Least Square. In [7], the authors propose a two-stage coding scheme based on Non-Negative Least Square representation. In [8], the author introduced a two phase test sample sparse representation (TPTSSR) method which is generally described as two steps. First, it represents the test sample as a linear combination of all the training samples, and determines the M nearest neighbors for the test sample according to the training samples that are the best suited to represent it. Then the TPTSSR method represents the test sample as a linear combination of all the M nearest neighbors and uses the representation result to perform classification. The two phase coding schemes described in [6,8,7] provide a way for selecting the examples. They use a user defined parameter without any way allowing to estimate it optimally and in advance. All two-phase strategies use different schemes for selecting the examples that should be handed over to the next coding phase. However, all of them, use a fixed and predefined number for these examples. Thus, the performance of the final classifier depends on this choice.

In this paper, we introduce three schemes for self-optimized TPTSSR that can overcome the tuning of the neighborhood used. The first scheme estimates the size value that maximizes a recognition score evaluated within the training set via a Leave One Out Cross Validation. The second scheme estimates the optimal value by seeking the largest discontinuity in the self representation measure. The third scheme seeks optimal and adaptive neighborhood.

The paper is structured as follows. In section 2, we briefly review the "two phase test sample sparse representation" (TPTSSR) method. In section 3, we introduce our proposed schemes for self-optimized TPTSSR. Section 4 contains the experimental results associated with face recognition problem performed on three face data sets. Finally, in section 5 we present our conclusions. In the sequel, capital bold letters denote matrices and small bold letters denote vectors.

2 Overview of Two Phase Test Sample Sparse Representation Method

In [8], a two phase strategy was proposed. This variant was coined "two phase test sample sparse representation" (TPTSSR) method. It has two stages. We assume that we have N samples $\mathbf{x}_1, \mathbf{x}_2 \ldots, \mathbf{x}_N$ belonging to C classes. Each class includes n_c training samples, D denotes the dimension of samples. The training samples are denoted by the D $\times$ N matrix $\mathbf{X} = (\mathbf{x}_1, \mathbf{x}_2 \ldots, \mathbf{x}_N)$. Let $\mathbf{y}$ denote the test sample. We assume that the test sample $\mathbf{y}$ and the training samples are represented as unit vectors.

First Phase. It assumes that the test sample $\mathbf{y}$ can be approximately represented as a linear combination of all training samples:

$$\mathbf{y} = \mathbf{X}\,\mathbf{a} \tag{1}$$

The objective is to estimate the coefficients, $\mathbf{a}$, that minimize the residual error $\|\mathbf{y} - \mathbf{X}\mathbf{a}\|^2$ using L_2 regularization. This can be expressed by:

$$\mathbf{a}^\star = arg\min_{\mathbf{a}} \|\mathbf{y} - \mathbf{X}\mathbf{a}\|^2 + \lambda \|\mathbf{a}\|^2$$

Using simple algebra, the solution to the above equation will be given by:

$$\mathbf{a}^\star = arg\min_{\mathbf{a}}(\mathbf{X}^T\mathbf{X} + \lambda\mathbf{I})^{-1}\mathbf{X}^T\mathbf{y}$$

where $\mathbf{I}$ and λ denote the identity matrix and a small positive constant, respectively. Equation (1) shows that every training sample makes its own contribution to represent the test sample. Thus, the contribution that the training sample $\mathbf{x}_i$ makes is $a_i\mathbf{x}_i$. According to [8], the following equation can be used in order to evaluate the contribution of the training samples $\mathbf{x}_i$ in representing the test sample.

$$e_i = \|\mathbf{y} - a_i\mathbf{x}_i\|^2 \tag{2}$$

A small e_i means a great contribution. Based on this fact, the M training samples that have the M largest contributions are selected and denoted by $\widetilde{\mathbf{X}} = (\widetilde{\mathbf{x}}_1, \widetilde{\mathbf{x}}_2, \ldots, \widetilde{\mathbf{x}}_M)$ $1 \leq M \leq N$. The matrix $\widetilde{\mathbf{X}}$ denotes the M selected training examples. These selected samples can be considered as the M nearest neighbors of the test sample.

Second Phase. The second phase seeks to represent the test sample $\mathbf{y}$ as a linear combination of the determined M nearest neighbors and uses the representation result to classify the test sample. This phase assumes that the following equation is approximately satisfied:

$$\mathbf{y} = \widetilde{\mathbf{X}}\mathbf{b} \tag{3}$$

This can be solved by using:

$$\mathbf{b}^\star = arg\min_{\mathbf{b}}(\widetilde{\mathbf{X}}^T\widetilde{\mathbf{X}} + \gamma\mathbf{I})^{-1}\widetilde{\mathbf{X}}^T\mathbf{y}$$

where γ is a positive constant and $\mathbf{I}$ is the identity matrix. At this stage, the label of the test sample $\mathbf{y}$ will be determined by using the SRC principle on the retained samples $\widetilde{\mathbf{X}}$ and the estimated coding vector $\mathbf{b}$. More precisely, suppose that there are t samples from the kth class and they are denoted by $\widetilde{\mathbf{x}}_1^k, \ldots, \widetilde{\mathbf{x}}_t^k$, and the corresponding coefficients are denoted by $b_1^k, \ldots, b_t^k$. The following equation can be used in order to evaluate the collaborative contribution, of the retained training samples of the kth class, in representing the test sample $\mathbf{y}$.

$$Dev(k) = \left\|\mathbf{y} - \sum_{j=1}^{t} \widetilde{\mathbf{x}}_j^k b_j^k\right\|^2$$

A smaller deviation $Dev(k)$ means a greater contribution to representing the test sample. The SRC affects the label of the test sample using the following:

$$l(\mathbf{y}) = arg\min_{k} Dev(k)$$

3 Proposed Schemes

As mentioned before, the TPTSSR needs a parameter that defines the number of the retained samples in the first stage denoted by M. In [8], the authors do not provide any mechanism that allows to choose M in a clever way. Instead, the authors apply the algorithm on test data using a large set of values for M. This is not a practical solution since by definition the test data are new examples that should be recognized once they are available. The obtained results in [8] show that the value of M can have a great impact on the performance of TPTSSR method. In this section, we propose three strategies allowing to estimate the size of retained samples using only the training set. For these three strategies, the whole associated computation is carried out offline once for all.

3.1 Optimal Size Based on Recognition Performance

The first strategy aims at estimating a single optimal value for the neighborhood size (defined by the TPTSSR method) by exploiting the training set and its labels. To this end, we use the training set in a Leave One Out Cross Validation scheme. Given an initial set of possible values for the algorithm parameter $M \in [M_{min}, M_{max}]$. The proposed strategy aims at computing the best values for M, named $M^\star$. For every possible value M, a scoring measure is estimated. This scoring measure is set to the recognition rate obtained by the TPTSSR where every training sample is recognized based on the rest $N-1$ samples. This is very similar to the Leave One Out Cross Validation. However, in our scheme only the training set is used in order to get an estimation of the best value for M that can be handed over to the testing. Thus, the best value of M is chosen as follows:

$$M^\star = arg \max_{M \in [M_{min}, M_{max}]} score(M),$$

3.2 Optimal Size Based on Self-representation

For a fixed value for M, we can define the contribution $e_{i,j}$ as the jth residual error resulting from representing the sample $\mathbf{x}_i$ by the rest of the samples after applying the second phase of coding. This is given by:

$$e_{i,j} = \|\mathbf{x}_i - \widetilde{\mathbf{x}}_j \, b_j\|^2$$

For a fixed value for M, we can define the average contribution over the training set by:

$$e(M) = \frac{1}{N.M} \sum_{i=1}^{N} \sum_{j=1}^{M} e_{i,j}$$

By studying the values of $e(M)$ over a predefined interval , we can select the optimal value of $M^\star$ as the value that gives the largest discontinuity in the function $e(M)$ This is motivated by the fact that the good self-representation of data is generally violated when the average contribution abruptly changes.

$$M^\star = arg \max_{M \in [M_{min}, M_{max}]} \mid e(M + \Delta M) - e(M) \mid$$

In the above equation, ΔM can be set as a function of the total size of the training set, N.

The whole scheme is summarized in Figure 1.

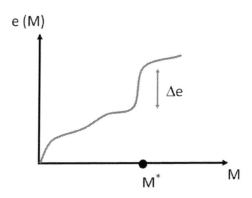

Fig. 1. The optimal value of M corresponds to the largest increase in the average contribution Δ

3.3   Adaptive and Optimal Size

in the above two schemes the objective was to compute an optimal value for the neighborhood size. This optimal parameter will be fixed at the stage of testing. Thus, it would be advantageous to make this optimal value as sample based. The sample can belong to the training set or to the testing one. The basic idea is to compute a neighborhood size for every training sample using a kind of jump detection in the neighbor cluster. At testing stage, the test sample will be associated to the nearest neighbor sample in the training set. The associated parameter will then be used by the TPTSSR algorithm in order to infer its label. The whole algorithm that estimates the optimal neighborhood size for every training sample is given in Algorithm 3.3.

In the above algorithm, $D(\mathbf{x}_p, \mathbf{x}_q)$ denotes the distance between two samples, and $d(\mathbf{x}_j, CurrentSet)$ means the minimal distance between $\mathbf{x}_j$ and the points in set $CurrentSet$. For η, experimentally, 0.25 to 0.33 will be suitable for most situations. The parameter K should be large enough in order to capture the local structure. In our implementation K was set to one fifth of training set size. Although Algorithm 1 has two parameters K and η, its output is a set

Data: A given training sample **x**
Result: Its optimal neighborhood size k

Initialize a large neighborhood size K;
Search the set of K nearest neighbors of **x**: $KNN(\mathbf{x}) = \{\mathbf{x}_i\}, i = 1, \ldots, K$;
Calculate the diameter of KNN (**x**): $d_{max} = arg \max_{\mathbf{x}_p; \mathbf{x}_q \in KNN(\mathbf{x})} D(\mathbf{x}_p, \mathbf{x}_q)$;
$CurrentSet = \{\mathbf{x}\}$;
$RemainSet = $ KNN $(\mathbf{x})$ - $\{\mathbf{x}\}$;
j = 1 ;
while $RemainSet \neq \emptyset$ **do**
    $\mathbf{x}_j = arg \min_{\mathbf{x}_i \in RemainSet} D(\mathbf{x}, \mathbf{x}_i)$;
    k = j ;
    if $d(\mathbf{x}_j, CurrentSet) < \eta \, d_{max}$ **then**
        $CurrentSet = CurrentSet \cup \{\mathbf{x}_j\}$;
        $RemainSet = RemainSet - \{\mathbf{x}_j\}$;
        j= j +1 ;
    else
        k = k-1;
    end
end

Algorithm 1. Neighborhood size selection for a training sample

of N optimal neighborhood sizes since it is invoked for every training sample **x**. Thus, every training sample will have its best neighbor size k. At testing time, the aim is to determine the label of a test sample **y**. We proceed as follows. First, the nearest neighbor to the test sample is selected among the training samples. Then, the optimal neighborhood size k_i of that neighbor, already known from the training stage, will be used by the TPTSSR algorithm.

4 Experimental Results

The performance of the proposed schemes is assessed in the face recognition problem under different challenges. Under the assumption that the face images to be tested can be reconstructed by the images from the same categories, sparse coding can also be used in face recognition[5,1]. The complexity in face recognition emerges from the variability of the appearance of a human face [9,10]. We have tested the proposed schemes on three benchmark face data sets: ORL, Yale, and FERET.

4.1 Datasets

- **ORL**[1]**:** There are 10 images for each of the 40 human subjects, which were taken at different times, varying the lighting, facial expressions (open/closed

---

[1] http://www.cl.cam.ac.uk/research/dtg/attarchive/facedatabase.html

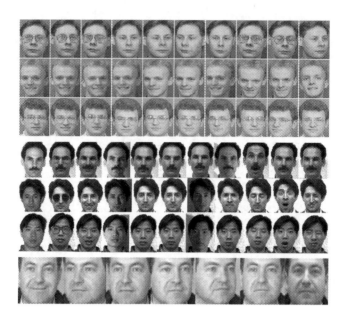

Fig. 2. Some samples of ORL, Yale, and FERET data sets

eyes, smiling/not smiling) and facial details (glasses/no glasses). The images were taken with a tolerance for some tilting and rotation of the face up to 20°.

- **Yale**[2]: The Yale face data set contains 165 images of 15 persons. Each individual has 11 images. The images demonstrate variations in lighting condition, facial expression (normal, happy, sad, sleepy, surprised, and wink). Each image is manually cropped and resized to $32{\times}32$ pixels.

- **FERET**[3]: We use a subset of FERET database, which includes 1400 images of 200 distinct subjects, each subject has seven images. The subset involves variations in facial expression, illumination and pose. In our experiment, the facial portion of each original image is cropped automatically based on the location of eyes and resized to $32{\times}32$ pixels.

Figure 2 illustrates some samples from ORL, Yale, and FERET face data sets.

4.2   Method Comparison

In the first group of experiments, we evaluated the TPTSSR performance on the face data sets. Each data set is split into a training part and a testing part. The training part was set to 50% of the whole data set. Then, the face

---

[2] http://see.xidian.edu.cn/vipsl/database_Face.html

[3] http://www.itl.nist.gov/iad/humanid/feret/

images in the testing part are recognized by the TPTSSR method. Figure 3 illustrates the recognition rate of the TPTSSR method as a function of the neighborhood size. As can be seen, the TPTSSR performance is highly dependent on the neighborhood size. For instance, in the case of FERET database, the variation of the recognition rate obtained at the worst value and the best value is more than 25%.

In the second group of experiments, we compare the TPTSSR with the proposed schemes with the classic TPTSSR and with the Nearest Neighbor (NN) classifier. To this end, every face data set is randomly split into eight train/test partitions. The performance (recognition rate) is averaged over these eight random splits. Since the performance of the classic TPTSSR depends on the neighborhood size, for every split, the performance was quantified over an exhaustive range for this parameter and then the average performance is retained for each split. Tables 1,2, and 3 illustrate the obtained average performance of the used classifiers for ORL, Yale and FERET datasets, respectively. As can be seen, the three proposed schemes have improved the average performance of the TPTSSR method. One can observe that even the unsupervised schemes (schemes 2 and 3 which do not exploit the labels) are also very useful in improving the recognition rate.

Table 1. Average recognition rate of different schemes obtained with the ORL dataset (See text for details)

ORL	Average	Stan. Dev.
NN classifier	87.58	2.51
TPTSSR	94.10	1.73
TPTSSR (Scheme1)	94.38	1.74
TPTSSR (Scheme2)	**95.10**	1.40
TPTSSR (Scheme3)	92.35	3.53

Table 2. Average recognition rate of different schemes obtained with the Yale dataset (See text for details)

Yale	Average	Stan. Dev.
NN classifier	80.38	8.14
TPTSSR	92.48	4.41
TPTSSR (Scheme1)	**94.97**	4.44
TPTSSR (Scheme2)	92.88	4.52
TPTSSR (Scheme3)	89.24	5.28

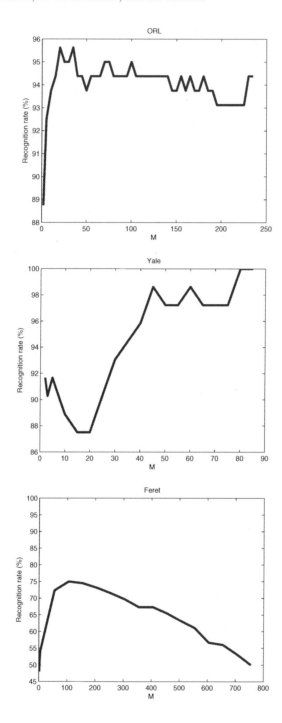

Fig. 3. Recognition rate of the TPTSSR method as a function of the neighborhood size M

Table 3. Average recognition rate of different schemes obtained with FERET dataset

FERET	Average	Stan. Dev.
NN classifier	37.08	12.83
TPTSSR	52.11	17.42
TPTSSR (Scheme1)	**60.94**	18.98
TPTSSR (Scheme2)	50.19	17.07
TPTSSR (Scheme3)	56.42	14.57

5   Conclusion

We proposed three schemes for an adaptive two phase test sample sparse representation (TPTSSR) method. The main advantage of these schemes is the offline estimation of an optimal neighborhood size for the two phase process. Experiments sowed that even the unsupervised schemes based on data exploration can enhance the recognition performance of the two phase test sample sparse representation method. Future work, may address the application of the proposed schemes on very large data sets of images and other types of signals.

Acknowlodgment. This work was supported by the projects EHU 13/40 and LNCSR 03-10-11.

References

1. Wright, J., Yang, A., Ganesh, A., Sastry, S., Ma, Y.: Robust face recognition via sparse representation. IEEE Trans. on Pattern Analysis and Machine Intelligence 31, 210–227 (2009)
2. Yang, M., Zhang, L., Yang, J., Zhang, D.: Robust sparse coding for face recognition. In: IEEE Int. Conf. Computer Vis. Pattern Recognition (2011)
3. Zhang, L., Yang, M., Feng, X.: Sparse representation or collaborative representation: Which helps face recognition? In: International Conference on Computer Vision (2011)
4. Waqas, J., Yi, Z., Zhang, L.: Collaborative neighbor representation based classification using l2-minimization approach. Pattern Recognition Letters 34, 201–208 (2013)
5. Shi, Q., Eriksson, A., Hengel, A., Shen, C.: Is face recognition really a compressive sensing problem? In: IEEE Int. Conf. Computer Vis. Pattern Recognition (2011)
6. Li, C., Guo, J., Zhang, H.: Local sparse representation based classification. In: IEEE Int. Conference on Pattern Recognition (2010)
7. He, R., Zheng, W., Hu, B., Kong, X.: Two-stage nonnegative sparse representation for large-scale face recognition. IEEE Transactions on Neural Networks and Learning Systems 24, 35–46 (2013)
8. Xu, Y., Zhang, D., Yang, J., Yang, J.Y.: A two-phase test sample sparse representation method for use with face recognition. IEEE Transactions on Circuits and Systems for Video Technology 21, 1255–1262 (2011)
9. Chai, X., Shan, S., Chen, X., Gao, W.: Locally linear regression for pose-invariant face recognition. IEEE Trans. on Image Processing 16, 1716–1725 (2007)
10. Zhang, X., Gao, Y.: Face recognition across pose: A review. Pattern Recognition 42, 2876–2896 (2009)

Automatic User-Specific Avatar Parametrisation and Emotion Mapping

Stephanie Behrens, Ayoub Al-Hamadi, Robert Niese, and Eicke Redweik

Institute for Information Technology and Communications,
Otto von Guericke University, Magdeburg, Germany
{Robert.Niese,Ayoub.Al-Hamadi}@ovgu.de
http://www.iikt.ovgu.de/

Abstract. In this paper an approach for automatic user-specific 3D model generation and expression classification is proposed. User performance-driven avatar animation is recently in the focus of research due to the increasing amount of low-cost acquisition devices with integrated depth map computation. Thereby challenging is the user-specific emotion classification without a complex manual initial step. Correct classification and emotion intensity identification can only be done with known expression specific facial feature displacement which differs from user to user. The use of facial feature tracking on predefined 3D model expression animations is presented here as solution statement for automatic emotion classification and intensity calculation. Consequently with this approach partial occlusions of a presented emotion do not hamper expression identification based on the symmetrical structure of human faces. Thus, a markerless, automatic and easy to use performance-driven avatar animation approach is presented.

Keywords: Avatar animation, face normalisation, automatic facial feature extraction, facial expression analysis, blendshape animation.

1 Introduction

One of the main challenging tasks in performance-driven avatar animation is related to automatic expression classification. Expressions and facial proportions differ from user to user wherefore facial feature movement is unknown. Secondary the definition of realistic facial emotion animation sets, expression intensity identification and mapping onto the 3D model is a sophisticated part due to unknown maximum feature displacement per expression. Therefore the aim is to introduce an approach for automatic expression extraction, classification and mapping with a low-cost acquisition device like the Microsoft Kinect sensor as input.

A vision-based approach in combination with a precomputed motion capture database is presented by Chai et al. [3]. Character animation is real-time user-controlled via a 2D video camera input whereat animation control parameter determined by the basis of feature tracking. Optical flow and gradient based motion estimation are used for tracking. Furthermore the motion capture database

J. Blanc-Talon et al. (Eds.): ACIVS 2013, LNCS 8192, pp. 192–202, 2013.

integrates a-priori knowledge and therefore facilitates the translation of 2D input into 3D facial expressions. As initial step 19 points have to be set inside the first frame whereof 15 control parameter are calculated.

The Kinect sensor as input device is also used in a performance-based work by Weise et al. [14]. Avatar animation is implemented as optimisation problem by blending user-specific expression animations together. The needed blendshape weights are estimated from 3D/2D input data matching the user-specific 3D model. An animation prior term is defined and learned from the user-specific expression animations for tracking support and weight calculation. This term is based on Mixtures of Probabilistic Principal Component Analysers (MPPCA). Prejudicial is the time-consuming initial step. Hereby the user performs several expressions and in each expression sequence feature points have to be set manually. Secondary pre-calculation of the expression model and prior term takes approximately 20 min.

Other approaches uses semi-automatic initialisation, special laser scanner or special make-up for feature extraction and tracking as well as extensive databases with pre-calculated expressions models. Furthermore automatic photofit techniques for user-specific avatar modelling are not integrated. The goal of this work is to present an approach without semi-automatic or marker-based initial steps.

2   System Overview

The proposed approach is a two step automatic system for real-time user controlled avatar expression animation. Firstly an off-line expression depending facial feature movement estimation is performed (see section 2.1). Therefore a user-specific 3D model is generated based on the Kinect sensor input and animated with the six basic emotions. A photofit technique is used for 3D model generation and finding an automatic method for the needed feature key-point calculation poses the most challenging part of this step. Secondary an on-line video analysis method for expression classification is applied (see section 2.2). This method consists of a feature tracking and expression detection step, expression classification with integrated occlusion handling and the avatar animation part. Figure 1 visualises the processing pipeline.

2.1   Image Analysis

Expression classification and intensity identification is one of most difficult parts in performance-driven avatar animation due to unknown facial feature shifting. The proposed system is a vision-based approach wherefore facial feature movement estimation is based on a user-specific 3D model which is used in the later process for expression classification. Hence, the first step is the generation of the user-specific 3D model. Therefore an image of the user is acquired, normalised and passed to the key-point extraction step. The photofit based user-specific 3D

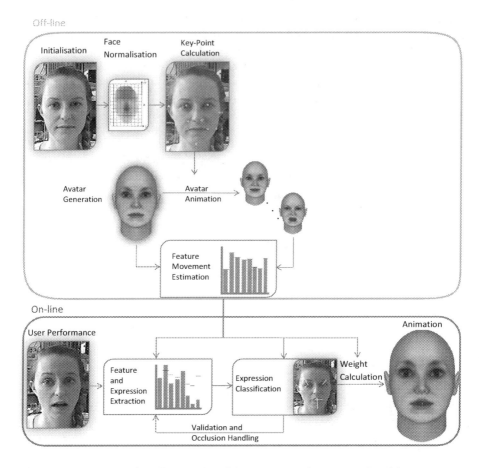

Fig. 1. Processing pipeline. During the off-line image analysis step a facial feature point displacement estimation is calculated. The values for facial feature shifting during emotion based facial deformation are estimated from an animated user-specific 3D model. At run-time the pre-calculated feature point positions and feature relationships are used for expression extraction and classification.

model reconstruction requires the definition of key-points for solving the correspondence problem between the user face image and a statistical average face model.

Key-Point Extraction: User image acquisition is implemented by placing the user in front of a Microsoft Kinect sensor in neutral expression. A frontal view of the reference face and/or an illumination uniformity environment is not mandatory since the face normalisation method will meet this challenge.

The face normalisation method of [11] contains face detection, background removal, frontal face view alignment and if needed illumination correction and is therefore optimal suited for simplifying the expression classification method. Thereby a 3D point cloud based on the Kinect depth map is generated and a colour based point clustering for face localisation is performed. Face position estimation is computed by a modified iterative closest point algorithm (ICP) what can be summarised in the following way:

- Initialization or reset of pose vector $t^{[0]}$.
- Let $W(1)$ be a cloud of face cluster points p_i and $M(5)$ an ICP model with vertices a_j and associated normals b_j.
- Repeat for $k = 1...k_{max}$ or until convergence:
  - Compute a set of closest correspondences S

$$S = \bigcup_{j=1}^{m} (a_j, f_{CP}(a_j(t^{[k-1]}), W)) \tag{1}$$

  with f_{CP} returning closest point p_i in W to any point a_j.
  - Compute new pose vector $t^{[k]}$ that minimises the fitting error function e w.r.t. to all pairs S.

Afterwards the detected face model is equal in orientation and position to the real face and a standard hardware based OpenGL rasterisation technique is used for frontal view generation. Consequential due to the standardised size and orientation of each user face changes result through expressions only. The normalised face image is the basis for the needed photofit key-point determination. Key-points represent important facial features which differ in size and position depending on the users ethnic group. Additionally key-points on the outer boundaries of the user's face for face size determination are needed. Therefore correct identification of these facial features is mandatory for user-specific 3D model generation. Other than in previous works like [14] or [3] an approach for automatic determination of 11 key-points for the eyes, wings of the nose, corners of the mouth, cheek bones, jawbones and chin is presented.

Initially the left eye e_l, right eye e_r, tip of the nose n_{mid} and the upper lip ul are detected via a trained Haar feature-based Cascade Classifier based on the work of [13] and [9] (see figure 2 a)). The classifier is trained on face images with edge, line and center-surround features. Subsequent a-priori knowledge about facial geometry and proportions of the human average face is utilised for the position estimation of the remaining points. The human face is sagittaly symmetrical and divisible in three parts: forehead and eyes, nose and the mouth and chin region. From this it follows that the search area for the key-points can be limited. Furthermore average values for distances between facial features exists whereby key-points calculation is simplified. For instance the position of the left nose wing n_l is computed in the following way:

$$d(n_{mid}, e_l) = d(e_l, e_r) * \left(\frac{2}{1 + \sqrt{5}} \right), \tag{2}$$

$$n_l = \left(\frac{d(n_{mid}, e_l)}{2} + e_l, e_l \right), \tag{3}$$

with the nose to eye distance $d(n_{mid}, e_l)$ and the distance between the eyes $d(e_l, e_r)$. Likewise computation of the residual points is accomplished what is

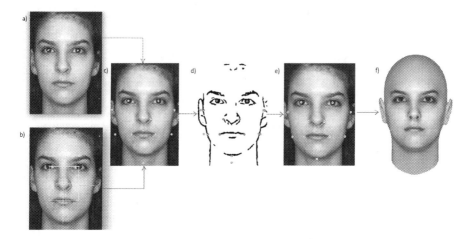

Fig. 2. Key-point calculation for automatic user-specific 3D model generation. a) Result of haar-cascade detection for eyes, tip of the nose and upper lip. b) A-priori knowledge about facial proportions serve as basis for seed point estimation. Similar line colours indicate equal line length. c) Seed point estimation on the basis of a) and b). d) Seed point improvement towards edges of facial features. Initial seed points are orange coloured and optimised points are visualised in blue. e) Input image with improved seed points for 3D model generation. f) Final user-specific 3D model.

illustrated in figures 2 b) and c). These points are used as seed points and are subsequently improved towards facial feature edges (see figure 2 d)). The edge image is generated by adaptive thresholding and several morphological operations. Finally a photofit technique for user-specific 3D model generation is applied to the facial user image with the optimised points as input (see figures 2 e) and f)).

The photofit method reconstructs a morphable 3D model like integrated into the FaceGen Modeller [5]. This 3D mesh is used as basis for avatar animation. Thereby new faces are generated as a modification of the co-efficients of a linear combination of an average face constrained by statistics:

$$f' = f^- + \sum_{j=1}^{N_s}(s_j f^j) + \sum_{k=1}^{N_a}(a_k u^k) \tag{4}$$

with the average model f^-, symmetric shape vector f^j, asymmetric shape vector u^k, the symmetric and asymmetric co-efficients s_j, a_k and the number of symmetric and asymmetric shapes N_s, N_a. The normalised face image is used as detailed texture map for the final 3D model.

Facial Feature Movement Estimation: The later in the process following online expression classification is build up on facial feature shifting, since Bassili et al. [1] have shown that a direct correlation exists between point displacement

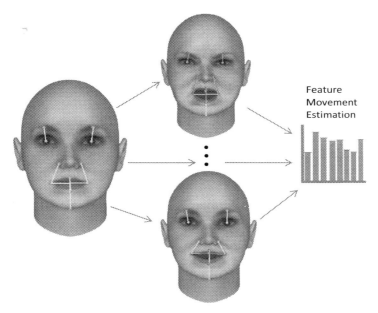

Fig. 3. Database build-up. Starting with a user-specific 3D model in neutral facial expression feature point shifting and relationship modifications for expression classification are calculated on an animated 3D model. Therefore the model is animated with all six basic emotions and for each facial expression feature point shifting is computed and stored in a database.

of facial features, the relationship of movements between these features and the shown facial expression. Therefore the extraction of facial features in neutral facial expression images and images with shown emotions is mandatory for point displacement calculation. Avoiding a high amount of user-interaction and abstain from marker-based methods is the intention of this approach wherefore the user-specific 3D model serves as foundation for feature shifting estimation.

The main idea for the presented vision based expression identification method is the change of relative distances of facial features to each other between neutral expression and shown emotions. Thereby a challenging aspect is the user-specific facial deformation per expression and the thereof individual facial feature movement. For feature movement estimation the identification of the eyes, eyebrows, wings of the nose, corners of the mouth, upper and lower lip is necessary since these facial features are involved forming the six universal basic expressions fear, anger, surprise, happiness, sadness and disgust (see [4]). An automatic solution for this task is realised through 3D model generation for each user and animation of this model with the six basic emotions of maximum amount. After each animation the facial features are detected on images of the model V_e via the afore mentioned key-point detection method and the point displacements as well as the changed relationships V_{dis} for each feature to each other are calculated based on the neutral expression model V_n:

$$V_{dis} = \sum_{i=1}^{N} V_e^i - \sum_{q=1}^{N} V_n^q, \qquad (5)$$

with the number of feature points N. Figure 3 illustrates this approach. For on-line classification these values are stored in a database. Consequently for each user the approximate value for feature point shifting per expression is estimated and a displacement threshold calculated. This threshold describes the percent value of the distance between a facial feature in the neutral 3D model and the same facial feature in the animated model. Thereby the minimum shifting value of each feature point per expression is calculated. Additionally informations about emotions which occur sagittal symmetric are saved. In the further process expressions are detected on the basis of the displacement threshold.

2.2 Video Analysis

The on-line expression detection and classification is simplified by the pre-calculated shifting values for facial features and build up a basis for expression mapping onto the avatar. At run-time facial features are detected and tracked over time. Then the feature position values are passed to the expression detection and classification step. In case of non-availability of all feature points an occlusion handling step is accomplished. Then a classified expression animates the avatar.

Tracking: The Lucas-Kanade method with pyramids [2] is used as optical flow algorithm for facial feature tracking and the computation of relative distances of facial features to each other what forms the basis for the presented vision based expression detection and classification method.

Expression Extraction and Classification: The detection and classification process is based on relationship alteration since expressions are the sum of facial feature shifting. At run-time features are tracked and the positions and relationships are compared to database values. Exceeds one or more feature points the pre-calculated displacement threshold (see section2.1) an expression is detected. The detected expression is passed to the expression classification step. Feature point displacement and feature relationship modifications are characteristic for each expression. Once feature positions and relationships have surpassed the according displacement thresholds and the positions as well as the relationships correlate to database entries expressions are derived.

Avatar Animation. Animations are implemented via a blendshape approach. Thereby a blendshape animation can be described as a linear weighted sum of k predefined facial animation meshes M [8]:

$$f = \sum_k w_k M_k, \tag{6}$$

with w_k specifying the weighting and M_k the blendshape animation mesh vector. The used animation meshes are based on the FaceGen animations but any other predefined animation meshes can be used as well. With a given set of animation target meshes a new facial expression can be synthesized via linear blending of different amounts of M_k. Avoiding implausible facial expressions is usually done by value restriction $w_k \in [0, 1]$.

With a known blendshape mesh and weighting factor blendshapes are easy to use and form a dense representation of predefined facial expressions [14]. Therefore the main challenging task in avatar animation is robust blendshape mesh identification and determination of the blendshape weights. Mesh identification is done via the aforementioned expression classification. The weight calculation is performed inside the mapping function.

The mapping function calculation is based on the amount of feature displacement. Given the maximum amount of movement on the basis of the predefined displacement database and the minimum from the neutral face the weighting factor can be approximated. The weighting is in accordance with the proportionately Euclidian distance between the neutral feature position and the expression feature point position.

Afterwards the expression corresponding blendshape mesh with the calculated weighting factor are added to the neutral avatar 3D model and displayed to the user.

Occlusion Handling: Most of the basic expressions appear sagittal symmetrically which can be used in terms of occlusion handling. Nevertheless if only the left or right part of the face is visible classification leads to correct expression identification due to the displacement database. In addition with the help of the pre-calculated animations expressions are mapped completely onto the avatar.

3   Results

Based on a 2D and 3D image acquisition with a low-cost 3D sensor the presented approach illustrated that automatic performance-driven avatar animation is realisable.

The presented approach was tested for the following 11 feature points: Eyebrows, eyes, wings of the nose, corners of the mouth, upper lip, lower lip and the chin. In figure 4 different actions and emotions can be seen: raising eyebrows, closed eyes, happiness and surprise. Occlusions with correct expression mapping are illustrated in figure 5. Expressions are detected according to relative distances between feature points, e.g. raised eyebrows are detected on the basis of the eyebrow-pupil distance. The used displacement threshold is set to

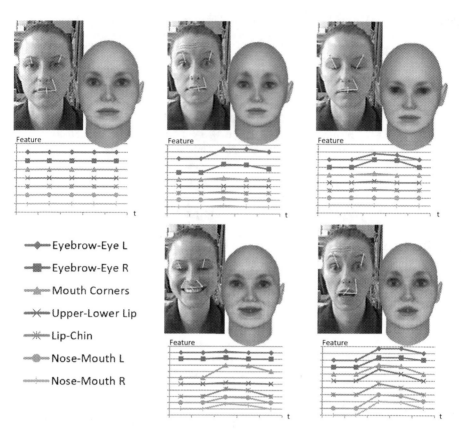

Fig. 4. Avatar animation results. A user animates an automatic generated user-specific 3D model. First row from left to right: neutral expression, raised eyebrows and closed eyes. Second row shows happiness and surprise. Diagrams represent absolute values of relationship changes between facial features.

10 percent of the distance between feature points. As soon as the feature point distance exceeds the computed threshold an expression is detected and classified related to the feature point position and distance value. The blendshape weight is proportional to the eyebrow-pupil distance.

Good results are obtained for eyebrow raising, happiness and surprise though detection and classification of the eye blinking action is more challenging. Optical tracking fails in terms of disappeared feature points whereby unusual results for distances and feature point locations occur. Thereby the threshold is not every time transcended although the expression is performed. In the case of an occlusion a similar issue appears but with a higher amount of point displacement rather exceedance of the threshold arises.

The generated output are blendshape weights and the identified expression. These data can be applied to every blendshape animated model whereby not only a user-specific avatar is conceivable non-humanoid avatar can be applied as well.

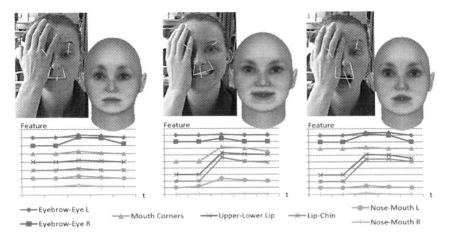

Fig. 5. Avatar animation results with correct expression mapping despite half-page occlusions. From left to right: raised eyebrows, happy and surprised.Diagrams represent absolute values of relationship changes between facial features.

4   Conclusion and Future Work

A complete automatic performance-driven avatar animation is still in the focus of computer vision research and a challenging task. The face normalisation solves the pose and illumination problem and therefore simplifies the avatar construction and expression extraction as well as the emotion classification. The frontal face view facilitates avatar model generation since photofit key-point calculation is done under the simplified assumption of an ideal face image. Avatar expression images which are based on the predefined blendshape meshes support frontal view and specify the probable feature displacement for each expression. The a-priori knowledge about feature displacement is then used for validation of feature extraction and expression classification. Collateral expression extraction and classification is limited by the symmetry assumption whereby occlusion handling is realised.

Other works presented marker based approaches or marked facial features manually inside the first frames. The proposed approach described a method for continuous automatic user-specific avatar animation based on a low-cost acquisition device. Thereby no marker or manually facial feature points have to be placed or annoying light pattern is needed.

For future work supporting individual expressions and re-usability on different 3D face models would be preferable. On the one hand blendshape animations offer a multitude of advantages but on the other hand only the transfer of pre-calculated expression animations to the avatar is possible. Extraordinary user specific expressions are not taken into account respectively mapped to one of the basic expressions. A higher amount of different blendshapes would also increase the level of user-specific expressions. The low resolution and the high noise level of the Kinect sensor is only usable of limited suitability for the photofit based avatar texturising. An adequate preprocessing of the input image would improve texture map quality. Overall the presented approach is a basis for automatic avatar animation as it is easy to use and modular constructed so that different extraction or emotion mapping methods can be tested in future work.

Acknowledgment. This work was supported by DFG-Transregional Collaborative Research Centre SFB/TRR 62.

References

1. Bassili, J.N.: Facial motion in the perception of faces and of emotional expression. Journal of Experimental Psychology: Human Perception and Performance 4(3), 373–379 (1978)
2. Bouguet, J.-Y.: Pyramidal implementation of the affine lucas kanade feature tracker description of the algorithm. Intel Corporation (2001)
3. Chai, J.-X., Xiao, J., Hodgins, J.: Vision-based control of 3d facial animation. In: Proceedings of the 2003 ACM SIGGRAPH/Eurographics Symposium on Computer Animation, pp. 193–206. Eurographics Association (2003)
4. Ekman, P., Friesen, W.V.: Constants across cultures in the face and emotion. Journal of Personality and Social Psychology 17(2), 124 (1971)
5. Facegen modeller (April 2013), http://facegen.com/modeller.htm
6. Fasel, B., Luettin, J.: Automatic facial expression analysis: a survey. Pattern Recognition 36(1), 259–275 (2003)
7. Joshi, P., Tien, W.C., Desbrun, M., Pighin, F.: Learning controls for blend shape based realistic facial animation. In: ACM SIGGRAPH 2005 Courses, p. 8. ACM (2005)
8. Lewis, J., Anjyo, K.-I.: Direct manipulation blendshapes. IEEE Computer Graphics and Applications 30(4), 42–50 (2010)
9. Lienhart, R., Kuranov, A., Pisarevsky, V.: Empirical analysis of detection cascades of boosted classifiers for rapid object detection. In: Michaelis, B., Krell, G. (eds.) DAGM 2003. LNCS, vol. 2781, pp. 297–304. Springer, Heidelberg (2003)
10. Liu, X., Xia, S., Fan, Y., Wang, Z.: Exploring non-linear relationship of blendshape facial animation. In: Computer Graphics Forum., vol. 30, pp. 1655–1666. Wiley Online Library (2011)
11. Niese, R., Al-Hamadi, A., Michaelis, B.: A novel method for 3d face detection and normalization. Journal of Multimedia 2(5), 1–12 (2007)
12. Pantic, M., Rothkrantz, L.J.M.: Automatic analysis of facial expressions: The state of the art. IEEE Transactions on Pattern Analysis and Machine Intelligence 22(12), 1424–1445 (2000)
13. Viola, P., Jones, M.: Rapid object detection using a boosted cascade of simple features. In: Proceedings of the 2001 IEEE Computer Society Conference on Computer Vision and Pattern Recognition, CVPR 2001, vol. 1, pp. I–511. IEEE (2001)
14. Weise, T., Bouaziz, S., Li, H., Pauly, M.: Realtime performance-based facial animation. ACM Trans. Graph. 30(4), 77 (2011)

Optimizing Contextual-Based Optimum-Forest Classification through Swarm Intelligence

Daniel Osaku[1], Rodrigo Nakamura[2], João Papa[2], Alexandre Levada[1],
Fábio Cappabianco[3], and Alexandre Falcão[4]

[1] Department of Computing, Federal University of São Carlos
danosaku@hotmail.com, alexandre@dc.ufscar.br
[2] Department of Computing, UNESP - Univ. Estadual Paulista
{rodrigo.mizobe,papa}@fc.unesp.br
[3] Institute of Science and Technology, Federal University of São Paulo
cappabianco@unifesp.br
[4] Institute of Computing, University of Campinas
afalcao@ic.unicamp.br

Abstract. Several works have been conducted in order to improve classification problems. However, a considerable amount of them do not consider the contextual information in the learning process, which may help the classification step by providing additional information about the relation between a sample and its neighbourhood. Recently, a previous work have proposed a hybrid approach between Optimum-Path Forest classifier and Markov Random Fields (OPF-MRF) aiming to provide contextual information for this classifier. However, the contextual information was restricted to a spatial/temporal-dependent parameter, which has been empirically chosen in that work. We propose here an improvement of OPF-MRF by modelling the problem of finding such parameter as a swarm-based optimization task, which is carried out Particle Swarm Optimization and Harmony Search. The results have been conducted over the classification of Magnetic Ressonance Images of the brain, and the proposed approach seemed to find close results to the ones obtained by an exhaustive search for this parameter, but much faster for that.

Keywords: Magnetic Resonance Images, Optimum-Path Forest, Markov Random Fields, Particle Swarm Optimization, Harmony Search.

1 Introduction

Image classification plays an important role in many magnetic resonance imaging (MRI) applications. Many classification techniques have been proposed, but most part of them assume that samples are identical independent distributed, and no information about the correlations between them is employed.

Recently, some works have exploited the concept of contextual information in order to improve the classification step using temporal and/or spatial information. For instance, Tarabalka et al. [15] proposed a hybrid approach composed by Support Vector Machines (SVM) and Markov Random Fields (MRF) for remote

J. Blanc-Talon et al. (Eds.): ACIVS 2013, LNCS 8192, pp. 203–214, 2013.

sensing image classification called SVM-MRF. Using a similar idea, Moser and Serpico [10] proposed a SVM-MRF approach for contextual classification using an one-step formulation for both SVM and MRF, since the work of [15] is carried out in two phases. Wu et al. [17] have also proposed a different version of the SVM-MRF classifier for mouse brain image segmentation. Therefore, the main idea behind these contextual classifiers concerns with how to model some *a priori* knowledge as a locally dependent MRF in order to hold a spatial smoothness assumption of the pixel labels [2,7,5].

In our previous work [11], we proposed the use of the Optimum Path Forest (OPF) [13,12] together with MRF for classification of MRI images, following the similar idea proposed by Tarabalka et al. [15], which extended the feature vectors using the Iterated Conditional Modes (ICM) [3] method to extract additional information from the label map generated by pixelwise classification. However, the ICM method is parameter-dependent and is not possible to find the optimal value since it can assume infinite solutions. As such, in this paper we propose an improvement regarding the work of Nakamura et al. [11], in which the ICM parameter, that defines the spatial content of the contextual classification, is obtained by means of a nature-inspired optimization algorithm. Thus, we propose to model the process of finding such parameter as an optimization problem, in which the fitness function to be maximized is the OPF accuracy over a validating set. We also introduce two well-known optimization techniques in order to find out the parameter used by ICM method.

The remainder of this paper is organized as follows. Section 2 presents a brief theoretical background regarding OPF and Markov Random Fields. Section 3 introduces the proposed approach and the two optimization techniques employed in this paper: Particle Swarm Optimization (PSO) and Harmony Search (HS). Sections 4 and 5 state the experiments and conclusions, respectively.

2   Concepts and Methods

This section briefly presents the theoretical background regarding the OPF classifier and Markov Random Fields.

2.1   Optimum-Path Forest

Assume we are given a dataset $\mathcal{D}(\mathcal{X}, \mathcal{Y})$, where $\mathcal{X}$ stands for set of features and $\mathcal{Y}$ a class associated with each sample. The OPF classifier models $\mathcal{D}$ as a graph $\mathcal{G}(\mathcal{V}, \mathcal{A})$ whose nodes are the samples in $\mathcal{V} = \mathcal{X}$, the arcs are defined by an adjacency relation $\mathcal{A}$, and weighted by a distance function between the feature vectors of the corresponding nodes.

Similarly to the community ordered formation, where groups of individuals are formed based on optimum connectivity relations to their leaders, OPF employs a role competition process between some key nodes (prototypes) in order to partition the graph into optimum-path trees according to some path-cost function. By analogy, the population is divided into communities, where each individual belongs to the group which offered to him/her the highest reward.

In addition, the dataset $\mathcal{D}$ is partitioned in three subsets $\mathcal{D} = \mathcal{D}_1 \cup \mathcal{D}_2 \cup \mathcal{D}_3$, standing for training, validation and test sets, respectively. Therefore, their corresponding graph formulation are $\mathcal{D}_1 = \mathcal{G}_1(\mathcal{V}_1, \mathcal{A}_1)$, $\mathcal{D}_2 = \mathcal{G}_2(\mathcal{V}_2, \mathcal{A}_2)$ and $\mathcal{D}_3 = \mathcal{G}_3(\mathcal{V}_3, \mathcal{A}_3)$. Now assume π_s be a simple path in the graph with terminal $s \in \mathcal{D}_1$, and $\langle \pi_s \cdot (s,t) \rangle$, an additive path defined by the concatenation between π_s and the arc (s,t). Let $\mathcal{S} \subset \mathcal{D}_1$ be a set of prototypes of all classes. Precisely, the main idea of Optimum-Path Forest algorithm is to minimize $\Psi(\pi_t)$, $\forall t \in \mathcal{D}_1$:

$$\Psi(\langle s \rangle) = \begin{cases} 0 & \text{if } s \in \mathcal{S} \\ +\infty & \text{otherwise,} \end{cases}$$
$$\Psi(\pi_s \cdot \langle s,t \rangle) = \max\{\Psi(\pi_s), d(s,t)\}. \tag{1}$$

More particularly, an optimal set of prototypes $\mathcal{S}^*$ can be found by exploiting the theoretical relation between minimum-spanning tree [4] and optimum-path tree for Ψ [1]. By computing a minimum-spanning tree in the complete graph $\mathcal{G}_1$, we obtain a connected acyclic graph whose nodes are all samples of $\mathcal{D}_1$ and the arcs are undirected and weighted by the distance function between adjacent samples. The spanning tree is optimum in the sense that the sum of its arc weights is minimum as compared to any other spanning tree in the complete graph. In addition, every pair of samples is connected by a single path, which is optimum according to Ψ. Moreover, the minimum-spanning tree contains one optimum-path tree for any selected root node. Therefore, the optimum prototypes are defined as the closest elements of the minimum-spanning tree with different labels in $\mathcal{D}_1$.

In the classification phase, for any sample $t \in \mathcal{D}_2$, we consider all arcs connecting t with samples $s \in \mathcal{G}_1$, as though t were part of the graph. Considering all possible paths from $\mathcal{S}^*$ to t, we find the optimum path $\mathcal{P}^*(t)$ from $\mathcal{S}^*$ and label t with the class $\lambda(\mathcal{R}(t))$ of its most strongly connected prototype $\mathcal{R}(t) \in \mathcal{S}^*$. In the evaluation phase, we follow the same idea but using $\mathcal{D}_3$ set. Note that this path can be identified incrementally, by evaluating the optimum cost $\mathcal{C}(t)$ as:

$$\mathcal{C}(t) = \min\{\max\{\mathcal{C}(s), d(s,t)\}\}, \ \forall s \in \mathcal{G}_1. \tag{2}$$

Suppose the node $s^* \in \mathcal{G}_1$ be the one which satisfies (2). Given that $\mathcal{L}(s^*) = \lambda(\mathcal{R}(t))$, the classification simply assigns $\mathcal{L}(s^*)$ as the class of t. Clearly, an error occurs when $\mathcal{L}(s^*) \neq \lambda(t)$.

2.2   Potts Model

The anti-ferromagnetic Potts model is a Markov Random Field which arose from statistical physics to generalize the Ising model to multiple discrete states [14,16]. The states are often thought of as colours, so that the ground state consists of a colouring where no two neighbours have the same colour [9]. In the context of image processing and pattern recognition, this model have been deeply used as a prior to hold the smoothness assumption, since neighbouring pixels are likely to have same label.

Given a system's neighbourhood $\mathcal{N}$, we can define a local condition density of Potts Models:

$$p(x_{ij} = m | x_{\mathcal{N}_{ij}}, \beta) = \frac{\exp\{\beta \mathcal{H}_{ij}(m)\}}{\displaystyle\sum_{l=1}^{|\mathcal{L}|} \exp\{\beta \mathcal{H}_{ij}(l)\}}, \qquad (3)$$

where $\mathcal{H}_{ij}$ stands for the number of pixels in $\mathcal{N}ij$ which have label equals a respective class l, β is a parameter representing the spatial dependencies between neighbours (namely inverse temperature) and m, the observed value for the central pixel x_{ij}. It is worth noting the higher value of β, higher spatial dependence between samples. In this paper, each sample $s \in D$ is modeled as an image pixel, and the parameter β is the one that will be chosen here by the nature-inspired optmization techniques.

3 Proposed Algorithm

The main idea behind using optimization methods is to find out reasonable values of β (Equation (3)) that maximize OPF accuracy over a validating set. It is worth noting that β considers the contextual information in the classification process, and $\beta = 0$ means we have no contextual information added to the learning procedure.

As aforementioned, Nakamura et al. [11] presented OPF-MRF, which combines OPF classification together with a contextual-based model given by MRF. However, the spatial-dependent parameter β has been empirically set in that work. In this paper, we propose to model the problem of finding suitable values for β as a swarm-based optimization task. For that, we have partitioned the original dataset in the training, validating and test sets. The training and validating sets are used to find out β values, and the test set is then used to assess the effectiveness of the proposed approach. Figure 1 displays the methodology employed in this work, which considers MRI classification.

The first step is to extract features from MRI images in order to build up a dataset composed by pixel-based samples. After that, this dataset is partitioned in a training, validating and test sets, being the training and validating sets used to estimate β values that maximizes the OPF accuracy over the validating set (red box at Figure 1). Further, the near-optimal value of β is then used to build the contextual-based model to be employed in the OPF learning process over the training set followed by traditional classification in the test set. Thus, we have an initial estimative called "Label map" (green box at Figure 1), which is essentially the image classified by naïve OPF.

The best β value found out at the design phase (red box at Figure 1) is then used to guide ICM algorithm to maximize the label map using Equation (3). After that, the feature vectors are extended with the labels of neighbourhood pixels using the ICM classified image (test set). Finally, the contextual-based classification is performed using traditional OPF. Algorithm 1 shows the OPF-MRF procedure, as proposed by Nakamura et al. [11].

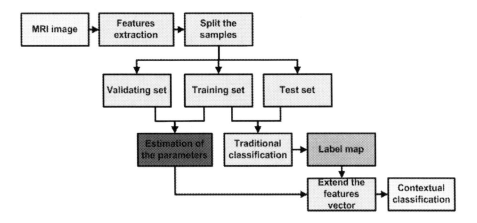

Fig. 1. Proposed scheme to find out β

Algorithm 1. OPF-MRF

INPUT: A λ-labeled training set $\mathcal{D}_1$, test set $\mathcal{D}_3$, number of ICM iterations n,
            and β obtained by some optimization algorithm.
OUTPUT: A labelled map $\mathcal{L}$

1.   Define a Markov Random Field model, $\mathcal{M}$ (e.g. Potts model).
2.   Train OPF using $\mathcal{D}_1$.
3.   Classify $\mathcal{D}_3$ generating a initial $\mathcal{L}$.
4.   Create new instances $\mathcal{D}_1'$ and $\mathcal{D}_3'$ by extending $\mathcal{D}_1$ and $\mathcal{D}_3$
5.   with the frequency of the neighbourhood labels given by $\mathcal{L}$.
6.   For each iteration i $(i = 1, \ldots, n)$, do
7. $[\mathcal{D}_1^*, \mathcal{D}_3^*] \leftarrow \text{ICM}(\mathcal{M}, \mathcal{D}_1', \mathcal{D}_3', \beta, \mathcal{L})$.
8.   Train OPF using $\mathcal{D}_1^*$.
9.   Classify $\mathcal{D}_3^*$ generating an updated label map $\mathcal{L}'$.
10. $\mathcal{L} \leftarrow \mathcal{L}'$, $\mathcal{D}_1' \leftarrow \mathcal{D}_1^*$ and $\mathcal{D}_3' \leftarrow \mathcal{D}_3^*$.

In Line 1 we defined a MRF model. In this paper, we have employed the Potts model described in Section 2.2. Lines $2-3$ train OPF classifier over the training set $\mathcal{D}_1$ and classify test set $\mathcal{D}_3$, respectively, generating an initial estimative (label map) $\mathcal{L}$. Lines $4-5$ create new training and test sets by extending the feature vector of each sample with the frequency of the labels that fall in its neighbourhood. Further, the loop in Lines $6-10$ is responsible for refining the solution using ICM algorithm (Line 7), which outputs $\mathcal{D}_1^*$ and $\mathcal{D}_3^*$, that are updated versions of $\mathcal{D}_1'$ and $\mathcal{D}_3'$, respectively. This means $\mathcal{D}_1^*$ stands for $\mathcal{D}_1'$ after energy maximization by ICM (the same is defined for $\mathcal{D}_3^*$).

Further, we apply OPF classifier over $\mathcal{D}_1^*$ (training) and $\mathcal{D}_3^*$ (classification step) in Lines $8-9$. Line 9 generates an updated label map (classified image) $\mathcal{L}'$, which is then used at the next ICM iteration. In this paper, we have set $n = 5$ based on empirical tests. Now, we explain how to implement the parameters estimation (red box at Figure 1) using PSO and HS.

3.1 Particle Swarm Optimization

The Particle Swarm Optimization [8] is an iterative method for global optimization, which works by maintaining a swarm of particles that move around in the search space influenced by the improvements discovered by the others particles.

We employed PSO in order to find out the value of β that maximizes the spatial/temporal dependences, trying to provide better accuracies than simple randomly chosen it. Algorithm 2 implements this procedure.

Algorithm 2. PSO PROCEDURE FOR FINDING β

INPUT: A λ-labeled training $\mathcal{D}_1$ and validating $\mathcal{D}_2$ sets, a particle set $\mathcal{P}$, MRF model $\mathcal{M}$, number of iterations T, number of particles U, and number of ICM iterations n.
OUTPUT: β value that maximizes OPF accuracy over the validating set.

1.   Define a swarm set $\mathcal{P}$.
2.   For each iteration i $(i = 1, \ldots, T)$, do
3.   For each particle k $(k = 1, \ldots, U)$, do
4.   Train OPF using $\mathcal{D}_1$.
5.   Classify $\mathcal{D}_2$ generating a initial $\mathcal{L}$.
6.   Create new instances $\mathcal{D}_1'$ and $\mathcal{D}_2'$ by extending $\mathcal{D}_1$ and $\mathcal{D}_2$
7.   with the frequency of the neighbourhood labels given by $\mathcal{L}$.
8.   For each iteration j $(j = 1, \ldots, n)$, do
9. $[\mathcal{D}_1^*, \mathcal{D}_2^*] \leftarrow$ ICM$(\mathcal{M}, \mathcal{D}_1', \mathcal{D}_2', p_k, \mathcal{L})$.
10.   Train OPF using $\mathcal{D}_1^*$.
11.   Classify $\mathcal{D}_2^*$ generating an updated label map $\mathcal{L}'$,
12.   and stores the accuracy in A.
13. $\mathcal{L} \leftarrow \mathcal{L}'$, $\mathcal{D}_1' \leftarrow \mathcal{D}_1^*$ and $\mathcal{D}_2' \leftarrow \mathcal{D}_2^*$.
14. $f_k \leftarrow A$.
15. $\beta \leftarrow \max(\boldsymbol{f})$.

Firstly, U possible values are randomly chosen in regular intervals and associated to a particle $p_k \in \mathcal{P}$ (Line 1), respecting the interval of possible values in the search space. Further, for each PSO iteration (loop in Lines $2 - 14$), we execute a similar procedure given by Algorithm 1, i.e., each particle k stores its own β value in p_k, which is then used as input to the ICM algorithm together with the label map $\mathcal{L}$, and training and validating sets (Line 9). After ICM execution, we have the accuracy over the last instance of the validating set, which is stored in f_k. The above procedure is executed over more $T - 1$ iterations, and the final β value is the one that maximizes the accuracies stored in $\boldsymbol{f}$ (Line 15).

3.2 Harmony Search

Harmony Search (HS) is a recently developed music-based metaheuristic optimization algorithm [6], which was inspired in the way the musicians create songs. At the improvisation musical process, a musician normally follows three rules: (a) plays any famous piece of music exactly from his/her memory; (b) plays something similar to a known piece, but adjusting the pitch slightly; or (c) composes new or random notes. These rules are implemented by using the Harmony Memory Consideration Rate (HMCR) and Pitch Adjustment Rate (PAR) parameters. Based on the above ideas, Algorithm 3 presents the proposed HS-based approach to find β.

Algorithm 3. HS PROCEDURE FOR FINDING β

INPUT: A λ-labeled training $\mathcal{D}_1$ validating $\mathcal{D}_2$ sets, a MRF model $\mathcal{M}$, Harmony Memory Considering rate (HMCR), Pitch Adjusting rate (PAR), number of Harmony Search iterations T, number of harmonies U, and number of ICM iterations n.
OUTPUT: β value that maximizes OPF accuracy over the validating set.

1.   Initialize the Harmony Memory (HM) with U harmonies.
2.   Train OPF using $\mathcal{D}_1$.
3.   Classify $\mathcal{D}_2$ generating a initial label map $\mathcal{L}$.
4.   For each iteration i $(i = 1, \ldots, T)$, do
5. $min \leftarrow$ find the harmony with the worst accuracy at MH.
6. $r \leftarrow$ Random[0,1].
7.   If (HMCR $> r$) Then
8. $h \leftarrow$ Random$[1, U]$.
9. $X_{new} \leftarrow$ MH$[h]$.
10. $r \leftarrow$ Random[0,1].
11.   If (PAR $> r$) Then
12. $X_{new} \leftarrow$ pitch(X_{new}).
13.   Else
14. $X_{new} \leftarrow$ Create a new harmony randomly.
15.   Create new instances $\mathcal{D}_1'$ and $\mathcal{D}_2'$ by extending $\mathcal{D}_1$ and $\mathcal{D}_2$
16.   with the frequency of the neighbourhood labels given by $\mathcal{L}$.
17.   For each iteration j $(j = 1, \ldots, V)$, do
18. $[\mathcal{D}_1^*, \mathcal{D}_2^*] \leftarrow$ ICM($\mathcal{M}$, $\mathcal{D}_1'$, $\mathcal{D}_2'$, X_{new}, $\mathcal{L}$).
19.   Train OPF using $\mathcal{D}_1^*$.
20.   Classify $\mathcal{D}_2^*$ generating an updated label map $\mathcal{L}'$,
21.   and stores the accuracy in f_i.
22. $\mathcal{L} \leftarrow \mathcal{L}'$, $\mathcal{D}_1' \leftarrow \mathcal{D}_1^*$ and $\mathcal{D}_2' \leftarrow \mathcal{D}_2^*$.
23.   If ($f_i >$ MH$[min]$) Then
24.   MH$[min] \leftarrow X_{new}$.
25. $\beta \leftarrow$ max($\boldsymbol{f}$).

Firstly, the Harmony Memory is initialized with values within β interval in Line 1. In Lines $2 - 3$, the traditional OPF classifier is trained over $\mathcal{D}_1$ and its effectiveness is evaluated over $\mathcal{D}_2$. The loop in Lines $4 - 24$ performs the HS algorithm, and Line 6 generates a random number within the interval $[0, 1]$. Lines $7 - 14$ are responsible to create a new harmony, which can be done using values from the Harmony Memory (Lines $8 - 12$), or can be created only with random values (Line 14).

Lines $15 - 16$ creates extended versions of $\mathcal{D}_1$ and $\mathcal{D}_2$ and employ them at the ICM algorithm in Lines $17 - 22$, as aforementioned in Algorithm 3. Further,

Lines $23-24$ are responsible to replace the worst harmony in HM by the new one whether it has a better fitness value. The above procedure is executed over more $T-1$ iterations, and the final β value is the one that maximizes the accuracies stored in f (Line 25).

4   Simulations and Results

In this section, we discuss the simulation results conducted to evaluate our approach. In order to illustrate the robustness of the proposed technique, we have used six magnetic resonance images of the Internet Brain Segmentation Repository[1].This dataset is composed by T1-weighted 3-dimensional coronal brain scans after they have been positionally normalized. A reference data is available as a result of semi-automated segmentation techniques providing a segmentation of the following regions: white matter (WM), gray matter (GM) and cerebrospinal fluid (CSF). Figures 3a and 3b show an example image and its ground truth version, respectively.

We have compared PSO and HS-based optimization results together with a Brute Force (BF) approach, i.e., an exhaustive search for β values within $]0, V]$, where $V = \ln(1 + \sqrt{c})$, being c the maximum number of possible classes. For that purpose, we have used 5 iterations for ICM algorithm. The training, validating and test sets percentages were 0.03%, 19.97% and 80.00%, respectively, being empirically chosen. In regard to the image description, we have extracted 27 features from each pixel (voxel), which stand for a 3×3 in a 3-D neighbourhood. The features are the pixels' gray values divided by the brightest pixel of the image.

As aforementioned, the proposed approach first iterates over the training/validating sets in order to find the best β value provided by optimization algorithms using 5 particles and 10 iterations for PSO, and 5 harmonies and 50 iterations for HS (we have used more iterations for HS because it has been consistently faster than PSO). Moreover, we use HMCR $= 0.9$ and PAR $= 0.6$ for HS method. Finally, we employed ICM algorithm over the training/test sets using the β value after it has been obtained by PSO/HS. In order to give more conclusive results, we have executed a four cross-validation over the training, validating and test sets. In regard to BF method, we used β values with steps of 0.1. Figure 2 shows the average results for BF method over the test set for images $01-06$. We can see the mean accuracy variations over different values of β, mainly for image 06, in which the mean accuracy has dropped from 89.06% to 84.59% with $\beta = 0.8$ and $\beta = 0.9$, respectively. It is worth noting to remind the reader that BF procedure has been carried out over training and test sets. The validating set has been employed just for PSO and HS for finding β.

Table 1 displays the accuracy results for each employed image regarding BF, PSO and HS approaches. In regard to BF results, we have employed the ones

---

[1] The description of data was provided by the Center for Morphometric Analysis at Massachusetts General Hospital and is available at http://www.cma.mgh.harvard.edu/ibsr/

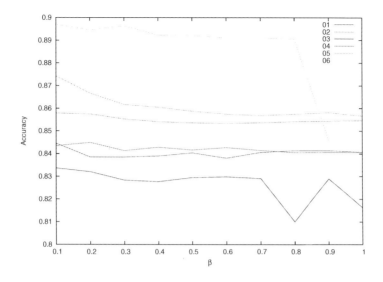

Fig. 2. Accuracy over the test set for different values of β using BF

with the best accuracies for each image, as shown in Figure 2. We can see BF has outperformed PSO and HS in 3 out 6 images, but is noticeable that all approaches have obtained close accuracies, which was the expected results. Figures 3d, 3e and 3e display the results for PSO, HS and BF approaches for one example image (Figure 3a), respectively.

Table 1. Average accuracy (AA) over the employed images. The most accurate techniques are bolded.

	01	02	03	04	05	06
HS	84.38%	85.84%	83.07%	**84.78%**	87.32%	89.81%
PSO	**84.61%**	85.81%	**83.95%**	84.77%	87.29%	89.83%
BF	84.50%	**86.05%**	83.36%	84.67%	**87.43%**	**89.91%**

However, the main point concerns with the execution times, which are displayed in Table 2 in the following format x:y:z, where x, y and z stands for hours, minutes and seconds, respectively. The execution times consider the whole learning algorithms for finding β in case of PSO and HS (Algorithms 2 and 3). We can clearly see the optimization methods have been faster than BF. For instance, if we consider image 03, PSO has been 71.56% faster than BF, being PSO still more accurate than BF for this same image (Table 1). A similar behaviour can be see for the remaining images.

Table 2. Mean execution time over the images. The fastest techniques are bolded

	01	02	03	04	05	06
HS	**3:21:40**	3:32:00	3:04:46	**2:55:11**	**3:01:45**	**3:44:31**
PSO	3:39:33	**3:31:29**	**2:18:58**	3:13:16	3:04:15	4:02:06
BF	4:24:36	4:32:00	3:58:25	4:11:12	3:53:43	4:52:56

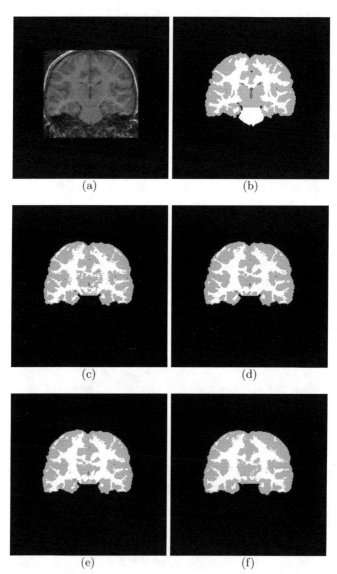

Fig. 3. MRI-T1 classification: (a) IBSR-04 slice 58, (b) reference data, (c) baseline, (d), (e) and (f) are the results obtained using PSO, HS and BF methods, respectively

5 Concluding Remarks

In this paper, we have presented a new approach for finding a Potts Model dependent parameter β, which encodes the contextual information for image classification. We have improved the previous work of Nakamura et al. [11], which proposed the OPF-MRF, a contextual-based approach that combines the Optimum-Path Forest classifier together with Markov Random Fields. In that paper, we authors have employed empirically chosen β values, which can be a hard task, since the interval of this parameter may contain infinite values.

The proposed approach can be used with any optimization algorithm, and in this paper we have employed two swarm-based approaches: Particle Swarm Optimization and Harmony Search. The experiments compared PSO and HS against a Brute Force (exhaustive) search over the range of allowed values for β in six MRI images of the brain. Another contribution of this paper is the methodology used to find out β, in which we have employed a training and validating sets for such purpose, being the image refined with the Iterated Conditional Modes algorithm.

We have concluded that PSO and HS can achieve similar results to the ones obtained by BF, but they can be much faster than the exhaustive search (sometimes up to 71%). This behaviour has been observed for all images. In regard to future works, we are planning to evaluate other swarm-based optimization techniques to this context.

References

1. Allène, C., Audibert, J.Y., Couprie, M., Cousty, J., Keriven, R.: Some links between min-cuts, optimal spanning forests and watersheds. In: Proceedings of the International Symposium on Mathematical Morphology, pp. 253–264. MCT/INPE (2007)
2. Besag, E.: Spatial interaction and the statistical analysis of lattice systems. Journal of the Royal Statistical Society B36, 192–236 (1974)
3. Besag, J.: On the statistical analysis of dirty pictures. Journal of the Royal Statistical Society, Series B (Methodological) 48(3), 259–302 (1986)
4. Cormen, T.H., Leiserson, C.E., Rivest, R.L., Stein, C.: Introduction to Algorithms, 2nd edn. The MIT Press (2001)
5. Greig, D.M., Porteous, B.T., Seheult, A.H.: Exact maximum a posteriori estimation for binary images. Journal of the Royal Statistical Society 51(2), 271–279 (1989)
6. Geem, Z.W.: Music-Inspired Harmony Search Algorithm: Theory and Applications, 1st edn. Springer Publishing Company, Incorporated (2009)
7. Geman, S., Geman, D.: Stochastic relaxation, gibbs distributions, and the bayesian restoration of images. IEEE Transaction on Pattern Analysis and Machine Intelligence 6(6), 721–741 (1984)
8. Kennedy, J., Eberhart, R.: Particle swarm optimization. In: Proceedings of the IEEE International Conference on Neural Networks, vol. 4, pp. 1942–1948 (November/December 1995)
9. Moore, C., Nordahl, M.G., Minar, N., Shalizi, C.R.: Vortex dynamics and entropic forces in antiferromagnets and antiferromagnetic potts models. Physical Review E 60, 5344–5351 (1999)

10. Moser, G., Serpico, S.B.: Combining support vector machines and markov random fields in an integrated framework for contextual image classification. IEEE Transactions on Geoscience and Remote Sensing PP(99), 1–19 (2012)
11. Nakamura, R., Osaku, D., Levada, A., Cappabianco, F., Falcão, A., Papa, J.: OPF-MRF: Optimum-path forest and markov random fields for contextual-based image classification. In: Wilson, R., Hancock, E., Bors, A., Smith, W. (eds.) CAIP 2013, Part II. LNCS, vol. 8048, pp. 233–240. Springer, Heidelberg (2013)
12. Papa, J.P., Falcão, A.X., Albuquerque, V.H.C., Tavares, J.M.R.S.: Efficient supervised optimum-path forest classification for large datasets. Pattern Recognition 45(1), 512–520 (2012)
13. Papa, J.P., Falcão, A.X., Suzuki, C.T.N.: Supervised pattern classification based on optimum-path forest. International Journal of Imaging Systems and Technology 19(2), 120–131 (2009)
14. Potts, R.B.: Some generalized order-disorder transformations. Mathematical Proceedings of the Cambridge Philosophical Society 48, 106–109 (1952)
15. Tarabalka, Y., Fauvel, M., Chanussot, J., Benediktsson, J.: SVM- and MRF-based method for accurate classification of hyperspectral images. IEEE Geoscience and Remote Sensing Letters 7(4), 736–740 (2010)
16. Wu, F.Y.: The potts model. Reviews of Modern Physics 54, 235–268 (1982)
17. Wu, T., Bae, M.H., Zhang, M., Pan, R., Badea, A.: A prior feature SVM-MRF based method for mouse brain segmentation. NeuroImage 59(3), 2298–2306 (2012)

A Mobile Imaging System
for Medical Diagnostics

Sami Varjo and Jari Hannuksela

The Center for Machine Vision Research
Department of Computer Science and Engineering
P.O. Box 4500, FI-90014 University of Oulu

Abstract. Microscopy for medical diagnostics requires expensive equipment as well as highly trained experts to operate and interpret the observed images. We present a new, easy to use, mobile diagnostic system consisting of a direct imaging microlens array and a mobile computing platform for diagnosing parasites in clinical samples. Firstly, the captured microlens images are reconstructed using a light field rendering method. Then, OpenCL accelerated classification utilizing local binary pattern features is performed. A speedup of factor 4.6 was achieved for the mobile computing platform CPU (AMD C-50) compared with the GPU (AMD 6250). The results show that a relatively inexpensive system can be used for automatically detecting eggs of the Schistosoma parasite. Furthermore, the system can be also used to diagnose other parasites and thinlayer microarray samples containing stained tumor cells.

1 Introduction

Parasites such as nematode Strongyloides and Schistosoma haematobium are infecting people in developing countries. In rural areas, where sanitation standards are poor, diagnosis is often difficult due to limited resources and knowledge. The resulting under or over medication leads to, for example, drug resistance in unnecessary mass treatments.

A traditional low cost method for detecting Schistosomiasis in urine has been visual inspection of blood in urine samples [7]. Parasitic infections are typically diagnosed using microscopes by detecting parasites, or their various states, in urine or stool samples. The samples for microscopy can be prepared at low cost using glass or even polymeric sample slides. However, the laboratory quality microscopes cost several thousand dollars or more. In addition, operating and maintaining the devices for laboratory diagnosis require expertise and the analysis of the viewed images require some level of parasitological training. There is a clear need for new tools that enable better diagnosis in challenging environments with low operating costs.

Zhu et al. have collected a review on imaging techniques for point-of-care diagnostics [11]. Attaching conventional microscope lenses to mobile phones have been suggested, for example, by Breslauer et al. [3]. Their system uses conventional microscope lenses which are expensive and limit the field of view to a few

J. Blanc-Talon et al. (Eds.): ACIVS 2013, LNCS 8192, pp. 215–226, 2013.

hundreds of micrometers. Tseng et al. have studied lens free holography based imaging in the mobile environment [8]. The results are very promising enabling a spatial resolution of several micrometers and a large field of view. On the other hand, holography based imaging techniques can be argued to be computationally intensive [6], and thus unsuitable for mobile environments.

Bogoch et al. have recently proposed a modified mobile phone camera to detect parasites in stool samples [2]. They utilized an iPhone 4S with an attached 3-mm ball lens for achieving the desired magnification. The image quality obtained with this approach is quite poor in comparison with a conventional microscope, but enabled the detection of some parasites. In addition to distorted images from the ball lens, the field of view is very limited when compared with the proposed imaging approach. In summary, there are several imaging techniques for point-of-care diagnostics, but these have not been utilized effectively as complete systems for parasite detection.

In this work, we present a new mobile imaging based diagnostic system. Schistosoma parasite eggs are used as an example case, where sample is imaged with the microlens array imaging setup. Figure (1) shows an example of a parasite egg obtained with our system. For comparison, an image captured with a conventional light microscope is presented. These parasite eggs have lengths ranging from 75 to 150 micrometers. In our solution, the images are first reconstructed using a light field rendering method. After that, Schistosoma parasite eggs are detected with cascade type classifiers and findings are visualized for the user. The selected computing platform compares to a midrange mobile phone. We present the diagnostic chain on embedded computing environment. The openCL framework is utilized to enable the better control of heterogeneous computing resources and to accelerate the classifier speed.

 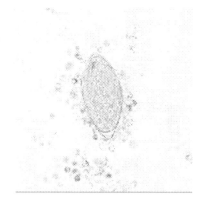

Fig. 1. An example of a Schistosoma parasite egg imaged with the direct microlens array imaging (left) and conventional light microscope using 5x magnification (right)

2   The System Description

The system consists of three main phases. The first phase is the image capturing part where a light field imaging method is utilized. The approach enables capturing images of relatively large areas at once with a resolution about 5 μm. The next phase is the image rendering where the raw data consisting of microimages is processed in order to reconstruct conventional images. The final phase is the detection of the parasites in the image followed by the result visualization and logging.

We have used a low end tablet, Acer Iconia W500, as a computing platform. The device has an AMD Fusion C-50 dual-core 1 GHz processor, an AMD Radeon HD 6250 GPU, 2 GB DDR-3 RAM, and a 10.1-inch display. This represents a typical midrange smartphone computing performance but with a bigger display for better viewing capabilities.

2.1   The Imaging System

A direct imaging microlens array system was build and utilized for capturing microscopic images. The imaging platform consists of five main parts: a camera sensor, a microlens array, a sample holder, a field aperture, and a light source. Figure (2) shows a conceptual view of the imaging setup [9].

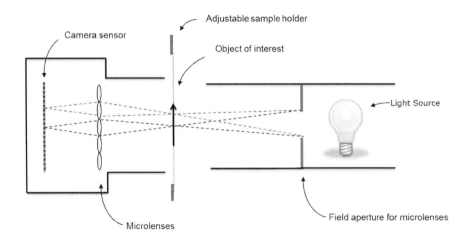

Fig. 2. A conseptual image of the imaging setup

Here a usb-camera (IDS UI-148xLE) was used. The imaging sensor area is 2560x1920 pixels, with a pixel size of 2.2 μm giving an active imaging area of 5.6x4.2 mm. The fused silica microlens array come from Süss MicroOptics (Art.Nr 18-00041). The aluminium body housing the camera, the adjustable sample holder, and the light source was build in-house. The 4 mm square aperture was cut using a laser on 75 μm thick brass which was fixed on a holder allowing distance adjustment. The light source consists of a blue led controlled with an in-house build PWM power supply and an opal diffusing glass (Edmund Optics Ltd, art NT43-717) between the led and the aperture.

The imaging approach is a form of light field imaging where the lens array is used as a light collecting element. The distance between the lens array and the light source is adjusted so that the square aperture is imaged by each microlens once without overlap, and the sample distance to the lenslets so that as sharp image as possible was obtained. A USAF resolution target (Edmund Optics, R209441-11069) was used for tuning. The distance from the sample to the microlenses also affects the overlap between imaged areas for neighboring microlenses. Here the image overlap was adjusted to minimal as the imaged objects are microscopically thin. Moreover, we are not interested in refocusing in different depths, but to cover as large area of the sample with as high resolution as possible.

The main difference with regard to a plenoptic camera, presented by Georgiev and Lumsdaine [5], is that there is no relay optics for microlenses but the imaging is done directly with the microlens array. As the images from each microlens are not allowed to overlap on the camera sensor there is no effective magnification from the optics. The achievable resolution is limited by the sensor pixel size via the sampling theorem and the quality of the microlenses. The achieved resolution, based on the resolution target, was about five micrometers. One clear benefit of this imaging approach over several other imaging approaches [2,3] is the possibility for capturing images with area limited by the camera sensor size rather than the optics.

2.2   Image Rendering

The raw images from the imaging system are arrays of microimages which are processed to produce conventional images Fig. (3). The rendering is based on mosaicing the micro images with adjustable overlap to achieve the in-focus image. The method is similar to blending rendering [5], but here no known subimage lattice is assumed. Also we do not require image reconstruction at multiple depths simultaneously as the samples are thin.

The lighting in raw data is normalised by dividing it pixelwise with an image of light source without any sample. The rendering algorithm (1) utilizes the locations of lens centers, $cdata$, so that the microimage in the middle of raw data was selected as an anchor C_a. The other microimages were warped towards this anchor image where the shift $\Delta(x, y)_i$ is the distance of the warped image C_i and the anchor divided by the micro image size S times the desired overlap o in x and y directions. The advantage of the selected approach is its speed compared with most other rendering techniques and it is not significantly limited by the microlens array and the rendering parameters.

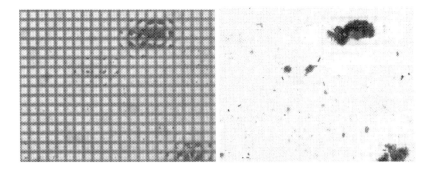

Fig. 3. An example of a raw image (left) and a rendered image (right). The image contains parasitic eggs and sample matrix.

Algorithm 1. mosaicSubImages

Require: calibration *cdata*, raw *data*, overlap *o*
    locate each lens center C_i from *cdata*
    calculate image size S from distances in C_i
    select anchor C_a from C_i
    for all lenses i in C_i **do**
        calculate $\Delta(x, y)_i = ((C_a - C_i)/S) * o$
        warp subimage in *data* at C_i by $\Delta(x, y)_i$
        update *accumulator* and *weight* image
    end for
    normalise *accumulator* for *result* image with *weight*

2.3   Parasite Detection

Rapid object detection in images can be performed using cascade classifiers [10]. Sets of weak classifiers are utilized to build up strong classifier stages. A classifier stage, consisting of a few weak classifiers, can efficiently reject a large number of input pixels while the probability for real detection increases with each passed cascading stage. The original cascade object detector utilized Haar-like features for weak classifiers but it is also possible to utilize other features calculated in the detection window. Fast alternatives for Haar-based features calculated using integral images include local binary patterns [1] and the modified census transform [4].

A lookup table (LUT) based classifier approach by Fröba and Ernst [4] was modified to use LBP features and was implemented with OpenCL. Unlike in typical approaches, where LBP codes are used to create histograms for classification [1], the LUT based approach do not rely on histograms. Instead, the classification is based on weak classifiers where the probability of the appearance of given LBP code at the given search window position is used. The training of such classifier can be carried out using AdaBoost style learning. Weighted probability distributions of code words in all the pixel positions of the search window are calculated for the positive and negative training samples. A weak classifier LUT is formed for the pixel position where the classification error is the smallest. LUT is a binary selector for each LBP-code associated with the AdaBoost training weight based on the classification error. For the next AdaBoost stage the training weight is updated and weights for correct and incorrect samples are adjusted and the process is repeated for the remaining pixel positions.

Strong classifier stages consist of a given number of weak classifiers where the lookup table based weights are summed and compared against a stage threshold. The comparison results in either a hit or a rejection of the pixel location. Positive detection is encountered if all the stages in a test window are passed. Here five to ten weak classifiers were selected per stage and eight stages were trained and used.

The training set consisted of 305 positive samples and 1000 negative samples. It is possible to increase the number of training samples by applying small amount of geometric distortions to the images, but it was not improving the results here. The positive samples were cropped from the rendered images captured with the same system and rotated to have a common orientation. Negative samples were selected from the areas not including the positive samples. For comparison, also classifiers with Haar-like features were trained. As neither the basic version of LBP nor the Haar-like features are rotation invariants, a set of the classifiers with four different, evenly distributed, orientations were trained.

2.4   Implementation

The implementation is divided into two main threads. The first one handles the image capturing and the other one is for image processing and displaying. The image capturing is clearly faster than the image processing part and thus double buffering at the capture is sufficient. The image processing thread listens for the new image events from the camera, gets the captured image buffer and triggers a new capture even at the buffer switch. The new image is first rendered which is followed by the object detection and displaying the result on the screen.

The OpenMP framework was used to parallelize the rendering loop where the sub images from the separate microlenses are handled separately followed by common normalization. The object detection with the different orientations was also parallelized as separate tasks.

The OpenCL framework was used to implement multiplatform compatible classifiers. The classifier using LBP features was based on the lookup table approach [4]. The LBP input image for a classifier is precomputed with a separate OpenCL kernel where each pixel is handled as a separate work instance. Image type was used for reading and writing the LBP source and result images to enable the efficient use of possible texture memory. The LBP value describes the 8-neighborhood relative to the center pixel as a binary vector [1]. The 8-bit value was obtained by comparing if the center pixel value has smaller value than the surrounding pixel at a given position and shifting the comparison result by the number of bits indicated by the comparison position. Apeendix A contains the OpenCL code for the LBP image calculation kernel. With Haar-like features, this stage corresponds to calculating an integral image.

Each of the cascade stages is launched as a separate kernel job parallellizing the computation at the pixel level. The hits at each cascade stage are collected into a common hit index vector indicating the positions of pixels that are left to process in the subsequent stages. Appendix B presents the first LBP classifier stage in openCL. Each kernel, or computing core, handles a row of detection window locations in the first stage. In the following stages the work determined by the number of hits from previous the stage is divided evenly among the available computing units. All the utilized kernels were precompiled and the classifier was preloaded to the computing device memory prior execution.

3 Results

The openCL based LBP classifier was tested with several image sizes using two GPUs on desktop, namely NVidia Quadro 600 and Ati Radeon 5450, desktop CPU (Intel Core i5-2400 @3.1GHz), the Acer Iconia table CPU (AMD C-50) and the tablet GPU (AMD 6250). The classification times for each image scale are plotted in Figure (4). Surprisingly, the tablet's GPU is the slowest with small image sizes but as the image size is increased the GPU clearly outperforms the tablet CPU. While the slow down with 64x64 images was 0.67 for the tablet GPU versus the CPU. For images sized 256x256, 512x512 and 1024x1024 the speedup was respectively 1.4, 2.7, and 4.6 favoring the GPU.

The state of art four core desktop CPU performs here clearly the best having about ten fold performance compared with the tablet. The old desktop GPUs have slightly worse performance compared with the CPU. However, the same trend, as with the tablet processing units, can be observed as the GPU performance closes the CPU with increasing image size.

Figure (5) shows a screen capture of the user interface of the implemented system. In this first implementation a library Haar cascade was utilized. Three circles indicate the successfully detected parasite eggs in captured and rendered image. The detection rate on the target platform with a library classifier was about 0.1-0.2 frames per second which is not real-time but acceptable for diagnostic applications in the field. For comparison, a desktop running Intel Core i5-2400 @ 3.1 GHz was about 15 times faster with the full image capturing and analyzing pipeline.

The image quality here is clearly better when compared with the work by Bogoch et al. [2]. In their work, the analysis part was done by trained laboratory technicians and senior microscopist and sensitivity of only 69.4% was reported. As the training data here was from a single sample from a single patient it would be unfair to report high sensitivity and accuracy values and we restrain to state that the approach appears to be very promising. Other experiments not reproduced here, showed that even an untrained person can easily see if a view contains hits or not. A further study with a larger number of both training and testing samples is required for benchmark values.

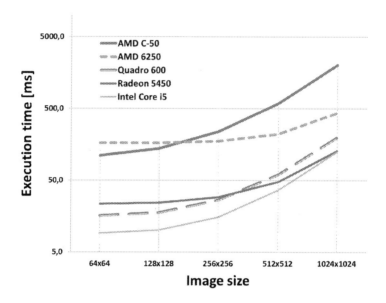

Fig. 4. The classification times with openCL accelerated LBP-cascade classifier using several computing platforms and input image sizes.

It must be noted that the parasite eggs were used as an example for the system usability. There are many other possible samples that could be also analyzed with the same approach. Figure (6) presents an image of the nematode Strongyloides parasite worm and an image of stained thinlayer microarray samples. In the latter, the dark dots indicate tumor infected cells. The level of tumor cell count versus healthy areas can be estimated.

4   Summary and Discussion

We have demonstrated a complete system for detecting parasites in physiological samples. The system consists of three main stages: the microlens array based image capturing, the image rendering, and finally the detection of the parasites with trained classifiers. The system demonstrates that the direct microlens array imaging and the mosaicing based light field rendering produces image quality suitable for classification.

Schistosoma parasite eggs were successfully detected with the automated system in a urine sample. We have demonstrated the proof of the concept for computer vision based helminth egg detection with portable system. The processing rate per captured image was about 0.1-0.2 frames per second on the mobile platform. Further work is required to test the classification performance with samples from numerous patients acuired at different stages of infection.

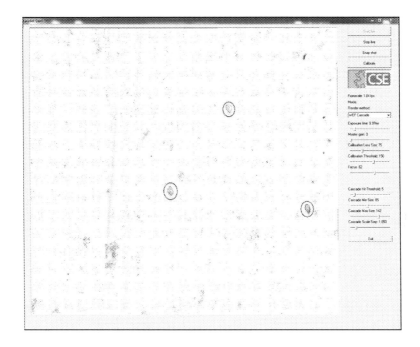

Fig. 5. A screen capture of the implemented system with three circles indicating detected parasite eggs

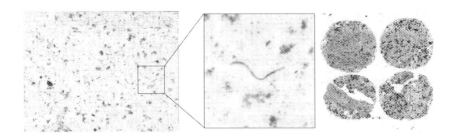

Fig. 6. (Left) Strongyloides parasite. (Rigth) Stained thinlayer microarray samples.

Cascade classification can be accelerated using OpenCL framework on the embedded platforms. While the AMD C-50 dual core CPU was faster with small image sizes, it was possible to achieve 4,6 fold speedup when the input size was increased from 64x64 images to 1024x1024. While some parallelization was utilized in the implementation, the computing resources of the system were not yet maximally utilized. We are further studying the possibility to improve the classification speed by optimizing the classifiers and increasing the parallellization level. OpenCL enables easy division of tasks between the CPU and GPU. This allows for example pipelining the raw image rendering, detection and result displaying more efficiently and it can be expected that concurrent utilization of CPU and GPU resources cut the image analysis time to about half of the current implementation.

While the parasite eggs were used as an example case we also showed that utilized approach could be used to detect parasites in other stages like hatched nematodes. The system is also suitable for detecting stained tumor cells in thin-layer microarray samples.

Acknowledgements. Professor emeritus Ewert Linder from Department of Microbiology, Tumor and Cell Biology (MTC), Karolinska Institutet, SE-171 77, Stockholm, Sweden, and Johan Lundin Institute for Molecular Medicine Finland (FIMM), P.O. Box 20, FI-00014, University of Helsinki, Finland, are thanked for the background information on parasitology and the inspiring feedback about the importance of the work as well as the parasite samples used in the work.

References

1. Ahonen, T., Hadid, A., Pietikainen, M.: Face description with local binary patterns: Application to face recognition. IEEE Transactions on Pattern Analysis and Machine Intelligence 28(12), 2037–2041 (2006)
2. Bogoch, I.I., Andrews, J.R., Speich, B., Utzinger, J., Ame, S.M., Ali, S.M., Keiser, J.: Short report: Mobile phone microscopy for the diagnosis of soil-transmitted helminth infections: A proof-of-concept study. The American Journal of Tropical Medicine and Hygiene, 12–0742 (2013)
3. Breslauer, D.N., Maamari, R.N., Switz, N.A., Lam, W.A., Fletcher, D.A.: Mobile phone based clinical microscopy for global health applications. PLoS ONE 4(7), e6320 (2009)
4. Froba, B., Ernst, A.: Face detection with the modified census transform. In: Proceedings of the Sixth IEEE International Conference on Automatic Face and Gesture Recognition, pp. 91–96 (2004)
5. Georgiev, T., Lumsdaine, A.: Focused plenoptic camera and rendering. Journal of Electronic Imaging 19, 021106 (2010)
6. Nebrensky, J.J., Hobson, P.R.: The reconstruction of digital holograms on a computational grid. In: Holography 2005: International Conference on Holography, Optical Recording, and Processing of Information. Proc. SPIE, vol. 6252, pp. 62521I–62521I-6 (2006)
7. Savioli, L., Mott, K.: Urinary schistosomiasis on pemba island: low-cost diagnosis for control in a primary health care setting. Parasitol Today 5(10), 333–337 (1989)

8. Tseng, D., Mudanyali, O., Oztoprak, C., Isikman, S.O., Sencan, I., Yaglidere, O., Ozcan, A.: Lensfree microscopy on a cellphone. Lab. Chip. 10, 1787–1792 (2010)
9. Varjo, S., Hannuksela, J., Silvén, O.: Direct imaging with printed microlens arrays. In: 21st International Conference on Pattern Recognition, pp. 1355–1358 (2012)
10. Viola, P., Jones, M.: Rapid object detection using a boosted cascade of simple features. In: Proceedings of the 2001 IEEE Computer Society Conference on Computer Vision and Pattern Recognition, vol. 1, pp. I–511–I–518 (2001)
11. Zhu, H., Isikman, S.O., Mudanyali, O., Greenbaum, A., Ozcan, A.: Optical imaging techniques for point-of-care diagnostics. Lab. Chip. 13, 51–67 (2013)

A   Appendix

```
__constant sampler_t sampler = CLK_NORMALIZED_COORDS_FALSE |
        CLK_ADDRESS_CLAMP  |  CLK_FILTER_NEAREST;

__kernel void lbp3x3_kernel(
                __read_only image2d_t imIn,
                __write_only image2d_t imOut)
{
  int x = (int)get_global_id(0);
  int y = (int)get_global_id(1);

  int2 coord = (int2)(x,y);
  uint4 center = (uint4)read_imageui(imIn,sampler, coord);
  uint4 val = 0;
  uint4 pixval;

  pixval = (uint4)read_imageui(imIn,sampler,(int2)(x+1,y-1));
  val.x |= (center.x < pixval.x)<<2;

  pixval = (uint4)read_imageui(imIn,sampler,(int2)(x+1,y));
  val.x |= (center.x < pixval.x)<<3;

  pixval = (uint4)read_imageui(imIn,sampler,(int2)(x+1,y+1));
  val.x |= (center.x < pixval.x)<<4;

  pixval = (uint4)read_imageui(imIn,sampler,(int2)(x,y+1));
  val.x |= (center.x < pixval.x)<<5;

  pixval = (uint4)read_imageui(imIn,sampler,(int2)(x-1,y+1));
  val.x |= (center.x < pixval.x)<<6;

  pixval = (uint4)read_imageui(imIn,sampler,(int2)(x-1,y));
  val.x |= (center.x < pixval.x)<<7;

  write_imageui(imOut, coord, val);
}
```

B Appendix

```
__kernel void classify_stage_1 (
          __global CascadeClassifierLBP  *cc ,  //Classifier
          __read_only   image2d_t imIn ,        //lbp image
          __global float *hits )                //hits vector
             (0/1)
{
  uint id   = get_global_id( 0 );
  uint cols = get_image_width( imIn ) - CASCADE_WINDOW_SIZE;
  uint rows = get_image_height( imIn ) - CASCADE_WINDOW_SIZE;

  uint r1 = id / cols ;
  uint c1 = id - r1 * cols ;

  __global AdaBoostLBPstage *pStage = &cc->AdaBoostStages[0];

  float value=0;

  for (uint weakId = 0; weakId < pStage->W; weakId++){

    // The position of weak classifier in window(LBP pixel):
    uint pIdx = pStage->pos[weakId];

    uint y = r1 + (pIdx/CASCADE_WINDOW_SIZE) ;
    uint x = c1 + (pIdx%CASCADE_WINDOW_SIZE) ;

    uint4 lbpValue = read_imageui(imIn, sampler, (int2)(x,y));
    value += pStage->weak[weakId].lut[lbpValue.x];
  }

  //The hits are compacted with prefix scan in the next stage
  if( id < ( cols * ( rows ) ) && value >= pStage->threshold )
     {
     hits[id] = 1;
  }
  else{
     hits[id] = 0;
  }
}
```

Fast Road Network Extraction
from Remotely Sensed Images

Vladimir A. Krylov and James D.B. Nelson

Dept. of Statistical Science, University College London, London, WC1E 6BT, UK
{v.krylov,j.nelson}@ucl.ac.uk

Abstract. This paper addresses the problem of fast, unsupervised road network extraction from remotely sensed images. We develop an approach that employs a fixed-grid, localized Radon transform to extract a redundant set of line segment candidates. The road network structure is then extracted by introducing interactions between neighbouring segments in addition to a data-fit term, based on the Bhattacharyya distance. The final configuration is obtained using simulated annealing via a Markov chain Monte Carlo iterative procedure. The experiments demonstrate a fast and accurate road network extraction on high resolution optical images of semi-urbanized zones, which is further supported by comparisons with several benchmark techniques.

Keywords: Road network, remote sensing, localized Radon transform, Markov chain Monte Carlo.

1 Introduction

In this paper we address the problem of road network extraction from aerial or satellite imagery. This problem has received a great deal of attention recently because of its important role in map production and updating. An ever growing volume and accessibility of remotely sensed imagery has motivated various applications, such as image coregistration, building detection, urban planning, and agricultural and forestry mapping— all of which can benefit greatly from the development of unsupervised, reliable, and computationally fast road network extraction methods. However the development of such techniques is hindered by the following problems: the heterogeneous nature of road materials results in different radiological patterns of roads; various types of occlusions (shadows, buildings, tree canopies); varying road width present in the same scene. As such, standard line, edge and ridge detection techniques [2] are inappropriate for road detection, see in [11, 17, 18].

A wide range of approaches have been taken to extract road networks: from human-assisted Bayesian filtering [18] and region growing [1], to dynamic programming [11], endpoint tracking [5], Hough transform-based detection with Gabor-filtering [4]. Another recent direction is junction-based road-network extraction. This is of particular interest for urban (i.e. highly structured) scenes [3]

J. Blanc-Talon et al. (Eds.): ACIVS 2013, LNCS 8192, pp. 227–237, 2013.
© Springer International Publishing Switzerland 2013

and special acquisition modalities such as SAR imaging systems [12]. It is common to consider the image as a stochastic configuration of various geometrical primitives (lines, circles, ellipses, etc.). This view has motivated a range of purely stochastic techniques, such as active contours [15], phase fields [14], marked point [9, 16] and jump-diffusion [10] processes. Whereas many can boast very accurate results, they either require operator input [1, 18] and/or require computationally expensive stochastic optimization [9, 14, 15]. Typically, processing of a medium sized 1000×1000 scene can take from several minutes (as in [10]) to over an hour (in [9]), which is restrictive for many applications. In view of this problem, our aim is to develop a fast road extraction technique that can arrive at sufficiently accurate results that, if need be, can be further improved by, e.g., initializing various stochastic techniques [9, 16].

In this paper we concentrate on the problem of automatic road detection with as little human interaction as possible (i.e., parameter specification). Our work is inspired by the positive results reported by noise-robust Radon and Hough transforms in line detection on remotely sensed imagery [4, 17]. Since road networks are comprised of line structures that are curved and significantly shorter than the image size, we employ a localized version of the Radon transform. We solve the problem of image partitioning, required for the localized transform, by defining an overlapping fixed-grid (or, equivalently, sliding window) of equally-sized image regions. Each of the regions undergoes a Radon transform separately from the rest of the image in order to extract a redundant set of road segment candidates. Note that compared to the birth-and-death process guided techniques [9, 16], the use of a deterministic candidate extraction approach such as the Radon transform facilitates a reduction in the amount of parameters employed which in turn significantly reduces the computational complexity albeit at the expense of some detection accuracy. In the second step of our approach, we extract a refined road structure of line segments by (i) favouring segments that have high contrast against the background segments, and (ii) imposing interactions in the local neighbourhood by invoking a Markov dependency structure over the grid. Optimization is then performed stochastically via simulated annealing [6] using a Markov chain Monte Carlo (MCMC) algorithm [6, 7]. This two step approach affords both fast and accurate road network extraction results.

The central contribution of this work is to consider an approach to combine the localized Radon maxima extraction with the optimization (network extraction). More specifically, in the first stage we allow several maxima at each node of the grid. This allows the method to adapt to the local contrast variations. In the second stage, the segments that interact strongly with the neighboring grid nodes are selected. This allows the method to significantly reduce the MCMC structure and optimization complexity as compared to methods like [4, 9]. Furthermore, it also allows the method to consider curved road-networks infeasible for junction- and Hough transform-based techniques.

The paper is organized as follows. In Section 2 we present our line segment candidate detection approach. In Section 3 we introduce the energy terms and describe the Markov chain Monte Carlo optimization procedure. In Section 4 we

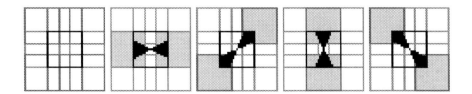

Fig. 1. Overlapping grid (with node region boundaries in different colours) and clique selection in a 3-by-3 neighbourhood that is performed based on orientation of the current segment. From left to right: the grid and cliques for the slope angle ranges $[0, 22.5) \cup [157.5, 180)$, $[22.5, 67.5)$, $[67.5, 112.5)$ and $[112.5, 157.5)$.

give the outline of the proposed road network extractor. In Section 5 we present the experiments and comparisons, and in Section 6 summarize the conclusions of this study.

2 Line Segment Detection

We begin the road structure extraction by building an exhaustive set of line segments that will be refined in the second stage of the algorithm. Although the Radon transform is a popular and efficient tool for linear structure extraction [2,4], it suffers two major drawbacks when applied to remotely sensed scenes. Firstly, it addresses only straight line detection, whereas most of the road structures demonstrate a certain degree of curvature. Secondly, the transform applied to the whole image favours longer lines over shorter ones. The first results in either complete or partial loss of curved lines, whereas the second restricts detection to solely long road segments. In order to overcome these shortcomings we employ a localized Radon transform on a grid. In this way, shorter lines receive the same treatment as longer lines and the curved road parts and junctions can be approximated by a set of shorter line segments.

The continuous Radon transform is defined by an integral of a two-dimensional function $f(x, y)$ over a straight line defined by ρ - its distance from the origin and θ - the angle its normal vector makes with the positive X-axis [2] (note, that it differs from the slope angle by 90 degrees):

$$Rf(\rho, \theta) = \int_{y=-\infty}^{\infty} \int_{x=-\infty}^{\infty} f(x, y)\delta(\rho - x\cos\theta - y\sin\theta)dxdy.$$

The discrete Radon transform follows the same idea by summing the image intensities along a specific angle and distance [2] in a bounded region of a digital image.

The fixed grid results in a lack of translation invariance, i.e., the detection of lines crossing grid boundaries is affected. We employ an overlapping fixed grid which partially overcomes this problem by allowing the points close to the boundaries to appear in several distinct regions of the grid, as illustrated in the left image in Fig. 1. The overlap ratio of the grid presented in Fig. 1 is of 33%. This means that the overlap between a current square and any one of its closest four neighbors (in vertical or horizontal directions) is equal to one third of its size. The scale of the grid should be chosen small enough to cover the expected minimal size of the road segments but large enough to tolerate partial road occlusions. Note as well that the finer the scale, the higher the possible curvature of the detected structures, since a finer fitting is achieved.

Each node of the grid corresponds to a square image region over which the Radon transform is taken. At every node we extract S-many line segment candidates, corresponding to the first S maxima of the Radon transform that are at least $\Delta\rho$ or $\Delta\theta$ apart. This segment detection strategy is locally contrast invariant and robust to histogram stretching.

3   Energy Terms and Optimization

The localized Radon transform employed in the first stage extracts the road segments along with a lot of false candidates of various origins, e.g., bright roofs, fields, etc. In order to select the relevant road segments from a largely redundant set of line candidates we allow not more than one segment to remain per grid node. Defined on the overlapping grid this choice allows a certain degree of overlap necessary for the crossroads modeling. To arrive at such refinement we consider a Markov Random Field (MRF) model for the local dependencies on the grid. For computational reasons, we consider a smaller 3 by 3 neighbourhood that consists of the current grid-location and its eight neighbouring nodes, as in Fig. 1. To reduce the computational complexity of considering all possible cliques, the relevant clique is selected adaptively based on the slope angle α of the current line segment l as demonstrated in Fig. 1. The MRF assumption and Hammersley-Clifford theorem [6,7] allow the probability of a grid configuration L can be written as a Gibbs distribution, namely

$$\mathbf{P}(L) = \frac{1}{Z}\exp\Big(-\sum_j U_j\Big),$$

where Z is a normalizing constant and the sum in the exponent gives the total energy with the summation taken over all nodes of the grid. The energy U_l at each node consists of a unitary data term $D(l)$ that evaluates the accuracy of the fit of its current line segment l (that changes as the configuration evolves) as well as the potential terms $V(l, l_n)$ that describe interactions of l with its neighbours l_n.

The unitary data term evaluates the dissimilarity of texture inside the line segment l and in the outer (background) region, which is constructed of two parallel lines located at distance p on both sides of the current line segment, see Fig. 2. The distance p should be chosen such that the outer stripes are outside of the road if the current segment is correctly placed. For this data term we employ the Bhattacharyya distance $d(l)$ [13] which measures the distributional

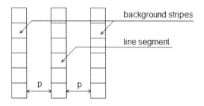

Fig. 2. Inner and outer (background) regions (at $\alpha = 90$ orientation) employed to calculate the distance $d(l)$

similarity of two continuous random variables. This choice is motivated by a good performance of this metric in various object detection applications, see in [16]. An alternative is, e.g., to consider the Student t-test statistic to estimate the dissimilarity in the means [9] which, however, is variance-insensitive. We assume that the pixel intensities over two separate short line regions originate from two independent Gaussian variables $N(\mu_{in}, \sigma_{in}^2)$ and $N(\mu_{out}, \sigma_{out}^2)$. The Bhattacharyya distance is then defined as

$$d(l) = \frac{1}{4}\frac{(\mu_{in} - \mu_{out})^2}{\sigma_{in}^2 + \sigma_{out}^2} - \frac{1}{2}\ln\frac{2\sigma_{in}\sigma_{out}}{\sigma_{in}^2 + \sigma_{out}^2},$$

where the means μ and variances σ^2 are replaced by their standard sample estimates $\bar{x}$ and S^2 [13]. The values of the distance range from 0 for the exact same distributions to $+\infty$ when the supports of the probability density functions do not overlap. We construct a unitary energy data term based on the Bhattacharyya distance as follows:

$$D(l) = \begin{cases} 1 - d(l)/d_0, & \text{if } d(l) < d_0; \\ \exp\left(1 - d(l)/d_0\right) - 1, & \text{otherwise.} \end{cases}$$

Here d_0 is a sensitivity parameter: the higher its value, the more selective the data term is. The distance $D(l)$ takes values between -1 for perfect radiometric contrast between the road and the background strips, and 1 for the exact same statistical patterns in the regions (poor candidate for the road).

To induce realistic road configurations we consider interaction terms of two types. Firstly, those that favour smooth configurations, i.e., similar orientations of the neighbouring segments. Secondly, terms that favour continuous line structure, i.e., intersection of the neighbours. Note that contrary to the purely stochastic approaches [9,16], we do not have to penalize overlap of the lines because of the deterministic grid-based generation of line candidates.

The first potential term favours similar orientation of the neighbouring segments, since such configurations are desirable for road networks. To this end we introduce a potential of the following form:

$$V_a(l_1, l_2) = -\left(1 - |\alpha_1 - \alpha_2|/90\right)^2,$$

where α_1, α_2 are the slope angles (in degrees) of the neighbouring line segments l_1 and l_2 respectively.

The second interaction term promotes continuous configurations by favouring segments that intersect:

$$V_d(l_1, l_2) = \begin{cases} -1, & \text{if segments } l_1 \text{ and } l_2 \text{ intersect;} \\ 0, & \text{otherwise.} \end{cases}$$

Thus, the energy U_l at the grid node containing line segment l is constructed as

$$U_l = D(l) + \gamma_a \Big[V_a(l^+, l) + V_a(l^-, l) \Big] + \gamma_d \Big[V_d(l^+, l) + V_d(l^-, l) \Big],$$

where neighbours l_+, l_- are selected according to Fig. 1, and (γ_a, γ_d) are the contribution weights of the potential terms.

To optimize the MRF configuration we employ a simulated annealing [6] procedure in a form of a Markov Chain Monte Carlo (MCMC) algorithm [7]. Note that this optimization method is chosen due to the non-regularity of the considered potential terms for the graph-cuts [8]. The MCMC procedure is initialized with the first Radon maximum at each grid node. It then proceeds iteratively by selecting randomly (uniformly over the grid) a node and randomly (uniformly over the segment candidates associated with the current node) proposing a new segment l_n, which is either accepted or rejected. The optimal configuration is the one that yields the lowest total energy. In accordance with this energy minimization rule, the new segment l_n is accepted and replaces the current l with the acceptance probability $\min(1, \exp((E - E_n)/T))$. The resulting chain of configurations corresponds to the Metropolis-Hastings procedure [7] with a uniform proposal distribution; the annealing temperature parameter T encourages more exploratory behaviour during the early stages but becomes more prohibitive as it converges to zero later on.

4   Road Network Extraction

The outline of the proposed detector is presented in Algorithm 1. The first part of the algorithm (Radon transform, lines 2-4) is parallelizable, whereas the second (MCMC, lines 6-16) has to be performed sequentially to ensure convergence of the MCMC procedure [6]. Note that a parallelization by dividing the scene into sub-scenes can be achieved due to the locality of the considered interactions, see [16]. One iteration of MCMC is completed when all of the grid nodes have been visited at least once. Theoretical considerations require the cooling schedule to be logarithmic [6], but as in [9, 16] we employ the geometric cooling to accelerate convergence. The iterative process is stopped when the configuration stabilizes, i.e. the proportion of accepted line candidates within a given MCMC iteration goes below a threshold M_{stop}.

In the developed algorithm the line segment candidates compete solely with those located at the same node of the grid. Accordingly, if no removal of undesirable segments is applied after the MCMC procedure each node of the grid will

---

Algorithm 1. Road network extractor

---

1 define an overlapping square grid on the input image;
  for all *grid nodes* (i, j) **do**
2   perform the discrete Radon transform Rf;
3   find the S maxima of the transform;
4   initialize MCMC by setting l as the first maximum;

5 set temperature $T := T_0$, acceptance ratio $\Delta := 1$;
  while $\Delta > M_{stop}$ **do**
6   reset counters $changed := 0$, $total := 0$;
     while *not all grid nodes have been visited* **do**
7 $total := total + 1$;
8   randomly select a node (i, j) of the grid;
9   randomly select a new candidate l_n in (i, j);
10   calculate energy U_l with clique based on l;
11   calculate energy U_{l_n} with clique based on l_n;
12   generate a uniform $u \sim U[0, 1]$;
      if $u < \min(1, \exp((U_l - U_{l_n})/T))$ **then**
13   accept the candidate $l = l_n$;
14 $changed := changed + 1$;

15   update acceptance ratio $\Delta := changed/total$;
16   apply geometric temperature decrease $T := \tau \cdot T$;

17 remove weak segments with $U_l < M_{\text{thresh}}$.

---

contain a line segment. Disjoint segments can survive when all the candidates at the given grid node interact weakly with their respective neighbours due to acquisition noise, non-road objects or incorrect grid-scale selection. To remove these, we introduce the final segment thresholding (line 17).

The fast performance of the developed approach is due to the use of a deterministic segment detection, use of a smaller 3-by-3 MRF neighbourhood with predefined clique selection, and the use of intersection-based interaction penalties instead of more time-consuming distance-based penalties. The generalization of the latter two can improve the MCMC results at the price of a computational complexity increase.

5 Experiments

In this section we present experiments on road network extraction in semi-urbanized zones on several 400×500 images from Google Maps (© Google) of about 0.5 meter per pixel resolution. The following complete set of parameters have been employed: overlapping square grid with side equal to 30 pixels with 33% of overlap (see Fig. 1); $[0, 180)$ angle range for the Radon transform with a step of one degree; distance between Radon maxima at least $\Delta\rho = 5$ or $\Delta\theta = 5$; $S = 5$ segments per region; cooling procedure with $T_0 = 0.75, \tau = 0.97$; MCMC stopping threshold of $M_{\text{stop}} = 0.01$; outer regions lines are taken $p = 10$

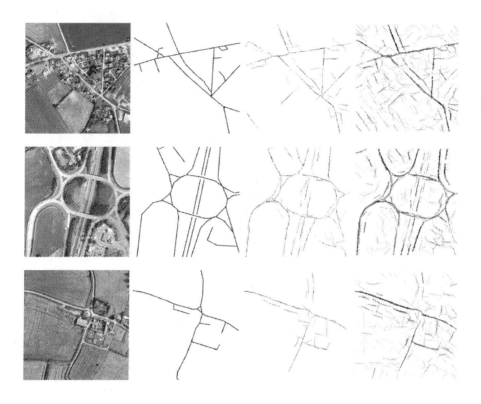

Fig. 3. From left to right: initial images, ground truth (manual extraction) of the road network, extraction results (total computation time of 3 sec) weighted with $\exp(-U_l)$, and the detected Radon segments maps (1 sec) weighted with $(1 - D(l))/2$,

pixels away from the line candidates; and the postprocessing threshold is set to $M_{\mathrm{thresh}} = -1$. The data sensitive parameters are the weights $(\gamma_a, \gamma_d) = (0.75, 0.5)$, and the unitary data term parameter $d_0 = 0.3$.

The experiments were performed in a MATLAB implementation with a CPU-parallelized Radon transform / maxima calculation part and sequential MCMC optimization. We have performed experiments on 15 images with various road networks and three typical extraction results are presented in Fig. 3. It is immediate that the segment extraction via Radon transform with weights attributed by the $D(l)$ distance identifies the necessary road structure well with very few undetected segments. Note that some of these undetected roads originate from occlusions or low contrast and can be identified by varying the grid scale. The designed MCMC-based approach performs the extraction with a good level of accuracy in just under 4 seconds on a Core-i7 2GHz, 6Gb RAM, Windows 7 system.

To provide a point of comparison with the benchmark techniques we perform experiments on a 650×900 'Road' image (©IGN) [16], see Fig. 4. The same parametric setting are used except for a smaller size of square grid (15 pixels),

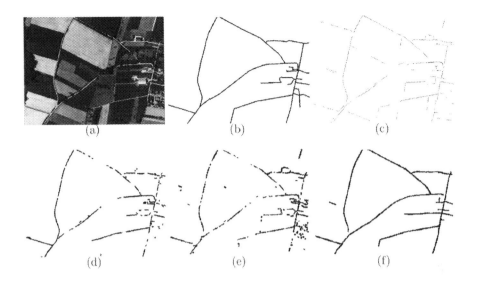

Fig. 4. (a) 'Road' image (©IGN), provided by courtesy of the authors of [16] and (b) the ground truth map. The detection results: (c) by the proposed method, (d) by Verdie et al. [16], (e) by Lafarge et al. [10] and (f) by Lacoste et al. [9].

an increased weight of the orientation term $\gamma_a = 1.2$, and the outer regions lines are taken $p = 3$ pixels away from the line candidates. This parameter adjustment is due to the thinness of roads on the considered scene and their low curvature. Note that this increased the grid from roughly 25-by-30 (in the above experiments) to 90-by-120 and resulted in a computation time increase as reported in Table 1. The obtained results are compared with three different line-detection techniques: two reversible jump MCMC-based techniques [9, 16] and a jump-diffusion approach [10].

All these techniques employ the marked point processes to describe the scene as a stochastic configuration of interacting geometrical objects, each of which is assigned a combination of labels, such as orientation, width/size, etc. (for more details see the 'Quality Candy' model [9]). The characteristic difference of the approach developed in this paper is the fixed number of objects in the analysed scene (equal to the number of grid nodes). In fact, the detected number of objects can only be reduced if none of the candidate segments at some of the grid locations is assigned a sufficiently strong energy. The considered benchmark techniques consider the number of objects as random and employ sophisticated optimization techniques to arrive at stable energy configurations. A numerical comparison can be drawn from Table 1 (the results of the benchmark techniques are reported as in [16]). Note that the approach developed in this paper does not estimate the sizes of the objects (widths). Therefore, to provide a fair comparison, the detected lines were dilated with radius $r = 4$. For the method proposed here, an increase in the reported true positive rate (TPR) at the expense of an increased false positive rate (FPR) can be observed.

Table 1. Numerical results obtained on the 'Road' image from [16]

Algorithm	TPR	FPR	FNR	Computation time
Proposed method	0.709	0.053	0.291	13 sec
Verdie et al. [16]	0.637	0.004	0.363	15 sec
Lafarge et al. [10]	0.658	0.013	0.342	381 sec
Lacoste et al. [9]	0.812	0.006	0.188	155 min

The most relevant improvement can be seen in computation time. Note that the computation times of the benchmark techniques appear in this paper as in [16], although they were obtained on a different hardware system and can therefore only serve as a rather rough comparison. It is immediate that the proposed approach performs significantly faster than methods [9, 10]. The technique in [16] gives a comparable computation time, however, its results were obtained in a massively parallelized CUDA-implementation with a specialized GPU. Whilst a similar kind of implementation is possible for the developed approach, it is beyond the scope of this work. It is also crucial to note that method in [16] employed a preliminary classification in order to obtain the 'classes of interest' which guaranteed the absence of (false) detection in the central (inside the large road circuit) and upper left side of the scene. This pre-classification was necessary to further reduce the computational load. However, it was not specified in detail in [16]. The method proposed in this paper has been employed without any preliminary classification and, thus, we believe that the increase of FPR is (partially) due to this important difference.

6   Conclusions

We have designed a fast approach to road network extraction from remotely sensed images. It combines a deterministic localized Radon transform on an overlapping image grid to draw a redundant set of line segment candidates and a stochastic Markov chain Monte Carlo process to extract the road network. The obtained result can be used to initialize the state-of-the-art approaches [9, 16] to further refine the extraction. The experiments demonstrate a fast and accurate extraction of continuous road networks with intersections and roads of varying width, degree of curvature and brightness. The performed comparisons demonstrate a very fast and competitively accurate performance of the developed technique.

Acknowledgments. This work was supported by the Engineering and Physical Sciences Research Council (grant number EP/J010081/1), UK. The authors thank Y. Verdie and F. Lafarge, INRIA Sophia Antipolis, for providing the benchmark comparison data.

References

1. Amo, M., Martinez, F., Torre, M.: Road extraction from aerial images using a region competition algorithm. IEEE Trans. Image Process 15(5), 1192–1201 (2006)
2. Bracewell, R.: Two-Dimensional Imaging. Prentice Hall, Englewood Cliffs (1995)
3. Chai, D., Forstner, W., Lafarge, F.: Recovering line-networks in images by junction-point processes. In: Proc. of IEEE Conf. Computer Vision and Pattern Recognition, Portland, US (2013)
4. Gao, R., Bischof, W.F.: Detection of linear structures in remote-sensed images. In: Kamel, M., Campilho, A. (eds.) ICIAR 2009. LNCS, vol. 5627, pp. 896–905. Springer, Heidelberg (2009)
5. Geman, D., Jedynak, B.: An active testing model for tracking roads in satellite images. IEEE Trans. Patt. Anal. Mach. Intell. 18(1), 1–14 (1996)
6. Geman, S., Geman, D.: Stochastic relaxation, Gibbs distributions, and the Bayesian restoration of images. IEEE Trans. Patt. Anal. Mach. Intell. 6, 721–741 (1984)
7. Hastings, W.: Monte Carlo sampling method using Markov chains and their applications. Biometrika 57, 97–109 (1970)
8. Kolmogorov, V., Zabih, R.: What energy functions can be minimized via graph cuts? IEEE Trans. Patt. Anal. Mach. Intell. 26(2), 147–159 (2004)
9. Lacoste, C., Descombes, X., Zerubia, J.: Point processes for unsupervised line network extraction in remote sensing. IEEE Trans. Pattern Anal. Mach. Intell. 27(10), 1568–1579 (2005)
10. Lafarge, F., Gimel'farb, G., Descombes, X.: Geometric feature extraction by a multimarked point process. IEEE Trans. Patt. Anal. Mach. Intell. 32(9), 1597–1609 (2010)
11. Merlet, N., Zerubia, J.: New prospects in line detection by dynamic programming. IEEE Trans. Patt. Anal. Mach. Intell. 18(4), 426–431 (1996)
12. Negri, M., Gamba, P., Lisini, G., Tupin, F.: Junction-aware extraction and regularization of urban road networks in high-resolution sar images. IEEE Trans. Geosci. Remote Sens., 2962–2971 (2006)
13. Papoulis, A.: Probability, Random Variables, and Stochastic Processes, 3rd edn. McGraw-Hill, New York (1991)
14. Peng, T., Jermyn, I., Prinet, V., Zerubia, J.: Incorporating generic and specific prior knowledge in a multiscale phase field model for road extraction from VHR images. IEEE J. Sel. Top. Appl. Earth Obs. Remote Sens. 1(2), 139–146 (2008)
15. Rochery, M., Jermyn, I., Zerubia, J.: Higher order active contours. Int. J. Comput. Vision 69, 27–42 (2006)
16. Verdié, Y., Lafarge, F.: Efficient monte carlo sampler for detecting parametric objects in large scenes. In: Fitzgibbon, A., Lazebnik, S., Perona, P., Sato, Y., Schmid, C. (eds.) ECCV 2012, Part III. LNCS, vol. 7574, pp. 539–552. Springer, Heidelberg (2012)
17. Zhang, Q., Couloigner, I.: Accurate centerline detection and line width estimation of thick lines using the Radon transform. IEEE Trans. Image Process 16(2), 310–316 (2007)
18. Zhou, J., Bischof, W., Caelli, T.: Road tracking in aerial images based on human–computer interaction and Bayesian filtering. ISPRS J. Photogramm. Remote Sens. 61(2), 108–124 (2006)

Partial Near-Duplicate Detection in Random Images by a Combination of Detectors

Andrzej Śluzek

Khalifa University, Abu Dhabi, UAE
andrzej.sluzek@kustar.ac.ae

Abstract. Detection of partial near-duplicates (e.g. similar objects) in random images continues to be a challenging problem. In particular, scalability of existing methods is limited because keypoint correspondences have to be confirmed by the configuration analysis for groups of matched keypoints. We propose a novel approach where pairs of images containing partial near-duplicates are retrieved if ANY number of keypoint matches is found between both images (keypoint descriptions are augmented by some geometric characteristics of keypoint neighborhoods). However, two keypoint detectors (Harris-Affine and Hessian-Affine) are independently applied, and only results confirmed by both detectors are eventually accepted. Additionally, relative locations of keypoint correspondences retrieved by both detectors are analyzed and (if needed) outlines of the partial near-duplicates can be extracted using a keypoint-based co-segmentation algorithm. Altogether, the approach has a very low complexity (i.e. it is scalable to large databases) and provides satisfactory performances. Most importantly, *precision* is very high, while *recall* (determined primarily by the selected keypoint description and matching approaches) remains at acceptable level.

Keywords: keypoint description, keypoint correspondences, partial near-duplicates, affine invariance, object detection, co-segmentation.

1 Introduction and Background Work

Detection of partial near-duplicates (e.g. retrieval of image pairs containing the same objects on diversified backgrounds) is a challenging problem for which a fully scalable solution has not been found yet. Because individual keypoint matches are usually incorrect in a (semi-)global context, post-processing operations have to be performed, where the spatial consistency over groups of preliminarily matched keypoints is verified. This is a computation-intensive task, no matter whether the Hough transform (e.g. [6], [9]), RANSAC-based methods (e.g. [1], [17]) or other less popular solutions (e.g. [19]) are used.

Currently, most of the *state-of-the-art* methods (e.g. [3], [5], [2]) seem to apply this approach, although they attempt to preliminarily reduce the numbers of analyzed image pairs using, for example, (*geometric*) *min-hashing* or *weak geometric*

J. Blanc-Talon et al. (Eds.): ACIVS 2013, LNCS 8192, pp. 238–249, 2013.

consistency. Nevertheless, with such approaches the size of visual databases cannot grow indiscriminately. In particular, there is always a need to process groups of matched keypoints in all pairs of preselected images (geometric verification).

In this paper, we attempt to solve the problem of partial near-duplicate detection using only individual keypoint matches. The basic idea is to incorporate into descriptions of individual keypoints selected visual and geometric characteristics of keypoint neighborhoods. Similar concepts of *keypoint bundling* have been discussed previously (e.g. [17], [10] and [12]). However, in most cases keypoint bundles are used as a pre-retrieval mechanism, i.e. matched bundles indicate for which image pairs (and at which locations within these images) geometric consistency of matched keypoints should be verified. Only in [12] keypoint bundles are represented by affine-invariant descriptions which are incorporated into descriptors of keypoints around which the bundles are built (such keypoints are referred to as bundle centroids). Then, a match between two bundles indicates that there is some photometric *and* geometric similarity between two groups of keypoints (incorporated into both bundles) so that the presence of partial near-duplicates can be assumed without any further geometric verification. This method, when using vocabularies of reasonable size to represent image contents and geometry, provides acceptable *precision* and *recall* (both reaching approx. 50% level, details in [12]).

We apply a very similar approach, i.e. keypoint description incorporating visual and geometric characteristics of keypoint neighborhoods. However, compared to [12], three significant changes have been introduced:

(a) The geometric model of keypoint bundles is simplified (in order to accept stronger distortions). On one hand, it improves *recall* of partial near-duplicate retrieval, but on another hand *precision* deteriorates.

(b) Two variants of the method using alternative types of keypoint detectors (Harris-Affine and Hessian-Affine, see [7]) are run simultaneously, and only pairs of images retrieved by both variants are preliminarily accepted. Thus, a high level of *recall* is maintained, while *precision* is much higher than achieved by individually applied variants.

(c) Finally, keypoint correspondences are accepted if similarly located keypoint correspondences exist for the other detector. This step further improves *precision*, which reaches nearly 100%.

Principles of keypoint description (both the previous version and the proposed improvements) are highlighted in Section 2. In Section 3, we describe details of partial near-duplicate retrieval by using a combination of Harris-Affine and Hessian-Affine results (including the post-processing operations mentioned in the above Step 3).

Section 4 presents exemplary verification results for the selected datasets. Finally, Section 5 concludes the paper and highlights the directions for current and future researches.

2 Keypoint Bundles

Assuming that keypoint matching is considered the main operation in partial near-duplicate retrieval, and accepting that individual *standard* (e.g. based on SIFT descriptors) keypoint correspondences are virtually useless in this problem (most of them are incorrect in (semi-)global image context, e.g. [10]) we propose to incorporate characteristics of keypoint neighborhoods into keypoint description. Obviously, neighborhoods of limited size (either the radius or the number of neighboring keypoints) should be used. However, we exclude from the neighborhoods keypoints which are too close to the center or are significantly smaller/larger than the central keypoint. Altogether (as shown in Fig.1a) given a keypoint K represented by E ellipse, its neighborhood contains other keipoints K_i (with E_i ellipses)for which the following conditions are satisfied:

1. The Mahalanobis distance $D_M(K, K_i)$ is between $0.5\sqrt{2}$ and 2 (where the unit distance is defined by the shape of E ellipse).
2. The area of E_i ellipse is between 0.5 and 1.5 of the area of E ellipse..

Additionally, if more that 20 keypoints fulfill Conditions 1 and 2, only 20 of them (the closest to K) are retained so that the computational complexity of neighborhood processing is constrained.

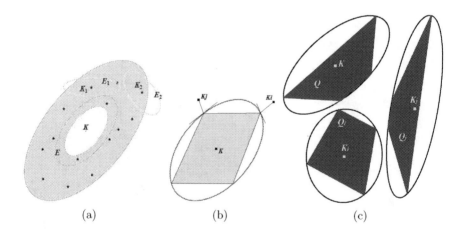

Fig. 1. Exemplary distribution of keypoints in the neighborhood of K keypoint (a). A trapezoid built in E ellipse in the context of K_i and K_j keypoints (b), and the trapezoids built in all three ellipses of a tuple (c).

Subsequently, all pairs of the neighborhood keypoints K_i and K_j (if they also are not too close to one another, see Condition 1 above) are used to form tuples $\{K, K_i, K_j\}$. The collection of such tuples is referred to as the *keypoint bundle* with K centroid. In practice, the average number of tuples in a bundle for typical images of fairly complex contents is approx. $60 - 70$ for both Harris-Affine and Hessian-Affine keypoints.

2.1   Description of Keypoint Bundles

Photometric characteristics of an individual tuple of keypoints can be invariantly represented by the corresponding SIFT descriptors (or SIFT words) of K, K_i and K_j keypoints. The (affine-)invariant representation of the tuple's geometry is more complicated. It has been shown in [12,14] how several shapes can be unambiguously built within a tuple $\{K, K_i, K_j\}$. We use only some of these shapes, namely the trapezoids found in ellipses in the context of two other keypoints. Fig.1b illustrates (more details in [14]) how a trapezoid is built inside E ellipse (centered in K keypoint), while Fig.1c shows the trapezoids Q, Q_i and Q_j correspondingly built for all keypoints of the tuple.

Since the shapes of such trapezoids change co-variantly with any affine mapping of the tuple, we use (following [12,14]) the simplest affine-invariant moment-based shape descriptor Inv (Eq. 2, details in [15]) computed over the three trapezoids to affine-invariantly represent the configuration of the tuple. Therefore, geometric characteristics of each tuple are described by a 3D vector

$$[Inv(Q), Inv(Q_i), Inv(Q_j)], \tag{1}$$

where

$$Inv = \frac{M_{20}M_{02} - M_{11}^2}{M_{00}^4} \tag{2}$$

(note that M_{pq} is the central moment of order $p + q$).

Altogether, the tuple is described photometrically and geometrically by a 6D vector

$$[Sift(K), Sift(K_i), Sift(K_j), Inv(Q), Inv(Q_i), Inv(Q_j)]. \tag{3}$$

Then, the whole bundle centered at K keypoint is represented by a list of such vectors (one for each tuple in a bundle). In practice, 5D vectors

$$[Sift(K_i), Sift(K_j), Inv(Q), Inv(Q_i), Inv(Q_j)] \tag{4}$$

can be used because $Sift(K)$ is the same for all tuples and it can be memorized only once.

3   Detection of Partial Near-Duplicates

3.1   Matching Keypoint Bundles

The proposed descriptions of keypoint bundles actually represent semi-local structures of images (i.e. keypoints with their neighborhoods). Thus, a match between bundles around two keypoints indicates similarity between image fragments much larger than individual keypoint ellipses. In other words, this is an indicator of partial near-duplicates in both images.

For convenience, the matching operation for two bundles built around key-points K and L, correspondingly, is divided into two phases. First, $Sift(K)$ and $Sift(L)$ are compared (i.e. we match the bundle centroids). Any typical approach can be used, e.g. *mutual-nearest-neighbor* or *the-same-visual-word*. In the conducted experiments, a SIFT vocabulary of 2^{16} words has been used.

If K and L match, their bundles are compared by matching tuples from both bundles. Finally, we assume that the bundles match, if at least A matching tuples are found for which

$$[Sift(K_i), Sift(K_j), Inv(QK), Inv(QK_i), Inv(QK_j)] \equiv \qquad (5)$$

$$\equiv [Sift(L_m), Sift(L_n), Inv(QL), Inv(QL_m), Inv(QL_n)].$$

We match tuples by *the-same-word* approach, where SIFT descriptors are quantized into a relatively small vocabulary of 2000 words, while *Inv* invariants are quantized into 12 words only. Note that the tuple geometry is represented by three values only (compared to 16D vectors in [12]) which are quantized very coarsely so that a wide range of geometric image deformations can be tolerated.

The number of matching tuples (A threshold) needed for a match between two bundles has been established experimentally. It has been finally decided to use $A = 2$ for both Harris-Affine and Hessian-Affine bundles (even though the former ones usually contain slightly more tuples).

3.2   Preliminary and Final Image Matching

Detection, bundling and matching operations are performed independently using Harris-Affine and Hessian-Affine keypoints. When compared images contain clearly visible partial near-duplicates, usually both approaches retrieve a number of matching bundle pairs (i.e. correspondences between bundle centroids and unspecified numbers of similar tuples) as shown in a simple example in Figs 2a and 2b. However, the number of such matches in hard to predict, and even images of random contents may be occasionally matched as well (although a close visual inspection always reveals some level similarity between the corresponding areas). Nevertheless, such correspondences are rather infrequent in random images and (in general) Harris-Affine and Hessian-Affine matches are found at different locations, as illustrated in Figs 2c and 2d. In images sharing actual partial near-duplicates, however, Harris-Affine and Hessian-Affine matches are usually located in the same areas (as seen in Figs 2a and 2b).

Since the numbers of matching keypoints (bundles) are unpredictable, we preliminarily assume that pairs of images with *any* number of matches may contains partial near-duplicates. However, if it is additionally requested that *both* Harris-Affine and Hessian-Affine matches (see Point (b) in Section 1) must exist in the image pair, the number of false correspondences is dramatically reduced.

A further reduction (see Point (c) in Section 1) is obtained by checking the locations of matched keypoints (bundle centroids). A pair of images is retained

(a)   (b)

(c)   (d)

Fig. 2. Matched keypoints (centroids of matched bundles) for images sharing the same object (using Hessian-Affine (a) and Harris-Affine (b)). The results for images of random contents are shown in (c) and (d).

if each pair of matched Harris-Affine keypoints (K_{har}, L_{har}) has at least one counterpart pair of matched Hessian-Affine keypoints (K_{hes}, L_{hes}) (and another way around) with similar coordinates, i.e.

$$K_{hes} \in E(K_{har}); \quad L_{hes} \in E(L_{har}); \quad Khar \in E(K_{hes}); \quad L_{har} \in E(L_{hes}) \quad (6)$$

where $E(K)$ and $E(L)$ are ellipses of the corresponding keypoints .

It can be seen that matched keypoints in Figs 2a and 2b clearly satisfy Eq.6, while the pairs of images from Figs 2c and 2d would be rejected.

The proposed method of detecting images with partial near-duplicates is very fast and efficient. Although matching using two types of keypoints is needed (i.e. the database memory for image representation is doubled), no geometric verification of keypoint matches (which is the bottleneck of existing solutions) is needed. Although some geometry-based calculations are performed in Eq.6, their complexity is negligible.

Experimental verification of this proposed method is presented in the following section.

4   Experimental Verification

4.1   Methodology

The experiment has been conducted using two publicly available datasets, i.e. VISIBLE and PASCAL 2007. VISIBLE[1] contains diversified views of 1, 2 or 3

---

[1] http://156.17.10.3/~visible/data/upload/FragmentMatchingDB.zip

locally planar objects on diversified backgrounds. The objects are manually outlined so that *ground-truth* (the presence of partial near-duplicates) is estimated.
Actually, other partial near-duplicates (outside the object outlines) also exist (see
examples below) so that this is a very conservative *ground-truth*. PASCAL 2007[2]
also provides *ground-truth* data but they are not partial near-duplicates (instead,
they are outlines of the same category objects, which may look very differently)
so that we consider this dataset a collection of confusing images. Therefore, we
assume only 511 *ground-truth* image pairs with partial near-duplicates (the number of VISIBLE image pairs sharing the same object(s)). The total number of
image pairs is 4,950 in VISIBLE only (these are used in the first part of the experiment) and 135,460 in the union of VISIBLE and PASCAL 2007 (the second
part of the experiment). Images in Fig.2 are actually from VISIBLE dataset.

Bundle centroids are matched by using thresholded difference between SIFT descriptors (the threshold obtained from over 50,000,000 *mutual-nearest-neighbor*
matches). Neighborhood keypoints are matched using a 2000 word SIFT vocabulary, while the tuple geometries are compared using the vocabulary of $12^3 = 1728$
words (*Inv* invariant quantization in Section 3.1).

4.2   Results

Full results obtained for VISIBLE dataset (i.e. matches between 4,950 image
pairs attempted) are summarized in Table 1, and exemplary correct matches
(both Harris-Affine and Hessian-Affine) are shown in Fig. 3. Note that matches
in Fig.2 are also from this experiment.

Table 1. Retrieved image pairs (total and correct, compared to *ground truth*) in
VISIBLE dataset

Method	Total	Correct	Precision	Recall
HarAff	536	306	57.09%	59.88%
HesAff	488	284	58.20%	55.58%
HarAff +HesAff	375	283	75.47%	55.38%
HarAff+ HesAff+Eq.6	304	283	93.09%	55.38%

Recall of the ultimate results is not perfect, but still better (55.38% *versus*
51.40%) than reported in [12] for the same dataset. *Precision*, however, is very
high and it effectively reaches almost 100%. This can be claimed because most of
false positives are actually correct (indicating near-duplicate fragments outside
the *ground truth* outlines of objects). Examples of such *correct false positives* are
provided in Fig. 4.

---

[2] http://pascallin.ecs.soton.ac.uk/challenges/VOC/voc2007/

Fig. 3. Matched centroids of bundles for VISIBLE images sharing the same object. Hessian-Affine (left column) and Harris-Affine (right column) detectors are used.

A limited *recall* value can be attributed to certain effects in the keypoint bundling process. Our experiments show that 35-40% of detected keypoints (both Harris-Affine and Hessian-Affine) have too few neighbors (as defined in Section 2, see Fig.1a) to form bundles with a sufficient (for prospective bundle matching) number of tuples. If matches between such keypoints are the only evidences of partial near-duplicity between two image fragments, those partial near-duplicates would be missed.

Fig. 4. Examples of *correct false positives*, i.e. near-duplicate fragments identified outside the *ground truth* objects

Results for the union of VISIBLE and PASCAL 2007 datasets (with $135,460$ image pairs to be matched) are presented in Table 2. It can be noticed that when only Harris-Affine keypoint bundles are matched *precision* is much lower than in the first experiment. This is understandable because stray partial near-duplicates (i.e. fragments with weakly seen visual similarity usually represented by only one match in the whole image) appear quite often, i.e. in approx. 2.5% of image pairs. However, such random matches usually happen for only Harris-Affine or Hessian-Affine keypoint. Thus, as shown in the table, the intersection of Harris-Affine and Hessian-Affine retrievals provides much higher *precision*. Eventually, after the verification by Eq. 6, *precision* is almost the same as in the first experiment (where the number of image pairs is $27\times$ smaller).

Table 2. Retrieved image pairs (total and correct, compared to *ground truth*) in VISIBLE and PASCAL 2007 datasets

Method	Total	Correct	Precision	Recall
HarAff	3,453	306	8.86%	59.88%
HarAff +HesAff	660	283	42.88%	55.38%
HarAff+ HesAff+Eq.6	318	283	88.99%	55.38%

Fig. 5. Examples of near-duplicate fragments identified outside the *ground truth* objects (VISIBLE + PASCAL 2007 datasets)

Similarly to Table 1, the actual *precision* in the last row of Table 2 is also almost 100%. Fig. 5 shows examples of fragments which are clearly partial near-duplicates, but which are not included into the *ground truth* (thus, considered *false positives*).

4.3   Additional Operations

The present method of partial near-duplicate retrieval returns only image pairs containing near-duplicate fragments and provides approximate locations of these fragments using coordinates of matched keypoints (i.e. centroids of matched bundles) in both images. If the outlines of near-duplicates are required, additional operations should be performed. Details of such operations are not discussed in this paper, but their exemplary outcomes are presented for completeness.

Although outlines of partial near-duplicates can be approximated by convex polygons using the methods proposed in [9], we prefer another technique based on the concept of *co-segmentation*.

Popular co-segmentation methods (e.g. [4,8]) use the graph-cut framework solved by minimizing a Markov Random Field energy function through a min-cut/max-flow algorithm. The method we apply has been adopted from an unpublished report [18]. This algorithm follows the standard approaches regarding the image energy (which consists of the *deviation penalty* and *separation penalty* functions). However, a novel foreground energy is proposed based in nonlinear mappings between co-segmented images. The mappings (based on TPS, i.e. *thin plate splines* warping) use the keypoint correspondences established in partial near-duplicate detection as the control points. In the report, the algorithm is benchmarked against alternative solutions, and its performances in co-segmentations of partial near-duplicates have been found superior to other methods. Fig.6 shows exemplary image fragments around matched keypoints, and the results of co-segmentation.

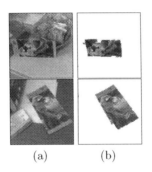

(a)   (b)

Fig. 6. Exemplary pair of approximately matched image fragments (a) and the co-segmentation results using the [18] algorithm

5   Summary

5.1   Discussion

The paper presents a novel method for detection of partial near-duplicates in large databases of unknown and unpredictable images. Using keypoint detection as a starting point, we build around detected keypoints *bundles of neighboring keypoints*. Bundles are described by 5D vectors invariantly representing photometric and geometric properties of the bundles.

The bundle descriptions are incorporated into descriptors of keypoints (bundle centroids) so that individual keypoint correspondences (found using such augmented descriptors) indicate without any geometric verification that images may contain partial near-duplicates around the locations of matched keypoints.

Performances of the method (*precision* in particular) are improved by intersecting results obtained by two independently applied affine-invariant keypoint detectors, i.e. Harris-Affine and Hessian-Affine.

The proposed description of keypoint bundles is effectively a *set-of-words* from a large vocabulary. If bundle centroids are matched using a SIFT vocabulary of 2^{16} words, while tuples are matched using two words from a 2000-word SIFT vocabulary and a vocabulary of 1728 words to represent geometry (see Section 4.1), the overall size of the vocabulary is more than 4.5×10^{14}. With such a huge vocabulary, sophisticated image indexing strategies and/or efficiently organized databases (e.g. [11,16]) can be implemented for prospective web-scale applications of the method.

A particularly attractive properties of the proposed approach is that, in spite of a huge vocabulary, a very good balance is maintained between *precision* and *recall*. Usually (see a discussion in [16]) too large vocabularies are unable to produce satisfactory *recalls*. In our method, the value of *recall* is acceptable and, actually, it can be further improved by modifying parameters for neighborhood building and bundling keypoints (see Section 4.2).

5.2 Future Works

The presented method can be considered fully developed in terms of its methodological principles. However, numerous technical improvements are possible. In particular, the method is currently implemented in Matlab so that we do not discuss its timing performances. They will be experimentally verified after an efficient C++ implementation (incorporating additional mechanisms, e.g. inverted indexing and distributed memory for inverted files, [13]) will have been developed.

Moreover, extensive experiments on much larger dataset sets are needed for fine-tuning parameters (e.g. the size and shape of keypoint neighborhoods, threshold values, etc.) and general evaluation. Many ideas will be borrowed from a recent Google project preliminarily presented in [16].

References

1. Chum, O., Matas, J.: Matching with prosac - progressive sample consensus. In: Proc. IEEE Conf. CVPR 2005, San Diego, CA, pp. 220–226 (2005)
2. Chum, O., Matas, J.: Large-scale discovery of spatially related images. IEEE PAMI 32(2), 371–377 (2010)
3. Chum, O., Perdoch, M., Matas, J.: Geometric min-hashing: Finding a (thick) needle in a haystack. In: Proc. IEEE Conf. CVPR 2009, pp. 17–24 (2009)
4. Hochbaum, D., Singh, V.: An efficient algorithm for co-segmentation. In: Proc. ICCV 2009, Kyoto, pp. 269–276 (2009)

5. Jegou, H., Douze, M., Schmid, C.: Improving bag-of-features for large scale image search. International Journal of Computer Vision 87(3), 316–336 (2010)
6. Lowe, D.G.: Object recognition from local scale-invariant features. In: Proc. 7th IEEE Int. Conf. Computer Vision, vol. 2, pp. 1150–1157 (1999)
7. Mikolajczyk, K., Schmid, C.: Scale and affine invariant interest point detectors. International Journal of Computer Vision 60, 63–86 (2004)
8. Mukherjee, L., Singh, V., Dyer, C.R.: Half-integrality based algorithms for cosegmentation of images. In: Proc. IEEE Conf. CVPR 2009, Miami Beach, pp. 2028–2035 (2009)
9. Paradowski, M., Śluzek, A.: Local keypoints and global affine geometry: Triangles and ellipses for image fragment matching. In: Kwaśnicka, H., Jain, L.C. (eds.) Innovations in Intelligent Image Analysis. SCI, vol. 339, pp. 195–224. Springer, Heidelberg (2011)
10. Romberg, S., August, M., Ries, C.X., Lienhart, R.: Robust feature bundling. In: Lin, W., Xu, D., Ho, A., Wu, J., He, Y., Cai, J., Kankanhalli, M., Sun, M.-T. (eds.) PCM 2012. LNCS, vol. 7674, pp. 45–56. Springer, Heidelberg (2012)
11. Sivic, J., Zisserman, A.: Efficient visual search of videos cast as text retrieval. IEEE PAMI 31(4), 591–606 (2009)
12. Śluzek, A.: Large vocabularies for keypoint-based representation and matching of image patches. In: Fusiello, A., Murino, V., Cucchiara, R. (eds.) ECCV 2012 Ws/Demos, Part I. LNCS, vol. 7583, pp. 229–238. Springer, Heidelberg (2012)
13. Śluzek, A.: Inverted indexing in image fragment retrieval using huge keypoint-based vocabularies. In: Proc. CBMI 2013, Veszprem, pp. 167–172 (2013)
14. Śluzek, A., Paradowski, M.: Detection of near-duplicate patches in random images using keypoint-based features. In: Blanc-Talon, J., Philips, W., Popescu, D., Scheunders, P., Zemčík, P. (eds.) ACIVS 2012. LNCS, vol. 7517, pp. 301–312. Springer, Heidelberg (2012)
15. Śluzek, A.: Zastosowanie metod momentowych do identyfikacji obiektów w cyfrowych systemach wizyjnych. WPW, Warszawa (1990)
16. Stewénius, H., Gunderson, S.H., Pilet, J.: Size matters: Exhaustive geometric verification for image retrieval. In: Fitzgibbon, A., Lazebnik, S., Perona, P., Sato, Y., Schmid, C. (eds.) ECCV 2012, Part II. LNCS, vol. 7573, pp. 674–687. Springer, Heidelberg (2012)
17. Wu, Z., Ke, Q., Isard, M., Sun, J.: Bundling features for large scale partial-duplicate web image search. In: Proc. IEEE Conf. CVPR 2009, Miami Beach, pp. 25–32 (2009)
18. Yang, D., Śluzek, A.: Co-segmentation by keypoint matching: Incorporating pixel-to-pixel mapping into mrf. Tech. rep., Nanyang Technological University, SCE, Singapore (2010)
19. Zhao, W.-L., Ngo, C.-W.: Scale-rotation invariant pattern entropy for keypoint-based near-duplicate detection. IEEE Trans. on Image Processing 2, 412–423 (2009)

Object Recognition and Modeling Using SIFT Features

Alessandro Bruno, Luca Greco, and Marco La Cascia

DICGIM, Università degli Studi di Palermo, Italy
{alessandro.bruno15,luca.greco,marco.lacascia}@unipa.it

Abstract. In this paper we present a technique for object recognition and modelling based on local image features matching. Given a complete set of views of an object the goal of our technique is the recognition of the same object in an image of a cluttered environment containing the object and an estimate of its pose. The method is based on visual modeling of objects from a multi-view representation of the object to recognize. The first step consists of creating object model, selecting a subset of the available views using SIFT descriptors to evaluate image similarity and relevance. The selected views are then assumed as the model of the object and we show that they can effectively be used to visually represent the main aspects of the object.

Recognition is done making comparison between the image containing an object in generic position and the views selected as object models. Once an object has been recognized the pose can be estimated searching the complete set of views of the object. Experimental results are very encouraging using both a private dataset we acquired in our lab and a publicly available dataset.

Keywords: Object Recognition, Pose Estimation, Object Model, SIFT.

1 Introduction

The problem of automatically learning object models for recognition is one of the classical challenges in the field of Computer Vision. Object recognition can be formulated in terms of shape, appearance, or feature matching. In this paper we address object recognition as a features model matching problem. More particularly, we analyze the matches between local keypoints in multiple views of the same object to extract a model of the object. The SIFT [1] keypoints descriptors are used to address object recognition problem. Research in object recognition is increasingly concerned with the ability to recognize specific instances or generic classes of objects. We focus our attention on the problem of the recognition of specific instances of objects into the images.

Many methods in object recognition separate processing into two main steps: feature extraction and matching. In the first stage, discrete primitives, or features are detected. In the second stage, stored models are matched against those features.

From a neuroscientific perspective, object recognition is one of the most fascinating abilities that humans possess. It is easy (for human being) to generalize from observing a set of objects to recognizing objects that have never been seen

J. Blanc-Talon et al. (Eds.): ACIVS 2013, LNCS 8192, pp. 250–261, 2013.

before. On the contrary, it is not simple to develop vision systems that match the cognitive capabilities of human beings. The relative pose of an object to a camera, the lighting variation of a scene, and generalization from a set of exemplar images are some of the development of a vision system for object recognition should cope with. A good object recognition system should be able to extract and recognize the regularities of images, taken under different lighting and pose conditions. Object models and representations capture the most important features of the same object; furthermore the models for object recognition should be as more compact as possible to allow a lower computational complexity in the recognition phase. The representations can be either 2D or 3D. The recognition process is carried out by matching the test image against the stored object representations or models.

In this paper we present a new method for automatically learning object models for recognition. We used a dataset in which each object is subjected to rotation of 180 degrees, in steps of 5 degrees along yaw-axis, and 90 degrees along pitch-axis, in steps of 5 degrees (703 image samples for each object). We analyze the number of matches between nearby images (rotations of 5 degrees) by choosing, as a model of the object, only the most representative images (the criterion of choice of the images will be described in greater detail in section 3). As result we create a model for each object that has a compact representation (a few images instead of 703). After the model is built, we use the models for object recognition; the pose of the object is also estimated with a good level of accuracy.

The contributions of this paper are a new method for automatically learning object models, and a new method for object recognition and pose estimation. The rest of the paper is organized as follows: section 2 gives an overview of the state of the art, sections 3 describe in detail the proposed method, and the datasets used for testing and training our system, in section 4 the experimental results are shown, section 5 ends the paper with conclusions e future works.

2   State of the Art

The most important object recognition approaches can be subdivided in three main categories:

1)Geometry-based approaches [2] [3];
2)Appearance-based algorithms [4];
3)Feature-based algorithms [5] [6].

In Geometric based approaches the main idea is that the geometric description of a 3D object allows the projected shape to be accurately analyzed in a 2D image under projective projection, thereby facilitating recognition process using edge or boundary information.

The most notable appearance-based algorithm is the eigenface method [4] applied in face recognition. The underlying idea of this algorithm is to compute eigenvectors from a set of vectors where each one represents one face image as a raster scan vector of gray-scale pixel values. The central idea of feature-based object recognition algorithms lies in finding interest points, often occurred at intensity discontinuity, that are invariant to change due to scale, illumination and affine transformation.

3D object recognition is an important area in computer vision and pattern recognition and mainly include two steps: Object Detection and Object Recognition.

Object recognition algorithms based on views or appearances are a hot research topic [7] [8]. In [9] Pontil et al. proposed a method that recognize the objects also if the objects are overlapped. In recognition system based on view, the dimensions of the extracted features may be of several hundreds. After obtaining the features of 3D object from 2D images, the 3D object recognition is reduced to a classification problem and features can be considered from the perspective of pattern recognition. In [10] the recognition problem is formulated as one of appearance matching rather than shape matching. The appearance of an object depends on its shape, reflectance properties, pose in the scene and the illumination conditions. Shape and reflectance are intrinsic properties of the object, on the contrary pose and illumination vary from scene to scene. In [10] the authors developed a continuous and compact representation of object appearance that is parameterized by object pose and illumination (parametric eigenspace, constructed by computing the most prominent eigenvectors of the set) and the object is represented as a manifold. The exact position of the projection on the manifold determines the object's pose in the image. The authors suppose that the objects in the image are not occluded by others objects and therefore can be segmented from the remaining scene.

In [11] the author developed an object recognition system based on SIFT descriptors [1]. The features of SIFT descriptors are invariant to image scaling, translation and rotation, partially invariant to illumination changes and affine or 3D projection. SIFT are efficiently detected through a filtering approach that extract stable points in scale space. The SIFT keypoints are used as input to a nearest-neighbor indexing method, this identifies candidate object matches.

In [12] the authors analyzed the features which characterize the difference of similar views to recognize 3D objects. Principal Component Analysis (PCA) and Kernel PCA (KPCA) are used to extract features and then classify the 3d objects with Support Vector Machine (SVM). KPCA-SVM, PCA-SVM performances on Columbia Object Image Library (COIL-100) have been compared. The best performance is achieved by SVM with KPCA. KPCA is used for feature extraction in view-based 3D object recognition. In [12] different algorithms are shown by comparing the performances only for four angles of rotation ($10°$ $20°$ $45°$ $90°$). Furthermore, the experimental results are based only on images with dimensions 128 x 128.

Peng Chang et al. [13] used the color co-occurrence histogram (that adds geometric information to the usual color histogram) for recognizing objects in images. The authors computed model of Color Co-occurrence Histogram based on images of known objects taken from different points of view. The models are then matched to sub-regions in test images to find the object. Moreover thy developed a mathematical probabilistic model for adjusting the number of colors in Color Co-occurrence Histogram.

Many object recognition methods perform also object pose estimation. In [14] Kouskorida et al. proposed a solution to the problem of 3D object pose estimation. More particularly, the authors build an architecture based on appearance and geometrical attributes. The feature extraction procedure is accompained by a clustering scheme over the key-points. The clusters are considered to establish representative manifolds. In [15] Viksten et al. performed comparison of local image descriptors for full 6 Degree-of-Freedom Pose Estimation. In [16] Pose Estimation is treated as a regression problem. In [17] the authors addressed the challenging problem of pose recognition using simultaneous color and depth information. They used a multi-kernel approach to incorporate depth information to perform more effective pose recognition on table-top objects.

Our method is a new object recognition algorithm based on visual object models, it also performs pose estimation of the object. In [11] SIFT keypoints and descriptors are used as input to a nearest-neighbor indexing method that identifies candidate object matches, we, instead, used SIFT for obtaining the object model for multiple views and multiple images of the same object. In our method the recognition of the object is performed by matching the keypoints of the query image only with the keypoints of the objects models. Similarly to the Peng Chang et al. method [13] we used object modeling for object recognition but we preferred to extract local features (SIFT) rather than global features such as the color Co-occurrence histogram.

Once recognition phase is done, we estimate the pose of the object by matching the SIFT of the query image with the SIFT keypoints of all the views of that object. On the other side, Kouskurida et al. [14] proposed a method for pose estimation in which appearance and geometrical attributes are extracted and clustered over keypoints.

3   Object Modeling and Recognition

The proposed method is a recognition algorithm based on visual object models. Object models are pre-calculated starting from a particular type of image dataset.

Fig. 1. Example of a car for -90, 0 and +90 degrees rotation on a turntable

3.1   Objects Image Dataset

The method works with a particular type of dataset, that is a collection of multi angle views of each objects. For each object, the dataset contains N views from a fixed camera generated rotating the object by a fixed angle, having only one degree of freedom (i.e. using a turntable). The same result can be obtained by taking image rotating uniformly around the fixed object. An example of this is show in Fig. 1.

If the N images cover only a specific range of views of the object (i.e. 0-180 degrees), the recognition algorithm is reliable on this range.

For each object, the model is obtained as follows:

1. SIFT keypoints and descriptors are calculated for every view;
2. For each view, only the union of the subsets of the keypoints that match with the previous and the next view is used as view descriptor;
3. Starting from image 1 to N, the number of matching keypoints of the selected subset and the subset of next view is calculated and associated to the current image;
4. The views corresponding to local minima and maxima of this sequence are selected as model of the object.

Fig. 2. Complete object view in our dataset. Squares are the subset of the image selected for the object model.

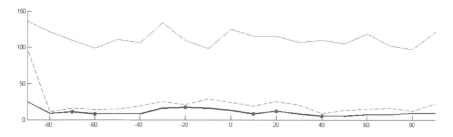

Fig. 3. The higher line is the number of detected SIFT keypoints, the middle line is the number of filtered keypoints, the lower line is the number of match between a view and the next. Circles represents maxima and minima included in the model.

Step 2 performs a filtering on keypoints keeping only those that are present in a filtering sliding window of 3 images. So only repeated and not occluded points are present in the resulting subset. In step 3 the visual continuity of the sequence is evaluated for each image looking at the match between the image and next view, so calculating the similarity in SIFT descriptors.

Taking local minima of this similarity, the corresponding images are the most dissimilar in their neighborhood, so representing views that contains a visual change of the object. Local maxima, conversely, correspond to images that contains common feature in their neighborhood, so being representative of this.

The views corresponding to local maxima and minima, so taking the images that contain "typical" views (maxima) and visual breaking views (minima). The number M of this image is lower than original N dimension of starting dataset. The value of M depends on the shape of the object.

Although the visual model for recognition is composed of the selected images, the filtered subset of descriptors is also stored to describe completely the objects and to perform pose estimation.

3.2   Dataset

To evaluate the performance of modeling objects, a dataset has been created. It contains 18 objects and 19 views for each of this, in the range [-90 90] degrees with a change of 10 degree at each step. An example of this dataset is shown in Fig. 2. The squares represent the images forming the model: the brighter ones are the one associated to local maxima, the darker ones those associated to minima.

The 18 objects are different in shape and color and so cover a very large number of possible typology of recognition scenarios.

Using this dataset the overall amount of images of the models is 93, starting from a full dataset dimension of 342.

3.3   Recognition

The recognition algorithm is based on the models of objects obtained with the procedure of the previous paragraph.

Having a new query image, containing (or not) an object present in the dataset, the recognition algorithm is:

1.   Calculate the SIFT keypoints and descriptors for the query image;
2.   Match the keypoints with all the filtered keypoints of the images of all models;
3.   Select the object referring to the best match (over a fixed threshold, 15 in our experiments) as the recognized object.

Using this method, the number of the match to calculate is reduced to the dimension of model dataset. In the case of our dataset, the reduction is from 342 to 93, so having only the 27% of matches to calculate compared to the full dataset. Object models on average are made of 5.1 images.

3.4   Pose Estimation

Having a well-defined type of dataset, where the pose of the object is known, it is possible to have a pose estimation of the recognized object without taking explicitly into account the shape characteristics of the query image (i.e. segmentation and 3d structure of the object). In fact, once the object is recognized this can be compared with the original full model of N images of the dataset (without model filtering) to recover the best match and so the pose.

In summary, given a query image, the process of recognition and pose estimation is the following:

1.   Calculate the SIFT of query image;
2.   Compare with models and recognize if there is a known object;
3.   If recognized, compare the query image with all images (N) of the original dataset for the recognized object and determine the pose with the largest number of matches.

The overall process consist of a number of comparison that is the sum of the models images and N. In our dataset this number is 112, so only the 33% of the comparison using the entire dataset.

Fig. 4. Result of recognition and pose estimation. Size and light condition are not the same than in dataset.

4   Results

Datasets are a key factor in recognition task when the method doesn't use external knowledge on objects (i.e. 3D information on shape and geometry). Ponce et al. in [19] shows that current datasets suffer some limitation in the number of objects available and in objects views variability. To avoid this limitation the presented method uses only a well-defined type of dataset. To analyze the recognition performance of the proposed method the algorithm has been tested on using the dataset present in [18]. This is composed of 16 object with views with 2 degrees of freedom: the object is rotated using a turntable with shifts of 5 degree from 0 to 180 and the camera is rotated from frontal view (0 degrees) to upper view (90 degrees) with shifts of 5 degree. So there are 37 images from 19 point of views, obtaining 703 images for each object.

In our test we used only the images from the middle (45 degrees) vertical camera position and all the horizontal camera position. The overall number of image of the extracted dataset is 592.

In [18], the same images are taken with a black background and a cluttered background. In this case the testset is composed by the cluttered images from the same or from shifted camera position. In Fig. 5 are shown images from dataset and testset.

Fig. 5. From left to right: House (0°), House (30°), Cluttered House (30°), Cluttered House (30°) and camera at 30° (15° shift than dataset)

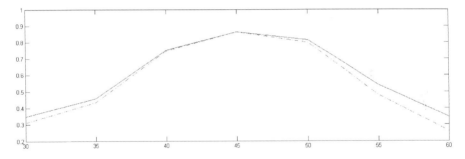

Fig. 6. Accuracy of recognition changing testsets. Solid line is recognition accuracy, dashed line is pose estimation accuracy. Best results are for testset whit the same camera angle of the original dataset. Accuracy decreases if test image are largely shifted from this angle.

4.1   Recognition and Pose Estimation Performances

The algorithm has been tested with our dataset and the reduced version of [18]. In the first case, testset is composed by query images containing objects of the dataset. Using this, the recognition performance is 80% and the pose estimation performance is 75%.

In the second case, testset is composed by cluttered images taken from vertical camera position in range [30 60], so having a displacement of 15 degrees from the fixed dataset point of view of 45 degrees. Recognition and pose estimation accuracy for central point of view is both 86%. Fig. 6 shows how performances change when the camera position of test image change respect to the original dataset position.

The same experiment was repeated with the same testset but with a random resize of the images with a proportion from 0.2 to 1. In Fig. 7 there is the plot of the results in this case. Accuracy is uniformly lower than in the first case (73% for recognition and 72% for pose estimation) but the trend of results is very similar.

Modeling the [18] dataset, the original (592) number of images for the recognition is reduced to 217 images, with an average value of 13,5 images for object. So, the recognition task is performed with only the 36% of the total comparison. The pose estimation step adds 37 match, so the total reduction of the complete elaboration is to 43%. Table 1 and 2 report the performance for the used datasets.

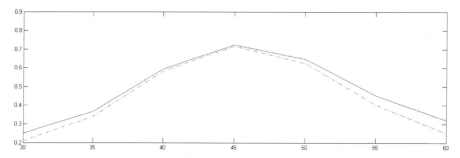

Fig. 7. Accuracy for randomly resized images of testset

Table 1. Performances of the proposed method

dataset	Recognition accuracy	Pose estimation accuracy
Our dataset	80%	75%
[18]	86%	86%
[18] random resize	73%	72%

Table 2. Comparison reduction of the proposed method

dataset	Images/model	reduction
Our Dataset	5,1	27%
[18]	13,5	37%

4.2   Limits of Recognition

Recognition by SIFT descriptors works reliably if object actually have recognizable features like texture, corners or writings. Results reported for the dataset [18] are calculated using the entire dataset, but not all the objects are really suited for recognition with proposed method.

As shown in Fig. 8 accuracy of recognition for each object is very close to one if it has shape characteristics recognizable by SIFT keypoints. Only a few objects show poor accuracy and actually they have not sufficient visual features to be recognized using SIFT. Removing these objects from the dataset the proposed recognition method performance increases. For example, using [18] testset without the two objects shown in Fig.8, recognition accuracy increases to 96% for the same camera point of view of dataset.

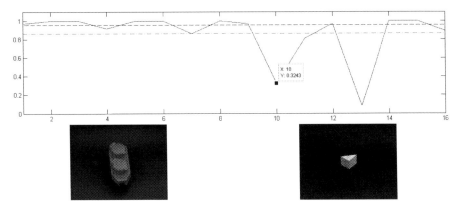

Fig. 8. Performance results versus object id number. Accuracy is low only with two objects (id 10 and 13, shown from left to right under the chart). Straights lines show average accuracy without (the higher) and with (the lower) these objects.

5   Conclusions and Future Works

We have presented an object recognition technique based on object modeling using local features. For this task, we used a multiview dataset of objects. The method performs modeling selecting only a subset of the views, creating in this way a compact representation. View selection is done by analyzing views similarity for each object by comparing SIFT descriptors.

Recognition is done by comparing a query image to the extracted models, reducing the number of comparisons with respect to the full dataset. Only pose estimation step needs to be performed using all views of the object.

Our method shows good performance in terms of accuracy for both object recognition and pose estimation. The construction of the model of objects with different shape and appearance was performed using the SIFT descriptors which extract informations only when the objects show texture surfaces, contours, edges, local maxima and minima of intensity. The worst results in term of precision for object recognition correspond to those objects that do not show regions with texture. As consequence, these objects include a few SIFT points and then it is not possible to construct a valid model for the object. In future work it would be appropriate to use descriptors of features that are present in objects that do not show texture (e.g. color descriptors, histogram, etc.) in the construction of the object model. The approach used in this paper may be easily extended to the recognition and modeling of objects in video or by using datasets with multiple degrees of freedom. Furthermore, it would be interesting to extend our work to a setting with different local keypoint descriptors such as ASIFT, MSER, Harris Affine, Hessian Affine and SURF, described in [20] [21]. A performance evaluation of different local descriptors could give important informations, in order, to know which of them works better. These possible extensions are currently under development in our lab.

Acknowledgement. This paper has been partially supported under the research program P.O.N. RICERCA E COMPETITIVITA' 2007-2013, project title SINTESYS - Security INTElligence SYStem, project code PON 01_01687.

References

1. Lowe, D.G.: Distinctive Image Features from Scale-Invariant Keypoints. International Journal of Computer Vision 60(2), 91–110 (2004)
2. Mundy, J., Zisserman, A.: Geometric invariance in computer vision. MIT Press, Cambridge (1992)
3. Mundy, J.L.: Object recognition in the geometric era: A retrospective. In: Ponce, J., Hebert, M., Schmid, C., Zisserman, A. (eds.) Toward Category-Level Object Recognition. LNCS, vol. 4170, pp. 3–28. Springer, Heidelberg (2006)
4. Turk, M., Pentland, A.: Eigenfaces for recognition. Journal of Cognitive Neuroscience 3, 71–86 (1991)
5. Sivic, J., Zisserman, A.: Video Google: a text retrieval approach to object matching in videos. In: Proceedings of IEEE International Conference on Computer Vision, pp. 1470–1477 (2003)
6. Nister, D., Stewenius, H.: Scalable recognition with a vocabulary tree. In: Proceedings of IEEE Conference on Computer Vision and Pattern Recognition, pp. 2161–2168 (2006)
7. Zhao, L.W., Luo, S.W., Liao, L.Z.: 3D object recognition and pose estimation using kernel pca. In: Proceedings of the Third International Conference on Machine Learning and Cybernetics, Shanghai, China, pp. 3258–3262 (2004)
8. Wang, X.Z., Zang, S.F., Li, J., et al.: View-based 3d object recognition using wavelet multi-scale singular value decomposition and support vector machine. In: Proceedings of the International Conference on Wavelet Analysis and Pattern Recognition, Beijing, pp. 1428–1432 (2007)
9. Pontil, M., Verri, A.: Support vector machines for 3D object recognition. IEEE Transactions on Pattern Analysis and Machine Intelligence 20(6), 637–646 (1998)
10. Murase, H., Nayar, S.K.: Visual learning and recognition of 3-D objects from appearance. International Journal of Computer Vision 14(1), 5–24 (1995)
11. Lowe, D.G.: Object recognition from local scale-invariant features. In: The Proceedings of the Seventh IEEE International Conference on Computer Vision, vol. (2), pp. 1150–1157 (1999)
12. Wu, Y.J., Wang, X.M., Shang, F.H.: Study on 3D Object Recognition Based on KPCA-SVM. In: International Conference on Information and Intelligent Computing IPCSIT, vol. 18, pp. 55–60 (2011)
13. Chang, P., Krumm, J.: Object recognition with color cooccurrence histograms. In: IEEE Computer Society Conference on Computer Vision and Pattern Recognition (1999)
14. Kouskouridas, R., Gasteratos, A.: Establishing low dimensional manifolds for 3D object pose estimation. In: IEEE International Conference on Imaging Systems and Techniques (IST), pp. 425–430 (2012)

15. Viksten, F., Forssén, P.-E., Johansson, B., Moe, A.: Comparison of local image descriptors for full 6 degree-of-freedom pose estimation. In: IEEE International Conference on Robotics and Automation, ICRA 2009, pp. 2779–2786 (2009)
16. Torki, M., Elgammal: A Regression from local features for viewpoint and pose estimation. In: IEEE International Conference on Computer Vision (ICCV), pp. 2603–2610 (2011)
17. El-Gaaly, T., Torki, M.: RGBD object pose recognition using local-global multi-kernel regression. In: IEEE 21st International Conference on Pattern Recognition, pp. 2468–2471 (2012)
18. http://www.isy.liu.se/cvl/research/objrec/posedb/datasets.html
19. Ponce, J., Berg, T.L., Everingham, M., Forsyth, D.A., Hebert, M., Lazebnik, S., Marszalek, M., Schmid, C., Russell, B.C., Torralba, A., et al.: Dataset issues in object recognition. Toward Category-Level Object Recognition, 29–48 (2006)
20. Morel, J.-M., Yu, G.: ASIFT: A new framework for fully affine invariant image comparison. SIAM Journal on Imaging Sciences 2(2), 438–469 (2009)
21. Bay, H., Ess, A., Tuytelaars, T., Van Gool, L.: Speeded-up robust features (SURF). Computer Vision and Image Understanding 110(3), 346–359 (2008)

Painting Scene Recognition
Using Homogenous Shapes

Razvan George Condorovici*, Corneliu Florea, and Constantin Vertan

The Image Processing and Analysis Laboratory, LAPI
University "Politehnica" of Bucharest,
Bucharest, Romania
rcondorovici@alpha.imag.pub.ro,
{corneliu.florea,constantin.vertan}@upb.ro

Abstract. This paper addresses the problem of semantic analysis of paintings by automatic detection of the represented scene type. The solution comes as an incipient effort to fill the gap already stated in the literature between the low level computational analysis and the high level semantic dependent human analysis of paintings. Inspired by the way humans perceive art, we first decompose the image in homogenous regions, follow by a step of region merging, in order to obtain a painting description by the extraction of perceptual features of the dominant objects within the scene. These features are used in a classification process that discriminates among 5 possible scene types on a database of 500 paintings.

Keywords: scene analysis, scene classification, perceptual segmentation, paintings.

1 Introduction

Since ancient times there was a close connection between human kind evolution and the form of art it produced. With the entering into the digital era and fostered by the growth of computer usage in daily life, there can be seen considerable efforts of creating automatic systems for facilitating a better understanding of art. As noted in the reviews of Stork et al. [18] and Cornelis et al. [4] such topics cover a very wide range, from systems used for high quality and accuracy digitization of paintings to image analysis and diagnostics or virtual restoration, color rejuvenation, pigment analysis, brush stroke analysis, lightning incidence, craquelure analysis or painting authentication and classification.

In most of the cases, adapting classical image processing techniques for art understanding offered good results, proving that computers are indeed able to help humans, experts or amateurs, to better comprehend art. However, art is fundamentally about humans and the way humans see and feel art is a major component in this understanding process. Following psycho-visually experiments,

* This work was supported by the Romanian Sectoral Operational Programme Human Resources Development 2007-2013 through the European Social Fund Financial Agreements POSDRU/107/1.5/S/76903.

J. Blanc-Talon et al. (Eds.): ACIVS 2013, LNCS 8192, pp. 262–273, 2013.

Ramachandran [15] concluded that the key for understanding the art perception are the human perceptual processes, rather than the analysis of the aesthetic properties, noting that *"the painter does not paint with his eyes, but with his brain"*. Subsequently, many works integrated the human perception principles and often concluded that a semantical interpretation of the painting is highly needed [8], [10], [16], [19]. The here proposed method follows the same line.

Regarding the analysis level, Wallraven et al. [19] observed that there are three possibilities: a low level of pictorial information (consisting in technique, thickness of brush strokes, type of painting material, color composition), a middle level about the information content (specific objects, type of painting or subject) and a high-level information containing background data (historical events or artist and period in general). While the first and third level are generally reserved for art experts, the mid-level content information is the most accessible for non-expert art viewers. By contrast, most of the computer aided painting analysis solutions known in the literature focus on the low-level features, as they are more suitable to be modelled with classical image processing techniques and the works focusing on mid-level features are rather scarce.

In this category we note the efforts in creating a system for mid-level painting analysis by Carneiro et al. [2]. They propose a solution for detecting the painting theme from a set of 27 types and for identifying human bodies in a database containing 988 grayscale images of paintings by exploring the accuracy of different state of the art inductive and transductive photographic image annotation methods. Yet, following [15], paintings are more perceptually constructed, when compared with natural photographs, which are more chaotic, thus motivating a perceptual approach on the scene analysis topic. Our current work is situated in the same mid-level, as it focuses on detecting the painting subject from five possible categories (portrait, nude, landscape, cityscape and still life) relying on a perceptual approach.

While we note the lack of relevant state of the art in painting scene analysis, nevertheless we stress that the literature holds many attempts of detecting the scene type in general photographic images. Lazebnik et al. [13] proposed a pyramidal decomposition of the scene in sub-regions described through histograms of local features. Oliva et al. [14] developed a spatial envelope model of perceptual features, constructing the now state of the art GIST feature image description for a detection rate of $\approx 90\%$ when classifying natural images from 4 classes. More recently, an unsupervised classification of 13 types of natural scenes, based on an hierarchical Bayesian model using codebooks, was proposed by Fei-Fei and Perona [9], reporting a detection rate of 76%. We note that, as a general direction, the query image is described by features that are salient with respect to a multi-resolution pyramidal, global decomposition, which, again, is different from the way humans perceive things.

The overview of the proposed painting scene detection algorithm is presented in section 2. The database and the classification method are discussed in section 3, while experiments and results, as well as a comparison with state of the art are presented in section 4. Finally, the last section is dedicated to conclusions.

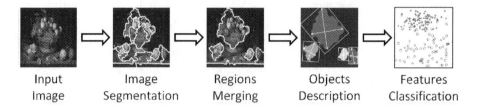

| Input | Image | Regions | Objects | Features |
| Image | Segmentation | Merging | Description | Classification |

Fig. 1. Algorithm's overview

2   Algorithm Description

The proposed solution is based on the Gestalt [20] visual perception principles. The Gestalt (shape) theory states that the human eye perceives objects in their entirety before detecting their individual parts. In other words, when watching a scene, or a painting, as in this paper, the component objects are immediately identified and have a greater meaning than point-level details such as paint, canvas, brush stroke or subregion of the objects. In order to model this behavior, our solution starts with a segmentation process that will offer the basic parts of the images. These components will be further grouped according to Gestalt principles in more meaningful regions, called *objects*. Further on, the objects are described by a set of perceptual features that will be used in detecting the scene type. The algorithm's overview can be seen in Figure 1.

2.1   Image Segmentation

In order to obtain the basic components of a scene, a segmentation process is performed on the input image. Considering the fact that we aim to mimic the Gestalt perception principles, the segmentation algorithm used is Normalized Cuts [17] as it was developed based on the Gestalt theory.

The segmentation solutions in the graph cut category are seen as a graph partitioning problem, where each pixel is a node of the graph that is interconnected with spatially neighboring pixels and the weight of the link (and respectively the cut cost) is given by a similarity measure of pixels intensities and by the quantity of edges in between. The normalized cut criterion considers the total dissimilarity between different groups normalized by the similarity within the group in what one may perceive as an adaptation of the Fisher discriminant. In our solution, we have used a derivation of the original Normalized Cut. This segmentation, proposed by Cour et al [5], optimizes the initial method by considering a multiscale spectral approach that exploits the isolation of the segmentation cues used to detect coherent regions within faint boundaries. The algorithm segments the input image in a given number of clusters that will be discussed later.

2.2   Perceptual Regions Merging

Considering the fact that the Normalized Cuts segmentation is based on Gestalt perception principles, the segmentation output should be consistent with the way

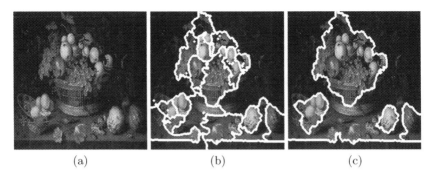

(a)   (b)   (c)

Fig. 2. Example of object detections (*a*) Original input image. (*b*) Segmented image (*c*) Image segmentation after regions merging.

the human eye perceives the scene. However, our experiments showed that this is not always true, especially due to the over-segmentation phenomenon caused by the usage of a higher number of classes compared to the number of objects in the scene. In order to overpass this issue we have introduced an intermediary step that merge adjacent regions according to the Gestalt principles. The merging algorithm is:

- **Repeat:**
  1. Compute the Region Adjacency Graph. This graph will denote all pairs of adjacent regions;
  2. For each pair of neighboring regions compute the compatibility features, that will be described later;
  3. Compute the compatibility matrix by evaluating whether two regions should be merged. As discussed further, four scores are computed and the merging decision is taken by a Naive Bayes classifier;
  4. Merge all regions marked as belonging to the same object;
- **Until** no regions were merged in step 4 or the maximum iteration number was achieved

The Gestalt theory states several principles that are followed by the human brain when it perceives different regions as belonging to the same object [20]:

- *Similarity*: Regions that share visual characteristics like shape, size, color, texture will be seen as belonging to the same object;
- *Proximity*: Objects or shapes that are close to one another appear to form groups;
- *Closure*: The effect of suggesting a visual continuity between sets of elements which do not actually touch each other or the phenomenon of seeing complete figures even when part of the information is missing;
- *Continuity*: The effect of continuing shapes beyond their ending points, to meet up with other shapes or the edge of the picture plane.

In order to mimic the behavior of the human brain we have developed a set of compatibility features that models the Gestalt principles in order to assess whether two adjacent regions should be merged.

The *similarity* between two regions was modelled through the difference of the mean color of the two regions.

The *closure* aspect of the Gestalt theory was modelled through a measure derived from the spatial segmentation component of the JSEG segmentation algorithm [7]. Considering a region R_1, the sum of distances from each of the region's points to the weighting center of mass is computed and denoted by J_{R1}. Having two regions, R_1 and R_2, the JSEG measure is computed for both regions, as well as for the merged region $R_1 \cup R_2$. The final closure measure, μ_{close}, is computed as:

$$\mu_{close} = \frac{J_{R1} + J_{R2}}{J_{R1 \cup R2}} \tag{1}$$

The *continuity* property is far more complex and difficult to model, as also observed by Zlatoff et al. [22] as it involves more high level concepts such as direction or shape. Thus, at this stage we have chosen to model only one aspect of the continuity principle by computing the percentage of common border between two adjacent regions. This way, if for example a region is encapsulated by a larger one, the percentage will be maximum, indicating that most likely the human eye will tend to group those two regions.

With regards to *proximity*, this principle is automatically taken into consideration through the fact that two regions are considered for merging only if they share a border.

Having computed the compatibility features, the next step is *to decide* whether two adjacent regions should be merged into the same object. For this step we have used a Naive Bayes classifier, for the ease of bias prior classes probability. This bias was needed because the usage of equiprobable classes lead to an over-merging phenomenon. For example, in the simple case of three regions, R_1, R_2 and R_3, let's say that R_1 and R_2, as well as R_2 and R_3 were marked as belonging to the same objects, but R_1 and R_3 were marked as belonging to different objects. Due to the transitive property of the merging operation, the R_1 and R_3 regions are falsely merged into the same object. In order to avoid this, it was preferred to decide that two regions should be merged only if the decision was very clear. This was achieved by giving a much higher prior probability to the decision of not merging. The classifier was trained using more than 2000 positive and negative examples of merging and offered a detection rate of 72% on the training set.

An example of segmented image after the regions merging process can be see in Figure 2 c).

2.3   Objects Description

The next step of the proposed solution is the description of the identified objects. Usually the segmented image, obtained according to the merging process, consists in an object corresponding to the background of the scene and one or more

Table 1. Features that describe an object description

Feature	Shape	Area	Perimeter	Color	Location
Size	8	1	1	3	9

foreground objects. Due to the composition rules that are in general followed in paintings, the position and the general shape of the objects are consistent for a certain scene type. For example, in case of a portrait, usually there are maximal two foreground objects corresponding to the subject or to the subject's face and body, and a darker background object around them.

Considering this, a set of features is proposed to describe the objects composing the scene: object area, object perimeter, object shape, object mean color and object location. The area, perimeter and the mean color are self explanatory. The shape of the object is described using a 8 bins histogram of orientations computed on the object edge (the classical HoG [6], but restricted only to the outer object edges).

With regards to the *location* of the object, the most obvious choice would be the usage of the coordinates of the weighting center of mass. However, given that one of the most basic rules of composition is the "rule of thirds", we set a location descriptor based on this rule. The painting was divided in a 3 × 3 grid and for each of the resulting 9 rectangles the percentage of space occupied by the current object was taken as feature. The vector of 9 sub-unitary values is taken as the final feature indicating the object position in the image.

One of the challenges encountered was the fact that the *number of final objects* presented in the final image could vary in a quite large interval. We preferred to overcome this problem by considering a fixed number (N) of objects for all scenes. In this case, if the scene contains less objects than the chosen number, the features vector will be filled with zeros. Otherwise, only the first N objects will be considered.

This leads to another issue regarding the way the objects are *ranked*. This aspect is very important not only when it comes to choosing the first N objects to be described, but also because the same type of object from multiple paintings should have the same rank in the classification process. For example, if in a landscape painting the first object is the sky and the second one corresponds to the ground, the same order should be applied for all the other landscape paintings containing two objects. As will be shown in section 4, the best results were obtained when the objects were ranked by their *size*.

The complete set of variables in a feature vector describing an image is presented in table 1.

Table 2. Average Detection Rate (ADR) for various segmentation algorithms: Normalize Cuts – NormCut, K-Means , Mean Shift, Graph Cuts

Method	NormCut	K-Means	MeanShift	GraphCut
ADR[%]	67.4	63.0	55.9	62.3

3   Database and Recognition Scheme

The vector of features describing the resulted N objects within a painting is presented to a classifier in order to determine the scene type. For the classification process we have used a 10-fold validation scheme over a database containing 500 paintings out of 5 scene types: portrait, nude, landscape, cityscape, still life. When choosing the scene types we wanted to test the most encountered scene types in the art history and to ensure as well that both very different classes (like portrait and landscape) and very similar classes (like landscape and cityscape) are present. The images were taken from the Yorck Project Database [21] and the scene type was manually marked for establishing the ground truth.

The classifier was chosen by experiment and it turned out that a bagged ensemble of 25 decision trees proved to offer the best performance.

The criterion used for measuring performance is the average correct detection rate (ADR).

4   Results

4.1   Algorithm's Parameters

In order to study the performance of our solution, we have investigated the influence of various parameters or algorithmic blocks onto the overall performance.

Segmentation Method. For the first stage of the solution we have also considered the usage of other widely used segmentation algorithms, but the non-perceptual solutions offered lower detection rates. The tested alternative segmentation solutions were K-Means, Mean Shift [3] and standard Graph Cuts [1], [12], leading to the detection rates presented in table 2.

Although the performance of the others methods were not very far behind, the chosen segmentation method (Normalized Cuts) offered the best results.

Number of Clusters. For the Normalized Cuts segmentation method we tested the usage of various initial numbers of clusters; the resulting average detection rates are showed in table 3. While a very small number of classes do produce enough separation and too many classes lead to over-segmentation, the best results are achieved with a medium number of classes. Because of the similarity in the average detection rates obtained for $N = 20$ and $N = 30$ segmentation clusters and taking into account the higher computation time necessary for $N = 30$ classes, we decided to continue the experiments using a $N = 20$ class segmentation.

Color Space. We have also considered several color spaces (RGB, HSV, HMMD, Lab) for the segmentation process and for objects description. The achieved results are presented in table 4. We note that although the results are similar, perceptual color spaces provide more accurate results, which confirms Ramachandran [15] hypothesis.

Table 3. Variation of overall Average Detection Rate (ADR) with respect to the initial number of clusters considered in the Normalized Cut algorithm

No of clusters	10	20	30	40
ADR[%]	64.6	67.4	67.4	64.7

Table 4. Average Detection Rate (ADR) achieved when considered various colorspaces

Color space	RGB	HSV	HMMD	Lab
ADR[%]	61.9	58.0	64.7	67.4

Region Merging. As stated in chapter 2, for the merging stage of the algorithm, when deciding whether two regions should be merged or not, it is very important to control the prior probability of the two decisions. Therefore, a series of tests were performed in order to determine the best prior probabilities for the Bayes Classifier that establish whether two regions are merged. The tests showed that the detection rate varied from a minimum of 54.8% for equal prior probabilities to a maximum of 67.4% when the decision to keep the two regions apart had a probability of 0.8.

Features. In order to assess the performance of our set of features models the Gestalt principles, we have implemented the set of features proposed by Zlatoff et al. [22], obtaining an average detection rate of 59.4%.

Furthermore, in order to assess the contribution of each group of features to the overall score, we independently removed each group from the object description and re-performed the classification. The results are presented in table 5. As the individual contribution of each set is small, we may conclude that features complement each other.

Object Selection. As previously described, once the main objects of the scene are detected, it is of great importance to find a consistent way of sorting them so that during the classification process corresponding objects from different scenes are situated at the same positions in features vector. In other words, for example in the case of a portrait, it is very important for the subject to be, the first object in the scene and the background the second. In order to achieve this order, we have tested several ordering criteria based on the features describing the objects; the results are presented in table 6. Although the sorting by size offered good results, we consider that this aspect might be a bottleneck in our solution, because often objects with similar sizes are detected in the scene and miss-sorting them might introduce classification errors. We suggest here that some graph matching algorithms might offer better results.

Number of Objects. Another aspect related to the objects description that had to be assessed was the optimal number of objects to be kept in the final feature vector. Our tests showed that keeping the largest two objects from the scene offer good results, as can be seen in Table 7. These findings are consistent with

Table 5. Contribution of each feature to the overall detection rate

Feature group	Shape	Area	Perimeter	Color	Location
Contribution[%]	1.2	1.2	0.4	10.0	7.0

Table 6. Average Detection Rate (ADR) achieved when different criteria was chosen for selecting the representative object

Sorting Criteria	Size	Intensity	Hue	Location
ADR[%]	67.4	55.4	46.9	55.4

Table 7. Average Detection Rate (ADR) when different number of objects were considered

No. Objects	1	2	3	4	5
ADR[%]	66.8	67.4	66.4	65.6	62.6

Table 8. Average Detection Rate (ADR) for tested classifiers (Logistic Regression – LR, Multilayer Perceptron – MLP, Sequential minimal optimization – SMO, Bagged ensemble of tress – Ba, LogitBoost – LB, Naive Bayes – NB, Random Forrest – RF). Details regarding the implementation of the classifiers are to be found in [11] and references therein.

Classifiers	LR	MLP	SMO	Ba	LB	DT	RF
ADR [%]	60	61.8	62.2	67.4	60.4	54	59.8

the human perception mechanism because usually the two biggest objects from a scene are a clear cue for the scene type.

Classifier Choice. For the last stage of the proposed solution, several classifiers implemented in the open-source machine learning library Weka [11] and presented in Table 8 were considered. The fact that all tested classifiers had very similar performance leads us to believe that the features space is consistent and that the results would remain in the same range no matter what classifier will be used.

4.2   Scene Detection Accuracy and Comparison with Prior Art

Having set the parameters values, we have performed another set of tests in order to assess the overall performance of the proposed solution.

In order to compare our work with state of the art, we have described the same database using the GIST image descriptor [14] alone. Basically, GIST provides a global description of the scene, while our method follows Gestalt principle that states objects are more important for scene understanding. As can be shown in

Table 9. Comparison with state of the art: average detection rate for the proposed algorithm and GIST solution

Proposed Solution	67.4 %
GIST [14]	61.4 %

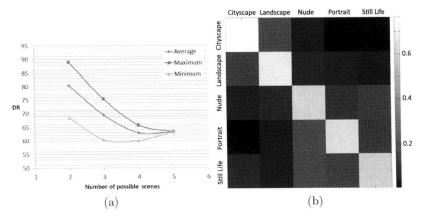

Fig. 3. (a) Detection rates for various number of classes; (b) Confusion Matrix

table 9 our algorithm outperforms the GIST solution for paintings scene classification. However, we consider that such a result is reasonable to expect only for painting analysis where human perception prevails to the nature randomness.

In order to assess how our solution performs for various number of possible scene types all possible combinations of the five scene types were tested. In Figure 3 a) the average, the lowest and the highest detection rates are presented for each possible number of classes. As expected, the overall detection rate decreases with the increase of possible scene types, but the results remain acceptable for all scene types.

Figure 3(b) shows the confusion matrix for the five scene types, where it can be seen that the lowest detection rate is obtained for the nude scenes that are sometimes confused with still life or portraits. Also, as it was expected, a slightly higher confusion occurs between cityscape and landscapes.

Figure 4 shows some examples of misclassified scenes. While for the cityscape and landscape examples a wrong classification might be expectable, for the nude example the justification might be not very visible at a first glance. However, this example of nude painting is not exactly a classical nude painting, compositionally speaking. Usually the nude paintings contained a skin-colored object in the middle of the paint, surrounded by a background. For the portrait painting the error's cause is much clear, the man's clothes having a color very similar to the skin's color.

Fig. 4. (a) Examples of misclassified scenes. (a.1) cityscape painting classified as landscape (a.2) landscape classified as cityscape (a.3) nude classified as cityscape (a.4) portrait classified as nude. (b) Examples of correctly classified paintings: (b.1) cityscape (b.2) landscape (b.3) nude (b.4) portrait

5   Conclusions and Continuation

In this paper we have proposed a method for the automatic recognition of the scene type in digitized paintings. As art is dedicated to humans, we inspired our method from the Gestalt perception theory, stressing that objects are more important in scene identification than the overall description. We successfully validated the robustness of our method on a 5-scene, 500 images database.

As continuation paths, we need to investigate more thoroughly criteria for selecting the most representative object from a scene and to extend the testing, by increasing both the database and the number of considered scenes.

References

1. Boykov, Y., Kolmogorov, V.: An experimental comparison of min-cut/max-flow algorithms for energy minimization in vision. IEEE Transactions on PAMI 26(9), 1124–1137 (2004)
2. Carneiro, G., da Silva, N.P., Del Bue, A., Costeira, J.P.: Artistic image classification: An analysis on the PRINTART database. In: Fitzgibbon, A., Lazebnik, S., Perona, P., Sato, Y., Schmid, C. (eds.) ECCV 2012, Part IV. LNCS, vol. 7575, pp. 143–157. Springer, Heidelberg (2012)
3. Comaniciu, D., Meer, P.: Mean shift: A robust approach toward feature space analysis. IEEE Trans. on PAMI 24(5), 603–619 (2002)
4. Cornelis, B., Dooms, A., Cornelis, J., Leen, F., Schelkens, P.: Digital painting analysis, at the cross section of engineering, mathematics and culture. In: Proc. of EUSIPCO, pp. 1254–1259 (2011)

5. Cour, T., Benezit, F., Shi, J.: Spectral segmentation with multiscale graph decomposition. In: Proc. of CVPR, vol. 2, pp. 1124–1131 (2005)
6. Dalal, N., Triggs, B.: Histograms of oriented gradients for human detection. In: Proc. of CVPR, pp. 886–893 (2005)
7. Deng, Y., Manjunath, B.S.: Unsupervised segmentation of color-texture regions in images and video. IEEE Trans. on PAMI 23, 800–810 (2001)
8. Durand, F.: An invitation to discuss computer depiction. In: Proc. International Symposium on Non-Photorealistic Animation and Rendering, NPAR. pp. 111–124. ACM (2002)
9. Fei-Fei, L., Perona, P.: A bayesian hierarchical model for learning natural scene categories. In: Proc. of CVPR, vol. 2, pp. 524–531 (2005)
10. Graham, D., Redies, C.: Statistical regularities in art: Relations with visual coding and perception. Vision Research 50(16), 1503–1509 (2010)
11. Hall, M., Frank, E., Holmes, G., Pfahringer, B., Reutemann, P., Witten, I.H.: The weka data mining software: an update. ACM SIGKDD Explorations Newsletter 11(1), 10–18 (2009)
12. Kolmogorov, V., Zabih, R.: What energy functions can be minimized via graph cuts? IEEE Trans. on PAMI 26(2), 147–159 (2004)
13. Lazebnik, S., Schmid, C., Ponce, J.: Beyond bags of features: Spatial pyramid matching for recognizing natural scene categories. In: Proc. of CVPR, vol. 2, pp. 2169–2178 (2006)
14. Oliva, A., Torralba, A.: Modeling the shape of the scene: A holistic representation of the spatial envelope. IJCV 42(3), 145–175 (2001)
15. Ramachandran, V.S., Herstein, W.: The science of art: A neurological theory of aesthetic experience. Journal of Consciousness Studies 6, 15–51 (1999)
16. Shamir, L., Macura, T., Orlov, N., Eckley, D.M., Goldberg, I.G.: Impressionism, expressionism, surrealism: Automated recognition of painters and schools of art. ACM Transactions on Applied Perception 7(2), 1–17 (2010)
17. Shi, J., Malik, J.: Normalized cuts and image segmentation. IEEE Trans. on PAMI 22(8), 888–905 (2000)
18. Stork, D.: Computer vision and computer graphics analysis of paintings and drawings: An introduction to the literature. In: Proc. of CAIP, pp. 9–24 (2009)
19. Wallraven, C., Fleming, R.W., Cunningham, D.W., Rigau, J., Feixas, M., Sbert, M.: Categorizing art: Comparing humans and computers. Computers & Graphics 33(4), 484–495 (2009)
20. Wertheimer, M.: Principles of perceptual organization. Readings in Perception, 115–135 (1958)
21. Yorck, P.: The yorck project (December 2012) http://commons.wikimedia.org/wiki/Category:PD-Art_(Yorck_Project)
22. Zlatoff, N., Tellez, B., Baskurt, A.: Image understanding and scene models: a generic framework integrating domain knowledge and gestalt theory. In: Proc. of ICIP, vol. 4, pp. 2355–2358 (2004)

A Novel Graph Based Clustering Technique for Hybrid Segmentation of Multi-spectral Remotely Sensed Images

Biplab Banerjee[1], Pradeep Kumar Mishra[2], Surender Varma[1],
and Buddhiraju Krishna Mohan[1]

[1] Satellite Image Processing Lab, CSRE, IITBombay
[2] Vision and Image Processing Lab, EE, IIT Bombay
{biplab.banerjee,gsvarma,bkmohan}@iitb.ac.in,
pkmishraiitb@ee.iitb.ac.in

Abstract. This paper proposes a novel unsupervised graph based clustering method for the purpose of hybrid segmentation of multi-spectral satellite images. In hybrid image segmentation framework, the source image is initially (over)segmented while preserving the fine image details. A region merging strategy has to be adopted next for further refinement. Here mean-shift (MS) based technique has been considered for initially segmenting the source image as it performs edge preserving smoothing beforehand hence eliminates noise. The objects found after this step are merged together in a low-level image feature space using the proposed graph based clustering algorithm. A graph topology combining k-nearest-neighbor (KNN) and minimum spanning tree has been considered on which the proposed iterative algorithm has been applied to eliminate the edges which span different clusters. It results in a set of connected components where each component represents a separate cluster. Comparison with two other hybrid segmentation techniques establishes the comparable accuracies of the proposed framework.

Keywords: Image Segmentation, Graph Based Clustering, Mean-Shift, Hybrid Segmentation.

1 Introduction

Image segmentation refers to the process of partitioning a given image into its constituent objects in such a manner that pixels belonging to a given region are **similar** with respect to a set of low level image features like color, texture, shape etc. This is usually achieved by defining a measure of similarity followed by a grouping of the image elements (pixels) based on the defined criterion. The problem of image segmentation is domain specific and unfortunately there is no single segmentation technique available till now which works well with different kinds of images. A detailed discussion on different segmentation techniques can be obtained in [9] [4] [6].

J. Blanc-Talon et al. (Eds.): ACIVS 2013, LNCS 8192, pp. 274–285, 2013.

The processing and analysis of satellite images have gained much popularity as these images, being an increasing important information source, are playing one of the leading roles in diverse fields like environment monitoring, resource management, urban planning, traffic analysis etc. Segmentation of remotely sensed satellite images has been assumed to be a difficult task due to variations in the image spatial and spectral resolution, lack of prior knowledge regarding the land-cover classes etc. Different approaches for satellite image segmentation can be obtained in [8]. Clustering based methods are particularly suitable in such a scenario due to their inherent unsupervised nature. [11] has proposed a symmetry based cluster validity index for unsupervised segmentation of satellite images. The index has been optimized by a genetic algorithm based clustering and the proposed technique is able to detect clusters of any shape and size as long as they are internally symmetrical. A hybrid method incorporating rough set based knowledge extraction, expectation maximization algorithm and spanning tree clustering for multi-spectral image segmentation has been proposed in [10]. [1] has combined mean-shift clustering with morphological operations for multi-spectral remotely sensed image segmentation. The spectral and spatial bandwidth parameters of mean shift are adaptively determined by exploiting differential morphological profile.

The main aim of hybrid segmentation techniques is to offer an improved solution to the segmentation problem by integrating a set of component methods. Object based image segmentation is a special case of hybrid techniques where an initially over-segmented version of the original image is generated by some method which is then followed by a region merging to produce the final segmentation. Although clustering based methods have been adopted for such cases, they usually fails to preserve the underlying image discontinuities. Spatial segmentation methods like watershed technique etc. can be considered as an alternative, but these kind of methods unnecessarily generate a large number of quasi-homogeneous regions. [7] has proposed an object based natural image segmentation methodology using super-pixels as a grouping cue. The super-pixels are fused in a bipartite graph partitioning framework. [2] has developed a hybrid segmentation method using watershed transform followed by a modified mean-shift (MS) [3] based merging.

MS algorithm is usually applied to perform discontinuity preserving smoothing followed by image segmentation. However, it is difficult to partition a remotely sensed image into different land-covers solely based on the MS algorithm as MS is unsupervised technique where the number and shape of the data clusters are unknown *a priori* though comparatively smaller values of the bandwidth parameter used for the kernel density estimator can assure (over)segmentation in the output. Hence, MS based method is a good choice to perform the initial over-segmentation.

Typical graph based segmentation methods are difficult to apply directly to image pixels, as the storage and computational costs become huge. Hence, for hybrid segmentation algorithms, graph based clustering is the usual choice for the final region merging purpose where the nodes of the graph represent the objects extracted from the initially over-segmented image (produced by some other algorithms like MS based segmentation) which are far less in number than the pixels present in the original image. Algorithms like C-means or Fuzzy c-means are generally not encouraged to be used for this final merging because they tend to produce hyperspherical clusters and they have the inherent parametric nature.

This paper proposes a hybrid multi-spectral satellite image segmentation incorporating mean-shift and a novel graph based clustering. The image is first (over)-segmented by the well-known MS based method by proper tuning of the bandwidth parameters. After that, a set of low level image features have been obtained from each object found in the previous step. These object, in the newly defined feature space, are merged further using the proposed graph based clustering. A k nearest neighbor (KNN)- minimum spanning tree (MST) based topology has been used to construct the graph from the given data points. Euclidean distance measure has been considered as the edge weight between a pair of graph nodes. A novel clustering validity index has been proposed which iteratively selects the optimum cluster number and accordingly breaks down the graph to produce that particular number of connected components.

The paper is organized as follows. Section II details the proposed segmentation process. Mean-shift based segmentation method has been discussed in section III. Feature extraction from the objects has been mentioned here. Section IV describes the proposed graph based clustering process. Section V deals with the experimental results. The paper concludes in Section VI with possible future directions.

2   The Proposed Satellite Image Segmentation Algorithm

Figure (1) depicts the flowchart of the proposed segmentation method. Broadly it is a three steps process.

– Apply the MS based segmentation algorithm to cluster the pixels of the input satellite image in the spectral domain.
– A feature extraction step is carried out to calculate some low level features from each of the objects found in the previous state.
– Considering each region as a node in the newly defined feature space, the proposed KNN-MST graph based non-parametric clustering method is applied for final region merging.

The steps are described in detail in subsequent sections.

3   Mean-Shift Based Image Segmentation

MS based segmentation has been considered here due to its non-parametric nature. The actual segmentation step here is preceded by an edge-preserving smoothing technique which keeps all the local discontinuities. The algorithm is

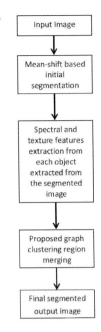

Fig. 1. Flowchart of the proposed segmentation algorithm

adaptive to the number of classes of pixels actually present and assigns each pixel to the nearest mode in the non-parametric kernel probability density plot.

Given a set of data points $\{x_1, x_2, \ldots x_n\}$, $(x_i \epsilon R^d)$ sampled from some distribution *iid* with unknown mixture densities $\{f_i\}$, the non-parametric kernel density estimator is defined as:

$$\hat{f}_h(x) = \frac{1}{n}\sum_{i=1}^{n}K_h(x - x_i) \quad = \frac{1}{nh^d}\sum_{i=1}^{n}K\left(\frac{x - x_i}{h}\right) \tag{1}$$

Here $K()$ is the kernel, which is symmetric but not necessarily a positive function, integrates to 1. $h > 0$ is called the bandwidth. The optimal value of the smoothing parameter h can be obtained by using the L2 risk criterion function. The kernel function satisfies the condition,

$$K(x) = C_{k,d}k(||x||^2) > 0 \tag{2}$$

$C_{k,d}$ is a normalization constant which assures that $K(x)$ integrates to 1. The modes of the density function are located at the zeros of the gradient function $\nabla \hat{f}_h(x) = 0$.

The gradient of the density estimator of Equation (1) is:

$$\nabla \hat{f}_h(x) = \frac{2C_{k,d}}{nh^{d+2}}\sum_{i=1}^{n}(x_i - x)g\left(||\frac{x - x_i}{h}||^2\right) \tag{3}$$

$$= \frac{2C_{k,d}}{nh^{d+2}} \left[\sum_{i=1}^{n} g(||\frac{x-x_i}{h}||^2) \right] \left[\frac{\left[\sum_{i=1}^{n} x_i g(||\frac{x-x_i}{h}||^2) \right]}{\left[\sum_{i=1}^{n} g(||\frac{x-x_i}{h}||^2) \right]} - x \right] \tag{4}$$

Here $g(x) = -k'(x)$. The first term of Equation (4) is proportional to the density estimate at x computed with kernel $G(x) = C_{g,d} g||x||^2$ and the second term

$$m_h(x) = \frac{\sum_{i=1}^{n} x_i g(||\frac{x-x_i}{h}||^2)}{\sum_{i=1}^{n} g(||\frac{x-x_i}{h}||^2)} - x \tag{5}$$

defines the mean-shift. The mean-shift vector thus points towards the direction of maximum increase in the density. The procedure is iterated by successive computation of the mean-shift vector and translation of the kernel $G(x)$ by the mean shift vector. It converges at a nearby point where the estimate has zero gradient.

Dense regions in feature space corresponds to local optima or modes. So for each data point, gradient ascent is performed on the local estimated density until convergence. The stationary points obtained via gradient ascent represent the modes of the density function. All the data items associated with the same stationary point belong to the same cluster.

The image segmentation using mean-shift can be summarized as,

- Use kernel density estimator to shift the means of pixels in the image.
- Stop when each mean sequence has converged.
- Use the converged means to delineate segments.
- Usually a pair of pixels belong to a given segment if their converged spectral and spatial components are within some given threshold.
- For segments with pixel count less than a given threshold, merge them with neighboring segments.

Now individual objects are extracted using connected component labeling technique with a neighborhood size of 8.

3.1   Feature Extraction from the Segmented Objects

The objects found after this step are further considered for feature extraction. Mean spectral value of the region and a set of statistical texture features have been considered for this purpose. Shape feature has not been considered here as a given land use class may have different size and shape at different geographical location.

Gray level co-occurrence matrix (GLCM) [5] based texture features have been considered as these kinds of features can classify images with micro-textural elements. This concept is key in classifying different land cover classes of remotely sensed satellite images. GLCM is defined as the distribution of the co-occurring values within a given offset in the image plane. It represents the distance and angular spatial relationship over an image sub-region of specific size. The GLCM used here is direction invariant. Hence the average of all four spatial arrangements depicting $0°$, $45°$, $90°$ and $135°$ has been used. A pixel offset of 1 and a quantization level of 256 have also been considered. From the co-occurrence matrix, many texture parameters [5] can be calculated. Entropy, energy, homogeneity and contrast have been selected for this case to capture the relative gray level randomness and brightness of a given region. Hence for a p- band image, the regions found after the previous step are represented in a $(p + 4)$-dimensional feature space which are further clustered using the proposed graph based clustering.

4   The Proposed Graph Based Clustering

Given a set of data points $X = \{x_i\}_{i=1}^n$, $x_i \in R^d$ (here $d = p + 4$), a graph $G(V, E)$ is constructed where data points represent the vertex set (V) of G and E defines a measure of similarity given a pair of adjoining vertices in term of their Euclidean distance. Here a KNN-MST based graph topology has been adopted which is capable of capturing the distribution of the data items in the feature space and it can be inferred easily by considering the weight of a edge whether the edge spans two different clusters or resides within a given cluster. The job now is to identify those edges which spans different clusters and remove them from the graph. It will result in a number of connected components where points belonging to a given component constitute a cluster. To achieve this goal, an iterative clustering algorithm has been proposed here where the edges are deleted recursively from the graph according to their weight measure and a proposed cluster validity measure is being evaluated. The particular instance (grouping) which optimizes the validity measure is considered to be the optimal clustering and the corresponding edges are removed from the graph accordingly.

4.1   Graph Construction

The method for constructing $G(V, E)$ given X are:

1. For each $x_i \in X$, add an edge E_{x_i, x_j} between x_i and x_j where x_j is in the first nearest neighbor of x_i. The edge is weighted $(W(x_i, x_j))$ by the Euclidean distance between x_i and x_j. E_{x_i, x_j} is then included to E.
2. Once step 1 is completed for all the points, the results will be a set of connected components.
3. For each component, find its nearest component using single linkage Euclidean distance (Equation 6).

$$w(C_{i1}, C_{i2}) = min\{W(\xi_{i1}, \xi_{i2})\}, i1 \neq i2 \tag{6}$$

Here C_{i1} and C_{i2} represent two separate connected components. ξ_{i1} and ξ_{i2} represent data points belonging to C_{i1} and C_{i2} respectively. Equation 6 essentially identifies the two closest data points of two given connected components. Hence, for a given C_{i1}, identify the particular C_{i2} for which $w(C_{i1}, Ci2)$ is the smallest. The closest pair of data points of C_{i1} and C_{i2} are now connected by an edge and the edge is included in E.

4. Step 3 is repeated until G is minimally connected.

The advantages of this graph topology are:

- The graph is minimally connected.
- The spatial distribution of the data items are completely captured with this kind of graph construction.
- Noisy data points can now be identified by checking the size of a connected component obtained after the KNN based graph construction.

4.2   Clustering G

Algorithm 1 depicts the clustering procedure.

Algorithm 1. Input: $G(V, E)$, A list $W1$ which stores the edge weights in descending order **Output:** Array L of labels of the vertices of G

1: **for** $index = 1$ to $size(W_1)$ **do**
2:     Find the sub-tree where $E_{W1(i)}$ is present and delete $E_{W1(i)}$. {Deletion of k edges from a minimally connected graph results in $k + 1$ connected components}
3:     Now for the forest obtained, calculate τ (According to Equation 7) and store the value in $\tau_{Array}(index)$. {A forest is a set of disconnected graphs}
4: **end for**
5: Find the $index$ for which τ_{Array} attains the maximum value.
6: Remove the largest $index - 1$ number of edges from G and the result will be $index$ number of clusters.

4.3   The Proposed Cluster Validity Index

τ is defined as:

$$\tau(index) = \frac{1}{\sum_{i=1}^{index} M_{C_{w_i}}} + \sum_{1 \leq i,j \leq index, i \neq j} D(S_{C_i}, S_{C_j}) + \frac{1}{\sum_{i=1}^{index} max_{C_{w_i}}} \quad (7)$$

The particular $index$ which maximizes $\tau(index)$ is considered as the optimal number of clusters. The first term of Equation (7) ensures that the summation of the edge weights of a connected component attains minimum possible value if the underlying cluster is compact and optimal (No under or over clustering involved). According to the second term, the single linkage distance between a cluster and its *most similar* cluster (1 nearest neighbor) attains the maximum possible value in the optimal scenario. The third term indicates the the maximum edge weight per connected component will be minimized at the point of optimal clustering.

5   Experimental Result

5.1   Study Areas and Experimental Setup

Three study areas have been presented here for analysis. The images considered here are primarily of the Maharashtra Area, India acquired by Indian Remote Sensing Satellite P6 Linear Imaging Self-Scanner IV (IRS P6 LISS (IV)(Figure 2(b)), QuickBird (Figure 2(c)), IRS 1B LISS II (Figure 2(a)). Spatial resolution of Figure 2(a) is $23.8m \times 23.8m$ each and for 2(b) the resolution is $5.8m \times 5.8m$. 2(c) is pan-sharpened and has a spatial resolution of $0.61m$.

GLCM calculation requires the generation of the corresponding gray level image given a multi-spectral image. Principal Component Analysis (PCA) based and uniform band averaging based methods have been explored for this purpose. The intensity image (mean of all the available bands) has been selected for texture analysis as PCA based technique has tendency to discard noise, hence, some of the texture components remain unnoticed.

For the initial MS based segmentation, a bandwidth value of 5 and a minimum allowable region size of 20 have fixed. These comparatively smaller values of these two parameters ensure over-segmentation in the output.

5.2   Validity Comparison of the Proposed MST Based Clustering

The objects extracted after the MS based segmentation undergo a feature extraction stage. The objects are further merged using the proposed graph based clustering technique. The efficiency of this clustering has been compared with some well known clustering techniques from the literature, i.e., normalized cut based graph clustering [12], adaptive mean-shift based clustering with data centric bandwidth estimation, C-means++ in term of Silhouette index. At the optimal clustering, the value of Silhouette index become maximum. Table I shows the results of the comparison based on cluster validity index. For normalized cut based clustering and C-means++, the number of clusters (N_c) has been set manually to the approximate number of classes present in the image based on expert opinion. The values mentioned here are the average of 50 realizations.

Table 1. Clustering efficiency comparison based on the mean Silhouette index (For images in Figure 2(a)-2(c))

Proposed graph based clustering	Normalized cut	Mean-shift	C-means
0.7232 ($N_{graph} = 7$)	0.6607 ($N_c = 7$)	0.6422	**0.7405** ($N_c = 7$)
0.5270 ($N_{graph} = 5$)	0.4698 ($N_c = 5$)	0.4687	**0.5325** ($N_c = 5$)
0.6429 ($N_{graph} = 9$)	**0.6196** ($N_c = 7$)	0.4821	0.6104 ($N_c = 7$)

N_{graph} denotes the number of clusters **generated** by the proposed graph based clustering. It can be observed from Table I that the proposed clustering technique performs near-optimal clustering in almost all the cases and is comparable to other popular clustering techniques. The problem with techniques like Normalized cut, C-means++ is that the approximate number of clusters needs to be supplied beforehand and even under-merging occurs with those methods. It is difficult to ascertain this information from remotely sensed satellite images a priori. The N_{graph} measures exhibit that the proposed method can detect the actual number of clusters. Problems due to cluster shape and size are well taken care of by the underlying tree structure.

5.3   Comparison of the Segmentation Results

The segmentation results of the proposed hybrid clustering based method have been compared with two recent object based clustering techniques [2] and [13]. Like [2], [13] is also a two step process where the objects extracted from the over-segmented output of the MS based clustering are merged using Normalized cut based clustering. The accuracy assessment for the segmentation technique is performed by comparing the results to the reference classified images obtained by expert annotation. Figures 2(d)-2(f) depicts the outputs of the initial mean-shift based segmentation. The results of proposed graph based region merging have been shown in Figures 2(g)-2(i). Figures 2(j)-2(l) and 2(m)-2(o) represent the results of [2] and [13] respectively.

These 3 segmentation methods have further been compared with respect to the reference manually classified image in term of overall classification accuracy. Table II shows the accuracy assessment of the proposed segmentation technique with respect to the other ones used in terms of the overall generalization accuracy.

Overall, the proposed segmentation algorithm is capable of segmenting a given satellite image into almost accurate number of land cover classes without any user intervention. Use of MS algorithm with properly tuned parameters guarantees an over-segmented image while keeping fine image details. The edge preserving smoothing property of MS based segmentation helps in removing unnecessary noise elements that may be present in the image due to improper sensing or environmental hazards. Hence, MS based clustering is a better option than the traditional watershed based segmentation in the initial stage. Now to merge these initially found objects, it is always better to adopt any pure non-parametric method due to lack of domain knowledge available for a given remotely sensed image. Non-parametric algorithms like MS are not encouraged to use for this merging stage as these algorithms are often stuck in local modes present in the feature space. The proposed graph based clustering does not suffer from such kind of problems and furthermore, the proposed separation predicate allows subdivision up to a level when the clusters under consideration and sufficiently far from each other.

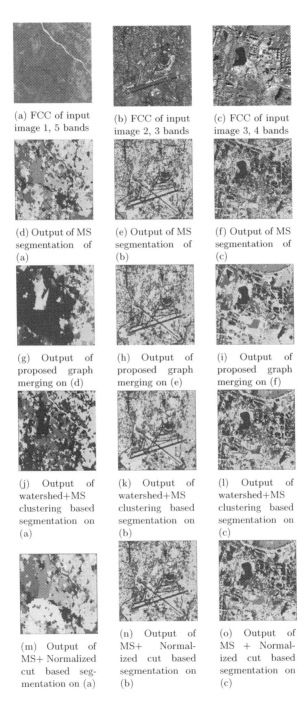

(a) FCC of input image 1, 5 bands

(b) FCC of input image 2, 3 bands

(c) FCC of input image 3, 4 bands

(d) Output of MS segmentation of (a)

(e) Output of MS segmentation of (b)

(f) Output of MS segmentation of (c)

(g) Output of proposed graph merging on (d)

(h) Output of proposed graph merging on (e)

(i) Output of proposed graph merging on (f)

(j) Output of watershed+MS clustering based segmentation on (a)

(k) Output of watershed+MS clustering based segmentation on (b)

(l) Output of watershed+MS clustering based segmentation on (c)

(m) Output of MS+ Normalized cut based segmentation on (a)

(n) Output of MS+ Normalized cut based segmentation on (b)

(o) Output of MS + Normalized cut based segmentation on (c)

Fig. 2. Comparison of segmentation outputs

Table 2. Comparison in terms of overall accuracy

Proposed method	Watershed + MS based	MS + Normalized cut based
84.71	73.68	77.24
82.69	81.11	82.33
80.41	76.29	80.70

6   Conclusion

This paper proposes a hybrid segmentation technique for multi-spectral images using mean-shift and a novel graph based clustering. Mean-shift based technique has been used for initial segmentation purpose as it preserves the underlying image discontinuities. The objects obtained here undergo a feature extraction step. These objects, in the newly defined feature space, are clustered using the proposed graph based clustering technique. The proposed graph based clustering is non-parametric and does not assume anything regarding the shape and size of the clusters. The current mode of work is to make the clustering much more robust by incorporating noisy cluster detection method with it.

References

1. Aytekin, Ö., Ulusoy, İ., Halici, U.: Segmentation of high resolution satellite imagery based on mean shift algorithm and morphological operations. In: Proc. SPIE Eur. Remote Sens., pp. 747704–747704 (2009)
2. Banerjee, B., Surender, V.G., Buddhiraju, K.M.: Satellite image segmentation: A novel adaptive mean-shift clustering based approach. In: 2012 IEEE International Geoscience and Remote Sensing Symposium (IGARSS), pp. 4319–4322 (July 2012)
3. Comaniciu, D.: An algorithm for data-driven bandwidth selection. IEEE Transactions on Pattern Analysis and Machine Intelligence 25(2), 281–288 (2003)
4. Fu, K.S., Mui, J.: A survey on image segmentation. Pattern Recognition 13(1), 3–16 (1981)
5. Haralick, R.M.: Statistical and structural approaches to texture. Proceedings of the IEEE 67(5), 786–804 (1979)
6. Haralick, R.M., Shapiro, L.G.: Image segmentation techniques. Computer Vision, Graphics, and Image Processing 29(1), 100–132 (1985)
7. Li, Z., Wu, X.M., Chang, S.F.: Segmentation using superpixels: A bipartite graph partitioning approach. In: 2012 IEEE Conference on Computer Vision and Pattern Recognition (CVPR), pp. 789–796. IEEE (2012)
8. Meinel, G., Neubert, M.: A comparison of segmentation programs for high resolution remote sensing data. International Archives of Photogrammetry and Remote Sensing 35(Pt. B), 1097–1105 (2004)
9. Pal, N.R., Pal, S.K.: A review on image segmentation techniques. Pattern Recognition 26(9), 1277–1294 (1993)

10. Pal, S.K., Mitra, P.: Multispectral image segmentation using the rough-set-initialized em algorithm. IEEE Transactions on Geoscience and Remote Sensing 40(11), 2495–2501 (2002)
11. Saha, S., Bandyopadhyay, S.: Application of a new symmetry-based cluster validity index for satellite image segmentation. IEEE Geoscience and Remote Sensing Letters 5(2), 166–170 (2008)
12. Shi, J., Malik, J.: Normalized cuts and image segmentation. IEEE Transactions on Pattern Analysis and Machine Intelligence 22(8), 888–905 (2000)
13. Tao, W., Jin, H., Zhang, Y.: Color image segmentation based on mean shift and normalized cuts. IEEE Transactions on Systems, Man, and Cybernetics, Part B: Cybernetics 37(5), 1382–1389 (2007)

Planar Segmentation by Time-of-Flight Cameras

Rudi Penne[1,4], Luc Mertens[1], and Bart Ribbens[1,2,3]

[1] Faculty of Applied Engineering, University of Antwerp, Salesianenlaan 30, B-2660 Antwerp, Belgium
[2] Laboratory of BioMedical Physics, University of Antwerp, Belgium
[3] Acoustics & Vibration Research Group, Department of Mechanical Engineering, Free University of Brussels, Belgium
[4] Department of Mathematics, University of Antwerp, Belgium
rudi.penne@uantwerpen.be

Abstract. This article presents a new feature for detecting planarity when using range images on the principle of Time of Flight (ToF). We derive homogeneous linear conditions for Time-of-Flight images of 3 or 4 points to be the projection of collinear or coplanar points respectively. The crucial part in our equations is played by the D/d-ratios of the ToF-distance $D(u, v)$ and the *internal radial distance* (IRD) $d(u, v)$ for each pixel (u, v). The knowledge of the IRD d may be a consequence of an accurate lateral calibration of the camera, but this IRD can also be directly obtained. Consequently, the proposed planarity condition holds in principle for uncalibrated camera's. The elegance, efficiency and simplicity of our coplanarity constraint is illustrated in experiments on planarity tests and the segmentation of planar regions.

1 Introduction

If cameras or other sensors are used in autonomous tasks such as navigation or manipulation, the understanding of the work space appears to be an important aspect. Man-made environments typically consist of many flat surfaces. From this point of view, it is useful to develop a reliable, simple and fast technique to decompose the sensored data into planar regions.

In the field of computer vision quite a few articles were published concerning the segmentation of planar regions. Usually, a segmentation algorithm has to cope with two questions.

1. How can we detect whether different pixels or image regions belong to the same plane in the observed scene?
2. What framework or strategy actually segments the given image by means of the chosen feature in (1).

Regarding (2), it seems that most strategies in the literature are some kind of clustering techniques ([3]). The clustering process can operate by means of merging or splitting or a combination of both as suggested by [8]. This combination, a split and merge procedure, has been succesfully applied for the segmentation

J. Blanc-Talon et al. (Eds.): ACIVS 2013, LNCS 8192, pp. 286–297, 2013.

of planar regions by [15] and [20]. The segmentation strategy might or might not be designed independently from the chosen planarity criterion. But in any case it is preferable to include a verification step that supports the evidence for the flatness of the clustered regions, often supplied by the total residue of some best fitting model (plane). Finally, a post processing is needed to take care for non-segmented pixels and fuzzy boundaries.

The decision on aspect (1) of the segmentation algorithm, i.e. the choice of the feature that recognizes planarity, depends on the nature of the used sensor. For a standard CCD camera one might use the projective invariant for five coplanar points as described by [19]. This technique however requires coping with point correspondences in stereo images or in an image sequence generated by a monocular automated guided vehicle. A refining of this method by means of planar homographies is represented by [11].

Due to the technological evolution in 3D-vision, new segmentation algorithms could be developed for range images containing depth information. In [20] the estimation of the planarity feature was done by a parameter model (least squares plane fitting). We also mention an interesting and fast plane segmentation developed by [9], using collinearity constraints for consecutive pixels. And recently, in [2] a *Gradient of Depth* feature was used to perform planar segmentation for Time of Flight cameras.

This article presents a new feature for detecting planarity when using range images on the principle of Time of Flight (ToF). Two types of ToF cameras are currently used. Both types are still growing in performance.

A first group uses a modulation wave of a near infrared light source (NIR wavelength = about 1 μm). For such systems each pixel (u, v) on the ToF-sensor is able to measure the distance D to a single world point by means of a phase shift calculation.

In contrast with phase shift measurements a second group of ToF-cameras is directly based on the time (e.g. in μs) needed for a light pulse to travel forth and back to a world point at a distance D.

For both ToF camera types the same geometrical properties hold. Every pixel delivers a measurement of a distance D (m) to the detected world point. On the other hand, independent from this 3D-measurement, we associate an *internal radial distance* d with each pixel (Figure 1), from now on denoted by IRD (Section 2). The IRD $d(u, v)$ is the distance (measured in pixel units) between the camera centre C and the sensor point with pixel coordinates (u, v). Notice that $d(u, v)$, unlike $D(u, v)$, is an intrinsic camera feature, constant for fixed camera settings, and that does not depend on the observed scene.

In Section 3 we derive simple and elegant equations for 4 coplanar points or for 3 collinear points. These are homogeneous linear equations in the d/D-ratios of the involved image points, from now on briefly called the d/D-test. The coefficients are computed by the **uncalibrated** images of the points. These coplanarity and collinearity constraints appear to be very appropriate as feature in a planar segmentation algorithm for ToF cameras. We list some arguments in favour of this d/D-test:

- The d/D-test is simple and elegant, both computationally as conceptually, especially for 4 pixels that form a rectangle or for 3 equidistant pixels (Section 3).
- The d/D-test is a constraint that can serve as a coplanarity test for 4 clustered pixels, but also for 4 pixels that are spreaded in the image. This might be useful when after some iterations larger regions must be evaluated during the clustering process. It enables more flexibility and possibilities in the design of clustering strategies, and might be useful if further verification of the detected planar regions is required. Furthermore, it is useful in applications where collinearity or coplanarity must be detected for non-adjacent regions, e.g. in the task of pallet finding and grasping.
- The feature uses no model fitting, hence there is no need for determining parameters.
- If the coplanarity constraint is performed for well chosen pixel configurations, it detects the boundaries of the segmented regions very well (Section 4). The need of postprocessing is reduced drastically.

In this article, the coplanarity and collinearity features are expressed by homogeneous linear equations in the d/D-ratios for the individual pixels. While the radial distance D to the viewed scene points is automatically provided by the ToF measurement, the IRD d is not directly available. An obvious way to compute the internal radial distance d for every single pixel is by way of the intrinsic calibration parameters, as described in Section 2. This means that the ToF camera must pass a lateral calibration step. Several suggestions have been published for finding the intrinsic parameters of a ToF camera, as there are [1,18,12]. From our own experiences we obtained accurate results by the recent calibration procedure presented in [7], using a parallel setting combining a ToF camera and a high resolution colour camera. Alternatively, we can suggest our own handy calibration technique ([13,14]), requiring only one camera and one image of a plane, without the need to extract specific features in the image.

Alternatively, one can choose to compute the IRD d without calibrating the camera first. In [17] we explain how in theory the coplanarity constraints of Section 3 can be used in combination of two images of a flat surface to build a system of homogeneous linear equations that determine the IRD d up to a global factor. As a matter of fact, in [17] we argue that the ratios d/D provide an alternative model for ToF cameras that is more natural than the intrinsic K-matrix of the pinhole model (see also [14]).

Furthermore, the data provided by the internal radial distances d can also be presented in more general camera models, as introduced in [6]. This means that our coplanarity constraints transcends the perspective pinhole model.

In spite of the listed arguments in favour, the d/D-test for 4 coplanar points or 3 collinear points comes with two warnings:

1. The homogeneous linear equations are derived while ignoring nonlinear lens distortions. As long as these distortions are rather small, they can be coped

with by an appropriate choice for the treshold in the setup of the segmentation criterion. To a restricted extent, the lens distortion can be compensated by small variations on the IRD d, if the latter has been directly obtained from reference images. Of course, if the nonlinear lens effects cannot be neglected, a preprocessing calibration step is necessary. e.g. to correct radial distortion.

2. The quality of the ToF measurement of the radial distances D has been improved during the last decade. The state-of-the-art accuracy (expressed as 6σ) is about 15 mm/m. Still, the depth measurements suffer from both systematic and casual errors. We refer to [16] for an overview of the sources of these inaccuracies. These might be cumbersome for our planarity test, that is sensitive to noise on D, because D appears in de denominators of the equation terms. A possible solution could be a (time consuming) depth calibration. Possible suggestions for correcting D can be found in [12,5,4,10]. However, we believe that a depth calibration is not essential in this application. Indeed, in our planar segmentation experiments we observed a limited distortion of the planarity feature when applied for 4 nearby pixels, not exceeding our segmentation treshold (Section 4).

2   Internal Radial Distances

Let C be the centre of a ToF camera. Assume that the sensor contains $H \times W$ pixels (H stands for "height", W stands for "width"). Using the conventional pixel coordinate axes, each pixel gets coordinates (u, v) with row index $v \in \{1, \ldots, H\}$ and column index $u \in \{1, \ldots, W\}$.

The *internal radial distance map* (IRD) d provides the distances from the centre C to the pixels of the ToF sensor in pixel units (Figure 1). It is represented as a function on the pixel grid:

$$d(u, v) = |C - p_{uv}|$$

(p_{uv} is the pixel with coordinates (u, v)). In case the aspect ratio of the sensor differs from 1, we agree to measure $d(u, v)$ in horizontal pixel units.

Notice that the IRD function d is an intrinsic property of the ToF camera, independent from its position in the world, and independent from the received signal as reflected by the environment.

Under the assumption of square pixels, the pinhole calibration is given by the principal point $c = (u_0, v_0)$ (the orthogonal projection of the camera centre C on the sensor plane) and the focal length f (the distance between C and the sensor plane, in pixel units). Observe that f is exactly the IRD of the principal point: $f = d(u_0, v_0)$. From these parameters, the 3D-reconstruction of a pixel point p_{uv} w.r.t. the camera reference frame can be computed by

$$P_{uv} = \frac{D(u, v)}{d(u, v)}(u - u_0, v - v_0, f)$$

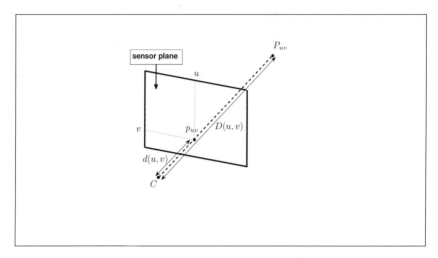

Fig. 1. The measured ToF-distance $D(u, v)$ is scene-sensitive, while the IRD $d(u, v)$ is an intrinsic camera feature

where the radial distance (in world unit)

$$D(u, v) = ||CP_{uv}||$$

is provided by the TOF sensor. Observe that in the square pixel case the IRD is obtained by

$$d(u, v) = \sqrt{(u - u_0)^2 + (v - v_0)^2 + f^2}$$

In general, in the traditional pinhole model the calibration matrix K contains the intrinsic camera parameters as follows:

$$K = \begin{pmatrix} f & s & u_0 \\ 0 & \tau f & v_0 \\ 0 & 0 & 1 \end{pmatrix}$$

f: focal length in horizontal pixel units
τ: aspect ratio
s: skewness
(u_0, v_0): pixel coordinates of the principal point

If we consider a "pixel" camera reference frame XYZ, as usual centered at C and Z equal to the focal axis, taking pixel units, then we observe that a pixel p_{uv} on the sensor has 3D coordinates in this frame, computed by

$$\begin{pmatrix} x_p \\ y_p \\ z_p \end{pmatrix} = f \cdot K^{-1} \begin{pmatrix} u \\ v \\ 1 \end{pmatrix}$$

Remark. If we cannot ignore lens distortions, then these should be removed in a preprocessing phase. From now on, we assume that (u, v) are "rectified" pixel coordinates.

Now we can state the relation between K and the IRD d:

$$d(u, v) = f \cdot \left\| K^{-1} \begin{pmatrix} u \\ v \\ 1 \end{pmatrix} \right\|$$

We conclude that the IRD d is known after a lateral calibration of the ToF camera.

However, it is also possible to compute the IRD d without the necessity to calibrate the camera first (e.g. see [17]). But this strategy has not been investigated yet at the same extent as intrinsic pinhole calibration, and there is still a lot of room for improving the accuray of the direct computation of d.

3 Coplanarity and Collinearity Constraints

Let p_1, p_2, p_3, p_4 be four given points in a ToF image with pixel coordinates $p_i = (u_i, v_i)$. To each of these image points we can associate two measurements:

- $d_i = d(p_i)$: the IRD value of p_i, which is independent from the world scene that is captured in the image, it only depends on the intrinsic camera settings.
- $D_i = D(p_i)$: the ToF measurement for the distance between the camera centre C and the scene point P_i that is reflected on the image point p_i.

The value d_i is assumed to be given in pixel units, while D_i is given in world units (meter). In general, a point P in the world scene can be described by world unit coordinates (x, y, z) in the standard camera reference frame, that can be obtained by rescaling the pixel unit coordinates of its ToF image $p = p_{uv}$ in this same camera frame:

$$\begin{pmatrix} x \\ y \\ z \end{pmatrix}_P = \frac{D}{d} \begin{pmatrix} x_p \\ y_p \\ z_p \end{pmatrix} = \frac{Df}{d} \cdot K^{-1} \begin{pmatrix} u \\ v \\ 1 \end{pmatrix}$$

where

$$D = D(p_{uv}) = \|P - C\| \quad \text{and} \quad d = d(p_{uv}) = \|p - C\|$$

If the ToF images p_1, p_2, p_3, p_4 are collinear then the scene points P_1, P_2, P_3, P_4 must necessarily be coplanar. But in case the images p_1, p_2, p_3, p_4 do not lie on one line, we get a nontrivial coplanarity equation for the world points P_1, P_2, P_3, P_4:

$$\begin{vmatrix} x_1 & x_2 & x_3 & x_4 \\ y_1 & y_2 & y_3 & y_4 \\ z_1 & z_2 & z_3 & z_4 \\ 1 & 1 & 1 & 1 \end{vmatrix} = 0$$

or, after expanding with respect to the last row,

$$\begin{vmatrix} x_2 & x_3 & x_4 \\ y_2 & y_3 & y_4 \\ z_2 & z_3 & z_4 \end{vmatrix} - \begin{vmatrix} x_1 & x_3 & x_4 \\ y_1 & y_3 & y_4 \\ z_1 & z_3 & z_4 \end{vmatrix} + \begin{vmatrix} x_1 & x_2 & x_4 \\ y_1 & y_2 & y_4 \\ z_1 & z_2 & z_4 \end{vmatrix} - \begin{vmatrix} x_1 & x_2 & x_3 \\ y_1 & y_2 & y_3 \\ z_1 & z_2 & z_3 \end{vmatrix} = 0$$

Each term in this equation can be rewritten as

$$\begin{vmatrix} x_i & x_j & x_k \\ y_i & y_j & y_k \\ z_i & z_j & z_k \end{vmatrix} = f^3 \cdot \frac{D_i \, D_j \, D_k}{d_i \, d_j \, d_k} \cdot \frac{1}{\det(K)} \cdot \begin{vmatrix} u_i & u_j & u_k \\ v_i & v_j & v_k \\ 1 & 1 & 1 \end{vmatrix}$$

Consequently, the coplanarity constraint can be translated in a homogeneous linear equation in the four ratios d_i/D_i:

$$[234]\frac{d_1}{D_1} - [134]\frac{d_2}{D_2} + [124]\frac{d_3}{D_3} - [123]\frac{d_4}{D_4} = 0 \tag{1}$$

with coefficients

$$[ijk] = \begin{vmatrix} u_i & u_j & u_k \\ v_i & v_j & v_k \\ 1 & 1 & 1 \end{vmatrix}$$

directly measurable in the uncalibrated image, hence independent from K.

In the special case that p_1, p_2 and p_3 are collinear (on line L), the coplanarity condition for the world points P_1, P_2, P_3, P_4 is equivalent to requiring that P_1, P_2, P_3 are collinear. Equation 1 now simplifies to

$$[23]\frac{d_1}{D_1} - [13]\frac{d_2}{D_2} + [12]\frac{d_3}{D_3} = 0$$

because $[123] = 0$ and $[ij4] = [ij]\cdot|p_4L|$. Here $[ij]$ stands for the "signed distance" between p_i and p_j ($1 \le i,j \le 3$), with the sign determined by the orientation of L that makes p_4 lie on the left of L.

The nice thing about ToF cameras is the availability of distance information in every pixel, without the need to perform any feature detection. This means that the coplanarity condition is often applied for self chosen pixels. A convenient choice consists of four pixels being the vertices of a rectangle. In this case (ordering $p_1, \ldots, p_4$ in counterclockwise sense): $[234] = [134] = [124] = [123]$ = area of this rectangle. Consequently, the coplanarity equation takes a more simple form, called *rectangular coplanarity equation*:

$$\frac{d_1}{D_1} - \frac{d_2}{D_2} + \frac{d_3}{D_3} - \frac{d_4}{D_4} = 0 \tag{2}$$

Another simplification occurs when we select three equidistant collinear points, p_1, p_2, p_3 (with p_2 the midpoint). So, $[13] = 2[12] = 2[23]$, and the collinearity equation simplifies to the so-called *midpoint equation*:

$$\frac{d_1}{D_1} - 2\frac{d_2}{D_2} + \frac{d_3}{D_3} = 0 \tag{3}$$

Remarks

- Because 1 is homogeneous, it holds equally well for a rescaled IRD. For example, the pixel p_{uv} can be represented by *angular coordinates* (φ, ψ), with lateral angle φ and inclination angle ψ given by

$$\tan \varphi = \frac{u - u_0}{f} \quad \text{and} \quad \tan \psi = \frac{v - v_0}{\tau f}$$

  This yields the following reconstruction formula:

$$P = \frac{D(u, v)}{d(\varphi, \psi)} (\tan \varphi, \tan \psi, 1)$$

  where we used a rescaled version of the IRD:

$$d(\varphi, \psi) = \frac{d(u, v)}{f} = \sqrt{\tan^2 \varphi + \tan^2 \psi + 1}$$

- In [17,14] we explain how the rectangular equations and the midpoint equations for coplanar quadruples and collinear triples can be used to determine the IRD d of a ToF camera up to a global factor, avoiding carrying out a lateral calibration first. To this end we need two non-parallel images of a plane that covers the whole ToF sensor (e.g. a wall).

4   Results and Experiments

We tested several variants of the d/D-coplanarity constraint. An excellent choice is given by the square $NSWE(u, v)$ consisting of the four adjacent pixels of a given pixel (u, v). We assume that (u, v) is not a boundary pixel. So, the four vertices are given by pixel coordinates

$$(u - 1, v), \quad (u + 1, v), \quad (u, v - 1), \quad (u, v + 1)$$

For testing the coplanarity of the four points that are measured by the vertices of $NSWE(u, v)$, the simplified 2 applies. We checked this out for images of several walls and for different cameras. A typical result is shown in Fig. 2.

In the example we used a 64×50 IFM camera and captured the image of a flat wall that completely covered the ToF sensor. For all the 2976 non-boundary pixels (u, v) we computed the coplanarity feature for the four neighbours $NSWE(u, v)$. As theoretically predicted all the 2976 values for 2 are close to zero (mean: -0.0060 ; standard deviation: 0.4747). The satisfying accuracy and stability of our d/D-coplanarity feature in our experiments is especially remarkable if you take into account that

- We did not correct for nonlinear lens distortions.
- We did not carry out any depth calibration. We used the (inaccurate) D-measurements directly given by the ToF camera.

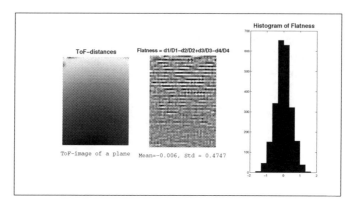

Fig. 2. The performance of the coplanarity test given by 2 for all possible choices of
$NSWE$-squares

- We only intrisically calibrated for the focal length ($f = 79$ for the 64×50 IFM
  camera). For the aspect ratio and the principal point we took the default
  values ($\tau = 1$, geometric centre as principal point). We observed that a more
  accurate lateral calibration did not significantly improve the performance of
  the coplanarity test for $NSWE$-squares.

This observation was confirmed by simulations. In Fig. 3 and Fig. 4 we show
the results of such a simulation (resolution 64×50, $f = 79$, $\tau = 1.003$ and $c = (27, 34)$). In Fig. 3 we assumed an exact ToF-measurement D, but we computed
the IRD d by means of inaccurate calibration parameters ($f = 82$, $\tau = 1$ and

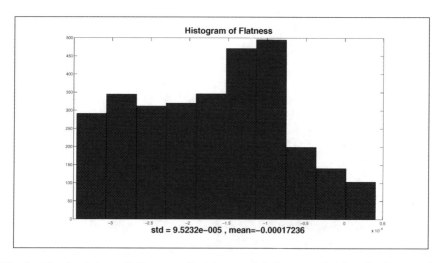

Fig. 3. We simulate a ToF-sensor that is completetly occupied by the image of a
plane. The errors on the d/D-coplanarity test are due to the use of inaccurate intrinsic
calibration parameters. Notice that the unit of the horizontal axis is 10^{-4}.

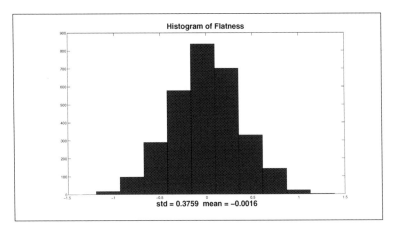

Fig. 4. We simulate a ToF-sensor that is completetly occupied by the image of a plane. The errors on the d/D-coplanarity test is due the ToF-noise on D.

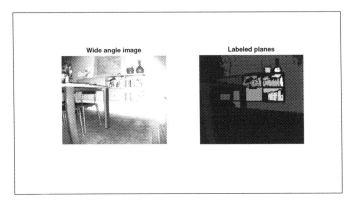

Fig. 5. The left diagram shows the *confidence image* of the scene (illuminence-distance ratio). The right image shows the segmentation of 17 planes by means of the coplanarity test given by 2. (Matlab cpu time equal to 0.0468 sec.)

$c = (25, 32)$). We observe that the resulting noise on the coplanarity equations for all the 2976 $NSWE$-squares is neglectable. We conclude that the game of careful lateral calibration is not worth the candle with respect to the detection of planar regions by our procedure.

In Fig. 4 we added simulated noise on the measured radial distances D. Now, the standard deviation of the coplanarity features is larger but still restricted, and of the same order of magnitude as in our real experiments. An apropriate choice of decision treshold still enables us to distinghuish flat from non-flat.

Finally, in Fig. 5 we illustrate our coplanarity test for an image of a typical indoor scene, taken by a wide angle ToF-camera (144×176). The planar regions were identified after a simple clustering technique, based on 2 applied on $NSWE$-squares.

5 Conclusions and Further Research

The key result of this paper is the proof of 1: the general coplanarity constraint for four points given by their ToF-images (both pixel coordinates as radial distance D). It is no coincidence that the resulting constraint is supported by the d/D-ratios. Indeed, it appears that each 3D-computation for a ToF-camera can be expressed in terms of these ratios.

Remarkable is the fact that we do not need calibrated coordinates in 1. However:

– The equation assumes the perspective model. So, in principle nonlinear lens distortions shoud be rectified in advance. If one chooses to do so, we recommend a simple one-parameter model to correct for radial distortion, because we experienced no profit in using a more advanced model.
– Knowledge of the IRD d is required, and the most obvious way to accomplish this is by way of a lateral calibration of the camera (determining the intrinsic parameters K). However, in [17,14] we present a linear procedure to compute the IRD d (up to a global scalar) avoiding this lateral calibration.

We also considered special cases in which the coplanarity condition reduces to its most simple form: 3 for 3 equidistant collinear points, and 2 for the 4 vertices of a rectangle. In particular, we applied this for $NSWE$-squares, yielding a stable and accurate feature for testing planarity and segmenting planar regions, as illustrated by our real experiments and simulations. This stability is demonstrated by observing high quality results in the application, **even without**

– correcting for radial and tangential distortions
– using accurate values for the principal point and the aspect ratio when computing the IRD d
– carrying out any depth calibration for the TOF-distances D.

In the future we expect an increasing interest for the use of Time-of-Flight cameras. This might imply the creation of a proper camera model, requiring a serious adaption of the pinhole model, in the spirit of [6]. In such a more general model, the concept of "internal radial distances" can be transferred, rather than the concept of "calibration matrix" K. We believe that the proportions d/D remain to play a crucial part in 3D-algorithms for TOF-cameras. It is important to develop accurate and stable methods to compute the IRD d **directly**, in the pinhole model as well as in more general models.

References

1. Beder, C., Koch, R.: Calibration of focal length and 3d pose based on the reflectance and depth image of a planar object. Int. J. of Intelligent Systems Technologies and Applications 5(3), 285–294 (2008)
2. Enjarini, B., Gräser, A.: Planar segmentation from depth images using gradient of depth feature. In: IROS, pp. 4668–4674 (2012)
3. Forsyth, D., Ponce, J.: Computer Vision: A Modern Approach. Prentice Hall (2002)
4. Fuchs, S., Hirzinger, G.: Extrinsic and depth calibration of tof-cameras. Computer Vision and Pattern Recognition, 1–6 (2008)
5. Fuchs, S., May, S.: Calibration and registration for precise surface reconstruction. In: Proceedings of the DAGM Dyn3D Workshop, Heidelberg, Germany (September 2007)
6. Grossberg, M., Nayar, S.: The raxel imaging model and ray-based calibration. Int. J. of Computer Vision 2(61), 119–137 (2005)
7. Hanning, T., Lasaruk, A., Tatschke, T.: Calibration and low-level data fusion algorithms for a parallel 2d/3d-camera. Information Fusion 12, 37–47 (2011)
8. Horowitz, S., Pavlidis, T.: Picture segmentation by a tree traversal algorithm. Journal of the ACM 23, 368–388 (1976)
9. Jiang, X., Bunke, H.: Fast segmentation of range images into planar regions by scan line grouping. In: Machine Vision and Applications, pp. 115–122 (1994)
10. Kahlmann, T., Remondino, F., Ingensand, H.: Calibration for increased accuracy of the range imaging camera swissranger. In: Image Engineering and Vision Metrology, vol. 36, pp. 136–141 (2006)
11. Liang, B., Pears, N.: Visual navigation using planar homographies. In: ICRA, pp. 205–210 (2002)
12. Lindner, M., Kolb, A.: Lateral and depth calibration of PMD-distance sensors. In: Bebis, G., et al. (eds.) ISVC 2006. LNCS, vol. 4292, pp. 524–533. Springer, Heidelberg (2006)
13. Mertens, L., Penne, R., Ribbens, B.: The lateral calibration of a time-of-flight camera by one image of a flat surface (submitted)
14. Mertens, L., Penne, R., Ribbens, B.: Time of flight cameras (3d vision). In: Buytaert, J. (ed.) Recent Advances in Topography. Nova Science Publishers (2013)
15. Parvin, B., Medioni, G.: Segmentation of range images into planar surfaces by split and merge. In: Computer Vision and Pattern Recognition (1986)
16. Pattinson, T.: Quantification and Description of Distance Measurement Errors of a Time-of-Flight Camera. Ph.D. thesis, University of Stuttgard (2011)
17. Penne, R., Mertens, L., Ribbens, B.: The internal radial distances of a time-of-flight sensor (submitted)
18. Schiller, I., Beder, C., Koch, R.: Calibration of a pmd-camera using a planar calibration pattern together with a multi-camera setup. In: Proceedings of the XXI ISPRS Congress (2008)
19. Sinclair, D., Blake, A.: Quantitative planar region detection. Int. Journal of Computer Vision 18(1), 77–91 (1996)
20. Taylor, R.W., Savini, M., Reeves, A.P.: Fast segmentation of range imagery into planar regions. Computer Vision, Graphics, and Image Processing 45(1), 42–60 (1989)

An Efficient Normal-Error Iterative Algorithm for Line Triangulation

Qiang Zhang[1,2], Yan Wu[1], Ming Liu[1], and Licheng Jiao[2]

[1] School of Electronic Engineering, Xidian University, Xi'an, 710071, China
[2] Key Laboratory of Intelligent Perception and Image Understanding of Ministry of Education of China, Xidian University, Xi'an, 710071, China
zhangqiang@xidian.edu.cn

Abstract. In this paper, we address the problem of line triangulation, which is to find the position of a line in space given its three projections taken with cameras with known camera matrices. Because of measurement error in line extraction, the problem becomes difficult so that it is necessary to estimate a 3D line to optimally fit measured lines. In this work, the normal errors of measured line are presented to describe the measurement error and based on their statistical property a new geometric-distance optimality criterion is constructed. Furthermore, a simple iterative algorithm is proposed to obtain suboptimal solution of the optimality criterion, which ensures that the solution satisfies the trifocal tensor constraint. Experiments show that our iterative algorithm can achieve the estimation accuracy comparable with the Gold Standard algorithm, but its computational load is substantially reduced.

Keywords: Line triangulation, Normal error, Iterative algorithm, Suboptimal solution.

1 Introduction

In computer vision, triangulation is one of fundamental problems and in the past many algorithms [1-11] have been proposed to solve point triangulation. But, as the reconstruction of manmade environment becomes hot spot topic, lines in space as reconstruction feature draw more and more attention. This is not only because lines exist largely in manmade environments, also because they have some advantages that points haven't [1]. For example, a line is extracted with more accuracy, it has less chance to be occluded but more information to represent geometric structure of object, and etc. However, line triangulation is more difficult than point triangulation. To construct overconstrained problem, line triangulation needs at least trilinear constraint of three projections, compared with bilinear constraint in the point triangulation [2]. Moreover, because a line in space has 4 degrees of freedom, there is no trivial representation [12].

Although there are many difficulties, some researchers have begun the research of line triangulation. In the early works [13-15], the algorithms are proposed to solve line triangulation for calibrated cameras. But it is difficult for these algorithms to deal

J. Blanc-Talon et al. (Eds.): ACIVS 2013, LNCS 8192, pp. 298–309, 2013.

with the practical problem in which just the affine or projective camera matrices are known. To solve the problem in practice, with Plücker coordinates, a simple linear algorithm [12] is proposed. Because of its algebraic-error cost function and the Plücker correction, the solution of this algorithm is not accurate enough. The optimal algorithm in [16] can give global solution, but its optimality criterion just describes the statistics property of image line coordinates and its computation is very intensive. In the Gold Standard algorithm [17], geometric errors in images can be utilized to construct cost functions. But, because none of these cost functions for the Gold Standard algorithm are convex, even though the LM iteration method has large computational load, their solutions are not optimal.

In this paper, a novel algorithm is proposed for line triangulation of three views, equally valid in the projective, affine and metric reconstruction. The main difference of our algorithm from the previous algorithms is that its optimality criterion has both geometric and statistic meaning. This is because the normal errors of measured line are defined to describe measurement error in image, and based on the statistical property of the normal error, the likelihood function of the normal error is used to construct cost function. Furthermore, because the trifocal tensor constraint in the optimality criterion is simplified via the linear normal-error representation of the estimated line, a simple iterative algorithm is proposed to find suboptimal solution of this optimality criterion, which makes the constraint satisfied in each iterative cycle. Experiments show that our algorithm not only has lower computational load than the Gold Standard algorithm, but also has almost the same estimation accuracy with the Gold Standard algorithm.

The remainder of this paper is organized as follows. Section 2 is about the definition of the normal error and the normal-error representation of line. In Section 3, we give the normal-error distribution and construct optimality criterion. Further on in Section 4, an iterative algorithm is described to solve the optimality criterion. Section 5 reports experimental results. Section 6 concludes this paper.

2   Normal-Error Representation of Line

In this paper, the discussed situation is that the measured lines in images correspond to same 3D line and just have measurement error, so it is reasonable to assume that the estimated lines are not far from the measured lines and the angles between them are far less than 90 degrees. As shown in Fig 1, this means that the distances λ_1 and λ_2, which are perpendicular to the measured line $\mathbf{l}$ and from the measured endpoints $\mathbf{x}, \mathbf{y}$ to the estimated line $\overline{\mathbf{l}}$, are finite. Because these two distances are measured along the normal direction of the measured line, we define them as normal errors between the measured line and the estimated line. Via the normal errors, two intersections $\overline{\mathbf{x}}, \overline{\mathbf{y}}$ on the estimated line can be obtained and we define them as the estimated endpoints of the estimated line, which are represented as follows:

$$\overline{\mathbf{x}} = \mathbf{x} + \lambda_1 \begin{pmatrix} \mathbf{n} \\ 0 \end{pmatrix}, \overline{\mathbf{y}} = \mathbf{y} + \lambda_2 \begin{pmatrix} \mathbf{n} \\ 0 \end{pmatrix} \tag{1}$$

where **n** is the vector including the normalized first two elements of the measured line **l** . Furthermore, via these two estimated endpoints, the normal-error representation of the estimated line $\overline{\mathbf{l}}$ can be written as

$$\overline{\mathbf{l}}(\lambda_1,\lambda_2) = \overline{\mathbf{x}}\times\overline{\mathbf{y}} = \mathbf{l} + \lambda_1\mathbf{g}_1 + \lambda_2\mathbf{g}_2$$

$$= \mathbf{x}\times\mathbf{y} + \lambda_1\begin{pmatrix}\mathbf{n}\\0\end{pmatrix}\times\mathbf{y} + \lambda_2\mathbf{x}\times\begin{pmatrix}\mathbf{n}\\0\end{pmatrix} \qquad (2)$$

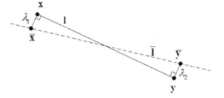

Fig. 1. Normal errors λ_1 and λ_2 between measured line **l** (solid line) and estimated line $\overline{\mathbf{l}}$ (dash line)

It is obvious that the normal-error representation (2) is a linear representation of the estimated line $\overline{\mathbf{l}}$ and its parameters are its two normal errors, which reduce the number of line coordinates and make the representation of error easier.

3   An Optimality Criterion about the Normal Error

3.1   Normal-Error Distribution

Before constructing the normal-error optimality criterion, it is necessary to give the statistical distribution of the normal error in this section. Therefore, two set of experiments are performed as follows. In these experiments, 1000000 random 3D lines are projected onto 1024×1024 image plane as standard lines. Then, each standard line is randomly sampled with 10 and 30 points (including two endpoints). It is common to assume that the extracted points in image are subject to Gaussian noise, we add Gaussian noise to these sampling points with zero mean and one-pixel standard deviation, the corresponding measured line is fitted to these noised sampling points using the least-squares and the measured endpoints are the nearest points from the two endpoints to the measured line. Thus, the normal error is the distance between the endpoint to the measured endpoint.

From Fig 2, we can see that no matter whether the experiment is about 10 or 30 sampling points, its histogram of the normal error can be perfectly approximated by a Gaussian distribution. Thus, it is reasonable to assume that each normal error of the measured line satisfies the Gaussian distribution.

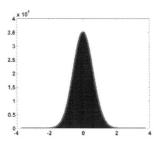 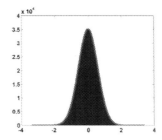

Fig. 2. The histograms of the normal error and their Gaussian distribution fittings for the 10-sampling-point experiment (left) and the 30-sampling-point experiment (right), where the horizontal axis represents the normal error level (pixel), the vertical axis represents the number of times each error level occurs.

Thus, based on maximum likelihood estimation, the most likely values for the normal errors in n images can be obtained by minimizing the function

$$L\left(\lambda_{11},\lambda_{12},\lambda_{21},\lambda_{22},\cdots,\lambda_{n1},\lambda_{n2}\right)=\sum_{i=1}^{n}\lambda_{i1}^{2}+\lambda_{i2}^{2} \tag{3}$$

where i stands for the i th image, subject to some constraint

$$T\left(\lambda_{11},\lambda_{12},\lambda_{21},\lambda_{22},\cdots,\lambda_{n1},\lambda_{n2}\right)=0 \tag{4}$$

Once these normal errors are known, the corresponding estimated line can be found via (2).

3.2   The Optimality Criterion for Three Views

For three-view line triangulation, the constraint (4) can be described with trifocal tensor [17]. Given the measured line correspondence $\left(\mathbf{l}_1,\mathbf{l}_2,\mathbf{l}_3\right)$ and their endpoints $\left\{\left(\mathbf{x}_1,\mathbf{y}_1\right),\left(\mathbf{x}_2,\mathbf{y}_2\right),\left(\mathbf{x}_3,\mathbf{y}_3\right)\right\}$ in three images, using the normal errors $\left(\lambda_{j1},\lambda_{j2}\right)$ on the j th image $\left(j=1,2,3\right)$, the estimated endpoints of the line on the first image can be written as

$$
\begin{aligned}
\left(\bar{x}_1,\bar{x}_2,1\right)^T &= \mathbf{x}_1+\lambda_{11}\left(\mathbf{n}_1^T,0\right)^T \\
\left(\bar{y}_1,\bar{y}_2,1\right)^T &= \mathbf{y}_1+\lambda_{12}\left(\mathbf{n}_1^T,0\right)^T
\end{aligned}
\tag{5}
$$

and the estimated lines $\bar{\mathbf{l}}_2,\bar{\mathbf{l}}_3$ on the last two images can be written as

$$
\begin{aligned}
\bar{\mathbf{l}}_2\left(\lambda_{21},\lambda_{22}\right) &= \mathbf{l}_2+\lambda_{21}\mathbf{g}_{21}+\lambda_{22}\mathbf{g}_{22} \\
\bar{\mathbf{l}}_3\left(\lambda_{31},\lambda_{32}\right) &= \mathbf{l}_3+\lambda_{31}\mathbf{g}_{31}+\lambda_{32}\mathbf{g}_{32}
\end{aligned}
\tag{6}
$$

where $\mathbf{n}_i$ is the vector including the normalized first two elements of the measured line $\mathbf{l}_i\left(i=1,2,3\right)$,

$$\mathbf{g}_{21} = \begin{pmatrix} \mathbf{n}_2 \\ 0 \end{pmatrix} \times \mathbf{y}_2 , \mathbf{g}_{22} = \mathbf{x}_2 \times \begin{pmatrix} \mathbf{n}_2 \\ 0 \end{pmatrix}$$
$$\mathbf{g}_{31} = \begin{pmatrix} \mathbf{n}_3 \\ 0 \end{pmatrix} \times \mathbf{y}_3 , \mathbf{g}_{32} = \mathbf{x}_3 \times \begin{pmatrix} \mathbf{n}_3 \\ 0 \end{pmatrix}$$

thus, the trifocal tensor constraint can be written as following point-line-line correspondence

$$C_1 (\lambda) = \overline{\mathbf{l}}_2^T (\overline{x}_1 \mathbf{T}_1 + \overline{x}_2 \mathbf{T}_2 + \mathbf{T}_3) \overline{\mathbf{l}}_3 = 0$$
$$C_2 (\lambda) = \overline{\mathbf{l}}_2^T (\overline{y}_1 \mathbf{T}_1 + \overline{y}_2 \mathbf{T}_2 + \mathbf{T}_3) \overline{\mathbf{l}}_3 = 0 \qquad (7)$$

where $(\mathbf{T}_1, \mathbf{T}_2, \mathbf{T}_3)$ is the trifocal tensor of the three images, $\lambda = (\lambda_{11}, \lambda_{12}, \lambda_{21}, \lambda_{22}, \lambda_{31}, \lambda_{32})^T$ is called normal-error vector. From (3) and (4), we have the normal-error optimality criterion for three views

$$\min \lambda^T \lambda$$
$$s.t. \quad C_1 (\lambda) = 0 \qquad (8)$$
$$C_2 (\lambda) = 0$$

Although via the normal-error representation of line, the degrees of both the two constraints in (8) are just three, the optimality criterion belongs to the nonlinear constraint quadratic programming and complex algorithm is needed to solve it but hardly to obtain the optimal solution. So, in next section, a simple iterative algorithm is proposed to obtain the suboptimal solution which satisfies the trifocal tensor constraint.

4   Iterative Algorithm

In this section, we regard the two constraints in the optimality criterion (8) as two 3-degree surfaces in the normal-error vector space, so the triangulation problem is converted to find the point on the intersection of the two surfaces and nearest to the origin. To simplify solving process and obtain the suboptimal solution, an iterative algorithm is used. In each iterative cycle, we define a pencil of lines through the origin, and the iteration solution is the nearest point to the origin, which is not only on the intersection of the two 3-degree surfaces but also on the pencil. Thus, the original criterion (8) can be converted to equation to solve and its process is stated as follows.

Suppose the solution λ^n of the n th iteration is known, where initial value $\lambda^0 = 0$, the pencil in the $n+1$ th iteration is defined by the linear span of the gradients of the two constraints at λ^n which are the normal vectors to the two degree 3 surfaces at point λ^n if $n \neq 0$. Therefore, the point λ on the pencil can be expressed

$$\lambda = x\mathbf{p}_1 + y\mathbf{p}_2 \qquad (9)$$

where

$$\mathbf{p}_1 = \partial C_1\left(\boldsymbol{\lambda}^n\right)/\partial\boldsymbol{\lambda} = \begin{bmatrix} \overline{\mathbf{l}}_2\left(\lambda_{21}^n,\lambda_{22}^n\right)^T (\sum_{i=1}^{2} n_{1i}\mathrm{T}_i)\overline{\mathbf{l}}_3\left(\lambda_{31}^n,\lambda_{32}^n\right) \\ 0 \\ \mathbf{g}_{21}^T(\sum_{i=1}^{3}\overline{x}_i^n\mathrm{T}_i)\overline{\mathbf{l}}_3\left(\lambda_{31}^n,\lambda_{32}^n\right) \\ \mathbf{g}_{22}^T(\sum_{i=1}^{3}\overline{x}_i^n\mathrm{T}_i)\overline{\mathbf{l}}_3\left(\lambda_{31}^n,\lambda_{32}^n\right) \\ \overline{\mathbf{l}}_2\left(\lambda_{21}^n,\lambda_{22}^n\right)^T (\sum_{i=1}^{3}\overline{x}_i^n\mathrm{T}_i)\mathbf{g}_{31} \\ \overline{\mathbf{l}}_2\left(\lambda_{21}^n,\lambda_{22}^n\right)^T (\sum_{i=1}^{3}\overline{x}_i^n\mathrm{T}_i)\mathbf{g}_{32} \end{bmatrix},$$

$$\mathbf{p}_2 = \partial C_2\left(\boldsymbol{\lambda}^n\right)/\partial\boldsymbol{\lambda} = \begin{bmatrix} 0 \\ \overline{\mathbf{l}}_2\left(\lambda_{21}^n,\lambda_{22}^n\right)^T (\sum_{i=1}^{2} n_{1i}\mathrm{T}_i)\overline{\mathbf{l}}_3\left(\lambda_{31}^n,\lambda_{32}^n\right) \\ \mathbf{g}_{21}^T(\sum_{i=1}^{3}\overline{y}_i^n\mathrm{T}_i)\overline{\mathbf{l}}_3\left(\lambda_{31}^n,\lambda_{32}^n\right) \\ \mathbf{g}_{22}^T(\sum_{i=1}^{3}\overline{y}_i^n\mathrm{T}_i)\overline{\mathbf{l}}_3\left(\lambda_{31}^n,\lambda_{32}^n\right) \\ \overline{\mathbf{l}}_2\left(\lambda_{21}^n,\lambda_{22}^n\right)^T (\sum_{i=1}^{3}\overline{y}_i^n\mathrm{T}_i)\mathbf{g}_{31} \\ \overline{\mathbf{l}}_2\left(\lambda_{21}^n,\lambda_{22}^n\right)^T (\sum_{i=1}^{3}\overline{y}_i^n\mathrm{T}_i)\mathbf{g}_{32} \end{bmatrix},$$

$$\left(\overline{x}_1^n,\overline{x}_2^n,\overline{x}_3^n\right)^T = \mathbf{x}_1 + \lambda_{11}^n\left(\mathbf{n}_1^T,0\right)^T, \left(\overline{y}_1^n,\overline{y}_2^n,\overline{y}_3^n\right)^T = \mathbf{y}_1 + \lambda_{12}^n\left(\mathbf{n}_1^T,0\right)^T, \left(n_{11},n_{12}\right) = \mathbf{n}_1^T.$$

Substituting $\boldsymbol{\lambda}$ into the two constraints of (8), we obtain two cubic equations in x, y

$$\begin{cases} a_1 x^3 + a_2 x^2 y + a_3 xy^2 + a_4 x^2 + a_5 y^2 + a_6 xy + a_7 x + a_8 y + a_9 \\ = \left(\mathbf{u}_1^T \mathbf{M}_1 \mathbf{v}_1\right)x^3 + \left(\mathbf{u}_1^T \mathbf{M}_1 \mathbf{v}_2 + \mathbf{u}_2^T \mathbf{M}_1 \mathbf{v}_1\right)x^2 y + \left(\mathbf{u}_2^T \mathbf{M}_1 \mathbf{v}_2\right)xy^2 + \left(\mathbf{u}_2^T \mathbf{M}_2 \mathbf{v}_2\right)y^2 \\ + \left(\mathbf{l}_2^T \mathbf{M}_1 \mathbf{v}_1 + \mathbf{u}_1^T \mathbf{M}_1 \mathbf{l}_3 + \mathbf{u}_1^T \mathbf{M}_2 \mathbf{v}_1\right)x^2 + \left(\mathbf{l}_2^T \mathbf{M}_1 \mathbf{v}_2 + \mathbf{u}_2^T \mathbf{M}_2 \mathbf{v}_2 + \mathbf{u}_2^T \mathbf{M}_1 \mathbf{l}_3 + \mathbf{u}_2^T \mathbf{M}_2 \mathbf{v}_1 \\ )xy + \left(\mathbf{l}_2^T \mathbf{M}_1 \mathbf{l}_3 + \mathbf{l}_2^T \mathbf{M}_2 \mathbf{v}_1 + \mathbf{u}_1^T \mathbf{M}_2 \mathbf{l}_3\right)x + \left(\mathbf{l}_2^T \mathbf{M}_2 \mathbf{v}_2 + \mathbf{u}_2^T \mathbf{M}_2 \mathbf{l}_3\right)y + \left(\mathbf{l}_2^T \mathbf{M}_2 \mathbf{l}_3\right) = 0 \\ b_1 y^3 + b_2 x^2 y + b_3 xy^2 + b_4 x^2 + b_5 y^2 + b_6 xy + b_7 x + b_8 y + b_9 \\ = \left(\mathbf{u}_2^T \mathbf{N}_1 \mathbf{v}_2\right)y^3 + \left(\mathbf{u}_1^T \mathbf{N}_1 \mathbf{v}_1\right)x^2 y + \left(\mathbf{u}_1^T \mathbf{N}_1 \mathbf{v}_2 + \mathbf{u}_2^T \mathbf{N}_1 \mathbf{v}_1\right)xy^2 + \left(\mathbf{u}_1^T \mathbf{N}_2 \mathbf{v}_1\right)x^2 \\ + \left(\mathbf{l}_2^T \mathbf{N}_1 \mathbf{v}_2 + \mathbf{u}_2^T \mathbf{N}_1 \mathbf{l}_3 + \mathbf{u}_2^T \mathbf{N}_2 \mathbf{v}_2\right)y^2 + \left(\mathbf{l}_2^T \mathbf{N}_1 \mathbf{v}_1 + \mathbf{u}_1^T \mathbf{N}_2 \mathbf{v}_2 + \mathbf{u}_1^T \mathbf{N}_1 \mathbf{l}_3 + \mathbf{u}_2^T \mathbf{N}_2 \mathbf{v}_1 \\ )xy + \left(\mathbf{l}_2^T \mathbf{N}_1 \mathbf{l}_3 + \mathbf{u}_2^T \mathbf{N}_2 \mathbf{l}_3\right)x + \left(\mathbf{l}_2^T \mathbf{N}_1 \mathbf{l}_3 + \mathbf{l}_2^T \mathbf{N}_2 \mathbf{v}_2 + \mathbf{u}_2^T \mathbf{N}_2 \mathbf{l}_3\right)y + \left(\mathbf{l}_2^T \mathbf{N}_2 \mathbf{l}_3\right) = 0 \end{cases} \quad (10)$$

where $\mathbf{u}_1 = p_{13}\mathbf{g}_{21} + p_{14}\mathbf{g}_{22}$, $\mathbf{u}_2 = p_{23}\mathbf{g}_{21} + p_{24}\mathbf{g}_{22}$, $\mathbf{v}_1 = p_{15}\mathbf{g}_{31} + p_{16}\mathbf{g}_{32}$,
$\mathbf{v}_2 = p_{25}\mathbf{g}_{31} + p_{26}\mathbf{g}_{32}$, $\mathbf{M}_1 = p_{11}n_{11}\mathrm{T}_1 + p_{11}n_{12}\mathrm{T}_2$, $\mathbf{M}_2 = x_1\mathrm{T}_1 + x_2\mathrm{T}_2 + \mathrm{T}_3$,

$N_1 = p_{22}n_{11} T_1 + p_{22}n_{12} T_2$, $N_2 = y_1 T_1 + y_2 T_2 + T_3$, $(x_1, x_2, 1)^T = \mathbf{x}_1$, $(y_1, y_2, 1)^T = \mathbf{y}_1$,

$(p_{11}, 0, p_{13}, p_{14}, p_{15}, p_{16})^T = \mathbf{p}_1$, $(0, p_{22}, p_{23}, p_{24}, p_{25}, p_{26})^T = \mathbf{p}_2$.

Then the following problem is to solve the two cubic equations. From (10), it can be seen that the highest degree of x in the second equation is 2. Therefore, we rewrite the second one as

$$(b_2 y + b_4) x^2 + (b_3 y^2 + b_6 y + b_7) x + (b_1 y^3 + b_5 y^2 + b_8 y + b_9) = 0 \tag{11}$$

And suppose y is known and $y \neq -b_4 / b_2$, the solutions of x are

$$x = \frac{-A(y) \pm \sqrt{B(y)}}{2C(y)} \tag{12}$$

where $B(y) = (b_3 y^2 + b_6 y + b_7)^2 - 4(b_2 y + b_4)(b_1 y^3 + b_5 y^2 + b_8 y + b_9)$, $C(y) = b_2 y + b_4$, $A(y) = b_3 y^2 + b_6 y + b_7$. Substituting (12) into the first equation of (10), we obtain the equation

$$\left(a_1 \left(-A(y)^3 - 3A(y)B(y) \right) + 2C(y)(a_2 y + a_4)\left(A(y)^2 + B(y) \right) \right.$$
$$\left. -4A(y)C(y)^2 (a_3 y^2 + a_6 y + a_7) + 8C(y)^3 (a_5 y^2 + a_8 y + a_9) \right)^2 \tag{13}$$
$$= \left(a_1 \left(3A(y)^2 + B(y) \right) - 4A(y)C(y)(a_2 y + a_4) + 4C(y)^2 (a_3 y^2 + a_6 y + a_7) \right)^2 B(y)$$

This is an equation in y of degree 12, which can be solved with companion matrix [19].

Based on the above discussion, our iterative algorithm is outlined in Table 1. Because the iterative algorithm ensures that each iterative solution satisfies the trifocal tensor constraint, the suboptimal solution can be used to determine a 3D line directly. Therefore, substituting the suboptimal solution into (5) and (6) to obtain the estimated endpoints in the first image and the estimated lines in the other images, the 3D line can be computed by linear algorithm [12] without the Plücker correction.

Table 1. The Normal-Error Iterative Algorithm

Initiation: given a termination threshold ε and let $n = 0, \lambda^0 = 0$

---

1. Compute $\mathbf{p}_1, \mathbf{p}_2$ in (9) with λ^n and the coefficients of cubic equations (10);

2. Construct equation (13) and solve it with the companion matrix, substitute roots of (13) which are different from $-b_4 / b_2$ into (12) to obtain x, and when $y = -b_4 / b_2$, $x = \left(b_1 b_4^3 - b_2 b_4^2 b_5 + b_2^2 b_4 b_8 - b_2^3 b_9 \right) / \left(b_2 b_3 b_4^2 - b_2^2 b_4 b_6 + b_2^3 b_7 \right)$;

3. Select the (x', y') from solutions that satisfies (10) and makes $\left\| x\mathbf{p}_1 + y\mathbf{p}_2 \right\|^2$ smallest, $\lambda^{n+1} = x'\mathbf{p}_1 + y'\mathbf{p}_2$;

4. If $\left\| \lambda^n - \lambda^{n+1} \right\| \leq \varepsilon$, then output λ^{n+1} and terminate; otherwise, let $n = n + 1$ and return to 1.

---

5   Experiments

Both simulated and real experiments are carried out to evaluate the different four algorithms using MATLAB on a PC with Intel Core2 2.33 GHz CPU and 2GB RAM. These compared algorithms include LIN(linear algorithm)[12], GS+d(Golden Standard method with the distance from the measured endpoint to the estimated line), GS+nd(Golden Standard method with the normal distance), NIA(our normal-error iterative algorithm). In NIA, the termination threshold ε is 10^{-7}.

5.1   Simulated Data

As shown in Fig.3, the simulated experimental setup includes three cameras looking inward to a cube. The size of the angle between the adjacent cameras is chosen as 15 degrees, 30 degrees respectively to carry out two experiments. In all of these experiments, the distance between each camera centre and cube is 10 units and the side length of cube is 1 unit. In cube, 28 lines connecting every two vertices are chosen as test lines, which are projected onto 1024×1024 image plane. The internal matrices of the three cameras are set as:

$$K = \begin{pmatrix} 700 & 0 & 512 \\ 0 & 700 & 512 \\ 0 & 0 & 1 \end{pmatrix}.$$

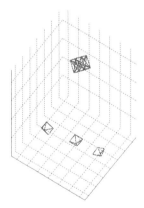

Fig. 3. Camera setup

In each of these experiments, 10 sampling points are extracted from test line randomly. After Gaussian noise with zero mean and standard deviation σ is added to each sampling point, the measured line is fitted to the 10 sampling points with the least-squares. The noise level σ varies from 0.4 to 2 with the steps of 0.4 pixels, 200 trails are performed at each noise level. The evaluated performances include: RMS (Root Mean Square) error of the normal distance; Average error of the space angle which is the angle between the real line and the estimated line in space; RMS error of the space distance which is the distance between the real line and the estimated line in space.

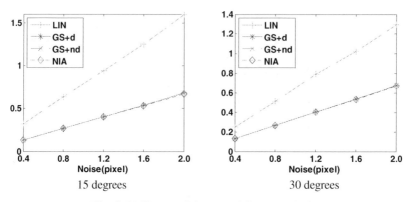

Fig. 4. RMS error of the normal distance (pixel)

Table 2. The difference between NIA and GS+nd for RMS error of the normal distance (pixel)

Noise (pixel)	0.4	0.8	1.2	1.6	2.0
15 degrees	1.68×10^{-7}	9.63×10^{-9}	2.08×10^{-12}	-0.007	-0.014
30 degrees	2.39×10^{-12}	8.67×10^{-9}	3.23×10^{-13}	-0.004	-0.007

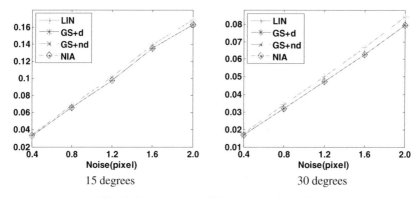

Fig. 5. Average error of the space angle (radian)

The error of normal distance in image and two errors of 3D reconstruction in space are shown in Fig.4, Fig.5 and Fig.6, respectively. From these errors, we can see that, in both experiments, the LIN has the worst performance and the other three geometric-distance algorithms have almost the same accuracy. In more detail, from Table2, it can be seen that the accuracy of the NIA is the similar to the GS+nd in the case of low noise level, but is better than it as the increase of noise level. From Table3 and Table4 which are about the differences of 3D reconstruction accuracy between the normal-distance algorithm (the NIA) and the point-line-distance algorithm (the GS+d), we can see that the NIA has better accuracy than the GS+d as the increase of noise level, not only in the case of the space angle but also in the case of the space distance.

Table 3. The difference between NIA and GS+d for average error of the space angle (radian)

Noise (pixel)	0.4	0.8	1.2	1.6	2.0
15 degrees	7.89×10^{-8}	-1.54×10^{-7}	9.66×10^{-8}	-6.94×10^{-5}	-0.00013
30 degrees	1.83×10^{-8}	-1.28×10^{-8}	-2.21×10^{-7}	-3.89×10^{-7}	-5.60×10^{-7}

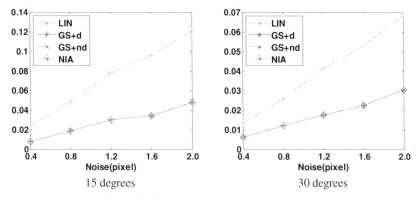

15 degrees   30 degrees

Fig. 6. RMS error of the space distance (unit)

Table 4. The difference between NIA and GS+d for RMS error of the space distance (unit)

Noise (pixel)	0.4	0.8	1.2	1.6	2.0
15 degrees	3.94×10^{-8}	1.94×10^{-8}	-1.84×10^{-7}	-5.85×10^{-7}	-2.37×10^{-6}
30 degrees	-4.12×10^{-8}	-2.25×10^{-8}	-3.87×10^{-7}	-1.57×10^{-6}	-1.17×10^{-5}

5.2 Real Data

In real experiments, two sets of real images are used to test the algorithms mentioned above. One of the two sets is indoor objects as shown in Fig.7(left), in which the 36 measured lines are fitted to the points extracted by hand; the other is Tsinghua school as shown in Fig.8(left), in which the 196 measured lines are extracted by Canny edge detector. Their right figures show the reconstructions of indoor objects and Tsinghua school by NIA, respectively.

From Table 5 and Table 6 we can see that the accuracy of NIA is just the same as GS+d and GS+nd. But the running times of NIA are all less than $1/3$ times of them. Although the running time of the LIN is the least of all, its worst accuracy indicates that the LIN is not suitable to be utilized in practice.

Table 5. Results of indoor objects

	LIN	NIA	GS+d	GS+nd
RMS error of the normal distance (pixel)	0.76	0.29	0.29	0.29
average of running time(10^{-4} s)	2.06	45.90	146.74	183.02

Table 6. Results of Tsinghua school

	LIN	NIA	GS+d	GS+nd
RMS error of the normal distance (pixel)	3.54	0.19	0.19	0.19
average of the running time(10^{-4} s)	2.13	38.87	146.24	177.00

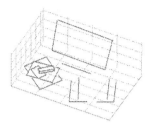

Fig. 7. Measured lines from indoor objects (white line) and its 3D reconstruction by NIA

Fig. 8. Measured lines from Tsinghua school (white line in the left of pictures, black line in the right of pictures) and its 3D reconstruction by NIA

6   Conclusions

This paper discusses the line triangulation for three images. The main contributions include: the normal error is defined to describe measurement error of measured line and construct a linear representation of image line; based on the statistical property of the normal error, an optimality criterion about the normal error is presented; furthermore, a simple iterative algorithm is proposed to solve this optimality criterion, which makes the trifocal tensor constraint satisfied in each iterative cycle. Experiments show that our iterative algorithm can achieve comparable estimation accuracy with the Gold Standard algorithm, but with much less computational load.

Acknowledgements. This work was supported by the Open Project Program of the National Laboratory of Pattern Recognition (NLPR)(201204243), the Fundamental Research Funds for the Central Universities(K5051302009), the Natural Science Foundation of China (No.61272281, No.61271297), and the Specialized Research Fund for the Doctoral Program of Higher Education (No. 20110203110001).

Reference

[1] Beardsley, P.A., Zisserman, A., Murray, D.W.: Navigation using affine structure from motion. In: Eklundh, J.-O. (ed.) ECCV 1994. LNCS, vol. 801, pp. 85–96. Springer, Heidelberg (1994)

[2] Hartley, R., Sturm, P.: Triangulation. Computer Vision and Image Understanding, 146–157 (1997)

[3] Wu, F., Zhang, Q., Hu, Z.: Efficient suboptimal solutions to the optimal triangulation. International Journal of Computer Vision, 77–106 (2011)

[4] Kanatani, K., Sugaya, Y., Niitsuma, H.: Triangulation from two views revisited: Hartley-Sturm vs. optimal correction. In: The British Machine Vision Conference, pp. 173–182. BMVC Press, Leeds (2008)

[5] Lindstrom, P.: Triangulation made easy. In: IEEE Conference on Computer Vision and Pattern Recognition, pp. 1554–1561. IEEE Press, New York (2010)

[6] Olsson, C., Kahl, F., Oskarsson, M.: Branch and bound methods for Euclidean registration problems. IEEE Trans. Pattern Anal. Mach. Intell., 783–794 (2009)

[7] Olsson, C., Kahl, F., Hartley, R.: Projective least-squares: global solutions with local optimization. In: IEEE Conference on Computer Vision and Pattern Recognition, pp. 1216–1223. IEEE Press, New York (2009)

[8] Lu, F., Hartley, R.I.: A fast optimal algorithm for L_2 triangulation. In: Yagi, Y., Kang, S.B., Kweon, I.S., Zha, H. (eds.) ACCV 2007, Part II. LNCS, vol. 4844, pp. 279–288. Springer, Heidelberg (2007)

[9] Hartley, R., Schaffalitzky, F.: L_∞ minimization in geometric reconstruction problems. In: IEEE Conference on Computer Vision and Pattern Recognition, pp. 504–509. IEEE Press, New York (2004)

[10] Ke, Q., Kanade, T.: Quasiconvex optimization for robust geometric reconstruction. IEEE Trans. Pattern Anal. Mach. Intell., 1834–1847 (2007)

[11] Kahl, F., Hartley, R.: Multiple-view geometry under the L_∞-norm. IEEE Trans. Pattern Anal. Mach. Intell., 1603–1617 (2008)

[12] Bartoli, A., Sturm, P.: Structure-from-motion using lines: representation, triangulation, and bundle adjustment. Computer Vision and Image Understanding, 416–441 (2005)

[13] Spetsakis, M., Aloimonos, J.: Structure from motion using line correspondences. International Journal of Computer Vision, 171–183 (1990)

[14] Weng, J., Huang, T., Ahuja, N.: Motion and structure from line correspondences: closed-form solution, uniqueness, and optimization. IEEE Trans. Pattern Anal. Mach. Intell. 318–336 (1992)

[15] Taylor, C.J., Kriegman, D.J.: Structure and motion from line segments in multiple images. IEEE Trans. Pattern Anal. Mach. Intell. 1021–1032 (1995)

[16] Josephson, K., Kahl, F.: Triangulation of Points, Lines and Conics. Journal of Mathematical Imaging and Vision, 215–225 (2008)

[17] Hartley, R., Zisserman, A.: Multiple view geometry in computer vision. Cambridge University Press, Cambridge (2003)

[18] Ressl, C.: Geometry, Constraints and Computation of the Trifocal Tensor. PhD thesis, Technical University of Vienna (2003)

[19] Horn, R., Johnson, C.: Matrix Analysis. Cambridge University Press, Cambridge (2005)

Moving Object Detection System in Aerial Video Surveillance

Ahlem Walha, Ali Wali, and Adel M. Alimi

REGIM: REsearch Groups on Intelligent Machines,
University of Sfax, National Engineering School of Sfax (ENIS),
BP 1173, Sfax, 3038, Tunisia
{walha.ahlem,ali.wali,adel.alimi}@ieee.org
http://www.regim.org

Abstract. Moving object detection in aerial video, in which the camera is moving, is a complicated task. In this paper, we present a system to solve this problem by using scale invariant feature transform(SIFT) and Kalman Filter. Moving objects are detected by a feature point tracking method based on SIFT extraction and matching algorithm. In order to increase the precision of detection, some pre-processing methods are added to the surveillance system such as video stabilization and canny edge detection. Experimental results indicate that the suggested method of moving object detection can be achieved with a high detection ratio.

Keywords: Moving object detection, Aerial surveillance, scale invariant feature transform(SIFT), Digital video stabilization.

1 Introduction

Unmanned Aerial Vehicle(UAV)based surveillance are used in several applications like reconnaissance, homeland security and border protection. They present many advantages such as wide field of view, free motion and ability to be controlled remotely. An important task of video surveillance is to identify and track all moving objects in the scene and to generate exactly one track per object. This may involve detecting the moving objects and tracking them while they are visible. In aerial surveillance this problem is very difficult. The challenges of moving object detection in mobile platform include camera motion, small object appearances of only few pixels in the image, changing object background, object aggregation,panning, and noise. Therefore, video stabilization has become essential in mobile surveillance systems. Also it is the first step in many aerial applications.

In this paper we demonstrate that Scale Invariant Feature Transform (SIFT) as features are robust for video stabilization and moving object detection purposes. Using SIFT point extraction and matching, we can locate regions of the image where a residual motion occurs. Our contribution in this paper is that we applied kalman filtering on this moving region and not on the whole of image in order to estimate the motion of the region.

J. Blanc-Talon et al. (Eds.): ACIVS 2013, LNCS 8192, pp. 310–320, 2013.

The paper is organized as follows. In Section 2 we provide a summary of the related work in the area of video stabilization and moving object detection. Section 3 gives the complete system framework of our proposed approach detailing the SIFT feature extraction and matching process and how it is adopted to the stabilization and motion detection problem. In Section 4 our detailed experimental evaluation. Finally, Section 5 concludes the paper along with future research directions.

2   Related Work

Automatic surveillance system generally begins with detection of moving objects in the scene with the hypothesis that nothing might occur in areas without any movement. Moving object detection can be used in the tracking process as initial positions [22] or used as regions to be classified in recognition. Also it can alert interesting areas where it is required to be focused on (intrusion, line cross, etc.). In this way moving objects detection is an important research topic of surveillance system.

In literature various approaches aim to extract moving object are reported. However, they mostly tackle stationary camera scenarios [20] [21] [3] [19]. Recently, there has been an increasing interest in studying motion from moving cameras [17]. Background subtraction technique is one of the most successful approaches to extract moving objects[6] [11]. In this technique statistical background model are built and moving objects are extracted by finding regions which do not have similar characteristics to the background model. However, they have limitation that they are only applicable with the stationary cameras in fixed fields of view. Detection of moving objects with moving cameras has been researched to overcome this limitation of installment and inefficiency to cover large arias.

Video stabilization is a pre-processing step that is usually applied to analyze aerial video surveillance. Different approaches have been introduced which are deviated into four groups: mechanical, optical, electronic and digital stabilization. In this paper we focused on digital image stabilization method. Battiato et al. [1] employed SIFT to detect the feature points and then their trajectory is evaluated to estimate inter frame motion. Iterative Least Squares method is used to avoid estimation errors. This method requires heavy computation. Wang et al.[25] proposed a realtime video stabilization method for aerial video surveillance by keypoints matching based on FAST corner detection. After that the matched keypoints are involved for estimation of affine transform to reduce false matching. They use affine transform model to perform motion estimation and Spline smoothing to compensate vibration. This method is able to achieve an average up to 30 frames per second (fps). Wang et al. [24] presented an approach for feature tracking based on a homography estimation and motion compensation using high degree B-spline smoothing. Hu et al [9] proposed a method based on SIFT with the combination of Gaussian kernel filtering and parabolic fitting for removing the vibrations.

Concerning moving object detection in video captured by moving camera, the most typical method for detecting moving objects with mobile cameras is the extension of background subtraction method [2] [4] [7] [16]. In these methods, panoramic background models are constructed by applying various image registration techniques [14] to input frames and the position of current frame in panoramas is found by image matching algorithms. Then, moving objects are segmented in a similar way to the fixed camera case. In[6] and [19] camera motion matrix is estimated foreground is segmented by comparing input frame to background mosaic. In these work different type of motion model are used, but both of them do not consider image registration error by parallax effect. Lin et al [12] proposed an ego-motion estimation and background/foreground classification method. The authors built their model focusing on the motion vectors obtained by using the SURF algorithm to extract the feature points and their correspondence between frames . There may be some problems for the reason that the feature points selected by the algorithm may lay on moving objects in the frame, as a result, the model built based on the feature motion vectors may fail to get the moving object. Kang et al. [4] built background mosaic considering internal parameters of cameras. But, camera internal parameters are not always available and possible stabilization errors are still not considered in this method. Deal with this problem of stabilization errors and segment moving object robustly, in[2] cylindrical mosaics are and in [15] spatial distribution of Gaussian is proposed. In [8]one pixel is considered as spatial mixture of random processes to solve possible registration errors.

The second method to detect moving objects with moving camera is optical flow [18] [26]. They assume that the motions of backgrounds and foreground objects are divided by different optical flows and reduce moving object detection to motion segmentation problem. This scheme has been adopted in the following approaches. In [26] map is used to segment moving objects in the scene. Thakoor et al. [18] used dense optical flow and detected moving objects by comparing it to the estimated camera motion. But detecting moving objects, dense optical flow requires heavy computation and camera motions should be relatively small. In [23] the authors obtain the motion model of the background by computing the optical flow between two adjacent frames in order to get motion information for each pixel. Cuntoor [5] use Histogram of oriented Gradients, Histogram of oriented optical Flow and Haar features to classify the motion segmentation into person vs. other and vehicle vs. other.

In this paper, we present a new system for video stabilization and moving object detection in aerial video to solve the existing problems in traditional approaches. Our problem is defined as Consider a particular pixel position. The pixel value is changing over time without a certain pattern in aerial video because the background is changing all the time using SIFT and Kalman filter.

3   Proposed Method for Moving Object Detection

Background modeling could not be applied to mobile surveillance system when background is fast moving. At the same time, camera vibration and noise enormously affects the accuracy of detection. SIFT feature extraction [13]can identify keypoint in order to be tracked over multiple frames of video and they are invariant to image translation, rotation and scale. For this reason, in this paper, we use the feature point tracking method to acquire a serial of features, which are then classified into three categories: undesired motion, moving object and static object. Our method consists of two steps: Video stabilization to eliminate camera vibration and noise and Motion detection and tracking using SIFT feature point extraction, matching and kalman filter. The flowchart of our method is illustrated in Fig. 1 and the details are explained as follows.

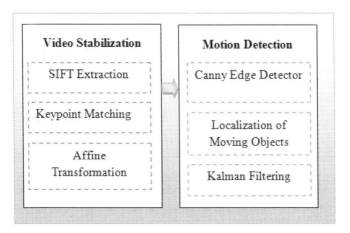

Fig. 1. Overview of the proposed method

3.1   Video Stabilization

The input of our system is a real video captured from UAV. First of all, SIFT keypoint are extracted and matching pairs are determined. Next, motion between two consecutive frames is estimated based on an affine transform model. Finally, the frames are compensated based on median filtering.

SIFT can provide robust matching in our case where change in 3D viewpoint, noise, and change in illumination are present. We use SIFT keypoints to estimate the global interframe motion vector where we extract SIFT from two successive frames and then we match two sets of feature points to obtain a local motion vector. Mathematically speaking, since absolute positions $P_1(x_1,y_1,1)$ and P'_2 $(x_2,y_2,1)$ of both first and second keypoint in both frames are known, the local motion vector can be estimated and represent how the feature has supposedly moved from the previous frame to the next one. We used RANSAC (Random Sample Consensus) to filter outliers that come from the imprecision of the SIFT model. RANSAC is a robust estimator where it was used to derive a usable model from a set of data. The whole set of local motion vectors do not contain useful information for effective motion compensation as it includes matches related to moving objects in the scene. We eliminate moving objects by assuming that the

Fig. 2. SIFT Keypoint extracted and matched for two consecutive frame

velocity of moving objects is very large as compared to other motions.Fig. 2 shows the result of matching.

Thus the transformation matrix is obtained. In this paper we adopt a four parameter 2D affine motion model to describe geometric transformation between two consecutive frames. If $P(x,y,1)$ is the point in frame n, and $P'(x',y',1)$ is the same point in the successive frame, then the transformation from P to P' can be represented as shown in Eq.(1).

$$\begin{pmatrix} x' \\ y' \\ 1 \end{pmatrix} = \begin{pmatrix} S\cos\theta & -S\sin\theta & T_x \\ S\sin\theta & S\cos\theta & T_y \\ 0 & 0 & 1 \end{pmatrix} \begin{pmatrix} x \\ y \\ 1 \end{pmatrix} \qquad (1)$$

The affine matrix can describe accurately pure rotation, panning, and small translations of the camera in a scene with small relative depth variations and zooming effects. S is the scale, θ is the rotation and T_x and T_y are the translations. This has only four free parameters compared to the full affine transform's six: one scale factor, one angle, and two translations. The linear Least Squares Method on a set of redundant equations is a good choice to solve this problem. It results in robust parameter estimation. We need to compensate the current frame to obtain stable images. Compensation of the images is calculated directly from the parameters estimated in Eq.(1). But undesired motion of the sensors and normal motion of the UAV should be separated. We used mediane filter to reduce noise and to estimate motion for the current frame. Specifically, the proposed method calculates the spatial correlation between the current motion vector and its neighboring motion vectors. If the current motion vector is not correlated with its neighboring motion vectors, we decide that the current motion vector is an outlier, and correct the motion vector into a new motion vector generated by the median filter. Hence, we can remove undesired motion in the frame caused by outliers, and improve the image quality of the frame.

3.2   Moving Object Detection

After removing the undesired motion of camera the first step of moving object detected is object edges detected by using canny edge detection algorithm [10]. The Canny operator is an optimal edge detector. It takes as input a gray scale image, and produces as output an image showing the positions of tracked intensity discontinuities. The Canny operator works in three steps. First of all, the image is smoothed by Gaussian convolution. Then, a simple 2-D first derivative operator (somewhat like the Roberts Cross) is applied to the smoothed image to highlight regions of the image with high first spatial derivatives. Edges give rise to ridges in the gradient magnitude image. The tracking process exhibits hysteresis controlled by two thresholds: T_1 and T_2, with $T1 > T2$. Tracking can only begin at a point on a ridge higher than T_1. Tracking then continues in both directions out from that point until the height of the ridge falls below T_2. This hysteresis helps to ensure that noisy edges are not broken up into multiple edge fragments.The results are shown in Fig.3.

The second step consists of using edged image to extract SIFT keypoint and determine matched pair. We fixed a threshold to detect moving objects by assuming that the velocity of moving objects is very large as compared to other motions.

In our method, we detected moving object for each frame. Therefore tracking becomes difficult. Because false detection and the presence of objects that enter and leave the scene can modify the number of detected object in consecutive frame. To resolve this problem, we used kalman filtering. In general Kalman filter is used for filtering a noisy dynamic system. It estimates the new states of the system and then corrects it by the measurements. In our case, the motion can be described as shown in Eq.(2) and (3).

$$\boldsymbol{x_k} = (\,x\,)_k \, \dot{x}_k = \begin{pmatrix} x_{k-1} \\ \dot{x}_{k-1} \end{pmatrix} \begin{pmatrix} 1 & 1 \\ 0 & 1 \end{pmatrix} + w_{k-1} \tag{2}$$

$$z_k = (\,1\,)\,0\boldsymbol{x_k} + v_k \tag{3}$$

with x_k is the position coordinate in one direction, z_k is the measured position, w_{k-1} is the process noise and v_k is the measurement noise. We assume zero to the acceleration because we do not have information about the control of the motion, also we modeled the change in velocity by the process noise. As it is shown in Eq.(2), we do not include the acceleration in the process equation, and the effect of the acceleration noise is described by the velocity noise.Result is shown in Fig.5

Fig. 3. Canny Edge Detection

Fig. 4. Localization of moving object

4   Experimental Results

We tested our method with UCF-ARG data set.The videos were taken in 60 frames per second with the resolution of 1920 x 1080 pixels [1]. The challenges composed by this dataset include characteristics of aerial videos such as different shapes, sizes and ethnicities of people, scale changes, shadows, cloth variations and different scenarios. Our first experiment consists of comparing our system to [25]. This system is based on FAST corner detection.

We used Peak Signal-to-Noise Ratio (PSNR), an error measure, to evaluate the quality of the video stabilization. $PSNR$ between frame n and frame $n + 1$ is defined as

$$PSNR(n) = 10 \log_{10} \frac{I_{MAX}}{MSE(n)} \tag{4}$$

---

[1] http://crcv.ucf.edu/data/UCF_Aerial_Action.php

Before Kalman Filtering   After Kalman Filtering

Fig. 5. Kalman Filtering

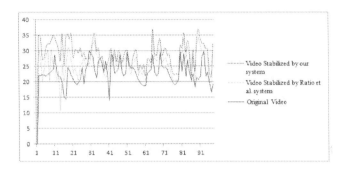

Fig. 6. Graph of the Peak Signal-to-Noise ratio of the original video and the stabilized video

Where $MSE(n)$ Mean-Square-Error between frames, I_{MAX} is the maximum intensity value of a pixel and N and M are frame dimensions. The $PSNR$ value for each frame of the original video and our stabilized version are shown in the graph in Fig.6 We find that our stabilization system is working well especially in the case where video sequences including moving objects. Due to the accuracy of detected keypoints and the use of adaptive RANSAC to remove outliers, our system gives a good results compared to wang *et al.* system [25]. We used Detection Ratio(DR) and False Alarm Ratio *(FAR)* to evaluate the performance of our detection method. In Eq.(5)and Eq.(6) TP is true positives of moving objects, *FP* is false positive of moving objects and *FN* is false negative (not detected). Results are shown in Table (1)

$$DR = TP/(TP + FN) \qquad (5)$$

$$FAR = FP/(TP + FP) \qquad (6)$$

318   A. Walha, A. Wali, and A.M. Alimi

Table 1. Quantitative analysis of our detection & tracking method

Video Stream	Moving Object	Detection	Detection Ratio	False Alarm Ratio
Video 1	2	4	1	0.2
Video 2	4	7	1	0.5
Video 3	3	7	1	0.6
Video 4	5	12	1	0.8
Video 5	7	14	1	0.34

Table 1 illustrates the performance of our system. The experimental results show that our system can achieve good performance in detection rate.

5   Conclusions

In this paper, a processing chain is presented for stabilization and moving object detection in UAV surveillance videos. For video stabilization, SIFT features are detected and matched for frame-to-frame to estimate the affinity matrix transformation. Using a stabilized video, SIFT features are then used for moving object detection by compensation of camera motion and moving features to cluster independent motion. Our result is improved by using filter kalman to estimate the motion of detected object. In application with our UAV data, we achieved 91% correctly detected moving objects.

Acknowledgments. The authors would like to acknowledge the financial support of this work by grants from General Direction of Scientific Research (DGRST), Tunisia, under the ARUB program.

References

1. Battiato, S., Gallo, G., Puglisi, G., Scellato, S., Catania, S.S.D.: Sift features tracking for video stabilization. In: 14th International Conference on Image Analysis and Processing, pp. 825–830 (2007)
2. Bhat, K.S., Saptharishi, M., Khosla, P.K.: Motion detection and segmentation using image mosaics. In: IEEE International Conference on Multimedia and Expo 2000 (ICME), pp. 1577–1580 (2000)
3. Chakroun, M., Wali, A., Alimi, A.M.: Multi-agent system for moving object segmentation and tracking. In: 2011 8th IEEE International Conference on Advanced Video and Signal-Based Surveillance (AVSS), pp. 424–429. IEEE (2011)
4. Cucchiara, R., Prati, A., Vezzani, R.: Advanced video surveillance with pan tilt zoom cameras. In: Proceedings of the Workshop on Visual Surveillance (VS) at ECCV 2006, Graz, Austria (May 2006)
5. Cuntoor, N.P., Basharat, A., Perera, A.G.A., Hoogs, A.: Track initialization in low frame rate and low resolution videos. In: 2010 International Conference on Pattern Recognition, pp. 3640–3644 (2010)

6. Elgammal, A., Duraiswami, R., Harwood, D., Davis, L.: Background and foreground modeling using nonparametric kernel density estimation for visual surveillance. Proceedings of the IEEE 90(7), 1151–1163 (2002)
7. Guillot, C., Taron, M., Sayd, P., Pham, Q.C., Tilmant, C., Lavest, J.-M.: Background subtraction adapted to ptz cameras by keypoint density estimation. In: Proceedings of the British Machine Vision Conference, pp. 34.1–34.10. BMVA Press (2010), doi:10.5244/C.24.34
8. Hayman, E., Eklundh, J.-O.: Statistical background subtraction for a mobile observer. In: Proceedings of the Ninth IEEE International Conference on Computer Vision, vol. 1, pp. 67–74 (2003)
9. Hu, R., Shi, R., Shen, I., Chen, W.: Video stabilization using scale-invariant features. In: The 11th International Conference Information Visualization, pp. 871–877 (2007)
10. Kitti, T., Jaruwan, T., Chaiyapon, T.: An object recognition and identification system using the harris corner detection method. International Journal of Machine Learning and Computing 2(4), 462–465 (2012)
11. Ko, T., Soatto, S., Estrin, D.: Warping background subtraction. In: 2010 IEEE Conference on Computer Vision and Pattern Recognition (CVPR), pp. 1331–1338 (2010)
12. Lin, C.-C., Wolf, M.: Detecting moving objects using a camera on a moving platform. In: 20th IEEE International Conference on Pattern Recognition, pp. 460–463 (2010)
13. Lowe, D.: Distinctive image features from scale-invariant keypoints. International Journal of Computer Vision 14(2), 91–110 (2004)
14. Lucas, B.D., Kanade, T.: An iterative image registration technique with an application to stereo vision (ijcai). In: Proceedings of the 7th International Joint Conference on Artificial Intelligence (IJCAI 1981), pp. 674–679 (April 1981)
15. Ren, Y., Chua, C.-S., Ho, Y.-K.: Motion detection with non-stationary background. In: Proceedings of the 11th International Conference on Image Analysis and Processing, pp. 78–83 (2001)
16. Robinault, L., Bres, S., Miguet, S.: Real time foreground object detection using PTZ camera. In: International Conference on Computer Vision, Theory and Applications (VISAPP 2009), pp. 609–614 (February 2009)
17. Teutsch, M., Kruger, W.: Detection, segmentation, and tracking of moving objects in uav videos. IEEE Ninth International Conference on Advanced Video and Signal-Based Surveillance 60(2), 91–110 (2012)
18. Thakoor, N., Gao, J.: Automatic object detection in video sequences with camera in motion (2004)
19. Walha, A., Wali, A., Alimi, A.M.: Support vector machine approach for detecting events in video streams. In: Hassanien, A.E., Salem, A.-B.M., Ramadan, R., Kim, T.-h. (eds.) AMLTA 2012. CCIS, vol. 322, pp. 143–151. Springer, Heidelberg (2012)
20. Wali, A., Alimi, A.M.: Incremental learning approach for events detection from large video dataset. In: Advanced Video and Signal Based Surveillance (AVSS), pp. 555–560 (2010)
21. Wali, A., Alimi, A.M.: Multimodal approach for video surveillance indexing and retrieval. Journal of Intelligent Computing 4(1), 165–175 (2010)
22. Wang, J., Bebis, G., Nicolescu, M., Nicolescu, M., Miller, R.: Improving target detection by coupling it with tracking. Mach. Vision Appl. 20(4), 205–223 (2009)

23. Wang, Y., Zhang, Z., Wang, Y.: Moving object detection in aerial video. In: 2012 11th International Conference on Machine Learning and Applications, pp. 446–450 (2012)
24. Wang, Y., Chang, R., Chua, T., Leman, K.: Video stabilization based on high degree b-spline smoothing. In: 21st International Conference on Pattern Recognition, pp. 3152–3155 (2012)
25. Wang, Y., Hou, Z., Leman, K., Chang, R.: Real-time video stabilization for unmanned aerial vehicles. In: IAPR Conference on Machine Vision Applications, pp. 825–830 (2011)
26. Zhang, Y., Kiselewich, S., Bauson, W., Hammoud, R.: Robust moving object detection at distance in the visible spectrum and beyond using a moving camera. In: Conference on Computer Vision and Pattern Recognition Workshop, CVPRW 2006, p. 131 (2006)

An Indoor RGB-D Dataset for the Evaluation of Robot Navigation Algorithms

Adam Schmidt, Michał Fularz, Marek Kraft,
Andrzej Kasiński, and Michał Nowicki

Institute of Control and Information Engineering
Poznan University of Technology
{adam.schmidt,michal.fularz,marek.kraft,andrzej.kasinski}@put.poznan.pl,
michal.k.nowicki@student.put.poznan.pl

Abstract. The paper presents a RGB-D dataset for development and evaluation of mobile robot navigation systems. The dataset was registered using a WiFiBot robot equipped with a Kinect sensor. Unlike the presently available datasets, the environment was specifically designed for the registration with the Kinect sensor. Moreover, it was ensured that the registered data is synchronized with the ground truth position of the robot. The presented dataset will be made publicly available for research purposes.

Keywords: robot navigation, SLAM, benchmark dataset, Kinect, RGB-D.

1 Introduction

In recent years, the advances in the field of sensor and algorithm development contributed to the introduction of successful visual odometry and simultaneous localization and mapping systems (SLAM). Moreover, the appearance of the Microsoft Kinect sensor allowed to propose new methods for robot navigation [5][6]. Those methods combine the already known vision-based approaches with the additional information about the scene depth from the RGB-D sensor. Additionally, the fact that the Kinect sensor is affordable made it very popular in the robotic research community.

However, the further progress of those methods relies on the publicly available benchmark datasets enabling comparison of the trajectory estimated using the researched algorithm against the ground truth. The novelty of the Kinect sensor is a reason some of the commonly used benchmark datasets do not contain the data registered using this sensor. An example is the Rawseeds database [3].

The few publicly available datasets containing the data registered using Kinect usually incorporate additional information from a wide spectrum of other sensors and the registration environment is not specially prepared for the registration carried out using the Kinect sensor. This is the case with the publicly available Freiburg datasets [8]. The Freiburg datasets contain the RGB and depth images registered with the handheld Kinect, Kinect mounted on the robot, as well as

J. Blanc-Talon et al. (Eds.): ACIVS 2013, LNCS 8192, pp. 321–329, 2013.
© Springer International Publishing Switzerland 2013

3D object recognition and dynamic object sequences. Unfortunately, in parts of the sequences registered by the moving robot, there are no physical objects visible in Kinect's working range (up to 6 meters). As a consequence, no proper depth information is available, and the systems relying on depth information for the inter-frame transformation estimation may not work properly. The dataset is therefore not appropriate for testing of simple Kinect SLAM algorithms or for the algorithms in the early development phase.

Additionally, the Freiburg database contains the timestamped Kinect data and the timestamped ground truth data, but their timestamps are not synchronized. In order to retrieve the information about a position of a robot for the chosen timestamp of the Kinect data, the interpolation of ground truth position must be used.

This paper presents the system used for the dataset acquisition and the ground truth generation allowing to retrieve precise information about position and orientation of the robot in the environment. The result produced by the described system is the publicly available, Kinect-dedicated dataset. In the presented system, the timestamps are synchronized for the Kinect's RGB and depth image and for the global ground truth system. Eliminating a need to interpolate robot position makes the reference information more credible. Moreover, the datasets described in this paper were registered in Kinect-friendly indoor bureau environment with an abundance of objects that can be tracked at all times in the Kinect sensor range.

The paper is organized in the following manner. The section 2 presents the registration system and the used mobile robot, the section 3 explains the registration procedure, the solution used for synchronization and shows the trajectory reconstruction procedure, while the section 4 presents the registered dataset. The section 5 contains conclusions and outlines the possible directions of further work.

2   Registration System

2.1   Motion Capture System

The system described in [7] was used for the data registration. The system is comprised of 5 high resolution Basler acA1600 cameras with low-distortion, aspherical 3.5mm lenses. The cameras were calibrated according to the rational function lens distortion model[4] using the functions provided with the OpenCV library[2]. The Table 1 presents the registration system cameras parameters as well as the average reprojection error obtained during the calibration process. The cameras are arranged in an X-shaped layout (Fig. 1). The field of view (FOV) of the central camera partially overlaps with FOVs of the peripheral cameras and the FOV of each of the peripheral cameras partially overlaps with FOVs of two other peripheral cameras. The coordinate frame of the central camera is considered to be coincident with the global coordinate system. The pose of the peripheral cameras was obtained by registering a set of images with the calibration marker visible simultaneously from at least two cameras (Fig. 2). The Levenberg-Marquardt algorithm was used to find the cameras pose by minimizing the reprojection error of calibration marker corners on all images.

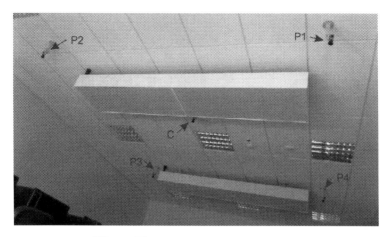

Fig. 1. The registration system cameras

Table 1. Intrinsic parameters, distortion coefficients and the average reprojection error of the registration system cameras

ID	f_u	f_v	u_0	v_0	k_1	k_2	k_3	k_4	k_5	k_6	p_1	p_2	error
C	832.3	832.3	808.5	597.1	-0.019	0.096	0.003	0.002	0.040	0.034	-0.025	0.101	0.18
P_1	822.3	823.1	810.8	605.3	0.008	0.055	-0.001	0.002	-0.030	0.041	-0.028	0.009	0.24
P_2	821.1	820.6	806.3	632.8	-0.017	0.072	0.001	-0.002	-0.004	0.031	-0.038	0.048	0.21
P_3	827.9	828.3	787.6	611.1	-0.104	0.001	0.001	-0.001	0.092	-0.048	-0.128	0.160	0.22
P_4	830.2	830.4	805.0	591.8	0.132	0.060	0.001	-0.000	0.063	0.188	-0.073	0.137	0.11

Fig. 2. The calibration marker observed by three cameras

Table 2. The Cartesian position and orientation represented with the Rodrigues' formula of the peripheral cameras

ID	$x[m]$	$y[m]$	$z[m]$	r_x	r_y	r_z
P_1	-1.288	1.769	0.039	-0.0183	0.2351	-3.1164
P_2	-1.381	-1.634	0.049	-0.1498	0.0869	0.0017
P_3	2.259	-1.825	-0.015	-0.1255	0.0392	-0.0070
P_4	2.365	1.624	-0.021	0.0652	-0.3374	3.1158

The position and orientation of the peripheral cameras with regard to the central camera's frame is presented in the Table 2.

2.2   Mobile Robot

The WiFiBot Lab V3 mobile platform was used to gather the data. The robot was equipped with a rigid frame with a calibration marker and Kinect sensor attached to it (Fig. 3).

As the robot's pose was calculated according to the observations of the marker it was assumed that the robot coordinate system is defined by the marker. The pose of the Kinect within this coordinates was calculated using an additional calibration marker and an external camera. The external camera was placed in location that allowed simultaneous observation of both the calibration markers while the Kinect recorded the image of the external marker. The Levenberg-Marquardt algorithm was used to find the Kinect pose minimizing the reprojection error of both the calibration markers corners on all recorded images. Table 3 presents the pose of the Kinect sensor in the robot coordinate system.

Fig. 3. The WiFiBot robot with the calibration marker and the Kinect sensor

Table 3. The Cartesian position and orientation represented with the Rodrigues' formula of the Kinect sensor

$x[m]$	$y[m]$	$z[m]$	r_x	r_y	r_z
1.364	-0.005	0.034	0.170	-0.126	-0.075

3   Registration Procedure

The registration system is divided into the mobile (the robot with the camera and the Kinect sensor) and the static (the overhead cameras) part. Two independent computers were used for capturing and saving the images. Block diagram of the configuration of the registration system is presented on Fig. 4.

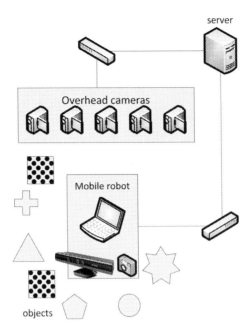

Fig. 4. Schematic of the registration system

The computer connected to the overhead cameras was acting as the central server and was supervising and synchronizing all the actions. Tests were conducted to choose the best way to synchronize the acquisition in the system and all the wireless solutions (using the Wi-Fi network and using the proprietary wireless modules) were dropped due to large variance in delays. In the end, synchronization using the TCP/IP protocol over the Ethernet cable connection was chosen. Throughout the experiments, the packet delay between the computers was monitored using a simple network analysis tool and was reported to be less than 1 ms. The system was working with maximum achievable frequency (approximately 9 frames per second for each camera). Whenever both parts of the system signaled that they are ready to capture new data, the trigger signal was sent to all the cameras to acquire the next set of images. Due to the large amount of data that need to be sent from the cameras to the server, the network card was specifically configured to facilitate additional receive buffers, use low interrupt moderation rate and use the biggest jumbo frames available [1]. The server software was created in C# and uses Pylon SDK version 3.1. The software takes advantage of multithreading and splits the workload into several separate tasks (synchronization, GUI and statistics, capturing the images and saving to disk). To be able to save all the acquired data (approx. 90MB/s) to disk, a fast SSD drive was used.

The robot trajectory was reconstructed offline after each trial. The pose of the robot at each timestamp was calculated independently according to the observations from the registration system cameras (Fig. 7). Depending on the position of

326 A. Schmidt et al.

the robot it could be visible on one or more cameras. The Levenberg-Marquardt algorithm was used to find the robot pose in the central camera's coordinate system that minimized the average reprojection error of the calibration marker corners on all images. Figure 5 presents an exemplary trajectory reconstructed from a single robot's run.

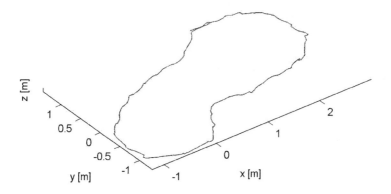

Fig. 5. An exemplary robot's trajectory

4 Dataset

4.1 Registered Data

The dataset contains the following common data:

- the calibration data (intrinsic parameters) for each individual camera in the system,
- the calibration data (extrinsic parameters) for the five cameras mounted on the ceiling,
- the images used for camera calibration, enabling the potential users of the datatbase to use their own camera calibration algorithms or models.

As mentioned before, data from all imaging devices for a single trajectory sampling point is acquired simultaneously. A complete set of data for such a sampling point contains of:

- one RGB camera image and one corresponding depth image (example images given in Fig. 6),
- current pose of the robot w.r.t. the reference frame given as six values (three translation vector components and three rotation components given in Rodrigues' representation),
- five images from the registration system cameras to give the potential users of the datatbase the possibility to use their own algorithms for marker tracking (example images given in Fig. 7).

All of the images contained within the dataset were saved using lossless compression.

Fig. 6. Sample RGB-D image pairs from the sequence contained in the datatset

Fig. 7. Images registered by the ceiling cameras at a sample trajectory point. In this particular case, the robot is visible in all five cameras.

It is worth noting that the environment was specifically design to provide useful data for the depth-based algorithms. Therefore, a number of various objects was placed in the laboratory to ensure that there are items in the working range of the Kinect sensor during the whole robot's run.

5   Conclusions

An indoor RGB-D dataset for evaluation of robot navigation algorithms has been described in this article. To overcome the shortcomings of the currently freely available datasets of RGB-D data used for the evaluation of visual navigation algorithms, special care was exercised to properly synchronize the imaging devices used for the acquisition. Moreover, the additional objects were introduced to the registration environments, so that physical objects are visible in the working range of the Kinect sensor throughout the whole registered sequences.

As the global optimization using the Levenberg-Marquard algorithm was utilized for the calibration of the relative pose of the ceiling cameras and for the estimation of the position of the marker associated with the robot, the robot's trajectory can be tracked very accurately. As a result, the ground truth data contained within the dataset is highly reliable.

The presented dataset is publicly available and can be freely downloaded and distributed according to the Open Access research model. As such, it can serve as a valuable common ground for the comparative studies of both currently available and prospective RGB-D and vision-based navigation algorithms.

In the future the benchmarking system will be extended to allow simultaneous tracking of multiple robots exploring shared environment. Moreover, the system will be adapted to track the movement of other platforms, e.g. a quadrocopter robot.

Acknowledgments. Adam Schmidt and Michał Fularz are scholarship holders within the project "Scholarship support for PH.D. students specializing in majors strategic for Wielkopolska's development", Sub-measure 8.2.2 Human Capital Operational Programme, co-financed by European Union under the European Social Fund.

This research was supported by the Polish National Science Centre grant funded according to the decision DEC-2011/01/N/ST7/05940, which is gratefully acknowledged.

References

1. Basler: Installation and setup guide for cameras used with Basler's Pylon API, 7th edn. (October 2012)
2. Bradski, G.: The OpenCV Library. Dr. Dobb's Journal of Software Tools (2000)
3. Ceriani, S., Fontana, G., Giusti, A., Marzorati, D., Matteucci, M., Migliore, D., Rizzi, D., Sorrenti, D., Taddei, P.: Rawseeds ground truth collection systems for indoor self-localization and mapping. Autonomous Robots 27(4), 353–371 (2009), http://dx.doi.org/10.1007/s10514-009-9156-5
4. Claus, D., Fitzgibbon, A.W.: A rational function lens distortion model for general cameras. In: IEEE Computer Society Conference on Computer Vision and Pattern Recognition, CVPR 2005, vol. 1, pp. 213–219. IEEE (2005)
5. Endres, F., Hess, J., Engelhard, N., Sturm, J., Cremers, D., Burgard, W.: An evaluation of the "RGB-D" slam system. In: 2012 IEEE International Conference on Robotics and Automation (ICRA), pp. 1691–1696 (2012)
6. G., Huang, S., Hu, L.Z., Alempijevic, A., Dissanayake, G.: A robust "RGB-D SLAM" algorithm. In: 2012 IEEE/RSJ International Conference on Intelligent Robots and Systems (IROS), pp. 1714–1719 (2012)
7. Schmidt, A., Kraft, M., Fularz, M., Domagał a, Z.: The registration system for the evaluation of indoor visual "slam" and odometry algorithms. Journal of Automation, Mobile Robotics & Intelligent Systems 7(2), 46–51 (2013)
8. Sturm, J., Engelhard, N., Endres, F., Burgard, W., Cremers, D.: A benchmark for the evaluation of rgb-d slam systems. In: 2012 IEEE/RSJ International Conference on Intelligent Robots and Systems (IROS), pp. 573–580 (2012)

Real-Time Depth Map Based People Counting

František Galčík* and Radoslav Gargalík**

Institute of Computer Science,
P.J. Šafárik University, Faculty of Science,
Jesenná 5, 041 54 Košice, Slovak Republic
frantisek.galcik@upjs.sk, radoslav.gargalik@student.upjs.sk

Abstract. People counting is an important task in video surveillance applications. It can provide statistic information for shopping centers and other public buildings or knowledge of the current number of people in a building in a case of an emergency. This paper describes a real-time people counting system based on a vertical Kinect depth sensor. Processing pipeline of the system includes depth map improvement, a novel approach to head segmentation, and continuous tracking of head segments. The head segmentation is based on an adaptation of the region-growing segmentation approach with thresholding. The tracking of segments combines minimum-weighted bipartite graph matchings and prediction of object movement to eliminate inaccuracy of segmentation. Results of evaluation realized on datasets from a shopping center (more than 23 hours of recordings) show that the system can handle almost all real-world situations with high accuracy.

Keywords: people counting, Kinect depth sensor, continuous tracking.

1 Introduction

People counting is an important task in a variety of video surveillance applications. Known approaches to realize people counting can be divided into the following groups: counting by detection, counting by regression and unsupervised tracker. Each of the mentioned approaches has some problems which impact negatively on either people counting performance or accuracy.

The main idea of counting by detection is using the multi-scale window slide over the image. To determine if there is a person within a window or not, a binary classifier is used [4, 13]. Counting by detection approach has two main unsolved problems. The first one is the situation where one object may correspond to different bounding boxes and it causes problems for non-maximum suppression [5,6] if people have interactions. The second one is the situation where some objects are occluded (either partially or wholly) so they are too difficult to detect.

Counting by regression approach is based on learning a map between features and the number of people in the training set, where the regression techniques are used to learn that map. Next, the map is used to estimate the number of people in test images

* Supported by the Slovak grant contracts VEGA 1/0479/12 and APVV-0035-10.
** Supported by the Slovak grant contracts APVV-0526-11 and VVGS-PF-2012-60.

J. Blanc-Talon et al. (Eds.): ACIVS 2013, LNCS 8192, pp. 330–341, 2013.

[8, 10]. The main disadvantage of counting by regression is that the performance always depends on training instances. If the number of training instances is large, then the labeling is very time consuming.

The final mentioned approach is based on using the unsupervised point tracker. The point tracker tracks the visual features and clusters their trajectories. In general, the number of cluster centers is the number of people. The main problem of this approach arises, when a person makes a long move. The result will be two clustered trajectories instead of one. Some people can also pass together which results in a single trajectory.

In [15] Zhang et al. presented a novel approach for people counting based on the Kinect depth sensor. They used simulation of water filling to find local minimum regions in an input depth map, which should correspond to heads of people located in the scene. The algorithm was tested on two datasets with impressive results. Note that the idea of using depth camera is not new in the field of people counting. In [1, 12] a vertical Time-of-Flight sensor was used to detect and track people. The Kinect depth sensor has two main advantages in comparison with the Time-of-Flight sensor. Firstly, the Kinect sensor is much cheaper and secondly, the Kinect sensor seems to provide better precision. Thus, the use of the Kinect sensor is a natural decision, because knowledge of a vertical depth of the scene is very helpful in the people counting process. In addition, the Kinect sensor positioned in the vertical position helps to avoid the occlusion problem.

The Kinect sensor uses structural light technique to generate the calibrated depth information of the scene [7]. The depth is estimated for every pixel in the scene. The acquired depth information is invariant to illumination, color and texture. The knowledge of such information in the people counting process is very useful and can speed up the process of counting and make it more precise. If we assume that the head should be closer to the sensor than any other body parts, we can reduce the head segmentation to finding local minimum regions. However, in real applications some serious problems arise, which make the segmentation process more complicated. First of all, the Kinect sensor is noisy. This results in discontinuities in a produced depth map - the presence of "holes" (pixels for which depth information was not estimated - black pixels in the depth map in Figure 1). In practice, some of the holes are quite huge. Secondly, the depth map of crowded people can contain multiple local extremum. Therefore, it is difficult to achieve satisfactory precision and fast performance with the traditional techniques sensitive to the threshold (mean shift, watershed, etc.).

In this paper, we describe an unsupervised real-time people counting system based on a vertical Kinect depth sensor. Although we use the Kinect depth sensor in our system, the Kinect depth sensor can be replaced with another depth sensor (e.g., Asus Xtion) without affecting algorithmical parts of the system. Since there are depth sensors that do not provide RGB data (e.g., one model of the Asus Xtion), the system uses only depth data to realize the people counting. Similarly to previous works (e.g., [7]), the core part of the system is identification of head segments in the input depth map. In contrast to other works, our head segmentation algorithm is based on a fast region-growing approach with thresholding. To deal with inaccuracy of segmentation for real-world scenes, we introduce a tracking algorithm that combines minimum-weighted bipartite graph matchings and prediction of object movement.

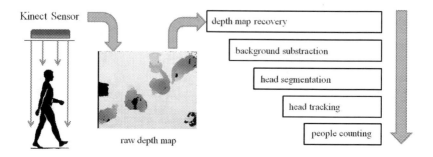

Fig. 1. Overview of our people counting system. The Kinect depth sensor is installed on the ceiling and pointing to the floor. The depth map produced by the sensor is processed by five components of the system.

Several datasets were published to evaluate people counting on. However, there is still a lack of some specific scenes which occur permanently in real life situations. For example, the following scene situations are obvious in shopping centers: parents guiding their children by hand, parents carrying their children on arms, people wearing either baseball caps or winter hats or some other sort of hats (which may have a negative impact on the head detection), wheelchair people, people with shopping baskets (either empty or not), people with strollers, etc. Although some algorithms and approaches to people counting give interesting results, most of them were not evaluated on the mentioned real life scenes. In order to evaluate our approach on real life scenes, we installed the Kinect depth sensor in a shopping center.

In Section 2, we discus the quality of input depth maps produced by the Kinect depth sensor in a real-world environment (entrances of buildings) and propose a simple preprocessing to improve the quality of depth maps. Section 3 describes our approach and details of algorithms forming the processing pipeline of the system. Practical experiments and evaluation tests of the proposed system are presented in Section 4. We evaluated segmentation accuracy and compared our results with those published in [15]. The counting accuracy was evaluated on recordings (over 23 hours) from a shopping center. Finally, Section 5 concludes the paper.

2   Depth Map Recovery

The Kinect depth sensor and other currently available depth sensors (e.g., Asus Xtion) use infrared (IR) pattern, which is projected onto the scene. Projected IR pattern can be seriously affected by direct sunlight. Therefore, depth sensors may not be functional in outdoor environments where the direct sunlight is present. Some modern shopping centers and other public buildings have entrances made of glass, which admits direct sunlight inside. Thus even if the depth sensor is located in the indoor environment, it is still possible that it will be affected by sunlight because of glass entrances and glass walls. In this case sunlight affects the IR pattern projected by the depth sensor which results in many missing values in the acquired depth map. An example can be seen in Figure 2. Such many missing depth values have negative impacts on our segmentation algorithm, so it is vital to improve the quality of acquired depth map in this case.

Several methods have been developed to improve the quality of depth maps. Some of them focus on the recovery of missing depth values. A joint-bilateral filtering framework to inpaint depth maps was presented in [2]. The depth value at each pixel in an image is replaced by a weighted average of depth values from nearby pixels. Filter weights are determined by considering RGB data, depth information and a temporal consistency map. In [11], the authors proposed a color-depth fusion strategy integrating conventional inpainting and a non-local filtering scheme. The color structure is exploited to compensate the depth map at object boundaries. Recovery of missing depth values caused by shadow regions was investigated in [14]. Utilizing a mathematical model based on the depth measurement of Kinect, the authors developed a method for detection and removal of shadow regions without the use of RGB data.

Fig. 2. Recovery of missing depth values. The left picture is the RGB view on the scene. The middle picture is the depth map with missing depth values (black pixels). The right picture depicts the result of the recovery algorithm applied on the upper part of the depth map.

In our people counting system we use a simple strategy to recover missing depth values without the use of RGB data. Indeed, experiments show that the produced recovery results are sufficient for utilized segmentation algorithm. As a consequence of the simple strategy, the recovery phase has small computational requirements. The recovery algorithm fills missing value regions ("holes") layer by layer in direction from the boundary of the region to its center. Initially, all pixels with missing depth values neighbouring to a pixel with known depth value are enqueued. Next, we iteratively dequeue and process pixels. The missing depth value of a pixel is computed as the average value of all known depth values in its 4-connected neighbourhood and all its neighbours with the missing depth value are enqueued to be processed in the next iteration. The algorithm stops when there are no pixels with the missing depth value.

3   People Counting

The processing pipeline of our people counting system (see Figure 1) consists of five components: the *depth map recovery*, the *background substraction*, the *head segmentation*, the *head tracking*, and finally the *people counting*. The input of the processing pipeline is the output of the Kinect depth sensor - a depth map that assigns depth information to large number of pixels in a scene.

The first component of the system recovers the missing depth values using the strategy described in the previous section. The result of the recovery component is passed to the second component realizing the background substraction. The Kinect sensor has a fixed position and orientation. During deployment (a calibration phase) with no people in the scene we compute the mean depth for each pixel position. The background substraction removes all pixels with depth close to the computed mean depth at their positions. The remaining pixels are classified as foreground pixels. After this step the input depth map I can be considered as a set of foreground pixels for which depth information was estimated. For an arbitrary pixel $p \in I$, we denote coordinates of p in the depth image by $(x[p], y[p])$ and its depth (distance from the projecting plane of the sensor) by $d[p]$. Recall that the Kinect depth sensor is pointing to the floor. It implies that pixels corresponding to upper parts of a human body (e.g. head) have smaller depth than pixels of lower parts (e.g. legs).

The third component, the head segmentation, and the fourth component, the head tracking, are described in more details in Section 3.1 and Section 3.2, respectively. The last component, the people counting, is based on a simple analysis of the trace of a moving head segment. Whenever the trace of a head segment goes from the in-area to the out-area (separated by a neutral "counting" area) the out-counter is incremented, and vice-versa. Note that there are monitored areas with more than one in- and out-areas in practice.

3.1 Head Segmentation

The segmentation process consists of two phases: the base segmentation and the head identification.

Base segmentation. First, we realize the base segmentation (see Algorithm 1) of the input depth map I adopting a region-growing approach with a threshold value T. Given a seed pixel s of a new region, we iteratively grown the region by adding each unallocated neighbouring pixel p with $d[p] < d[s]+T$ to the region. We choose an unallocated pixel with the smallest depth as a seed for a new region. Note, that the base segmentation algorithm can be implemented in such a way that the total processing time is $O(n)$ where n is the number of image pixels (utilizing CountingSort algorithm and Breadth-first search).

Fig. 3. The right picture shows regions that form the result of the base segmentation

---

Algorithm 1. Base segmentation

Input: set I of foreground pixels with depth information
Output: set of segmented regions

$Q \leftarrow I$;
while $Q \neq \emptyset$ **do**
    choose a pixel s from Q, s.t., $d[s]$ is minimal;
    remove s from Q;
    $R \leftarrow \{s\}$;
    repeatconstruct a region R with s as a seed
        $N(R) \leftarrow$ neighbours of all pixels in R ;
        $C \leftarrow \{p \in Q \cap N(R) | d[p] < d[s] + T\}$;
        if $C \neq \emptyset$ **then**
            $p \leftarrow$ an arbitrary point from C;
            move p from Q to R;
        end
    until $C = \emptyset$;
    add new region R to the segment set;
end

In our application we use 4-connected neighbourhood to grow a region and 100 millimeters as the threshold value T. Our approach follows from the observation that the majority of pixels of a human head that are observable from top-down (ceiling) view have usually their depths not greater that 100 millimeters from the highest point of the head. As a conseqence, we expect that the result set of the base segmentation contains exactly one region of reasonable size for each human head in the scene.

Head identification. We choose regions that represent human heads during the second phase of the segmentation. A set of descriptors is computed for each segment. The set of descriptors was choosen to be able to distingush regions that correspond to human heads from other regions corresponing to other parts of the body, shopping carts, bags, etc. In our algorithm we use the following three descriptors: the normalized area of a region, the roundness of a region, and the box test.

The area of a region (number of pixels) does not provide good description of real size of the region. The input depth map is a result of camera projection, i.e., closer objects have bigger area. Hence, the real area of the region must be computed. To effectively estimate the real area, we use the assumption that head segments are roughly parallel to the floor plane (whose coordinates can be a priori computed using RANSAC). We orthogonally project all pixels of the region to the floor plane. The area of the region projected on the floor plane, the normalized area, is then used as one of the descriptors.

The next descriptor is the roundness of a region. Since the shape of a head is close to a sphere, one can expect that the shape of a head segment is close to a circle. The roundness of a region with area A is computed as percetage of region pixels with distance smaller than $\sqrt{A/\pi}$ from the center of gravity of the region.

The last descriptor is the box test descriptor. A head segment is expected to be a local extrema in view of its neighbouring regions. Let us denote by $P_l(R)$ a set of pixels that are in distance l from the perimeter of a region R and do not belong to R. Let us consider the value $d_l = min\{d[p]|p \in P_l(R)\}$, i.e., the depth of the highest pixel close to the perimeter of R. Given a positive value r, if R is a head segment, the size of the set $\{p \in R|d[p] < d_l - r\}$ is expected to be close to $|R|$ and the value $|\{p \in R|d[p] < d_l - r\}|/|R|$ is taken as the value of the descriptor. Intuitively, if we put a box around the perimeter of a head (see Figure 4), the bottom edge of the box will be placed at the shoulders. Now, if we consider the set of pixels in the box that are r millimeters above the bottom edge of the box, the majority of head pixels must belong to this set. Due to noise in input data, we compute descriptor not only for $l = 1$, but also for few other values l ($l \le 12$) and we choose the value l for which the highest ratio is achieved. We used r equal to 50 millimeters in our experiments.

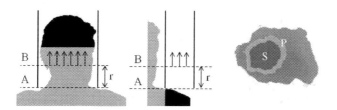

Fig. 4. The basic idea of the box test follows from an expectation that allmost all pixels of a head segment are more than r millimeters (Line B) above the bottom edge of a box (Line A) placed around the perimeter of the region. Black pixels correspond to pixels of the tested region. In the left picture all pixels are above Line B (test passed), in the middle picture no pixels are above Line B (test failed) - so the shoulder is not recognized as a head segment. The right picture depicts the perimeter P of a region S used to identify the location (bottom edge) of a box, i.e., the smallest pixel depth on the perimeter.

As a result, we have three descriptor values. In order to smooth thresholding, we translate each descriptor value to the interval $(0, 1)$ by applying the logistic function $\frac{1}{1+e^{-c\cdot(d-T)}}$ where d is a value of a descriptor, T is a threshold value for a descriptor and c is a smoothness parameter (T and c for the normalized area are set manually during deployment, for the other descriptors we use $T = 75$ and $c = 1$ in our experiments). For each region we compute the "probability", correctness of head segmentation, that the region corresponds to a head segment by multiplying descriptor values after applying the logistic function. Regions with correctness below a given minimal value (0.7 in our case) are not considered to be head segments [1].

3.2   Tracking

The segmentation process identifies heads including their locations and descriptors in a frame (depth map). In order to count the number of incoming and outcoming people, a sort of head segment tracking is realized. Since the input for tracking is a series

---

[1] Parameters were set and fixed to given values as a result of analysis of initial experiments. Later experiments (several instalations) showed stability of chosen parameters.

of continuous frames including segmentation results, the tracking algorithm can work with much more information than the segmentation. Hence, the tracking process can eventually correct inaccuracy of segmentation results.

Let $F_i = \{H_1, H_2, ...\}$ be a set of objects (head segments) recognized in the frame i. Since the segmentation process estimates for each head segment a correctness parameter, we denote by $p(H_j)$ correctness of head segment estimation. It denotes the probability of existence of an object (a head segment in our case). The goal of tracking is to identify objects in F_i with objects in F_{i+1}. Due to inaccuracy of segmentation, it can happen that the set F_{i+1} does not contain an object which can be identified with $H_j \in F_i$, although an underlaying real object is present in F_{i+1} (see Figure 5). As a consequence, the trace of an object (used by the counting component) can be broken by one or more frames with inaccurate segmentation results. Another problem caused by incorrect segmentation appears when a segment not corresponding to a real head is recognized on few frames. There is a chance of incorrect identification of objects between frames and thus incorrect trace of a head segment movement can be produced.

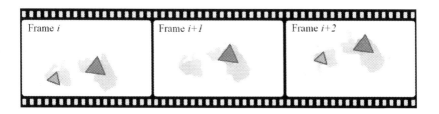

Fig. 5. Inaccuracy of segmentation causes a missing real object in the frame $i + 1$. As a consequence, the left object in the frame i cannot be identified with an object in the frame $i + 1$. Similarly, the left object in the frame $i + 2$ is not identified with an object in the frame $i + 1$. Hence, the trace of the left moving object is broken.

In this section we propose a tracking algorithm that will treat the problem of inaccurate segmentation. The key element of our approach is the use of *ghosts*. A ghost is an object that is created for each object in F_i (called a *source object*) and added to the set F_{i+1}. Probability assigned to a ghost is smaller by a multiplicative factor p_f than the probability of its source object. A ghost is created at a position predicted by the previous trace of its source object. To predict the position of the ghost we adopted the constant velocity model.[2]

Due to introducing ghosts, each object in F_i with reasonable probability can be identified with an object in F_{i+1} (at least with its ghost). Moreover, an object in F_i can be identified only with a ghost for which it is a source object.

An algorithm for minimum-weighted bipartite graphs is utilized to identify objects in F_i with objects in F_{i+1}. The sets F_i and F_{i+1} form two partitions of a bipartite graph. An edge is only between objects whose Euclidian distance is less than a given threshold max_{dist}. The value max_{dist} can be given as a parameter of the algorithm or

---

[2] The prediction can be improved utilizing the Kalman filter. However, experiments show that even the simple prediction method is sufficient for tracking people.

Algorithm 2. Tracking

Input: set of objects in frame F_i and frame F_{i+1}
Output: matching between objects in F_i and F_{i+1}

```
/* create ghosts                                                        */
```
foreach $H \in F_i$ **do**
  $(x_H, y_H) \leftarrow$ predicted position of H in F_{i+1};
  $H_G \leftarrow$ copy of H at position (x_H, y_H);
  $p(H_G) \leftarrow p_f \cdot p(H)$;
  if $p(H_G) \geq p_{min}$ **then** add H_G to F_{i+1} ;
end

create a weighted bipartite graph $G = (F_i \cup F_{i+1}, E)$;
foreach $H \in F_i$, $H' \in F_{i+1}$ **do**
  if $dist(H, H') > max_{dist}$ **then** continue ;
  if H' *is a ghost* $\wedge$ H' *is not a ghost of H* **then** continue ;
  create edge $e = (H, H')$;
  $(x_H, y_H) \leftarrow$ predicted position of H in F_{i+1};
  $w(e) \leftarrow dist((x_H, y_H), H') + (1 - p(H) \cdot p(H') \cdot similarity(H, H')) \cdot Penalty$;
end

compute minimum-weighted bipartite matching in G;
remove from F_{i+1} all unmatched ghosts;

---

can be upperbounded by mean and expectation of speed of objects [3]. Weight of an edge (H, H') is computed as a function (see Algorithm 2) of Euclidian distance between predicted position of H in F_{i+1} and the position of $H' \in F_{i+1}$, $p(H)$, $p(H')$, and similarity between H and H' $(similarity(H, H') \in \langle 0, 1 \rangle)$. The similarity of head segments is computed as Euclidian distance of two vectors formed by their segment descriptors (area of the segment, the average distance from the floor plane, i.e., estimated height of a person). Decreasing probabilities of ghosts and the weight formula imply that identification of objects with non-ghost (real) objects is preferred. We apply the Hungarian algorithm [9] to compute minimum-weighted bipartite matching in G. The time complexity of this algorithm is $O(n^3)$ for a graph of order n. Since the algorithm is applied on a graph built from head segments, this time complexity is acceptable for us (only a small number of head segments is expected in one frame). After computing the matching, we remove from F_{i+1} all ghosts that were not matched to an object in F_i.

Note that segments resulting from inaccurate segmentation can be removed by removing all object traces (including objects) that do not appear on prescribed number of frames, i.e., we remove objects with short traces.

4 Experiment

Our algorithm was evaluated on four datasets. Dataset A is a dataset used to evaluate the approach from [15]. We evaluated only the accuracy of our head segmentation algorithm on this dataset. Whereas the ground truth of segmented heads is included in the dataset, the evaluation was quite straightforward.

Table 1. Experimental results for head segmentation

Dataset	Dataset A.1			Dataset A.2		
Method	Recall	Accuracy	F-score	Recall	Accuracy	F-score
Our algorithm	99.78%	99.89%	99.84%	99.23%	99.62%	99.42%
Water filling [15]	98.82%	98.83%	98.79%	99.47%	99.57%	99.52%

The next three datasets consist of data recorded in a shopping center. The datasets were recorded during different days. Dataset B consists of data recorded during a business day, when the people flow is considered to be average. The length of this dataset is 12 hours. Dataset C consists of randomly selected parts of recorded data, where the people flow was quite low. The length of Dataset C is 45 minutes. Finally, Dataset D consists of data recorded during a Saturday, when the people flow was quite huge. The length of this dataset is 11 hours. We evaluated only the people counting on Dataset B, C, and D. Our algorithm calculated the IN and OUT flows and then we manually checked the precise counts.

Our algorithm assumes that the whole head of a person in the scene is visible by the Kinect sensor. Due to technical limitations of a place where the Kinect depth sensor was mounted, there were locations close to the left and the right side where the head of a walking person was out of the sensor range. Therefore, the people whose heads are not completely visible for the sensor are not counted in the number of real people.

4.1 Evaluation of the Head Segmentation

We evaluated our head segmentation algorithm only on Dataset A used for evaluation in [15]. This dataset consists of two subdatasets. The first one includes 2834 images with 4541 heads and the second one includes 1500 images with 1553 heads.

Similarly as in [15], we use three measurements to compare the performance: recall rate, accuracy and F-score, where recall rate is the fraction of people that are detected; accuracy is the fraction of detected result that are people, and F-score is the average of recall rate and accuracy. The results are stated in Table 1.

4.2 Evaluation of the People Counting

Our people counting system was evaluated on three datasets, which consist of recorded data in a shopping center. The total length of all three datasets is 23 hours and 45 minutes. In Dataset B the total number of recorded people is 6352, in Dataset C it is 221 people and in Dataset D the total number of recorded people is 7501.

4.3 Results

The results of the evaluation can be seen in Table 2. The evaluation showed that our algorithm works properly also in many problematic situations such as interaction between people, people with baseball caps, winter hats and all other sorts of hats. Our algorithm also correctly tracks children and small babies, even if they are carried in arms of their

Table 2. Experimental results for people counting on Dataset B, C, and D

Dataset	Real		Counted		Score		Average Score
	# In	# Out	# In	# Out	In	Out	
Dataset B	3525	2827	3495	2810	98.962%	98.936%	98.949%
Dataset C	108	113	107	114	99.206%	99.346%	99.276%
Dataset D	4117	3384	4102	3369	99.189%	99.227%	99.209%

parents. Also the wheelchair people, people with shopping baskets (either empty or not) and people with strollers are not a problem for our algorithm.

Although the algorithm gives satisfactory results for practical applications, we identified several drawbacks. The major drawback concerns small children, who are guided by an adult by hand. The problem is that in some cases the child walks too near to the adult and its small head blends with some part of the body of the adult - in most cases with a leg - so the head of the child could not be identified.

Our algorithm assumes that the head is the highest part of a person from the floor. If this assumption is not fulfilled, then our algorithm will give in the most cases a wrong result. But in practice, we did not notice this problem during the evaluation of the people counting in a shopping center.

All tested algorithms were implemented in C# (Microsoft .NET Framework 3.5). The speed of the processing pipeline is over 60 frames (size 640×480) per second on a PC with Intel Xeon CPU (2.4 GHz) and 6 GB RAM without use of multithreading. [3]

5   Conclusions

In this paper, we described a real-time people counting system utilizing a vertical Kinect depth sensor. The proposed system includes a novel heuristic approach to head segmentation that combines region-growing segmentation and classification based on three descriptors. Experimental comparison with algorithms in [15] showed that the presented head segmention approach provides comparable results. To treat the problem of inaccuracy of head segmentation (due to real-world scenes and noise in input data), we introduce a tracking algorithm based on minimum-weighted bipartite matching and prediction of object movement. Experimental evaluation of the people counting system realized on real-world datasets from a shopping center (length of recordings over 23 hours) shows high accuracy of the system. It turns out that the main drawback of a Kinect based system for real-world applications is a restricted field of view of the sensor. It can be difficult to cover wider entrances in such a way that the head of each person can be recorded by the sensor. Hence, a counting system that is not based on head tracking and the data fusion from multiple Kinect sensors to cover more large horizon are the main challenges.

---

[3] Performance of the solution presented in [15] is 30 FPS for smaller depth maps (320×240) on a comparable PC configuration. In latest tests on a PC with Intel Core i5-3210M 2.5GHz CPU (dual core with HTT) and 4G of RAM we achieve 47% of CPU usage when using two Kinect sensors (two different entrances) and parallelized processing pipeline (2 threads for one Kinect sensor).

Acknowledgements. We thank to Xucong Zhang for accessing datasets. Our thanks also go to company Novitech for support and cooperation on experimental evaluation.

References

1. Bevilacqua, A., Di Stefano, L., Azzari, P.: People tracking using a time-of-flight depth sensor. In: IEEE International Conference on Video and Signal Based Surveillance, AVSS 2006, pp. 89–89 (2006)
2. Camplani, M., Salgado, L.: Efficient spatio-temporal hole filling strategy for kinect depth maps. In: Proc. SPIE 8290, Three-Dimensional Image Processing (3DIP) and Applications II (2012)
3. Chowdhury, A.S., Chatterjee, R., Ghosh, M., Ray, N.: Cell tracking in video microscopy using bipartite graph matching. In: 2010 20th International Conference on Pattern Recognition (ICPR), pp. 2456–2459 (2010)
4. Dalal, N., Triggs, B.: Histograms of oriented gradients for human detection. In: IEEE Computer Society Conference on Computer Vision and Pattern Recognition, CVPR 2005, vol. 1, pp. 886–893 (2005)
5. Desai, C., Ramanan, D., Fowlkes, C.: Discriminative models for multi-class object layout. International Journal of Computer Vision 95, 1–12 (2011)
6. Felzenszwalb, P., Girshick, R., McAllester, D., Ramanan, D.: Object detection with discriminatively trained part-based models. Pattern Analysis and Machine Intelligence 32(9), 1627–1645 (2010)
7. Han, J., Shao, L., Xu, D., Shotton, J.: Enhanced computer vision with microsoft kinect sensor: A review. IEEE Transactions on Cybernetics (2013)
8. Kong, D., Gray, D., Tao, H.: Counting pedestrians in crowds using viewpoint invariant training. In: British Machine Vision Conf. Citeseer (2005)
9. Kuhn, H.W.: The hungarian method for the assignment problem. Naval Research Logistics Quarterly 2(1-2), 83–97 (1955)
10. Marana, A., Costa, L.F., Lotufo, R., Velastin, S.: On the efficacy of texture analysis for crowd monitoring. In: International Symposium on Proceedings of the Computer Graphics, Image Processing, and Vision, SIBGRAPI 1998, pp. 354–361 (1998)
11. Qi, F., Han, J., Wang, P., Shi, G., Li, F.: Structure guided fusion for depth map inpainting. Pattern Recognition Letters 34(1), 70–76 (2013)
12. Tanner, R., Studer, M., Zanoli, A., Hartmann, A.: People detection and tracking with tof sensor. In: IEEE Fifth International Conference on Advanced Video and Signal Based Surveillance, AVSS 2008, pp. 356–361 (2008)
13. Viola, P., Jones, M., Snow, D.: Detecting pedestrians using patterns of motion and appearance. In: Proceedings of the Ninth IEEE International Conference on Computer Vision, vol. 2, pp. 734–741 (2003)
14. Yu, Y., Song, Y., Zhang, Y., Wen, S.: A shadow repair approach for kinect depth maps. In: Lee, K., Matsushita, Y., Rehg, J., Hu, Z. (eds.) ACCV 2012, Part IV. LNCS, vol. 7727, pp. 615–626. Springer, Heidelberg (2013)
15. Zhang, X., Yan, J., Feng, S., Lei, Z., Yi, D., Li, S.: Water filling: Unsupervised people counting via vertical kinect sensor. In: 2012 IEEE Ninth International Conference on Advanced Video and Signal-Based Surveillance (AVSS), pp. 215–220 (2012)

Tracking of a Handheld Ultrasonic Sensor
for Corrosion Control on Pipe Segment Surfaces

Christian Bendicks, Erik Lilienblum, Christian Freye, and Ayoub Al-Hamadi

Institute for Information Technology and Communications,
Otto von Guericke University, Universitätsplatz 2, D-39106 Magdeburg, Germany
christian.bendicks@ovgu.de

Abstract. The article describes a combination of optical 3-d measurement technique and ultrasonic testing for areawide acquisition of wall thickness on piping segments. It serves the purpose to match automatically ultrasonic measurements to their 3-d positions at the examined pipe segment. The sensor, which is normally occluded by hand, is equipped with a cap with a number of attached LEDs. A model based approach is presented to track these LEDs and to visualise the measured wall thickness at a three-dimensional surface. Therefore the model of the cap is fitted to the segmented image data, so that the 3-d position of the ultrasonic sensor can be derived from computed model orientation. Our approach works robustly and can build the basis for further applications in real industrial environments.

Keywords: tracking, photogrammetry.

1 Introduction

To guarantee security of piping systems on industrial arrangements like refineries a restricted number of wall thickness measurements to the corrosion control is carried out up to now regularly, however, only random check-wise. Beside radiographic testing the conventional ultrasonic technology [1] is used as measuring procedure, because it is safe for human examiners. Nevertheless, on this occasion, one receives only a fraction of the surface of a pipe segment. The wall thickness is captured, but the precise location of the measurement on the pipe segment is documented insufficiently. A mapping of the wall thickness is a plausible wish because thereby a pictorial representation of the corrosion course becomes also possible for a long period. Regarding to this there is a need by industry to localize and track ultrasonic measurements accurately.

For the area-wide ultrasonic check of work pieces there are already mechanical solutions available, e.g. RapidScan 3-d system [2]. Here, a co-ordinate measuring arm is used capturing the three-dimensional position of the ultrasonic measurement. Disadvantages of this attempt are a high mechanical expenditure and wear, a low flexibility in particular in hardly accessible areas, a limited measuring volume (depending on the size of the co-ordinate measuring arm) and furthermore difficulties to get repeatable measurement results by repositioning

J. Blanc-Talon et al. (Eds.): ACIVS 2013, LNCS 8192, pp. 342–353, 2013.

the co-ordinate measuring arm. Therefore, such an approach seems not suitable for outdoor applications on a refinery.

To the determination of orientation and geometry of work pieces in particular optical systems are suited. Main aspect of this article is the tracking of a hand-held ultrasonic sensor to create a 3-d point cloud of the measured pipe segment surface linked with information of wall thickness. Tracking algorithms can be classified into color based and model based approaches, whereupon this article brings a model based approach for sensor tracking into focus. In [8] an overview of monocular model based approaches and available tracking techniques is given. Some real-time tracking procedures are also presented in [6] and [7], which are tested under laboratory conditions and it is not assessable how they work in an outdoor environment. Other interesting approaches especially to 3-d measuring technology in industrial applications are mentioned in [4].

Although the fields of 3-d tracking and 3-d measuring is widely investigated, no directly applicable procedure for the problem of tracking and mapping of an ultrasonic sensor at an outdoor pipework system is found. This article will attach at this point and presents a straightforward approach, which can be used for industrial measurement applications. Note, it would also work if only one camera is available – but for the need of measurement accuracy and reliable detection of the sensor in an outdoor environment, this approach uses a stereo camera head and an additional cap with LEDs around the sensor.

The remainder of the article is structured as follows: section 2 describes the components of the evolved system. In section 3 an overview of the optical tracking system is given and it provides detailed information of the LED segmentation and localisation, as well as the camera model. Furthermore the two approaches for detecting and tracking of the half cube model are specified. In section 4 an examination of the model fitting accuracy is presented, followed by a presentation of aspects for the visualisation of the measurement results in section 5. The article finishes in section 6 with a conclusion.

2 System Components

The components of the measurement system consists of a portable ultrasonic flaw detector for wall thickness gauging and a calibrated stereo camera head to detect and track the position of the ultrasonic contact transducer which is normally covered by hand. Both cameras have a monochrome 1/3"-CMOS sensor inside with resolution of 752×480 pixels and 10 mm lenses are used. The working distance is about 1 m.

To locate the position the transducer is equipped with a cap which is similar to a half cube consisting of two side faces and one top face (see fig. 1). Each face contains a set of LEDs (SMD type 603, white, 690 mcd, viewing angle 120°) located near to the corners serving as optical markers. The top face contains an additional LED in the middle which is used for identification. In the further text this cap is referenced as target. A human operator should be able to lead the transducer with target comfortably over the surface of the test object.

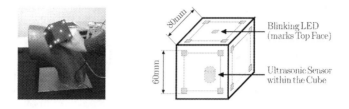

Fig. 1. Ultrasonic sensor equipped with optical target

Data acquisition for both ultrasonic data and stereo imaging data is synchro-nized by a trigger box (see fig. 2). At each trigger event the wall thickness value is directly grabbed from the serial port. Simultaneously, each acquired stereo image pair is processed by the tracking software, which will be described in the following section. The trigger rate is 15 Hz, limited by the ultrasonic flaw detec-tor. The geometry of pipe segments e.g. with information about pipe diameters and bending radii is stored in a database. This kind of a priori information is used to be fit in the measured 3-d point cloud of sensor positions and also used to create a normalized unwind of pipe segment surface to map colour coded wall thickness values.

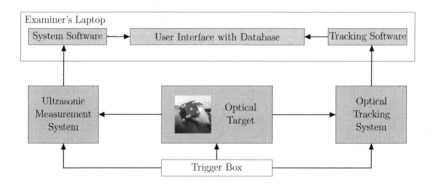

Fig. 2. Overview of the system components

3   Optical Tracking System

The algorithm of the optical tracking system is outlined as flow chart in figure 3. It starts with the image acquisition of stereo images and continues with their preprocessing, segmentation and location of the LEDs, which is described further below. The optical tracking system implements two basic concepts to label and track the target, called top-down and bottom-up approach.

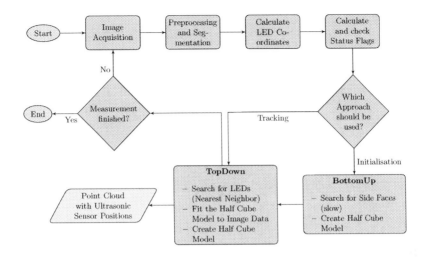

Fig. 3. Flow chart of the tracking algorithm

Which strategy to choose depends on the system state which is described by following indicators:

- maximum rotation or translation of the cube model between two frames is greater than a predetermined threshold,
- mean deviation between current projected cube model and segmented LED marker is within a predetermined limit,
- maximum deviation between current projected cube model and segmented LED markers is within a predetermined limit,
- blinking LED was found on one of the cube side faces.

As shown in figure 4 and according to the recognition state the tracking system may follow one of the two strategies to label the markers. The high-level description at the top represents the half cube model with its 3-d co-ordinates of vertices and LED locations. At the bottom is the low-level description representing the image data from which the LED markers and their image co-ordinates are extracted. The bottom-up approach will label LED markers based on their image locations by trying to group them to a set for each side face. Then it can be tested if the recognized side faces are neighboured according to their vertices. At the end the faces are assembled in that way to fit the half cube model. The top-down strategy, will track already labelled marker image co-ordinates from a previous time frame to label the co-ordinates in the current frame by e.g. a nearest neighbour mapping.

Both strategies are essential. The top-down approach is fast but leads to confusions in labelling when approximated locations of the LED markers from previous locations are bad or don't exist. For example such situation will appear when the target orientation or position has changed too much, at the beginning of the measurement, or in case of occlusion. If the top-down approach doesn't work, the bottom-up approach is needed to re-assemble the correct side faces

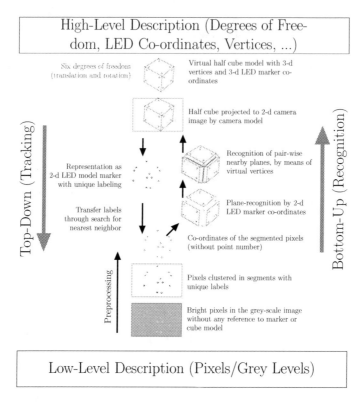

High-Level Description (Degrees of Freedom, LED Co-ordinates, Vertices, ...)

Six degrees of freedom
(translation and rotation)

Virtual half cube model with 3-d vertices and 3-d LED marker co-ordinates

Half cube projected to 2-d camera image by camera model

Representation as 2-d LED model marker with unique labeling

Recognition of pair-wise nearby planes, by means of virtual vertices

Transfer labels through search for nearest neighbor

Plane-recognition by 2-d LED marker co-ordinates

Co-ordinates of the segmented pixels (without point number)

Top-Down (Tracking)

Bottom-Up (Recognition)

Preprocessing

Pixels clustered in segments with unique labels

Bright pixels in the grey-scale image without any reference to marker or cube model

Low-Level Description (Pixels/Grey Levels)

Fig. 4. High-level and low-level concept for optical tracking

from co-ordinates of detected LED segments. The bottom-up runs in each camera channel separately whereas the top-down approach considers both camera channels simultaneously.

Since the relative position of ultrasonic sensor to the half cube model is known, the contact location of the sensor at the surface is computed from the location and orientation of the fitted model in both images. Hence, the system delivers one 3-d world co-ordinate per frame which is linked to the measured wall thickness at this place. While the sensor is lead over the surface of e.g. a pipe bend segment a growing 3-d point cloud is created and stored together with wall thickness information.

3.1 LED Marker Segmentation and Location in Images

Because of the use of small LEDs as tracking markers, which appear much brighter on camera images than other objects in natural environments, automated segmentation of these markers is easily realized. Working with small apertures and short exposure times ensures that only LED markers are recognisable, all other regions of the scene should appear dark (grey value < 10).

To segment LED markers in grey-scale images adaptive thresholding is applied. It works robustly, even under changing lighting conditions. Pixels with values above threshold t are assumed to belong to marker regions. The threshold t is computed by histogram analysis expressed by eq. 1 and eq. 2.

$$t = \begin{cases} \max(G) & \text{, if } \quad G \neq \emptyset \\ t_{min} & \text{, else} \end{cases} \tag{1}$$

$$G = \left\{ i \Big| \sum_{j=i}^{255} H(j) > n_h \wedge i \in [t_{min}, 255] \right\} \tag{2}$$

A set G of grey-scale pixels is selected by eq. 2 using the histogram H of the current image. t_{min} is a user specified threshold, that marks the lower grey-scale border. n_h is also a user specified threshold and identifies the amount of pixels, which are taken into account (in this case $n_h = 0.35\%$ of all pixels). For each i are the histogram values $H(j)$ summed up. According to eq. 1 t results in the maximum value of set G, if its not an empty set. Otherwise it will be t_{min}. Here it is taken into advantage that projections of the LEDs are small and bright. In fact, threshold t should be found near to the right border of the histogram.

Now, bright areas can be separated from background easily and pixels belonging to different LED-regions are assigned to pixel lists as shown in figure 5. Assuming the image origin is defined at the upper left corner, each pixel is analysed from the left to the right and from the top to the bottom. Pixels in the first line and first row are ignored. If the value of active pixel (fig 5. red cross) is above t (grey pixels in figure) then its left and top neighbour are tested whether they already belong to a pixel list or not.

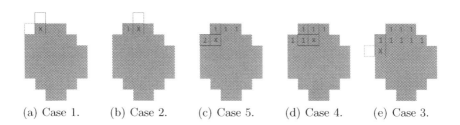

(a) Case 1.   (b) Case 2.   (c) Case 5.   (d) Case 4.   (e) Case 3.

Fig. 5. Cases for segmenting an LED marker by a pixelwise check of the top and left neighbour. Grey area corresponds to pixels above threshold t.

Pixels in a pixel list are declared as 'assigned'. There are five different cases and assignment is performed in the following manner:

– Case 1, left and top neighbour are not assigned: Create a new pixel list and add active pixel.
– Case 2, left neighbour is assigned but not the top neighbour: add active pixel to the pixel list the left neighbour belongs to.

- Case 3, top neighbour is assigned but not the left neighbour: add active pixel to the pixel list the top neighbour belongs to.
- Case 4, left and top neighbour belong to same pixel list: add active pixel to this list.
- Case 5, left and top neighbour belong to different pixel lists: merge this two pixel lists to one and add active pixel.

Each pixel list represents a segmented LED projection. Subpixel image co-ordinates (x, y) of an LED marker are computed from integer co-ordinates (x_i, y_i) and corresponding intensity values $I(x_i, y_i)$ of all n pixels contained in a list by using the centre of mass method, eq. 3. These co-ordinates are used for model fit in camera images as described in the next subsections.

$$
x = \frac{\sum_{i=0}^{n-1}(x_i \cdot I(x_i, y_i))}{\sum_{i=0}^{n-1} I(x_i, y_i)}; y = \frac{\sum_{i=0}^{n-1}(y_i \cdot I(x_i, y_i))}{\sum_{i=0}^{n-1} I(x_i, y_i)} \tag{3}
$$

3.2 Camera Model

For projecting the 3-d target model into camera images, a specific camera model is needed. The perspective projection of 3-d world co-ordinates x, y, z to the image plane is expressed by the mathematical formulation shown in equations 4 and 5 which is based on the pinhole camera model.

$$
x' = x'_p + c \cdot \left(\frac{r_{11}(x - x_o) + r_{21}(y - y_o) + r_{31}(z - z_o)}{r_{13}(x - x_o) + r_{23}(y - y_o) + r_{33}(z - z_o)} \right) + \Delta x'_{rad} \tag{4}
$$

$$
y' = y'_p + s_y c \cdot \left(\frac{r_{12}(x - x_o) + r_{22}(y - y_o) + r_{32}(z - z_o)}{r_{13}(x - x_o) + r_{23}(y - y_o) + r_{33}(z - z_o)} \right) + \Delta y'_{rad} \tag{5}
$$

So called extrinsic parameters describe camera's position and orientation by the location of the projective centre (x_o, y_o, z_o) and rotation angles $\varphi_x, \varphi_y, \varphi_z$ about co-ordinate axes in world frame. The rotation angles determine the entries $r_{i,j}$ of a three by three rotation matrix. Additionally, so called intrinsic parameters characterise imaging properties of lens and sensor. These are co-ordinates x'_p, y'_p of the principle point, the calibrated focal length c, a scaling factor s_y for pixel ratio, as well as two parameters to express radial lens distortion contained in terms $\Delta x'_{rad}$ and $\Delta y'_{rad}$. For detailed information how to model some kind of lens distortion we refer to [5].

Extrinsic and intrinsic parameters of each camera are obtained by camera calibration before measurement, which is a well known photogrammetric technique. In particular we use a calibration target with coded circles and the standard bundle block adjustment technique [3].

3.3   Bottom-Up Approach for Initialisation

The method for initialisation tries to find a consistent numbering of the segmented LED marker. That happens without a 3-d model, just based on geometric image-based features, which is a complex issue, because all LED markers
looks the same.

After segmentation all LED marker co-ordinates are unsorted and unnum-
bered. One can now select three arbitrary marker points $(\mathbf{p}_0, \mathbf{p}_1, \mathbf{p}_2)$. As shown
in figure 6(a) a forth marker point $\mathbf{p}_3$ should be near to the predicted location
$\mathbf{p}_0 + \vec{u} + \vec{v}$. If this is true, all four points are potentially part of a side face of the
half cube model. Due to some improvements, this idea leads to a fast and robust
search method for side faces. In the first phase, an affine model (2-d) of the cube
side faces is used to save all reasonable combinations of four LED markers in a
sorted list (weighted according to their quality). The second phase attempts to
compose the found side faces to a consistent half cube model.

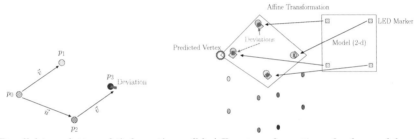

(a) Parallel translation of $\vec{v}$ along $\vec{u}$ (b) Affine transformation of cube model

Fig. 6. Geometric relations between 2-d model and extracted features

The expected vertices of the cube in the image can be predicted approximately
using the affine model parameter of the side faces, as shown in figure 6(b).
Because two side faces of the half cube model have two common vertices, should
the vertex of one side face lie near the vertex of the other. This criteria can be
used to check, if two planes in the sorted list are nearby. If such a neighbourhood
is identified, the same criteria can be used to search a third plane, which fits to
the already found pair. After that the half cube model is deemed to be found.

Because the LEDs on each side face are arranged at the same positions, a
cyclic permutation of the three side faces can occur at this kind of recognition.
This permutation can be corrected by a rotation, if the blinking LED is found,
which is attached at the centre of the top face (see fig. 1).

3.4   Model Based Top-Down Approach

This method is called top-down approach, because it seeks LED marker segments
(low-level description) on the assumption of a high-level optical target description.
The basis for this approach is, that the model is already well fitted to the image

data. Then the markers can be labelled by a quick search for the nearest neighbouring LED segments. Even small errors are usually corrected after convergence of the process, e.g. if the side face is in a very steep angle to the observing camera and therefore the LED segments are very close together. If the observation angle between camera and normals of the side faces becomes too big, the appropriate LED markers can be weighted lesser or entirely turned off.

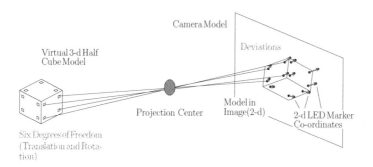

Fig. 7. Relation between target model and camera model

This model based approach allows the introduction of many a priori information and thereby a high robustness and reliability. The method uses a well defined 3-d model of the target (3-d co-ordinates of the LED markers) and a model of the previously calibrated camera (see fig. 7). Also the position of the ultrasonic sensor within the optical target is deemed to be known. Are the pose- and orientation parameters of the model correct, should the m LED marker positions $\vec{p}_i$ (projected to the image by the camera model) lay approximately near the m segmented LED marker positions $\vec{s}_i$. If this is not the case (see red deviations in fig. 7), the parameter vector $\boldsymbol{\theta} = (\theta_0, \theta_1, \ldots, \theta_5)^T$ of the optical target projection $f(p, \boldsymbol{\theta})$ have to be modified until the deviations in the image becomes minimal (see eq. 6). The parameter vector $\boldsymbol{\theta}$ contains three translation and three rotation parameters of the model. This model fitting is solved by the Levenberg-Marquardt algorithm [9], which is an iterative procedure. The needed initial guess for the parameter vector $\boldsymbol{\theta}$ is given by the tracked half cube model. The time to convergence of this algorithm is short enough to fulfil the real-time conditions of this application.

$$S(\boldsymbol{\theta}) = \sum_{i=1}^{m} [s_i - f(p_i, \boldsymbol{\theta})]^2 \qquad (6)$$

However, a typical disadvantage of this method is, that for every projected marker of the target model just one segmented marker can be denoted as target co-ordinate. If errors occur at the assignment of the segmented LEDs, e.g. caused by bad observation angles or a too high acceleration of the target during the measurement, it may lead to serious systematic errors. In this situation the system has to switch into the bottom-up mode for re-initialisation.

4   Accuracy Examination

In principle, the presented technique to track the target also works, if only one camera is available, by reason of known target geometry and calibrated camera model parameters. Using two or more cameras increases accuracy and robustness, but also computing time. The following accuracy evaluation is done by considering our setup using two cameras.

The accuracy of the ultrasonic sensor position depends on the actual output of the model fitting. Two possible criteria for estimating the accuracy of the model approximation are the mean residuals of all LED markers and the maximum residual at each frame. The graph in figure 8 shows a measurement of a pipe bend segment and the resulting residuals (measured in pixels) for the model fitting of the half cube. Note, each frame is a measurement on a different position.

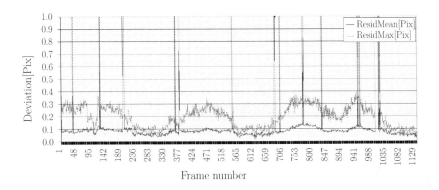

Fig. 8. Residuals between half cube model and LED markers

The achieved mean deviation of the model and the segmented LED markers lies at approximately 0.1 pixel. The maximum residual deviates in general around 0.1 to 0.4 pixel. The displayed outliers arises, if just an insufficient number of LED markers could be segmented and labelled to the target co-ordinates. At a scale of 1 mm per pixel, this leads to an accuracy of the sensor position about 1 mm, which is sufficient for the actual industrial applications at this project.

5   Visualisation

Essential for the applicability of the overall system is the preparation and presentation of the measured sensor positions in a comprehensible form to the controller. The optical measuring system typically yields not only the position of the ultrasonic sensor at a particular time, but also its normal vector. This already allows the presentation of the sensor position as disc-shaped objects, whose colour encodes the wall thickness measured by the ultrasonic sensor. Because the display is in real-time and 3-d, the controller is able to consider the point cloud from all directions, rotate the view and zoom in if necessary, after the first measurement. An example measurement of a pipe bend is illustrated in figure 9(a). The view gives the controller a feedback about already measured regions and supports him to fill white spaces.

For the comparison of an actual measurement of the same pipe segment against a measurement done in the past, 2-d visualisations of the surface may be more useful than 3-d visualisations. With known pipe geometry it is possible to obtain a normalized unwind of the pipe segment surface. In case of a pipe bend segment the stretched and compressed phase (so the controller denotes the interior and exterior of the pipe bend) are always located at the same point of the map in this presentation. The surface of the pipe bend can be divided into sections, that represents the same part of the surface at every inspection. By the implementation of appropriate matching algorithms it is possible to attach the measuring results of the optical tracking system with the previously defined pipe segment model (e.g. diameter, bending radius). This fitting of the point cloud and the pipe bend model can be seen in figure 9(b). Thereby, the pipe regions from different inspections are identically allocated at the pipe segment

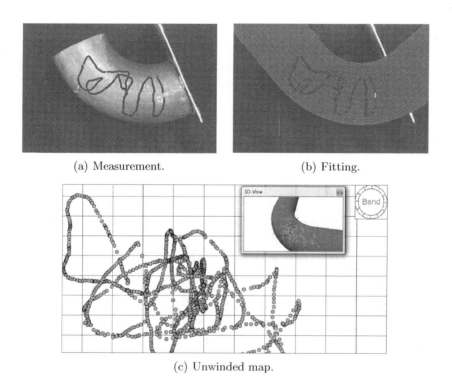

(a) Measurement.   (b) Fitting.

(c) Unwinded map.

Fig. 9. Visualisation of measurement results on a pipe bend. (a) Examiner's view on test object with overlaid ultrasonic measurements. (b) Pipe bend model fitted at current 3-d point cloud. (c) An unwinded map representation constructed from fitted bend model and measurements.

model with help of predefined anchor points. Figure 9(c) shows the map of a colour-coded normalized unwind of a pipe bend model with measured ultrasonic positions and an additional 3-d model view.

6 Conclusion

Under laboratory conditions the combination of ultrasonic testing and optical 3-d measurement satisfies industrial requirements in terms of accuracy and reliability. The use of a-priory information about pipe segment geometry, camera system and optical target offers the ability for a control of success and to perform optimization in each time step. To investigate corrosion over time, it is preferable to use the 2-d unwinded representation of the measurements against the 3-d visualisation. Also first field trials were promising, but the current system is only a prototype for now, and has to be protected against water, if it wants to be used outdoors.

Our approach works robustly and can build the basis for further applications in real industrial environments, for instance the automated inspection of cylindrical storage tank roofs.

Acknowledgement. This work was funded by the German Federal Ministry of Economics and Technology (KF2188302JT0).

References

1. Blitz, J., Simpson, G.: Ultrasonic Methods of Non-Destructive Testing. Chapman & Hall, London (1996)
2. Open Access NDT Database, www.ndt.net/search/docs.php3?id=6806&content=1
3. Luhmann, T., Robson, S., Kyle, S., Harley, I.: Close Range Photogrammetry: Principles, Techniques And Applications, Whittles Publishing, Caithness (2006)
4. Shortis, M.R., Fraser, C.S.: State of the Art of 3D Measurement Systems for Industrial and Engineering Applications, 21st International Congress of FIG, Commission 6, Brighton (1998), www.geomsoft.com/markss/papers/ShortisFraserFIG1998.pdf
5. Kraus, K.: Photogrammetry: Geometry from Images and Laser Scans, 2nd ed., Walter de Gruyter, Berlin (2007)
6. Park, Y., Lepetit, V., Woontack, W.: Multiple 3D Object tracking for augmented reality, Proceedings of the 7th IEEE/ACM International Symposium on Mixed and Augmented Reality, 117–120 (2008)
7. Prisacariu, V., Reid, I.: PWP3D: Real-Time Segmentation and Tracking of 3D Objects, Int. J. Comput. Vision, vol. 98, 335–354 (2012)
8. Lepetit, V., Fua, P.: Monocular model-based 3D tracking of rigid objects, Found. Trends. Comput. Graph. Vis., vol. 1, 1–89 (2005)
9. Hanke-Bourgeois, M.: Grundlagen der Numerischen Mathematik und des Wissenschaftlichen Rechnens, Vieweg + Teubner, Wiesbaden (2009)

Extended GrabCut
for 3D and RGB-D Point Clouds

Nizar K. Sallem[1,2,*] and Michel Devy[1,2]

[1] CNRS, LAAS, 7 avenue du colonel Roche, F-31400 Toulouse, France
[2] Université de Toulouse, LAAS, F-31400 Toulouse, France
nksallem,michel@laas.fr

Abstract. GrabCut is a renowned algorithm for image segmentation. It exploits iteratively the combinatorial minimization of energy function as introduced in graph-cut methods, to achieve background foreground classification with fewer user's interaction. In this paper it is proposed to extend GrabCut to carry out segmentation on RGB-D point clouds, based both on appearance and geometrical criteria. It is shown that an hybrid GrabCut method combining RGB and D information, is more efficient than GrabCut based only on RGB or D images.

Keywords: segmentation, graph-cut, GrabCut, RGB-D, max-flow.

1 Introduction on Image Segmentation

Image segmentation is the pillar of almost all the computer vision processes. It is aimed at separating a whole image I into connex regions $\{R_1, R_2 \ldots R_n\}$ according to some criteria, hoping that this segmentation could make easier a semantical interpretation, e.g. separate objects set on a table, detect obstacles on the ground,etc. It, formally, can be stated as :

$$I = \bigcup_{i=1}^{i=n} R_i, \forall i \neq j R_j \cap R_i = \emptyset \tag{1}$$

Segmentation algorithms can be divided, according to the support, into histogram based, contour based, region based, model based, training based, graph based and any combination of the above.

A full review is beyond the scope of this paper. So briefly, histogram segmentation methods extract peaks and valleys in an histogram to infer position of clusters. Contour based methods, first determine the boundaries - using edges for instance - to then extract regions using some operators in order to close contours. Region based techniques seeks for an uniformity criterion to identify connected pixels associated to the same group. Training based methods acquire the ability to differentiate one or several entities through user interaction or non

---

* N.K. Sallem was funded mainly by the project ASSIST ANR-07-ROBO-011 and partially by the projet ICARO ANR-10-CORD-0025.

J. Blanc-Talon et al. (Eds.): ACIVS 2013, LNCS 8192, pp. 354–365, 2013.

supervised learning in different situation, pose change, light change, etc. Graph based methods see the image as a connected network where pixels are nodes connected to their neighbors through capacitated edges and look for a criterion to cut through edges to create sub-graphs which will represent the regions. Grab-Cut belongs to the broad graph based category, extending the generic graph-cut segmentation algorithm.

GrabCut has been extensively used in order to segment color images; we applied this method [11] in order to detect objects on tables from color images acquired from a camera embedded on a robot. Now our robot is equipped with a RGB-D sensor; so it is proposed here to combine color and depth information in the GrabCut method. It is shown using some test images, that this hybrid algorithm makes more efficient the segmentation method.

The following section describes the graph-cut algorithm, so that the paper would be self contained. Then the section 3 presents the GrabCut variant of graph-cut. The section 4 applies the GrabCut method on 3D data, using criterion on the normal orientation in order to segment 3D images. The section 5 proposes our hybrid approach, using both color and normal orientation as uniformity criteria to define regions. Finally the section 6 summarizes our contribution and mentions some on-going works.

2   Graph-Cut Segmentation

Graph-cut was first presented by [5] and later renewed by [1]. When used to segment an image I, it is a combinatorial optimization technique which minimizes Gibbs energy function given by :

$$E(f) = \sum_{p \in I} D_p(f_p) + \sum_{(p,q) \in \mathcal{N}} V_{p,q}(f_p, f_q) \tag{2}$$

with $f = \{f_p, p \in I\}$ a set of labels, assigned to pixels p; $D_p(f_p)$ a weight function computed upon the observed value of the intensity at pixel p, which measures the cost of assigning f_p to p; $V_{p,q}$ is an interaction potential which determines the cost of simultaneously assigning f_p to p and f_q to q where p and q belong to the same vicinity $\mathcal{N}$. $V_{p,q}$ is a penalty function that ensures the spatial consistency by reprimanding labeling discontinuity for neighboring pixels.

We shall first consider the question of graph representation of such a function as a prior to solving it.

Graph Representation. The former problem Equation 2 is generalized in the work of [7] as a $\mathcal{F}^2$ class energy function :

$$E(x_1 \dots x_n) = \sum_i E^i(x_i) + \sum_{i<j} E^{i,j}(x_i, x_j) \tag{3}$$

where $x_i, 0 \leq i \leq n$ are binary variables, $E^i(x_i)$ is the energy contribution of single variable x_i and $E^{i,j}(x_i, x_j)$ is the energy contribution of the pair (x_i, x_j).

Kolmogorov presented some regularity conditions required for the class function $E(f)$ to be represented by a graph $\mathcal{G} =< \mathcal{V}, \mathcal{E} >$ where $\mathcal{V}$ is the set of vertices and $\mathcal{E}$ is the set of edges. $\mathcal{V}$ is defined by:

$$\mathcal{V} = \mathcal{V}_P \cup \{s, t\} \tag{4}$$

$\mathcal{V}_P$ is the subset of $\mathcal{V}$ where each node correspond to an image pixel, s and t are virtual nodes named, respectively, *source* and *sink*. Each edge $(u, v) \in \mathcal{E}$ such as $u, v \in \mathcal{V}$ is a capacitated edge of weight $c_{(u,v)}$.

For $u \in P$, edges (s, u) and (u, t) are called terminal edges and represent $D_p(s)$ and $D_p(t)$ in the equation 2. If s stands for the *foreground* and t for the *background*, then $c_{(s,u)}$ would be the cost of u belonging to the foreground and $c_{(u,t)}$ the cost of u belonging to the background. Analogously, (u, v) where $u, v \in P$ represent the term $V_{p,q}$ and $c_{(u,v)}$ is the weight of the two neighboring pixels wearing distinct labels.

The graph layout is given by connecting E^i and $E^{i,j}$ sub-graphs. For simplification reason, let us note $edge(u, c)$ the edge (s, u) of capacity c if $c > 0$ or the edge (u, t) of capacity $-c$ if $c < 0$. First, E^i representation involves three nodes $\mathcal{V} = s, u, t$ and one single edge $edge(u, E(1) - E(0))$ and is given in Figure 1.

$$E^i(1) - E^i(0) \qquad\qquad\qquad E^i(0) - E^i(1)$$

(a) $E^i(0) < E^i(1)$ (b) $E^i(0) \geq E^i(1)$

Fig. 1. E^i graph representation. If $E^i(0) < E^i(1)$ edge (s, v_i) is added (a) else edge (v_i, t) is added (b).

$E^{i,j}$ sub-graph on the other involves four nodes $\{v_i, v_j, s, t\}$ and three edges:

- $edge(v_i, E(1, 0) - E(0, 0))$;
- $edge(v_j, E(1, 1) - E(1, 0))$;
- (v_i, v_j) with weight $-\pi(E) = - \displaystyle\sum_{x_1 \in \{0,1\}, x_2 \in \{0,1\}} \left(\prod_{i=1}^{2} (-1)^{x_i} \right) E(x_1, x_2)$.

On the Figure 2, we depict $E^{i,j}$ sub-graph when $E(1, 0) > E(0, 0)$ and $E(1, 0) > E(1, 1)$.

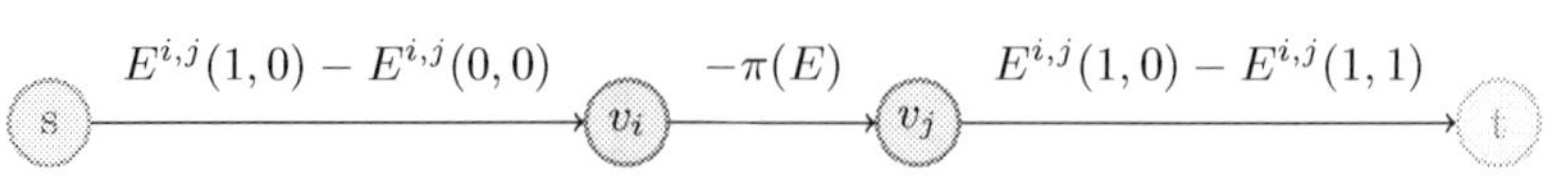

$$E^{i,j}(1, 0) - E^{i,j}(0, 0) \qquad -\pi(E) \qquad E^{i,j}(1, 0) - E^{i,j}(1, 1)$$

Fig. 2. $E^{i,j}$ graph representation. Case where $E(1, 0) > E(0, 0)$ and $E(1, 0) > E(1, 1)$.

Energy Minimization. Let E the energy function to be minimized, represented by a graph $\mathcal{G}$ and a subset $\mathcal{V}_0$. It is then possible to find the exact minimum of E, in polynomial time computing the min-cut $s - t$ of $\mathcal{G}$.

Thanks to the equivalence of the min-cut and max-flow problems, max-flow algorithms can be employed to minimize $E(f)$. In the literature, two methods are commonly used to solve it : the Goldberg-Tarjan and derived *push-relabel* methods and the Ford-Fulkerson and derived *augmenting paths* methods. A computational complexity comparison shows that this last one is the more efficient with a complexity of $O(\mathcal{E}.f_{max})$. But, even if efficient, this method is not adapted to the computer vision context where the problem is nearly N-P hard locally.

A more suitable alternative is given by the Boykov-Kolmogorov algorithm depicted in [2]. Authors maintain two distinct trees $\mathcal{S}$ of root s and $\mathcal{T}$ of root t. $\mathcal{S}$ is formed by all the edges $(s, u), u \in \mathcal{V}_P$ and $\mathcal{T}$ by all the edges $(u, t), u \in \mathcal{V}_P$. First $\mathcal{S}$ and $\mathcal{T}$ are grown till a path $s \to t$ is found. Active nodes attract neighboring by exploring non saturated edges. Acquired nodes will form the new frontier of the tree and become *active*. Once all the outcoming edges of a node are exploited it becomes *passive*. If during the cruise, a node from the other tree is encountered the growth step is halted. The found path is augmented which may lead to saturated edges. In this case the node become *orphan*. Second the orphans are adopted either through an unsaturated edge or - if none qualifies - they are requalified as *free* and removed from the search trees leaving all their successors *orphans* and the adoption step starts over. Finally, the growth stage is reinitiated. The algorithm stops once it is not possible to expand $\mathcal{S}$ or $\mathcal{T}$ i.e. there is no more active nodes and the frontier is formed by only saturated edges which means that the maximum flow is reached.

Graph-Cut Segmentation. Graph-cut was successfully applied by [5] for binary image restoration and then by [3] for both automatic and interactive 2D and 3D image segmentation.

[5] formulated the energy function as a Maximum A Posteriori estimation of a Markov Random Field :

$$E(f) = \lambda \sum_{p \in P} ln Pr(I_p|I^o) + \sum_{\{p,q\} \in \mathcal{N}} \delta_{I_p \neq I_q} \text{ where } \delta_{I_p \neq I_q} = \begin{cases} 1 & \text{if } I_p \neq I_q \\ 0 & \text{if } I_p = I_q \end{cases} \quad (5)$$

with $I = \{I_p | p \in P\}$ the set of unknown original binary intensity values of the image and I^o is the observed intensity of a pixel.

[3] stated their energy function as:

$$E(f) = \lambda \sum_{p \in P} R_p(f_p) + \sum_{\{p,q\} \in \mathcal{N}} B_{p,q}.\delta_{f_p \neq f_q} \text{ where } \delta_{f_p \neq f_q} = \begin{cases} 1 & \text{if } f_p \neq f_q \\ 0 & \text{if } f_p = f_q \end{cases} \quad (6)$$

$$= \lambda \sum_{p \in P} R_p(f_p) + \sum_{\{p,q\} \in \mathcal{N}} exp\left(-\frac{(I_p - I_q)^2}{2\sigma^2}\right).\frac{1}{dist(p,q)}.\delta_{f_p \neq f_q} \quad (7)$$

with $f_p \in \{\text{"}obj\text{"}, \text{"}bkg\text{"}\}$ a binary label and $\begin{cases} R_p(\text{"}obj\text{"}) = -ln Pr(I_p|\text{"}obj\text{"}) \\ R_p(\text{"}bkg\text{"}) = -ln Pr(I_p|\text{"}bkg\text{"}) \end{cases}$.

The decision for a pixel to be classified either as "obj" or "bkg", is made upon automatic process using a precomputed histogram model of the object or through user interaction who selects a region of the image to contain the object.

So far, we described the graph-cut segmentation basics, in the following section we will describe the GrabCut segmentation algorithm.

3   Segmentation of RGB Images: GrabCut

GrabCut was introduced in [9] and defined as "an iterative graph-cut". In our point of view, authors made three significant improvements to graph-cut interactive segmentation :

1. the use of a trimap with three labels: "background", "object" and "unknown" in contrast with the binary "object", "background";
2. the iterative application of graph-cut: at each step, min-cut is computed and labels are updated till stabilization;
3. the exploitation of the RGB space instead of intensity values.

User delimits a region on the image, pixels inside are labeled "unknown" while outsiders are labeled "background". Two Gaussian Mixture Models (GMM) of K components are then built, one for the background and one for the foreground to model the color distribution $\underline{\theta}$. This approach is the same used by [10].

$$\theta = \{\pi(\alpha, k), \mu(\alpha, k), \Sigma(\alpha, k), \alpha = 0, 1, k = 1 \ldots K\} \qquad (8)$$

with π, Σ and μ respectively weight, covariance and mean of each one of the $2K$ gaussians.

The Orchard-Bouman algorithm [9] is then applied to assign each pixel to the corresponding gaussian. This leads to a composite energy function:

$$E(\underline{\alpha}, k, \underline{\theta}, z) = U(\underline{\alpha}, k, \underline{\theta}, z) + V(\underline{\alpha}, z). \qquad (9)$$

4   Segmentation of Depth Images: 3D GrabCut

Extension of GrabCut to handle geometric data is based on observation of normals direction. Given a small enough support region $\mathcal{N}$, on a plane, a geometric uniform region, normals direction will be almost the same which is a good coercion indicator while edges will be the location of a normals direction change. These observations are schematized on Figure 3.

Another fact is that Ruzon et al. [10] ascertainment for colors i.e. the observed color of a pixel p is the combination of the true pixel color altered by colors of pixel in its vicinity inversely proportional to their distance to p, apply similarly to normals direction i.e normal direction at a point p, computed using its 3D coordinates, is affected by the coordinates of its neighbors hence the use of GMMs is justified. Let us consider P a 3D point cloud of computed normals $N = \{n_0..n_i..n_n\}$ then we can build a normals distribution model:

$$\underline{\theta_N} = \{\pi(\alpha, k), \mu(\alpha, k), \Sigma(\alpha, k), \alpha = 0, 1, k = 1 \ldots K\} \qquad (10)$$

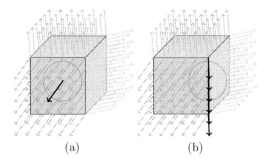

(a)   (b)

Fig. 3. Normal direction on a plane and on an edge. On a planar surface (a) normals directions are parallel while on edge (b) the variation of normal directions indicates the presence of a border.

with π, Σ and μ respectively weight, covariance and mean of each one of the $2K$ gaussians representing foreground and background normals distributions. Energy function can then be expressed, analogously to Equation 9:

$$E(\underline{\alpha}, k, \underline{\theta_N}, \boldsymbol{n}) = U(\underline{\alpha}, k, \underline{\theta_N}, \boldsymbol{n}) + V(\underline{\alpha}, \boldsymbol{n}). \tag{11}$$

Replacing *red*, *green* and *blue* color components used in GrabCut with n_x, n_y and n_z the 3 axis projections of a normal $\boldsymbol{n}$, we can apply the GrabCut routines to segment, geometrically, an object from its background.

4.1   Experimental Results

To evaluate the performance of 3D GrabCut we acquired an image of a scene with a RGB-D camera. The output consists of a point cloud P and a color image I. User performs initialization on I since it is the natural way to distinguish object from background. Thanks to the mapping between points and pixels, we run GrabCut and 3D GrabCut on the same region. At each run we measure the number of iterations before convergence. We expect a less or equal number of iterations since the discontinuity in normals direction should be more perceptible according to the visual representation of Figure 4.

GrabCut and 3D GrabCut implementation is the one described in [12]. We used the Boykov-Kolmogorov implementation of **maxflow v2.02** library. Normals computation is performed according to [6]. The scene contains three easy to distinguish objects. Table 1 summarizes the number of iterations for each object prior to convergence. We notice that the number of iterations is comparable and 3D GrabCut performs better when there is fewer loss in 3D data on the surface of the object.

The visual result of the above segmentations is reported on Figure 5. To ease comparison we projected back the segmentation result on the color image. From a normals point of view the 3D GrabCut performs much better than GrabCut on color images but when projected back we notice the irregular borders due to the strong variation on the edges.

(a)   (b)

Fig. 4. Scene acquired by a RGB-D camera. (a) color image, (b) normals representation in color such us $[r\ g\ b]^T = [\boldsymbol{n_x}\ \boldsymbol{n_y}\ \boldsymbol{n_z}]^T$.

Table 1. Comparison between GrabCut and 3D GrabCut based on the necessary iterations to achieve segmentation of three object from the scene

Object	Selection $< x_{min}, y_{min}, x_{max}, y_{max} >$	GrabCut	3D GrabCut
1	$< 220, 428, 336, 241 >$	6	8
2	$< 388, 418, 502, 211 >$	14	12
3	$< 81, 349, 204, 172 >$	13	9

The major inconvenient for the 3D GrabCut is that computation of normals depend on 3D data presence. The sensor used in our experiments has a limited $[0.5m\ 3m]$ and induces artifacts as a result of the adoption of infra-red for the light projector. The other drawback is the coarseness of borders which is explained by the strong variation of normals along edges. We propose a second extension that will operate on the **N-RGB** space to overcome these issues.

5   Segmentation of RGB-D Images: Hybrid GrabCut

Correlation between colorimetric and geometric data in RGB-D allows for a **N-RGB** space consideration:

$$\mathbb{R}^3 \to \mathbb{R}^6$$
$$\boldsymbol{p} \mapsto < \boldsymbol{n}, \boldsymbol{z} >$$
$$[x\ y\ z]^T \mapsto [n_x\ n_y\ n_z\ r\ g\ b]^T \qquad (12)$$

with $\boldsymbol{p}$ 3D coordinates of p, $\boldsymbol{n} = [n_x\ n_y\ n_z]^T$ normal of p and $\boldsymbol{z} = [r\ g\ b]^T$ the color of the corresponding pixel in the image.

We build a composite model of normals/colors distribution of the point cloud:

$$\underline{\theta_H} = \underline{\theta_N} + \underline{\theta} = \{\pi_n(\alpha, k), \mu_n(\alpha, k), \Sigma_n(\alpha, k), \pi_z(\alpha, k), \mu_z(\alpha, k), \Sigma_z(\alpha, k)\} \quad (13)$$

with π, Σ and μ respectively the weights, the covariances and means of the $2 \times 2K$ gaussians. The separation of the gaussians is made possible by the independence of colors and normals. The challenge is to be able to assign a unique gaussian to each point.

Fig. 5. Objects segmentation with GrabCut and 3D GrabCut. Objects (1st column) are selected by user on the image. GrabCut segmentation result is shown on 2nd column. 3D GrabCut applied to the corresponding area of N is displayed on the 3rd column then result is projected back on the image (4th column). Projected segmentation leaves rough edges because of the strong normals variation on borders but when reported to normals, 3D GrabCut is better than GrabCut on image.

5.1 Modified Orchard-Bouman

In [8], authors employ statistics of second order to build a binary decision tree to divide an initial set of data into two clusters and so on till the desired number of clusters K is reached. First all the points are gathered in a single C_1 cluster. Then, for each $C_k, \{1 \le k \le K\}$ we compute the mean μ_k, covariance Σ_k. Next the cluster is divided by a plane perpendicular to the direction of the greates variation into two groups C_{2k} and C_{2k+1} and so on. Direction of the variation is obtained through the eigenvalues decomposition (**EVD**) of Σ_k. Direction is given by e_k, the eigenvector corresponding to the largest eigenvalue λ_k. The split is formalized in Equation 14 and Orchard-Bouman algorithm is outlined in Algorithm 1.

$$
\begin{aligned}
C_{2k} &= \{p \in C_k, e_k^\mathsf{T}.\boldsymbol{p} \le e_k^\mathsf{T}.\mu_k\} \\
C_{2k+1} &= \{p \in C_k, e_k^\mathsf{T}.\boldsymbol{p} > e_k^\mathsf{T}.\mu_k\}
\end{aligned}
\tag{14}
$$

Input: set of points to classify S, number of groups K
Output: clusters $\{C_k\}_{1 \le k \le K}$
$C_1 = S$
Compute covariance Σ_1
Compute mean μ_1
Compute cardinal N_1
for $k = 2$ **to** K **do**
  Find leaf k which maximises λ_k
  Form leaves $2k$ and $2k+1$ from Eq. 14
  Compute Σ_{2k}, μ_{2k} and N_{2k}
  Deduce Σ_{2k+1}, μ_{2k+1} and N_{2k+1}
  $\Sigma_{2k+1} = \Sigma_k - \Sigma_{2k}$
  $\mu_{2k+1} = \mu_k - \mu_{2k}$
  $N_{2k+1} = N_k - \mu_{2k}$
end

Algorithm 1. Orchard-Bouman algorithm for data clustering

The original Orchard-Bouman algorithm is tuned to account for variations in color and normals. For each cluster C_k we compute two covariance matrices Σ_{n_k}, Σ_{z_k} and two means, μ_{n_k}, μ_{z_k} accounting for normals and colors. We perform EVD on both Σ_{n_k} and Σ_{z_k} to retrieve (λ_{n_k}, e_{n_k}) and (λ_{z_k}, e_{z_k}). Decision for a point $p \in C_k$ to be in C_{2k} or C_{2k+1} is made upon a double condition:

$$
\begin{aligned}
C_{2k} &= \{p \in C_k, e_{z_k}^\mathsf{T}.\boldsymbol{z} \le e_{z_k}^\mathsf{T}.\mu_{z_k} \vee e_{n_k}^\mathsf{T}.\boldsymbol{n} \le e_{n_k}^\mathsf{T}.\mu_{n_k}\} \\
C_{2k+1} &= \{p \in C_k, e_{z_k}^\mathsf{T}.\boldsymbol{z} > e_{z_k}^\mathsf{T}.\mu_{z_k} \vee e_{n_k}^\mathsf{T}.\boldsymbol{n} > e_{n_k}^\mathsf{T}.\mu_{n_k}\}
\end{aligned}
\tag{15}
$$

Except from the split criteria and the computation of $(\Sigma_n, \mu_n, \lambda_n, e_n, N_n)$ and $(\Sigma_z, \mu_z, \lambda_z, e_z, N_z)$, the remaining of the algorithm remains the same.

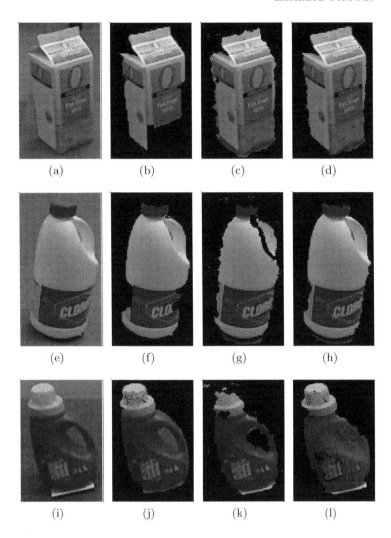

Fig. 6. Segmentation output from GrabCut, 3D GrabCut and Hybrid GrabCut. User selection is on the 1st column. GrabCut output is on the 2nd column, 3D GrabCut projected on the image is visible on 3th column and Hybrid GrabCut segmented objects are displayed on the 4th column. Hybrid GrabCut proofs to outline smoother contours and correcter segmentation.

Fig. 7. Hybrid GrabCut handling of color only data. User's selection (a) is a pure color region (b) so 3D GrabCut is unable to perform segmentation (c) while Hybrid GrabCut behaves as a classic GrabCut.

5.2   Experimental Results

We run the same experimental protocol as in Section 4.1 on the same selections. We notice that the number of iterations is reduced because of the double variation computation: the minimum energy is reached faster.

Table 2. Number of iterations required by Hybrid GrabCut to achieve convergence on the three objects of scene in Fig. 4

Objet	Slection $< x_{min}, y_{min}, x_{max}, y_{max} >$	Hybrid GrabCut
1	$< 220, 428, 336, 241 >$	5
2	$< 388, 418, 502, 211 >$	10
3	$< 81, 349, 204, 172 >$	9

We report the segmentation result on the image to compare outputs of Grab-Cut, 3D GrabCut and Hybrid GrabCut. We notice the regularity of borders when compared to 3D GrabCut and the enhanced results when compared to GrabCut, especially for the first object where GrabCut lays out a part of the milk box due to the difference of color.

In a second experiment we try to segment the bottle cap on the bottom left corner of Figure 4. This is beyond the abilities of 3D GrabCut since the data is out of range of the sensor but we expect Hybrid GrabCut to perform equally to GrabCut thanks to the presence of RGB data. Results are shown on Figure 7.

6   Conclusion

In this paper we proposed two extension of GrabCut to handle segmentation of 3D and RGB-D point clouds. Our approach prooves to be as reliable as GrabCut and behaves even better when combining colors and geometric data. The extension mechanism is based on observation of normals direction on surfaces and edges. The parallelism of normals directions on planar surfaces is a good region coercion criterion while the strong variation on edges is a clear indication for borders. The second order statistics used in the clustering algorithm catche these subtilities and allows, inside a composite model, to build the distribution model integrated into the energy function to be minimized in a graph-cut subprocess.

References

1. Boykov, Y.Y., Jolly, M.P.: Interactive graph cuts for optimal boundary & region segmentation of objects in N-D images 1, 105–112 (2001)
2. Boykov, Y., Kolmogorov, V.: An experimental comparison of min-cut/max-flow algorithms for energy minimization in vision. IEEE Transactions on Pattern Analysis and Machine Intelligence 26, 359–374 (2001)
3. Boykov, Y., Funka-Lea, G.: Graph cuts and efficient n-d image segmentation. Int. J. Comput. Vision 70(2), 109–131 (2006)

4. Ford, L.R., Fulkerson, D.R.: Flows in Networks. Princeton University Press (1962)
5. Greig, D.M., Porteous, B.T., Seheult, A.H.: Exact Maximum A Posteriori Estimation for Binary Images (1989)
6. Holzer, S., Rusu, R.B., Dixon, M., Gedikli, S., Navab, N.: Adaptive neighborhood selection for real-time surface normal estimation from organized point cloud data using integral images. In: 2012 IEEE/RSJ International Conference on Intelligent Robots and Systems (IROS), pp. 2684–2689. IEEE (2012)
7. Kolmogorov, V., Zabin, R.: What energy functions can be minimized via graph cuts? IEEE Transactions on Pattern Analysis and Machine Intelligence 26(2), 147–159 (2004)
8. Orchard, M.T., Bouman, C.A.: Color quantization of images. IEEE Transactions on Signal Processing 39(12), 2677–2690 (1991)
9. Rother, C., Kolmogorov, V., Blake, A.: "grabcut": interactive foreground extraction using iterated graph cuts. In: ACM SIGGRAPH 2004 Papers, SIGGRAPH 2004, pp. 309–314. ACM, New York (2004)
10. Ruzon, M., Tomasi, C.: Alpha Estimation in Natural Images. In: Proc. IEEE Conf. Comp. Vision and Pattern Recog., pp. 18–25 (2000)
11. Sallem, N., Devy, M.: Modélisation d'objets 3D en vue de leur reconnaissance et leur manipulation par un robot personnel. In: Proc. ORASIS 2009 - Congrès Des Jeunes Chercheurs En Vision Par Ordinateur, Trégastel, France (2009)
12. Talbot, J.F., Xu, X.: Implementing GrabCut (April 2006)

A Resource Allocation Framework for Adaptive Selection of Point Matching Strategies*

Quentin De Neyer and Christophe De Vleeschouwer

Université Catholique de Louvain, 1348 Louvain-La-Neuve, Belgique
quentin.deneyer@uclouvain.be

Abstract. This report investigates how to track an object based on the matching of points between pairs of consecutive video frames. The approach is especially relevant to support object tracking in close-view video shots, as for example encountered in the context of the Pan-Tilt-Zoom (PTZ) camera autotracking problem. In contrast to many earlier related works, we consider that the matching metric of a point should be adapted to the signal observed in its spatial neighborhood, and introduce a cost-benefit framework to control this adaptation with respect to the global target displacement estimation objective. Hence, the proposed framework explicitly handles the trade-off between the point-level matching metric complexity, and the contribution brought by this metric to solve the target tracking problem. As a consequence, and in contrast with the common assumption that only specific points of interest should be investigated, our framework does not make any a priori assumption about the points that should be considered or ignored by the tracking process. Instead, it states that any point might help in the target displacement estimation, provided that the matching metric is well adapted. Measuring the contribution reliability of a point as the probability that it leads to a crorrect matching decision, we are able to define a global successful target matching criterion. It is then possible to minimize the probability of incorrect matching over the set of possible (point,metric) combinations and to find the optimal aggregation strategy. Our preliminary results demonstrate both the effectiveness and the efficiency of our approach.

Keywords: active tracking, point matching, cost-benefit optimization.

1 Introduction

Tracking represents an important task within the field of computer vision. It has been studied intensively for a broad range of applications including surveillance, sport, traffic monitoring, augmented reality etc. Among these applications, active tracking [9,12,6], also named autotracking in the literature, offers challenges in both control and computer vision: a camera is commanded (pan, tilt, zoom)

---

* Part of this work has been funded by the european FP7 SV3D project, and by the Belgian NSF.

J. Blanc-Talon et al. (Eds.): ACIVS 2013, LNCS 8192, pp. 366–377, 2013.

automatically to follow a target, based on its own captured video stream. It thus forms a closed-loop system where the error signal is measured by the tracking of the target across successive frames. Recent advances in the ad hoc technology have made it possible to command cameras accurately at high frequency, with small delays. In addition recent computers can now process video streams in realtime for heavy tasks such as tracking. As a result, it now becomes possible to support active tracking over large areas, collecting close-up sequences while keeping camera locked on the object of interest.

In this paper, we are primarily interested in tracking close-up views of a target across a video stream. Since only a fragment of the target might be visible (due to the close-up nature of the view, but also to potential occlusions), we model the target based on the texture locally surrounding a set of points. Hence, our problem consists in inferring a correct target displacement, by analysing the correspondance probability distributions computed for a given set of points in two successive frames. The points and their matching metric should be jointly selected to maximize the chance of correct target displacement inferrence. This is in contrast with many previous works that use a single matching strategy and restrict their investigation to points of interest, which are characterized by highly discriminant and/or highly invariant features [4,7,1]. In addition, when performing tracking in real-time, the computational resources to handle each pair of consecutive frames are limited. Therefore, we introduce a cost-benefit framework to maximize the chance to infer a correct target displacement, under some global computational complexity constraint. The deployment of this framework ends-up in selecting the points to match, and in adapting their respective matching metrics to their textured neighborhood. It implies a formal definition of the notion of point matching benefit, defined to reflect the contribution of each individual point to a reliable estimate of the target displacement. The presented matching framework can then be embedded in an active tracking process [2].

To conclude this introduction, it is worth pointing out that the proposed framework, unlike most popular matching methods, does not make any a priori assumption about the characteristics of the points that should be considered to support the tracking. Instead, it provides a methodology to estimate whether a given point neighborhood is worth being matched with some given metric. Any point is potentially relevant to infer the target displacement between two frames. Specifically, its relevance is estimated in terms of matching reliability, as a function of the spatial neighborhood and of the envisioned matching metric.

The rest of the report is organized as follows. Section 2 motivates the approach in comparison with state-of-art tracking methods. Next, Section 3 introduces the notion of matching metric, and explains how points should be selected, and how their distance maps aggregated, so as to maximize the chance of correct target displacement inference. Section 4 then defines the cost-constrained target displacement estimation problem, and proposes a heuristic method to select the points and their matching metrics in a so called cost-reliability (CR) optimal way. Eventually, Section 5 presents how the CR-optimal points matching process can be used in practice. Section 6 presents preliminary experimental results, whilst Section 7 concludes.

2   Related Works

A very common way to track objects in videos captured with still cameras consists in modeling the background and comparing every new image to this model, in order to detect foreground activity [13]. When the camera moves, it is possible to reconstruct a sort of puzzle background, by compensating the camera motion between frames. The performance of this method is, however, severely degraded by the inaccuracies of the compensations (inaccuracy of detected motion and optical geometry compensation). Therefore, the authors in [10] use background subtraction methods that are robust to small spatial drifts. However, these methods really break down in case of zoom changes.

Because the tracked objects in our applications undergo severe global deformations, while remaining locally quite invariant, we focus our investigations on techinques using local descriptors and do not study trackers using global descriptors like shape, contours or histograms. Moreover, for computational efficiency reasons, we adopt a sparse representation of the object and do not consider motion analysis over the whole frame [3] or target [5].

Discrete local features have received a significant amount of attention in the computer vision research community over the past 15 years. Among the numerous developed algorithms, the most popular and intensively used methods are certainly the Harris corner detector[4], the SIFT keypoints detector/descriptor [7] and the similar speeded-up version SURF [1], but there exist plenty of them. These approaches work symetrically by detecting key features in two images and then perform discrete associations [11]. Although these methods have shown to be very performant in multiple viewpoints matching, panoramic recontruction, object recognition, and other matching tasks, their performances in object tracking (especially for deformable objects) are questionable. One practical reason is that keypoints are frequently located at the boundary of the object to track and therefore include background information in their description, with the risk that points drift into the background. The boundaries of a target also undergo non-affine transformation because of their 3D nature, making them uncertain source of information. More fundamentally, the use of a saliency criterion to select the points to match between frames supposes that one knows what point will be good for tracking a priori. In contrast, we relax this assumption, and consider that any point could be useful to infer information about target displacement, provided that it is matched with an appropriated metric. In the following, we use matching metric to denote the combination of a point neighborhood descriptor (e.g. a squared grid of pixels) and its associated distance metric (e.g. euclidian distance). By allowing the use of multiple strategies to match multiple points, we also increase the system's capability in handling specific problems. As a prime example, a gradient-based descriptor will be sensible to motion blur on an image, but not color histogram based descriptors, while these are led to mistake in presence of similarly coloured background.

3   Points Selection and Distance Maps Aggregation for Reliable Target Displacement Estimation

In this section, we investigate the procedure for aggregating information arising from multiple points, and derive an objective criterion for point and associated matching metric selection. Section 3.1 first defines the notion of matching metric and formalizes the point matching process, providing the material to understand the subsequent developments. Section 3.2 then considers how to best aggregate distance maps, in order to maximize the chance of correct target displacement inference, while Section 3.3 introduces the additive metric that is used to quantify the reliability of the target displacement estimate resulting from the aggregation of the distance maps computed for a set of target points. This metric is fundamental because it allows to order a given set of points according to their respective contribution to a reliable target displacement estimation. It will be the core of the cost-reliability optimal selection method presented in Section 4.

3.1   Matching Metric and Distance Map

We consider the matching of a point p from a reference image I to a query image J. In the case of video tracking, I and J are two successive frames in the sequence. The matching metric includes (1) the function $rep(p, I)$ that computes a feature vector (descriptor) describing the point p and its neighborhood in image I, (2) the distance used to evaluate the similarity between two feature vectors and (3) the search region S in frame J. A patch of pixels luminance around p, a SAD-distance and a square search window define a simple example of matching metric.

Let $\mathcal{P}$ be a set of N points representing an object of interest. Considering that a matching metric is assigned (arbitrarily) to each point in P, N distance maps are computed by applying the matching metrics between the reference points in I and every point belonging to the corresponding search region in J. For every point in $\mathcal{P}$, the minimum of the distance corresponds to the most probable point displacement.

3.2   Aggregation of Distance Maps for Reliable Target Registration

For a given set $\mathcal{P}$ of N points, this section considers aggregation of N distance maps $dm_i(x)$, $i = 1...N$, $x \in S$ = search region. For the sake of simplicity and without loss of generality, we restrict the developments to $S = \{X, \bar{X}\}$, which means that there are only two possible displacements X and $\bar{X}$ of the target between frame I and J, X being the actual target displacement. The N points of $\mathcal{P}$ belong to the same object, and are thus assumed to follow the same translation, up to some deformation noise.

The N observations, corresponding to the matching of N points, are considered to be independent. The most probable displacement $\hat{X}$ is given below:

$$\hat{X} = \underset{x \in \{X, \bar{X}\}}{\text{argmax}} \; P(d = x | dm_i(X), dm_i(\bar{X})_{|i=1...n})$$

By using the (conditional) independance of the observations and the Bayes formula, after some developments, we get (f denoting the pdf)

$$\hat{X} = \underset{x\in\{X,\bar{X}\}}{\text{argmax}} \prod_{i=1}^{N} f(dm_i(x)|d=x)f(dm_i(\bar{x})|d=x)$$

$$= \underset{x\in\{X,\bar{X}\}}{\text{argmax}} \prod_{i=1}^{N} \frac{f(dm_i(x)|d=x)}{f(dm_i(x)|d=\bar{x})} \underbrace{f(dm_i(\bar{x})|d=x)f(dm_i(x)|d=\bar{x})}_{equal\ for\ x=X\ and\ x=\bar{X}}$$

We assume that $f(dm_i(x)|d=x)$ and $f(dm_i(x)|d=\bar{x})$ are normally distributed with parameters $N(\mu_{i1},\sigma_{i1})$ and $N(\mu_{i0},\sigma_{i0})$ respectively. For the sake of simplicity, we also consider that $\sigma_{i0}=\sigma_{i1}=\sigma_i$. This is not a strong assumption, as the standard deviation reflects the variability of the distance, as a result of the deformations of the tracked object. Hence, by taking the logarithm of the product and after simplifications, we get

$$\hat{X} = \underset{x\in\{X,\bar{X}\}}{\text{argmin}} \sum_{i=1}^{N} \frac{(dm_i(x)-\mu_{i1})^2}{\sigma_i^2} - \frac{(dm_i(x)-\mu_{i0})^2}{\sigma_i^2}$$

using relation $a^2-b^2=(a+b)(a-b)$ and developing, we have

$$\hat{X} = \underset{x\in\{X,\bar{X}\}}{\text{argmin}} \sum_{i=1}^{N} 2dm_i(x)\frac{(\mu_{i0}-\mu_{i1})}{\sigma_i^2} - \underbrace{\frac{(\mu_{i1}+\mu_{i0})(\mu_{i0}-\mu_{i1})}{\sigma_i^2}}_{constant\ term}$$

$$= \underset{x\in\{X,\bar{X}\}}{\text{argmin}} \sum_{i=1}^{N} \frac{(\mu_{i0}-\mu_{i1})}{\sigma_i^2}dm_i(x) = \underset{x\in\{X,\bar{X}\}}{\text{argmin}} \underbrace{\sum_{i=1}^{N} \frac{\mu(D_i)}{\sigma^2(D_i)}dm_i(x),}_{g(x)} \qquad (1)$$

where $D_i = dm_i(\bar{x})-dm_i(x) \propto N(\mu_{i0}-\mu_{i1},\sigma_{i0}^2+\sigma_{i1}^2)$. The likeliest displacement, given N distance metrics two observations in two candidate displacements X and $\bar{X}$, is thus the one that minimizes $g(x)$, a weighted sum of the distance maps computed in the candidate positions.

3.3   Selection of Points for Reliable Target Displacement Estimation

Now that we have found how to aggregate the maps (when they are just composed of two measurements for each point, see Section 3.2), we have to figure out how to select the points whose maps should be aggregated to best estimate the target displacement. The points selection problem is formulated as follows: given a set $\mathcal{P}$ of P points, find the subset of indices Φ_N such that $\{p_i, i \in \Phi_N\} \subset \mathcal{P}$ of points that minimizes the risk of wrong target displacement inference, given the aggregation rule deduced in Section 3.2. Let D_{Φ_N} be the difference of aggregated observations at the wrong and the right displacement,

$$D_{\Phi_N} = g(\bar{X}) - g(X) = \sum_{i=1}^{N} \frac{\mu(D_i)}{\sigma^2(D_i)} \underbrace{(dm_i(\bar{X}) - dm_i(X))}_{\propto N(\mu(D_i), \sigma^2(D_i))}. \qquad (2)$$

Given the decision rule defined by Equation (1), the probability of having an error is equal to the probability that D_{Φ_N} is negative. It must be minimized. Because D_{Φ_N} is a weighted sum of gaussian variables, it also follows a gaussian distribution and the probability of error is the lowest when maximizing its mean versus standard deviation ratio, or the square of it:

$$\hat{\Phi}_N = \underset{\Phi_N}{\operatorname{argmax}} \frac{\mu(D_{\Phi_N})^2}{\sigma(D_{\Phi_N})^2} = \underset{\Phi_N}{\operatorname{argmax}} \sum_{i \in \Phi_N} \frac{\mu_i^2}{\sigma_i^2} = = \underset{\Phi_N}{\operatorname{argmax}} \sum_{i \in \Phi_N} r_i^2$$

Hence, the objective function to maximize when selecting the points to aggregate appears to be the squared sum of the ratio between the mean and the standard deviation of the variables D_i associated to the selected points. The ratio $r_i = \mu_i^2/\sigma_i^2$ denotes the ith point matching reliability.

4   Cost-Reliability Optimal Target Registration

The developments of section 3 consider a simplified registration problem, observing the distances in two displacement candidates for a set of N points, with predefined matching metrics. In the proposed application, we are interested in estimating the most reliable displacement within a predefined search window S, for a given amount of computational resources. Therefore, in this section, we extend the set of candidates to an arbitrary search area, and consider that the matching metric of each point can be selected within a set of metrics, so as to achieve an optimal trade-off between displacement estimation reliability and computational cost. Section 4.1 formulates the cost-benefit optimization problem, while Section 4.2 proposes a heuristic to compute an approximated solution.

4.1   Cost-Constrained Target Registration Problem Definition

By definition, we consider that a target is registered between two frames once its (translational) displacement between the two frames has been estimated. We showed that for two displacement assumptions X_1 and X_2, under some reasonable hypotheses, this is done by minimizing the weighted sum of observations $dm_i(X_1)$ and $dm_i(X_2)$ associated to a set of points $\Phi_N = \{p_i, i = 1...N\}$. In Section 3.3, we have explained that the probability of incorrect target registration can be minimized by maximizing the sum of the points matching reliabilities r_i. In practice, of course, the matching process generates more than 2 observations for each point. Those are spread over the search area S, resulting in a distance map (see Section 3.1). According to the results of section 3.3 and considering observation of the whole distance maps, minimizing the error risk is equivalent to minimizing the probability of error in any location $j \neq X$ (X denotes the correct displacement) of the search region. This is achieved by maximizing the sum of ratios $r_i(j) = \mu_i^2(j)/\sigma_i^2(j)$, as estimated in the most ambiguous candidate displacement $j \in S$. In other words, to minimize the error likelihood, the set of N points $\hat{\Phi}_N$ should be selected so as to maximize the smallest (over all positions j) sum of reliabilities, i.e.

$$\hat{\Phi}_N = \underset{\Phi_N}{\operatorname{argmax}} \min_j \sum_{i \in \Phi_N} r_i(j) \tag{3}$$

Estimating $r_i(j)$ for every possible $j \in S$ is, however, too expensive in practice. Moreover, even if the $r_i(j)$ and underlying $\mu_i(j)$ and $\sigma_i(j)$ had been estimated for all positions j surrounding the ith point in the query image, they could not be used for summing the distance maps, since, in practice, the actual position of the ith point in the target frame is not known. In order to simplify the problem and to make it solvable, we approximate the map $r_i(j)$ by a constant r_i multiplied by a binary mask $b_i(j)$. This means that for each point p_i, we consider that the r_i function is characterized by two regions in the search window: one region where $r_i(j)$ is small, i.e. where the distance map has low values, and another region where it has high values. The distance map dm_i corresponding to the point p_i primarily helps in rejecting the displacements j corresponding to high distance map values, i.e. to position j for which $b_i(j) = 1$. Fig. 1 illustrates this approximation on several typical instances of distance maps, showing that the hypothesis is reasonably justified in practice.

Fig. 1. Distance maps are often divided in two contrasted regions of likely and unlikely matching, so that $r_i(j)$ can be approximated by a constant r_i multiplying a binary mask

Two consequences arise from the above binary approximation. The first one is a simplification of the distance maps aggregation process. The distance maps $dm_i(j)$ can now be aggregated through a weighted sum, with a weight $r_i = \mu_i/\sigma_i^2$, assigned to each point p_i, that does not depend on j. The second consequence results from the fact that the area associated to large reliability values $r_i(j)$, for which $b_i(j) = 1$, is the one that helps the system to discriminate between the wrong displacement candidates and the correct one. To complement each others, points have thus to be selected so that they have complementary binary masks, i.e. so that they best disambiguate (reinforce the "wrong" status of) points that do not correspond to the target displacement. This notion of complementarity will be further discussed in Section 5.

Now that we have introduced our binary approximation, we come back to our target registration problem. For increased generality, instead of considering the selection of a set Φ_N of N points among P points to best estimate the target displacement, we consider that we have to assign, to each point p_i in $\mathcal{P}$, a matching metric $m(i) = m_k$, selected in the set $\mathcal{M} = \{m_k, k = 1...K\}$ of K admissible matching strategies. Interestingly, assuming that the point skipping decision defines a zero-complexity/zero-benefit matching metric option in $\mathcal{M}$, finding the optimal points matching strategies also implicitly provides a natural solution to select Φ_N, i.e. select the (number of) points that are worth to be matched, with respect to the global complexity constraint C. Hence, our problem writes as finding the optimal metric assignment m^*, that solves

$$m^* = \operatorname*{argmax}_{m \in \mathcal{M}^N} \min_j \sum_{i=1}^{P} r_{ik} b_{ik}(j) \quad \text{subject to} \quad \sum_{i=1}^{P} c_{ik} < C, \qquad (4)$$

where the matching reliability r_{ik}, the mask $b_{ik}(j)$, and the cost c_{ik} are associated to the pair (p_i, m_k), as defined in Section 3 and 4. This problem can be shown to be NP-hard, by reduction of the Knapsack problem [8].

4.2 Heuristic Technique for Approximate Solution

A first simplification for solving (4) is to consider for each point only the best matching metric m_{k^*}, regarding the benefit/cost ratio. This metric satisfies $k^* = \operatorname{argmax}_k r_{ik}/c_{ik}$. The ith point reliability is $r_i = r_{ik^*}$ and every point can be either matched with its optimal metric or not matched.

A natural way to solve problem (4) heuristically is to start from an empty set of points $\Phi = \{\}$ and add points one after one, selecting each point so as to disambiguate the matching at the most ambiguous location j on the distance map, assuming that the actual target displacement moves the ith point to the center of the search range. Algorithm 1 presents the pseudo code of our solution. At each step, the most ambiguous location j^* is determined (line 3). Next the point that best disambiguate at location j^* is computed and added to Φ.

Algorithm 1. Heuristic point selection method

1: $\Phi = \{\}$; $N = 0$

2: **while** $\sum_{i \in \Phi_N} c_i < C$ and $N < P$ **do**

3:    $j^* = \operatorname{argmin}_j \sum_{i \in \Phi_N} r_i(j) b_i(J)$

4:    $i^* = \operatorname{argmax}_{i \notin \Phi_N} \frac{r_i}{c_i} b_i(j^*)$

5:    $\Phi = \{\Phi, p_{i^*}\}$; $N = N + 1$

6: **return** Φ

---

5 Towards Practical Implementation

This section aims at giving a better understanding of the theoretical results derived in Sections 3 and 4 through the discussion of practical implementation recommendations. Section 5.1 explains the implications of the choices of the initial points set, and motivates the partition of the search region for solving problem (4). It also proposes a method for estimating the parameters that are required to solve the problem. Section 5.2 gives an example of system implementation.

5.1 Principles to Select the Points Set, and to Estimate Their Associated Distance Map Parameters

The only hypothesis to keep in mind when choosing the initial set $\mathcal{P}$ is that the observations should be mutually independant, conditionally to the target displacement (as requested in Section 3.2). This is achieved by selecting points that are not too close to each other. The set must be chosen, however, with $|\mathcal{P}| = P$ large enough to be certain to include enough points that are worth to be matched and can bring the variety/diversity of information required to solve (4), by maximizing the sum of reliabilities in every part of the search region.

When solving problem (4), using the heuristic approach described in Section 4.2 to select a point that disambiguate the matching in the most ambiguous location of the search region, it is quite cumbersome to consider each pixel j in S separately, while the distance maps and the associated reliability metrics $r_i(j)$ appear to be constant over large regions, and could be simplified by grouping pixels into subregions of S. Fig.2 shows three ways for partitioning the search region and their effect on the approximation of the pixel-precise mask $B(j)$ introduced in Section 4.1, and illustrated on Fig. 1. Hence, using this approximation, in the 3rd line of algorithm 1 in Section 4.2, the most ambiguous *location* j^* becomes the most ambiguous *region* J^*. Note that these approximations only affect the choice of points to match and not the inference of the global target motion.

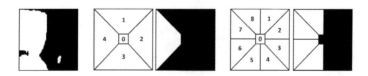

Fig. 2. The binary mask (left) approximation depends on the chosen partition

The solution presented in Section 4 to select the points and their associated matching metrics, but also to compute the weights for the optimal summation of the points distance maps require to know, for each possible association (p_i, m_k), the mean μ_{ik} and standard deviation σ_{ik} of the random variable D_{ik}, denoting the difference between the point matching distances computed in incorrect and correct positions. The optimal points subset selection also requires to estimate $b_{ik}(J)$. We propose to estimate those parameters based on the observation of the point neighborhood. This can be done, for instance, by computing the auto-correlation of point p_i in the reference image I, generating a distance map. This map can be thresholded to define the binary mask $b_{ik}(J)$, and the mean and variance parameters can then be computed over the sets of correct and incorrect matching distances.

5.2 Example of Practical Implementation

In this section, we show an example of implementation of the proposed frame-work. The method is then evaluated in Section 6. In order to fully exploit the possibilities of the approach, we consider a set $\mathcal{M} = \{m_1, m_2\}$ containing only two matching metrics, and a random set $\mathcal{P}$ with a large number of points. This contrasts with many solutions that seek for a small set of very strong points to match very precisely. The metric m_1 adopts a simple descriptor: a vector of pixel luminance values on a vertical line centered at the point location in the reference image. It performs a search in a square search region S.

Equivalently, m_2 considers a horizontal line as descriptor. Both matching met-rics use the sum of absolute difference as distance for similarity evaluation. For the estimation of parameters μ_{ik} and σ_{ik}, k denoting the index of the matching metric, we compute the autocorrelation of point p_i on frame I divide the auto-correlation map according to the first partition represented on Fig. 2. All the μ_{ik}, σ_{ik} and $b_{ik}(J)$ are computed over these sets.

6   Experimental Validation

This section aims at validating the proposed framework throuhg simple experi-ments on two successive frames of a video. The tests focus on frame registration and not on tracking, which involves too many other parameters. The experiment is set up as follows: given two successive video frames I and J, given the position of the target in I (mask), the method should infer the translational displacement of the target with a limited computational power ($=$ complexity constraint) C. The method that is evaluated here is the one described in 5.2. A set of 12 pairs of frames, with different kind of manually tagged targets (people) is used as validation set. The displacement of the target between two frames is computed as the median displacement of several manually matched points pairs.

The performances are measured by comparison with a method that chooses a points set randomly and then assigns the vertical matching metric to half of the points and the horizontal one to the second half.

Fig. 3 (left) compares both methods in terms of averaged motion error (in pixels) for several complexity constraints $C = [2, 4, 6, 9, 12]$, the complexity unit being the matching of one point. The motion errors have been computed over the whole validation set and the tests were repeated to generate this averaged error measure. Because the search region is a square of side equal to 80 pixels, a mean error superior to 30 pixels is not better than a random guess of the displacement.

In order to further reduce the complexity, we have tested the framework with the same two matching metrics m_1 and m_2, but reducing the search window to a vertical (horizontal for m_2) line. A single distance line is thus computed to approximate the whole distance map. Surprisingly, the framework is able to select points and associated metrics such that few tens of points are sufficient to predict the target displacement sufficiently well (with a matching complexity for each point that is considerably reduced). Fig. 3 (right) shows the results using this particular metrics set. Again, the complexity unit corresponds to the matching of one point.

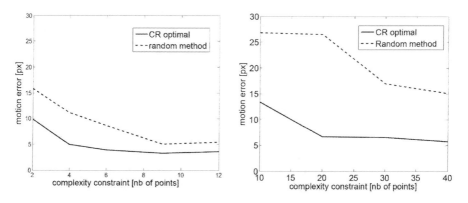

Fig. 3. Adapting the matching metric to the point neighborhood and selecting only reliable points allows infering a correct displacement at a lower computational cost

These results demonstrate the benefit of using the presented framework, particularly when the cost constraint is critical. Indeed, in the first approach, 4 points are sufficient for estimating the displacement with the CR-optimal method against 9 with the random method. In the second test case, 20 points generally suffice for a good motion estimation with the proposed method, while 30 points are needed with the random approach to perform significantly better than a simple guess on the displacement.

Interestingly, the results are even better for estimation the motion of a car between two pairs of frames, which is not surprising considering the number of visual structures of the vehicles. On the contrary, the performances are degraded when the method is applied on sequences where the target undergoes severe deformations compared with the target size.

7   Conclusion

We have presented a formulation of the tracking problem within a points matching framework. We showed that it was possible to optimize the reliability of the target displacement estimation, under some complexity constraint, by adapting the point matching strategy to each point regarding its neighborhood content. The approach differs from classical methods in that points are not selected based on some intuitive criterion, but are chosen so as to minimize the probability of erroneous target global displacement inference. We have shown the validity of our approach on a practical example, in which the combination of a few points and associated "cheap" matching metrics were sufficient to infer the targets displacements correctly between pairs of consecutive video frames.

References

1. Bay, H., Ess, A., Tuytelaars, T., Van Gool, L.: Speeded-up robust features (surf). Computer Vision and Image Understanding 110(3), 346–359 (2008)
2. De Neyer, Q., Sun, L., Chaudy, C., Parisot, C., De Vleeschouwer, C.: Demo: Point matching for ptz camera autotracking. In: ICDSC. IEEE (2012)
3. Denman, S., Fookes, C., Sridharan, S.: Improved simultaneous computation of motion detection and optical flow for object tracking. In: Digital Image Computing: Techniques and Applications, DICTA 2009, pp. 175–182. IEEE (2009)
4. Harris, C., Stephens, M.: A combined corner and edge detector. In: Alvey Vision Conference, Manchester, UK, vol. 15, p. 50 (1988)
5. Hu, W.C.: Adaptive template block-based block matching for object tracking. In: Eighth International Conference on Intelligent Systems Design and Applications, ISDA 2008, pp. 61–64. IEEE (2008)
6. Lalonde, M., Foucher, S., Gagnon, L., Pronovost, E., Derenne, M., Janelle, A.: A system to automatically track humans and vehicles with a ptz camera. In: Defense and Security Symposium. International Society for Optics and Photonics (2007)
7. Lowe, D.: Object recognition from local scale-invariant features. In: ICCV, pp. 1150–1157 (1999)
8. Martello, S., Toth, P.: Knapsack problems: algorithms and computer implementations. John Wiley & Sons, Inc. (1990)
9. Papanikolopoulos, N.P., Khosla, P.K., Kanade, T.: Visual tracking of a moving target by a camera mounted on a robot: A combination of control and vision. IEEE Transactions on Robotics and Automation 9(1), 14–35 (1993)
10. Sun, L., De Neyer, Q., De Vleeschouwer, C.: Multimode spatiotemporal background modeling for complex scenes. In: EUSIPCO (2012)
11. Veenman, C.J., Reinders, M.J.T., Backer, E.: Resolving motion correspondence for densely moving points. IEEE Transactions on Pattern Analysis and Machine Intelligence 23(1), 54–72 (2001)
12. Xie, Y., Lin, L., Jia, Y.: Tracking objects with adaptive feature patches for ptz camera visual surveillance. In: 2010 20th International Conference on Pattern Recognition (ICPR), pp. 1739–1742. IEEE (2010)
13. Zhang, Y., Liang, Z., Hou, Z., Wang, H., Tan, M.: An adaptive mixture gaussian background model with online background reconstruction and adjustable foreground mergence time for motion segmentation. In: IEEE International Conference on Industrial Technology, ICIT 2005, pp. 23–27. IEEE (2005)

VTApi: An Efficient Framework for Computer Vision Data Management and Analytics

Petr Chmelar[2], Martin Pesek[2], Tomas Volf[2],
Jaroslav Zendulka[1,2], and Vojtech Froml[2]

[1] IT4Innovations Centre of Excellence,
[2] Faculty of Information Technology, Brno University of Technology
Bozetechova 1/2, 612 66 Brno, Czech Republic
{chmelarp,ipesek,ivolf,zendulka}@fit.vutbr.cz, xfrom100@stud.fit.vutbr.cz

Abstract. VTApi is an open source application programming interface designed to fulfill the needs of specific distributed computer vision data and metadata management and analytic systems and to unify and accelerate their development. It is oriented towards processing and efficient management of image and video data and related metadata for their retrieval, analysis and mining with the special emphasis on their spatio-temporal nature in real-world conditions. VTApi is a free extensible framework based on progressive and scalable open source software as OpenCV for high- performance computer vision and data mining, PostgreSQL for efficient data management, indexing and retrieval extended by similarity search and integrated with geography/spatio-temporal data manipulation.

Keywords: VTApi, computer vision, data management, similarity search, clustering, API, methodology, spatio-temporal.

1 Introduction

Ever expanding multimedia content necessitates the research of new technologies for content understanding and the development of a wide variety of academic, commerce and government applications [10]. The main objective of the VideoTerror (the Ministry of the Interior) project is to create a prototype of a system warehousing image and video accomplished with computer vision and video analytics for preventing and protecting against illegal activities and natural or industrial disasters affecting citizens, organizations or infrastructure. The basic requirements include image and video feature extraction, storage and indexing to enable (content-based) retrieval, summarization and data mining in the meaning of object detection and activity recognition in an interactive and iterative process.

In addition to the technology, we also target usual aspects of the research – to unify and accelerate it by choosing an appropriate design methodology and architectural framework for the composition of domain and application specific tools focusing on open source software. In particular, we propose a solution

J. Blanc-Talon et al. (Eds.): ACIVS 2013, LNCS 8192, pp. 378–388, 2013.

that will enable the development and adaptation of a complex computer vision application at a reduced cost in terms of time and money. We target this goal by (re)using and integrating tool chains of (CV) methods and (multimedia) data and metadata in an arbitrary combination as simple and versatile as possible.

The VT methodology is based on the fact, that most methods of the same purpose have similar types of inputs and outputs, so there may be chains of them. Moreover, the input of a process (a running instance of a method) can be seen as another process's output (e.g., annotation, feature extraction, classification) including media data creation as illustrated in Figure 1. The VT project is not limited to specific methods or data - they are created by users of (VideoTerror API) VTApi.

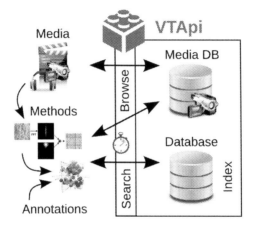

Fig. 1. The illustration of VTApi and the concept of methods' chaining

In this paper, we present the most general part of the system and methodology – VTApi[1], open source C++ and Python code. At the moment, VTApi is technologically based on a (remote) file-system media storage (with multimedia scraping capability) and PostgreSQL database for metadata management extended by our vector-based simililarity search (distance) metrics, originaly developed for efficient local (invariant) features search (pgDistance). We have integrated GEOS and PostGIS to be able of multi-dimensional indexing of the geography/spatio-temporal nature of real-world multimedia data acquired by (phones' and surveillance) cameras and appearing objects (trajectories). OpenCV is used as the primary vision framework. In the future, we plan to integrate other technologies and databases (SQLite at the moment) and a NoSQL storage.

2 State of the Art

In the past decade multimedia technology has become ubiquitous. There is an instantly growing tendency of multimedia data produced by many applications in

---

[1] http://gitorious.org/vtapi, http://vidte.fit.vutbr.cz/ inCzech

today's world. It requires to organize and manage this data and to provide support for its processing. First, image processing and data management have been a great challenge for researchers. So far, OpenCV supports only (XML/YAML) file storages, which are flexible, but not really efficient. Content-based image retrieval (CBIR) emerged as an important area in computer vision and information retrieval. Later, the video database management systems were supported by the SQL/MM standard. Its Part 5 Still Image provides structured user-defined types both for still images and their features that allow to store images into a database, retrieve them, modify them and to locate them by applying various "visual" predicates [9]. These data types are implemented in several commercial database products, e.g., in Oracle Multimedia and IBM DB2 Image Extender. There are also some extensions to open source database products to facilitate CBIR system development. For example, PostgreSQL-IE [1] extends the architecture of PostgreSQL.

MPEG-7 standard (Multimedia Content Description Interface [8]) published in 2002 has brought a standard model of multimedia content. However, most of XML-enabled and native XML databases ignore management of time intervals, vectors and matrix data types, which MPEG-7 defines as the extent to the XML. The MPEG-7 model has been adopted or supported by several multimedia database management systems, for example, BilVideo-7 [3]. It supports multimodal queries, video indexing and retrieval and spatio-temporal queries. MPEG-7 Multimedia Database System (MPEG-7 MMDB) [6] is another example. It is based on extensibility services of Oracle 10g. It maps MPEG-7 schema types to database types and introduces new indexing and querying of similarity. Cortina [2] is another CBIR system based on MySQL. Besides image search, retrieval, classification and duplicate detection, it offers the face detection, image annotation and relevance feedback. Another example of a CBIR system is our TRECVid Search 2009 Demo (http://minerva3.fit.vutbr.cz:8080/).

3   Concepts and Specifications

The VTApi framework is based on the following fundamental concepts that grow from both computer vision and data management:

- *Dataset* is a named set of (multimedia) data along with metadata (descriptive data). Datasets can be organized hierarchically, i.e., one may be based on several others. Each dataset contains sequences.
- *Sequence* is a named ordered set of frames. There are two types of sequences - *Video* and *Images*. The ordering of frames in video is time-based. There can be intervals defined for a sequence.
- *Interval* is any subsequence of *Video* or *Images* whose elements share the same metadata (and thus may define their order). Naturally, it can be a video shot or any sequence of frames containing the monitored object in the video or scene. Metadata of an interval are created by a process.
- *Process* (task or operation) is a named run of a method. *Method* defines the custom algorithm and the structure of metadata consumed and produced by

its processes. Such a way, processes represent all activities of a VTApi-based application related to video and image data processing. Implementation of a specific method may or may not be included in VTAPI, it is created by developers, who can share the code using VTCli.

- *Tag* is a term representing an ontology class (in hierarchy). Tags are assigned to the multimedia data as descriptor or annotation of a scene, object or action.
- *Selection* is a set of logically related metadata specified by developers as means of doing operations on metadata effectively and making it possible to chain processes. This concept is related to the effective implementation and access to metadata in the database. A common example of a *Selection* is *Interval*.
- *Key-Value* is the basic way of metadata organization in VTApi. It is a generic data structure (associative array) that allows to store data as <key, value> pairs, so changes in data definition do not imply changes of the VTApi code.

In VTApi, all these concepts are mapped to classes as it is shown in Figure 2. Our approach is not based directly on MPEG-7 XML descriptors and description schemes, because they do not provide the flexibility for efficient streaming and database storage and they are tree structured. Thus, we focus more on the BiM (Binary Format for MPEG-7 [8]). We generally support all structures of descriptors including operations as the first order temporal interpolation, spatial transformation and coordinate mapping, including their indexing using GiST and GIN [7]. The same states about MPEG-A (Multimedia application format) Part 10: Surveillance application format.

3.1 Data Model

The simplified class diagram of VTApi is illustrated in Figure 2. It follows the concepts given in the previous section and operations that logically belong to. Most classes inherit from the class *KeyValues* that provides the basic operations needed to manage key-value pairs, on which the VTApi model is based. The *KeyValues* class is crucial to ensure the functionality and generality of the framework by the main function *next()*, which includes not only navigation over data structures, but also executes database queries, commits changes made by setter methods and commits new data added by adder methods. It uses the lazy approach – accessing objects only when they are needed by using caches and batches where possible.

Classes derived from *KeyValues* contain only functionality related to the consistency of data and to make some operations easier for VTApi users and factory methods. For instance, *getLocation()* returns the physical data location (e.g., a dataset or a directory with pictures). The method *newSequence()* of the *Dataset* class object is an example of a factory method. It creates a new object of the class *Sequence*, with all necessary parameters. So, then it is possible to access all the current dataset's sequences identified by *getName()* by calling the *next()* method. This is illustrated in the sample code in Section 4.1.

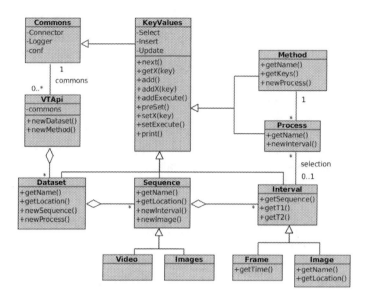

Fig. 2. The simplified class diagram of VTApi

VTApi is strongly typed. The following description uses notation of X referring to any data type implemented as integers, floating points, strings, 4D geometry points, lines and polygons and their structures, vectors, arrays and (OpenCV) matrices. For instance, $getX(k)$ or $setX(k,v)$ operates key k and its value v of type X.

The entry point to the application is the *VTApi* class based on a configuration file and command-line arguments. This class is used to implement the additional command line interface (VTCli[1]), which can give you an insight into the managed data and metadata.

There are several other important classes, some of them nested in the class KeyValues (shown as its attributes) in Figure 2:

- *Commons* class provides a very basic functions such as loading configuration file and command line parameters. It provides a connection to the database (PostgreSQL), a data storage (remote file system) and provides some centralized services, as error processing and logging.
- *Select* class is used to construct queries that as a part of the first call of the function *next()* retrieves the required data from the database. There are special functions to simplify the construction of queries available. Other functions simplify the work with selections, keys and their values to filter queries, use functions and indexes.
- *Insert* class provides insertion of data by the function $addX(k,v)$ into the database. There are two possible ways of inserting – immediate (*addExecute()*) or batch (implicitly) by calling *next()*.

- *Update* class allows modification of the current element using the typed family of functions $setX(k,v)$. The approach is similar to the one described in the *Insert* class.

A *Selection* can be either a relational table or a storage in a non-SQL database (using modified *KeyValues* class) for storing data as image features, trajectories or tags. The database schema is available at the project page[1].

4 Use Cases

We have chosen three simple use-cases demonstrating the use of VTApi for common tasks based on TRECVid evaluations and an object trajectory extraction and transformation experiment. The first use-case is a simple CBIR and the second presents trajectory clustering. It is followed by a performance experiment. The fourth example is the TRECVid Surveillance Event Detection task software.

4.1 Content-Based Image Retrieval

The OpenCV library provides powerful feature extraction and classification techniques. However, it doesn't have capabilities to store the data to be efficiently searched and processed further. This is especially useful for tools like Google Image Search or developed within TRECVid [10], where the retrieval is based on multiple types of (low to high-level, local and global) features related to any object together with annotations (tags).

Thus, we have implemented various similarity-based distance functions. The pgDistance extension (included in the VTApi code) performs the similarity queries measuring distances of feature vectors in PostgreSQL database, e.g., Cosine or Euclidean distance. So that we can employ the feature-based similarity search supported by efficient indexing techniques (SP-)GiST and GIN [7] using Heap and Bitmap indexes, Quad-Tree, KD-Tree, R-Tree, Inverted Document Index and other general indexing structures, supporting containment and nearest neighbor search on vectors (using @> and <-> operators). However, the example in Figure 3 is quite simple. Assume you have a large dataset of images called "search" already populated in the database, and we want to perform MPEG-7 Color layout descriptor based CBIR.

4.2 Object Tracking, Trajectory Querying and Analysis

In the surveillance video, it is important to be able to track moving objects and to extract their visual and spatio-temporal features. Such extracted metadata then should be cleaned, stored and indexed to be able to query and analyze.

Object tracking is a complex task, especially in crowded scenes. We created a tracker based on OpenCV blobtrack demo that we extended with feature extraction as in [5]. The outputs of such methods include spatio-temporal locations in the form of trajectories, blobs and other features of moving objects.

```
// VTApi entry point, using Dataset "search"
VTApi* vtapi = new VTApi(argc, argv);
Dataset* dataset = vtapi->newDataset("search");
dataset->next();
// code of the ColorLayout Method, using Selection "image"
Image* image = new Image(&dataset, "image");
while (image->next()) {
    int[32] color = colorLayout(image->getDataLocation());
    image->setIntA("color", color, 32);
}
// retrieve Image(s) according to their similarity to "Q.jpg"
Image* nearest = new Image(&dataset);
nearest->select->from("image", "distance_square_int4(color, "
    + toString(colorLayout("Q.jpg")) + ")");
nearest->select->orderby("distance_square_int4");
nearest->next(); // is the most similar image
```

Fig. 3. A simple CBIR code example

The features might be used and searched for similarity by VTApi. A trajectory query may relate either to relationships between moving objects or a specific spatio-temporal region. Such an analysis can be performed both on VTApi clients and server, because we have adopted the OpenGIS GEOS library, that has been adopted by PostGIS. In order to perform these operations efficiently, VTApi adds a binary access to geometry types and n-dimensional cubes that are used as spatio-temporal minimum bounding boxes of (moving) objects.

Data mining and machine learning techniques can be performed on moving objects metadata. Such an analysis may involve trajectory clustering, classification, object recognition, outliers detection and so on. The following example shows a clustering of trajectories using VTApi and an OpenCV implementation of Expectation-maximization (EM) algorithm, which estimates parameters of a Gaussian mixture model (GMM) [4]. First, feature vectors representing trajectories are read from the database and training samples for the EM algorithm are prepared (see Figure 4). Suppose that trajectories are stored in selection "tracks" in this example. Second, GMM is trained by the EM algorithm and appropriate cluster labels are stored in the database.

We performed the trajectory clustering on a set of trajectories extracted from the second dataset of videos forming the i-LIDS dataset used for NIST evaluations (http://www.homeoffice.gov.uk/science-research/hosdb/i-lids/) it comes from five cameras at the LGW airport. An example of visualization of some obtained results is shown in Figure 5. There is a result of clustering trajectories from the first camera using the EM algorithm mentioned above. Different colors of trajectories refer to different clusters. We have prepared also an outliers analysis within the VideoTerror project.

```
Mat samples; // cv::Mat of training feature vectors
VTApi* vtapi = new VTApi(argc, argv);
Dataset* dataset = vtapi->newDataset("train");
dataset->next();
Sequence* sequence = dataset->newSequence();
while (sequence->next()) { // for each video
  Interval* track = new Interval(*sequence, "tracks");
  while (track->next()) { // for each trajectory
    Mat sample; // cv::Mat for feature vector of trajectory
    float feature = track->getFloat("feature");
    // ... read features and fill feature vector
    samples.push_back(sample);
  }
}


CvEM model, labels; // GMM-EM model and cluster labels
CvEMParams params; // EM parameters
// ... set EM parameters including number of clusters
model.train(samples, Mat(), params, labels);
// ... choose dataset and sequences according to code above
while (track->next()) {
  Mat sample;
  // ... read features and fill feature vector
  int cluster = (int)model.predict(sample); //get cluster label
  track->setInt("cluster", cluster); // store cluster label
}
```

Fig. 4. Sample code reading trajectories and preparing training samples (first block), training GMM and storing cluster labels (second block)

4.3   Real-Time Tracking and Trajectory Indexing

Because processing trajectories often relates to the real-time, we have performed experiments focused on how much time and resources are needed for the trajectory management. In the experiment (see Table 1), we transformed tracked trajectories, we stored them in the database as vectors capable of the first order temporal interpolation even stored as discrete points, and we index them using 3D bounding-cube and GiST (bitmap index), so that they can be retrieved very efficiently. The similarity query was performed by the containment operator (@>) returning 4 trajectories contained in a spatio-temporal bounding box (selected randomly).

At this simple demonstration we dealt with 7269 trajectories, tracked of about 4 hours of video (49:17 minutes by 5 cameras in parallel) in a very crowdy airport traffic of the i-LIDS dataset. According to the table, we show that this system

Table 1. A simple performance test of insertion and querying trajectory data

	insert/update (7269)	select (7269)	find similar (4)	total network data
(a) local	220 ± 1 s	43 ± 1 s	0.1 s	0
(b) remote	220 ± 5 s	74 ± 1 s	0.2 s	334 MB

Fig. 5. Examples of trajectory clustering results obtained by EM algorithm on trajectories from the first camera (left) and by k-means algorithm on trajectories from the third camera (right)

can eventually run in real-time both on: (a) 13" notebook (dual 1.4 GHz ULV processor, 2 GB RAM, 128 GB SSD) including both the trajectory processing part and the local database and (b) the same machine connected using Ethernet network to a remote VTApi database server, where the network delivery time must be taken into consideration in favor of the server hardware.

4.4 TRECVid Surveillance Event Detection

The main goal of NIST TRECVid (TREC Video Retrieval Evaluation) is to promote progress in content-based analysis and retrieval from digital video via open, metrics-based evaluation that attempts to model real world situations or significant component tasks involved in such situations [10]. The goal of the 2012 Interactive Surveillance Event Detection (SED) evaluation track is to support the development of interactive (i.e., human in the loop) technologies to detect visual events (people engaged in particular activities) in a large collection of streaming video data.

The Surveillance Network Augmented by Retrieval (SUNAR) Event Detection system, inherits the single-camera functionality of SUNAR - an information retrieval based wide area (video) surveillance system [5] being developed at FIT, Brno University of Technology. It contains both standard and experimental techniques evaluated at the AVSS 2009/10 Multi-Camera Tracking Challenge and TRECVid 2012 (SED pilot). We have deployed active learning functionality based on moving objects' trajectory statistics and shape classification using VTApi, which proved the acceleration of the the intelligent vision applications development by the factor of 4 (each person-month work was done within a single week).

You can get the open SUNAR-ED system including its source codes at http://sourceforge.net/projects/sunar-ed, VTApi at http://gitorious.org/vtapi[1].

Fig. 6. SED12 Annotator in the automatic mode at the Round 2 of the active learning process – a human annotator is supposed press "1" if the object highlighted is running

5   Conclusion

In the paper, we present an innovative open source computer vision data and metadata management framework we offer to the public. The main advantages of the proposed API is the reduction of effort and time to produce high-quality distributed intelligent vision and mining applications by unified and reusable methods and multimedia data and metadata sets on all levels. Above that, we offer novel data and methods interfaces and methodology to be used by researchers and developers of both academic and commercial sectors to collaborate and chain their efforts.

We have selected, integrated and extended a set of progressive and robust open source tools to be efficient for multimedia data and related metadata storage, indexing, retrieval and analysis. The system uses the best from (post)relational databases, it offers alternative storages and data structures we need to manage (e.g. vectors or matrices) to make the data access more efficient, especially for rapidly changing geography/spatio-temporal data of a very complex nature in the binary form that can be now processed both on VTApi clients and in the database.

Also, we plan to extend VTApi with the MPEG-7 Library to provide a standardized framework for methods' performance evaluation, followed by the KALDI audio and speech processing framework and some others to enable further multimedia analysis and mining.

Acknowledgment. This work was partially supported by the research plan MSM0021630528, the specific research grant FIT-S-11-2, the VG20102015006 grant of the Ministry of the Interior of the Czech Republic and the IT4Innovations Centre of Excellence CZ.1.05/1.1.00/02.0070.

References

1. Guliato, D., et al.: POSTGRESQL-IE: An image-handling extension for post-greSQL. Journal of Digital Imaging 22, 149–165 (2009)
2. Gelasca, E.D., et al.: CORTINA: Searching a 10 million + images database. Tech. rep. (September 2007),
   http://vision.ece.ucsb.edu/publications/elisa_VLDB_2007.pdf
3. Bastan, M., et al.: BilVideo-7: An MPEG-7- compatible video indexing and retrieval system. IEEE Multimedia 17, 62–73 (2010)
4. Bishop, C.M.: Pattern Recognition and Machine Learning. Springer, Singapore (2006)
5. Chmelar, P., Lanik, A., Mlich, J.: SUNAR surveillance network augmented by retrieval. In: Blanc-Talon, J., Bone, D., Philips, W., Popescu, D., Scheunders, P. (eds.) ACIVS 2010, Part II. LNCS, vol. 6475, pp. 155–166. Springer, Heidelberg (2010)
6. Döller, M., Kosch, H.: The MPEG-7 multimedia database system (MPEG-7 MMDB). J. Syst. Softw. 81(9), 1559–1580 (2008)
7. Hellerstein, J.M., Naughton, J.F., Pfeffer, A.: Generalized search trees for database systems. In: VLDB 1995, Zurich, Switzerland, pp. 562–573. Morgan Kaufmann (1995)
8. Kosch, H.: Distributed Multimedia Database Technologies: Supported MPEG-7 and by MPEG-21. CRC Press, Boca Raton (2004)
9. Melton, J., Eisenberg, A.: SQL multimedia and application packages (SQL/MM). SIGMOD Rec. 30(4), 97–102 (2001)
10. Smeaton, A.F., Over, P., Kraaij, W.: Evaluation campaigns and trecvid. In: MIR 2006: Proc. of the 8th ACM Int. Workshop on Multimedia Information Retrieval, pp. 321–330. ACM Press, New York (2006)

Computational Methods for Selective Acquisition of Depth Measurements: An Experimental Evaluation

Pierre Payeur[1], Phillip Curtis[1], and Ana-Maria Cretu[2]

[1] School of Electrical Engineering and Computer Science,
University of Ottawa 800 King Edward, Ottawa, ON, Canada
{ppayeur,pcurtis}@eecs.uOttawa.ca
[2] Department of Computer Science and Engineering,
Université du Québec en Outaouais 101 Saint-Jean-Bosco, Gatineau, QC, Canada
ana-maria.cretu@uqo.ca

Abstract. Acquisition of depth and texture with vision sensors finds numerous applications for objects modeling, man-machine interfaces, or robot navigation. One challenge resulting from rich textured 3D datasets resides in the acquisition, management and processing of the large amount of data generated, which often preempts full usage of the information available for autonomous systems to make educated decisions. Most subsampling solutions to reduce dataset's dimension remain independent from the content of the model and therefore do not optimize the balance between the richness of the measurements and their compression. This paper experimentally evaluates the performance achieved with two computational methods that selectively drive the acquisition of depth measurements over regions of a scene characterized by higher 3D features density, while capitalizing on the knowledge readily available in previously acquired data. Both techniques automatically establish which subsets of measurements contribute most to the representation of the scene, and prioritize their acquisition. The algorithms are validated on datasets acquired from two different RGB-D sensors.

Keywords: 3D imaging, depth measurement, RGB-D cameras, computational intelligence, selective sampling, neural gas.

1   Introduction

The ever increasing 3D acquisition capabilities of vision sensors now provide advanced possibilities to generate textured 3D models of an environment or specific objects. However, a large fraction of the data acquired by sensors such as RGB-D cameras, laser range finders, LIDARs or stereo-cameras contain substantial correlation, which leads to redundant information, large model size, lengthy acquisition, and heavy data processing. Acquiring, coding, interpreting and transmitting all of this information is a complex task, which contributes to what is known as the 'Big Data Challenge' [1]. Reducing the complexity of datasets proves essential to perform subsequent decisions on the resulting data at a reasonable

J. Blanc-Talon et al. (Eds.): ACIVS 2013, LNCS 8192, pp. 389–401, 2013.

computational cost. Current solutions for dimensionality reduction in range data rely either on predefined pattern-based or random subsampling, where a user input is expected as to the desired sampling density, or the minimum distance between samples. This proves difficult as the user is not always aware of the appropriate level of accuracy required for a given model to be further processed adequately.

However, a reduction of the redundancy in the data, immediately upon acquisition, can also be accomplished by initiating the acquisition with only a coarse collection of depth measurements, and then selecting regions of interest, characterized by rich depth features, within this acquisition to focus on for further refinement. In order to perform such selective sensing, regions of similar stochastic properties and continuity must be separated from each other in order to determine what areas need to be enhanced in the model. This research focuses on the design and evaluation of innovative approaches to achieve automatic selection of regions of acquisition for range and RGB-D sensors, in order for a sensor to collect only the most relevant measurements without human guidance, and as a result, expedite the acquisition process. The relevant regions of interest are extracted from 3D point clouds during the acquisition procedure to prevent an avalanche of data.

Two original and different computational methods recently introduced by the authors in [2, 3] are reported and experimentally compared in the context of RGB-D imaging to determine their relative performance and to develop guidelines for the implementation of automated selective depth acquisition procedures. Both methods begin with an initial sparse and rapidly acquired subset on 3D points over the surface of a scene. In the first method, the regression process of a neural gas network in the training phase is used to adaptively identify areas of interest for further scanning in order to improve the accuracy of the model. In the second method, a formal improvement measure, which expands on the classical interpolation technique of ordinary Kriging [4], is applied to automatically establish which regions within the field of view of a depth camera would provide the most improvement to a model of the scene if further acquisitions were concentrated in priority over those regions. Both methods are evaluated from datasets acquired with the popular Kinect multi-modal imaging sensor and a custom RGB-D structured light sensor, but are designed to be inherently independent of the depth sensing technology used.

2   Literature Review

Three sampling policies have been largely explored in the literature in relation with 3D point clouds [5, 6, 7]. Uniform sampling favors a sample distribution where the probability of a surface point to be sampled is equal for all. In random sampling, each point over an object has an equal chance of being selected, but only a lower number of points are collected. As the percentage of sampled points increases, the cost gets higher and eventually reaches that of uniform sampling. Stratified sampling subdivides the sampling domain into non-overlapping partitions and generates evenly spaced samples by sampling independently from each partition. Alternatively, Kalaiah and Varshney [8] propose a scheme to compactly decimate and represent point clouds using Principal Component Analysis (PCA). Coherent regions exhibit similar PCA parameters (orientation, frame, mean, variance) and can therefore be classified using clustering and quantization. These methods are not meant to be part of the actual sampling procedure, but rather operate as post-processing on collected data.

Pai *et al.* [9, 10] merge the sampling procedure into the measurement process, for modeling deformable objects. The probing procedure considers a known mesh of the object along with parameters such as the maximum force exerted on the object, the probing depth and the number of steps for the deformation measurement. An algorithm generates the next pose for the probe based on the specifications and the object mesh. However, the procedure is not selective and therefore reaches similar complexity as collecting data for all points over the mesh. Shih *et al.* [11] develop different techniques to guide a non-uniform data acquisition process based on a hierarchal tree representation, with error between actual values at the leaf nodes and the estimated values at those points, calculated from the next layer up, being used to determine if new points within each sub-division are worthwhile to acquire. The resulting point locations define the optimal scanning pattern for that particular object.

In a different perspective, numerous publications have addressed the next best view (NBV) problem which consists of dynamically defining a configuration where a sensor should be positioned and oriented in order to maximize the coverage and quality of the model of a scene, while minimizing the amount of separate acquisitions required. Connolly [12] proposed a method based on octrees generated from multiple views to determine optimal viewing vectors based on the current knowledge of the scene. Active view selection was investigated by several researchers [13, 14]. Morooka *et al.* [15] define a discretized shell around a region to limit the number of possible viewing vectors, which allows the use of lookup tables to optimize the entire process. Mackinnon *et al.* [16] rely on several additional fields of data provided by a laser range sensor to derive a quality metric for each acquisition point in order to drive the NBV process and optimize the quality of the overall model.

There has also been research that looked into optimal fixed scanning patterns for various scenarios. Ho and Saripalli [17] investigate scanning patterns for autonomous underwater vehicles (AUV) which attempt to maximize coverage and quality, while minimizing energy use from the AUV propulsion system. English *et al.* [18] use three different patterns, a Lissajous, a rosette, and a spiral scanning pattern, along with an adaptive algorithm to swap between them depending on the characteristics and objects detected in the scene, with the goal of optimizing the estimation of position and orientation for automated space docking operations.

3   Measurement Selection with Neural Gas

An adaptive computational approach for intelligent depth acquisition was developed by the authors in [2]. Meant to be an active part of the sampling procedure, the automated selective scanning scheme builds upon a self-organizing neural network to select regions of interest for further refinement. A self-organizing architecture is chosen for its ability to quantize a given input space into clusters of points with similar properties, leading to an efficient way to compress data. The neural gas network is selected over other self-organizing architectures due to its capability to capture fine details, unlike other architectures that tend to smooth them. The neural gas algorithm can be described as follows [19]: A set S of network nodes is initialized to contain N units c_i with the corresponding reference vectors $w_{c_i} \in \Re^n$ (each unit c has an associated n-dimensional reference vector that indicates its position in the input space) chosen randomly according to a probability density function $p(x)$ or from a set $D = \{x_1, x_2, ..., x_M \mid x_i \in \Re^n\}$. The winning neuron, namely the one that best matches an input vector x is identified using the minimum Euclidean distance:

$$s(x) = argmin_{c \in S}\|x - w_c\|, \tag{1}$$

where $\|.\|$ denotes the Euclidean vector norm. The neurons to be adapted during the learning procedure are selected according to their rank in an ordered list of distances between their weights and the input vector. When a new input vector x is presented to the network, a neighborhood ranking indices list is built $(j_0, ..., j_{N-1})$, where w_{j_0} is the weight of the closest neuron to x, w_{j_1} the weight of the second-closest neuron, and w_{j_k} is the reference vector such that k vectors w_i exist with: $\|x - w_i\| \leq \|x - w_{j_k}\|$. The weights of the neurons to be updated are calculated as follows:

$$w_j(t+1) = w_j(t) + \alpha(t)h_\lambda\left(k_j(x, w_j)\right)\left[x(t) - w_j(t)\right], \tag{2}$$

where $\alpha(t) \in [0, 1]$ describes the overall extent of the modification, and h_λ is 1 for $k_j(x, w_j) = 0$ and decays to zero for higher values according to:

$$h_\lambda\left(k_j(x, w_j)\right) = exp\left(-k_j(x, w_j)/\lambda(t)\right), \tag{3}$$

where $k_j(x, w_j)$ is a function that represents the ranking of each weight vector w_j. If j is the closest to input x then $k = 0$, for the second closest $k = 1$ and so on. The learning rate $\alpha(t)$ and the function $\lambda(t)$ are both time-dependent. These parameters are decreased slowly during the learning process in order to ensure that the algorithm converges. The following time dependencies are used, as in [19]:

$$\alpha(t) = \alpha_o(\alpha_T/\alpha_o)^{t/T}, \lambda(t) = \lambda_o(\lambda_T/\lambda_o)^{t/T}, \tag{4}$$

where the constants α_o and λ_o are the initial values for $\alpha(t)$ and $\lambda(t)$, α_T and λ_T are the final values, t is the time step and T the training length. The algorithm continues to generate random input signals x while $t<T$.

Starting from an initial sparsely scanned sample of 3D points over an object, the neural gas network with a predefined number of nodes is trained to adapt its nodes to the point cloud. The number of nodes is chosen according to the size of the initial scan [2]. In the current work, it varies from 1400 to 3000 for the different objects. Through this process, the nodes in the neural gas map converge toward regions where features and edges are located, which produces clusters of points in regions where more pronounced variations are present in the geometric shape. The training is stopped early by reducing the number of training epochs, to ensure that the nodes capture details rather than becoming uniformly distributed.

Regions that require additional sampling to ensure an accurate model are detected by finding higher density areas in the neural gas output map. A Delaunay triangulation is first applied to the neural gas map. Areas of high density of nodes are represented by small triangles in the tessellation. The mean value of the length of vertices between every pair of nodes for every triangle is set as a threshold. Subsequently, all the edges of triangles that are larger than this threshold are removed from the tessellation. The removal of these edges ensures the identification of close points and, therefore, dense areas of features. The subset of remaining nodes extracted from the neural gas map drives the rescanning over the regions of interest to acquire extra samples of 3D points. A model can then be constructed by selectively augmenting the initial sparse point cloud with the extra data samples.

4   Measurement Selection with Improvement Metric

More recently, an alternative computational method was introduced by the authors [3] that extends on the interpolation formalism of Kriging [4] to formulate an original and computationally efficient improvement metric which serves to dynamically guide further acquisition of depth measurements over regions of interest. By monitoring a relative improvement map which gets computed solely on the basis of data acquired at any given stage in the acquisition process, the data can be effectively compressed at acquisition time, while ensuring both an appropriate level of coverage of the scene and a sufficient level of quality in the 3D model created.

Kriging is an estimation technique that uses the stochastic properties of current measurements to estimate the measurements at other locations, while minimizing the estimation variance. Its advantage to the context of selective sampling of measurements is that it provides both an estimate of a value at a location, and an estimate of the variance on that estimate. Ordinary Kriging relies on the estimation of a semivariogram model, which is a graph that relates how much variation to expect over a given distance. In order to have the semivariogram be related to measured data, the semivariogram model is fit to the empirical semivariance of the measured data.

Capitalizing on this framework, and in order to determine optimal locations to acquire future range measurements, a formal measure of potential improvement that any particular point can contribute to the overall 3D representation of the scene is derived. Since it is desired to have an estimation of how the error in the estimation is reduced when a previously unknown point is acquired, the measure of error that is used as the basis in determining the estimation of improvement measure is the variance to mean ratio (VMR), $vmr(\hat{p}_j)$. This takes advantage of the fact that ordinary Kriging provides both the estimated depth, $\hat{z}(\hat{p}_j)$, and the estimated variance of the estimation, $\hat{\sigma}^2(\hat{p}_j)$, for an unmeasured point, $\hat{p}_j$. The VMR also appropriately reflects the fact that typically, and for most range sensors, as a depth measurement is located further from the sensor, the error on the measurement increases, and is inherently normalized in the formulation of the VMR, defined as follows:

$$vmr(\hat{p}_j) = \frac{\hat{\sigma}^2(\hat{p}_j)}{\hat{z}(\hat{p}_j)}. \tag{5}$$

Now, if in the future, an acquisition is made at a point, p_s, it will result in a depth measurement, $z(p_s)$. In order to predict the effects of this acquisition before it occurs, the assumption is made that the estimated depth value for that point is the actual value, namely that $p_s = \hat{p}_s$ and $z(p_s) = \hat{z}(\hat{p}_s)$. This assumption leads to the formulation of eq. (6), which represents the new VMR at unmeasured point, $\hat{p}_j$, given the previous assumption on point p_s. The difference between the former and the new VMR values leads to the formulation of a measure of improvement, eq. (7), indicating how much the knowledge acquired on $\hat{p}_s$ via a future range acquisition will improve the estimates of all points, $\hat{p}_j$, in the neighborhood of $\hat{p}_s$, or how much improvement in the model of the scene is estimated to be achieved by the acquisition of $\hat{p}_s$.

$$vmr(\hat{p}_j | \hat{p}_s) = \frac{\hat{\sigma}^2(\hat{p}_j | \hat{p}_s)}{\hat{z}(\hat{p}_j | \hat{p}_s)} . \tag{6}$$

$$imp(\hat{p}_s) = \sum_{j=1}^{m} vmr(\hat{p}_j) - vmr(\hat{p}_j | \hat{p}_s) . \tag{7}$$

Combining the semivariogram model fitted on readily available data with the improvement measure based on the variance to mean ratio, a final 'unrolled' estimated improvement, eq. (8), is developed [3] for all locations in the field of view of a range sensor, which leads to a bi-dimensional improvement map where areas of higher potential improvement are put in evidence, similarly to the clusters of nodes obtained with the neural gas approach described in section 3:

$$imp(\hat{p}_s) =$$

$$\frac{1}{\hat{\sigma}^2(\hat{p}_s)} \left(\lambda^T(\hat{p}_s) \left(\sum_{j=1}^{m} \frac{k(\hat{p}_j)k^T(\hat{p}_j)}{\hat{z}(\hat{p}_j)} \right) \lambda(\hat{p}_s) - \left(2a(\hat{x}_s^2 + \hat{y}_s^2) + 2b \right) \left(\sum_{j=1}^{m} \frac{k^T(\hat{p}_j)}{\hat{z}(\hat{p}_j)} \right) \lambda(\hat{p}_s) - \right.$$

$$2a \left(\sum_{j=1}^{m} \frac{k^T(\hat{p}_j)(\hat{x}_j^2 + \hat{y}_j^2)}{\hat{z}(\hat{p}_j)} \right) \lambda(\hat{p}_s) + 4a\hat{x}_s \left(\sum_{j=1}^{m} \frac{k^T(\hat{p}_j)\hat{x}_j}{\hat{z}(\hat{p}_j)} \right) \lambda(\hat{p}_s) + 4a\hat{y}_s \left(\sum_{j=1}^{m} \frac{k^T(\hat{p}_j)\hat{y}_j}{\hat{z}(\hat{p}_j)} \right) \lambda(\hat{p}_s) +$$

$$\left(a^2(\hat{x}_s^2 + \hat{y}_s^2)^2 + 2ab(\hat{x}_s^2 + \hat{y}_s^2) + b^2 \right) \left(\sum_{j=1}^{m} \frac{1}{\hat{z}(\hat{p}_j)} \right) +$$

$$\left(2a^2(\hat{x}_s^2 + \hat{y}_s^2) + 2ab \right) \left(\sum_{j=1}^{m} \frac{(\hat{x}_j^2 + \hat{y}_j^2)}{\hat{z}(\hat{p}_j)} \right) - \left(4a^2(\hat{x}_s^2 + \hat{y}_s^2)\hat{x}_s + 4ab\hat{x}_s \right) \left(\sum_{j=1}^{m} \frac{\hat{x}_j}{\hat{z}(\hat{p}_j)} \right) - \tag{8}$$

$$\left(4a^2(\hat{x}_s^2 + \hat{y}_s^2)\hat{y}_s + 4ab\hat{y}_s \right) \left(\sum_{j=1}^{m} \frac{\hat{y}_j}{\hat{z}(\hat{p}_j)} \right) + a^2 \left(\sum_{j=1}^{m} \frac{(\hat{x}_j^2 + \hat{y}_j^2)^2}{\hat{z}(\hat{p}_j)} \right) - 4a^2\hat{x}_s \left(\sum_{j=1}^{m} \frac{(\hat{x}_j^2 + \hat{y}_j^2)\hat{x}_j}{\hat{z}(\hat{p}_j)} \right) -$$

$$4a^2\hat{y}_s \left(\sum_{j=1}^{m} \frac{(\hat{x}_j^2 + \hat{y}_j^2)\hat{y}_j}{\hat{z}(\hat{p}_j)} \right) + 4a^2\hat{x}_s^2 \left(\sum_{j=1}^{m} \frac{\hat{x}_j^2}{\hat{z}(\hat{p}_j)} \right) + 8a^2\hat{x}_s\hat{y}_s \left(\sum_{j=1}^{m} \frac{\hat{x}_j\hat{y}_j}{\hat{z}(\hat{p}_j)} \right) + 4a^2\hat{y}_s^2 \left(\sum_{j=1}^{m} \frac{\hat{y}_j^2}{\hat{z}(\hat{p}_j)} \right) \right) +$$

$$\frac{2b}{\hat{z}(\hat{p}_s)} - \frac{b^2}{\hat{\sigma}^2(\hat{p}_s)\hat{z}(\hat{p}_s)} .$$

where m is the number of points in the neighborhood of $\hat{p}_s$, $\hat{p}_s$ and $\hat{p}_j$ are located at the coordinates $(\hat{x}_s, \hat{y}_s)$ and $(\hat{x}_j, \hat{y}_j)$ respectively, a and b are the fitting parameters of the semivariogram model, $\lambda(\hat{p}_j)$ is the ordinary Kriging weight vector corresponding to point $\hat{p}_j$, and $k(\hat{p}_j)$ is the ordinary Kriging measured-points-to-estimated-point semivariance vector corresponding to point $\hat{p}_j$.

5   Depth Sensing Technologies and Datasets

The evaluation of the proposed computational methods is performed here using a series of range images acquired, on one side, from the popular Microsoft Kinect for Xbox 360 platform, and on the other side, from a custom RGB-D sensor called Adaptive Structured Light Sensor (ASLS) developed in our laboratory that supports a larger depth of field. The Kinect RGB-D camera uses an IR camera and an IR projector to generate a structured light pattern. Data acquisition was accomplished using the open source OpenNI drivers, with the depth sensor resolution set at 640x480. The Kinect sensor has a 57° horizontal, and a 43° vertical field of view and depth sensing provides reliable data between 0.8m and 3.5m, with a depth resolution at 2m being about 10mm [20, 21]. The ASLS [22, 23] capitalizes on adaptive structured light sensing with a visible marching pseudo-random pattern projected onto a scene to generate features that are imaged by a stereoscopic pair of cameras. A time-domain multiplexing strategy projects a three-color pattern, where any 3x3 code block is unique and supports reliable stereo matching. Multi-focal capability is also integrated to further increase the operational range of the sensor. The configuration of the ASLS creates a maximum field of view of approximately 41.4°x31.7°, and a theoretical quantization error of 39.5mm at 10m depth. Due to its adaptive characteristics, the sensor can provide depth readings over a wide variety of surfaces, but takes longer to acquire a scene in high detail, which further substantiates the need for selective sensing.

Three different scenes are considered here to support the experimental evaluation. The first case consists of a standard computer workstation exhibiting various planar surfaces with different reflectance characteristics, as shown in Fig. 1a. The second scene is that of a large exercise ball, shown in Fig. 1b, which is selected for its curved and smooth surface. Finally, a more elaborate scene, composed of a fire hose station surrounded by pipes over a flat wall, shown in Fig. 1c, supports the validation of the computational methods over complex shapes and a wider range of depth values. All scenes are initially acquired with both sensors in order to provide datasets from which a coarse collection of depth measurements is extracted via uniform subsampling, at various densities, to initialize the selective sensing procedure. The datasets for the three scenes are also displayed in Fig. 1, respectively for the Kinect sensor and for the adaptive structured light sensor (ASLS).

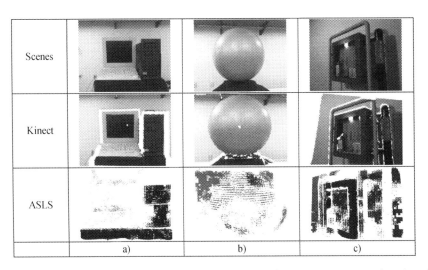

Fig. 1. Three scenes supporting the experimental evaluation: a) computer workstation, b) exercise ball, c) fire hose station, and RGB-D data acquired with Kinect and ASLS sensors

Comparing the two datasets, one easily notices the completeness and sharpness of the RGB-D information generated by the Kinect sensor. In comparison, the ASLS did not provide a similar density of depth measurements. White regions in the second and third rows of Fig. 1 correspond to locations where RGB-D measurements were not acquired over the scenes. The ASLS sensor also generated a large number of outliers in its datasets which have been removed here to better support the comparative evaluation, as they would otherwise have appeared as features and erroneously attracted the attention of the measurement selectors. Nevertheless it is interesting to study the performance of the two measurement selection techniques over datasets with different characteristics in order to monitor their ability to accommodate various means of acquisition.

6   Experimental Evaluation

This section examines the behavior and performance of both measurement selection techniques, while assuming an initial coarse scan of depth measurements is available. For comparison purposes, initial uniform subsampling is performed over the raw data to extract uniformly distributed 3D point clouds composed of 32x32, 64x64, and 128x128 depth measurements over each of the three scenes, and for both the Kinect and ASLS datasets respectively. This subsampling plays the role of an initial rough acquisition of a few measurements to initialize the measurements selection procedure, given that the methods rely on a priori acquired knowledge about a scene and not on user selected parameters to drive the acquisition. This makes the computational approaches fully automated and adaptive to the contents and nature of any scene.

In the case of the improvement metric method, an improvement map is computed for each of the three initial subsampling densities, following the methodology described in section 4 and the resulting improvement maps are displayed in the second and third columns of Fig. 2-4, respectively for the computer, exercise ball, and fire hose station datasets acquired with the Kinect and ASLS sensors. Brighter (white) areas represent those with the highest potential for contributing to increase the knowledge about a scene, and darker regions (black) are those where further time and energy spent at acquiring depth measurements is not likely to contribute significantly to knowledge and accurate modeling of the scene. Gray pixels map intermediate improvement potential on a continuous 0-1 (black-to-white) scale.

The approach based on neural gas is similarly applied on every dataset, initially subsampled at the same densities, and the resulting location of dense neural gas nodes highlights the regions of interest where further acquisitions are worthwhile to be performed to refine the definition of the scene. In this case the regions identified for further exploration are marked by dark triangles in the two last columns of Fig. 2-4.

One can notice in the set of comparative figures that the two methods succeed to consistently identify, in spite of their different approaches, most of the areas that require additional scanning to improve the model. In the current implementations, only depth information is used to monitor regions of interest over which further acquisition should be prioritized. This is motivated by the fact that the methods were developed to accommodate a diversity of range sensors, including laser triangulation and LIDAR sensors that do not provide color or texture information. In the special case where full RGB-D content is available, such as with the Kinect and ASLS sensors, this extra dimensionality of the data space can be taken advantage of to further refine the clustering of regions of interest. This aspect is not considered in the experimental tests reported in this section.

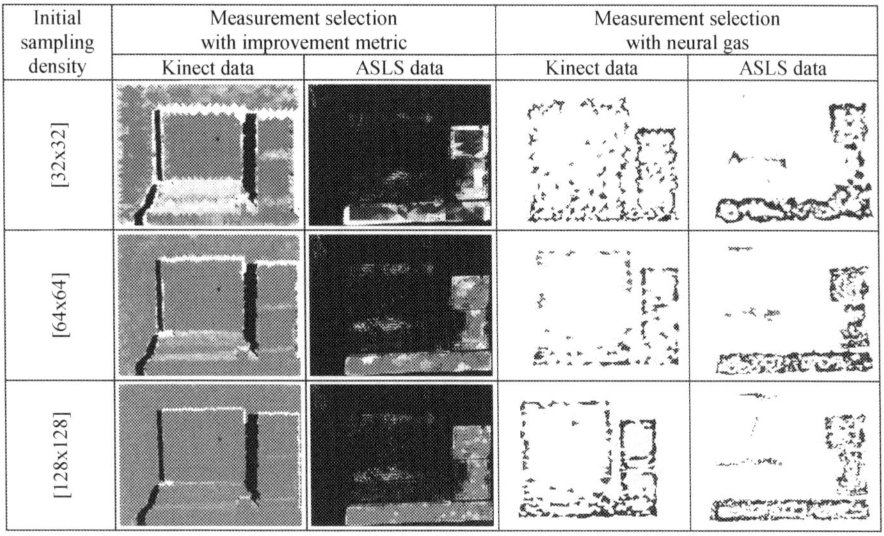

Initial sampling density	Measurement selection with improvement metric		Measurement selection with neural gas	
	Kinect data	ASLS data	Kinect data	ASLS data
[32x32]				
[64x64]				
[128x128]				

Fig. 2. Measurement selection computational methods applied on computer workstation acquired with Kinect and ASLS sensors

Initial sampling density	Measurement selection with improvement metric		Measurement selection with neural gas	
	Kinect data	ASLS data	Kinect data	ASLS data
[32x32]				
[64x64]				
[128x128]				

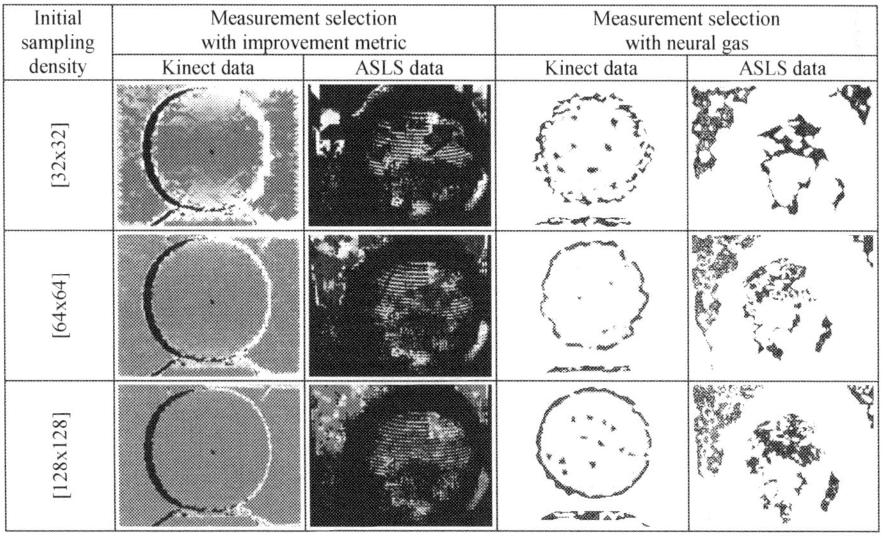

Fig. 3. Measurement selection computational methods applied on exercise ball acquired with Kinect and ASLS sensors

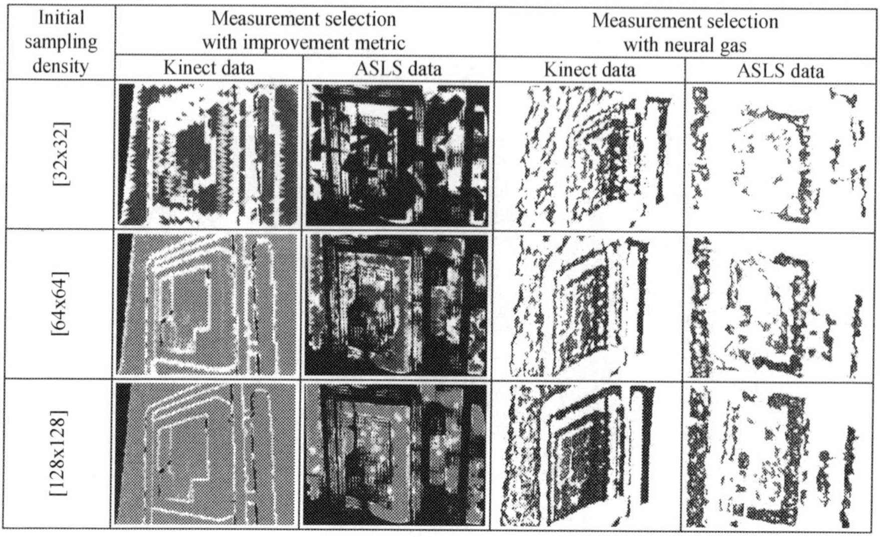

Initial sampling density	Measurement selection with improvement metric		Measurement selection with neural gas	
	Kinect data	ASLS data	Kinect data	ASLS data
[32x32]				
[64x64]				
[128x128]				

Fig. 4. Measurement selection computational methods applied on fire hose station acquired with Kinect and ASLS sensors

Close examination of Fig. 2-4 confirms that the sharpness of the regions of interest identified by both measurement selection methods improves with the density of the coarse scan of the scene used to initialize the process. The results also demonstrate that the techniques adapt well to the datasets, independently from their completeness. In the case of the Kinect sensor, the original data is cleaner and denser than with the ASLS, ensuring for both methods a sharper definition of areas of interest. For the neural gas nodes distributions, the smaller the density of the initial scan, a smaller number of nodes is needed to extract the topology of the scene, but more training epochs are required in general to ensure the correct identification of regions.

In cases where a larger number of areas are not properly acquired by the sensor, as can be observed for the computer and the ball scenes acquired with the ASLS, both measurement selection methods focus their mapping over regions where knowledge is available. This behavior is expected given that depth features are only detectable over those areas. A modification to the improvement map method that is currently under development aims at addressing this issue by introducing a mechanism to force a balance between accuracy (improving knowledge over already acquired areas) and coverage (improving knowledge over missed areas).

The correspondence between regions of interest identified by both methods is evidenced in all sets of results. However, the improvement metric method tends to highlight the edges and contours of components of the scene, where depth transitions occur, as denoted by white pixels in all improvement maps, especially those with finer initialization provided by 128x128 initial subsampling density. The method therefore concentrates in the areas of transition between the shape of the object and the background, or between various components of the scene at different depths, resulting in a clean definition of the object boundaries. On the other hand, the neural gas method concentrates clusters of points over sections of the surface of the objects. The complex fire hose station scene exemplifies this behavior. The neural gas nodes tend to obtain regions that are overall more uniformly spread, resulting in the identification of regions over the surface of the object. As a result, the improvement metric method appears as a very efficient technique for edge detection in depth maps or 3D models. Alternatively, the neural gas measurement selector provides an efficient approach to rapidly acquire a compact representation of a scene from only a very sparse set of measurements. Both methods can therefore find application in rapid scene understanding and object recognition, beyond their suitability to dynamically drive the acquisition process with random access range or RGB-D sensors.

Table 1. Computing time for obtaining the improvement map (ImpMap) and neural gas nodes distribution (NG) from various initial sampling densities on objects acquired with each sensor

	Sensor	Computer		Exercise ball		Fire hose	
		ImpMap	NG	ImpMap	NG	ImpMap	NG
[32x32]	Kinect	0.68 s	9.5 s	0.66 s	9.6 s	0.66 s	9.3 s
[64x64]	Kinect	0.82 s	37.2 s	0.83 s	37.5 s	0.85 s	36.5 s
[128x128]	Kinect	1.39 s	153.0 s	1.41 s	153.9 s	1.41 s	150.0 s
[32x32]	ASLS	13.4 s	9.8 s	16.7 s	8.9 s	19.5 s	8.8 s
[64x64]	ASLS	25.5 s	36.8 s	19.8 s	35.8 s	40.0 s	32.3 s
[128x128]	ASLS	42.4 s	161.6s	15.2 s	142.3s	81.7 s	140.2s

Table 1 summarizes the computation time required to obtain respectively the improvement map and neural gas node distribution that mark regions of interest. A significant difference is observed in between the computing time required to obtain improvement maps and neural gas nodes distribution. As can be observed from Table 1, the NG method scales near linearly with the number of points acquired in the subsampling, while the ImpMap method scales sub-linearly, although the NG method provides more consistent timing results regardless of the dataset and source processed. When acquisition is performed with slower range scanners, the methods are efficient enough to be embedded in the sensor and dynamically drive the acquisition process to collect measurements in priority over regions that contribute the most to increase the knowledge about the scene, that is, focus on regions that are rich in depth features. On the contrary, when used in conjunction with rapid RGB-D sensors, like the Kinect technology, advantage can be taken of the proposed computational methods to rapidly acquire an understanding of the content of a scene.

7   Conclusion

This experimental evaluation of two computational methods for the selective acquisition of measurements with RGB-D sensors demonstrates the effectiveness of the proposed techniques to selectively and automatically determine which regions of a scene best support the acquisition of supplementary data to progressively enhance knowledge about that scene while reducing the amount of data required to understand the nature of a scene. Such a capability proves essential when operating slower RGB-D sensors, such as the ASLS, or random access laser range sensors, as the acquisition can be interrupted at an earlier stage, when points that truly contribute to knowledge about the scene are already acquired. The methods also find applications with faster range sensors to efficiently detect the location and shape of objects, and support the operation of recognition processes when used as contour extractors from depth data.

References

1. Weiss, L.G.: Autonomous Robots in the Fog of War. IEEE Spectrum, 30-34 & 56-57 (2011)
2. Cretu, A.-M., Payeur, P., Petriu, E.M.: Selective Range Data Acquisition Driven by Neural Gas Networks. IEEE Trans. on Instrumentation and Measurement 58(8), 2634–2642 (2009)
3. Curtis, P., Payeur, P.: A Method for Dynamic Selection of Optimal Depth Measurements Acquisition with Random Access Range Sensors. In: Canadian Conf. on Computer and Robot Vision, pp. 311–318 (2013)
4. Bohling, G.: Kriging, University of Kansas,
   http://people.ku.edu/~gbohling/cpe940/Kriging.pdf
5. Pauly, M., Gross, M., Kobbelt, L.P.: Efficient Simplification of Point-Sampled Surfaces. IEEE Conf. on Vizualization, 163–170 (2002)
6. Uesu, D., Bavoil, L., Fleishman, S., Shepherd, J., Silva, C.T.: Simplification of Unstructured Tetrahedral Meshes by Point Sampling. In: Groller, E., Fujishio, I. (eds.) IEEE Intl. Workshop on Volume Graphics, pp. 157–238 (2005)
7. Nehab, D., Shilane, P.: Stratified Point Sampling of 3D Models, Eurographics. In: Alexa, M., Rusinkiewicz, S. (eds.) Symp. on Point-Based Graphics, pp. 49–56 (2004)
8. Kalaiah, A., Varshney, A.: Statistical Point Geometry.Eurographics. In: Kobbely, K., Schroder, P., Hoppe, H. (eds.) Symp. on Geometry Processing, pp. 107–115 (2003)
9. Pai, D.K., van der Doel, K., James, D.L., Lang, J., Lloyd, J.E., Richmond, J.L., Yau, S.H.: Scanning Physical Interaction Behavior of 3D Objects. Computer Graphics and Interactive Techniques, 87-96 (2001)
10. Lang, J., Pai, D.K., Woodham, R.J.: Acquisition of Elastic Models for Interactive Simulation. Intl. Journal of Robotics Research 21(8), 713–733 (2002)
11. Shih, C.S., Gerhardt, L.A., Williams, C.-C., Lin, C., Chang, C.-H., Wan, C.-H., Koong, C.-S.: Non-uniform Surface Sampling Techniques for Three-dimensional Object Inspection. Optical Engineering 47(5), 053606 (2008)
12. Connolly, C.I.: The Determination of Next Best Views. In: IEEE Intl. Conf. on Robotics and Automation, pp. 432–435 (1985)
13. Sequeira, V., Goncalves, J.G.M., Ribeiro, M.I.: Active View Selection for Efficient 3D Scene Reconstruction. In: IEEE Intl. Conf. on Pattern Recognition, vol. 1, pp. 815–819 (1996)
14. Maver, J., Bajcsy, R.: Occlusions as a Guide for Planning the Next View. IEEE Trans. on Pattern Analysis and Machine Intelligence 15(5), 417–433 (1993)
15. Morooka, K., Zha, H., Hasegawa, T.: Computations on a Spherical View Space for Efficient Planning of Viewpoints in 3-D Object Modeling. In: IEEE Intl Conf. on 3-D Digital Imaging and Modeling, pp. 138–147 (1999)
16. MacKinnon, D., Aitken, V., Blais, F.: Adaptive Laser Range Scanning using Quality Metrics. In: IEEE Instrumentation and Measurement Technology Conf., pp. 348–353 (2008)

17. Ho, C., Saripalli, S.: Where Do You Sample? - An Autonomous Underwater Vehicle Story. In: IEEE Intl. Symposium on Robotic and Sensors Environments, pp. 119–124 (2011)
18. English, C., Okouneva, G., Saint-Cyr, P., Choudhuri, A., Luu, T.: Real-Time Dynamic Pose Estimation Systems in Space: Lessons Learned for System Design and Performance Evaluation. Intl. Journal of Intelligent Control and Systems 16(2), 79–96 (2011)
19. Martinetz, T.M., Berkovich, S.G., Schulten, K.J.: Neural-Gas Network for Vector Quantization and its Application to Time-Series Prediction. IEEE Trans. on Neural Networks 4(4), 558–568 (1993)
20. Khoshelham, K.: Accuracy Analysis of Kinect Depth Data. In: ISPRS Workshop Laser Scanning (2011)
21. Macknojia, R., Chávez-Aragón, A., Payeur, P., Laganière, R.: Experimental Characterization of Two Generations of Kinect's Depth Sensors. In: IEEE Intl. Symposium on Robotic and Sensors Environments, pp. 150–155 (2012)
22. Boyer, A., Curtis, P., Payeur, P.: 3D Modeling from Multiple Views with Integrated Registration and Data Fusion. In: Canadian Conf. on Computer and Robot Vision, pp. 252–259 (2009)
23. Boyer, A.: Adaptive Structured Light Imaging for 3D Reconstruction and Autonomous Robotic Exploration, University of Ottawa, Thesis (2009)

A New Color Image Database TID2013: Innovations and Results

Nikolay Ponomarenko[1], Oleg Ieremeiev[1], Vladimir Lukin[1], Lina Jin[2],
Karen Egiazarian[2], Jaakko Astola[2], Benoit Vozel[3], Kacem Chehdi[3],
Marco Carli[4], Federica Battisti[4], and C.-C. Jay Kuo[5]

[1] National Aerospace University, Dept of Transmitters, Receivers and Signal Processing,
17 Chkalova St, 61070 Kharkov, Ukraine
`nikolay@ponomarenko.info`, `ol.eremeev@mail.ru`,
`lukin@ai.kharkov.com`
[2] Tampere University of Technology, Institute of Signal Processing, P.O.Box-553,
FIN-33101 Tampere, Finland
`{lina.jin,karen.egiazarian,jaakko.astola}@tut.fi`
[3] University of Rennes 1 - IETR, CS 80518, 22305 Lannion Cedex, France
`{benoit.vozel,kacem.chehdi}@univ-rennes1.fr`
[4] University of Rome III, via Ostiense , 161, Rome, Italy
`{marco.carli,federica.battisti}@uniroma3.it`
[5] Media Communications Lab, USC Viterbi School of Engineering, SAL 300, USA
`cckuo@sipi.usc.edu`

Abstract. A new database of distorted color images called TID2013 is designed
and described. In opposite to its predecessor, TID2008, this database contains
images with five levels of distortions instead of four used earlier and a larger
number of distortion types (24 instead of 17). The need for these modifications
is motivated and new types of distortions are briefly considered. Information on
experiments already carried out in five countries with the purpose of obtaining
mean opinion score (MOS) is presented. Preliminary results of these
experiments are given and discussed. Several popular metrics are considered
and Spearman rank order correlation coefficients between these metrics and
MOS are presented and discussed. Analysis of the obtained results is performed
and distortion types difficult for assessment by existing metrics are noted.

Keywords: full reference metrics, image visual quality, mean opinion score,
color image database, subjective experiments.

1 Introduction

Image quality assessment (IQA) is a hot research topic nowadays [1,2]. IQA plays a key
role in many applications of digital image and video processing such as lossy
compression of still images and video [3,4], watermarking [5], multimedia [6], image
denoising [7], image printing, etc. All these applications require quality, in the first
order, visual quality metrics able to adequately characterize images. Full-reference
metrics for which a reference image (or frame sequence) is available with respect to
which an impact of distortions is evaluated are studied better till the moment [6,8,9]. A
large number of full-reference metrics has been proposed and tested. However, tests

J. Blanc-Talon et al. (Eds.): ACIVS 2013, LNCS 8192, pp. 402–413, 2013.

have demonstrated that there is no universal metric corresponding to human perception perfectly and applicable equally well in different areas [10].

D. Chandler in his excellent work [9] stresses that creation of databases for metric testing and verification is one of challenges in current research. In fact, more than twenty image databases have been already created [9] including such databases as LIVE [11,12], Toyama [13], TID2008 [14], etc. A good database has to meet a set of requirements and to provide multiple opportunities for its designers and users (note that making such databases freely available has become a good tradition in community of IQA metric and database designers). First of all, MOS determined with a high accuracy and in a reliable manner is to be provided. Second, quite many types and levels of distortions, in particular, those ones typical for practice and emerging applications are to be taken into account and simulated in a proper manner. Third, different means for convenience of analysis and comparisons have to be offered.

For almost five years, TID2008 [14] was the world largest freely available database according to the number of distorted images, number of distortion types and the number of volunteers who participated in experiments thus ensuring high accuracy of MOS estimation. Although this database was originally created and intended for design and verification of full-reference IQA metrics, it has been intensively exploited by image processing community for other purposes as testing and efficiency analysis of blind methods for noise variance estimation [15], color image denoising techniques [16], verification of no-reference metrics [17], etc., due to availability of already distorted color images.

Concerning its main intention, TID2008 has been intensively used and, actually, has become a standard mean for metric verification and performance analysis. In particular, TID2008 has been exploited to increase Spearman rank order correlation coefficient (SROCC) [18] between metrics and MOS. Whilst in 2009 the largest SROCC for TID2008 was observed for the metric MSSIM [19] and it was approximately equal to 0.85, the SROCC has reached 0.95 for the combined metric BMMF [20] in 2012. This has been, in particular, achieved due to aggregating advantages of the metrics FSIM [21] and PSNR-H(M)A [22] proposed in 2011. Thus, near-optimum performance of the metrics that take into account peculiarities of human visual system (HVS) has been gained for TID2008 (maximal attainable SROCC approaches to unity). This means that the most advanced modern metrics are able to manage types and levels of distortions present in TID2008 quite well.

This was one motivation for creating a new database of distorted color images that we have called TID2013 to show the year of its creation and that TID2008 has served as the basis. Compared to TID2008, TID2013 contains seven new types of distortions. They have been added to account for new emerging applications and specific interest to color distortions (see Section 2 for more details). Besides, TID2008 was criticized [23] for having mainly distorted images for which distortions can be easily noticed (observed) compared to reference (distortion-free) images. To get around this shortcoming, we have also added images with one more (fifth) level of distortions to TID2013. For these images, distortions are not apparent (can be noticed not always). Under these modifications, TID2013 now has 3000 distorted images. Below we give its more detailed description and present some preliminary results of experiments carried out using TID2013. In particular, we give SROCC values for several known HVS-metrics and pay a special attention to IQA for new types of distortions.

2   TID2013 Description

TID2013 (available at http://ponomarenko.info/tid2013.htm) includes the same 25 reference color images as TID2008 where 24 distortion-free images are obtained (by cropping) from the Kodak database available at http://r0k.us/graphics/kodak/ and one more reference image (25th) is an artificially created (synthetic) image. All the images (reference and distorted) are of the same fixed size equal to 512x384 pixels. This size is chosen to simultaneously display three images (a reference image below and two distorted ones created on basis of the given reference in the upper part) at the monitor screen for performing pair-wise comparisons.

The database TID2013 contains 3000 distorted images where 120 distorted images (five levels for each of twenty four types of distortions) have been obtained for each reference image. As already said, there are five levels of distortions. They have been mainly simulated in such a way that the first level (added to TID2013 compared to TID2008) approximately corresponded to peak signal-to-noise ratio (PSNR) equal to 33 dB and four remainder levels related to 30, 27, 24, and 21 dB, respectively. Note that PSNR was successfully exploited for level setting in TID2008 and the use of PSNR for this purpose does not give benefit to any visual quality metric.

TID2013 contains images with all seventeen distortion types earlier present in TID2008, namely: additive white Gaussian noise (#1), additive white Gaussian noise which is more intensive in color components than in the luminance component (#2), additive Gaussian spatially correlated noise (#3), masked noise (#4), high frequency noise (#5), impulse noise (#6), quantization noise (#7), Gaussian blur (#8), image denoising (residual noise, #9), JPEG lossy compression (#10), JPEG2000 lossy compression (#11), JPEG transmission errors (#12), JPEG2000 transmission errors (#13), non-eccentricity pattern noise (#14), local block-wise distortions of different intensity (#15), mean shift (#16), contrast change (#17). In addition, the following seven types of distortions have been added after thorough discussions between teams of authors of this paper: Change of color saturation (#18), Multiplicative Gaussian noise (#19), Comfort noise (#20), Lossy compression of noisy images (#21), Image color quantization with dither (#22), Chromatic aberrations (#23), Sparse sampling and reconstruction (#24).

The motivations for including just these types of distortions were the following. First of all, three types of introduced distortions (## 18, 22, 23) somehow relate to color. Note that color information and color distortions are paid sufficient attention by humans in IQA. However, TID2008 as well as other databases do not contain many distorted images that relate to possible distortions of color. Besides, color distortions are valuable for such application as color image printing [24] and others. Meanwhile, many HVS metrics are not adapted to accounting for color distortions and recent results clearly demonstrate [21, 25] that it is worth doing so.

Second, existing databases contain images corrupted by additive or impulse noise but, to the best of our knowledge, none database has images corrupted by signal-dependent noise. Different types of signal-dependent noise might be met in practice. We have chosen multiplicative Gaussian spatially uncorrelated noise (#19) as a marginal (specific) representative of signal-dependent noise. Note that the recent results [26] show that existing HVS-metrics are unable to adequately characterize visual quality of images corrupted by signal-dependent noise.

Comfort noise (#20) takes into consideration a specific HVS feature that humans often do not distinguish images corrupted by different realizations of the noise added to the same reference image. Besides, human often do not recognize changes in textural regions. These properties are, e.g., exploited in lossy compression of color images and video when noise with the same characteristics as in original image or video is added after decompression to provide natural appearance [27].

TID2008 and other databases have been criticized for considering only "pure" types of distortions while distortions of several types can be present in real-life images jointly. To partly fill this gap, we introduced distortion type #21 – images with noise are subject to lossy compression [4, 28]. Obviously, analysis for such type of multiple distortions is important for several modern applications.

The last introduced distortion type (#24) relates to sparse sampling and reconstruction (also called compressive sensing) of images. This is a hot topic nowadays [29, 30]. Although visual quality of reconstructed images is of great importance, HVS-metrics have not been yet used in this application. And we expect that they will be exploited soon. Note that there are many techniques of compressive sensing. For generating distorted images, the method [29] of compressive sensing available at our disposal has been used. Due to a limited space, we do not present details of distorted image generation here.

Certainly, a larger number of distortion types could be included in the new database. However, we have to take into account several obstacles. First, we needed to have even number of distortion types to have equal number of pair-wise comparisons for each distorted image. Second, by increasing the number of distorted images for a given reference one, we make larger the time needed for carrying out each subjective experiment. Note that it is desirable and recommended to have a limited time for performing one experiment to avoid tiredness of observers (volunteers, experiment participants). In our case, average time spent for one experiment was about 17 minutes.

Similarly to the methodology used for TID2008, the experiments have been performed in tristimulus manner. A reference image and two distorted images have been displayed simultaneously. An observer had to choose a higher visual quality image between two distorted ones by clicking on it. The preferred image got one point. Nine comparisons were done for each distorted image, the winning points were summed-up. In fact, "quality competition" was organized in a manner of Swiss system in chess competitions where "approximately the same strength players" compete. In other words, after a few starting rounds, images of approximately the same visual quality were displayed for comparing them.

After getting the results for all observers, they were processed in a robust manner to reject abnormal ones. Such outliers occurred with probability about 2%. Then, the results were averaged for each tested image. Therefore, the obtained MOS varies from 0 to 9 where greater values of MOS relate to better visual quality assessed. Note that protocol (results of pair-wise comparisons) for each experiment has been documented and saved. This allows carrying out additional studies for determining and analyzing MOS.

Before starting the experiment, the participants were instructed concerning preferred conditions and a methodology of experiments. For TID2013, the experiments were conducted in five countries (Ukraine, Finland, Italy, France, USA).

The obtained results were in good agreement. The experiments were carried out both in laboratory conditions under tutor's control and distantly via Internet. Approximately equal number of experiments was performed for each reference image. Three persons outside aforementioned countries took part in experiments. Some other data concerning experiments and accuracy of the obtained MOS can be found in Table 1.

Table 1. Comparison characteristics of Databases LIVE, TID2008 and TID2013

N	Main characteristics	Test image database		
		LIVE Database	TID2008	TID2013
1	Number of distorted images	779	1700	3000
2	Number of different types of distortions	5	17	24
3	Number of experiments carried out	161 (all USA)	Totally 838 (437 - Ukraine, 251 - Finland, 150 - Italy)	Totally 971 (602 - Ukraine, 116 - Finland, 101 - USA, 80 - Italy, 72 - France)
4	Methodology of visual quality evaluation	Evaluation using five level scale (Excellent, Good, Fair, Poor, Bad)	Pair-wise sorting (choosing the best that visually differs less from original between two considered)	
5	Number of elementary evaluations of image visual quality in experiments	25000	256428	524340
6	Scale of obtained estimates of MOS	0..100 (stretched from the scale 1..5)	0..9	0..9
7	Variance of estimates of MOS	250*	0.63	0.69
8	Normalized variance of estimates of MOS	0.083*	0.031	0.035
9	Variance of MOS	-	0.019	0.018

3   Preliminary Results for a Limited Set of HVS-Metrics

Since the values of MOS are available and they have been obtained for a large number of conducted experiments (i.e., MOS values are accurate enough), it is possible to determine SROCC and Kendall rank order correlation coefficient (KROCC) for some known HVS-metrics. We have done this for the following metrics: FSIM [21] that has both component-wise and color versions, the latter is further denoted as FSIMc; MSSIM [19], NQM [31], SSIM [32], VIFP [33], VSNR [34], and WSNR [35]. All the latter metrics have been calculated for intensity component and computed using the software tool [36]. We have calculated SROCC and KROCC for the metrics PSNR-HVS [37], PSNR-HVS-M [38] and conventional PSNR computed for color image intensity as well. Finally, rank order correlation coefficients have been determined for the metrics PSNR-HA and PSNR-HMA [22]. These metrics are able to take into consideration different sensitivity of HVS to distortions in different color components. The metric PSNRc has been analyzed as well which is the color version of PSNR. This version is adapted to color images in the same manner as the aforementioned metrics PSNR-HA and PSNR-HMA [22].

To analyze the obtained results, the values of SROCC and KROCC are presented for all 24 types of distortions as well as for a subset of distortions that includes only the 7 newly introduced types of distortions (see data in Table 2). This is done to evaluate how "difficult" are the new types of distortions for the existing metrics.

Recall that maximally possible SROCC values approach to unity and they are commonly larger than corresponding KROCC values. Meanwhile, as it follows from analysis of data in Table 2, a smaller SROCC usually corresponds to a smaller KROCC. Thus, conclusions drawn from analysis of these rank order correlation coefficients are in proper agreement. Due to this, we will basically analyze SROCC.

As it is seen, even for the best HVS-metrics (the first three best results are indicated by bold) SROCC and KROCC are smaller than for the database TID2008 (e.g., SROCC for TID2008 is equal to 0.884 for FSIMc [21]). Moreover, the best (largest) SROCC values for new distortions subset are even smaller than for all distorted images in TID2013. This shows that, as the result, we have reached our main goal – created the database which is "difficult" for existing HVS-metrics. To our opinion, this will serve the goal of designing new metrics or modifying existing ones to provide better rank correlation, i.e. better adequateness of metrics to MOS.

Table 2. Rank order correlation coefficients of HVS-metrics and MOS

Metric Analyzed	Color or not	All distorted images		New distortion subset	
		SROCC	KROCC	SROCC	KROCC
FSIM		0.8007	0.6300	0.6494	0.5236
FSIMc	+	**0.8510**	**0.6669**	**0.7878**	**0.6120**
MSSIM		0.7872	0.6079	0.6314	0.4952
NQM		0.6349	0.4662	0.6258	0.4831
PSNR		0.6395	0.4700	0.6190	0.4728
PSNRc	+	0.6869	0.4958	**0.7772**	**0.5761**
PSNR-HA	+	**0.8187**	**0.6433**	0.7008	0.5416
PSVR-HMA	+	**0.8128**	**0.6316**	0.7382	0.5723
PSNR-HVS		0.6536	0.5077	0.6471	0.5169
PSNR-HVS-M		0.6246	0.4818	0.6474	0.5179
SSIM		0.6370	0.4636	0.5801	0.4226
VIFP		0.6084	0.4567	0.5921	0.4512
VSNR		0.6809	0.5077	0.5888	0.4374
WSNR		0.5796	0.4463	0.6471	0.5150

It is also interesting that there are many HVS-metrics for which SROCC and KROCC for all distorted images in TID2013 are smaller than for standard PSNR and PSNRc. This confirms the fact that it is difficult to create a universal metric applicable to various types of distortions. One more valuable observation is that all metrics that are adapted to color (sign + in the column "Color or not") perform considerably better than other their intensity counterparts. Success of FSIMc can be explained by its ability to react to color distortions as well as by the fact that it takes into account human's attention to edges and details in images.

Fig. 1 presents the histogram of MOS for the created database. As it is seen, there are no images the quality of which has been perceived as perfect by observers (for which MOS approaches to 9). Meanwhile, there is certain percentage of images the visual quality of which is very poor (that possess MOS smaller than 1).

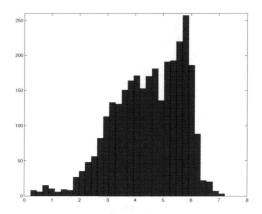

Fig. 1. Histogram of MOS values for TID2013

4   Analysis for Different Types of Distortions in TID2013

Distorted image databases can also serve several particular purposes (in additional to the main purpose of HVS-metrics verification). One of them is to analyze what types of distortions are perceived as more annoying than others. In this sense, it is interesting to consider dependence of MOS on distortion type and level. Such dependence is presented in Fig. 2.

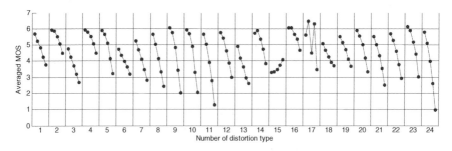

Fig. 2. Dependence of MOS on distortion type and level

For each number (index) of distortion type (horizontal axis), there are five points indicating MOS values for five levels of distortions starting from the smallest level (that corresponds to PSNR=33 dB and is indicated by the leftmost point in each group). For almost all types of distortions, MOS decreases if distortion level becomes larger. The exceptions are distortion type #14 (non-eccentricity pattern noise) for which MOS values for first two levels are approximately the same, distortion type #15 (local block-wise distortions of different intensity) for which MOS is mainly determined by the number of inserted homogeneous blocks but not by their intensities (see [14] for more details), and distortion type #17 (contrast change) for which contrast enhancement (stretching dynamic range of image representation) leads to better perception of images. Note that for all introduced types of distortions (## 18…24) MOS values are smaller for larger level of distortions.

The plot in Fig. 2 also allows determining what are the most annoying types of distortions (MOS for them is the smallest). For the first level, the most annoying are distortion types #3 (additive Gaussian spatially correlated noise). #6 (impulse noise), and #15 (local block-wise distortions of different intensity). On the contrary, for large levels of distortions, the most annoying are distortion types #11 (JPEG2000 lossy compression) and #24 (Sparse sampling and reconstruction).

Fig. 3 presents MOS root mean square errors (RMSEs) for different types and levels of distortions in the same manner as Fig. 2. It is seen that for most types and levels the RMSEs are about 0.3, i.e. opinions of observers concerning visual quality coincide well. Meanwhile, there are several types and levels of distortions for which RMSE values are sufficiently larger. For example, this happens for distortion types #11 (JPEG2000 lossy compression), #12 (JPEG transmission errors), and #23 (Chromatic aberrations), especially if distortion level is high. In these cases, observers mainly judge are they able to retrieve the image content from distorted images [9] and their opinions in this sense vary a lot.

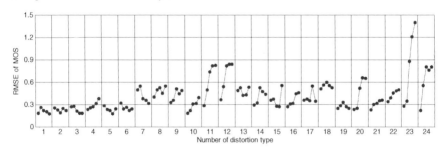

Fig. 3. RMSEs of MOS for different types and levels of distortions

An opportunity to analyze data in subsets allows determining what types of distortions are "the hardest" for a given metric. For this purpose, a subset is formed of two types of distortions where additive white Gaussian noise (distortion type #1) is the first type and the second type is a considered one. Then, SROCC is calculated and analyzed. The values of SROCC for such subsets are presented in Table 3 for the database TID2013 for the metric FSIMc which has been found the best according to data in Table 2. In each cell of Table 3, we first give index of distortion type and then present the obtained SROCC. It follows from analysis that the hardest distortion type for FSIMc is #18 (Change of color saturation) for which SROCC is the smallest. Distortion types # 17 (Contrast change) and #15 (Local block-wise distortions of different intensity) are quite hard as well. These results show that either FSIMc should not be applied if these types of distortions are observed (are predicted to appear) in the processed images or this metric should be modified to better cope with these types of distortions.

Table 3. SROCC for FSIMc and MOS for subsets containing two types of distortions

-	6) 0.791	11) 0.949	16) 0.876	21) 0.926
2) 0.913	7) 0.907	12) 0.870	17) 0.668	22) 0.892
3) 0.935	8) 0.932	13) 0.924	18) 0.535	23) 0.894
4) 0.875	9) 0.900	14) 0.81	19) 0.886	24) 0.934
5) 0.921	10) 0.946	15) 0.721	20) 0.917	

There is also one more way to present the metric values upon MOS. For this purpose, scatter-plots can be used and points of different colors represent estimates for different distorted images. If these points form a common cluster for the two considered types of distortions, a metric describes visual quality for both types similarly. If clusters are separate, there is a problem for a metric for one (or both) types. Since FSIMc is adequate for additive white Gaussian noise (AWGN), we can make scatter-plots for AWGN and any other type of distortions. As an example, a scatter-plot for AWGN (blue circles) Change of color saturation (distortion type # 18, red diagonal crosses) is presented in Fig. 4.

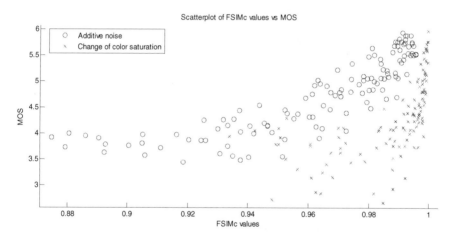

Fig. 4. Scatter-plots of MOS vs FSIMc for two types of distortions

As it is seen, the clusters do not coincide and this is the reason why SROCC for these pair of distortions is so small (see data in Table 3). FSIMc overestimates visual quality of images distorted by color saturations.

Finally, it is also possible to analyze SROCC (and KROCC) between a given metric and MOS for distorted images generated on basis of a given reference image. The corresponding plot is given in Fig. 5 where horizontal axis corresponds to index of the reference image. The smallest SROCC is observed for image #13 which is the most textural. Quite small SROCC values also take place for images ## 1 and 5 which are textural as well. Meanwhile, the largest SROCC are observed for images ## 3 and 12 that are quite simple. This shows that the most complicated task, even for a good HVS-metric, is to adequately characterize visual quality of textural images.

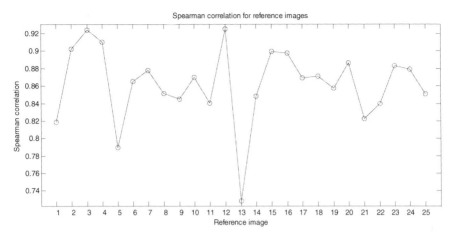

Fig. 5. SROCC vs image index in database for FSIMc

5   Conclusions

The paper presents the recently created database TID2013 that contains images with seven new types and one additional (fifth) level of distortions. The motivations for introducing these distorted images are given. It is shown that the introduced distortion types make IQA a more difficult task for most of known HVS-metrics. To our opinion, this can stimulate further design of HVS-metrics and/or improving their performance. Several ways of analyzing the obtained data are described and illustrated. These ways show distortion types for which IQA is a difficult task for observers, i.e. their assessments vary a lot. Besides, analysis allows determining what types of distortions is difficult for a given HVS-metric and, thus, what are possible directions of its modifying to provide better performance. Analysis has also demonstrated that quality evaluation for the metric FSIMc is a more difficult task for highly textural images. Similar analysis can be done for other HVS-metrics and it might clarify ways of their further improvement.

References

1. Keelan, B.W.: Handbook of Image Quality. Marcel Dekker, Inc., New York (2002)
2. Wu, H.R., Lin, W., Karam, L.: An Overview of Perceptual Processing for Digital Pictures. In: Proceedings of International Conference on Multimedia and Expo Workshops, Melbourne, pp. 113–120 (2012)
3. Larson, E.C., Chandler, D.M.: Most apparent distortion: full-reference image quality assessment and the role of strategy. Journal of Electronic Imaging 19(1), 011006 (2010)
4. Ponomarenko, N., Krivenko, S., Lukin, V., Egiazarian, K.: Lossy Compression of Noisy Images Based on Visual Quality: A Comprehensive Study. EURASIP Journal on Advances in Signal Processing, 13 (2010), doi:10.1155/2010/976436
5. Carli, M.: Perceptual Aspects in Data Hiding. Thesis for the degree of Doctor of Technology, Tampere University of Technology (2008)

6. Moorthy, A.K., Bovik, A.C.: Visual Quality Assessment Algorithms: What Does the Future Hold? Multimedia Tools and Applications 51(2), 675–696 (2011)
7. Fevralev, D., Lukin, V., Ponomarenko, N., Abramov, S., Egiazarian, K., Astola, J.: Efficiency analysis of DCT-based filters for color image database. In: Proceedings of SPIE Conference Image Processing: Algorithms and Systems VII, San Francisco, vol. 7870 (2011)
8. Wang, Z., Bovik, A., Sheikh, H., Simoncelli, E.: Image quality assessment: from error visibility to structural similarity. IEEE Transactions on Image Processing 13(4), 600–612 (2004)
9. Chandler, D.M.: Seven Challenges in Image Quality Assessment: Past, Present and Future Research. In: ISNR Signal Processing, vol. 2913, pp. 1–53 (2013)
10. Jin, L., Egiazarian, K., Jay Kuo, C.-C.: Perceptual Image Quality Assessment Using Block-Based Milti-Metric Fusion (BMMF). In: Proceedings of ICASSP, Kyoto, pp. 1145–1148 (2012)
11. Sheikh, H.R., Wang, Z., Cormack, L., Bovik, A.C.: LIVE Image Quality Assessment Database Release 2, http://live.ece.utexas.edu/research/quality/subjective.htm
12. Sheikh, H.R., Sabir, M.F., Bovik, A.C.: A Statistical Evaluation of Recent Full Reference Image Quality Assessment Algorithms. IEEE Transactions on Image Processing 15(11), 3441–3452 (2006)
13. Horita, Y., Shibata, K., Parvez Saddad, Z.M.: Subjective quality assessment toyama database, http://mict.eng.u-toyama.ac.jp/mict/
14. Ponomarenko, N., Lukin, V., Zelensky, A., Egiazarian, K., Carli, M., Battisti, F.: TID2008 - A Database for Evaluation of Full-Reference Visual Quality Assessment Metrics. Advances of Modern Radioelectronics 10, 30–45 (2009)
15. Uss, M., Vozel, B., Lukin, V., Abramov, S., Baryshev, I., Chehdi, K.: Image Informative Maps for Estimating Noise Standard Deviation and Texture Parameters. EURASIP Journal on Advances in Signal Processing, 961–964 (2011)
16. Lukin, V., Ponomarenko, N., Egiazarian, K.: HVS-Metric-Based Performance Analysis of Image Denoising Algorithms. In: Proceedings of EUVIP, pp. 156–161 (2011)
17. Vu, C.T., Phan, T.D., Chandler, D.M.: S_3: a Spectral and Spatial Measure of Local Perceived Sharpness in Natural Images. IEEE Transactions on Image Processing 21(3), 934–945 (2012)
18. Kendall, M.G.: The advanced theory of statistics, vol. 1. Charles Griffin & Company limited, London (1945)
19. Wang, Z., Simoncelli, E.P., Bovik, A.C.: Multi-scale structural similarity for image quality assessment. In: IEEE Asilomar Conference on Signals, Systems and Computers, pp. 1398–1402 (2003)
20. Jin, L., Egiazarian, K., Jay Kuo, C.-C.: Performance comparison of decision fusion strategies in BMMF-based image quality assessment. In: Proceedings of APSIPA, Hollywood, pp. 1–4 (2012)
21. Zhang, L., Mou, X., Zhang, D.: FSIM: a feature similarity index for image quality assessment. IEEE Transactions on Image Processing 20(5), 2378–2386 (2011)
22. Ponomarenko, N., Eremeev, O., Lukin, V., Egiazarian, K., Carli, M.: Modified image visual quality metrics for contrast change and mean shift accounting. In: Proceedings of CADSM, Polyana-Svalyava, pp. 305–311 (2011)
23. Larson, E.C., Chandler, D.M.: Most apparent distortion: full-reference image quality assessment and the role of strategy. Journal of Electronic Imaging 19(1), 011006 (2010)

24. Pedersen, M., Bonnier, N., Hardeberg, J.Y., Albregtsen, F.: Attributes of Image Quality for Color Prints. Journal of Electronic Imaging 19(1), 011016-1–011016-13 (2010)
25. Hassan, M., Bhagvati, C.: Structural Similarity Measure for Color Images. International Journal of Computer Applications 43(14), 7–12 (2012)
26. Ponomarenko, N.N., Lukin, V.V., Ieremeyev, O.I., Egiazarian, K., Astola, J.: Visual quality analysis for images degraded by different types of noise. In: Proceedings of SPIE Symposium on Electronic Imaging, San Francisco, vol. 8655, p. 12. SPIE (2013)
27. Oh, B.T., Jay Kuo, C.-C., Sun, S., Lei, S.: Film Grain Noise Modeling in Advanced Video Coding, SPIE Proceedings, Vol. In: SPIE Proceedings, San Jose, vol. 6508, p. 12 (2007)
28. Petrescu, D., Pincenti, J.: Quality and noise measurements in mobile phone video capture. In: SPIE Proceedings, San Francisco, vol. 7881, p. 14 (2011)
29. Danielyan, A., Foi, A., Katkovnik, V., Egiazarian, K.: Spatially adaptive filtering as regularization in inverse imaging: compressive sensing, upsampling, and super-resolution. In: Milanfar, P. (ed.) Super-Resolution Imaging, CRC Press / Taylor & Francis (2010)
30. Paredes, J.L., Arce, G.R.: Compressive Sensing Signal Reconstruction by Weighted Median Regression Estimate. IEEE Transactions on Signal Processing 59(6), 2585–2601 (2011)
31. Damera-Venkata, N., Kite, T., Geisler, W., Evans, B., Bovik, A.: Image Quality Assessment Based on a Degradation Model. IEEE Transactions on Image Processing 9, 636–650 (2000)
32. Wang, Z., Bovik, A., Sheikh, H., Simoncelli, E.: Image quality assessment: from error visibility to structural similarity. IEEE Transactions on Image Processing 13(4), 600–612 (2004)
33. Sheikh, H.R., Bovik, A.C.: Image Information and Visual Quality. IEEE Transactions on Image Processing 15, 430–444 (2006)
34. Chandler, D.M., Hemami, S.S.: VSNR: A Wavelet-Based Visual Signal-to-Noise Ratio for Natural Images. IEEE Transactions on Image Processing 16(9), 2284–2298 (2007)
35. Mitsa, T., Varkur, K.: Evaluation of contrast sensitivity functions for the formulation of quality measures incorporated in halftoning algorithms. In: IEEE International Conference on Acoustic, Speech, and Signal Processing, Minneapolis, vol. 5, pp. 301–304 (1993)
36. Gaubatz, M.: Metrix MUX Visual Quality Assessment Package, http://foulard.ece.cornell.edu/gaubatz/metrix_mux
37. Egiazarian, K., Astola, J., Ponomarenko, N., Lukin, V., Battisti, F., Carli, M.: New full-reference quality metrics based on HVS. In: Proceedings of the Second International Workshop on Video Processing and Quality Metrics, Scottsdale, p. 4 (2006)
38. Ponomarenko, N., Silvestri, F., Egiazarian, K., Carli, M., Astola, J., Lukin, V.: On between-coefficient contrast masking of DCT basis functions. In: Proc. of the Third International Workshop on Video Processing and Quality Metrics, USA, p. 4 (2007)

Performance Evaluation of Video Analytics for Surveillance On-Board Trains

Valentina Casola[2], Mariana Esposito[1,2], Francesco Flammini[1],
Nicola Mazzocca[2], and Concetta Pragliola[1]

[1] Ansaldo STS, Via Argine 425, Naples Italy
{francesco.flammini,concetta.pragliola}@ansaldo-sts.com
[2] Department of Electrical Engineering and Information Technology,
University of Naples Federico II,
via Claudio 21, Napoli, Italy
{valentina.casola,mariana.esposito,nicola.mazzocca}@unina.it

Abstract. Real-time video-surveillance systems are nowadays widespread in several applications, including public transportation. In those applications, the use of automatic video content analytics (VCA) is being increasingly adopted to support human operators in control rooms. However, VCA is only effective when its performances are such to reduce the number of false positive alarms below acceptability thresholds while still detecting events of interest. In this paper, we report the results of the evaluation of a VCA system installed on a rail transit vehicle. With respect to fixed installations, on-board ones feature specific constraints on camera installation, obstacles, environment, etc. Several VCA performance evaluation metrics have been considered, both frame-based and object-based, computed by a tool developed in Matlab. We compared the results obtained using a commercial VCA system with the ones produced by an open-source one, showing the higher performance of the former in all test conditions.

Keywords: Rail security, Video Content Analysis, Intelligent video surveillance.

1 Introduction

CCTV (Closed-Circuit TeleVision) is widespread in the security surveillance of mass-transit systems. Terroristic attacks and several other threats are unfortunately common in railway domain. In this context, heterogeneous sensors are used in integrated manner [14],[15],[17],[19]. Very often, the sequence of events is heterogeneous, geographically distributed and the visual surveillance and sensor alarms provided by security systems do not provide accurated observation of threats [16], [18]. Automatic Video Content Analysis (VCA) is becoming increasingly adopted to overcome the limitations of visual inspection of multiple video sources in real time. However, in real environments where a high number of visual sensor are installed, the use of VCA can be critical for events detection,

J. Blanc-Talon et al. (Eds.): ACIVS 2013, LNCS 8192, pp. 414–425, 2013.

in particular in terms of false alarms. The main VCA problems arise in presence of waiving trees, daylight change, camouflage, shadows, etc. To reduce the effect of those phenomena, it is very important to carefully evaluate the performance of VCA system during the testing phase, in particular in environments which are as close as possible to the real infrastructure where the system will be finally installed. The evaluated performance of different VCA alarms is a driver to decide which alarms can be used in a certain scenario, like on-board surveillance installations. Also, simulation can help to optimize/customize system parameters or even modify the detection algorithms to best fit the specific scene.

While several studies address VCA systems in public transportation, including metro railways (see e.g. references [1],[21] [2], [11] and [13]), the scientific literature seem to miss works specifically addressing on-board surveillance, which is particularly challenging in terms of performances, due to critical installation and environmental constraints. The reference [6] analyses some gaps about video analytics for critical infrastructure protection, including transportation system. Gaps are due to high volume of moving clutter or when the activity-of-interest is defined by more complicated interactions between persons, vehicles, or objects. As we said, though VCA for security on-board vehicles is not evaluated anywhere in the literature, to the best of our knowledge, motion tracking and object detection techniques are widespread for different assets or objectives [7]. The essential point is the reliability of the automatic VCA system: the metrics used in this paper are the same largely described and used in reference [1], where a motion tracker has been evaluated considering false-negative and false-positive rates applied to videos captured in metro-railway environments.

In this paper we report an evaluation of a Commercial Off-The-Shelf (COTS) VCA system using different metrics both frame-based and object-based (not limited to false-negative and false-positive), computed by specific tool developed in Matlab. The evaluation has been performed in a real on-board surveillance environment, i.e. on a vehicle used for rail-based mass-transit. The evaluation methodology is based on the manual generation of the Ground Truth (GT) and on its comparison with the Algorithm Results (AR) automatically generated by the VCA software. The results obtained by the COTS software have been compared with the ones provided by an open-source system, on order to validate the choice of the former, which showed higher performance in all test conditions. The remainder of paper is structured as follow: Section 2 describes the reference architecture of the system; Section 3 introduces the metrics used to compare the COTS and open-source systems and implemented in the Matlab tool; Section 4 presents the evaluation method and discusses the results; finally, Section 5 provides the conclusions and hints about future work.

2   Reference VCA Architecture and Alarms

The architecture of the VCA system under test is sketched in the diagram of Figure 1 ([21]). First of all, the frames of the video stream are elaborated to generate the background model. The Background Model Generation module labels pixels into different classes of foreground and background, and produces a foreground mask as the input for the Blob Generation module. The Blob Generation module clusters the foreground pixels in different regions, namely blobs. The Tracking module identifies blobs in each frame and hence the Classification module classifies them in different categories (i.e. Video Metadata). The Video Metadata are used as input for the Event Detection module that is able to recognize the events of interest basing on user configuration parameters. The alarms implemented and activated in the COTS VCA software tested in this paper are the following, which are all relevant in mass-transit security applications:

- **Cover:** it detects camera occlusion/blurring with paint or obstacles.
- **Tamper:** it detects the manumission of the camera by moving it.
- **Stop:** it detects still objects in the scene.
- **Presence:** it detects objects/people moving in the scene.
- **Crowd:** it raises an alarm when the scene is overcrowded.

Fig. 1. VCA Architecture

3   Reference VCA Metrics

For the VCA performance evaluation, several metrics are proposed in the literature, almost all starting from the building of a Ground Truth (GT) [3], in which the expected (correct) results are stored. GT values are then compared with the Algorithm Result (AR), which contains the results obtained from system under test. Different tools exist which are able to support the building of a valid GT (e.g. Viper-GT, Video Annex, Anvil, etc.) and some allowing (semi)automatic generation; however, when feasible, the manual generation is more reliable, hence that is the approach we have adopted. The GT includes information about the objects present in the scene. In the GT file, the labels and coordinates of the bounding boxes for each frame are reported. In order to quantitatively evaluate performance, we use a set of frame-based and object-based metrics [4]. The former measure the performance on individual frames of a video stream and do not consider the preservation of the objecting identifier over its lifetime: the blobs are evaluated in their size and location and compared with GT. The latter considers the whole trajectory of each object in the scene and preserves its lifetime. In this case, in order to quantify the matching between the GT and the AR, it is necessary to introduce the concepts of spatial and temporal overlaps. The spatial overlap represents the overlapping of bounding boxes $A(GT_i, AR_j)$ tracks, in a specific frame k (equation (1)):

$$A(GT_{ik}, AR_{jk}) = \frac{Area(GT_{ik} \cap AR_{jk})}{Area(GT_{ik} \cup AR_{ik})} \qquad (1)$$

GT and AR bounding-boxes are associated if is verified the spatial overlap condition, where N is the number of overlap frames and T_{os} is a threshold (equation (2)):

$$\frac{\sum_{k=1}^{N} A(GT_{ik}, AR_{jk})}{N} \geq T_{os} \qquad (2)$$

The temporal overlap associates AR tracks to GT tracks according to the following condition (equation (3)):

$$\frac{L(GT_i \cap AR_j)}{L(G_i)} \geq T_{ot} \qquad (3)$$

in which the upper term represents the number of frames of intersection between GT track i and AR track j, while the bottom term represents the number of frames of GT track i; T_{ot} is a specific threshold. In the following, we introduce the metrics used and implemented in the Matlab tool to evaluate the performance of the system under test. For the frame based analysis, the following metrics have been considered and implemented.

True Positive (TP). Number of frames where both GT and AR agree on the presence of one or more objects, and the bounding boxes of one or more objects coincide.

False Negative (FN). Number of frames where GT contains at least one object, while AR either does not contain any object or none of the AR objects fall within the bounding box of any GT object.

False Positive (FP). Number of frames where AR contain at least one object, while GT either does not contain any object or none of the GT objects fall within the bounding box of any system object.

For the object based analysis, the following metrics have been considered and implemented.

Correct Detected Track (CDT). A GT track is considered to have been detected correctly if it satisfies both the following conditions:

- The temporal overlap between GT Track i and AR track j is larger than a predefined track overlap threshold .
- The system track j has sufficient spatial overlap with GT track i.

Track Detection Failure (TDF). A GT track is considered to have not been detected, if it satisfies any of the following conditions:

- A GT track i does not have temporal overlap larger than with any system track j.
- A GT track i does not have any sufficient spatial overlap with any system track, although it has enough temporal overlap with system track j.

False Alarm Track (FAT). We consider a system track as a false alarm if the system track meets any of the following conditions:

- A system track j does not have temporal overlap larger than with any GT track i.
- A system track j does not have sufficient spatial overlap with any GT track although it has enough temporal overlap with GT track i.

Track Fragmentation (TF). Fragmentation indicates the lack of continuity of system track for a single GT track. We allow multiple associations between GT tracks and AR tracks, therefore fragmentation is measured from the track correspondence results.

ID Change (IDC). It counts the number of ID changes for each AR_j track. For each frame k, the bounding box $D_{j,k}$ of AR_j may be overlapped with, GT areas:

$$N_{D_{j,k}} = \sum O(GT_{ik}, D_{jk}) \qquad (4)$$

We take into account only the frames for which $N_{D_{j,k}} = 1$, which means that the track AR_j is associated (spatially overlapped) with only one GT track for each of these frames. We use these frames to estimate the ID changes of AR_j as the number of changes of associated GT tracks. We can estimate the total number of IDC changes in video sequences as:

$$IDC = \sum_j IDC_j \qquad (5)$$

Starting from these metrics, some performance indices will be calculated such as: Accuracy, False Alarm Rate (FAR), Positive Prediction (PP), False Negative Rate (FNR), Fragmentation Index (FI), Frame Merging (FM); see Table 1.

4   Performance Evaluation

The method used for performance evaluation is showed in figure 2. The GT and AR files are organized in cell arrays whose row number indicates the object while the columns contain: the list of frames in which the object is present (vectors long as the number of frames of the track) and bounding-box coordinates (top-left and bottom-right). The other inputs are the thresholds used for spatial and temporal overlap, which are set to 15%. Starting from these information, the Matlab tool we have developed is able to compute the metrics by verifying conditions on spatial and temporal overlaps. The performance of the COTS VCA system has been compared with an open-source tool called i-SPY [5]. The videos selected to evaluate system performance are taken from a camera installed on a real vehicle [20]. The alarms we tested are those listed in Section 2. In the scene, events of interest have been simulated, together with light changes, shadows and object intersections.

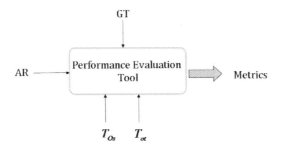

Fig. 2. Tool for performance evaluation

In both VCA systems, the same Min and Max threshold have been configured for the objects to detect. Furthermore, the same background elaboration area (see Figure 3) has been set, excluding the zones which could be potentially prone

Table 1. Performance Indices

Performance Index	Description
$FAR = \frac{FP}{TP+FP}$	Percent of false alarms
$PP = \frac{TP}{TP+FP}$	Percent of true positive
$FNR = \frac{FN}{FN+TP}$	Rate of false negative
$FI = \frac{TP}{FRAGM}$	Ratio of TP and objects detected by the system.
$FM = \frac{OBJ_{AR}-FP}{MERGE}$	Evaluates the merging of blobs in the system

Fig. 3. Background Area Selection

to problems (e.g. windows, doors, etc.). The video stream has been analysed for
a time of 1 minute at a frame rate of 10 fps.

4.1   Frame-Based Results

In the reference scenario, the tool elaborates the GT and AR files and generates
the results showed in Table 2 (a). The video has 1510 objects and it is divided
into 600 frames. The COTS VCA detects less objects than i-SPY, but it is far
more reliable regarding false positive (84 vs 2168), with a FAR of 6% instead of
41% (clearly unacceptable). Regarding Merging and Fragmentation, it is worth
noticing that COTS object fragmentation is less than a half with respect to
i-SPY, while merging is similar and acceptable for both systems.

4.2   Object-Based Results

The Object-Based results are reported in Table 2 (b). The FP and PP rates
reveal a higher reliability of the COTS tracker. Furthermore, the COTS tracker
performance in terms of TF (though the result is not very high in general due
to the many obstacles in the scene) is much higher than the i-SPY one. The TF
is a very important performance parameter since alarms are generated after a
certain persistence of events, therefore a high fragmentation of a track is very
likely to prevent the generation of alarms.

4.3   Alarm Testing

While preliminary frame-based and object-based metrics allow a low level evaluation and possible improvement of VCA algorithms, black-box results are essential to evaluate system performance against end-user requirements. Alarms
were tested on a real vehicle for light railways and tramways, using the COTS
VCA system. The hardware includes a dome network camera connected to a
Network Video Recorder (NVR) which runs the VCA software. The reference

Table 2. Frame-Based Results (a) and Object-Based results (b)

600 frames 1510 obj	COTS	i-SPY
TP	1307	1324
FN	203	186
FP	84	2168
OBJ-AR	1288	3680
BlobFragm	2589	6214
BlobMerge	1638	1699
Accuracy	86%	87%
FAR	6%	41%
PP	94%	60%
FNR	13%	11%
FI	50%	21%
FM	73%	89%

(a)

600 frames 8 GT Tr	COTS Tracks	i-SPY Tracks
AR Tracks	74	375
TP	7	8
FN	1	0
FP	9	213
TF	11	17
IDC	0	0
Accuracy	88%	1%
FAR	56%	96%
PP	44%	3%
FNR	13%	0%

(b)

alarms have been described in Section 2. The reference metrics for evaluating alarm generation performance are (acronyms are as usual):

- **TP:** alarm generated in a predefined time range (MaxDelay, set to 2s), starting from event simulation.
- **PD:** alarm generated with a delay more than MaxDelay.
- **FN:** event simulated but no alarm generated.

The reference performance index are FAI and POD:

$$FAI = \frac{\#FalseAlarms}{\#RealAlarms} \tag{6}$$

$$POD = \frac{TP}{FN + TP + PD} \tag{7}$$

Events were simulated in different environmental conditions (including light variations, occlusions, etc.), ranging from best to worst cases. Configuration parameters for each alarm are described in Table 3, while test conditions for each alarm are summarized in Table 4.

In Figure 4, examples of COVER and PRESENCE alarms are presented. The green line represents the area of background elaboration. An instance of Cover alarm is presented, with a 'Coverage percentage'= 95% and 'Time of coverage'= 10 s. In Figure 5 the results of alarm performance evaluation in terms of POD and FAR are reported. The POD is higher than the min threshold (67%) required in practical applications, and in some cases it is close to 100%. The results are even better if we consider the very low FAR (nearly 0%).

Table 3. Alarm Configuration Parameters

Alarm	Parameters
COVER	**Cover Percentage:** threshold of coverage to generate an alarm (95% min). **Cover Time:** time of coverage to generate an alarm (10 s).
TAMPER	**Elaboration area:** area of alarm elaboration. **Tampering Threshold:** threshold in area percentage to generate a tamper alarm. **Check Time (sec):** time between two consecutive checks.
STOP	**Elaboration area:** orange area in Figure 4 . **Movement Threshold:** threshold of object movement. **Min/ Max Object Size (%)** to generate an alarm. **Stop Time:** min time of object permanence.
PRESENCE	**Elaboration area:** green area in 3. **Min / Max Object Size (%)** to generate an alarm.
CROWD	**People Density:** min percentage to raing an alarm. **Threshold:** Low Crowded (20%), Crowded (60%), Very Crowded (90%) **Crowd Time:** min time of crowd permanence to generate an alarm.

Table 4. Alarm Test Conditions

Alarm	Test Conditions
COVER	Good lighting condition. The camera is covered by a dark object. The coverage percentage is varied.

TAMPER	Good lighting condition.
	
	– TEST 1
	  • Check Time=10 s
	  • Tampering Threshold: 20%, 30% , 40%
	– TEST 2
	  • Check Time= 5, 10, 15 s
	  • Tampering Threshold = 30%

STOP	Good lighting condition. Objects of different colours and size: grey bag, red backpack, green envelope. A person enters the scene and leaves the object.
PRESENCE	Good and bad lighting conditions. The person in the scene has an average height and wears dark clothes.
CROWD	Good lighting condition. Growing density of people starting from 3 persons.

Fig. 4. Example of COVER and PRESENCE alarm

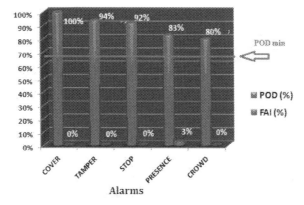

Fig. 5. Performance Evaluation of Alarm

5   Conclusions

In this paper we have presented the preliminary performance evaluation of a
COTS VCA system developed for video surveillance on-board mass-transit vehicles. The aim was to assess the robustness of VCA algorithms to environmental
conditions as well as their overall reliability and time of response. In fact, though
on-board VCA is increasingly requested in recent metro railway tenders, with
strict performance requirements, we are aware of no known system currently installed, or at least whose performance has been tested on real vehicles. To enable
the analysis, we used an automatic tool developed in Matlab which allowed us
to calculate the performance indices quickly and reliably. In order to understand
whether the COTS system was worth the acquisition with respect to open-source
solutions, we started comparing the results of the two VCA systems. The evaluation proved a good performance in object recognition for both systems; however,
the COTS one showed much higher reliability in terms of low number of false
positive. Another important advantage of the COTS system was the low fragmentation rate of single blobs. Those results allowed to go on with the testing
of high-level alarms associated to event recognition on the vehicle. The black-
box performance evaluation results were good in terms of both probability of

detection and false alarm rate, the latter close to 0% in our test conditions. Regarding the generality of the approach, it is important to highlight that the evaluation method used in this paper applies equally well to other vehicles and testing environments. Also, the tool we have developed can be easily extended to any other relevant metrics (e.g. Track Matching Error, Latency of System Track, Track Completeness, etc.). Finally, we intend to extend the testing campaign to evaluate the system in extreme conditions (e.g. vehicle moving during night time with heavy rain and fog) and considering the effect of other variables (e.g. resolution, frame rate) or disturbs (e.g. vibrations, electro-magnetic interference, etc.).

References

1. Cozzolino, A., Flammini, F., Galli, V., Lamberti, M., Poggi, G., Pragliola, C.: Evaluating the effects of MJPEG compression on motion tracking in metro railway surveillance. In: Blanc-Talon, J., Philips, W., Popescu, D., Scheunders, P., Zemčík, P. (eds.) ACIVS 2012. LNCS, vol. 7517, pp. 142–154. Springer, Heidelberg (2012)
2. Piero, J.C.: Intelligent Video Results of testing 4 technologies on Madrid Metro. In: Procs. Joint UITP-CUTA International Security Conference, Montreal, Canada, November 11-12 (2009)
3. Lookingbill, A., Antunez, E.R., Erol, B., Hull, J.J., Qifa, K., Moraleda, J.: Ground-Truthed Video Generation from Symbolic Information. In: Multimedia and Expo IEEE International Conference (2007)
4. Yin, F., Makris, D., Velastin, S.A., Orwell, J.: Quantitative evaluation of different aspects of motion trackers under various challenges. In: Quantitative Evaluation of Trackers, Annual of the BMVA (2010)
5. http://www.ispyconnect.com/
6. Thornton, J., Baran-Gale, J., Yahr, A.: An assessment of the video analytics technology gap for transportation facilities. In: IEEE Conference on Technologies for Homeland Security, vol. 135(142), pp. 11–12 (2009)
7. Sacchi, C., Regazzoni, C.S.: A distributed surveillance system for detection of abandoned objects in unmanned railway environments. IEEE Transactions on Vehicular Technology 49(5), 2013–2026 (2000)
8. Faisal, B., Porikli, F.: Performance evaluation of object detection and tracking systems. In: PETS, vol. 6 (2006)
9. Baumann, A., Boltz, M., Ebling, J., Koeing, M., Loors, H.S., Merkel, M., Niem, W., Warzelhan, J.K., Yu, J.: A Review and Comparison of Measures for Automatic Video Surveillance Systems. EURASIP Journal on Image Video Processing (2008)
10. de Titta, S., Gera, G., Marcenaro, L.: VTrack: Video analytics for automatic video-surveillance. In: 2011 8th IEEE International Conference on Advanced Video and Signal-Based Surveillance (AVSS), pp. 536–538 (2011)
11. Kamijo, S., Takahashi, T., Naito, T., Yoshimitsu, Y.: Framework Study on Behavior Understandings Based on Posture and Location State Transition for Railway Station Security. International Journal of Intelligent Transportation Systems Research, 1–8 (2012)
12. Manohar, V., Soundararajan, P., Raju, H., Goldgof, D., Kasturi, R., Garofolo, J.: Performance evaluation of object detection and tracking in video. In: Proceedings of the 7th Asian Conference on Computer Vision, Hyderabad, India, January 13-16 (2006)

13. Monitzer, A.: Using video surveillance to detect dangerous situations in underground stations by computer vision. In: Proceedings of Scientific Presentation and Communication (2006)
14. Casola, V., Esposito, M., Mazzocca, N., Flammini, F.: Freight train monitoring: A case-study for the pSHIELD project. In: Proceedings of 6th International Conference on Innovative Mobile and Internet Services in Ubiquitous Computing, IMIS (2012)
15. Casola, V., Gaglione, A., Mazzeo, A.: A reference architecture for sensor networks integration and management. In: Trigoni, N., Markham, A., Nawaz, S. (eds.) GSN 2009. LNCS, vol. 5659, pp. 158–168. Springer, Heidelberg (2009)
16. Amato, F., Casola, V., Gaglione, A., Mazzeo, A.: A semantic enriched data model for sensor network interoperability. Journal of Simulation Modelling Practice and Theory 19(8), 1745–1757 (2011)
17. Bocchetti, G., Flammini, F., Pragliola, C., Pappalardo, A.: Dependable integrated surveillance systems for the physical security of metro railways. In: Third ACM/IEEE International Conference on Distributed Smart Cameras, pp. 1–7. IEEE (2009)
18. Flammini, F., Mazzocca, N., Pappalardo, A., Pragliola, C., Vittorini, V.: Augmenting surveillance system capabilities by exploiting event correlation and distributed attack detection. In: Tjoa, A.M., Quirchmayr, G., You, I., Xu, L. (eds.) ARES 2011. LNCS, vol. 6908, pp. 191–204. Springer, Heidelberg (2011)
19. Flammini, F., Gaglione, A., Ottello, F., Pappalardo, A., Pragliola, C., Tedesco, A.: Towards wireless sensor networks for railway infrastructure monitoring. In: Electrical Systems for Aircraft, Railway and Ship Propulsion (ESARS), pp. 1–6. IEEE (2010)
20. Buemi, F., Esposito, M., Flammini, F., Mazzocca, N., Pragliola, C., Spirito, M.: Empty Vehicle Detection with Video Analytics. In: Petrosino, A. (ed.) ICIAP 2013, Part II. LNCS, vol. 8157, pp. 731–739. Springer, Heidelberg (2013)
21. Garibotto, G., Murrieri, P., Capra, A., De Muro, S., Petillo, U., Flammini, F., Esposito, M., Pragliola, C., Di Leo, G., Lengu, R., Mazzino, N., Paolillo, A., Durso, M., Vertucci, R., Narducci, F., Ricciardi, S., Savastano, M.: White-paper: Industrial Applications of Computer Vision and Pattern Recognition CVPR. To appear in Proceedings of 17th International Conference on Image Analysis and Processing (2013)

GPU-Accelerated Human Motion Tracking Using Particle Filter Combined with PSO

Boguslaw Rymut[2], Bogdan Kwolek[1], and Tomasz Krzeszowski[2]

[1] AGH University of Science and Technology, 30 Mickiewicza Av.,
30-059 Kraków, Poland
bkw@agh.edu.pl
[2] Rzeszów University of Technology, W. Pola 2,
35-959 Rzeszów, Poland
brymut@prz.edu.pl

Abstract. This paper discusses how to combine particle filter (PF) with particle swarm optimization (PSO) to achieve better object tracking. Owing to multi-swarm based mode seeking the algorithm is capable of maintaining multimodal probability distributions and the tracking accuracy is far better than accuracy of PF or PSO. We propose parallel resampling scheme for particle filtering running on GPU. We show the efficiency of the parallel PF-PSO algorithm on 3D model based human motion tracking. The 3D model is rasterized in parallel and single thread processes one column of the image. Such level of parallelism allows us to efficiently utilize the GPU resources and to perform tracking of the full human body at rates of 15 frames per second. The GPU achieves an average speedup of 7.5 over the CPU. For marker-less motion capture system consisting of four calibrated cameras, the computations were conducted on four CPU cores and four GTX GPUs on two cards.

1 Introduction

Particle filtering is a widely used framework for visual object tracking since it offers the flexibility to handle non-linearity and non-normality of the object models. However, the huge number of particles, which is needed in applications like 3D model based articulated motion tracking limits their wide application, particularly if the tracking should be done in real-time. In typical applications of particle filters, the resampling is needed because of undesirable degeneracy problem, where all but one particle will have negligible weight after a few iterations. The widely used resampling algorithms in the particle filters are sequential in essence [5]. In [6] a shared-memory resampling algorithm was proposed. In the discussed work a left and right boundary was employed in the systematic resampling [1]. The two introduced variables remove the data dependency that keeps the systematic resampling serial. In our approach to parallel resampling we utilize the binary search algorithm [8] for selecting the particle indices.

To reduce the number of the particles, Deutscher and Reid [4] developed an annealed particle filter (APF), which adopts an annealing scheme to achieve

J. Blanc-Talon et al. (Eds.): ACIVS 2013, LNCS 8192, pp. 426–437, 2013.

better concentration of the particles and shift them towards the modes of the probability distribution. Additionally, a crossover operation was proposed to achieve better diversity of the particles. Compared with the ordinary particle filter (PF), the annealed particle filter greatly enhances the tracking accuracy. However, since the particles do not exchange information they have reduced capability of focusing the search on the promising areas. In contrast, the particle swarm optimization (PSO) [9] has better capability of exploration of the search space owing to combining the local search (by self experience) and global one (by neighboring experience).

In this paper we discuss how to combine a particle filter with a particle swarm optimization to reduce the number of particles that is needed to achieve the desirable tracking accuracy. Owing to multi-swarm based mode seeking the tracker is capable of maintaining multimodal probability distributions and the tracking accuracy is far better than accuracy of PF or PSO. We show the efficiency of our parallel PF-PSO algorithm on 3D model based human motion tracking.

2   GPU Computing

The programming of GPU has been considerably simplified through introducing CUDA framework by NVIDIA. In CUDA the parallel portions of an application are executed on GPU as kernels. A CUDA kernel is executed by an array of threads. Blocks of threads are organized into a one-dimensional or two-dimensional or three-dimensional grid of thread blocks. Blocks are mapped to multiprocessors and each thread is mapped to a single core. A warp is a group of threads within a block that are launched together and usually execute together. When a warp is selected for execution, all active threads execute the same instruction but operate on different data. A unique set of indices is assigned to each thread to determine to which block it belongs and its location inside it.

In order to obtain the best computing performance on GPU, we have to keep all processors occupied and hide memory latency. In order to achieve this aim, CUDA supports running hundred or thousands of lightweight threads in parallel. The benefit of having multiple blocks per multiprocessor is that the scheduling hardware is capable to swap out a block that is waiting on a high-latency instruction and replace it with a block that has threads ready to execute. The context switch is very fast because everything is stored in registers and thus there is almost no data movement. To achieve good performance both high density of arithmetic instructions per memory access as well as several hundreds of threads per block are needed. This permits the GPU to execute arithmetic instructions while certain threads are waiting for access to the global memory.

The global memory resides off chip and has a large data bus resulting in very large bandwidth. It is accessible from different blocks. Its latency can be hidden by careful design of control flow and adequate design of kernels. The shared memory resides on chip. It is shared between all processors of a multi-processor block, but two threads from different blocks cannot cooperate via shared memory. Its latency is several times shorter than the latency of the global memory.

3   3D Model-Based Human Motion Tracking

The articulated model of the human body has a form of a kinematic chain consisting of 11 segments. The 3D model is constructed using truncated cones (frustums) that represent the pelvis, torso, head, upper and lower arm and legs. The model has 26 DOF and its configuration is determined by position and orientation of the pelvis in the global coordinate system and the relative angles between the limbs. Each truncated cone is parameterized by the center of base circle A, center of top circle B, bottom radius $r1$, and top radius $r2$. Given the 3D camera location C and 3D coordinates A and B, the plane passing through the points is determined. Since the vectors AB and AC lie in the plane, their cross product, which is perpendicular to the plane of AB and AC, is the normal. The normal is used to determine the orientation of the trapezoid to be projected into 2D plane. Each trapezoid of the model is projected into 2D image of each camera via modified Tsai's camera model. The projected image of the trapezoid is obtained by projecting the corners and then a rasterization of the triangles composing the trapezoid. The main task of a filling rasterizer is to seek all pixels that are covered by a triangle. Though projecting all truncated cones we obtain the image representing the 3D model in a given configuration.

For each set of frames acquired simultaneously by the synchronized cameras, the 3D human pose is reconstructed through matching the current image observations with the projected human body model into each camera view. In most of the approaches to articulated object tracking a background subtraction algorithms are employed to extract the subject undergoing tracking. Additionally, image cues such as edges, ridges and color are often employed to improve the extraction of the person. In the presented approach the human silhouette is extracted via background subtraction. Afterwards, the edges are located within the extracted silhouette. Finally, the edge distance map is extracted. The matching score reflects (i) matching ratio between the extracted silhouette and the projected 3D model and (ii) the normalized distance between the model's projected edges and the closest edges in the image [11]. The objective function of all cameras is the sum of such matching scores.

3.1   Rasterization of the 3D Model

In PF-based or PSO-based 3D motion tracking a single particle represents a hypothesis about possible subject pose. In such approaches the most computationally and time demanding operation is evaluation of the particles' score. Since every particle represents a hypothesis about possible subject pose the CPU-time needed for the rasterizing the 3D models for all particles can be considerable. As we already mentioned, the image of the projected model is obtained by rasterization of the triangles composing the trapezoids. In our approach the triangles that are closer to the camera are rasterized first. During the rendering of a next triangle the algorithm checks if a triangle has already been rasterized. If yes, it skips the rasterization, i.e. the triangle already rasterized is not painted over. Such an operation is performed for each triangle.

In the evaluation of the particles' score the projected and rasterized 3D model is matched with the current image observation. The fitness score depends on the degree of overlap between the extracted silhouette in the current image and the projected and rasterized 3D model in the hypothesized pose. The overlap degree is calculated through checking the overlap from the silhouette to the rasterized model as well as from the rasterized model to the silhouette. The larger the degree overlap is, the larger is the fitness value. The objective function reflects also the normalized distance between the model's projected edges and the closest edges in the image. It is calculated on the basis of the edge distance map [11].

3.2 Parallelization of Model Rasterization

In the evaluation of particles scores we employ two kernels. In the first one the 3D models are projected into 2D image of each camera. In the second one we rasterize the models and evaluate the objective functions. In our approach, in every block we rasterize the model in the pose represented by a single particle as well as we calculate its fitness score. Thus, the number of blocks is equal to the number of the particles, see Fig. 1. Each thread is responsible for rasterizing the model in single column and summing the fitness values of the pixels in that column. The number of threads in each block is equal to the image width, whereas the number of running threads in each block is equal to the number of cores per multiprocessor, see Fig. 1.

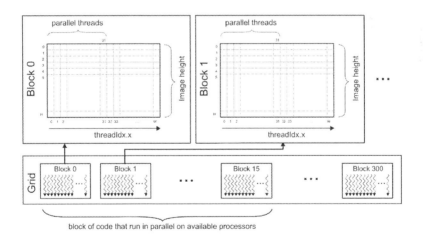

Fig. 1. Parallelization of the cost function

The cost values of the objective function are summed using parallel reduction. The results from each column of the threaded block are stored in the shared memory. In the next stage, $W/2$ consecutive threads determine the sums of the two adjacent memory cells of the shared memory and then store the results in the shared memory. The next iteration employs $W/4$ threads to add the results of the previous iteration, and so on. In order to speedup the triangle rasterization, for each triangle a rasterization area is determined. The rasterization is then only performed for pixels belonging to such a constrained area.

4   Parallel PSO for Object Tracking

Particle Swarm Optimization [9] is a bioinspired meta-heuristic for solving complex global optimization problems. The PSO is initialized with a group of random particles (hypothetical solutions) and then it searches for optima by updating all particles locations. The particles move through the solution space and undergo evaluation according to some fitness function. Each particle iteratively evaluates the candidate solutions and remembers the personal best location with the best objective value found so far, making this information available to its neighbors. Particles communicate good positions to each other and adjust their own velocities and positions taking into account such good locations.

In the ordinary PSO algorithm the update of particle's velocity and position can be expressed by the following equations:

$$v_j^{(i)} \leftarrow w v_j^{(i)} + c_1 r_{1,j}^{(i)} (p_j^{(i)} - x_j^{(i)}) + c_2 r_{2,j}^{(i)} (p_{g,j} - x_j^{(i)}) \tag{1}$$

$$x_j^{(i)} \leftarrow x_j^{(i)} + v_j^{(i)} \tag{2}$$

where w is the positive inertia weight, $v_j^{(i)}$ is the velocity of particle i in dimension j, $r_{1,j}^{(i)}$ and $r_{2,j}^{(i)}$ are uniquely generated random numbers with the uniform distribution in the interval $[0.0, 1.0]$, c_1, c_2 are positive constants, $p^{(i)}$ is the best position that the particle i has found so far, p_g denotes best position that is found by any particle in the swarm.

The velocity update equation (1) has three main components. The first component, which is often referred to as inertia models the particle's tendency to continue the moving in the same direction. In effect it controls the exploration of the search space. The second component, called cognitive, attracts towards the best position $p^{(i)}$ previously found by the particle. The last component is referred to as social and attracts towards the best position p_g found by any particle. The fitness value that corresponds $p^{(i)}$ is called local best $p_{\text{best}}^{(i)}$, whereas the fitness value corresponding to p_g is referred to as g_{best}.

Our parallel PSO algorithm for object tracking consists of five main phases, namely initialization, evaluation, p_best, g_best, update and motion, see Fig. 2. Before each optimization cycle, in the initialization stage an initial position $x^{(i)}$ and velocity $v^{(i)}$ is assigned to each particle. In the evaluation phase the fitness value of each particle is calculated using a cost function. In the p_best stage the determining of $p_{\text{best}}^{(i)}$ as well as $p^{(i)}$ takes place. The operations mentioned above are computed in parallel using available GPU resources. Afterwards, the g_{best} and its corresponding p_g are calculated in a sequential task. Finally, the update stage is done in parallel. That means that in our implementation we employ

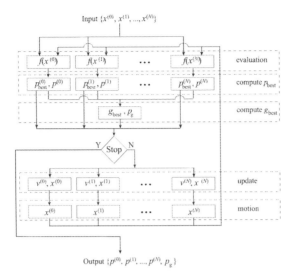

Fig. 2. Decomposition of synchronous particle swarm optimization algorithm on GPU

the parallel synchronous particle swarm optimization. The synchronous PSO algorithm updates all particle velocities and positions at the end of each iteration. In contrast to synchronous PSO the asynchronous algorithm updates particle positions and velocities continuously using currently accessible information.

In order to decompose an algorithm onto GPU we should identify data-parallel portions of the program and isolate them as CUDA kernels. In the initialization kernel we generate pseudo-random numbers using the curand library provided by the CUDA^{TM} SDK. On the basis of the uniform random numbers we generate normally distributed pseudorandom numbers using Box Mueller transform based on trigonometric functions [3]. The normally distributed random numbers are generated at the beginning of each frame to initialize the particles' velocities. Then the uniform random numbers r_1, r_2 for the optimal pose seeking are generated. This means that for every particle we generate $2 \times D \times K$ normally distributed random numbers, where D is dimension and K denotes the maximum number of iterations. They are stored in the memory and then used in the update kernel. At this stage the computations are done in $\lceil N/(2 \times W) \rceil$ blocks and W threads on each of them, where W denotes the number of cores per multiprocessor. In the compute p_{best} kernel and the update kernel the number of blocks is equal to $\lceil N/W \rceil$, whereas the number of threads in each block is equal to W. In the update kernel we constrain the velocities of the particles to the assumed maximal velocity values. In the motion stage the model's bone hierarchy is recursively traversed and the internal transformation matrices are updated according to the state vector of the particle.

4.1   Fitness Score for Particle Swarm Optimization

The fitness score for i-th camera's view is calculated on the basis of following expression: $f^{(i)}(\mathbf{x}) = 1 - ((f_1^{(i)}(\mathbf{x}))^{w_1} \cdot (f_2^{(i)}(\mathbf{x}))^{w_2})$, where w denotes weighting coefficients that were determined experimentally. The function $f_1^{(i)}(\mathbf{x})$ reflects the degree of overlap between the extracted body and the projected 3D model into 2D image corresponding to camera i. The function $f_2^{(i)}(\mathbf{x})$ reflects the edge distance-based fitness in the image from the camera i. The objective function for all cameras is determined according to the following expression: $f(\mathbf{x}) = \frac{1}{4}\sum_{i=1}^{4} f^{(i)}(\mathbf{x})$. The images acquired from the cameras are processed on CPU and then transferred onto the device.

5   Parallel PF for Object Tracking

The particle filter simulates the behavior of the dynamical system. Each sample predicts future behavior of the system in a Monte-Carlo fashion, and the samples that match the observed system behavior are kept, whereas ones that are unsuccessful in predicting tend to die out. The evolution of the state of the target as well as its measurement process is modeled by a set of (possibly non-linear) equations perturbed by (possibly non-Gaussian) i.i.d. noise:

$$\mathbf{x}_k = f_k(\mathbf{x}_{k-1}, \mathbf{v}_k) \tag{3}$$

$$\mathbf{z}_k = h_k(\mathbf{x}_k, \mathbf{n}_k) \tag{4}$$

where $\mathbf{x}_k$ denotes the state of the target at discrete time k, $\mathbf{v}_k$ is the process noise vector, $\mathbf{z}_k$ is the measurement vector, and $\mathbf{n}_k$ is the measurement noise vector. The aim is to estimate the distribution of the target state given all the previous measurements, that is, $p(\mathbf{x}_{k-1}|\mathbf{z}_{1:k-1})$, where $\mathbf{z}_{1:k-1} = \{\mathbf{z}_1, \ldots, \mathbf{z}_{k-1}\}$. The recursive Bayesian filter first calculates the *a priori* density $p(\mathbf{x}_k|\mathbf{z}_{1:k-1})$ using the system model and then evaluates *a posteriori* density $p(\mathbf{x}_k|\mathbf{z}_{1:k})$ given the new measurement.

In the PF, the distribution $p(\mathbf{x}_{k-1}|\mathbf{z}_{1:k-1})$ is approximated by a set of M particles $\{\mathbf{x}_{k-1}^i\}_{i=1\ldots M}$ and associated weights $\{w_{k-1}^i\}_{i=1\ldots M}$ in the following manner: $p(\mathbf{x}_{k-1}|\mathbf{z}_{1:k-1}) \approx \sum w_{k-1}^i \delta(\mathbf{x}_k - \mathbf{x}_{k-1}^i)$, where $w_k^i \propto w_{k-1}^i \frac{p(\mathbf{z}_k|\mathbf{x}_k^i)p(\mathbf{x}_k^i|\mathbf{x}_{k-1}^i)}{q(\mathbf{x}_k^i|\mathbf{x}_{k-1}^i,\mathbf{z}_k)}$, whereas $\sum w_{k-1}^i = 1$ and $\delta(\cdot)$ denotes the Kronecker delta function. The term $q(\mathbf{x}_k^i|\mathbf{x}_{k-1}^i, \mathbf{z}_k)$ stands for an importance density, which is typically obtained by approximating $p(\mathbf{x}_k|\mathbf{x}_{k-1}, \mathbf{z}_k)$ with a Gaussian distribution, or alternatively by using $p(\mathbf{x}_k|\mathbf{x}_{k-1})$.

One of the practical difficulties that is associated with particle filters is degeneration of the particle population after a few iterations because weights of several particles are negligible, and, eventually, only a very small number of particles contributes to the posterior distribution. To mitigate this problem the resampling should be used in order to eliminate particles with low importance weights and multiply particles with high importance weights. Resampling can be carried out at every iteration or only when a substantial amount of degeneracy is observed [5]. The algorithm can be expressed by the pseudo-code:

1. For $i = 1, 2, \ldots, M$ sample or propose particles using $p(\mathbf{x}_k | \mathbf{x}_{k-1})$
2. For $i = 1, 2, \ldots, M$ calculate the weights, $\tilde{w}_k^i = w_{k-1}^i p(\mathbf{z}_k | \mathbf{x}_k^i)$
3. Normalize the weights w_k^i using $\tilde{w}_k^i$
4. Calculate the state estimates, $\hat{\mathbf{x}}_k = \sum_{i=1}^{M} w_k^i \mathbf{x}_k^i$
5. Resample $\{\mathbf{x}_k^i, w_k^i\}$ to get new set of particles $\{\mathbf{x}_k^j, w_k^j = 1/M\}$

The resampling step can be expressed as follows:

1. Given the normalized weight, calculate an array of the cumulative sum of the weights.
2. Randomly generate a number and determine which range in that cumulative weight array to which the number belongs.
3. The index of that range would correspond to the particle that should be selected.
4. Repeat until the desired number of samples is selected.

The cumulative sum of the weights has been computed in parallel using all-prefix-sum operation [2]. The all-prefix-sums operation takes a binary associative operator $\oplus$, and an ordered set of n elements $a_0, a_1, \ldots, a_{n-1}$ and returns the ordered set $a_0, (a_0 \oplus a_1), \ldots, (a_0 \oplus a_1 \oplus, \ldots, \oplus a_{n-1})$. The cumulative sum was calculated using CUDA implementation of all-prefix-sums operation [7].

Given the cumulative sum of the weights, we randomly generate a number and then determine which range in that cumulative weight array to which the

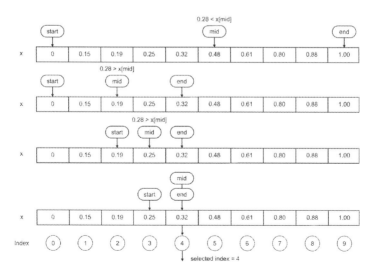

Fig. 3. Binary Search Algorithm - selecting indices based on uniform random numbers. Search for index corresponding to value 0.28 (generated by RNG).

number belongs. The search for the particle index corresponding to the generated random number was done in parallel using the binary search operation from Thrust parallel algorithms library [8], see also illustrative example on Fig. 3.

5.1   Observation Model of Particle Filter

In a particle filter the observation model describes the likelihood of a given observation given the considered object state. It assumes the following form: $p(\mathbf{z}_k|\mathbf{x}_k) = \exp(-f(x)^2/(2\sigma^2))$.

6   Parallel PF-PSO for Object Tracking

The strength of particle filter lies in their ability to represent multi-modal probability distributions and to maintain multiple hypotheses about target state. However, the number of particles that is required to adequately approximate the underlying probability distribution in the pose space might be huge. To mitigate this limitation, Deutscher and Reid [4] developed an annealed particle filter (APF).

Compared with the ordinary particle filter, the annealed particle filter greatly enhances the tracking accuracy. However, considerable number of particles is still required. Because the particles do not exchange information they have reduced capability of focusing the search on the promising areas. In contrast, owing to combining the local search (by self experience) and global one (by neighboring experience), the PSO algorithm has better capability of exploration of the search space. In [10] we demonstrated that a particle filter combined with a particle swarm optimization is better than each of them in terms of quality of tracking. In this work we present a modified PF-PSO, which has better capability of dealing with multimodal distributions. On the other hand, through the use of multiple swarms the diversity of PSO is also better.

In order to utilize the advantages of both algorithms, to emphasize their complementarities, and in particular to achieve real-time 3D motion tracking of full

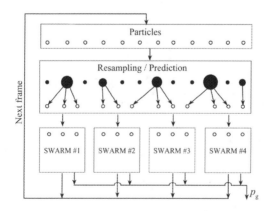

Fig. 4. PF-PSO algorithm

human body we elaborated a parallel PF-PSO algorithm. A flowchart of the algorithm is depicted in Fig. 4. At the beginning of each frame a PF with parallel resampling is executed.

After the resampling a diversification of the particles takes place. The particles are then assigned to four swarms and each self-optimizing swarm executes a specified number of iterations. In consequence, owing to multi-swarm optimization the algorithm is able to maintain the multimodal distributions. In the last stage the particles are propagated over time to cover the promising object poses in the next frame.

7   Experimental Results

The proposed PF-PSO algorithm has been evaluated on image sequences from [11]. They were acquired by four calibrated and synchronized cameras with 25 frames per second. The first pair of the cameras was approximately perpendicular to the second camera pair. The input images of size 1920×1080 were resized to 480×270 resolution. A commercial motion capture (MoCap) system from Vicon Nexus was employed to provide the ground truth data. The MoCap system delivers the data with rate of 100 Hz. The synchronization between MoCap and multi-camera system was accomplished using hardware from Vicon Giganet Lab. In the above mentioned work we demonstrated sample images with walking actors as well as the layout of the scene.

The execution time of the proposed algorithm was measured on a PC computer equipped with Intel Xeon X5690 3.46 GHz CPU (6 cores), with 8 GB RAM, and two NVidia GTX 590 graphics cards, each with 16 multiprocessors and 32 cores per multiprocessor. Each card has two GTX GPUs, each equipped with 1536 MB RAM and 48 KB shared memory per multiprocessor. Table 1

Table 1. Computation time [ms] and speedup for marker-less MoCap system consisting of 4 cameras. The times are for images from single cameras' shot.

	#particles	it.	Seq. 1			Seq. 2		
			GTX590	CPU	speedup	GTX590	CPU	speedup
PF	1000		14.5	143.1	9.9	15.2	141.6	9.3
	2000		26.7	264.6	9.9	26.3	263.0	10.0
	3000		40.0	387.1	9.8	39.6	388.5	9.8
	4000		52.2	515.8	9.9	54.5	517.7	9.5
PSO	100	10	30.7	138.7	4.5	30.5	139.0	4.6
	200	10	41.5	253.3	6.1	42.3	254.2	6.0
	300	10	58.5	368.0	6.3	58.8	370.0	6.3
	400	10	70.8	484.0	6.8	72.1	482.7	6.7
PF-PSO	100	10	33.3	139.3	4.2	31.2	138.5	4.4
	200	10	45.8	255.5	5.6	45.4	253.5	5.6
	300	10	57.7	371.3	6.4	55.5	367.7	6.6
	400	10	67.8	487.1	7.2	68.5	484.1	7.1

shows the computation time that we obtained on CPU and GPU for a MoCap configuration with four cameras. The processing times are in milliseconds. It contains the time needed for processing four images from single cameras' shot.

We compared the execution time of a generic particle filter (PF), synchronous Particle Swarm Optimization (PSO) and particle filter combined with PSO (PF-PSO) as well as the speedup of the GPU over GPU. The number of evaluations of the cost function by the considered algorithms was the same. For instance, the PF consisting of 4000 particles was compared with PSO consisting of 400 particles and executing 10 iterations. In the evaluation tests we used 4 CPU cores and 4 GPUs, i.e. on each GPU or CPU we processed the images from a single camera. The input images were preprocessed off-line and then transferred frame by frame to the GPU. As we can notice, the speedup of the algorithm executed on GPU over the CPU implementation is considerable. The speedup of PF does not vary much with the number of particles. For PSO and PF-PSO the speedup grows with the number of the particles. The speedup achieved by the PF is slightly better in comparison to speedup achieved by PSO and PF-PSO. As we can see, the full body motion can be tracked at frames larger than 15 frames by PSO or PF-PSO consisting of 300 particles and executing 10 iterations.

In Tab. 2 are shown the tracking accuracies that were obtained by the discussed algorithms. The errors were calculated using 39 markers. For each frame they were computed as average Euclidean distance between individual markers and the recovered 3D joint locations. For each sequence they were then averaged over ten runs of the algorithm with unlike initializations. As we can observe, the PF-PSO allows us to achieve superior tracking accuracy. Only for a PSO consisting of 100 particles and executing 10 iterations the tracking accuracy of the PSO is better than the accuracy of the PF-PSO. Moreover, the standard deviation achieved by the PF-PSO is far smaller in comparison to the standard deviation

Table 2. Average errors for $M = 39$ markers in two image sequences acquired by four synchronized and calibrated cameras

	#particles	it.	Seq. 1 error [mm]	Seq. 1 std. dev. [mm]	Seq. 2 error [mm]	Seq. 2 std. dev. [mm]
PF	1000		98.9	60.5	105.3	69.9
	2000		74.1	46.1	92.9	61.6
	3000		72.3	41.5	75.3	49.0
	4000		65.7	35.7	66.8	40.5
PSO	100	10	51.1	37.2	63.0	40.3
	200	10	59.1	49.6	65.0	48.2
	300	10	59.8	50.0	62.7	45.4
	400	10	55.2	44.1	53.9	37.5
PF-PSO	100	10	58.8	52.5	71.5	54.9
	200	10	49.4	34.8	58.2	39.0
	300	10	48.6	29.3	58.7	40.8
	400	10	49.9	36.0	53.9	35.5

achieved by the PF and the PSO. This means, that the PF-PSO algorithm copes better with the multimodal distributions than PSO algorithm.

8   Conclusions

We presented a PF-PSO algorithm, which has superior tracking accuracy to PF and PSO. Owing to multi-swarm based optimization the algorithm is capable of maintaining multimodal probability distributions. We proposed a parallel resampling scheme for particle filtering. The tracking of full human body can be performed at frame-rates of 16 frames per second using a two high-end graphics cards and images acquired by four cameras. The algorithm running on GPU is about 7.5 times faster in comparison to algorithm running on CPU. The average error is below 55 mm.

Acknowledgment. This work has been partially supported by the National Science Center (NCN) within the research project N N516 483240 and Ministry of Science and Higher Education within the grant U-206/DS/M.

References

1. Arulampalam, M., Maskell, S., Gordon, N., Clapp, T.: A tutorial on particle filters for online nonlinear/non-Gaussian Bayesian tracking. Trans. Sig. Proc. 50(2), 174–188 (2002)
2. Blelloch, G.E.: Prefix sums and their applications. Tech. Rep. CMU-CS-90-190, School of Computer Science, Carnegie Mellon University (November 1990)
3. Box, G.E.P., Muller, M.E.: A note on the generation of random normal deviates. The Annals of Mathematical Statistics 29(2), 610–611 (1958)
4. Deutscher, J., Blake, A., Reid, I.: Articulated body motion capture by annealed particle filtering. In: IEEE Int. Conf. on Pattern Recognition, pp. 126–133 (2000)
5. Doucet, A., Godsill, S., Andrieu, C.: On sequential Monte Carlo sampling methods for bayesian filtering. Statistics and Computing 10(1), 197–208 (2000)
6. Gong, P., Basciftci, Y.O., Ozguner, F.: A parallel resampling algorithm for particle filtering on shared-memory architectures. In: IEEE Int. Parallel and Distributed Processing Symposium, pp. 1477–1483. IEEE Computer Society (2012)
7. Harris, M., Sengupta, S., Owens, J.D.: Parallel prefix sum (scan) with CUDA. In: Nguyen, H. (ed.) GPU Gems 3. Addison Wesley (August 2007)
8. Hoberock, J., Bell, N.: Thrust: A parallel template library, version 1.3.0 (2010), http://www.meganewtons.com/
9. Kennedy, J., Eberhart, R.: Particle swarm optimization. In: Proc. of IEEE Int. Conf. on Neural Networks, pp. 1942–1948. IEEE Press, Piscataway (1995)
10. Krzeszowski, T., Kwolek, B., Wojciechowski, K.: Articulated body motion tracking by combined particle swarm optimization and particle filtering. In: Bolc, L., Tadeusiewicz, R., Chmielewski, L.J., Wojciechowski, K. (eds.) ICCVG 2010, Part I. LNCS, vol. 6374, pp. 147–154. Springer, Heidelberg (2010)
11. Kwolek, B., Krzeszowski, T., Gagalowicz, A., Wojciechowski, K., Josinski, H.: Real-time multi-view human motion tracking using particle swarm optimization with resampling. In: Perales, F.J., Fisher, R.B., Moeslund, T.B. (eds.) AMDO 2012. LNCS, vol. 7378, pp. 92–101. Springer, Heidelberg (2012)

Modelling Line and Edge Features Using Higher-Order Riesz Transforms[*]

Ross Marchant[1,2] and Paul Jackway[2]

[1] James Cook University
[2] CSIRO Computational Informatics

Abstract. The 2D-complex Riesz transform is an extension of the Hilbert transform to images. It can be used to model local image structure as a superposition of sinusoids, and to construct 2D steerable wavelets. In this paper we propose to model local image structure as the superposition of a 2D steerable wavelet at multiple amplitudes and orientations. These parameters are estimated by applying recent developments in super-resolution theory. Using 2D steerable wavelets corresponding to line or edge segments then allows for the underlying structure of image features such as junctions and edges to be determined.

Keywords: Riesz transform, 2D steerable filter, super-resolution, semi-definite program, local feature analysis.

1 Introduction

Low-level image features arise from interesting structures such as lines, edges, corners and junctions. Detection, classification and parametrisation of such features is a useful first step in the image analysis pipeline, providing input for higher-level pattern recognition. One approach is to project the local image patch onto a particular signal model. The model may be as simple as edge detection, or a more complex description with geometric information, e.g. [1]. The monogenic signal [2] locally models an image as an oriented sinusoid with a certain amplitude, phase and orientation, using the 1st order Riesz transform (RT). This representation is useful as amplitude encodes feature strength and phase encodes feature type, e.g. line or edge. Higher-order RTs are used for more complex signal models in [3] [4] and [5], and recent research has shown RTs can be used to construct 2D steerable wavelets [6], [7].

In this paper we propose to extend this work to model local signal structure as the superposition of a particular 2D steerable wavelet at multiple amplitudes and orientations. This is an inverse problem where these parameters must be optimised such that the model describes as much of the signal as possible. Our novel approach is to use the theory of super-resolution of spike trains via semi-definite programming [8], [9] to solve for the wavelet parameters. The choice of wavelet

[*] The first author is supported by JCU and CSIRO scholarships. This research is part of the CSIRO Transformational Biology Capability Platform.

depends on the feature of interest. For example, if a wavelet corresponding to a line segment or wedge segment is used, then the amplitude and orientation of individual line or wedge segments that make up more complex features, such as junctions or edges, can be determined.

2   Signal Model

2.1   Riesz Transform

The RT is an extension of the Hilbert transform to two or more dimensions [2]. The n-th order 2D complex RT, $\mathcal{R}^n$, is a complex-valued operator that can be expressed as either a convolution in the spatial domain, or multiplication in the Fourier domain. We shall use the following definition from [7], which differs from [4], [10] only in sign changes and the position of $i = \sqrt{-1}$,

$$\mathcal{R}^n f(\mathbf{z}) \quad \overset{\mathcal{F}}{\longleftrightarrow} \quad \left(\frac{u_x + iu_y}{\|\mathbf{u}\|} \right)^n \hat{f}(\mathbf{u}) \tag{1}$$

where $f(\mathbf{z}) \in L_2(\mathbb{R}^2)$, $\hat{f}(\mathbf{u}) = \mathcal{F}f(\mathbf{u})$ is its Fourier transform, and $\mathbf{u} = [u_x, u_y]$. Also $\mathcal{R}^{n*} = \mathcal{R}^{-n}$ and $\mathcal{R}^0$ is the identity operator. The vector valued multi-order RT, $\boldsymbol{\mathcal{R}}^N$, maps the $-N$ to N-th order RT responses to a vector valued signal [7],

$$\boldsymbol{\mathcal{R}}^N f(\mathbf{z}) = \{\mathcal{R}^n f(\mathbf{z}) \,|\, n \in \mathbb{Z}, |n| \leq N\} \tag{2}$$

We shall refer to the response at one point as an RT vector in the rest of this paper. The higher-order RT is a unitary operator that is translation and scale invariant [2], [7], and appears as a spherical harmonic in the Fourier domain. Local signal structure with a particular rotational symmetry gives the greatest response for an RT of the same order, e.g. an 'X' junction responds most to the 4-th order RT. Therefore describing local signal structure using larger order RTs allows for more complex structures to be analysed.

2.2   2D Steerable Wavelet

The RT is also used to construct 2D steerable wavelets that are self-reversible and polar separable in the Fourier domain, [6], [7]. A 2D steerable wavelet, $s(\mathbf{z}; \theta)$, given by the weighted summation of different order RTs of an isotropic bandpass filter kernel, $p(\mathbf{z})$, is

$$s(\mathbf{z}; \theta) = \sum_{n=-N}^{N} e^{in\theta} u_n \mathcal{R}^n p(\mathbf{z}) \tag{3}$$

where θ is the orientation of the wavelet, and $\mathbf{u}$ is the weights. Let $\mathbf{f}^N(\mathbf{z}) = \boldsymbol{\mathcal{R}}^N(p * f)(\mathbf{z})$. The 2D steerable wavelet, $s_f(\mathbf{z})$, whose RT vector is the same as the signal at $\mathbf{z} = \mathbf{0}$, i.e. $\mathcal{R}^N s_f(\mathbf{0}) = \mathbf{f}^N(\mathbf{0})$, is given by

$$s_f(\mathbf{z}) = \frac{1}{p(0)} \sum_{n=-N}^{N} f_n^N \mathcal{R}^{-n} p(\mathbf{z}) \tag{4}$$

Thus a particular 2D steerable wavelet is an approximation of local signal structure up to the Nth order of symmetry. The RT is similar to the derivative operator; however, it does not change the magnitude of the filter spectrum and thus increasing the number of orders used increases the spatial extent of the filter. In contrast, 2D derivative-based steerable filters maintain spatial extent with increasing order, e.g. [11], [12]. The bandpass filter used should be smooth, with a fast rate of decay, and a large number of vanishing moments [13].

2.3   Model

Let $f(\mathbf{z}) \in L^2(\mathbb{R}^2)$ be a 2D image and $p(\mathbf{z})$ be an isotropic bandpass filter kernel chosen to restrict the analysis to a particular scale, such as a log-normal filter [14]. Assuming a local coordinate system centred on a point of interest at $\mathbf{z} = \mathbf{0}$, we propose to model the local signal structure as

$$(p * f)(\mathbf{z}) = \sum_{k=1}^{K} \alpha_k s(\mathbf{z}; \theta_k) + \epsilon(\mathbf{z}) \tag{5}$$

where $s(\mathbf{z}; \theta)$ is a real valued 2D steerable wavelet with amplitude $\alpha \in \mathbb{R}$ and orientation $\theta \in [-\pi, \pi)$, and $\epsilon(\mathbf{z})$ is a residual component. Let $\mathbf{f}^N = \mathcal{R}^N (p * f)(\mathbf{0})$ be the signal RT vector at the point of interest, and $\mathbf{s}^N = \mathcal{R}^N s(\mathbf{0}; 0)$ be the wavelet RT vector at orientation 0 degrees. Then

$$\mathbf{f}^N = \sum_{k=1}^{K} \alpha_k \mathbf{R}_{\theta_k} \mathbf{s}^{N\mathsf{T}} + \epsilon^N \tag{6}$$

where $\mathbf{R}_\theta$ is the diagonal matrix $\{R_{\theta_{n,n}}^N = e^{in\theta} | n \in \mathbb{Z}, |n| \leq N\}$. A single component of the signal RT vector is therefore

$$f_n^N = s_n^N \sum_{k=1}^{K} \alpha_k \, e^{in\theta_k} + \epsilon_n^N \tag{7}$$

2.4   Super-Resolution

The problem of estimating the amplitude and orientation parameters of the model is similar to that of the super-resolution of spike trains developed in [8], [9]. This involves finding the location and amplitude of complex-valued spikes in a spike train signal from the low-frequency Fourier series components [8] even when corrupted by noise [9].

To briefly restate the problem in [8], let $x(t)$ be a signal composed of the super-position of a number of complex-valued spikes restricted to the domain $t \in [0, 2\pi)$, and $\mathcal{F}^N$ be an operator that maps a signal to its $-N$ to Nth Fourier series coefficients. Given the Fourier series coefficients, $\mathbf{y} = \mathcal{F}^N x(t)$ the position and amplitude of the spikes can be found by solving

$$\min_{\tilde{x}} \|\tilde{x}(t)\|_{\mathrm{TV}} \quad \text{subject to} \quad \|\mathcal{F}^N \tilde{x}(t) - \mathbf{y}\|_{L_1} < \delta \tag{8}$$

where $\tilde{x}(t)$ is the estimated spike train, and $\|\tilde{x}(t)\|_{\mathrm{TV}}$ is the total-variation norm which selects for the solution which has the smallest number of large valued spikes. The parameter, δ, allows for noise. For an ideal spike train with no noise and $\delta = 0$, total variation minimisation will give the *exact* solution so long the wrap-around distance is greater than $4\pi/N$ for complex spikes, and $3.74\pi/N$ for real valued spikes [8]. Numerical simulations in [8] suggest that the minimum distance required may be as low as $2\pi/N$ if there are a low number of spikes compared to N. Furthermore, for real spikes all of the *same* sign, the minimum distance is practically zero. The maximum number of spikes that can be resolved is N [8]. Importantly, the super-resolution problem does not need to be made discrete. It can be solved using just the Fourier coefficients via a semi-definite program to arbitrary precision. Example MATLAB code is given in [8].

2.5   A Solution

Returning to our problem, the n-th order RT is similar to the n-th order Fourier series component of the angular portion of the signal spectrum, and eq. (7) is equivalent to the Fourier series of a spike train weighted by $\mathbf{s}^N$. Let

$$g_n^N = f_n^N / s_n^N \tag{9}$$

$$r_n^N = \sum_{k=1}^{K} \alpha_k e^{in\theta_k} \tag{10}$$

where $|n| \leq N$. Note that $\mathbf{g}^N$ is the signal RT vector normalised by the 2D wavelet coefficients; this division is the crucial step that converts the problem from a super-position of wavelets to a super-position of spikes. The RT vector $\mathbf{r}^N$ corresponds to the desired solution. According to the super-resolution theory we may then solve

$$\min_{\boldsymbol{\alpha}} \|\boldsymbol{\alpha}\|_{\mathrm{TV}} \text{ subject to } \|\mathbf{r}^N - \mathbf{g}^N\| < \delta_\epsilon \tag{11}$$

to obtain the amplitudes and orientations of the component wavelet. Since the maximum number of spikes that can be recovered is N, we have $K \leq N$.

We have assumed the signal can be reasonably modelled by our choice of wavelet. If it cannot, there is no guarantee the signal will be angularly band-limited in the same way the wavelet is. Thus if for some n, s_n^N is small, g_n^N can be potentially quite large and have a disproportionate effect on the results. The wavelets we shall consider have coefficients with unity magnitude however, i.e. $|s_n^N| = 1$. If no solution is found, δ_ϵ, should be increased.

3 Feature Types

The main application of this work is to parametrise image features that are
made up of a particular feature component overlaid at different amplitudes and
orientations. For example, finding the amplitude and orientation of line segments
that make up a 'Y' junction, or the angle of the edges that make up a corner.
A junction or corner feature located at the point of interest, $\mathbf{z} = \mathbf{0}$, of an image
signal $f(\mathbf{z})$ can be described by

$$f(\mathbf{z}) = \sum_{k=1}^{K} \alpha_k t(\mathbf{z}; \theta_k) \tag{12}$$

where $t(\mathbf{z})$ is the feature component, such as a line segment. If $s_t(\mathbf{z}; 0)$ is the 2D
steerable wavelet approximation of $(p * t)(\mathbf{z})$, then we have

$$(p * f)(\mathbf{z}) = \sum_{k=1}^{K} \alpha_k s_t(\mathbf{z}; \theta_k) \tag{13}$$

Using the super-resolution method the amplitude and orientation of the wavelets
can be found, and thus so can the amplitude and orientation of the underlying
component $t(\mathbf{z})$. We shall consider features composed of line segments and wedge
segments.

3.1 Line Types

We define a line segment as a line radiating from a point with a constant amplitude and orientation. Local features such as 'Y' or 'X' junctions are composed
of multiple line segments.

An idealised line segment radiating from $\mathbf{z} = \mathbf{0}$ can be described in polar
coordinates, $\mathbf{z} = [r\cos\phi, r\sin\phi]$, by the function

$$t_{\text{line}}(r, \phi; \theta) = \alpha \frac{\delta(\phi - \theta)}{r} \tag{14}$$

where α is the amplitude and θ is the orientation. Modifying our previous results
in [10] to account for the different form of the RT used in this paper, the n-th
order RT at origin is

$$\mathcal{R}^n(p * t_{\text{line}})(\mathbf{0}) = (-\mathrm{i})^{|n|}\alpha e^{\mathrm{i}n\theta} \int_0^\infty \hat{p}(w)dw \tag{15}$$

where $\hat{p}(w)$ is the Fourier transform of the bandpass filter expressed in polar
coordinates, $w = \|\mathbf{u}\|$. The corresponding wavelet decomposition is

$$s_{\text{line}}(\mathbf{z}; \theta) = \frac{1}{p(\mathbf{z})} \sum_{n=-N}^{N} \mathcal{R}^n(p * t_{\text{line}})(\mathbf{0}) \cdot \mathcal{R}^{-n}p(\mathbf{z}) \tag{16}$$

$$= \frac{\alpha C}{p(\mathbf{0})} \sum_{n=-N}^{N} e^{\mathrm{i}n\theta}\mathcal{R}^{-n}p(\mathbf{z}) \tag{17}$$

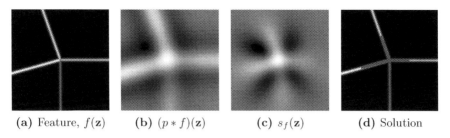

(a) Feature, $f(\mathbf{z})$ (b) $(p * f)(\mathbf{z})$ (c) $s_f(\mathbf{z})$ (d) Solution

Fig. 1. Estimating the amplitude and orientation of a line feature (a). Bandpassed signal shown in (b) with wavelet approximation (c). Amplitude (length of line) and orientation solution shown in (d).

where C is a constant dependent on the filter used. Finally, the normalised RT vector we shall use when solving for a line feature is

$$t_{\text{line}}^N = \{(-i)^{|n|} \mid n \in \mathbb{Z}, |n| \leq N\} \tag{18}$$

3.2 Edge Types

Consider a feature composed of wedge segments, such as chequerboard or a corner where solid planes meet. A wedge segment with edge angles θ_1, θ_2 may be represented in polar coordinates by

$$t_{\text{wedge}}(r, \phi; \theta_1, \theta_2) = \begin{cases} \alpha & \text{where } \phi \in [\theta_1, \theta_2) \\ 0 & \text{otherwise} \end{cases} \tag{19}$$

Solving this is a little more difficult. We begin by considering the RT response of the wedge segment without the bandpass filter, using the spatial expression for the RT in [7],

$$\mathcal{R}^n t_{\text{wedge}}(\mathbf{0}) = \langle (\mathcal{R}^n \delta)(-\mathbf{z}), t_{\text{wedge}}(\mathbf{z}) \rangle \tag{20}$$

$$= \int_0^\infty \int_0^{2\pi} \frac{n i^{|n|}}{2\pi} \frac{e^{in(\phi - \pi)}}{r^2} t_{\text{wedge}} \, d\theta \, r dr \tag{21}$$

$$= n \, i^{|n|} (-1)^n \frac{\alpha}{2\pi} \int_0^\infty \int_{\theta_1}^{\theta_2} \frac{e^{in\phi}}{r^2} \, d\theta \, r dr \tag{22}$$

$$= (-i)^{|n+1|} \frac{\alpha}{2\pi} (e^{in\theta_2} - e^{in\theta_1}) \int_0^\infty \frac{1}{r} dr \tag{23}$$

$$= (-i)^{|n+1|} \frac{\alpha}{2\pi} (e^{in\theta_2} - e^{in\theta_1}) \lim_{a \to 0} \int_a^\infty \frac{1}{r} dr \tag{24}$$

The limit in the above equation tends to infinity, however the main result is that the magnitude of the response has the same bounds regardless of RT order, n. For example, the magnitude of the response of the 1st order kernel to an edge

$(\boldsymbol{\theta} = [0, \pi])$ is the same as a 2nd order kernel to a corner $(\boldsymbol{\theta} = [0, \pi/2])$. If the signal is bandpassed using a filter kernel that decays to zero fast enough, then we may still write

$$\mathcal{R}^n(p * t_{\text{wedge}})(\mathbf{0}) = (-i)^{|n+1|} D(e^{in\theta_2} - e^{in\theta_1}) \tag{25}$$

where D is a constant dependent on the filter used. The corresponding wavelet is given by

$$s_{\text{wedge}}(\mathbf{z}; \theta_1, \theta_2) = \frac{D}{p(\mathbf{0})} \sum_{n=-N}^{N} (-i)^{|n+1|} (e^{in\theta_2} - e^{in\theta_1}) \mathcal{R}^{-n} p(\mathbf{z}) \tag{26}$$

Rewriting as the sum of two wavelets, s_{edge},

$$s_{\text{wedge}}(\mathbf{z}; \theta_1, \theta_2) = s_{\text{edge}}(\mathbf{z}; \theta_2) - s_{\text{edge}}(\mathbf{z}; \theta_1) \tag{27}$$

$$\text{where} \quad s_{\text{edge}}(\mathbf{z}; \theta) = \frac{D}{p(\mathbf{0})} \sum_{n=-N}^{N} (-i)^{|n+1|} e^{in\theta} \mathcal{R}^{-n} p(\mathbf{z}) \tag{28}$$

we obtain the normalised edge RT vector,

$$\mathbf{t}_{\text{edge}}^N = \{(-i)^{|n+1|} \mid n \in \mathbb{Z}, |n| \le N\} \tag{29}$$

which is the component that will be used to analyse edge features such as corners.

3.3   Smoothed Features

Line or edge features often appear smoothed in images. Let $g(\mathbf{z})$ be an band-limited isotropic smoothing kernel, such as a Gaussian, applied to our idealised line or edge feature, e.g. $(g * f)(\mathbf{z})$. Substituting $p_g(\mathbf{z}) = (p * g)(\mathbf{z})$ for the wavelet generating kernel, $p(\mathbf{z})$, in the previous two sections yields the same normalised line and edge RT vectors. The super-resolution method therefore remains the same.

3.4   Procedure

A general procedure resolving a line or edge feature is as follows:

1. Choose bandpass filter and maximum order, N, of RTs to be used.
2. Calculate RT vector at point of interest using eq. (2).
3. Determine whether local structure is a line or edge type. One method is compare the 0-th order RT response to that of the other orders. If it is around the same magnitude it is a line type, if it is closer to 0 it is an edge type.
4. Choose RT vector corresponding to the type, $\mathbf{t}_{\text{line}}(\mathbf{z})$ for positive lines, $-\mathbf{t}_{\text{line}}(\mathbf{z})$ for negative lines, $\mathbf{t}_{\text{edge}}(\mathbf{z})$ for edge types.
5. Solve eq.(11) using the super-resolution method to get the relative amplitudes and orientations. Increase δ_ϵ and re-evaluate if no solution is returned.

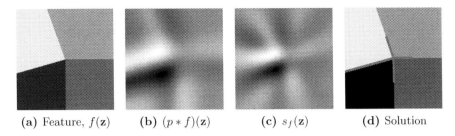

(a) Feature, $f(\mathbf{z})$ (b) $(p * f)(\mathbf{z})$ (c) $s_f(\mathbf{z})$ (d) Solution

Fig. 2. Estimating the amplitude and orientation of an edge feature (a). Bandpassed signal shown in (b) with wavelet approximation (c). Amplitude (length of line) and orientation solution shown in (d).

From the solution, one can classify the feature according to the number of components with amplitude above a certain threshold. Figures 1 and 2 show the wavelet approximation and super-resolution solution for a line and edge feature, respectively.

4 Experiments

4.1 Minimum Distance

The minimum distance condition needed for accurate super-resolution requires the segments of a line or edge feature to be separated by a given angle, which depends on the maximum order RT used. The minimum angle required for an exact solution was numerically evaluated for different numbers of segments. An ideal signal comprised of from three to five real valued spikes (segments) was solved from its Fourier series coefficients (RTs), using the super-resolution method with $N \in [2, 9]$. The minimum distance between adjacent spikes of the same sign, and of the opposite sign, that gave an accurate solution is shown in Figure 3. Generally for all N, the minimum distance required between spikes of the same sign was less than 0.1 radians, even if the signal contained opposite sign spikes. For opposite sign spikes, a minimum distance of π/N radians was needed. Knowing the expected minimum angle between segments in a line or edge feature can therefore guide the maximum order RT required.

4.2 Running Time

Average running time to calculate a solution in MATLAB, using one core of a 3GHz Core2 Quad Intel processor, ranged approximately linearly from 0.56s ($N = 2$) to 1.04s ($N = 10$).

4.3 Noise Sensitivity

A 'T' junction image, $f(\mathbf{z})$, consisting of 1-pixel wide line segments orientated at 0, 90 and 180 degrees was corrupted with varying levels of Gaussian noise.

The angle and orientation of the lines were found using our method with $\delta_\epsilon = 0.1 \times |\mathbf{f}^N|$, $N \in [2, 10]$, and a log-normal filter of wavelength 32 pixels and $\sigma = 0.65$. The average error is shown in Figure 4 (a) and (b). Figure 4 (c) shows the same experiment but with $N = 5$, and δ_ϵ ranging from 0.1 to $0.7 \times \|\mathbf{f}^N\|$. Increasing N decreases the amplitude and orientation error at the expense of longer computation time. For low noise values, increasing δ_ϵ increases the amplitude and orientation errors proportionally. However, if N is also increased these errors are reduced (not shown). In contrast, the percentage of solutions correctly classified as having three line segments (above 10% of maximum amplitude) improved with increasing δ_ϵ, because a larger value reduces the need for spurious components to compensate for noise.

4.4   Comparison

A recent method to estimate the orientation of line and edge segments is multi-steerable matched filters (MSMF) [12]. We tested the performance of our method (log-normal filter, $\sigma = 0.65$, wavelength $= [19, 10]$ for $N = [6, 12]$, respectively) against MSMFs (maximum derivative order of 28) for orientation estimation of a two line-segment feature. Orientation from the two maxima of the angular response of the component line-segment 2D steerable wavelet was also compared. The feature was constructed as two one-pixel wide line segments smoothed using a Gaussian kernel ($\sigma = 1.25$) with added Gaussian noise ($\sigma = 1$). Figure 5 shows the results. Our method using only six RT orders performs similarly to MSMFs using 28 derivative orders, and performs better for 12 RT orders. For small differences in line-segment orientation, super-resolution gives less error than simply rotating the line-segment wavelet and finding the local maxima of the response. This is because super-resolution can often resolve two line segments when there is only one peak in the angular response.

4.5   Example Images

Figure 6 shows the analysis of bee-wing vein junctions found using our method. Amplitude and orientation of the line segments were found using the negative line-segment RT vector ($-\mathbf{t}_{\text{line}}$, $N = 7$, $\delta_\epsilon = 0.3 \times |\mathbf{f}^N|$) using a log-normal filter with wavelength 16 and $\sigma = 0.65$. Each junction was classified according to the number of component line-segment wavelets with amplitude above 0.15 times the maximum amplitude.

A few of the junctions are misclassified, highlighting a challenge with practical application. Firstly, our signal model assumes that the line or edges of the image feature are radiating from the centre of the feature; therefore, the locations chosen must be as close to the centre of the feature as possible. Secondly, as the signal model only uses one particular component, i.e. line segment or edge segment, the solution given by the super-resolution method may return extra components to compensate for other types of structures present.

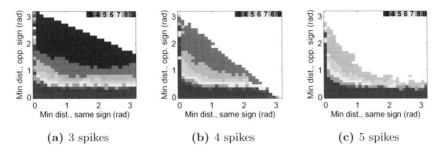

(a) 3 spikes   (b) 4 spikes   (c) 5 spikes

Fig. 3. Minimum distances between same sign spikes, and opposite sign spikes, for three to five spikes solved with $N \in [3, 9]$. Coloured areas indicate values where the solution was accurate for a particular order N. Areas for large N include that of smaller N. Grey areas indicate no accurate solution found for all evaluated orders.

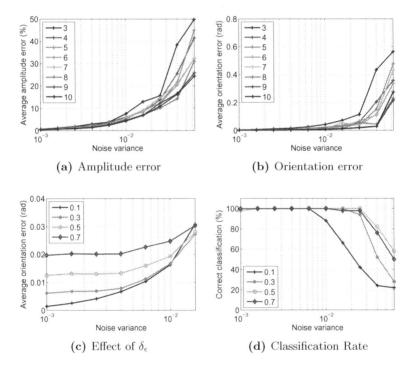

(a) Amplitude error   (b) Orientation error

(c) Effect of δ_ϵ (d) Classification Rate

Fig. 4. Effects of noise, order (N) and δ_ϵ: Amplitude error (a) and orientation error (b) vs increasing noise for different N (coloured lines) with $\delta_\epsilon = 0.1 \times |\mathbf{f}^N|$; amplitude (solid line) and orientation (dashed line) error (c) and classification rate (d) vs noise for different δ_ϵ (coloured lines) with $N = 5$

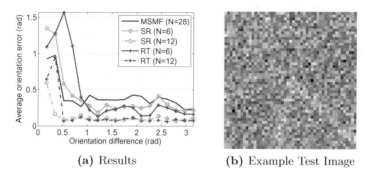

(a) Results   (b) Example Test Image

Fig. 5. Our method (SR) compared to multi-steerable matched filters (MSMF), and local maxima of the wavelet angular response (RT), for estimating the orientations of two line segments (a), with example shown in (b)

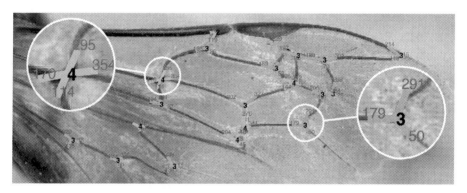

Fig. 6. Bee-wing vein junctions classified by number of line segments (black number). Lines indicate amplitude and orientation of line segments, with the angle shown in degrees (red numbers).

5   Conclusion

In this paper we have presented a novel method of representing local image structure as the superposition of either a line- or edge-type 2D steerable wavelet at multiple amplitudes and orientations. This provides a description of local image structure with rich geometric information, enabling junction or corner features to be classified by the number and position of their components. Steerable wavelets are used because they are generated using RTs, which maintain the scale of analysis when the order, N, is increased. In our experiments, the method compares favourably with multi-steerable matched filters, which use derivatives, for estimating line orientation.

Estimating the amplitudes and orientations using the super-resolution method allows for arbitrary accuracy without needing to discretise the problem, as would be necessary if solving using linear programming. For an ideal feature with any number of line or edge segments the solution will be exact, regardless of N, provided the minimum distance criteria is met. In the presence of noise, increasing N decreases error. Representing local image structure using 2D steerable wavelets with non-unitary RT vectors is the subject of future work.

References

1. Newell, A., Griffin, L.: Natural Image Character Recognition Using Oriented Basic Image Features. In: Proc. Int. Conf. Digital Image Computing Techniques and Applications, pp. 191–196 (December 2011)
2. Felsberg, M., Sommer, G.: The monogenic signal. IEEE Trans. Signal Process. 49(12), 3136–3144 (2001)
3. Zang, D., Sommer, G.: The Monogenic Curvature Scale-Space. In: Reulke, R., Eckardt, U., Flach, B., Knauer, U., Polthier, K. (eds.) IWCIA 2006. LNCS, vol. 4040, pp. 320–332. Springer, Heidelberg (2006)
4. Wietzke, L., Sommer, G.: The Signal Multi-Vector. J. Math. Imaging and Vision 37(2), 132–150 (2010)
5. Fleischmann, O., Wietzke, L., Sommer, G.: Image Analysis by Conformal Embedding. J. Math. Imaging and Vision 40(3), 305–325 (2011)
6. Unser, M., Van De Ville, D.: Wavelet steerability and the higher-order Riesz transform. IEEE Trans. Image Process. 19(3), 636–652 (2010)
7. Unser, M., Chenouard, N.: A unifying parametric framework for 2D steerable wavelet transforms. SIAM J. Imaging Sci. 6(1), 102–135 (2012)
8. Candes, E., Fernandez-Granda, C.: Towards a mathematical theory of super-resolution. arXiv preprint arXiv:1203.5871 (2012)
9. Candes, E., Fernandez-Granda, C.: Super-resolution from noisy data. arXiv preprint arXiv:1211.0290 (2012)
10. Marchant, R., Jackway, P.: Feature detection from the maximal response to a spherical quadrature filter set. In: Proc. Int. Conf. Digital Image Computing Techniques and Applications (December 2012)
11. Freeman, W.T., Adelson, E.H.: The design and use of steerable filters. IEEE Trans. Pattern Anal. Mach. Intell. 13(9), 891–906 (1991)
12. Mühlich, M., Friedrich, D., Aach, T.: Design and Implementation of Multisteerable Matched Filters. IEEE Trans. Pattern Anal. Mach. Intell. 34(2), 279–291 (2012)
13. Ward, J., Chaudhury, K., Unser, M.: Decay properties of Riesz transforms and steerable wavelets. arXiv preprint arXiv:1301.2525 (2013)
14. Boukerroui, D., Noble, J., Brady, M.: On the Choice of Band-Pass Quadrature Filters. J. Math. Imaging and Vision 21(1), 53–80 (2004)

Semantic Approach in Image Change Detection

Adrien Gressin[1,2], Nicole Vincent[2], Clément Mallet[1], and Nicolas Paparoditis[1]

[1] IGN/SR, MATIS, 73 Avenue de Paris, 94160 Saint-Mande, France
firstname.lastname@ign.fr
[2] LIPADE - SIP, Paris-Descartes University, 45 Rue des Saint-Pères, Paris, France
nicole.vincent@mi.parisdescartes.fr

Abstract. Change detection is a main issue in various domains, and especially for remote sensing purposes. Indeed, plethora of geospatial images are available and can be used to update geographical databases. In this paper, we propose a classification-based method to detect changes between a database and a more recent image. It is based both on an efficient training point selection and a hierarchical decision process. This allows to take into account the intrinsic heterogeneity of the objects and themes composing a database while limiting false detection rates. The reliability of the designed framework method is first assessed on simulated data, and then successfully applied on very high resolution satellite images and two land-cover databases.

Keywords: change detection, updating, classification, image, database.

1 Introduction

Geographic databases are nowadays almost complete in most developed countries. However, their update remains challenging, even if spatial imagery allows to cover, in a cost-effective way, large areas with higher and higher resolutions. More generally, image change detection is a large subject of research, in various domain such as video surveillance, civil infrastructure or medical diagnostic [13]. A large body of literature about change detection exists : between image pairs [10,11], time-series [14,7,12], using very-high-resolution images [1]. In the remote sensing field, very few papers study the discrepancies between a database and more recent images. For instance, [9] matches database objects with image saliencies. In fact, most methods are designed for very specific object types (road, building, etc.) [3], and manual photo-interpretation methods remain the most efficient tool [2].

In this paper, we propose a general framework for change detection, effective on various database types, by remaining independent of the object characterisation. Thereby, our method is able to deal with every kind of object (road, building, crop, forest ...). With a careful inspection of the database, our method provides a probability change map that allows to focus on change areas for subsequent and specific database update. In Section 2, we describe our hierarchical approach in the context of imagery. Then, we assess our method with several

J. Blanc-Talon et al. (Eds.): ACIVS 2013, LNCS 8192, pp. 450–459, 2013.

experiments on simulated data (Section 3), and successfully apply it on real remote sensing data, namely very high resolution satellite images and geographic
databases (Section 4). Finally, conclusions are drawn in Section 5.

2   Methodology

Geographic database are structured in a hierarchical manner : objects (namely
2D polygons) are grouped by themes (e.g., roads, forests, crops, etc.), themselves
composing the database (DB, cf. Figure 1a). The objects of all the themes of
a DB may not provide a full coverage of given area: the complementary part is
called background. In order to detect changes, the whole database needs to be
inspected and therefore the whole structure of the database. Thus, a hierarchical
analysis is designed at three different levels: the object level, the theme level,
and the database level (Figure 1b). At last, this database inspection allows to
obtain a change probability map. Our approach is based on the Support Vector
Machines (SVM) classifier because (1) it can handle a large number of features,
(2) it has a high generalisation ability, and (3) it is fast enough to perform as
many classifications as required (see below). A supervised approach is chosen
since we consider that only minor changes exist between the DB and the image,
meaning that the DB can be used to learn the appearance of the object and the
themes that compose it (Figure 1).

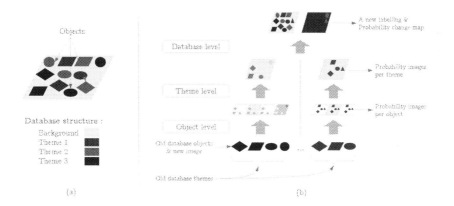

Fig. 1. (a) Database covering part of the image. (b) General view of our hierarchical
methodology (see text for more details).

2.1   Object Level

The aim of the object level analysis is to learn the different appearances of a
theme in the most recent image in order to consolidate the decision taken at

the theme level. This inspection is based on a supervised classification using features derived from the image, trained on a restricted but efficient subset of pixels. The selection of the training points is based on a two-step maximization of the classification recall [5]. Two selections are successively performed: one for the current object (*foreground*) and another one for the rest of the DB (*background*).

First, a background subset is randomly drawn among pixels out of the current theme. Such pixels may correspond to any other theme of the DB or may belong to the DB background (Figure 1a). Several foreground subsets are then randomly retrieved among pixels composing the current object. A Gaussian kernel soft-margin SVM is trained for each foreground subset, coupled with the background subset, and applied on all object pixels. The subset maximizing the recall of the object is selected. Similarly, the background subset is chosen by randomly selecting several subsets of pixels out of the current theme.

The optimal training set is finally defined as the union of the two best *background* and *foreground* subsets, and used to perform a classification of the full image. As for the subset selection step, a grid search method is applied to select the best hyper-parameters (C & γ) that maximize the cross-validation accuracy. Finally, a probability estimate to belong to the current object theme [17] is obtained for each pixel.

2.2   Theme Level

Probability images obtained for each object of a given theme are merged in order to obtain a single probability image per theme. This confidence map allows to define, for each pixel, the probability of this pixel to belong to the current theme.

Various methods have been tested in order to fuse those probability results, such as minimum or maximum values. Finally, the mean of all the probability images for each object of one theme gives the most satisfactory results. In practice, the mean value weighted by the size of each object is used in order to give more confidence on large objects that are less supposed to change.

2.3   Database Level

The database level is composed of two steps. First, a fusion of all probability images per theme is performed. Secondly, a decision process allows to obtain a unified probability change map (for each pixel, its new label accompanied with a confidence measure). Thereby, the label is obtained by keeping the theme with the maximum of probability computed at the theme level. Then, two measures of confidence are proposed and described below.

The maximum of probability provides a good absolute measure of how confident we are on the labelling. However, if at least two theme probability measures have high values, then the maximum of probability is high but the confidence is low. Thus, another measure, called *margin*, is proposed.

The *margin* is defined as the difference between the two highest probability values. This measure allows to assess the superiority of one labelling on the second most important.

The final labels are then compared with the initial database, resulting in a map of changes. This map is weighted by the maximum of probability confidence measures in order to obtain a probability change map. Such image is a traditional useful asset for final manual correction and checking before irreversible database update.

3   Experiments on Simulated Data

Simulated data have been generated in order to study the behaviour of our proposed method, while remaining independent of the method used to characterize objects of the database on the image (i.e. features). Simulated data are first introduced. Then, three experiments are described and analyzed. The first one is performed on ideal data and the next ones are designed to analyze the robustness of the method with respect to three possible degradations, the low discrimination between themes, the lack of homogeneity in a theme and the blur that can be present in the data.

3.1   Simulated Data Description

Our simulated data are composed of two parts, first of *initial database* (to be updated), secondly of the *simulated image* (used to update the database). For convenience of the presentation, the database is modelled by an image, figuring the labels and the objects associated with each label. Each object is coloured according to his theme. In the simulated image, each object has a single feature, its gray-level, the same as in the database image (Figure 2a-b). The initial database is composed of one hundred objects, equally distributed in ten themes. Objects are dispatched on a regular grid (Figure 2a).

Light gray-blue areas surrounding the image (columns 0 & 11 and lines 0 & 11) model unlabelled areas that may exist. The simulated image is composed of one hundred and one objects of various sizes (Figure 2b). Several changes are introduced between the initial database and the simulated image (Figure 2c). Four objects disappear while fifteen appear. Objects of each line change in the same way in increasing proportion from 10% to 100%. Four experiments have been set up. The method is first applied to the simulated data, without any modification, and provides a reference for the next experiments. Then, three different kinds of modifications are introduced on the simulated image to assess how the method is robust to: similar themes, inhomogeneous themes, and blurred data.

3.2   Ideal Condition

The three levels of inspection described in Section 2 are first evaluated on the default configuration (Figure 2b).

First, the object level inspection is performed on each object of each theme of the database. Recall and precision are measured for each object. Since each

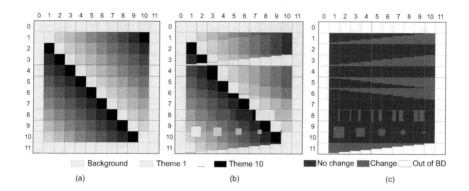

Fig. 2. (a) Initial database (to be updated), (b) Simulated image (used to update the database) and (c) Ground truth change map. Each cell (i, j) is 100×100 pixels.

theme is represented by a single gray-level, recall is always equal to 1 in this case. However, precision may not be equal to 1. For instance, in case of object size decrease (e.g., any cell of line 1), there is a confusion between the current object theme and the substituting theme. It results in lower precision values, ranging from 0.21 to 0.6, depending on the global surface of the replacing theme (from 30% to less than 10%, respectively).

Then, theme level inspection is performed. Results of this step allow to correctly classify each theme despite some confusion at the object level.

Next, the database level inspection is performed. Results are shown in Figure 3. One can notice all themes are correctly retrieved. The background is merged with theme 1 since no background class is learned in our method and its gray-level is the closest of this theme. However, the two confidence measures (b) and (c) have low values in this area. Moreover, confidence measures show variation between different themes, enhancing their variable surfaces of change. Thus, our probability change map (Figure 4 a) allows to correctly separate true changes from less confident areas. An additional active learning step using manual inputs would allow to provide a binary map of changes [4].

Finally, a precision metric is introduced in order to provide quantitative assessments. First, the probability change map is classified into three classes: change, no-change, and out of BD (Figure 5 f). The classification is simply retrieved by introducing two thresholds on the probability change value. In next experiments, the two thresholds have been arbitrary fixed to -0.2 and 0.2. Then, those classification is compared with the ground truth (Figure 2 c). Under these ideal conditions, the precision is equal to 100%.

3.3   Similar Themes

This second experiment aims to study the ability of our method to separate two themes with almost similar appearance. For this purpose, three themes have been selected: themes 2, 3 and 4 whose gray-scale values are 204, 179 and 153,

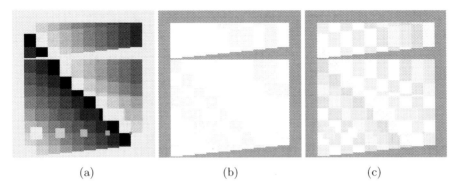

(a)   (b)   (c)

Fig. 3. (a) Theme fusion (one gray-scale per theme), (b) Maximum of probabilities and (c) Margin (orange:0→white:1). Each pixel is correctly labelled (a), except in surrounding areas where the two confident measures (b & c) have low values.

respectively. Then, the value of theme 3 is iteratively changed with values ranging from 169 to 153, so as to come closer to theme 4 (in this last case, themes 3 and 4 are identical).

The classification process manages to separate the two themes 3 and 4, except when they are equal. Figure 4 (b) shows the final probability change map result when theme 3 is close to theme 4 (gray-scale value:154) and (c) when themes 3 and 4 are identical. Results show that our method is able to deal with similar appearance themes, through the introduction of a confusion measure in addition to the supposed label. The precision is about 86% when themes 3 and 4 are identical, and of 100% otherwise.

3.4   Inhomogeneous Theme

The purpose of the third experiment is to assess whether our method is sensitive to non homogeneous objects. Some objects may indeed have two or more distinct appearances. This often happens in geographical databases when an object may include several entities of varying characteristic. Thus, we select the same three themes as previously, and apply two different gray values to pixels of theme 3 objects.

Two different configurations have been tested: one with two gray values between theme 2 and 4 (166 and 191), and one with two values out of these ranges (140 and 217). Then, proportion of the two colors ranges from 10 to 50%.

Results show that our training point selection method is able to efficiently deal with the inhomogeneity of the theme even if a few percent of the theme is different of the rest of the theme. Moreover, the Gaussian kernel of the SVM allows to differentiate theme 3, even if not linearly separable from the other themes. Finally, the probability change map (Figure 4d) allows to mostly discriminate changing / not changing areas (*blue/red* regions). The precision is about 99% for proportion of 10% in the two different configurations, and of 100% otherwise.

3.5 Blurred Data

Since edge between objects are often unclear in remote sensing data, the last experimentation aims to assess our method on blurred data. Thus, a Gaussian filter, with a standard deviation (σ) ranging from 5 to 100 pixels, has been applied on the simulated image.

In this case, classification at the object level and fusion at theme level are both slightly confused. However, the training point selection method allows to minimize this effect. The probability change map for a σ of 10 pixels, shown on Figure 4 (e), allows anyway to determine the majority of real changes. Results precision range from 88% ($\sigma = 100$ pixels) to 98% ($\sigma = 5$ pixels), assessing the efficiency of the method.

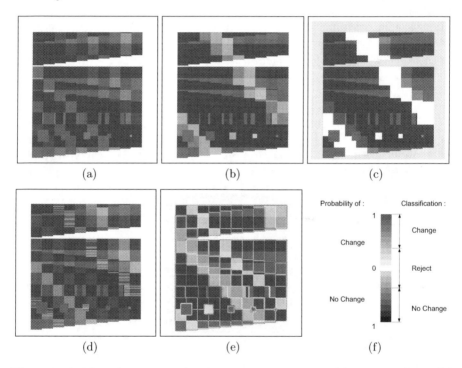

Fig. 4. Probability change maps for the various experiments: (a) Ideal condition, (b) and (c) Similar theme, (d) Inhomogeneous theme and (e) Blurred data. Dark blue cells correspond to areas that are likely not to have changed, whereas red ones indicate the most probable changes. White areas show undefined decisions. (f) show the color map and the thresholds for change / no change classification and a reject class corresponding to area out of the database has been also added.

4 Application to Geographical Database Update

The hierarchical method is applied on remote sensing data in order to update two different land cover databases. Very high satellite imagery is used as input.

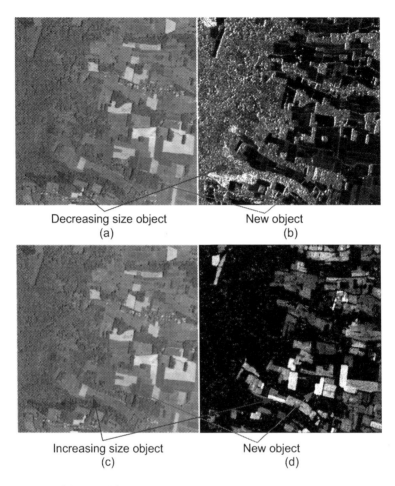

Fig. 5. Images (a) and (c) show the image used for change detection and the old database objects in green. Images (b) and (d) are giving the probability of the two themes Douglas and bread wheat respectively. The white part indicate a high probability. From these maps and initials databases the changes can be deduced and are indicated with the arrows.

Two databases are inspected in our study. First, the French Forestry Database is composed of about fifty themes. We focus here on the Theme *Douglas fir closed forest*. The second one describes the French agricultural crops (about thirty different themes). The Theme *bread wheat* is studied here. These two themes have been selected since they are representative of land-cover classes that should at least yearly monitored. For forested areas, both private companies and national authorities are highly interested in biomass estimation, deforestation or in assessing the impact of meteorological events. In case of agricultural themes, urban sprawl surveillance and crop diversity respect monitoring for sustainable development are among the main straightforward applications of such change detection work-flow. A very high resolution optical satellite image, acquired by the Pléiades sensor in August 2012, has been used to update those databases (Figure 5 a & c, South-West of France). Images are composed of four spectral bands (red, green, blue and near-infrared) with a 0.5 m resolution.

Classification is computed using four spectral features (the four channels) and two texture features, derived from the spectral ones : (1) the entropy of the histogram of gradient directions [16] and (2) a dense SIFT descriptor is computed, and the first three components of the principal component analysis (PCA) are kept [8].

The mean of the probability estimated for the *Douglas fir closed forest* theme are shown on Figure 5b, and the mean values for the *bread wheat* theme are depicted in Figure 5d. The forest theme is composed of two objects, so that results on this theme are more noisy than results on the crops theme (composed of 7 objects).

Nevertheless, our training point selection and hierarchical inspection have allowed to correctly discriminate those themes despite existing changes between initial databases and the image. Indeed, several objects have decreasing size, but do not compromise the classification result. Conversely, newer objects are correctly detected.

5   Conclusion

Since geographical databases need to be quickly and inexpensively updated, automatic methods, efficient at large-scales, have to be developed. In this paper, we have proposed a hierarchical inspection method that allows to compute a change probability map from an old database using a new image at equivalent resolution. This method is based on a carefully designed per object training point selection and a generic decision fusion, that can be applied on various datasets. Our methodology was first assessed on simulated data. Finally, we successfully applied the method on real remote sensing data and land cover databases. Since our method remains independent to any characterisation procedure, it can be straightforwardly applied on various databases and datasets. In addition, the proposed workflow offers a suitable basis for further extensions in geographical database analysis and processing. Therefore, in future works, we will work on the database update process and on transfer learning. This should allow to both deal with large datasets and propose land-cover classifications in countries where no database exists. Thereafter, our method is planned to be improved by introducing a feature selection step at the object level step, allowing to automatically adapt the process to the nature of the classified objects.

References

1. Bruzzone, L., Bovolo, F.: A Novel Framework for the Design of Change-Detection Systems for Very-High-Resolution Remote Sensing Images. Proceedings of the IEEE 101(3), 609–630 (2013)

2. Buttner, G., et al.: Corine Land Cover update 2000. Technical guidelines. European Environment Agency, Copenhagen (2002)
3. Champion, N., Boldo, D., Pierrot-Deseilligny, M., Stamon, G.: 2D building change detection from high resolution satellite imagery: A two-step hierarchical method based on 3D invariant primitives. PRL 31(10), 1138–1147 (2010)
4. Demir, B., Minello, L., Bruzzone, L.: An Effective Strategy to Reduce the Labeling Cost in the Definition of Training Sets by Active Learning (2013)
5. Forman, G.: An extensive empirical study of feature selection metrics for text classification. JMLR 3, 1289–1305 (2003)
6. Gomez-Chova, L., et al.: A review of kernel methods in remote sensing data analysis. In: Optical Remote Sensing, pp. 171–206. Springer, Heidelberg (2011)
7. Goyette, N., Jodoin, P.-M., Porikli, F., Konrad, J., Ishwar, P.: A changedetection.net: A new change detection benchmark dataset. In: Proc. IEEE Workshop on Change Detection (CDW 2012) at CVPR 2012, Providence, RI (2012)
8. Le Bris, A.: Extraction of vineyards out of aerial ortho-image using texture information. In: ISPRS Annals of Photogrammetry, Remote Sensing and the Spatial Information Sciences, Melbourne, Australia (2012)
9. Marcal, A., Borges, J., Gomes, J., Pinto Da Costa, J.: Land cover update by supervised classification of segmented ASTER images. IJRS 26(7), 1347–1362 (2005)
10. Miller, O., Pikaz, A., Averbuch, A.: Objects based change detection in a pair of gray-level images. PR 38(11), 1976–1992 (2005)
11. Nemmour, H., Chibani, Y.: Change detector combination in remotely sensed imagery. In: Advanced Concepts for Intelligent Vision Systems Conference, August 31-September 3, pp. 373–380. ACIVS, Brussels (2004)
12. Petitjean, F., Inglada, J., Ganarski, P.: Satellite image time series analysis under time warping. IEEE TGRS 50(8), 3081–3095 (2012)
13. Radke, R.J., Andra, S., Al-Kofahi, O., Roysam, B.: Image change detection algorithms: a systematic survey. IEEE TIP 14(3), 294–307 (2005)
14. Robin, A., Moisan, L., Hegarat-Mascle, S.: An a-contrario approach for subpixel change detection in satellite imagery. IEEE TPAMI 32(11), 1977–1993 (2010)
15. Schölkopf, B., Smola, A.J.: Learning with kernels: support vector machines, regularization, optimization and beyond. The MIT Press (2002)
16. Trias-Sanz, R., Stamon, G., Louchet, J.: Using colour, texture, and hierarchical segmentation for high-resolution remote sensing. ISPRS Journal of Photogrammetry and Remote Sensing 63(2), 156–168 (2008)
17. Wu, T.F., Lin, C.J., Weng, R.C.: Probability estimates for multi-class classification by pairwise coupling. JMLR 5, 975–1005 (2004)

Small Target Detection Improvement in Hyperspectral Image

Tao Lin, Julien Marot, and Salah Bourennane

Institut Fresnel / CNRS-UMR 7249
Ecole Centrale Marseille, Aix-Marseille Université
13013 MARSEILLE, France

Abstract. Target detection is an important issue in the HyperSpectral Image (HSI) processing field. However, current spectral-identification-based target detection algorithms are sensitive to the noise and most denoising algorithms cannot preserve small targets, therefore it is necessary to design a robust detection algorithm that can preserve small targets. This paper utilizes the recently proposed multidimensional wavelet packet transform with multiway Wiener filter (MWPT-MWF) to improve the target detection efficiency of HSI with small targets in the noise environment. The performances of the our method are exemplified using simulated and real-world HSI.

Keywords: Hyperspectral image, small target detection, multiway Wiener Filter.

1 Introduction

HSI consists of spatial locations and spectral signatures [4]. The additional spectral signature information makes it a suitable tool for target detection in many military and civilian applications, such as military vehicle detection and mine detection [15]. However, the HSI is always impaired by noise from radiation, atmospheric scattering and thermal noise in the sensor instrument [10], which can degrade the detection performances, therefore it is necessary to use denoising techniques for improving the detection efficiencies.

The classical denoising methods rearrange the HSI into a matrix whose columns contain the spectral signatures of all the pixels and principal component analysis (PCA) is used to estimate the signal subspace [17]. These methods own the convenience of using matrix algebra, however they neglect the HSI data structure which also contains useful information. To preserve the data structure, a multiway Wiener filter (MWF) [3, 12, 13, 16] is proposed to process a HSI as a whole entity based on TUCKER3 decomposition [7, 8]. In MWF, the filter in each mode is computed as a function of the filters in other modes, which reflects its capability in integrally utilizing the information in each mode of the multidimensional data.

Though MWF preserves the data structure of HSI, it also has some negative side effects in preserving small targets in the denoising process. In fact,

J. Blanc-Talon et al. (Eds.): ACIVS 2013, LNCS 8192, pp. 460–469, 2013.

MWF is essentially an optimal low-pass filter while small targets are high frequency signals in Fourier basis, therefore MWF might remove small targets in the denoising process. A multidimensional wavelet packet transform with multidimensional Wiener filter (MWPT-MWF) is recently proposed to reduce noise in a jointly filtering component way [14]. It decomposes the HSI into different coefficient tensors (components) by wavelet packet transform [6], and jointly filter each component by MWF. In [14], we have discussed the SNR improvement performance of MWPT-MWF. In the subsequent study, we find MWPT-MWF also performs well in preserving small targets in the denoising process. In fact, since large target and small target are separated into different components, the latter can be preserved in the denoising process.

Since small target detection is an important issue in the HSI processing field [1, 11], in this paper, MWPT-MWF is used to reduce noise in HSI with small targets and hence improve the target detection performances in the noise environment. The experiments of simulated and real-world images are given to present the performances of target detection after denoising by MWPT-MWF.

The remainder of the paper is as follows: Section 2 introduces some basic knowledge about the multilinear algebra. Section 3 introduces the signal model. Section 4 shows how to use MWF to jointly filter the data component tensor. Section 5 presents some experimental results and finally section 6 concludes this paper.

2   Multilinear Algebra Tools

2.1 n-mode Unfolding

$\mathbf{X}_n \in \mathbb{R}^{I_n \times M_n}$ denotes the n-mode unfolding matrix [5] of a tensor $\mathcal{X} \in \mathbb{R}^{I_1 \times \dots \times I_N}$, where $M_n = I_{n+1} \dots I_1 I_N \dots I_{n-1}$. The columns of $\mathbf{X}_n$ are the I_n-dimensional vectors obtained from $\mathcal{X}$ by varying index i_n while keeping the other indices fixed. Here, we define the n-mode rank K_n as the n-mode unfolding matrix rank, *i.e.*, $K_n = \text{rank}(\mathbf{X}_n)$.

2.2 n-mode Product

The n-mode product [5] is defined as the product between a data tensor $\mathcal{X} \in \mathbb{R}^{I_1 \times \dots \times I_N}$ and a matrix $\mathbf{B} \in \mathbb{R}^{J \times I_n}$ in mode n. It is denoted by $\mathcal{C} = \mathcal{X} \times_n \mathbf{B}$, whose entries are given by $c_{i_1 \dots i_{n-1} j i_{n+1} \dots i_N} \triangleq \sum_{i_n=1}^{I_n} x_{i_1 \dots i_{n-1} i_n i_{n+1} \dots i_N} b_{j i_n}$ where $\mathcal{C} \in \mathbb{R}^{I_1 \times \dots \times I_{n-1} \times J \times \dots \times I_N}$

3   Signal Model

A noisy HSI is modeled as a tensor $\mathcal{R} \in \mathbb{R}^{I_1 \times I_2 \times I_3}$ resulting from a pure HSI $\mathcal{X} \in \mathbb{R}^{I_1 \times I_2 \times I_3}$ impaired by an additive noise $\mathcal{N} \in \mathbb{R}^{I_1 \times I_2 \times I_3}$. The tensor $\mathcal{R}$ can be expressed as:

$$\mathcal{R} = \mathcal{X} + \mathcal{N} \tag{1}$$

In this paper, only the thermal noise is considered, which means that the noise is modeled as independent white Gaussian noise with noise variance σ.

4   Noise Reduction by Joint Component Filtering

4.1   Multidimensional Wavelet Packet Transform

By performing wavelet packet transform (WPT) in each mode, the multidimensional wavelet packet transform (MWPT) can be written in tensor form as:

$$\mathcal{C}^R = \mathcal{R} \times_1 \mathbf{W}_1 \times_2 \mathbf{W}_2 \times_3 \mathbf{W}_3 \tag{2}$$

and the reconstruction can be written as:

$$\mathcal{R} = \mathcal{C}^R \times_1 \mathbf{W}_1^T \times_2 \mathbf{W}_2^T \times_3 \mathbf{W}_3^T \tag{3}$$

where $\mathbf{W}_n \in \mathbb{R}^{I_n \times I_n}, n = 1, 2$ indicate the wavelet packet transform matrices. When the transform level vector is $\mathbf{l} = [l_1, l_2, l_3]^T$, where $l_n \geq 0$ denotes the wavelet packet transform level in mode n, the coefficient tensor $\mathcal{C}^{\mathcal{R}}_{\mathbf{l},\mathbf{m}}$, which is also called a component in this paper, of scale $\mathbf{m} = [m_1, m_2, m_3]$, where $0 \leq m_n \leq 2^{l_k} - 1$, can be extracted by:

$$\mathcal{C}^{\mathcal{R}}_{\mathbf{l},\mathbf{m}} = \mathcal{C}^R \times_1 \mathbf{E}_{m_1} \times_2 \mathbf{E}_{m_2} \times_3 \mathbf{E}_{m_3} \tag{4}$$

and the corresponding inverse process is:

$$\mathcal{C}^R = \sum_{m_1} \sum_{m_2} \sum_{m_3} \mathcal{C}^{\mathcal{R}}_{\mathbf{l},\mathbf{m}} \times_1 \mathbf{E}_{m_1}^T \times_2 \mathbf{E}_{m_2}^T \times_3 \mathbf{E}_{m_3}^T \tag{5}$$

where the extraction operator $\mathbf{E}_{m_n}$ is defined as:

$$\mathbf{E}_{m_n} = [\mathbf{0}_1, \mathbf{I}_{\frac{I_n}{2^{l_n}} \times \frac{I_n}{2^{l_n}}}, \mathbf{0}_2] \in \mathbb{R}^{I_n/2^{l_n} \times I_n} \tag{6}$$

where $\mathbf{0}_1$ is a zero matrix with size $\frac{I_n}{2^{l_n}} \times \frac{m_n I_n}{2^{l_n}}$ and $\mathbf{0}_2$ is a zero matrix with size $\frac{I_n}{2^{l_n}} \times \frac{(2^{l_n}-1-m)I_n}{2^{l_n}}$.

4.2   Joint Component Filtering

As proposed in [14], the signal coefficient tensor $\mathcal{C}^{\mathcal{X}}_{\mathbf{l},\mathbf{m}}$ can be estimated by filtering the noisy data coefficient tensor $\mathcal{C}^{\mathcal{R}}_{\mathbf{l},\mathbf{m}}$ with MWF.

$$\hat{\mathcal{C}}^{\mathcal{X}}_{\mathbf{l},\mathbf{m}} = \mathcal{C}^{\mathcal{R}}_{\mathbf{l},\mathbf{m}} \times_1 \mathbf{H}_{1,\mathbf{m}} \times_2 \mathbf{H}_{2,\mathbf{m}} \times_3 \mathbf{H}_{3,\mathbf{m}} \tag{7}$$

where $\mathbf{H}_{n,\mathbf{m}}$ is the mode-n MWF filter:

$$\mathbf{H}_{n,\mathbf{m}} = \mathbf{V}^{(n)}_{s,\mathbf{m}} \mathbf{\Lambda}^{\gamma}_{\mathbf{m}} \left[\mathbf{\Lambda}^{\Gamma}_{\mathbf{m}} + \sigma_n^{\Gamma^2} \mathbf{I}_{K_n} \right]^{-1} \mathbf{V}^{(n)}_{s,\mathbf{m}}{}^T \tag{8}$$

where $\mathbf{V}^{(n)}_{s,\mathbf{m}}$ is the n-mode signal subspace basis, $\mathbf{\Lambda}^{\gamma}_{\mathbf{m}}$ and $\mathbf{\Lambda}^{\Gamma}_{\mathbf{m}}$ are the eigenvalues of $\gamma^{(n)}_{RR} = E \left[\mathbf{C}^{\mathcal{R}}_n \mathbf{q}^{(n)} \mathbf{C}^{\mathcal{R}}_n{}^T \right]$ and $\Gamma^{(n)}_{RR} = E \left[\mathbf{C}^{\mathcal{R}}_n \mathbf{Q}^{(n)} \mathbf{C}^{\mathcal{R}}_n{}^T \right]$ respectively, and $\sigma_n^{\Gamma^2}$

is the n-mode noise variance which can be estimated as the mean of the $I_n - K_n$ smallest eigenvalues of $\Gamma_{RR}^{(n)}$ with K_n the rank of $\gamma_{RR}^{(n)}$.

After each signal coefficient tensor being estimated, the signal estimate can be obtained by:

$$\hat{\mathcal{X}} = \hat{\mathcal{C}}^{\mathcal{X}} \times_1 \mathbf{W}_1^T \times_2 \mathbf{W}_2^T \times_3 \mathbf{W}_3^T \tag{9}$$

where

$$\hat{\mathcal{C}}^{\mathcal{X}} = \sum_{m_1} \sum_{m_2} \sum_{m_3} \hat{\mathcal{C}}_{1,\mathbf{m}}^{\mathcal{X}} \times_1 \mathbf{E}_{m_1}^T \times_2 \mathbf{E}_{m_2}^T \times_3 \mathbf{E}_{m_3}^T \tag{10}$$

Notice that the large and small targets are separated into the approximation and detail coefficient tensors respectively, which makes it possible to avoid removing the small target in filtering noise. Therefore, MWPT-MWF outperforms MWF in preserving the small targets.

5   Experimental Results

In the experiments, MWPT-MWF and MWF are compared in the aspect of improving target detection performances. The results obtained both on simulated and real-world data are presented in this section. The HSI is modeled as a three-dimensional tensor, where the first two dimensions indicate the spatial field and the third dimension indicates the spectral bands. Wavelet db3 is used to do MWPT-MWF with transform levels $[l_1, l_2, l_3] = [1, 1, 0]$.

SAM detector [9] is used in the experiments to detect targets in the image. As Spectral Angle Mapper (SAM) does not require the characterization of background, it can avoid the inaccuracy of the comparison result caused by the noise covariance matrix estimation error. The SAM detector can be expressed as:

$$\mathrm{T_{SAM}}(\mathbf{x}) = \frac{\mathbf{s}^T \mathbf{x}}{(\mathbf{s}^T \mathbf{s})^{1/2} (\mathbf{x}^T \mathbf{x})^{1/2}} \tag{11}$$

where $\mathbf{s}$ is the reference spectrum, $\mathbf{x}$ is the pixel spectrum. To assess the performances of detection, the probability of detection (Pd) is defined as:

$$\mathrm{Pd} = \frac{\sum_i^{n_s} N_i^{rd}}{\sum_i^{n_s} N_i} \tag{12}$$

and the probability of false alarm (Pfa) is defined as:

$$\mathrm{Pfa} = \frac{\sum_i^{n_s} N_i^{fd}}{\sum_i^{n_s} (I_1 \times I_2 - N_i)} \tag{13}$$

where n_s is the number of spectral signatures, N_i the number of pixels with spectral signature i, N_i^{rd} the number of rightly detected pixels, and N_i^{fd} the number of falsely detected pixels.

5.1   Results on Simulated Data

The simulated data is generated with the spectral signatures presented in Fig. 1 and it has 100 rows, 100 columns and 220 spectral bands, which can be modeled as a $100 \times 100 \times 220$ tensor. There are six target types and three different spatial sizes 9×9, 3×3, 1×1 of each type, which are shown in Fig. 2(a). These targets are mixed to the background by using the linear mixing model with target abundance being 80%. The band 6 of the noisy image with SNR=20dB is shown Fig. 2(b), from which one can see that the small targets are almost disappeared in the noise.

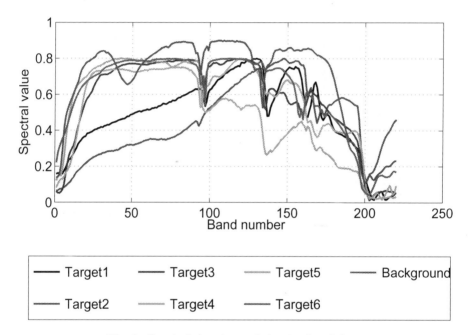

Fig. 1. Spectral signatures of the simulated data

Fig. 2(c) shows the detection result under Pfa $= 10^{-4}$ after denoising by MWF. In this figure, it is obvious that most of the 1×1 targets are not detected and there are two false alarm neighbors with the detected 1×1 targets. On the contrast, the detection result after denoising by MWPT-MWF is much better. The 2×2 targets are all detected and only one 1×1 target is dismissed. The experiment result in Fig. 2 implies that MWPT-MWF owns the capability in preserving the small targets in the denoising process.

To make the experimental results more convincing and show the subtle changes of the detection results, the receiver operating characteristic (ROC) values are given in Table 1 in the noise environments from 15dB to 25dB. In 15dB, Pd after denoising by MWPT-MWF is much greater than that by MWF under the same

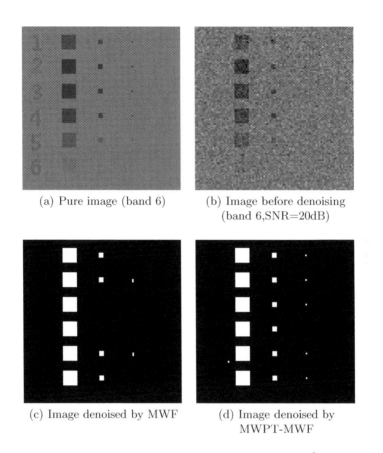

(a) Pure image (band 6)

(b) Image before denoising (band 6,SNR=20dB)

(c) Image denoised by MWF

(d) Image denoised by MWPT-MWF

Fig. 2. Detection results of HYDICE, Pfa=10^{-4}

Table 1. ROC values of MWF and MWPT-MWF for the simulated HSI

Pfa	Pd of MWF			Pd of MWPT-MWF		
	15dB	20dB	25dB	15dB	20dB	25dB
0.0001	0.5458	0.9597	0.9963	0.7125	0.9982	1.0000
0.0002	0.5714	0.9597	0.9963	0.7271	0.9982	1.0000
0.0003	0.5897	0.9597	0.9963	0.7381	0.9982	1.0000
0.0005	0.6190	0.9597	0.9982	0.7637	1.0000	1.0000
0.0008	0.6630	0.9597	0.9982	0.7821	1.0000	1.0000
0.0013	0.7088	0.9615	0.9982	0.8004	1.0000	1.0000
0.0022	0.7271	0.9615	0.9982	0.8132	1.0000	1.0000
0.0036	0.7601	0.9615	0.9982	0.8462	1.0000	1.0000
0.0060	0.8059	0.9689	0.9982	0.8956	1.0000	1.0000
0.0100	0.9011	0.9945	1.0000	0.9908	1.0000	1.0000

Pfa. From the comparison of ROC in Table 1, it shows that MWPT-MWF can improve the target detection performances more greatly than MWF can in different noise environments.

5.2   Results on Real-World Data

One high spatial resolution HSI HYDICE [2] is denoised by MWF and MWPT-MWF to compare their target detection improvement ability in noise environment. The HYDICE image contains 100 rows, 100 columns and 158 spectral bands, which is modeled as a $100 \times 100 \times 158$ tensor. Three types of target spectral signatures are considered, and these targets are mixed to the background with respect to the linear mixing model when target abundance is 80%;

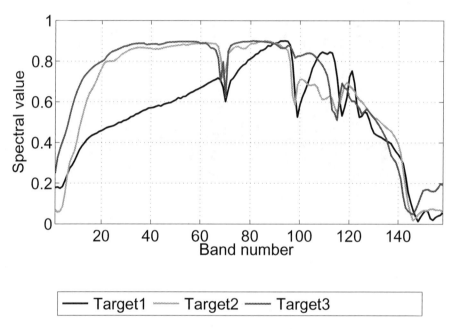

Fig. 3. Spectral signatures of targets

Fig. 4(a) and Fig. 4(d) are the pure and noisy images in band 50. The targets are placed in the field, beside the road and in the trees respectively to contain the usual target situations in HSI. The detection results after denoising by MWF and MWPT-MWF are shown in Fig. 4(c) and Fig. 4(d) respectively. In Fig. 4(d), 1×1 targets in the field and beside the road are detected. The only dismissed 1×1 target is in the trees, which is always a difficult situation to detect small target in it. On the contrast, in Fig. 4(c) all the 1×1 targets are dismissed and a 2×2 target in the trees is also lost. The comparison between Fig. 4(c) and Fig. 4(d) shows that MWPT-MWF owns better capability in preserving small targets than MWF as expected.

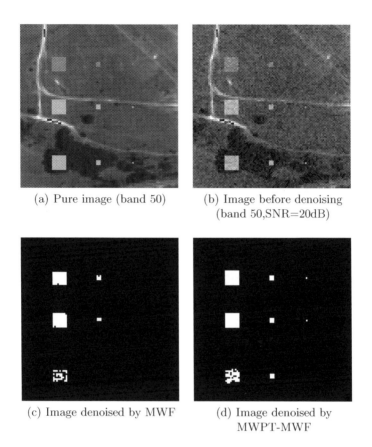

(a) Pure image (band 50)

(b) Image before denoising (band 50,SNR=20dB)

(c) Image denoised by MWF

(d) Image denoised by MWPT-MWF

Fig. 4. Detection results of HYDICE, Pfa=10^{-4}

Table 2. ROC values of MWF and MWPT-MWF for HYDICE

Pfa	Pd of MWF			Pd of MWPT-MWF		
	15dB	20dB	25dB	15dB	20dB	25dB
0.0001	0.6593	0.8828	1.0000	0.7289	0.8851	1.0000
0.0002	0.6593	0.9048	1.0000	0.7399	0.9084	1.0000
0.0003	0.6630	0.9121	1.0000	0.7546	0.9451	1.0000
0.0005	0.6703	0.9121	1.0000	0.7912	0.9634	1.0000
0.0008	0.6740	0.9487	1.0000	0.7985	0.9670	1.0000
0.0013	0.6777	0.9634	1.0000	0.8315	0.9707	1.0000
0.0022	0.6850	0.9780	1.0000	0.8498	0.9853	1.0000
0.0036	0.6923	1.0000	1.0000	0.8755	0.9927	1.0000
0.0060	0.7106	1.0000	1.0000	0.9341	0.9927	1.0000
0.0100	1.0000	1.0000	1.0000	1.0000	1.0000	1.0000

Apart from the binary target detection results in Fig. 4, to better compare the performances of MWF and MWPT-MWF, the ROC values are also presented in Table 2. As expected, the Pd of MWPT-MWF is better than that of MWF in the same Pfa. The comparison of the ROC values implies that MWPT-MWF performs better than MWF in improving the target detection result of the real-world data as well.

6   Conclusion

The performances of MWF and MWPT-MWF in improving the target detection in the noise environment are discussed in this paper. Though MWF performs well in reducing noise in HSI, it might also remove targets in the image, especially when the target is small. The reason leading to this phenomenon is that MWF treats directly HSI as a whole entity by filtering each mode of the HSI in a Wiener filter like way. Since the energy of the small target is thin, it is easy to be removed in the filtering process. However, MWPT-MWF decompose the HSI into several components (coefficient tensors) and filter each one by MWF. As small and large targets are separated into different components, the small ones can be preserved in the filtering process. This is why MWPT-MWF performs better than MWF in improving target detection performance when there exist small targets in the image.

Simulated and real-world HSIs are considered in the experiments to compare the performances of MWF and MWPT-MWF in improving target detection in the noise environment. The experimental results highlight that MWPT-MWF outperforms MWF in improving the target detection results in the presence of small targets.

References

1. Acito, N., Diani, M., Corsini, G.: A new algorithm for robust estimation of the signal subspace in hyperspectral images in the presence of rare signal components. IEEE Trans. Geosci. Remote Sens. 47(11), 3844–3856 (2009)
2. Basedow, R.W., Carmer, D.C., Anderson, M.E.: Hydice system: Implementation and performance. In: SPIE's 1995 Symposium on OE/Aerospace Sensing and Dual Use Photonics, pp. 258–267. International Society for Optics and Photonics (1995)
3. Bourennane, S., Fossati, C., Cailly, A.: Improvement of classification for hyperspectral images based on tensor modeling. IEEE Geosci. Remote Sens. Lett. 7(4), 801–805 (2010)
4. Bourennane, S., Fossati, C., Cailly, A.: Improvement of target detection based on tensorial modelling (2010)
5. Cichocki, A., Zdunek, R., Phan, A., Amari, S.: Nonnegative matrix and tensor factorizations: applications to exploratory multi-way data analysis and blind source separation. Wiley, New Jersey (2009)
6. Daubechies, I.: Ten lectures on wavelets. SIAM (2006)
7. De Lathauwer, L., De Moor, B., Vandewalle, J.: A multilinear singular value decomposition. SIAM J. Matrix Anal. Appl. 21(4), 1253–1278 (2000)

8. De Lathauwer, L., De Moor, B., Vandewalle, J.: On the best rank-1 and rank-(r1, r2,..., rn) approximation of higher-order tensors. SIAM J. Matrix Anal. Appl. 21(4), 1324–1342 (2000)

9. Jin, X., Paswaters, S., Cline, H.: A comparative study of target detection algorithms for hyperspectral imagery. In: SPIE Defense, Security, and Sensing, p. 73341W–73341W. International Society for Optics and Photonics (2009)

10. Kerekes, J., Baum, J.: Hyperspectral imaging system modeling. Linc. Lab. J. 14(1), 117–130 (2003)

11. Kuybeda, O., Malah, D., Barzohar, M.: Rank estimation and redundancy reduction of high-dimensional noisy signals with preservation of rare vectors. IEEE Trans. Signal Process. 55(12), 5579–5592 (2007)

12. Letexier, D., Bourennane, S.: Noise removal from hyperspectral images by multidimensional filtering. IEEE Trans. Geosci. Remote Sens. 46(7), 2061–2069 (2008)

13. Letexier, D., Bourennane, S., Blanc-Talon, J.: Nonorthogonal tensor matricization for hyperspectral image filtering. IEEE Geosci. Remote Sens. Lett. 5(1), 3–7 (2008)

14. Lin, T., Bourennane, S.: Hyperspectral image processing by jointly filtering wavelet component tensor. IEEE Trans. Geosci. Remote Sens. 51(6), 3529–3541 (2013)

15. Manolakis, D., Marden, D., Shaw, G.A.: Hyperspectral image processing for automatic target detection applications. Linc. Lab. J. 14(1), 79–116 (2003)

16. Muti, D., Bourennane, S.: Multidimensional filtering based on a tensor approach. Signal Process. 85(12), 2338–2353 (2005)

17. Renard, N., Bourennane, S.: Improvement of target detection methods by multiway filtering. IEEE Trans. Geosci. Remote Sens. 46(8), 2407–2417 (2008)

The Objective Evaluation of Image Object Segmentation Quality

Ran Shi, King Ngi Ngan, and Songnan Li

Department of Electronic Engineering, The Chinese University of Hong Kong, Hong Kong
{rshi,knngan,snli}@ee.cuhk.edu.hk

Abstract. In this paper, a novel objective quality metric is proposed for individual object segmentation in images. We analyze four types of segmentation errors, and verify experimentally that besides quantity, area and contour, the distortion of object content is another useful segmentation quality index. Our metric evaluates the similarity between ideal result and segmentation result by measuring these distortions. The metric has been tested on our subjectively-rated image segmentation database and demonstrated a good performance in matching subjective ratings.

Keywords: Object segmentation, Objective metric, Distortions.

1   Introduction

Object segmentation is an important prior processing step for a variety of applications, such as content-based image retrieval, image retargeting and image compression, etc. The object segmentation quality directly influences their performances. Human subjective quality judgment is a reliable approach to evaluate the object segmentation quality. However, the subjective evaluation is time-costing and cumbersome. Therefore, there is a great demand for designing objective metrics which can automatically evaluate segmentation quality and be in close agreement with human judgments.

F-measure is a classical and popular segmentation metric [1]. It compares segmentation results with manually labeled ground truths to find the mismatching regions. The mismatching regions are then classified as false positive and false negative ones, respectively. Two indexes called precision and recall are adopted to measure these two types of distortions, and they are combined in F-measure to evaluate the overall segmentation quality. In [2], Jaccard index was proposed, which used a region-merging strategy to measure segmentation accuracy. Like F-measure, Villegas and Marichal's metric [3] also classified segmentation errors into false positive and false negative ones. Distance information was introduced to weight these two types of errors. In [4], Erdem and Sankur adopted shape information as an empirical discrepancy measures. Fragmentation was introduced in [5] to measure discrepancy in terms of the quantity of objects. A new fuzzy Jaccard index is proposed in [6] to capture the intrinsic uncertainty in the edge positions in order to

J. Blanc-Talon et al. (Eds.): ACIVS 2013, LNCS 8192, pp. 470–479, 2013.
© Springer International Publishing Switzerland 2013

evaluate boundary accuracy. In [7, 18], Gelasca classified all possible segmentation errors into four different types: added region, added background, inside holes and border holes. Each type was assigned a weight which was derived from psychophysical experiments. Although this approach exploited perceptual information, it only used the area and distance information to describe segmentation errors. Furthermore, all these metrics mentioned above do not consider the distortions of the segmented object content.

In this paper, we propose a new objective quality metric to evaluate the subjective quality of the individual object segmentation. The proposed metric measures the similarity between the ground truth and segmentation result in four aspects: quantity, area, external contour and content. Section 2 describes them in detail. Experimental results are presented in Section 3. Finally, conclusion is drawn in Section 4.

2   Proposed Metric

For object segmentation, the image is partitioned into two segments, i.e., object and background. However, the segmented object may have more than one region. Suppose the segmented object consists of $\{R_1, R_2, ... R_n\}$, and $R_i \cap R_j = \varnothing$ for $i \neq j$. We group these regions into two sets:

$$R_{external-region} = \{R_i \mid R_i \cap R_{ground-truth} = \varnothing\} \tag{1}$$

$$R_{object-region} = \{R_j \mid R_j \cap R_{ground-truth} \neq \varnothing\} \tag{2}$$

where $R_{ground-truth}$ represents the ideal segmentation result as exemplified in Fig.1(a). Fig.1 (b) shows these two region sets in the segmentation result. The regions surrounded by red and blue lines are $R_{external-region}$ and $R_{object-region}$, respectively.

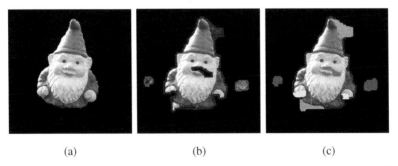

| (a) | (b) | (c) |

Fig. 1. Different kinds of regions and segmentation errors. (a) ground truth; (b) two kinds of regions; (c) four kinds of segmentation errors.

As aforementioned, in [7, 18] segmentation errors are classified into four types which is illustrated in Fig.1(c). Different types of segmentation errors distort the object differently. From Fig.1(c), we can observe that added regions (red) increase object's area and quantity; added background (green) increases object's area and changes object's external contour; border holes (yellow) decrease object's area and destroys object's external contour and content; inside hole (pink) decreases object's area and destroy content. A summary of these observations is given in Table 1. Our metric evaluates segmentation quality based on four aspects of the object, i.e., quantity, area, external contour and content. Higher metric score indicates better segmentation quality.

Table 1. The distortions produced by types of segmentation errors

	Quantity	Area	External Contour	Content
Added region	√	√		
Added background		√	√	
Border hole		√	√	√
Inside hole		√		√

2.1   The Quantity of Object

Number of objects in the segmentation result should be equal to that in the ground truth. In other words, a substantial disagreement of the object number can be used to indicate a large discrepancy [9]. For individual object segmentation, there is only one object. Since the human visual system (HVS) does not pay attention to very small errors [6, 8], those isolated points should not be treated as external regions. "Opening" and "Closing" operation (the mask is 3×3) is performed first on the segmentation result in order to remove isolated points and fill the very tiny holes. Then, we use the following equation to measure similarity in terms of the object quantity :

$$S_{quantity} = \frac{1}{1 + \dfrac{Area(R_{external-region})}{Area(R_{object-region})} \cdot card(R_{external-region})} \tag{3}$$

where $Area(\cdot)$ and $card(\cdot)$ is operation of computing the region area and quantity, respectively. Different from [5], we introduce relative sizes of added regions in Eq. (3) to replace the scaling parameters used in [5]. With this modification, larger area of added regions will lead to worse segmentation results.

2.2   The Area of Object

Area is another important index for segmentation quality measure. We use $R_{true-object}$ to denote the portion of object that has been correctly segmented.

The measure S_{area} is used to measure the area accuracy :

$$S_{area} = \frac{Area(R_{true-objcet})}{Area(R_{object-region} \cup R_{ground-truth})}$$

(4)

The above formula is like Jaccard Index [2]. Due to the area of added regions have been considered in Eq. (3), here we only consider the area variation caused by added background, border holes and inside holes.

2.3   The External Contour of Object

According to [7], segmentation quality will be quite different when errors are uniformly distributed along the object boundaries from that when errors concentrate in parts of the object boundaries. As shown in Fig.2, although the two pictures have the same area of added background, Fig.2 (a) has a better quality since its contour Fig.2 (b) maintains the shape of the ideal object contour.

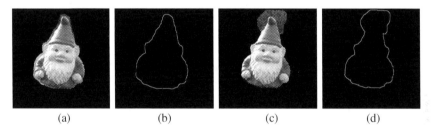

(a)   (b)   (c)   (d)

Fig. 2. Different kinds of object's external contour

According to the fuzzy set theory [6, 15], each pixel x is assigned two probabilities values, $f_{\Omega_G}(x)$ and $f_{\Omega_S}(x)$, Ω_G and Ω_S represent fuzzy sets for the ideal external contour and the segmented one, respectively. $f_{\Omega_G}(x)$ is the membership function of Ω_G, and is defined as :

$$f_{\Omega_G}(x) = \frac{refdis_G}{refdis_G + D_G(x)}$$

(5)

$$refdis_G = k \cdot length_G$$

(6)

where $D_G(x)$ is the shortest distance from x to the ideal external contour. k is a scaling value, and $refdis_G$ is a reference distance. $length_G$ is the diagonal of the ideal external contour's bounding box. If $D_G(x)$ is shorter than $refdis_G$, it means x has a high probability belonging to Ω_G. Furthermore, the probability of a pixel belonging to a contour is not only related to the distance between the pixel and the contour, but also related to the scale of the contour, or equivalently, the size of the object. Therefore, we introduce $refdis_G$ as a relative distance rather than using absolute distance as in [6], since $refdis_G$ is adaptive to different sizes of the object

The membership function $f_{\Omega_S}(x)$ of Ω_S can be similarly defined. We compare probability of elements in these two fuzzy sets to describe the similarity between the ideal contour and segmented contour:

$$S_{contour} = \frac{\sum\limits_{x} \min(f_{\Omega_G}(x), f_{\Omega_S}(x))}{\sum\limits_{x} \max(f_{\Omega_G}(x), f_{\Omega_S}(x))} \tag{7}$$

where $x \in R_{true-objcet} \oplus R_{ground-truth}$. From Eq. (7), we can see that for a good segmentation which maintains the shape of ideal contour, the two probabilities for each pixel should be similar, which can be satisfied by Fig. 2(b) and violated by Fig. 2(d).

The overall measure for the similarity of object region is defined as follows:

$$S_{object-region} = S_{area} \cdot S_{contour} \tag{8}$$

2.4   The Content of Object

Based on our observations on a subjective dataset to be introduced in Section 3, it is found that the segmented object without border holes or inside holes usually gets a higher subjective score than those with border holes or inside holes. As shown in Fig.3, the "cake" in the right image obtains a lower subjective score (1.04) than "sun flower" (2.08), even though it has a better external contour and smaller error area.

Fig. 3. The segmentation results of "sun flower" and "cake"

The reason is that the content information of object itself is lost due to border holes and inside holes, which makes the segmented object less recognizable. For example, in "sun flower", object itself is the yellow flower without green leaves. Subjects trend to prefer complete objects which can be easily recognized. We measure the completeness of object content in terms of area and texture :

$$S_{content} = S_{object-area} \cdot S_{object-texture} \tag{9}$$

Different from S_{area}, $S_{object-area}$ does not consider the error area of added background. It only measures the area variation which could lead to loss of object content. A lower value of $S_{object-area}$ indicates that the segmented object losses more content information. $S_{object-area}$ is given by

$$S_{object-area} = \frac{Area(R_{true-object})}{Area(R_{ground-truth})} \tag{10}$$

The texture information is crucial for object recognition [8]. We convert the original color image into a gray image. Then, Sobel operator is applied to this gray image. The magnitude of gradient values is used to approximate the texture information. $S_{object-texture}$ is defined as

$$S_{object-texture} = \frac{\sum Sobel(x)}{\sum Sobel(y)} \tag{11}$$

where pixel $x \in R_{true-object}$ and $y \in R_{ground-truth}$. A higher value of $S_{object-texture}$ indicates the segmented object could be easily recognized.

Finally, the overall objective quality metric by using spatial weighted pooling [10] for individual object segmentation is given as follows:

$$S_{overall} = \frac{\alpha \cdot S_{quantity} + S_{object-region} + \lambda \cdot S_{content}}{1+\alpha+\lambda} \tag{12}$$

where α and λ are balancing weights among three terms. The values of three parameters α, λ and k are determined by training as discussed in Section 3.

3   Experimental Results

Our dataset consists of a testing set and a training set. The testing set has 76 original images and 152 segmentation images which are generated by using Achanta's [11] and Rahtu's [12] segmentation algorithms. The training set has 18 original images and 18 segmentation images which are also generated by using the same segmentation algorithms. The original images are selected from Microsoft Research Asia salient object database (Image Set B). Each image includes only one object to be segmented. The ground truth is provided by Achanta [11]. One original image and its corresponding ground truth and segmentation results compose an image group. Since there are no prescribed standards for the subjective evaluation of object segmentation, we incorporate the simultaneous double stimulus for continuous evaluation (SDSCE) method and double-stimulus continuous quality-scale (DSCQS) method [13] to design our subjective assessment. The subjective assessment interface is shown in Fig.4. The original images are provided to help viewers to understand images' content. The viewers can press the "arrow button" to do the switchover among ground truths and segmentation results, and then they can select the subject ratings. The difference of the subjective assessment in this paper is the use of the absolute category rating (ACR) scale [19] which employs a five-grade discrete (5: excellent, 4: good, 3: fair, 2: poor, 1: bad) segmentation quality scale. In [17], the experimental data has demonstrated that there are no obvious overall statistical differences between different rating scales. Therefore, the five-grade discrete is employed to reduce the viewers' fatigue and make the subjective rating more distinguishable. Totally 16 subjects (10 males and 6 females, from 23 to 26 years old) participate in the subjective test to evaluate perceptual quality of each segmented image, where 8 viewers are experts in image processing and the others are not. Each viewer begins with a brief introduction about this subjective study and how to do the quality evaluation. During the subjective assessment, the first five image groups' assessments are treated as a training session which is used to stabilize the viewers' opinion. These images do not belong to testing set or training set, and their ratings are not taken into account in the results of the assessment. The subjective ratings are processed to calculate the Differential Mean Option Score (DMOS) which indicates the quality difference between the ground truth segmentation and the algorithm segmentation result. Outliers are rejected by a standard screening procedure [13]. The three parameters of proposed metric are automatically chosen by maximizing the Spearman Rank-Order Correlation Coefficients (SROCC) using the training set. The training result is $k = 0.03$, $\alpha = 0.5$ and $\lambda = 0.7$.

Fig. 4. The subjective evaluation interface

Following the Video Quality Expert Group's work [14], each metric score is mapped to $Q(x)$ firstly using the following fitting function to obtain a linear relationship between $Q(x)$ and the subjective scores:

$$Q(x) = \beta_1 \times (0.5 - \frac{1}{1 + \exp(\beta_2 \times (x - \beta_3))}) + \beta_4 \times x + \beta_5 \qquad (13)$$

To evaluate its performance, we use two common performance evaluation criteria, i.e., the Linear Correlation Coefficient (LCC) and the Spearman Rank-Order Correlation Coefficients (SROCC), which use Q(x) and DMOS as their inputs [16]. Our metric is compared against two popular image object segmentation quality metrics $F_\beta measure$ ($\beta = 0.3$) which is used in [11, 12] and Jaccard Index [2]. We also evaluate our metric's performance without $S_{content}$. The comparison results are shown in the Table 2:

Table 2. Overall performances of four different segmentation metrics

		$F_\beta measure$	Jaccard Index	Our (without $S_{content}$)	Our
76 images by	SROCC	0.74	0.80	0.80	**0.82**
Achanta	LCC	0.70	0.80	0.82	**0.84**
76 images by	SROCC	0.84	0.88	0.88	**0.88**
Rahtu	LCC	0.85	0.89	0.89	**0.91**
Overall 152	SROCC	0.81	0.87	0.87	**0.89**
images	LCC	0.82	0.86	0.87	**0.88**

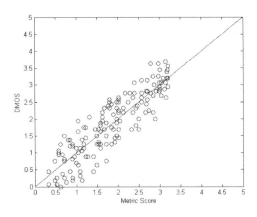

Fig. 5. Scatter plots of the proposed object segmentation quality metric on our dataset (after the nonlinear mapping)

From Table 2, we can see that our metric achieves higher SROCC and LCC with $S_{content}$. On the other hand, the experimental results demonstrate that the design of $S_{content}$ is reasonable. The object content is an important measure for segmentation quality evaluation. Fig. 5 shows the scatter plots of the proposed object segmentation quality metric on our databases. In the graph, each circle represents a test image (total 152 images). The vertical axis denotes the DMOS and the horizontal axis denotes the nonlinearly mapped metric outputs.

4   Conclusion

In this paper, we propose an objective quality metric for individual object segmentation in images. Our metric is designed based on describing four types of distortions. Relative size of added regions is considered to measure the quantity of object. We use fuzzy set theory to describe the similarity of object's contour, and introduce reference distance to adapt different sizes of the object. Meanwhile, the completeness of object content is treated as an important measure in our metric. The experimental results demonstrate that our metric has a good performance on our individual object segmentation dataset.

References

1. Powers, D.: Evaluation: From Precision, Recall and F-Factor to ROC, Informedne, Markedness & Correlation. Journal of Machine Learning Technologies 2(1), 37–63 (2011)
2. Ge, F., Wang, S., Liu, T.: New benchmark for image segmentation evaluation. Journal of Electronic Imaging 16(3), 33011 (2007)
3. Villegas, P., Marichal, X.: Perceptually-weighted evaluation criteria for segmentation masks in video sequences. IEEE Trans. Image Process 13(8), 1092–1103 (2004)
4. Erdem, C., Sankur, B.: Performance evaluation metrics for objectbased video segmentation. In: Proc. X Eur. Signal Process Conf., Tampere, Finland, vol. 2, pp. 917–920 (2000)
5. Strasters, K., Gebrands, J.: Three-dimensional image segmentation using a split, merge and group approach. Pattern Recognit. Lett. 12(5), 307–325 (1991)
6. McGuinness, K., O'Connor, N.: A comparative evaluation of interactive segmentation algorithms. Pattern Recognition 43(2), 434–444 (2010)
7. Gelasca, E.D.: Full-reference objective quality metrics for video watermarking, video segmentation and 3D model watermarking. In: Ph.D. dissertation, EPFL, Lausanne, Switzerland (2005)
8. Correia, P., Pereira, F.: Objective evaluation of video segmentation quality. IEEE Trans. Image Process 12(2), 186–200 (2003)
9. Zhang, Y.J.: A Survey on Evaluation Methods for Image Segmentation. Pattern Recognition 29(8), 1335–1346 (1996)
10. Li, S., Mak, L.C.-M., Ngan, K.N.: Visual Quality Evaluation for Images and Videos. In: Lin, W., Tao, D., Kacprzyk, J., Li, Z., Izquierdo, E., Wang, H. (eds.) Multimedia Analysis, Processing and Communications. SCI, vol. 346, pp. 497–544. Springer, Heidelberg (2011)
11. Achanta, R., Hemami, S., Estrada, F., Susstrunk, S., Frequency-tuned, M.S.: salient region detection. In: Proc. IEEE CVPR, Miami, USA, pp. 1597–1604 (2009)
12. Rahtu, E., Kannala, J., Salo, M., Heikkilä, J.: Segmenting salient objects from images and videos. In: Daniilidis, K., Maragos, P., Paragios, N. (eds.) ECCV 2010, Part V. LNCS, vol. 6315, pp. 366–379. Springer, Heidelberg (2010)

13. Internal Telecommunication Union Radio communication Sector, C.: ITU-R Recommendation BT.500-13, Methodology for the Subjective Assessment of the Quality of Television Pictures (2012)
14. Video Quality Expert Group (VQEG) S.: Final Report From the Video Quality Experts Group on the Validation of Objective Models of Video Quality Assessment I (2010)
15. Zadeh, L.: Fuzzy sets and systems. Information and Control 8(3), 338–353 (1965)
16. Li, S., Zhang, F., Ma, L., Ngan, K.N.: Image quality assessment by separately evaluating detail losses and additive impairments. IEEE Trans. Multimedia 13(5), 935–949 (2011)
17. Huynh-Thu, Q., Garcia, N.N., Speranza, F., Corriveau, P., Raake, A.: Study of rating scales for subjective quality assessment of high-definition video. IEEE Trans. Broadcasting 57(1), 1–14 (2011)
18. Gelasca, E.D., Karaman, M., Ebrahimi, T., Sikora, T.: A Framework for Evaluating Video Object Segmentation Algorithms. In: Proc. IEEE CVPR Workshop, New York, USA, pp. 198–198 (2006)
19. Internal Telecommunication Union Telecommunication Standardization Sector, C.: ITU-T Recommendation P.910, Subjective video quality assessment methods for multimedia applications (2012)

A Modification of Diffusion Distance for Clustering and Image Segmentation

Eduard Sojka and Jan Gaura

VŠB - Technical University of Ostrava,
Faculty of Electrical Engineering and Computer Science,
Department of Computer Science,
17. listopadu 15, 708 33 Ostrava-Poruba, Czech Republic
{eduard.sojka,jan.gaura}@vsb.cz

Abstract. Measuring the distances is an important problem in many image-segmentation algorithms. The distance should tell whether two image points belong to a single or, respectively, to two different image segments. The simplest approach is to use the Euclidean distance. However, measuring the distances along the image manifold seems to take better into account the facts that are important for segmentation. Geodesic distance, i.e. the shortest path in the corresponding graph or k shortest paths can be regarded as the simplest way how the distances along the manifold can be measured. At a first glance, one would say that the resistance and diffusion distance should provide the properties that are even better since all the paths along the manifold are taken into account. Surprisingly, it is not often true. We show that the high number of paths is not beneficial for measuring the distances in image segmentation. On the basis of analysing the problems of diffusion distance, we introduce its modification, in which, in essence, the number of paths is restricted to a certain chosen number. We demonstrate the positive properties of this new metrics.

Keywords: Image segmentation, diffusion distance, geodesic distance.

1 Introduction

In many image-segmentation algorithms, measuring the distances play an important role. The distance is usually needed as a quantity the value of which expresses the fact that two points should belong to a single or, respectively, to two different image segments. The use of the Euclidean distance measuring the "direct straight-line distances" is often considered. In the case of image segmentation, however, the input data (image) define certain manifolds in some space (e.g. the brightness function defines such a manifold). The key question then is whether or not it could have some sense to measure the distances along this manifold. Another question is what metric should be used.

Consider two points, denoted by A and B, respectively, on the manifold in the situations as follows (Fig. 1). In Fig. 1a, A and B both lie in one area with

J. Blanc-Talon et al. (Eds.): ACIVS 2013, LNCS 8192, pp. 480–491, 2013.

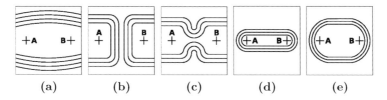

Fig. 1. On the problems arising when measuring the distances between two points (A, B): The images are depicted by the contour lines (isolines) of brightness similarly as in a map; various situations (a – e) are discussed in text

a constant brightness. The distance we expect in this case is small since both points should belong to a single resulting image segment. In Fig. 1b, although the points have the same brightness, they apparently should not belong to one image segment since the areas in which they lie are separated by a "mountain ridge" created by the manifold. Therefore, the distance we expect in this case is big. Fig. 1c shows two areas with the same brightness that are connected by a "channel" (the areas are separated by a weak boundary). The width of the channel usually determines whether or not the areas should be regarded as one segment. In Figs. 1d, 1e, two situations are depicted in which we would probably say that the points A and B belong to one area and have similar distances in both cases, in spite of the fact that one area is narrow and the other is wide.

The *Euclidean distance* measures the direct-line distances between the points that can be in general positions (i.e. including the positions outside of the manifold). Since the distance is not measured along the manifold, it can neither reveal the separation by the mountain ridge (Fig. 1b) nor quantify the width of a possible channel between the areas with similar brightness (Fig. 1c), which may deteriorate the quality of algorithms. The distance does not depend on the width of the areas (Figs. 1d, 1e), which is desirable. The *geodesic distance* measures the length of the shortest path lying entirely on the manifold including both endpoints. It reveals the mountain ridges (Fig. 1b) correctly. No hint about the channel width (Fig. 1c) is given; even a thin channel causes that a short distance is reported. Therefore, the areas may be connected incorrectly. From [3], the possibility of computing k shortest paths in graphs follows, which can by used for measuring the width of channel. Nevertheless, the problems with distinguishing the situations depicted in Fig. 1c and 1d remain.

The *resistance distance* is a metrics on graphs introduced by Klein and Randic [8] and further developed also by others [1]. The resistance distance between two vertices of a simple connected graph is equal to the resistance between two corresponding points in an equivalent electrical network (regular grid in this case). The resistances of edges in the network increase with the increasing local image contrast. Intuitively, the resistance distance explores many parallel (in electrical sense) paths whereas the geodesic distance, in contrast, explores only the shortest of them. The resistance distance is able to reveal the mountain ridges correctly. It also measures the width of channels. The wider the channel is, the higher number of conductive parallel paths runs through the channel, which decreases the resistance between the points.

The *diffusion-based methods* are known in image processing for more than twenty years [13], and are studied up to now [4]. Diffusion is a process during which a substance, e.g. heat or electric charge diffuses from the places of its greater concentration to the places where the concentration is lower. Mathematical description can be build on the diffusion equation that is connected with some physically-based problem or on the basis of the Markov matrices describing the random walker technique [6]. The diffusion maps were systematically introduced in [12,2]. Although further papers appear (e.g [10]), not so much is reported about convincingly positive results of practical use of diffusion distance for segmentation. This can be regarded as surprising since, at a first glance, the method has the properties that are useful. Simply speaking, the method can be viewed in such a way that many paths on the image manifolds are checked. Moreover, the sizes of image areas are measured.

In this paper, we show that examining a high number of paths (limited only by the size of image itself) need not be beneficial for measuring distances in segmentation. On the basis of analysing the problems of diffusion distance, we introduce its modification in which the number of paths is restricted to a certain chosen number. The computational technique remains similar as is usually presented for diffusion distance, i.e. it can be based on spectral decomposition of Laplacian matrix.

The paper is organised as follows. In the following section, we recall the needed theoretical background. In Section 3, the problems of diffusion distance are explained. Our proposed improvement is presented in Section 4. Section 5 is devoted to experimental results.

2   Diffusion Embedding, Distance, and Clustering

The diffusion-based methods are usually formulated by making use of the diffusion equation that can be written in the form of

$$\frac{\partial f(t,x)}{\partial t} = \text{div}\left(g(f(t,x),x)\nabla f(t,x)\right),\tag{1}$$

where $f(t,x)$ is a potential function (e.g. concentration, temperature, charge) evolving in time; $g(.)$ is a diffusion coefficient (function). In some applications, the coefficient does not depend on $f(t,x)$. If $g(.)$ reduces to a constatnt G, the right-hand side of Eq. (1) reduces to $G\nabla^2 f(t,x)$. In our context, $f(t,x)$ has the meaning of evolving image brightness or colour. The process of evolving starts at $t = 0$; $f(0,x)$ is a given input image.

In the discrete case, the problem is described by a graph. The diffusion properties are represented by edge weights that can be understood as proximity between the nodes connected by the corresponding edge (neighbouring nodes). The weights of edges may again be considered evolving in time or constant. In this paper, we follow the latter option. The diffusion equation can now be written in the form of

$$\frac{\partial \boldsymbol{f}(t)}{\partial t} = \mathbf{L}\boldsymbol{f}(t)\,, \tag{2}$$

where $\mathbf{L}$ is the Laplacian matrix created from the weights of edges; $\boldsymbol{f}(t)$ is a vector whose entries correspond to the potential in the particular graph nodes, i.e. $\boldsymbol{f}(t) = (f_1(t), \ldots, f_n(t))^\top$ (we suppose a graph with n nodes). The weight, denoted by $w_{i,j}$, of the edge connecting the nodes i and j is often considered according to the formula

$$w_{i,j} = e^{-\frac{\|c_{i,j}\|^2}{2\nu^2}}\,, \tag{3}$$

where $c_{i,j}$ denotes the grey-scale or colour contrast between the nodes. Let neighb(i) stand for the set of all neighbours of i. If $j \in$ neighb(i), $\mathbf{L}$ contains the weight $w_{i,j}$ at the position i, j. At the diagonal position i, i, $\mathbf{L}$ contains the value $-\sum_{j \in \text{neighb}(i)} w_{i,j}$. $\mathbf{L}$ is symmetric, positive semi-definite, and singular. Image processing problems usually lead to regular meshes in which each inner node (node corresponding to an inner image pixel) is connected with its four neighbours. Therefore, $\mathbf{L}$ has 5 entries in its corresponding row, i.e. $\mathbf{L}$ is sparse.

The solution of Eq. (2) can be found in the form of

$$\boldsymbol{f}(t) = \mathbf{H}(t)\boldsymbol{f}(0)\,, \tag{4}$$

where $\mathbf{H}(t)$ is a diffusion operator (a matrix). The entry $h_t(p, q)$ of $\mathbf{H}(t)$ expresses the amount of a substance that is transported from the q-th node into the p-th node (or vice versa since $h_t(p, q) = h_t(q, p)$) during the time interval $[0, t]$. It can be shown that the following formula for $\mathbf{H}(t)$ ensures that Eq. (2) is satisfied

$$\mathbf{H}(t) = \sum_{k=1}^{n} e^{-\lambda_k t} \boldsymbol{u}_k \boldsymbol{u}_k^\top\,, \tag{5}$$

where λ_k and $\boldsymbol{u}_k$, respectively, stand for the k-th eigenvalue and the k-th eigenvector of $\mathbf{L}$. Let $u_{i,k}$ be the i-th entry of the k-th eigenvector. For each graph vertex, the following vector of new coordinates can be introduced

$$\boldsymbol{x}_i(t) = \left(e^{-\lambda_1 t} u_{i,1}, e^{-\lambda_2 t} u_{i,2}, \ldots, e^{-\lambda_n t} u_{i,n}\right)\,. \tag{6}$$

If the coordinates are assigned in this way, we call it *diffusion map* or diffusion embedding (we note that the first coordinate can be omitted since $\lambda_1 = 0$ and $\boldsymbol{u}_1 = 1$) [2,9]. This vector can be used for clustering the vertices, which will be discussed later. By making use of this vector, also the entries of the diffusion matrix can be expressed as a dot product

$$h_{2t}(p, q) = \langle \boldsymbol{x}_p(t), \boldsymbol{x}_q(t) \rangle. \tag{7}$$

The square of diffusion distance is defined as a sum of squared differences of the concentrations caused by putting the unit concentration into the p-th node and into the q-th node, respectively, which corresponds to the formula

$$d_t^2(p, q) = \sum_{i=1}^{n} [h_t(i, p) - h_t(i, q)]^2\,. \tag{8}$$

After some effort, the following formula can be deduced from Eq. (8)

$$d_t^2(p,q) = h_{2t}(p,p) - 2h_{2t}(p,q) + h_{2t}(q,q) = \|\boldsymbol{x}_p - \boldsymbol{x}_q\|^2, \tag{9}$$

which shows that introducing the coordinates according to Eq. (6) may be seen as creating a *diffusion map*, which is a map created in a similar sense as was introduced in [15], where the idea was presented that measuring the distance along a data manifold in some space can be done by transforming the problem into a new space in such a way that the Euclidean distance in the new space is equal to the distance measured on the data manifold in the original space. It is believed that much less than n coordinates will be needed in practice. From Eq. (6), it is clear that the importance of coordinates decreases with the increasing values of their corresponding eigenvalues and with increasing time.

Despite time obviously plays an essential role in diffusion, it might be interesting to get rid of it in a further distance definition based on summing d_t^2 over time (*commute-time distance*, [5,16,14]) according the formula (the first eigenvector is not included since its corresponding eigenvalue is equal to zero and its entries are the same for all nodes)

$$d_{\mathrm{CTD}}^2(p,q) = \int\limits_{t=0}^{\infty} d_t^2(p,q)\,\mathrm{d}t = \sum_{k=2}^{n}\left(\frac{u_{p,k}-u_{q,k}}{\sqrt{\lambda_k}}\right)^2. \tag{10}$$

By analogy with the relation that exists between $d_t^2(p,q)$ and $\boldsymbol{x}_i(t)$ (Eqs. (6) and (9)), the vertex coordinates $\boldsymbol{x}_i = \left(u_{i,2}/\sqrt{\lambda_2}, u_{i,3}/\sqrt{\lambda_3}, \ldots, u_{i,n}/\sqrt{\lambda_n}\right)$ can be introduced and used for clustering. Eq. (10) shows again that the coordinates create a map, i.e. $d_{\mathrm{CTD}}^2(p,q) = \|\boldsymbol{x}_p - \boldsymbol{x}_q\|^2$. It is known that the commute-time distance is equivalent to *resistance distance* that was discussed earlier. In similar spirit, a biharmonic distance had been introduced in [10]. The map for the biharmonic embedding is created by assigning the coordinates by the following formula $\boldsymbol{x}_i = (u_{i,2}/\lambda_2, u_{i,3}/\lambda_3, \ldots, u_{i,n}/\lambda_n)$.

Diffusion clustering is based on the idea to use the coordinates introduced in Eq. (6) for clustering the graph nodes, i.e. the image pixels [12,9,7]. Clustering may be done in such a way that a certain clustering method is applied onto the diffusion coordinates. The time t can be used to set the level of details that is desired. Not too much is reported about diffusion clustering. Usually, the k-means method is mentioned [9,7], which copies the approaches used in spectral clustering.

3   The Problems with Diffusion Distance in Segmentation

In this section, we show that the diffusion distance has the properties that make it difficult to use this distance for segmentation and clustering. These observations will be exploited for its modification, which will be done in the next section.

We start from considering two points (denoted by p, q) in a certain image area that is separated, due to a very high resistance (low conductivity) along its boundary, from the rest of the image (Fig. 2). We claim that the following is true: (i) if the width of the area decreases (see the figure), the diffusion distance between p and q increases for certain values of t and vice versa; (ii) if the height of the area decreases, the diffusion distance increases again for certain values of t (and vice versa); (iii) if the area is split by an edge, the diffusion distance between p and q increases for certain values of t too. The claims (i) and (iii) can be easily seen for the case of commute-time distance, i.e. resistance distance (see the previous section). If the width of area decreases, fewer resistor links (connected in parallel) connect p with q. In the case of splitting the area with an edge, the number of links remains unchanged, but the resistance of at least one edge in each link increases. Since, according to Eq. (10), the commute-time distance is an integral of diffusion distance, the same must also hold for diffusion distance at least for some values of t. The claim (ii) can also be explained by making use of resistance distance in a similar way. Consider a continuous resistor network (with finite resistances) and the resistance between its points (p, q). If we remove an arbitrary part of the network (such that both the points are still present in the network, Fig. 2(ii)), the resistance between the points will increase.

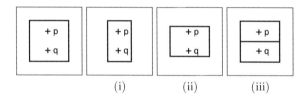

(i)   (ii)   (iii)

Fig. 2. On the problems arising when measuring the diffusion distance between the points (p, q). See text for further explanation

For image segmentation (and for clustering generally) the properties (i) and (ii) are unpleasant. In images, we would like to have image segments of various sizes. The goal of measuring distances in segmentation and clustering is to decide whether or not two points belong to one image segment (cluster). From the claims stated above, it follows that the existence of edge that should separate segments (clusters) may be overshadowed by the differences in the size of segments or clusters, i.e. the influence of various cluster sizes may be greater then is the influence of possible edge. As a result, the edge might not be detected.

In the rest of this section, we illustrate the problems with diffusion distance on more practical images (Figs. 3-7; please, read texts below the images). Probably the most important observation is presented in Fig. 4. It shows that the use of standard diffusion distance is problematic since the distance between two points in one image segment can be higher than the distance between two points lying in two different segments although the segments can be easily distinguished visually. The remaining figures show that the problem cannot be overcome by choosing a suitable value of t in Eq. (6) or ν in Eq. (3).

Fig. 3. An illustration of the problems hidden in diffusion distance. The diffusion distance from the center point of image (denoted by x in Fig. 4) are measured to all remaining image points. The image without noise (black=0, white=1, grey=0.6), and the images with added Gaussian noise ($\sigma = 0.1$, $\sigma = 0.2$) are considered (*left*, *middle*, and *right* image, respectively). The computed distances are shown and discussed in the subsequent figures.

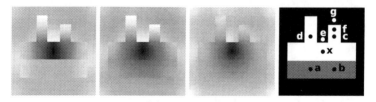

Fig. 4. For each image from Fig. 3, the diffusion distances from the image center (point x) are expressed by brightness (bigger brightness indicates a higher distance of the corresponding pixel). The computation was done for $t = 100$, and for $\nu = 0.1$, $\nu = 0.2$, and $\nu = 0.3$, respectively (*first*, *second*, and *third* image). It can be seen that the diffusion distance does not express what is needed for segmentation. The exact numerical computation shows, for example, that the following holds in all shown cases (d stands for the distance, the positions of points are shown in the *right* figure): $d(x,b) < d(x,c)$, $d(x,b) < d(x,f)$, $d(x,d) < d(x,c)$, $d(x,g) < d(x,e)$, which may be regarded as surprising and not suitable for segmenation.

4   The Proposed Improvement

In this section, we propose an improvement that, into a substantial extent, reduces the problems mentioned in the previous section. For convenience, we introduce the term *proximity* instead of *distance*. Clearly, distance and proximity are inverse notions. Let prox(p,q) stands for proximity of p and q. The following is required: prox$(p,q) \geq 0$, prox$(p,q) =$ prox(q,p), prox$(p,q) \geq$ prox$(p,r)+$prox(r,q).

The new measure we propose is inspired by the problems encountered for the diffusion distance from Eq. (8). In diffusion distance, the difference of the responses to unit sources placed at p and q, respectively, are measured over a big area, theoretically over the whole image. The first problem is that many unimportant contributions to the sum from Eq. (8) may substantially influence the final value of the distance, which was reflected in the claims (i) and (ii) in the previous section.

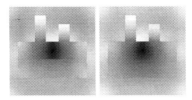

Fig. 5. The figure shows that the problems with diffusion distance cannot be solved by using a certain optimal value of ν in Eq. (3). The values of distances from the image centerpoint (the image with noise $\sigma = 0.1$) are presented here (higher brightness expresses a higher distance) for $\nu = 0.15$ (*left* image) and for $\nu = 0.3$ (*right* image) (the result for $\nu = 0.2$ was shown in Fig. 4, *middle* image). It can be seen that none of the presented distance maps brings any improvement.

Fig. 6. The figure illustrates that the problems with diffusion distance can hardly be overcome by using an optimal value of t in Eq. (6). The maps of distances from the image centerpoint are presented here for the image with noise ($\sigma = 0.1$) for $t = 10$ (*left* image), for $t = 1000$ (*middle* image), and for $t = 10000$ (*right* image) (the result for $t = 100$ has already been shown in Fig. 4, *middle* image). It can be seen again that none of the presented distance maps is usable without problems. From exact computation, it follows that in the *middle* image, for example, we have $d(x,b) < d(x,c)$, $d(x,b) < d(x,f)$, $d(x,d) > d(x,c)$, $d(x,g) < d(x,e)$.

The approach we propose can be described as follows: We can say that two points, denoted by p, q, are close to each other if we have a reasonable number of points, denoted by i, that are close both to p as well as to q. It can be easily understood that the number of such points cannot be unrestricted since it cannot be higher than is the size (in pixels) of the segment containing p and q (if we suppose for a while that p and q lie in one segment). For evaluating the ability of the i-th point to confirm a high value of proximity between p and q, we use the values $h_t(i,p)$ and $h_t(i,q)$ whose meaning was explained in Section 2. A point i confirms the hypothesis about a high value of proximity between p and q only if the values of $h_t(i,p)$ and $h_t(i,p)$ are both high; otherwise, i does not confirm the mentioned fact. It follows that the decision ability of i can be expressed by $\min(h_t(i,p), h_t(i,q))$. Let $\sum_{\text{top}_Q} \{\text{collection}\}$ stand for the sum of the highest Q elements from a collection of real numbers. We now define the *diffusion proximity* between p and q at the time t as follows

$$\text{prox}_t(p,q) = \frac{1}{Q} \sum_{\text{top}_Q} \left\{ \min\left(h_t(i,p), h_t(i,q)\right) \right\}_{i=1}^{n}. \tag{11}$$

Fig. 7. Quite often, the computation of diffusion distances is advised to be done by making use of spectral decomposition of the Laplacian matrix of image. The approach relies on the expectation that only several eigenvalues and eigenvectors should be enough to compute the new coordinates and the diffusion distance. This figure shows that the lower numbers of coordinates may provide the result that is substantially different from the exact solution. The figure shows the distances from the image centerpoint obtained from 5 coordinates (*left* image), 10 coordinates (*middle* image) and 20 coordinates (*right* image) for the image with noise ($\sigma = 0.1$) and for $t = 100$. The figure shows the need for a higher number of coordinates if the results corresponding to the formulas are to be obtained. The results shown in the previous images were computed by making use of 250 eigenvectors (coordinates).

We recall that Q is a parameter (number of points) whose value should not be higher than is the smallest expected size of one segment (cluster).

The proximity between two image areas can be defined in a similar manner. Let A and B stand for the areas. Their proximity can be defined by the formula

$$\text{prox}_t(A, B) = \frac{1}{Q} \sum_{\text{top}_Q} \left\{ \min \left(\frac{1}{R} \sum_{\text{top}_R} \{h_t(i,p)\}_{p\in A}, \frac{1}{R} \sum_{\text{top}_R} \{h_t(i,q)\}_{q\in B} \right) \right\}_{i=1}^n .$$

(12)

The rationale behind the formula can be easily seen. We can say that the areas A and B are close if a certain sufficient number (Q) of points exist that are close to A and B simultaneously. A point is regarded as close to an area if it is close to a certain sufficient number (R) of points of that area.

The rightfulness of constructing the proximities as was described above is illustrated in Figs. 8 and 9. The figures show the behaviour of the new metric in the same situations as were studied for the diffusion distance before. In contrast with diffusion distance, the new proximity behaves correctly. Please, read texts below the figures. Remember that proximity gives the values that are inversely proportional to distance.

5   Experimental Results

For testing the new metrics more practically, we have used the problem of seeded segmentation and a region growing algorithm. The algorithm starts from the seeds that were determined manually. The remaining pixels are marked as not yet decided. The seeds iteratively grow into the final image segments (in each iteration step, a certain estimation of all segments is available). In each iteration step, the algorithm does the following: For each pixel that has not been

Fig. 8. The proximities between the centre points of images from Fig. 3 and all remaining image points are computed and depicted by the level of brightness for $t = 100$, $Q = 100$ (higher brightness means a bigger proximity). The values of proximity behave according to the expectations, no surprising cases can be seen. With the increasing level of noise, the step in proximity between the white and grey area becomes less apparent in the presented images. The numerical results, however, show that the expected relations, e.g. $\text{prox}(x,c) < \text{prox}(x,b)$ are still preserved. (Please, compare these results with the behaviour of diffusion distance shown in Fig. 4; remember that proximity is inversely proportional to distance.)

Fig. 9. On the influence of the value of Q. For the image with noise ($\sigma = 0.1$), the distances from the image center points are computed for $Q = 10$ (*left* image), $Q = 100$ (*middle* image), and $Q = 1000$ (*right* image). The values of proximities exhibit more or less stable behaviour.

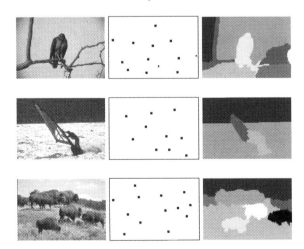

Fig. 10. Various images segmented using the region growing algorithm. From the left to the right: source image, initial seeds, and the result of region growing segmentation using the introduced proximity

decided yet, the proximities to all segment estimations are computed according to Eq. (12) for a certain predefined value of t. The maximal proximity is taken and checked whether it is greater that a chosen threshold. If so, the pixel is assigned to the corresponding segment. If no pixel is assigned in one iteration step, the algorithm stops. The results obtained for several images from The Berkeley Segmentation Dataset [11] are shown in Fig. 10. We note that we did not aim at comparing this segmentation process with other known approaches. We only wanted to show that the metrics we propose have the properties that make it possible to use the metrics for image segmentation.

6   Conclusions

We have discussed the problem of measuring the distances for image segmentation. Measuring the distances along the image manifold seems to take into account the properties that are important for segmentation. At a first glance, one would say that the resistance and diffusion distance should give the properties that are better since all the paths are checked, but the opposite is true. In this paper, we showed that an unlimited number of paths given only by the sizes of particular areas and the image itself need not be useful for measuring the distances for segmentation. We introduced a modification of diffusion distance, in which, in essence, the number of paths is restricted to a certain chosen number. Othrewise, the computational technique remains similar as is usually presented for diffusion distance, i.e. it is based on spectral decomposition of Laplacian matrix. As a disadwantage of the proposed metrics, we should mention its high time complexity. We are currenty working on the modifications that are computationally less expensive.

Acknowledgements. This work was partially supported by the grant SP 2013/185 of VŠB - Technical University of Ostrava, Faculty of Electrical Engineering and Computer Science.

References

1. Babić, D., Klein, D.J., Lukovits, I., Nikolić, S., Trinajstić, N.: Resistance-Distance Matrix: A Computational Algorithm and Its Applications. Int. J. Quant. Chem. 90, 166–176 (2002)
2. Coifman, R., Lafon, S.: Diffusion Maps. Applied and Computational Harmonic Analysis 21, 5–30 (2006)
3. Eppstein, D.: Finding the k Shortest Paths. J. Comp. 28(2), 652–673 (1999)
4. Fiorio, C., Mercat, C., Rieux, F.: Adaptive Discrete Laplace Operator. In: International Symposium on Visual Computing, pp. 567–577 (2011)
5. Fouss, F., Pirotte, A., Renders, J.M., Saerens, M.: Random-Walk Computation of Similarities between Nodes of a Graph with Application to Collaborative Recommendation. Trans. on Knowledge and Data Engineering 19, 355–369 (2007)
6. Grady, L.: Random Walks for Image Segmentation. TPAMI 28(11), 1768–1783 (2006)

7. Huang, H., Yoo, S., Qin, H., Yu, D.: A Robust Clustering Algorithm Based on Aggregated Heat Kernel Mapping. In: International Conference on Data Mining, pp. 270–279 (2011)
8. Klein, D., Randić, J.M.: Resistance Distance. J. Mat. Chem. 12, 81–95 (1993)
9. Lafon, S., Lee, A.B.: Diffusion Maps and Coarse-Graining: a Unified Framework for Dimensionality Reduction, Graph Partitioning, and Data Set Parameterization. TPAMI 28(9), 1393–1403 (2006)
10. Lipman, Y., Rustamov, R.M., Funkhouser, T.A.: Biharmonic Distance. ACM Transactions on Graphics 29, 1–11 (2010)
11. Martin, D., Fowlkes, C., Tal, D., Malik, J.: A Database of Human Segmented Natural Images and its Application to Evaluating Segmentation Algorithms and Measuring Ecological Statistics. In: International Conference of Computer Vision, pp. 416–423 (2001)
12. Nadler, B., Lafon, S., Coifman, R.R., Kevrekidis, I.G.: Diffusion Maps, Spectral Clustering and Eigenfunctions of Fokker-Planck Operators. Advances in Neural Information Processing Systems 18, 955–962 (2005)
13. Perona, P., Malik, J.: Scale-Space and Edge Detection Using Anisotropic Diffusion. TPAMI 12(7), 629–639 (1990)
14. Qiu, H., Hancock, E.R.: Clustering and Embedding Using Commute Times. TPAMI 29(11), 1873–1890 (2007)
15. Tenenbaum, J.B., de Silva, V., Langford, J.C.: A Global Geometric Framework for Nonlinear Dimensionality Reduction. Scienc. 290, 2319–2323 (2010)
16. Yen, L., Fouss, F., Decaestecker, C., Francq, P., Saerens, M.: Graph Nodes Clustering Based on the Commute-Time Kernel. In: Pacific-Asia Conference on Knowledge Discovery and Data Mining, pp. 1037–1045 (2007)

Flexible Multi-modal Graph-Based Segmentation

Willem P. Sanberg, Luat Do, and Peter H.N. de With

Eindhoven University of Technology, The Netherlands
w.p.sanberg@tue.nl

Abstract. This paper aims at improving the well-known local variance segmentation method by adding extra signal modi and specific processing steps. As a key contribution, we extend the uni-modal segmentation method to perform multi-modal analysis, such that any number of signal modi available can be incorporated in a very flexible way. We have found that the use of a combined weight of luminance and depth values improves the segmentation score by 6.8%, for a large and challenging multi-modal dataset. Furthermore, we have developed an improved uni-modal texture-segmentation algorithm. This improvement relies on a clever choice of the color space and additional pre- and post-processing steps, by which we have increased the segmentation score on a challenging texture dataset by 2.1%. This gain is mainly preserved when using a different dataset with worse lighting conditions and different scene types.

Keywords: Multi-modal Signal Analysis, RGBD Segmentation, Graphs.

1 Introduction

Segmentation of images has been a topic of research for many years in the field of computer vision. Over the years, increasingly complicated features or texture descriptors have been developed to improve the segmentation of interesting objects in two-dimensional (2D) texture images. This segmentation often serves as a basis for semantic labeling in applications such as object recognition, object tracking and event detection in security or sports video, cancer detection, etc.

However, texture segmentation has two fundamental limitations. First, a key issue in texture segmentation is that not all objects have clear, distinctive texture borders, leading to under-segmentation. For example, its is hard to a isolate a white cabinet in front of a white wall. Second, not all texture borders correspond to interesting object contours, depending on the application. For instance, shadows or texture with high variance can lead to over-segmentation.

These problems can be partially addressed by using multi-modal signal analysis. Recently, there has been a growth in multi-modal visual sensor systems that capture depth signals alongside 2D texture images, providing information on the geometry or shape of a scene. This facilitates, inter alia, detecting the white cabinet and neglecting the shadows, based on the change and invariability of the local geometry, respectively. To realize these benefits, new multi-modal

J. Blanc-Talon et al. (Eds.): ACIVS 2013, LNCS 8192, pp. 492–503, 2013.

segmentation algorithms are required. For this purpose, we need a segmentation structure in which we can flexibly incorporate texture and shape information. Segmentation graphs meet these demands. A graph consists of vertices and edges that connect these vertices. Vertices can contain RGB or grayscale values [4, 5], feature values [3], or shape information such as depth or orientation with respect to a viewpoint [9]. The edges have one or more weights, reflecting (dis)similarity between the connected vertices. Weights can be customized in many ways [3–5, 9]. Graphs can be defined over multiple scales [5], or provide hierarchical segmentation [5]. This makes graphs flexible to incorporate information from multiple signal modi. Moreover, graph structures can be implemented and segmented efficiently [4]. In the survey of Peng *et al.* [6], several graph-based texture segmentation methods are discussed and compared. From their quantitative analysis, the authors conclude that the method of Felzenszwalb and Huttenlocher [4] (Local Variance Segmentation, LVS) performs best in extracting the key structures in an image, especially when there are many objects present, and has the best average segmentation quality. Furthermore, the complexity of LVS is low, making it an attractive method to build upon.

By extending the LVS method, this paper addresses two related contributions. First, we extend the uni-modal segmentation method (LVS) to perform multi-modal analysis, such that any number of signal modi available can be incorporated in a very flexible way. Second, we experiment with several preprocessing steps for the texture information, which improves the results of the uni-modal LVS algorithm.

The remainder of this paper is divided as follows. The uni-modal baseline method is explained in Section 2 and we present our improvements in Section 3. We evaluate our contributions with several quantitative experiments, described in Section 4, the results of which are presented in Section 5. Our conclusions, a discussion and recommendations for future work are presented in Section 6.

2   LVS for Uni-modal Segmentation

A graph $G = (V, E)$ consists of vertices $(v_i \in V)$ that are connected by edges $(e = (v_i, v_j) \in E)$ that all have a weight $w(e)$. Segmenting a graph is the problem of finding disjoint subsets S_i such that $\bigcup_i S_i = V$. Ideally, the segments S_i represent areas of interest. In general, the first step of graph-based segmentation is to initialize V and E. The second step consists of selecting one or more seed points. The last step is the merging and labeling process. In the context of 2D texture images, the vertices are pixels that have edges to their neighbors. The weights are typically a measure of dissimilarity of the connected vertices, such as, e.g., the absolute difference in pixel intensity.

Felzenszwalb and Huttenlocher [4] designed their algorithm to result in a segmentation that is neither too coarse nor too fine, using the following definitions: (1) a segmentation is too fine when, among S_i, there are neighboring segments without evidence of a border between them; (2) a segmentation is too coarse if there is evidence of a boundary in at least one S_i. To generate this segmentation, Felzenszwalb *et al.* define the difference between segments, $\text{Ext}_T(S_1, S_2)$, as the minimal edge weight connecting the segments. Furthermore, they define the variation within a segment, $\mathrm{Int}_T(S_1)$, as the maximum edge weight in the Minimal Spanning Tree (MST) of the segment. Note that we add the subscript T of 'Texture' here for clearer notation later in the paper.

Let us now describe the principal steps of their segmentation algorithm in more detail. First, the graph is initialized with one vertex per pixel, where each vertex has an edge to each of its 8 neighbors. The edges are weighted with the intensity difference of the connected pixels. Furthermore, the segmentation is initialized with one segment per vertex, all having an initial threshold of K_T, which is a user parameter. In the next step, which is the *seeding step*, the edges are sorted to their weight w_T. Sorting is a crucial step, since it guarantees two requirements for proper execution. First, the edge under evaluation is always the connection with the lowest weight between two segments, which is equal to $\mathrm{Ext}_T(S_1, S_2)$. Second, the edge under evaluation is always the connection with the highest weight within the new segment, which is equal to $\mathrm{Int}_T(S_1)$.

The last step, i.e. the *merging step*, executes a boundary check for all edges in order of increasing weight. The boundary check $B_T(S_1, S_2)$ is false when the following inequality holds:

$$\mathrm{Ext}_T(S_1, S_2) \leq \min\left(\mathrm{Int}_T(S_1) + \frac{K_T}{|S_1|}, \mathrm{Int}_T(S_2) + \frac{K_T}{|S_2|}\right), \qquad (1)$$

where $|S_i|$ denotes the size of a segment in pixels. If the boundary check is false, the segments will be merged and the threshold of the new segment will be set accordingly. From Eq. (1) we can see that parameter K_T enables small segments to grow. For instance, when a segment contains just one pixel, its internal difference is zero, so that merging is only allowed along edges with a weight of zero. Choosing a large K_T makes it easier for segments to merge. Using an appropriate K_T, regions with high detail can be segmented in small segments, and regions with low detail can be segmented in large segments.

2.1 Shortcomings of LVS

The LVS algorithm suffers from two shortcomings. Firstly, LVS is a region-growing algorithm that merges segments when a single low-weight edge connects them. This can lead to under-segmentation, due to merging of adjacent pixels with similar intensity, but belonging to different objects (leakage). This is particularly difficult to prevent when two objects share a smooth border. Secondly, LVS allows small segments around noise and long thin segments around edges to exist, which leads to over-segmentation. This can happen due to noise in pixel intensities and blurry edges in combination with the seeding strategy of LVS.

3 Extending LVS to Multi-modal Segmentation (MLVS)

Let us now look at the integration of information from multiple signal modi into the LVS segmentation algorithm. Since in multi-modal systems multiple signals need to be processed simultaneously, it is necessary to adapt the initialization, seeding and merging and labeling steps accordingly. First of all, in the initialization stage of LVS, each vertex $v \in V$ of graph $G(V, E)$ is assigned an extra value per mode in addition to its texture image pixel intensity. As a consequence, each edge obtains one extra weight per mode. For example, an extra weight could be the Euclidian distance between vertex normal vectors or depth values. Then, for the seeding and merging steps of multi-modal signals, we identify two key strategies: (1) defining partial boundary functions for each signal mode, and (2) combining the different weights into a single weight and using a single boundary function. In the following subsections, we will analyze these two strategies in more detail.

3.1 Strategy 1: Partial Boundary Functions

In this approach, we first define a separate partial boundary function B_m for each of the available M modes such that each partial boundary function should reflect the nature of the signal. For example, when a depth signal is available, a boundary check similar to Eq. (1) cannot be applied, since the depth value of a single object varies, in contrast to its texture value. A better alternative is to define a boundary check based on a constant threshold, instead of an adaptively growing approach.

Second, we integrate these separate partial boundary functions in the framework by defining a general boundary function $B(B_1, ..., B_M)$. This boundary function is application-specific and should be designed carefully by the user. For example, if a high boundary detection rate is required and all modi are equally important, B can be implemented with a logical OR-function:

$$B(B_1, ..., B_M) = B_1 \vee B_2 \vee \ldots \vee B_M. \tag{2}$$

However, we are aware of the unequal nature of the partial boundary functions for different modi. Due to this inequality, combining different signal modi into a single boundary function will always be a compromise.

Since edges now have multiple weights, the sorting procedure in the *seeding step* is no longer straight-forward. We have explored two methods for sorting the weights: (1) sorting to the weights of a single mode, neglecting the other weights, or (2) hierarchical sorting by ordering to the weights of one mode, and within that list, sorting to the second mode. Both methods do not guarantee that the edges are handled in order of non-decreasing edge weight Ext(.) in all modi simultaneously, since the modi contain fundamentally different data. However, the strength of combining multi-modal signals is in exploiting partly conflicting information in different modi. The consequence of multi-modal sorting is that the segmentation is no longer unique: each sorting strategy can result in a different segmentation.

After a merge of two segments, the internal differences of the new segment are updated using the weights of the edge under evaluation. This is independent of the sorting method. Therefore, Int(.) only corresponds to the maximum value in the MST for the mode that is sorted.

3.2   Strategy 2: Combining Weights

Our second approach to incorporate multiple weights is to combine them into a single weight w_C:

$$w_C = \sum_{m=1}^{M} \alpha_m \frac{w_m}{A_m}, \qquad (3)$$

where M is the number of modi and A is a factor to normalize the weights of a mode to unity. For example, $A = 255$ for the luminance weight. The factor α ($\sum \alpha_m = 1$) expresses the importance of a mode. In our experiments, we have adopted $\alpha_m = 1/M$ for all m.

In the *seeding step*, the edges are sorted to the value of w_C. In the *merging step*, a boundary check analogous to Eq. (1) is applied, specified by:

$$\text{Ext}_C(S_1, S_2) \leq \min\left(\text{Int}_C(S_1) + \frac{K_C}{|S_1|}, \text{Int}_C(S_2) + \frac{K_C}{|S_2|}\right). \qquad (4)$$

An advantage of this approach is that adding additional signals only requires normalizing signal values and a difference metric that matches the nature of the signal. In our experiments, we have obtained good results when we use the absolute distance for scalar values and the Euclidian distance for vector values.

3.3   Pre- and Post-processing

Color Space. In the LVS algorithm, graph edges are weighted by the difference between pixel intensity values. A commonly used multi-modal capturing device is the Kinect camera. The Kinect RGB sensor uses a Bayer mosaic filter, resulting in a lower quality of the blue and the red signal component. This leads to over-segmentation in the LVS algorithm. To reduce the effect of the Bayer filter, we have adopted the luminance values (Y) of the YUV color space as the signal mode used for texture.

Filtering. The pre-processing step should reduce the noise within a segment but not smoothen object borders, which is referred to as *edge-preserving smoothing*. We have compared and evaluated three filtering approaches with an experiment in Section 5.

The first approach is the well-known median filter. It is a nonlinear smoothing filter that is often used to remove speckle noise, but it can also introduce false contours. There are two key parameters: the size of the neighborhood and the number of iterations that should be performed.

The second approach is Bilateral Filtering, which is a filtering technique that convolves an adaptive kernel with the input image. For each pixel under evaluation, the kernel weights decrease with the spatial distance and with the intensity difference (both compared to the kernel center), providing the possibility to smoothen texture variation in areas on both sides of an edge separately. This enhances the homogeneity of the region and at the same time preserves the edge.

Third, Nonlinear diffusion filtering (NLDF) evolves an image L through increasing scale levels. For edge-preserving smoothing, the authors of [7] and [10] propose to make the diffusion a function of the local image gradient magnitude. We test three of their NLDF approaches, using the implementation of [1].

Post-processing. The results of LVS may contain segments of only a few pixels, which are often not of interest. Therefore, if a segment is smaller than $minSegSize$, it is merged with its neighboring segment with the smallest Ext_T.

4   Segmentation Experiments

We have performed several experiments to show that we improve (1) the results of LVS on texture with our adaptations and (2) the segmentation degree further by using our extension to multi-modal signal analysis.

Texture Segmentation. We analyze our texture segmentation performance on the challenging Berkely Segmentation Data Set 500 (BSDS)[1], presented in [2] and consisting of RGB images with a wide variation of subjects (animals, landscapes, buildings, people, etc.). The dataset contains 200 training and 200 test images with multiple, manually annotated ground truths. The final score is the average score over all ground truths of an image. We will use this dataset to evaluate our texture segmentation and to train the texture pre-processing settings for the multi-modal signal analysis.

Multi-modal Segmentation. NYU Depth dataset V2 (NYU)[2], presented in [8], contains aligned texture/depth/normal-frames from a variety of indoor scenes (kitchens, bedrooms, office spaces, stores, etc.), split into 795 training and 654 test frames. The texture and depth images are captured with a Kinect camera. To create dense depth images, a hole-filling/inpainting algorithm is employed. The normal images are estimated from the individual depth images, by back-projecting depth points to 3D space and performing local plane fitting. For quantitative analysis, this dataset also includes a ground-truth labeling.

Segmentation Metric. To compare our results to the ground truth, Arbeláez *et al.* provide several boundary-based and segment-based metrics [2]. We will focus on the score on boundary detection but provide our final scores on all measures for completeness. We measure Recall (R) and Precision (P) scores on edge pixels, where R is the ratio of true boundary pixels that are detected by the segmentation and P is the ratio of detected boundary pixels that match true boundary pixels. We adopt the evaluation technique from [2], in which boundary pixels match when they are within a distance of 2 pixels of each other.

However, in the NYU dataset, the ground-truth annotation is inaccurate at object boundaries. The influence of inaccurate boundaries is low when the recall

---

[1] BSDS dataset at http://www.eecs.berkeley.edu/Research/Projects/CS/vision/grouping/resources.html

[2] NYU dataset at http://cs.nyu.edu/~silberman/datasets/nyu_depth_v2.html

of ground-truth regions is measured, as is performed by Silberman *et al.* [8]. In addition, over-segmentation in boundary areas will not considerably degrade the precision score. However, it is our opinion that inaccurate boundaries and over-segmentation in boundary regions should not be ignored. Therefore, we pre-process the ground-truth annotations by thinning borders that are not annotated. Hence, since we have modified the dataset in this aspect, we cannot compare ourselves anymore to experiments of others with the original dataset. Instead, we can compare the mutual results of our different segmentation strategies with the modified dataset.

Parameter Selection and Validation. We have performed a parameter-range search for each pre-processing method on the training set of BSDS. After this training step, we select two sets of parameter settings: Θ_{T,F_u}, a setting with the highest unweighted harmonic mean F_u for the improved texture segmentation, and Θ_{T,F_w}, a setting with the highest weighted harmonic mean F_w. We select Θ_{T,F_w} such that it promotes P as a basis for multi-modal segmentation and aim at increasing R by including detected boundaries from other modi.

To validate our training, we run our texture segmentation with Θ_{T,F_u} and Θ_{T,F_w} on the test sets of both BSDS and NYU and compare it to the results of the LVS method, all using the luminance Y as texture input. Next, we execute our two multi-modal segmentation methods on the NYU test set. For this, we use Θ_{T,F_w} and a number of different settings for depth, normal and angle modi.

5   Segmentation Results

Uni-modal Segmentation. In our training results, Nonlinear Diffusion Filtering with the Weickert Diffusivity function outperforms the other filtering methods. We have selected Θ_{T,F_u} as the tenth level of the evolution with a contrast factor of 0.5 and $K_T = 300$, and Θ_{T,F_w} as the thirteenth level of the evolution with a contrast factor of 0.5 and $K_T = 1000$.

We have executed both settings on the full test sets of BSDS and NYU to check how generic the settings are. To provide precision-recall curves instead of points, we have performed a range search over K_T while keeping the pre- and post-processing settings constant. As a baseline reference, we also show the score of the LVS method with luminance values Y as texture input. The results are shown in Fig. 1, indicating that our trained settings perform consistently on the BSDS test data. For the NYU test set, the results are less distinctive, but still a slight improvement is achieved. This shows the robustness of our method, as the parameters were not trained on the NYU images and this dataset has worse lighting conditions and degraded image quality and also contains different types of scenes. More importantly, it has an inaccurate ground truth.

The results of all metrics provided in [2] are presented in Table 1. Using Y values instead of RGB triplets as texture input, increases the scores of LVS significantly. Our pre- and post-processing steps augment the score on the boundary

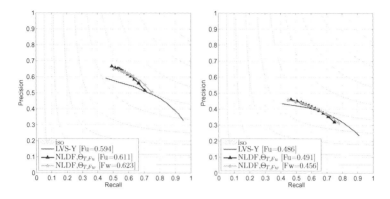

Fig. 1. Boundary detection results on the BSDS (left) and NYU (right) test sets. The settings used are Θ_{T,F_u} and Θ_{T,F_w}, with a range search over K_T to provide a curve.

Table 1. Boundary and region metrics of [2] on the BSDS test set

	Boundary	Region Covering	Region PRI	Region VI
LVS-RGB	0.55	0.46	0.79	3.27
LVS-Y	0.59	0.50	0.75	2.47
Θ_{T,F_u}	0.62	0.49	0.75	2.45

metric further, which is expected since we optimize our algorithm on boundary detection. Simultaneously, our extensions do not degrade the scores on the region-based metrics significantly. This again confirms the robustness of our method.

To illustrate our contributions visually, we show the results on several BSDS test images in Fig. 2. It is clear that our approach gives a cleaner and generally more accurate segmentation than the LVS method for various scenes. The rightmost image, for which we score the lowest F_u, is difficult for this LVS-based method, as the regions have high texture variation and no clear edges.

Multi-modal Segmentation. The quantitative results are summarized in Table 2. Overall, our method based on the combined weight clearly outperforms the method of using partial boundary functions. Using a combined weight of luminance and depth values provides the best results.

However, several improvements are small or even negative. The cause of this is analyzed with the graphs in Fig. 3 (b), where we plot the increase (or decrease) for F_u, R and P for each individual image and several different multi-modal methods, with the texture segmentation Θ_{T,F_w} as a reference. No image-index correspondences exist, since the images are sorted on their score for each graph separately. By plotting the scores in a sorted fashion, the graphs clearly show that although we generally achieve an increase in recall, we decrease the precision at the same time. This limits the increase in the overall F_u. Since we have designed the multi-modal segmentation to increase the recall of a high-precision

Fig. 2. Images of the BSDS test set. For each image, we show the original image (top), the result of LVS-Y (middle) and our result using Θ_{T,F_u} (bottom). The three images at the left are selected from the top 6 (ranked on F_u), right is the bottom one.

Table 2. Multi-modal Segmentation Results

Method	Key settings	F_u-score	increase
LVS-Y	max F_u on BSDS	0.480	
$B(Y)$	Θ_{T,F_u}	0.490	2.1%
	Θ_{T,F_w}	0.484	0.8%
$B(Y,D)$	$maxDist = 0.01$	0.478	-0.4%
	$maxDist = 0.15$	0.490	2.1%
$w_C(Y,D)$	$D^{-1}; K_c = 2$	0.512	6.8%
$B(Y,N)$	$K_N = 20$	0.440	-8.4%
$w_C(Y,N)$	$K_c = 2$	0.497	3.6%
$w_C(Y,A)$	$K_c = 2$	0.502	4.5%
$B(Y,D,N)$	$maxDist = 0.01; K_N = 20$	0.425	-11.5%
	$maxDist = 0.15; K_N = 20$	0.439	-8.6%
$w_C(Y,D,N)$	$D^{-1}; K_c = 2$	0.500	4.2%
$w_C(Y,D,A)$	$D^{-1}; K_c = 2$	0.510	6.3%

texture segmentation, this confirms our expectations. However, it also shows that our multi-modal segmentation methods are not applicable to all images. For example, setting a $maxDist$ in the partial boundary function helps distinguishing foreground from background objects when they have a similar texture. At the same time, it introduces false boundaries on surfaces that are at an angle with respect to the viewpoint. Similarly, normals provide additional object boundaries, but introduce false detections easily, on e.g. wrinkled surfaces. This is especially problematic in the noisy NYU data. Furthermore, it is striking that using more than two signals does not increase the performance further. From the $w_C(Y,A)$ (green) and $w_C(Y,D,A)$ (cyan, dashed) curves in Fig. 3 (b), it can

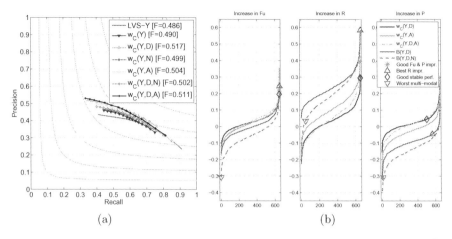

(a)   (b)

Fig. 3. (a): Boundary detection results on the NYU test set, using the combined weight with different modi. (b): Individual increase in F_u (left), Recall (middle) and Precision (right) by using additional signal modi with $K_c = 2$. Values pare sorted for clarity, so no image-index correspondences between graphs exist. The four images of Fig. 4 are marked.

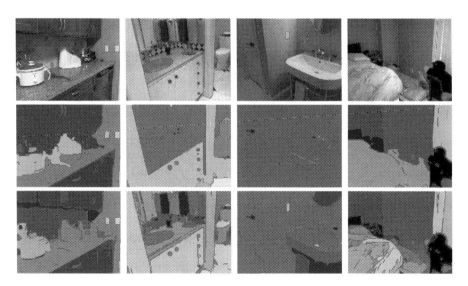

Fig. 4. Images of the NYU test set. For each image, we show the original image with ground truth (top), our texture segmentation result (Θ_{T,F_w}, middle) and a multi-modal result of interest (bottom); from left to right: $w_C(Y, A)$, $B(Y, D)$, $w_C(Y, D)$, $B(Y, D, N)$.

be seen that adding the third mode increases P but decreases R. This indicates that a more sophisticated way of combining the different modi can potentially boost the performance.

We show several practical results on NYU test images with our MLVS in Fig. 4. This figure displays four images with ground-truth overlay. For each image, we present the result of our texture segmentation and compare it to the result of our multi-modal segmentation. Each image is marked in the graphs of Fig. 3 (b). The leftmost image of Fig. 4 shows an example on which a good increase in both F_u and P is achieved, by using the combined weight of the luminance and angle signals. The highest increase in recall is obtained with the second image, using partial boundary functions on the texture and the depth signals. The third image shows a good performance of the most stable multi-modal approach (using a combined weight of luminance and depth values). The multi-modal segmentation performs worst on the fourth image, mainly due to the normal signal that causes false boundaries on the wrinkled blanket.

6   Conclusions, Discussion and Future Work

This paper aims at improving the well-known local variance segmentation method by adding extra signal modi and specific processing steps. To achieve this, we have developed an improved uni-modal texture-segmentation algorithm. With our choice of color space and additional pre- and post-processing steps, we have increased the harmonic mean of recall and precision (F_u) on the BSDS test set from 0.59 to 0.62, based on training with the BSDS training set. The same settings have improved the F_u metric on the NYU test set from 0.480 to 0.484, even though this dataset has worse lighting conditions, degraded image quality and also features different types of scenes.

Our second contribution extends this uni-modal segmentation method to perform multi-modal analysis, by introducing a method that can process any number of signal modi that are available in a flexible way. Based on the quantitative analysis on the NYU dataset, the use of a combined weight of luminance and depth values improves the F_u metric additionally from 0.484 to 0.512.

To assess the value of some of the aforementioned results, it should be noted that our uni-modal texture segmentation method does not outperform the state-of-the-art method of Arbeláez et al. [2] on the BSDS test set. We have selected an alternative graph-based method as a basis to extend it to multiple signal modi, since the full framework of Arbeláez et al. [2] is elaborate and complicated for multi-modal extensions.

We envision several possibilities for further improvement. First, although we have improved the results of LVS with pre- and post-processing steps, we consider that the seeding stage allows further optimization, such that all edges are evaluated with a parallel, more global approach to avoid border isolation. Second, the multi-modal algorithm should better exploit the different characteristics of signal modi. For example, the depth signal should primarily be used for separating foreground from background objects, and normals should mainly be applied to detect object surface boundaries. To this end, the boundary check or mode weight can be enhanced with e.g. the local confidence in a mode.

References

1. Alcantarilla, P.F., Bartoli, A., Davison, A.J.: KAZE Features. In: Fitzgibbon, A., Lazebnik, S., Perona, P., Sato, Y., Schmid, C. (eds.) ECCV 2012, Part VI. ECCV, vol. 7577, pp. 214–227. Springer, Heidelberg (2012)
2. Arbeláez, P., Maire, M., Fowlkes, C., Malik, J.: Contour detection and hierarchical image segmentation. IEEE Trans. on Pattern Analysis and Machine Intelligence (PAMI) 33(5), 898–916 (2011)
3. Cour, T., Benezit, F., Shi, J.: Spectral segmentation with multiscale graph decomposition. In: IEEE Comp. Soc. Conf. on Computer Vision and Pattern Recognition (CVPR), vol. 2, pp. 1124–1131. IEEE (2005)
4. Felzenszwalb, P.F., Huttenlocher, D.P.: Efficient Graph-Based Image Segmentation. Int. Journal of Computer Vision 59(2), 167–181 (2004)
5. Kropatsch, W., Haxhimusa, Y., Ion, A.: Multiresolution image segmentations in graph pyramids. Applied Graph Theory in Computer Vision and Pattern Recognition 41(2), 3–41 (2007)
6. Peng, B., Zhang, L., Zhang, D.: A survey of graph theoretical approaches to image segmentation. Pattern Recognition 46(3), 1020–1038 (2013)
7. Perona, P., Malik, J.: Scale-space and edge detection using anisotropic diffusion. IEEE Trans. on Pattern Analysis and Machine Intelligence (PAMI) 12(7), 629–639 (1990)
8. Silberman, N., Hoiem, D., Kohli, P., Fergus, R.: Indoor segmentation and support inference from RGBD images. In: Fitzgibbon, A., Lazebnik, S., Perona, P., Sato, Y., Schmid, C. (eds.) ECCV 2012, Part V. LNCS, vol. 7576, pp. 746–760. Springer, Heidelberg (2012)
9. Strom, J., Richardson, A., Olson, E.: Graph-based segmentation for colored 3D laser point clouds. In: IEEE/RSJ Int. Conf. on Intelligent Robots and Systems, pp. 2131–2136. IEEE, Taipei (2010)
10. Weickert, J.: Efficient image segmentation using partial differential equations and morphology. Pattern Recognition 34(9), 1813–1824 (1998)

The Divide and Segment Method for Parallel Image Segmentation

Thales Sehn Körting, Emiliano Ferreira Castejon,
and Leila Maria Garcia Fonseca

Brazil's National Institute for Space Research – INPE
Image Processing Division – DPI Av. dos Astronautas, 1758
São José dos Campos, Brazil
{thales,castejon,leila}@dpi.inpe.br

Abstract. Remote sensing images with large spatial dimensions are usual. Besides, they also include a diversity of spectral channels, increasing the volume of information. To obtain valuable information from remote sensing data, computers need higher amounts of memory and more efficient processing techniques. The first process in image analysis is segmentation, which identifies regions in images. Therefore, segmentation algorithms must deal with large amounts of data. Even with current computational power, certain image sizes may exceed the memory limits, which ask for different solutions. An alternative to overcome such limits is to employ the well-known divide and conquer strategy, by splitting the image into chunks, and segmenting each one individually. However, it arises the problem of merging neighboring chunks and keeping the homogeneity in such regions. In this work, we propose an alternative to divide the image into chunks by defining noncrisp borders between them. The noncrisp borders are computed based on Dijkstra algorithm, which is employed to find the shortest path between detected edges in the images. By applying our method, we avoid the postprocessing of neighboring regions, and therefore speed up the final segmentation.

1 Introduction

Remote sensing images are the only source capable of providing a continuous and consistent set of information about the Earth's land and oceans [8]. Combined with ecosystem models, remotely sensed data offers an unprecedented opportunity for predicting and understanding the behavior of the Earth's ecosystem [26]. Since the 1970s, the Landsat series of satellites have provided optical images of the land's surface of the Earth every 16 days at a resolution of 30 meters. The Landsat archive at the United States Geological Survey contains about 1 petabyte and is fully accessible worldwide [9]. From 2013 onwards, a new generation of optical remote sensing satellites from USA, China, Brazil, India and Europe will produce in one year as much data as 10 years of the Landsat-7 satellite.

However, our methods to analyze and understand massive datasets lag far behind our ability to produce and store this data [10,13,28]. And besides, it is

J. Blanc-Talon et al. (Eds.): ACIVS 2013, LNCS 8192, pp. 504–515, 2013.

still far from easy to search across large collections of satellite images for pictures containing a golf course, or a hurricane [14]. Therefore image analysis over large databases needs to be in the research agenda of the remote sensing community.

During the 1980s and 1990s, most remote sensing image analysis techniques were based on per-pixel statistical algorithms [7]. These techniques aimed at representing the knowledge about land cover patterns by a limited set of parameters, such as average and standard deviation values of groups of individual pixels. Recently, Object-Based Image Analysis (OBIA) has shown to be a good alternative to traditional per-pixel and region based approaches. Differently, OBIA approaches first identify regions in the image using segmentation, extract neighborhood, spectral and spatial descriptive features and afterwards combine regions and features for object classification. Although segmentation has a large tradition in image processing [16] and remote sensing [9], OBIA took a long time to reach mainstream users. This approach became popular when it combined image segmentation with good labeling methods that match the features to those of user-defined classes. However, remote sensing image analysis using OBIA can be lengthy and complex because of the difficulties related to image segmentation, the large number of features to be resolved [21] and the many different methods needed to model the semantic networks [17].

Segmentation of remote sensing images is a challenging field. Their results are expected to describe the regions found in images, allowing a deeper interpretation by experts or classification algorithms. The work of [16] defined segmentation as a way to separate the image into simple regions with homogeneous behavior. To partition automatically one image into regions, algorithms must consider the context, scale, neighborhood, meaning, and computational resources. In accord to [28], good quality results often come at the price of high computational cost. For example, the collection rate for IKONOS satellite is about 890 megapixels each minute [10]; for CBERS-2B is about 120 megapixels each minute. Considering current technology, even a tuned sequential segmentation algorithm is far slower than these rates.

Remote sensing images often present large sizes. A typical Landsat scene contains at least 7800×7100 pixels, and 6 spectral channels with 30m resolution (bands 1 to 5, and 7), that results in more than 300 million individual pixels. The variety of spectral channels, that in one side adds rich information about the land targets, in the other side increases the volume of information. Even with current computational power, certain sizes may exceed the memory limits, claiming new solutions. Research in segmentation techniques for large images points out the division of the image into blocks of predefined sizes, hereby called *chunks*. These chunks are segmented independently, and a postprocessing step is needed to merge the segmentation results into a single one. The problem of this approach is to merge the neighboring chunks without prejudicing the homogeneity in bordering regions. Figure 1 shows one example of this problem. The image was divided into crisp chunks and afterwards each one was segmented independently. The postprocessing in this case would not merge the regions highlighted in red (note the object of the type *roof*), because they present different attributes, like

Fig. 1. Example of the traditional parallel segmentation. Regions highlighted in red will not be merged properly.

average pixel value or standard deviation of pixels. The piece of the roof in the top region was too small to create an individual region, and therefore was merged in the region containing trees. Due to this problem, the bottom region with the rest of the roof will not be merged, because the spectral difference between these two regions is too high.

Another problem of this approach is the time processing. For example, suppose one image with 5000×5000 pixels, divided in two chunks of 2500 lines $\times$ 5000 columns, and a segmentation which created regions with an average area of 100×100 pixels. The border between these chunks will have at least 50 regions for each chunk, and the regions from one chunk will touch at least 2 regions from the other chunk. In this case, the algorithm will have to perform 100 tests between these regions to check whether they must be merged or not. Such comparisons include data access to evaluate average pixel values, vector differences, check if candidate merged regions will comply the segmentation parameters and so on. We argue that this step does not produce good results, and improve significantly the processing time. Our proposal is to convert this postprocessing into a preprocessing stage, cutting out the need to perform exhaustive tests in resultant regions.

In this article we tackle the problem of creating chunks for parallel segmentation. Instead of creating crisp chunks using the block strategy (which creates crisp borders), we analyze the image contours in the chunks' neighborhood, and create adaptive chunks defined by these contours. We argue that by defining noncrisp borders between the chunks we avoid the postprocessing of neighboring regions, remove the segmentation errors in the borders, and speed up the final segmentation.

2   Related Work

Several image segmentation techniques arise from the well-known "region grow-ing" strategy, relying on the similarity of near pixels. The method starts by defining candidate pixels (called seeds) in random positions of the image. Such seeds are compared to neighboring pixels, and according to their similarity, they are merged into homogeneous regions, therefore the pixels grow into larger regions. This process is repeated until all pixels are processed. [6] applied this approach in remote sensing images. Their method is based on the likeness between neighboring pixels and the smallest area allowed for a region. [2] is another example of region growing technique. In this approach, the algorithm minimizes the average heterogeneity of the regions. The heterogeneity balances the object's smoothness and compactness, resulting in more regular objects. It deals with the standard deviation of pixels for each band as well. We suggest the reading of [20] for a comparison of these two algorithms and alternatives for remote sensing segmentation.

To take advantage of the spatial similarity between neighboring pixels, the graph-based techniques create region adjacency graphs considering pixels as edges, and the differences between neighbor pixels as the edges. The work [12] presented the image foresting transform (IFT), a generalization of Dijkstra's algorithm, which is a graph-based approach to the design of image processing operators based on connectivity. This method considers one image as a directed graph whose nodes are the image pixels and whose arcs are the neighboring pixel pairs. It was applied to find homogeneous regions in 3D images and to perform boundary tracking, whose goal is to estimate an optimal curve, constrained to a given sequence of landmarks on the object's boundary.

[24] proposed an approach that extracts the global impression of an image, by treating image segmentation as a graph partitioning problem. The authors proposed a novel global criterion, called the normalized cuts, that measures both the total dissimilarity between the different groups of pixels as well as the total similarity within the groups. The algorithm has been tested in static images as well as motion sequences. The main idea is to create an adjacency matrix connecting all pixels in the image, and after perform the bipartitioning of the graph through normalized cuts, where the partitions will define the homogeneous regions in the image.

In the area of merging for creating mosaics of remote sensing images, [4] presented a blending technique, based on multi-resolution decomposition. The authors defined a cut line, considering texture information from overlapping regions of mosaicking images. The method found automatically the transition zone size and the cutting line on satellite and aerial images based on the minimum path using Dijkstra's algorithm.

The work of [5] presented one algorithm based on the morphological image compositing technique and applied to automatically generate a European wide image mosaic based on over 800 Landsat ETM+ scenes. A quantitative measure was also developed to estimate the quality of automatically delineated borders.

According to [19], parallel architectures are becoming a standard for handling complex operations that need significant computational power. Large size images include medical data sets of magnetic resonance imaging (MRI) [23], or remote sensing hyperspectral and multitemporal images [27,22]. Therefore parallel algorithms arise as an alternative to overcome those limits. As previously stated, such methods usually split the image into chunks, and segment each one individually.

The chunks often present regular sizes to be assigned equally among the processors [3]. However, according to [28] the results of coupling chunks are not acceptable because border objects are not correctly handled. A common solution is to adopt overlapping chunks, which is also inadequate because there is no upper bound on the size of objects of interest (e.g. rivers or roads). [25] proposed a parallel method for the seeded region growing algorithm ([1]), based on spreading seeds in different threads, each one growing in parallel. The authors needed to deal with simultaneous access for the same pixels. To avoid this problem, images were divided in square windows, employing a postprocessing step to join regions.

The technique proposed by [15] employed the traditional parallel segmentation. Each chunk was processed by a different thread, through a sequential algorithm based on [2]. This method falls on the same problem of treating boundary segments. The number of boundary objects, which depends on the image, can be prohibitive in certain cases.

3   Method

This work extends our previous research in parallel segmentation [18]. In the present approach, the algorithm finds automatically optimal cutting lines to divide the image into noncrisp chunks. Traditional parallel schemes first divide the image into crisp chunks, and after treat bordering regions in a postprocessing step. Some methods create chunks with overlapping regions, but fall into the same problem of postprocessing. Figure 2 describes our approach, and as follows we describe each step in detail.

3.1   Create Image of Edges

The first step is to obtain an image of edges based on the input data. From the basics of image processing, the well-known method to estimate the magnitude of the edges is the gradient function. Considering that in one image every pixel can be described as a function $f(x, y)$, where x and y are the coordinates of the pixel, the gradient is computed as the two-dimensional column vector:

$$\nabla \mathbf{f} = \begin{bmatrix} \frac{\delta f}{\delta x} \\ \frac{\delta f}{\delta y} \end{bmatrix} \tag{1}$$

which is a vector that indicates, for each pixel, the intensities of the border in horizontal and vertical directions. The magnitude of this vector points out the border's strength, and is computed by the following equation:

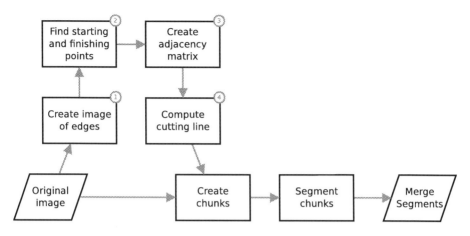

Fig. 2. Main diagram to find the optimal cutting line that divides the image into noncrisp chunks

$$mag(\nabla \mathbf{f}) = \left[\left(\frac{\delta f}{\delta x}\right)^2 + \left(\frac{\delta f}{\delta x}\right)^2\right]^{\frac{1}{2}}. \tag{2}$$

By applying these equations to all pixels of the image we obtain an image of edges. This image will be processed to find the optimal cutting line. The chunks must be defined with an average size (width and height) and a cutting line will be adapted according to the image of edges. Figure 3 shows one example of input image and its image of edges. Suppose this example image will be divided into 2 chunks. Therefore, a middle line (shown in yellow in Figure 3) is the candidate line. This candidate line will adapt to the shortest path between left and right edges. We also define a *region of interest*, limited by a maximum displacement between this candidate line to avoid chunks with very different sizes (shown in red in the Figure).

Fig. 3. The example input image (left) and its image of edges (right)

510 T.S. Körting, E.F. Castejon, and L.M. Garcia Fonseca

3.2 Find Starting and Finishing Points

To compute the cutting line, we must previously define starting and finishing points. We use the maximum value in the image of edges (higher magnitude in the gradient stands to the strongest border) at the beginning and end of the chunk. Considering the image of edges in Figure 3, they are represented by the higher values in the first and last columns, highlighted in green.

After, we create an adjacency graph (represented by a matrix) that connects all pixels in the candidate region. The Dijkstra's algorithm will be used to find the best path between starting and finishing points. This path will define the cutting line used to divide the image into noncrisp chunks.

3.3 Create Adjacency Matrix

The adjacency matrix is a graph, whose nodes are the image pixels and whose arcs are defined by an adjacency relation between pixels. The cost of a path in this graph, according to [12], is determined by an application-specific path-cost function, which usually depends on local image properties along the path, such as color, gradient, and pixel position. In our approach, the adjacency between the pixels is defined by 5 connections, including top, top-right, right, bottom-right and bottom pixels, as shown in Figure 4.

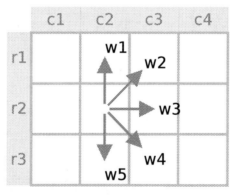

Fig. 4. The 5 weights associated to each pixel to build the adjacency matrix. The directions are top, top-right, right, bottom-right and bottom (w1 to w5).

The associated cost to each weight is defined by the magnitude of the gradient, therefore the highest magnitude has a lower cost. Since we defined 5 connections, we rank the cost with values in the interval $[1, 5]$, where 1 is the highest magnitude and 5 is the lowest. The choice of using 5 connections is to remove the adjacency between a pixel and its left side, so the discovered path will always have the direction tending to the right[1].

---

[1] This method is easily extensible to vertical cutting lines. In this case, the adjacency graph will be created to maintain a direction tending to the bottom, and the starting and finishing points will be defined in the top and in the bottom of the chunk.

3.4 Compute Cutting Line

Since we defined the starting and finishing points, and the adjacency matrix, it is possible to compute the best path between these two points. For this, we employ the Dijkstra's algorithm [11] using the weights between the pixels to find the best cutting line. This line will define the noncrisp border between the chunks, and will allow the segmentation algorithm to run independently in both chunks. The resulting segmentation will be the simple merge of regions detected in all chunks.

4 Results and Discussion

To evaluate the method we performed 2 experiments using images with different spatial and spectral resolutions. The purpose of the following experiments is to show that the resultant cutting line divided the image into independent chunks, in terms of the resultant regions from segmentation. For the sake of comparison, we tested our previous approach [18] in the same images, using equivalent parameters.

In the first experiment we used an image crop of a World View 2 scene from São José dos Campos, Brazil, with 3200×2400 pixels. The pixels of this image have a spatial resolution of 0.5m. The image was obtained in 2012. We defined the region of interest with a size of 120 pixels. Figure 5 (top) shows the detected cutting line. After this step, we applied segmentation (based on [6]) in both chunks and obtained the regions depicted in Figure 6.

Comparing our results, the cutting line created by our previous approach is shown in Figure 5 (bottom). It is possible to see that both results followed the edges inside the region of interest. By applying the Dijkstra's algorithm the cutting line got a smoother transition between pixels, while the previous approach resulted in a line with several spikes. It is noticeable that the cutting line divided the road (in the left part of the image) in two pieces, which is a limit of our method. When the object does not follow the direction of the cutting line (in this example, horizontal direction), the segmentation will produce divided regions. The second mistake is in the grass field; however this mistake were caused because of the size of the region of interest.

The second experiment used an image crop of a Quickbird scene from São Paulo, Brazil, with 1000×1175 pixels. The pixels of this image have a spatial resolution of 0.6m. We defined the region of interest with a size of 150 pixels. Figure 7 (top) shows the resultant cutting line. After this step, we applied the segmentation in both chunks (also using the approach based on [6]) and obtained the regions depicted in Figure 8. The cutting line produced by our previous approach is shown in Figure 7 (bottom). It is possible to see that in this result, the cutting line is not smooth, and presents high and low peaks along the line.

Fig. 5. First experiment: the cutting line created by our approach (top), in comparison to our previous method (bottom).

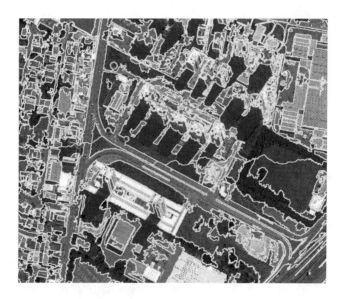

Fig. 6. Detail of the resulting segmentation, after merging segments from both chunks

Fig. 7. Second experiment: the cutting line created by our approach (top), in comparison to our previous method (bottom)

Fig. 8. The resulting segmentation, after merging segments from both chunks

5   Conclusion

This article tackled the specific problem of defining chunks for parallel segmentation. Current methods create crisp chunks, needing postprocessing steps to get final regions. In certain cases, such methods create inconsistent objects, demanding computational power to deal with bordering regions. Postprocessing detects the bordering regions, testing the best combination of regions to merge. This step aims to keep the consistence of the new regions to specific segmentation parameters, as spectral homogeneity and size. Our method proposes to change this postprocessing step into a preprocessing stage, by creating adaptive cutting lines and dividing the images into chunks without crisp borders.

However, the shape of certain objects near the cutting line does not allow creating a proper cutting line, like homogeneous regions whose size extrapolates the region of interest defined by the region of interest. Therefore dealing with these regions still remains an open problem, currently unsolved by our approach. Albeit in the results section we showed only horizontal chunks, this method easily extendable to vertical cutting lines. Another point is that Dijkstra's method is a greedy algorithm, which depending on the size of the adjacency matrix, can become a bottleneck in this operation. Future works on this issue include subdividing the cutting line into smaller subsets, and applying our approach individually on each subset, then recomposing the final cutting line by merging all subsets.

Acknowledgments. The authors acknowledge Digital Globe for providing the WorldView 2 imagery used in this article.

References

1. Adams, R., Bischof, L.: Seeded region growing. Pattern Analysis and Machine 16 (1994)
2. Baatz, M., Schape, A., Schäpe, M.: Multiresolution segmentation: an optimization approach for high quality multi-scale image segmentation. In: Wichmann-Verlag (ed.) XII Angewandte Geographische Informationsverarbeitung, pp. 12–23. Herbert Wichmann Verlag, Heidelberg (2000)
3. Bader, D., Jaja, J., Harwood, D., Davis, L.: Parallel algorithms for image enhancement and segmentation by region growing with an experimental study. In: Proceedings of International Conference on Parallel Processing, pp. 414–423 (1996)
4. Bagli, V., Fonseca, L.: Seamless mosaicking via multiresolution analysis and cut line definition. In: Signal and Image Processing. ACTA Press (2006)
5. Bielski, C., Grazzini, J., Soille, P.: Automated morphological image composition for mosaicing large image data sets. In: IEEE International Geoscience and Remote Sensing Symposium, IGARSS 2007, pp. 4068–4071 (2007)
6. Bins, L., Fonseca, L., Erthal, G., Ii, F.: Satellite imagery segmentation: a region growing approach. Simpósio Brasileiro de Sensoriamento Remoto 8, 677–680 (1996)
7. Blaschke, T.: Object based image analysis for remote sensing. ISPRS Journal of Photogrammetry and Remote Sensing 65(1), 2–16 (2010)
8. Bradley, B., Jacob, R., Hermance, J., Mustard, J.: A curve fitting procedure to derive inter-annual phenologies from time series of noisy satellite NDVI data. Remote Sensing of Environment 106(2), 137–145 (2007)
9. Câmara, G., Souza, R., Freitas, U., Garrido, J., Li, F.: Spring: Integrating remote sensing and gis by object-oriented data modelling. Computers and Graphics 20(3), 395–403 (1996)
10. Dial, G., Bowen, H., Gerlach, F., Grodecki, J., Oleszczuk, R.: IKONOS satellite, imagery, and products. Remote Sensing of Environment 88(1-2), 23–36 (2003)
11. Dijkstra, E.: A note on two problems in connexion with graphs. Numerische mathematik, 269–271 (1959)

12. Falcão, A., Stolfi, J., Lotufo, R.: The Image Foresting Transform: Theory, Algorithms, and Applications. IEEE Transactions on Pattern Analysis and Machine Intelligence 26(1), 19–29 (2004)
13. Fayyad, U., Shapiro, G., Smyth, P.: The KDD process for extracting useful knowledge from volumes of data. Communications of the ACM 39(11), 27–34 (1996)
14. Goodchild, M.F.: Geographic information systems and science: today and tomorrow. Annals of GIS 15(1), 3–9 (2009)
15. Happ, P., Ferreira, R., Bentes, C., Costa, G., Feitosa, R.: Multiresolution segmentation: a parallel approach for high resolution image segmentation in multicore architectures. In: The International Archives of the Photogrammetry, Remote Sensing and Spatial Information Sciences (2010)
16. Haralick, R., Shapiro, L.: Image segmentation techniques. Applications of Artificial Intelligence II 548, 2–9 (1985)
17. Hay, G., Castilla, G.: Geographic Object-Based Image Analysis (GEOBIA): A new name for a new discipline. In: Blaschke, T., Lang, S., Hay, G. (eds.) Object-Based Image Analysis: Spatial Concepts for Knowledge-Driven Remote Sensing Applications, chap. 1.4, pp. 75–89. Springer, Heidelberg (2008)
18. Körting, T., Castejon, E., Fonseca, L.: Divide and Segment - An alternative for parallel segmentation. In: Proceedings of XII GeoINFO, pp. 97–104. INPE, Campos do Jordão (2011)
19. Lenkiewicz, P., Pereira, M., Freire, M., Fernandes, J.: A new 3D image segmentation method for parallel architectures. In: 2009 IEEE International Conference on Multimedia and Expo, pp. 1813–1816 (June 2009)
20. Meinel, G., Neubert, M.: A comparison of segmentation programs for high resolution remote sensing data. International Archives of Photogrammetry and Remote Sensing 35(Part B), 1097–1105 (2004)
21. Pinho, C., Silva, F., Fonseca, L., Monteiro, A.: Intra-urban land cover classification from high-resolution images using the C4.5 algorithm. ISPRS Congress Beijing 7 (2008)
22. Plaza, A., Plaza, J., Paz, A., Sanchez, S.: Parallel Hyperspectral Image and Signal Processing. IEEE Signal Processing Magazine 28, 119–126 (2011)
23. Prassni, J., Ropinski, T., Hinrichs, K.: Uncertainty-aware guided volume segmentation. IEEE Transactions on Visualization and Computer Graphics 16(6), 1358–1365 (2010)
24. Shi, J., Malik, J.: Normalized cuts and image segmentation. IEEE Transactions on Pattern Analysis and Machine Intelligence 22(8), 888–905 (2000)
25. Singh, D., Heras, D., Rivera, F.: Parallel Seeded Region Growing Algorithm. In: VIII Simposium Nacional de Reconocimiento de Formas y Análisis de Imágenes, Bilbao, Spain (1999)
26. Tan, P., Steinbach, M., Kumar, V., Potter, C., Klooster, S., Torregrosa, A.: Finding Spatio-Temporal Patterns in Earth Science Data. Earth Science, 1–12 (2001)
27. Valencia, D., Lastovetsky, A., O'Flynn, M., Plaza, A., Plaza, J.: Parallel Processing of Remotely Sensed Hyperspectral Images on Heterogeneous Networks of Workstations Using HeteroMPI. IJHPCA, 386–407 (November 2008)
28. Wassenberg, J., Middelmann, W., Sanders, P.: An efficient parallel algorithm for graph-based image segmentation. In: Jiang, X., Petkov, N. (eds.) CAIP 2009. LNCS, vol. 5702, pp. 1003–1010. Springer, Heidelberg (2009)

Unsupervised Segmentation for Transmission Imaging of Carbon Black

Lydie Luengo[1–3], Hélène Laurent[2,3], Sylvie Treuillet[3], Isabelle Jolivet[1], and Emmanuel Gomez[1]

[1] CDR HUTCHINSON, rue Gustave Nourry, 45120 Châlette sur loing, France
[2] Laboratoire PRISME, ENSI de Bourges, 88 boulevard lahitolle, 18020 Bourges, France
[3] Laboratoire PRISME, PolytechOrleans, 45067 Orléans cedex 2, France
{lydie.luengo,isabelle-c.jolivet,
emmanuel.gomez}@cdr.hutchinson.fr,
helene.laurent@ensi-bourges.fr,
sylvie.treuillet@univ-orleans.fr

Abstract. During the last few years, the development of nanomaterials increases in many fields of sciences (biology, material, medicine…) to control physical-chemical properties. Among these materials, carbon black is the oldest one and is widely used as reinforcement filler in rubber products. Nevertheless, the interaction between nanoparticles and polymer matrix is poorly understood. In other words carbon black aggregate's characteristics are usually obtained by poorly official indirect analyses. This article presents an image processing chain allowing subsequent characterization of the carbon black aggregates. A database of several hundred samples of carbon black images has been collected using transmission electron microscopy. A significant selection of images has been manually expertised for ground truth. Using supervised evaluation criteria, a comparative study is performed with state-of-the-art carbon black segmentation algorithms, highlighting the good performances of the proposed algorithm.

Keywords: carbon black, image processing, segmentation, transmission electron microscopy.

1   Introduction

Produced by various thermic processes (furnace, lamp, tunnel, gas), carbon black is one of the fillers mostly used in the rubber industry. It can be described at macroscopic and nanometric scales, with pellets put into blend and primary particle, respectively. Its own characteristics modify reinforcing, conductive or protective properties of the final product [1].

However, fundamental relationships between properties, structure and morphology are difficult reachable. Methods based on chemical analyses allow measurement of surface area and structure of the carbon black in the dry state [2]. However, these measures are indirect and not satisfactory for a full characterization of the nanoscale phenomenon.

J. Blanc-Talon et al. (Eds.): ACIVS 2013, LNCS 8192, pp. 516–525, 2013.
© Springer International Publishing Switzerland 2013

To achieve such characterization, the most appropriate technique remains transmission electron microscopy (TEM), which allows the observation of spherical units, their organization and the aggregate distribution in rubber blends. In the sixties and seventies, especially through many works of Medalia [3] [4] and Hess [5] [6], this TEM method has been used to describe carbon black aggregates. Nowadays, ASTM 3849 [7] is the primary reference. This standard describes a simple analytical method for the morphological characterization of carbon black aggregates from the processing of transmission electron microscope images. Studies based on this standard have been carried out to investigate further the analysis of primary structure, using skeletons [8] or fractal geometries [9].

In order to study a larger number of samples and to decrease user intervention and subjectivity, some authors focused on the development of analysis techniques presenting higher automation. In 1969, the first "automatic" processing for electron micrographs (QUANTIMET) [10] is designed. It allows for the first time to carry out basic measures on large numbers of aggregate samples. Recently, Lopez and coworkers [11] developed a method allowing automatic characterization of aggregates morphology (branched, linear, ellipsoidal and spheroidal) on TEM images. Based on ASTM 3849 standard [7], they propose to set the magnification according to carbon black aggregates and to isolate them through gaussian smoothing and Otsu's thresholding method [12]. Morphological operations are finally applied. A major flaw of this proposal is its semi-automatic processing relying on user intervention. Moreover, the last morphological step results in aggregate distorsion due to the used structural element.

All the techniques mentioned above ultimately stay mostly manual and time-consuming, reducing their practical applicability. In order to automatically extract carbon black descriptive indices from transmission electron imaging, an effective segmentation step is necessary. The goal of this paper is to present the segmentation tool developed purpose. Next section presents the analytical method used and the considered samples. Section 3 describes the carbon black segmentation algorithm proposed. Finally, section 4 is dedicated to performance evaluation, including the results of the conducted comparative study.

2   Materials

To get good nanometer observations of carbon black, the specimen preparation and the image acquisition protocol have to be carefully laid-out.

2.1   Specimen Preparation

Based on ASTM 3849 [7], we have developed a preparation protocol facilitating the dispersion of the aggregates. Firstly, pellets are ground between two glass slides cleaned beforehand with acetone in an ultrasonic bath. Then 8 to 10 mg of carbon black are suspended in a test tube with 1 mL of tetrahydrofuran (THF). Prior to dispersing the solution in ultrasonic bath for 5 minutes, the test tube is put into ice to decrease the temperature and favor the dispersion of the aggregates. A second dilution of a few drops of the first solution is needed in 1mL of THF repeating the agitation step. Then, a drop of the solution is put on TEM coated carbon membrane grid. The grid is placed on a filter paper to absorb the solvent and dried in an oven at 80 ° C in a view to evaporate residual solvent. Finally, the grid is placed on the STEM[1] sample holder.

In this study, we analyzed five standard carbon blacks: N115, N330, N550, N772 and N990, therefore sweeping a whole group of carbon blacks, from the smallest to the biggest rank.

2.2   Electron Microscopy Device

The images are acquired by using a Zeiss Supra 35 field emission gun scanning electron microscope (FEG-SEM), equipped with a STEM retractable detector, which allows transmission observations at nanoscopic scale (0.8 nm at 30 KV). This detector is an excellent alternative to transmission electron microscope with optimal resolution of 0.1 nm (300 KV), since it offers better "transparency" views with better contrast and resolution because of lower acceleration voltage [13]. High-resolution SEM-STEM provides satisfactory and complementary visualizations in transmission and scanning of carbon black aggregates. Figure 1 shows two examples of TEM and SEM-STEM images. All database images of carbon blacks are acquired at acceleration voltage of 20KV.

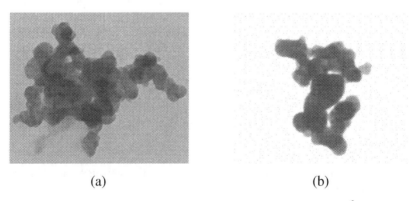

(a)   (b)

Fig. 1. Images of carbon black aggregate N772- acquired with (a) TEM-CTμ[2] Lyon FRANCE and (b) SEM-STEM-CDR Hutchinson

---

[1] STEM : Scanning transmission electron microscopy.
[2] CTμ : Centre Technologique des Microstructures.

2.3   Image Database

The database is composed of two series of 20 images for each carbon black: the first one acquired at low magnification (20,000 X with pixel size 5.6 nm), to study geometric properties of aggregates (shape factor, size ...); the second one at high magnification (80,000X with pixel size 1.4 nm) for a better observation of aggregates morphology (primary particles, branches...). All images have a resolution of 1024 × 768 pixels by pixels. Despite the care applied to the preparation, image artifacts remain. Among all images from the database, 32 were selected. The selection was made according to two criteria: the goal was to consider representatives of almost all carbon black types and to include a large panel of "imperfections" such as the presence of membrane, pollution, contamination of hydrocarbons and grid. These 32 images were manually segmented thus constituting the corresponding ground truth (GT). These ideal segmentations consist in artefact removal and aggregate delineation, preserving contours and cavities within aggregates. Figure 2 presents examples of the expertised images and corresponding GT. This expert information was used to define a specific image segmentation method which is detailed in the following section.

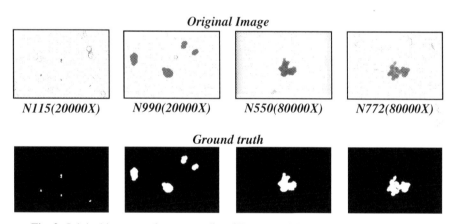

Fig. 2. Original images and corresponding GT extracted from the expertised database

3   Proposed Segmentation for Carbon Black Transmission Imaging

The objective of the proposed segmentation algorithm is to automatically separate carbon black aggregates from STEM images background. Segmentation methods [7], [11], conventionally used for carbon blacks characterization which are applicable to STEM images. Nevertheless, they give unsatisfactory results, requiring manual adjustment, taking into account pollutions, deleting smallest aggregates and distorting aggregate shape.

The new segmentation method is based on 3 steps: firstly, the image is partitionned using an unsupervised classification method, then an adaptive binarization is performed, followed by a cleaning step based on morphological and texture properties of the potential aggregates.

For the first step, several state-of-art methods have been tested to obtain an unsupervised segmentation of carbon black images. According to the comparative study proposed in the next section, a KMEANS algorithm is adopted.

In the second step, the algorithm analyzes all regions to realize an adaptive binarization. An area R is declared as background if the following condition satisfies:

$$m_b - \sigma_b \leq P(R) \leq m_b + \sigma_b \qquad (1)$$

with $(R) = \frac{1}{\sigma_b\sqrt{2\pi}}\exp\left[-\frac{1}{2}\left(\frac{R-m_b}{\sigma_b}\right)^2\right]$, and m_b, σ_b , respectively, represent the mean and standard deviation of the grey levels extracted from the background reference histogram. This histogram was obtained taking advantage of the expertised image database and considering all background areas manually extracted by the experts. Then we define a binary image containing potential aggregates as background complement.

Finally, a cleaning phase is realized. In order to retrieve aggregates, each connected component is analyzed to extract measurements and calculate shape index. The different stages of cleaning are described below:

— Suppression of small pollutions having a diameter lower than 85 nm, which is the minimal referenced diameter of aggregates [15]

— Shape study by thresholding according to the following three indices:
surface convexity: $SC = \frac{A}{A(C_H)}$, geodesic extension: $GE = \frac{4}{\pi}\frac{A}{D_G^2}$ and porosity index: $P_t = \frac{A}{A_t}$, where A is the surface of shape S, C_H its convex hull, D_G its geodesic diameter (biggest geodesic distance between two points of S) and A_t the empty areas within S.

These three indices were selected thanks to a preliminary study conducted on an expert database listing on the one hand "aggregates" and on the other hand "imperfections". Different shape indices such as the ones mentioned in Thibault's studies [16] were tested. Thresholding techniques applied on the three indices mentioned above led to the best results to separate individuals according to their class.

— Distribution analysis of regions' gray level.
For the aggregates selection, the same procedure is applied as for the selection of background. A R region is declared as aggregate part if:

$$m_a - \sigma_a \leq P(R) \leq m_a + \sigma_a \qquad (2)$$

where $(R) = \frac{1}{\sigma_a\sqrt{2\pi}}\exp\left[-\frac{1}{2}\left(\frac{R-m_a}{\sigma_a}\right)^2\right]$, m_a and σ_a respectively represent the mean and standard deviation of the grey levels extracted from aggregates reference histogram. This histogram was obtained taking into account all aggregates manually labelled by the experts.

— Elimination of aggregates that touch the outside edge, to avoid subsequent structure analysis distortion

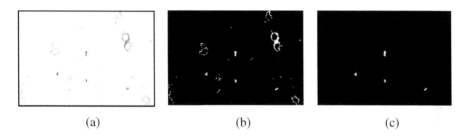

(a)   (b)   (c)

Fig. 3. Examples of results obtained after the different steps of the proposed method (a) STEM image at 20,000X on carbon black N115, (b) KMEANS segmentation of the image, (c) final segmentation result

Figure 3 shows results obtained after the different steps of the proposed segmentation algorithm. The next section is dedicated to the quantitative performance evaluation of the method including a comparative study with other segmentation algorithms previously introduced in the literature.

4   Performance Evaluation

4.1   Metrics for Comparison with GT

Evaluation protocol is based on GT established by experts as ideal image segmentation. Several metrics are available to quantify performances of algorithms in a such supervised context. Each of these metrics relies on overlap measures combined in different ways. In order to check if the evaluation metric choice highly influences the final conclusions, we implemented four metrics commonly used for the evaluation of segmentation and object detection methods: Matthews Correlation Coefficient (MCC), Martin's criteria (LCE and GCE) and Hafiane's criterion (HAF).

Relying on the set theory, MCC [19] analyses two segmentations (in our case, one segmentation result and the GT) as two sets and computes a correlation coefficient that takes into account the true positives and the false negatives. This criterion varies between -1 and 1 where 1 corresponds to a perfect correlation between the two considered sets. Martin and al. defined in [20] a local measure error between two segmentation results which is not symmetric. Given this local refinement error in each direction at each pixel, they combine the values, in two different ways, into error measures for the entire image: the global consistency error (GCE) and local consistency error (LCE). In order to facilitate the comparison, these criteria have been redisplayed to evolve between 0 and 1, 1 corresponding to a perfect correspondence between the segmentation result and the GT. Finally, based on overlap measures, HAF gives less influence to small classes than to large ones [21]. It also penalizes over and under-segmentations.

4.2   Segmentation Results

As mentioned above, first step of the developed method relies on an unsupervised region segmentation. We focus on three state-of-art algorithms for a comparative study.

K-means method [14] which is a conventional classification tool that divides a set of data into a K predefined number of homogeneous classes, JSEG algorithm [17] which uses color and texture information for classification and GBS algorithm [18] which is a graph-based segmentation method.

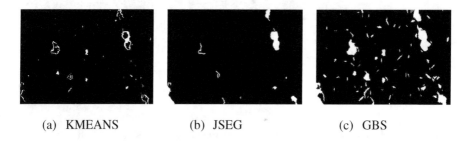

(a) KMEANS   (b) JSEG   (c) GBS

Fig. 4. Examples of results obtained at the end of the clustering step (a) KMEANS with k=3, (b) JSEG where l =10, m=0.2, q=2, (c) GBS $\sigma = 0.5$ $k = 200$ $min = 100$

Figure 4 shows results of each method whose parameters have been optimised to get best aggregates segmentation. Since the classification methods used do not provide at the end the same number of classes, the largest region has been considered as background. The mean results obtained using the different evaluation methods are presented in table 1. These results give the K-Means algorithm with parameter K = 3 as yielding the best results. JSEG and GBS algorithms underperformance can be explained by the lack of texture within the considered images. Since the metric results had similar trends, we decided in this article to solely consider the MCC criterion.

Table 1. Evaluations of the three tested clustering methods on 20000X and 80000X images using different evaluation metrics

		MCC	GCE	LCE	HAF
	KMEANS	**0,756**	**0,995**	**0,996**	**0,991**
20000X	JSEG	0,475	0,984	0,988	0,963
	GBS	0,453	0,980	0,990	0,911
	KMEANS	**0,832**	**0,993**	**0,996**	**0,991**
80000X	JSEG	0,675	0,943	0,988	0,963
	GBS	0,652	0,943	0,990	0,911

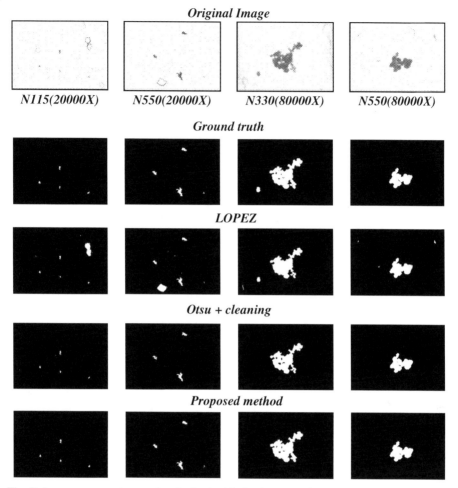

Fig. 5. Some segmentation results obtained with the three tested methods. Pictures in the first and second rows respectively represent original images and corresponding GT, while the other rows consist in segmentation results.

4.3   Comparison with Existing Works on Carbon Blacks

We compared the proposed algorithm with methods conventionally used for carbon blacks characterization through TEM images. This includes Otsu's thresholding completed with cleaning stage and the algorithm developed by Lopez and al. [11]. Pictures shown in figure 5 illustrate segmentation results obtained from the three compared methods on several original images, while mean quantitative evaluation obtained using MCC is presented in table 2. Actually, Lopez and Otsu's methods are penalized by oversegmentation errors due to pollution detection and by undersegmentation errors because of the loss of some parts in the objects' boundaries. On the opposite, our method achieves unscattered carbon black region segmentation correlated with aggregate shape, detecting cavities within the aggregates and removing automatically "imperfections".

Table 2. Evaluations of the three tested segmentation methods on 20000X and 80000X images using MCC metric

		KMEANS K=3	KMEANS K=3 + Cleaning	OTSU + Cleaning	LOPEZ
20000X	MCC	0.78 +/-0.1	**0.91** +/-0.06	0.86 +/-0.08	0.81 +/-0.09
80000X	MCC	0.96 +/- 0.02	**0.97** +/- 0.02	0.94 +/-0.03	0.94 +/-0.02

1   Conclusion and Future Works

Characterization of carbon black aggregates is essential to understand blends, since the morphology of this filler highly influences the mechanical properties and qualities of the final product. Many studies described carbon black, but none of them allowed filler routine control because of insufficient automation. The work presented in this article tries to fill this gap by contributing to the creation of automatic tools allowing to extract carbon black aggregates morphological characteristics.

In this paper, we proposed to focus on the first part of this problem, namely the automatic extraction of carbon black aggregates. The segmentation is carried out on STEM images. Based on KMEANS partitioning, the proposed algorithm includes a cleaning phase thanks to which artefacts can be removed through aggregates shape and histogram study. Compared with existing segmentation algorithms through a supervised evaluation protocol detailed in this paper, the defined algorithm achieves in interesting performance regardless of the considered magnification.

We plan in future works to complete the process for automatic aggregate characterization, including the extraction of nodule size, branch index, shape index... The veracity or adequacy of values obtained with STEM analysis, on the basis of the above principles, will be checked through 3D electron tomography.

References

1. Donnet, J.B., Bansal, R.C., Wang, M.J.: Carbon Black Science and Technology, 2nd edn. Marcel Dekker, New York (1993)
2. ASTM D 2663 - 08: Standard Test Methods for Carbon Black – Dispersion in Rubber (2008)
3. Medalia, A.I.: Morphology of aggregates. I. Calculation of shape and bulkiness factors; application to computer-simulated random flocs. Journal of Colloid and Interface Science 24, 393–404 (1967)
4. Medalia, A.I., Heckman, F.A.: Morphology of aggregates—II. Size and shape factors of carbon black aggregates from electron microscopy. Cabot Corporation 567–568 (1969)
5. Burgess, K.A., Scott, C.E., Hess, W.M.: Carbon black morphology. New techniques for characterization. Rubber World 164, 48–53 (1971)
6. Hess, W.M., McDonald, G.C., Urban, E.: Specific Shape Characterization of Carbon Black Primary Units. Rubber Chemistry and Technology 46(1), 204–231 (1973)

7. ASTM D3849 - 07: Standard Test Method for Carbon Black—Morphological Characterization of Carbon Black Using Electron Microscopy (2011)
8. Herd, C.R., McDonald, G.C., Smith, R.E., Hess, W.M.: The Use of Skeletonization for the Shape Classification of Carbon Black Aggregate. Rubber Chemistry and Technology 66(4), 491–509 (1993)
9. Herd, C.R., McDonald, G.C., Hess, W.M.: Morphology of carbon-black aggregates: fractal versus euclidean geometry. Rubber Chemistry and Technology 65(1), 107–129 (1992)
10. Hess, W.M., Ban, L.L., McDonald, G.C.: Carbon Black Morphology: I. Particule Microstructure. II. Automated em analysis of aggregate size and shape. Rubber Chemistry and Technology 42(4), 1209–1234 (1969)
11. López-de-Uralde, J., Ruiz, I., Santos, I., Zubillaga, A., Bringas, P.G., Okariz, A., Guraya, T.: Automatic Morphological Categorisation of Carbon Black Nano-aggregates. In: Bringas, P.G., Hameurlain, A., Quirchmayr, G. (eds.) DEXA 2010, Part II. LNCS, vol. 6262, pp. 185–193. Springer, Heidelberg (2010)
12. Otsu, N.: Threshold Selection Method from Gray-Level Histograms. IEEE Trans. Syst. Man. Cybern. SMC-9, 62–66 (1979)
13. Bogner, A., Jouneau, P.-H., Thollet, G., Basset, D., Gauthier, C.: A History of Scanning Electron Microscopy Developments: Towards 'wet-STEM' Imaging. Micron 38(4), 390–401 (2007)
14. MacQueen, J.B.: Some Methods for Classification and Analysis of MultiVariate Observations. In: Proceedings of 5th Berkeley Symposium on Mathematical Statistics and Probability, pp. 281–297. University of California Press (1967)
15. Carbon Black User's Guide, Safety, Health, & Environmental Information (2004)
16. Thibault, G.: Indices de Textures: Application au Classement de Noyaux de Cellules. Doctorale Thesis, University Aix-Marseille (2009)
17. Deng, Y.: Unsupervised Segmentation of Color-Texture Regions in Images and Video. IEEE Transactions on Pattern Analysis and Machine Intelligence 23(8), 800–810 (2001)
18. Felzenszwalb, P.F., Huttenlocher, P.D.: Efficient Graph-Based Image Segmentation. Int'l Conf. Computer Vision 59(2), 167–181 (2004)
19. Matthews, B.W.: Comparison of the Predicted and Observed Secondary Structure of T4 phage lysozyme. Biochimica and Biophysica Acta 405, 442–451 (1975)
20. Martin, D., Fowlkes, C., Tal, D., Malik, J.: A Database of Human Segmented Natural Images and its Application to Evaluating Segmentation Algorithms and Measuring Ecological Statistics. In: Proc. 8th Int'l Conf. Computer Vision, vol. 2, pp. 416–423 (2001)
21. Hafiane, A., Chabrier, S., Rosenberger, C., Laurent, H.: A New Supervised Evaluation Criterion for Region Based Segmentation Methods. In: Blanc-Talon, J., Philips, W., Popescu, D., Scheunders, P. (eds.) ACIVS 2007. LNCS, vol. 4678, pp. 439–448. Springer, Heidelberg (2007)

Tree Symbols Detection
for Green Space Estimation

Adrian Sroka and Marcin Luckner

Faculty of Mathematics and Information Science
Warsaw University of Technology
Koszykowa 75, 00-662 Warsaw, Poland
suvroc.adrian@gmail.com,
mluckner@mini.pw.edu.pl
http://www.mini.pw.edu.pl/~lucknerm/en/

Abstract. Geodetic base maps are very detailed sources of information. However, such maps are created for specialists and incomprehensible to non–professionals. An example of information that can be useful for citizen is change of urban green spaces. Such spaces, valuable for a local society can be destroyed by developers or a local government. Therefore, a monitoring of green areas is an important task that can be done on the basis of maps from Geodetic Documentation Centres. Unfortunately, the most popular form of digital documentations is a bitmap. This work presents a feasibility study of green areas estimation from scanned maps. The solution bases on symbols detection. Two kinds of symbols (coniferous and deciduous trees) are recognised by the following algorithm. Dots from centres of symbols are detected and their neighbourhood is extracted. Specific features are calculated as an input for neural networks that detect tree symbols. The accuracy of the detection is 90 percent, which is good enough to estimate green areas.

Keywords: Maps understanding, image understanding, image processing, pattern recognition.

1 Introduction

The main subject of this work is a detection of green spaces on geodetic base maps. Geodetic base maps are a source of information for many professions (e.g. architects, cartographers). They provide a precision image of a ground surface. Each object on them should be measured in the reality. This precision is very useful in many applications (c.f. spatial planning). Most of currently used maps are available only in a paper version. They were drawn by draughtsmen by hand. Due to a global computerisation today, many of them are converting to an electronic version. A segment of scanned map is given in Figure 1.

A visualisation of green areas on maps can help the user with an easy and quick identification of those areas. This paper describes image processing and classification methods to convert specialist symbols into generalised information. Section 2 presents a motivation for this work and Section 3 presents state of art.

J. Blanc-Talon et al. (Eds.): ACIVS 2013, LNCS 8192, pp. 526–537, 2013.

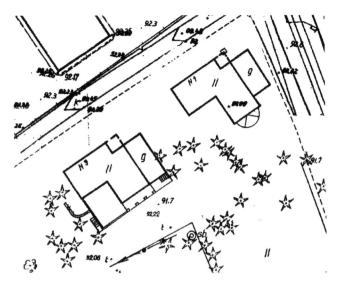

Fig. 1. A segment of geodetic map

The generalisation is based on a detection of tree symbols. The specialist symbols are described in Section 4.1. The first step of detection is an extraction of potential candidates from an image for a further classification in order to verify its membership to specific group of symbols. The main part of each symbol is a dot situated in its centre. The detection of dots (presented in Section 4.2) is a very useful tool to detect positions of trees. Next, symbols are extracted as segments of the whole map. The extraction described in Section 4.3 results in noised symbols. Therefore, the most important part of the entire solution is a selection of such features that allow a classifier to separate tree symbols from the others in spite of distortions. The proposed features are presented in Section 4.4. Finally, neural networks are used as a classifier (Section 4.5) and the classification results are given in Section 5. Conclusions are presented in Section 6.

2   Motivation

Economic and social changes bring massive expansion, redevelopment, and restructuring of cities. The changes influence on urban green spaces. The green spaces are important part of urban ecosystem in opinion of experts [11]. In addition, resident's perception of the importance of ecosystem services generated by green spaces is high [7]. Therefore, change of green area should be monitored.

Unfortunately, the automatic monitoring of green spaces is made hard by a form of information collected in Geodetic Documentation Centres [9]. First, interpretation of geodetic maps is a problem for a common citizen. Data are collected as geodetic maps at a scale of 1:500-1:5000. Usually, maps are hand–drawn under some regulation, but by many draughtsmen. The map contains

Fig. 2. Examples of tree symbols on real maps

information about localisation of real objects (buildings, roads, trees), real estates, a laying of pipes/sewers/power lines, and a terrain. After digitalisation, for publication in the Internet, all these objects create hard analysed image [12].

A vectorisation of all resources can be a solution of the problem. However, even current documents are very often created in a paper form and the vectorisation of archive resources is too expensive. Therefore, an alternative solution has to be proposed.

3   State of Art

The discussed problem is a part of maps understanding issue [8,10,14,12]. Our proposition is to detect tree symbols on maps and create a generalised projection of green spaces. Series of archival and current maps can be used to monitor changes in green areas.

Several works are focused on the map symbols recognition. In work [13], good results were obtained for several symbols. However, the recognition of tree symbols was only tested on 5 examples and the trees were represented by a solid symbol not a multi–part as in this work.

In work [3], 27 map symbols were recognised by a neural network and the recognition rate was 94.44 percent. However, examples of symbols are only partially given and the extraction process is omitted in that work.

The extraction process is discussed in work [5]. Among others the greenery symbols are extracted. However, in that work colours of layers are used to separate symbols. This solution cannot be used in this work because scanned maps are black and white.

4   Trees Detection

4.1   Symbols Description

The model tree symbols (examples are presented in Figure 2) are precisely described in the specification. It gives all sizes of symbol. Cartographers try to draw it according to that model. However, there are many variations of original symbols, still based on guidelines. For this reason, we make the main analysis relying on specification with a number of improvements to increase the efficiency of recognition. Another problem is that symbols overlap (example in Figure 1). Our research is based on the assumption of local image processing - work on image fragments. Looking on image fragments makes overlapped symbols not recognisable even for human. Only view on the neighbourhood of the symbol and its context can help. A global image processing could help with this, but it will also make many new problems.

4.2 Dots Detection

At the beginning of trees recognition, it is necessary to locate all possible dots (with the specified size) on the map. This is very useful information because all matched symbols have dot in the centre as we can see in Figure 2. The easiest way is to find all dots in specified size. It can be done using Hough transformation [2]. Next, several factors (a radius, a filling) are calculated to determine precisely the correctness of symbols.

The procedure was tested on four maps that contain 264 dots. Among them 226 (over 87 percent) was detected. Additionally, 342 other objects were detected as dots. That shows the enormous number of false positives. Therefore, the number of false negatives cannot be easy reduced. However, the dot detection is only the initial phase of the tree detection process. The number of false positives can be reduced in the symbol recognition process. On the other hand, not all rejected dots are parts of tree symbols. Therefore, the accuracy of the whole system cannot be settled yet.

4.3 Extraction

The first step in the symbol classification process is an extraction from the map. The task is quite hard, because of interaction of symbols [6]. We decide to simplify this phase. For each detected dot, an image is cropped to a specified size. As a result, a limited neighbourhood of dot is created.

Typical methods of symbol extraction [8] cannot be applied in this task. The segmentation based on a colour attribute of pixel was rejected because a processed image has only two colours (black and white). Therefore, we use simply cropping without determination the belonging of segments to symbols. The optimal size of the examined area was chosen as a maximal size of tree symbols with an additional margin of error. Thanks to this, we are sure that entire symbol is inside the fragment. Additionally, we place the centre of the dot on the centre of the extracted fragment to standardise objects. This approach to the extraction process results in noises (for example fragments of other trees), but the problem can be handled on the next phase.

4.4 Features

In the next stage, extracted fragments are transformed to collections of features. The extracted images cannon be just transformed into bitmaps, because of a high level of noises created by other symbols. Therefore, features that allow a filter to detect correct symbols should be defined.

When we look at some of the examples (Figure 2) we can notice the following qualities of that symbols:

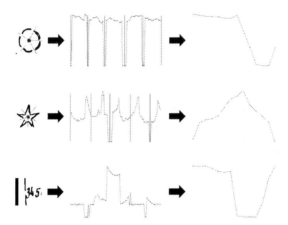

Fig. 3. Consecutively: dot neighbourhood, inner contour, averaged characteristic

- both symbols are built around the dots,
- both symbols are circular,
- each of the symbol have different, but specific appearance, either in terms of sizes and angles.

In the following sections, features based on those qualities are presented.

Inner Contour. This characteristic was chosen because of the listed attributes. It is calculated as a distance from the centre of the dot, which is also the centre of the processed fragment, to the first black pixel that does not belong to the dot.

The distance is computed for radii drawn across the circle with a given angle. The dot is estimated by a small circle on the centre and the calculation of the distance starts from this circle.

In Figure 3, characteristics for both deciduous and coniferous trees as well as for another symbol are presented. This characteristic stresses a variation of an outer part of the symbol. For trees, we can easily notice their cyclical nature. We can divide it in five similar parts, which are corresponding to five parts of a tree symbol. A natural idea is to check similarity between parts, because human should draw these fragments at the same style. However, after a few experiments we decide that due to many noises in a image (e.g. other symbols) these segments are not similar enough. This is a significant disadvantage of this characteristic, but we can reduce impact of that by using averages.

As noticed earlier, the characteristic for model symbol is repeatable. In addition, parts have equal sizes and are similarly oriented on the map. It is sufficient to process fragments in specified ranges defined a priori. The process results in a new feature that is the average calculated from five parts. The characteristic of obtained shape is presented in Figure 3. To reduce an impact of noises it is worth to cut off some boundary values of this characteristic.

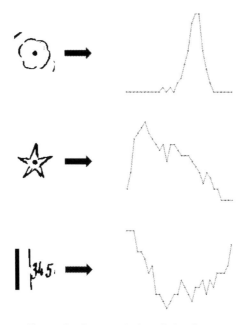

Fig. 4. Example characteristics of circular occupancy

This characteristic satisfies the assumptions of a simple classification: a reliance on human observations and clear rules to distinguish classes.

In the final classifier, the inner contour is only used to recognise coniferous trees. The results of classification for deciduous trees are nearly the same for classifiers based on description with and without that attribute (see section 5). Therefore, according to main rule of this work - simplicity, we dismissed it without prejudice to the results. For coniferous trees, this feature gives a significant increase of effectiveness.

Circular Occupancy. The main motivation to build this characteristic is a circular nature of the symbols. The feature is calculated as percentage occupancy of pixels on a circle with a specified radius and centre in the centre of the processed fragment (the centre of dot).

Figure 4 shows some examples of this characteristic. We can see that for a deciduous tree it is a simply peek of function and for a coniferous tree - an initially rapid increase and then a gently descent. In this case, image and symbol noises make problems, but they are not critical and visible in the results.

Ring Occupancy. Another notice during visual analysis is that each symbol is always evenly placed around the dot. Each has five similar segments. An analysis of the segments is done in eight separate circular fragments (this is assumed value; it should be not less than 5 and no more than 10). Examples are presented in Figure 5. For a proper symbol, each piece should contain at least one black pixel.

Fig. 5. Examples of checking ring occupancy

Border parts of a symbol are usually placed in a specified distance from the dot centre. Therefore, in this characteristic, we process only specified rings close to estimated positions of border parts. The rings are divided into eight equal segments. Then the inside of each ring is examined. If there is any fragment of the ring without black pixels, the symbol will be not circularly consistent.

To reduce a possibility of mistakes this test should be repeated with some offset, starting from *previous starting angle* $+\frac{1}{16}\pi$. If this test will be also failed, we will be sure that the processed symbol does not satisfy the basis requirements.

This feature helps in an elimination of negative effects of inner contour averaging, which may cause a loss of information about the circular consistency.

Radius of Maximal Circular Occupancy. This characteristic is closely related with the circular occupancy. We try to find a radius, which has the bigger number of black pixels within. This tells us about a distance from the centre to the shape around. Some noises cause a very small value of this distance. That results in a simply method of rejection of the noises. This is a simple but powerful factor.

Primary Tests. In the previous sections, the characteristics used in a classification were described. Working according to the simplification idea, tests were made with using the simplest minimum distance classifier. For factors (ring occupancy and radius of maximal occupancy), some conditions were not fulfilment. Therefore, correct symbols were not classified as a tree. For other features, a series of tests was made. On the beginning, we tried to use the minimum distance classifier, but it gave completely wrong results. It was happen because of more dimensions of this characteristics, and more variety between the symbols and image noises. The classifiers correctly detected tree symbols, but it was prone to an acceptance of bad symbols. Because of that, it was made another try with more complex classifier – a neural network.

4.5   Neural Networks

Neural network approximates human perception and models recognition of patterns. In chosen characteristics, a human eye is able to notice a regularity and a connection between a type of symbol and an appearance of specific feature fast and easy. Used mechanism was a Multi Layer Perceptron (MLP) with the back propagation learning method [1].

Input Data and Its Model Appearance. An input of neural network strictly depends on a modelled classification task. Below, a model appearance for each classification task is described. Two tasks are discussed: recognition of coniferous and deciduous trees. Both classifiers work on normalised features. The classifier of deciduous trees bases on the circular occupancy that should be given as one clear peek of the function. In the case of the coniferous trees classifier, the circular occupancy should rapidly increase and then slowly decrease and the inner contour has gentle and regular rises and falls.

Architecture. A scheme of architecture and a description of neural networks can be found in [4]. The entire solution has two pieces responsible for a detecting of a single type of trees. A size of input data depends on symbol type. We decide to use a simply architecture of multilayered neural network with one hidden layer. During the research, we decided how many neurons were suitable for the hidden layer and how many learning cycles were necessary.

An output layer of this network is designed as as single neuron that can determine membership to a class specific for the network.

5 Results

Methods of Tests. The effectiveness of networks was tested on manual prepared data. Dots detected on maps was manual classified and divided in two subsets. For deciduous tree, 250 examples created the learning set and 650 examples created the testing set. For coniferous tree, 400 examples created the learning set and 1800 examples created the testing set. All tests were made on that collection.

Major parameters of a Multi Layer Perceptron with one hidden layer that project on results are a size of the hidden layer and the number of learning epoch. Because of that test was made to set up these parameters.

Number of Neurons in Hidden Layer. The tables 1 and 2 show the relation between effectiveness of symbol recognition and the number of neurons in hidden layers. Tests were made for the fixed number of learning epochs and a variable value of hidden neurons. Tests were performed repeatedly and the results were averaged. The degree of correctness is percentage of correctly recognised symbols. At the first glance, we can see the difference between correctness for deciduous and coniferous trees. However, now we are interesting in a selection of the number of hidden neurons. The correctness reaches the maximum for 25 neurons. Therefore, this value was chosen for further research as the best value for both neural networks.

Number of Learning Epochs. Tables 3 and 4 shows for what number of learning epochs networks gives the best results. We try to find the moment with the best correctness. Too small number of epochs may cause an under fitting, but too many results in an over fitting. Tests were made for the fixed number

Table 1. Correctness of neural network for deciduous trees depending on number of hidden neurons

Hidden layer	Correct	Incorrect	False negative	False positive
5	92.44%	7.56%	6.19%	1.37%
10	92.34%	7.66%	6.10%	1.56%
15	92.32%	7.68%	6.20%	1.48%
20	92.31%	7.69%	5.96%	1.74%
25	92.35%	7.65%	5.99%	1.66%
30	92.28%	7.72%	5.97%	1.76%
Average	92.33%	7.67%	6.06%	1.61%

Table 2. Correctness of neural network for coniferous trees depending on number of hidden neurons

Hidden layer	Correct	Incorrect	False negative	False positive
5	87.04%	12.96%	4.97%	7.99%
10	89.07%	10.93%	4.61%	6.32%
15	88.35%	11.65%	4.51%	7.14%
20	88.15%	11.85%	4.61%	7.24%
25	88.79%	11.21%	4.35%	6.86%
Average	88.24%	11.76%	4.64%	7.12%

of hidden neurons and a variable value of learning epochs. The research was performed repeatedly and the results were averaged. Initially, the correctness is increasing, but it is slowly decreasing from the specified point. Therefore, once again we choose the maximum value. For deciduous tree, the maximum value is after 150 epochs and for coniferous trees, the maximum value is after 550 epochs. This divergence is consistent with our conjectures, because the neural network for coniferous trees has much bigger input data and logically their learning should take more time.

Number of Input Data for Deciduous Trees Classification. Comparative tests were performed for neural networks trained on the input created from characteristics described in Section 4.4. The better results were obtained by the neural network trained on a single characteristic. It can be justified by the fact that too many inputs can reduce the quality of recognition due to introducing unnecessary data.

5.1   Results from Tests

The recognition results are different for coniferous and deciduous trees. The ratio of positive recognised coniferous trees is 88.24 percent and 7.12 percent of other

Table 3. Deciduous trees - correctness depends on number of epochs

Epochs	Correct	Incorrect	False negative	False positive
50	91.59%	8.41%	7.56%	0.85%
100	92.82%	7.18%	5.44%	1.74%
150	93.03%	6.97%	5.41%	1.56%
200	92.85%	7.15%	5.54%	1.62%
300	92.85%	7.15%	5.74%	1.41%
350	92.49%	7.51%	6.00%	1.51%
400	92.23%	7.77%	5.92%	1.85%
450	92.31%	7.69%	6.38%	1.31%
500	92.01%	7.99%	6.17%	1.82%
550	92.09%	7.91%	6.15%	1.75%
600	91.97%	8.03%	6.28%	1.75%
650	92.09%	7.91%	6.03%	1.88%
700	92.09%	7.91%	6.09%	1.82%
Average	92.33%	7.67%	6.06%	1.61%

Table 4. Coniferous trees - correctness depends on number of epochs

Epochs	Correct	Incorrect	False negative	False positive
50	81.94%	18.06%	2.57%	15.49%
100	86.78%	13.22%	5.87%	7.35%
150	86.93%	13.07%	4.89%	8.18%
200	87.92%	12.08%	5.14%	6.94%
300	89.20%	10.80%	4.16%	6.64%
350	89.20%	10.80%	4.89%	5.91%
400	89.95%	10.05%	2.81%	7.24%
450	89.17%	10.83%	5.14%	5.69%
500	89.14%	10.86%	5.20%	5.65%
550	90.84%	9.16%	2.49%	6.67%
600	88.69%	11.31%	5.72%	5.59%
650	88.68%	11.32%	5.72%	5.60%
700	88.54%	11.46%	5.43%	6.03%
Average	88.24%	11.76%	4.64%	7.12%

objects were recognised as trees. The ratio of positive recognised coniferous trees is 92.33 percent and 1.61 percent of other objects were recognised as trees.

Based on all performed tests we obtained the average ratio of positive recognised tree symbols on the level of 90 percent with relative small percent of false positives (about 4 percent).

This is a very good result when we remember about all difficulties. The majority of not recognised symbols are intersected with other objects on the input

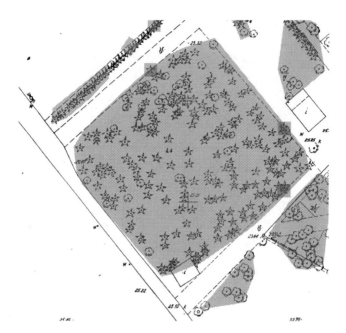

Fig. 6. The result of a green space detection

image (particularly with other trees). The issue of overlapping symbols was a problem for local methods, but (as we checked in practice) this caused a difficulty even for humans. Moreover, some tree symbols are not important in the generalisation process.

6   Conclusions

The presented results of tree detection are good enough to create a generalised image of green spaces. In Figure 6 detected green areas are presented. Several symbols are not detected, but the global picture is clear. Therefore, it may be assumed that a recognition of tree symbols on the level of 90 percent is good enough to create a green areas generalisation on the basis of scanned geodetic maps.

Apart from improving the detection accuracy two future possible directions of research are proposed. Detected area can be divided by types coniferous, deciduous, and mixed. Moreover, other kinds of greenery (bushes, lawns) can be recognised. However, their presentation on maps has a completely different character and new image processing methods should be used.

References

1. Bishop, C.M.: Neural Networks for Pattern Recognition. Oxford University Press (1995)
2. Chia, A., Leung, M., Eng, H.L., Rahardja, S.: Ellipse detection with hough transform in one dimensional parametric space. In: IEEE International Conference on Image Processing, ICIP 2007, vol. 5, pp. 333–336 (2007)
3. Choi, K.S., Ahn, D., Lee, S.H., Kong, Y.H.: Automatic recognition of map symbols for gis input module. In: 1997 IEEE Pacific Rim Conference on Communications, Computers and Signal Processing, 10 Years PACRIM 1987-1997 - Networking the Pacific Rim, vol. 2, pp. 543–546 (1997)
4. Costa, L.: Shape Classification and Analysis: Theory and Practice, 2nd edn. CRC, Boca Raton (2009)
5. Dhar, D., Chanda, B.: Extraction and recognition of geographical features from paper maps. International Journal of Document Analysis and Recognition (IJ-DAR) 8(4), 232–245 (2006), http://dx.doi.org/10.1007/s10032-005-0010-9
6. Fletcher, L.A., Kasturi, R.: A robust algorithm for text string separation from mixed text/graphics images. IEEE Transactions on Pattern Analysis and Machine Intelligence 10(6), 910–918 (1988)
7. Jim, C., Chen, W.: Perception and attitude of residents toward urban green spaces in guangzhou (china). Environmental Management 38(3), 338–349 (2006)
8. Lu, W., Okuhashi, T., Sakauchi, M.: A proposal of efficient interactive recognition system for understanding of map drawings. In: Proceedings of the Third International Conference on Document Analysis and Recognition, vol. 1, pp. 520–523 (1995)
9. Luckner, M., Izdebski, W.: Publication of geodetic documentation center resources on internet. In: Ralyté, J., Franch, X., Brinkkemper, S., Wrycza, S. (eds.) CAiSE 2012. LNCS, vol. 7328, pp. 533–548. Springer, Heidelberg (2012)
10. Mariani, R., Deseilligny, M.P., Labiche, J., Lecourtier, Y.: Geographic map understanding, attributes computation for hydrographic network. In: Proceedings of the IEEE Southwest Symposium on Image Analysis and Interpretation, pp. 252–257 (1996)
11. Miller, R.W.: Urban forestry: Planning and managing urban greenspaces. Prentice-Hall (1997)
12. Stapor, K.: Geographic map image interpretation - survey and problems. Machine GRAPHICS & VISION 9(1/2), 497–518 (2000)
13. Szendrei, R., Elek, I., Fekete, I.: Automatic recognition of topographic map symbols based on their textures. In: Tan, Y., Shi, Y., Chai, Y., Wang, G. (eds.) ICSI 2011, Part II. LNCS, vol. 6729, pp. 299–306. Springer, Heidelberg (2011), http://dblp.uni-trier.de/db/conf/swarm/icsi2011-2.html#SzendreiEF11
14. Zhou, C.: Map recognition for automatic information generation in an am/fm system. In: Proceedings of the Intelligent Information Systems, IIS 1997, pp. 376–380 (1997)

Hierarchical Layered Mean Shift Methods

Milan Šurkala, Karel Mozdřeň, Radovan Fusek, and Eduard Sojka

Faculty of Electrical Engieneering and Informatics,
17. listopadu 15, 708 33 Ostrava-Poruba, Czech Republic
{milan.surkala,karel.mozdren,radovan.fusek,eduard.sojka}@vsb.cz

Abstract. Many image processing tasks exist and segmentation is one
of them. We are focused on the mean-shift segmentation method. Our
goal is to improve its speed and reduce the over-segmentation problem
that occurs with small spatial bandwidths. We propose new mean-shift
method called Hierarchical Layered Mean Shift. It uses hierarchical pre-
processing stage and stacking hierarchical segmentation outputs together
to minimise the over-segmentation problem.

Keywords: layer, segmentation, image, mean shift, hierarchical.

1 Introduction

Segmentation is one of the constantly developing image processing tasks. The
goal is to improve not only the accuracy and the segmentation quality but also
the speed of algorithms. We are focused on the one of the most popular segmentation methods, the Mean Shift. It was released in 1975 [7], but it started to be
developed more 20 years later, in 1995 [2]. The most important papers about
this method are, for example, [3], [5], and [4].

The main idea of the mean-shift method is in iterative motion of data points
to the position of their highest density. We are segmenting images, therefore,
these data points are image pixels. For each pixel, a kernel density estimate is
computed and it is shifted according to this estimate. It is repeatedly computed
until the point converges to an attractor, the place of the highest density of
pixels. In general MS [7], we need two datasets. The first one is the original
dataset that is used to compute the density estimate of the data points and the
second one holds the shifted values (the actual data points for which the density
estimate is computed). If we use Blurring MS [1], only one dataset is needed.
The source dataset is replaced by the computed values after each iteration. The
BMS method also has the smaller number of iterations per data point.

The hierarchical approaches [11] [10], [6] showed to be a very fast way to
accelerate the algorithms with a very small influence on the segmentation quality.
They use more stages of the algorithm with different bandwidths and they use the
output from the first stage as the input for the following one. A small bandwidth
in the first stage ensures fast computation as well as the smaller input for the
next one.

The layered approaches [9], on the other hand, run several MS computation
and stack them together. If the pair of pixels belongs to the same segment

J. Blanc-Talon et al. (Eds.): ACIVS 2013, LNCS 8192, pp. 538–545, 2013.

in more resultant segmentations (threshold has to be set, for example, in two segmentations of the three processed), they are merged together.

We present Hierarchical Layered Mean Shift (HLxMS) methods that use the hierarchical approach and stacking of segmentations to reduce the over-segmentation problem. In the next two sections, Mean Shift basics and our HLxMS approach will be discussed. In the Section 4, experiments will be carried out and the last section is devoted to the conclusion.

We are going to describe hierarchical layered mean-shift method that use the Blurring Mean Shift (BMS) method as its base. Therefore, we will denote it as HLBMS (the "B" standing for blurring is replacing the general "x" in HLxMS notation covering all hierarchical layered versions). We will also describe only the BMS method deeply, although the experiments will be also carried out with general MS [2] (HLMS) and Evolving Mean Shift [12] (HLEMS) method too.

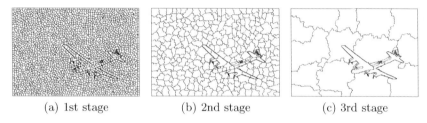

(a) 1st stage   (b) 2nd stage   (c) 3rd stage

Fig. 1. Stages of the HBMS method

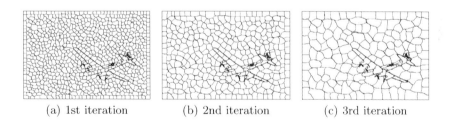

(a) 1st iteration   (b) 2nd iteration   (c) 3rd iteration

Fig. 2. Iterations of the LBMS method

2   Mean Shift Methods

If $X = \{x_i\}_{i=1}^n \subset R^d$ is a dataset of n points in the d-dimensional space, the *kernel density estimator* for BMS method is given by the following equation

$$p(x) = \frac{1}{n\sigma^d} \sum_{i=1}^n K\left(\frac{x - x_i}{\sigma}\right),$$ (1)

where the first fraction is a normalisation constant and σ is the bandwith. It sets the diameter of the searching window (kernel function $K(x)$). In digital images, we use two types of bandwidths. The spatial bandwidth σ_s is limiting the neighbourhood of the processed pixel in x and y axis (usually, it has the same values for both axes). The range bandwidth σ_r indicates the maximum possible luminance difference between the processed pixel and the pixels in its neighbourhood. MS can use broad kernels (for example, the *Gaussian*) that cover all the data points and σ parameters change only the shape of kernel as all pixels are involved in computation. If we use truncated kernels (for example, the *Epanechnikov, uniform*), the bandwidth parameters really limit the size of kernel. In our algorithm, we use only truncated kernels, because it is based on using the small kernels that improve the speed of the algorithm. The Epanechnikov kernel is given by the equation

$$K(x) = \begin{cases} 1 - x^2, & \text{if } \|x\| \leq 1 \\ 0, & \text{otherwise} \end{cases} . \tag{2}$$

The *mean-shift vector* that is iteratively needed for each pixel in the processed image, is given by

$$m_{\sigma,k}(x) = \frac{\sum_{i-1}^{n} x_i k \left(\left\| \frac{x-x_i}{\sigma} \right\|^2 \right)}{\sum_{i-1}^{n} k \left(\left\| \frac{x-x_i}{\sigma} \right\|^2 \right)} - x \,, \tag{3}$$

where the function $k(x)$ is a derivative of the kernel $K(x)$. This equation indicates the difference between the former position of the processed pixel x (on the right-hand side of the equation) and a new position of the processed pixel x (estimate of the position with the highest density of data points). In each iteration, the point is moved to the new computed position until the movement is zero or close to zero (smaller than a preset threshold). Each iteration consists of moving all the points according to their mean-shift vectors, then the output of this iteration is converted to the input for the next one.

3 Hierarchical Layered Mean Shift

Our new method called Hierarchical Layered Mean Shift (HLxMS in general) combines the hierarchical [11] [10], [6] and layered approach [9]. The hierarchical approach divides the segmentation of the image into several stages. The first stage use very small spatial bandwidth and, therefore, it is carried out very fast. It creates a large number of small segments. We consider the segment as one data point with the weight proportional to the number of points it contains. This output is used as the input for the next stage with a larger spatial bandwidth. Because this input is smaller (due to preprocessing in the first stage), the next stage can be carried out very fast too even if the larger spatial bandwidth is used (the dataset is smaller). The number of stages is not limited, mostly two or three stages are enough (it depends on the size of the processed image). HBMS results can be seen in Fig. 1.

The layered approach uses a larger number of stages on the same dataset (not for outputs from the previous stages). We carry out computation with several

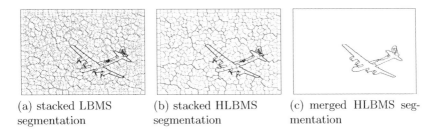

(a) stacked LBMS segmentation (b) stacked HLBMS segmentation (c) merged HLBMS segmentation

Fig. 3. Stacked LBMS and HLBMS (hierarchical LBMS) image and the result after merging the HLBMS segments

small, but different bandwidths. Each result has the same boundaries around the significant objects but it has variously shaped segments in the flat areas of the image. If we stack the segmentation results, the most significant boundaries would be clearly seen (Fig. 3(a)). The *merging algorithm* is straightforward. If two random pixels are, for example, twice in the same segment in two different segmentations of three processed segmentations, they are assigned to one bigger segment. The number of segmentations does not necessarily need to be 3. In practice, some images could be processed with three segmentations very well, but mostly four segmentations are better.

We can carry out much more segmentations and we need to set the threshold t lower than this number to denote the number of segmentations, where two random pixels need to be in the same segment in order to assign them to the same final segment. We have to check all the pairs of pixels that are in the distance equal or lower than the maximal used spatial bandwidth (we do not need to check all the pairs of pixels in the processed image). It greatly reduces the computational cost of the algorithm with no influence to the segmentation result.

This approach needs to compute several very fast segmentations (because of small σ_s) and almost completely reduces the problem of over-segmentation. The flat areas are merged together. It can be used with BMS and EMS, but the character of MS (general Mean Shift) segments is not very suitable for this approach - much larger initial bandwidth is necessary.

HLxMS combines both approaches together. It carries out one very fast initial segmentation with a very small bandwidth. Its output is used as the input for two or more layered segmentations. That is the difference. General layered approach uses the original image as an input, whereas the hierarchical layered approach uses the first preprocessing stage for creating its input as in the hierarchical versions of mean-shift methods. Simply, the hierarchical approach makes one over-segmented image and the layered segmentation post-processing will decide which segments should be grouped and which boundaries should be preserved. Of course, more hierarchical stages can be executed in order to minimize the computational time if we process very large images.

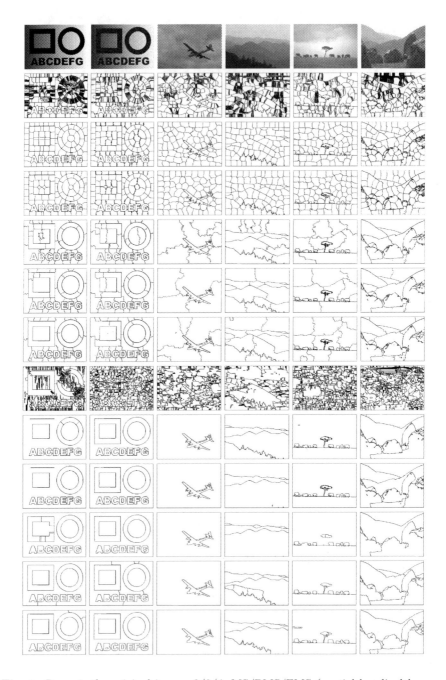

Fig. 4. Rows 1: the original image; 2/3/4: MS/BMS/EMS (spatial bandiwdth $\sigma_s = 15$); 5/6/7: HMS/HBMS/HEMS ($\sigma_s = 4/16/64$); 8/9/10: LMS/LBMS/LEMS ($\sigma_s = 4$, multiplier of the bandwidth $mul = 1.4$); 11/12/13: HLMS/HLBMS/HLEMS ($\sigma_s = 3.5$, $mul = 1.35$).

4   Experiments

For comparison, we present the achieved results with various mean-shift methods, especially general MS, Blurring MS and Evolving MS as our method is aimed as an improvement to Mean Shift. Therefore, we will compare it only with several mean-shift methods. All their hierarchical (HxMS) and layered versions (LxMS) are presented too. Our hierarchical layered versions are denoted by HLxMS. As it was already said, in all cases, the "x" letter stands for arbitrary MS method (general, blurring or evolving). Because each type of algorithms has another properties, they will be used with different spatial bandwidths that will be mentioned and deeply described later. Testing images are presented in the first row of Fig. 4, we use the images from Berkeley Image Dataset [8] and our synthetic image in noise-free and noisy version. All images were downscaled to the resolution 320×214 pixels.

Table 1. The comparison of speed depending on algorithm

	synthetic	syn. noise	airplane	hills	savana	bird
MS	1948.3 s	983.6 s	1199.3 s	1923.6 s	1564.7 s	1411.1 s
HMS	127.1 s	37.3 s	37.8 s	36.6 s	39.2 s	42.1 s
LMS	3472.9 s	498.6 s	1139.4 s	2148.9 s	782.4 s	1307.9 s
HLMS	261.8 s	46.5 s	57.1 s	55.5 s	56.6 s	62.7 s
BMS	31.8 s	37.5 s	34.7 s	40.2 s	34.7 s	52.4 s
HBMS	8.7 s	10.1 s	9.6 s	8.9 s	8.2 s	9.9 s
LBMS	42.2 s	43.4 s	46.1 s	44.3 s	41.1 s	45.7 s
HLBMS	6.4 s	5.6 s	6.1 s	6.4 s	6.1 s	6.9 s
EMS	812.2 s	603.8 s	168.3 s	198.9 s	160.9 s	184.9 s
HEMS	29.7 s	33.8 s	18.8 s	17.3 s	20.4 s	20.6 s
LEMS	561.5 s	440.2 s	149.2 s	156.2 s	153.2 s	158.7 s
HLEMS	20.3 s	20.7 s	16.8 s	17.0 s	17.8 s	17.3 s

In Fig. 4, the results of all mentioned methods are clearly visible. The computational times are listed in Table 1. All algorithms used the range bandwidth $\sigma_r = 24$, the spatial bandwidths are clearly described in the caption of Fig. 4. We will justify our choice of the bandwidth in the following paragraphs.

Original methods (MS, BMS, and EMS) used the spatial bandwidth of only $\sigma_s = 15$. It is obvious that the result suffers from a heavy over-segmentation and the computational times are very long even with such a small bandwidth. Hierarchical approaches (HMS, HBMS, and HEMS) started with $\sigma_{s_1} = 4$ and ended with $\sigma_{s_3} = 64$, fast three-staged versions of the algorithm was used (2-staged versions are usually slower). Because of the better speed of the algorithm, we could afford to enlarge the final spatial bandwidth to 64 in order to lower the over-segmentation problem.

Layered algorithms (LMS, LBMS, and LEMS) used the initial bandwidth $\sigma_s = 4$ and each following stage used enlarged bandwidth by the multiplier of 1.4. All algorithms were run in 4-staged mode, where pixels that were three times in the same segmentation, were merged. Even though 3-staged type of the algorithm can be successfully used too, we chose the 4-staged version because of its lower sensitivity to the parameter settings and greater stability.

Hierarchical layered version (our new presented algorithm) used even smaller initial bandwidth $\sigma_s = 3.5$ and the slightly smaller multiplier 1.35. This multiplier is applied once more for the first layered stage. Therefore, the initial stage used $\sigma_s = 3.5$, the first layered stage ran with $\sigma_s = 3.5 \times 1.35 \times 1.35 = 6.4$, the second layered stage used $\sigma_s = 6.4 \times 1.35 = 8.6$ and the last one ran with the bandwidth $\sigma_s = 8.6 \times 1.35 = 11.6$ in our tests. Note that only three layered segmentations are sufficient in the hierarchical layered approach.

General MS is very good algorithm for filtration but its segmentation results are not great in digital images, especially in the flat areas with a small spatial bandwidth. Blurring MS and Evolving MS are much faster but suffer from the over-segmentation problem too. We can enlarge their spatial bandwidth but the computation time will enlarge too. Hierarchical approaches can use much larger bandwidths and achieved dramatically better computational times.

Layered MS is unusable with the general MS as its base method when using small kernel sizes as many variously shaped segments emerge. Layered BMS and Layered EMS give very nice segmentation results and their computational times are comparable with the original methods. Note that we used 4-staged algorithm but we can also use only 3 stages that would lead to much faster time. The drawback is in the need of careful setting of parameters in order to get properly segmented results (4 stages are more robust).

Hierarchical methods (HLxMS) are more robust and faster than the layered versions (LxMS). HLMS is slower than HMS, but it solves its over-segmentation problem. On the other hand, HLBMS and HLEMS are faster than original hierarchical methods and, moreover, also lower the problem of over-segmentation. We can say that our new method successfully suppresses the over-segmentation problem and also improves the speed when using Blurring MS or Evolving MS as its base method.

5   Conclusion

We have shown that the layered approaches can almost eliminate the over-segmentation problem in a reasonable time. The general layered versions are a little bit sensitive to parameter settings and the use of general MS is very problematic. Both BMS and EMS algorithms are useful in their layered versions. Hierarchical layered versions that we have presented in this paper do not suffer from the need of proper setting of parameters and they work very well with general MS even when the lower number of stages is used. It outperforms the hierarchical mean-shift methods in both areas of the speed and the segmentation quality. Even when the hierarchical versions use very large final bandwidth, they are not able to merge all segments in large flat areas.

References

1. Carreira-Perpiñán, M.: Fast nonparametric clustering with Gaussian blurring mean-shift. In: Proceedings of the 23rd International Conference on Machine Learning, ICML 2006, pp. 153–160. ACM, New York (2006)
2. Cheng, Y.: Mean shift, mode seeking, and clustering. IEEE Transactions on Pattern Analysis and Machine Intelligence 17, 790–799 (1995)
3. Comaniciu, D., Meer, P.: Mean shift analysis and applications. In: The Proceedings of the Seventh IEEE International Conference on Computer Vision, vol. 2, pp. 1197–1203 (1999)
4. Comaniciu, D., Meer, P.: Mean shift: a robust approach toward feature space analysis. IEEE Transactions on Pattern Analysis and Machine Intelligence 24(5), 603–619 (2002)
5. Comaniciu, D., Ramesh, V., Meer, P.: The variable bandwidth mean shift and data-driven scale selection. IEEE International Conference on Computer Vision 1, 438 (2001)
6. DeMenthon, D., Megret, R.: Spatio-Temporal Segmentation of Video by Hierarchical Mean Shift Analysis. Tech. Rep. LAMP-TR-090,CAR-TR-978,CS-TR-4388,UMIACS-TR-2002-68, University of Maryland, College Park (2002)
7. Fukunaga, K., Hostetler, L.: The estimation of the gradient of a density function, with applications in pattern recognition. IEEE Transactions on Information Theory 21(1), 32–40 (1975)
8. Martin, D., Fowlkes, C., Tal, D., Malik, J.: A database of human segmented natural images and its application to evaluating segmentation algorithms and measuring ecological statistics. In: Proc. 8th Int'l Conf. Computer Vision, vol. 2, pp. 416–423 (2001)
9. Šurkala, M., Mozdřeň, K., Fusek, R., Sojka, E.: Layered mean shift methods. In: Pack, T. (ed.) SSVM 2013. LNCS, vol. 7893, pp. 465–476. Springer, Heidelberg (2013)
10. Vatturi, P., Wong, W.-K.: Category detection using hierarchical mean shift. In: Proceedings of the 15th ACM SIGKDD International Conference on Knowledge Discovery and Data Mining, KDD 2009, pp. 847–856. ACM, New York (2009)
11. Šurkala, M., Mozdřeň, K., Fusek, R., Sojka, E.: Hierarchical blurring mean-shift. In: Blanc-Talon, J., Kleihorst, R., Philips, W., Popescu, D., Scheunders, P. (eds.) ACIVS 2011. LNCS, vol. 6915, pp. 228–238. Springer, Heidelberg (2011), http://dl.acm.org/citation.cfm?id=2034246.2034270
12. Zhao, Q., Yang, Z., Tao, H., Liu, W.: Evolving mean shift with adaptive bandwidth: A fast and noise robust approach. In: Zha, H., Taniguchi, R.-i., Maybank, S. (eds.) ACCV 2009, Part I. LNCS, vol. 5994, pp. 258–268. Springer, Heidelberg (2010)

Globally Segmentation Using Active Contours and Belief Function

Foued Derraz[1,3], Miloud Boussahla[3], and Laurent Peyrodie[2]

[1] Facult Libre de Mdicine
Institut Catholique de Lille
Universit Catholique de Lille
46 rue du Port de Lille, France
foued.derraz@icl-lille.fr
[2] Hautes Etudes d'Ingenieur
Universit Catholique de Lille
46 rue du Port de Lille, France
laurent.peyrodie@hei.fr
[3] Telecommunication Laboratory
Technology Faculty
Abou Bekr Belkaid University, Tlemcen, Algeria
BP 230, Tlemcen 13000, Algeria
m_boussahla@mail.univ-tlemcen.dz

Abstract. We study the active contours (AC) based globally segmentation for vector-valued image incorporating both statistical and evidential knowledge. The proposed method combine both Belief Functions (BFs) and probability functions in the same framework. In this formulation, all features issued from vector-valued image are integrated in inside/outside descriptors to drive the segmentation process based AC. In this formulation, the imprecision caused by the weak contrast and noise between inside and outside descriptors issued from the multiple channels is controlled by the BFs as weighted parameters. We demonstrated the performance of our segmentation algorithm using some challenging color biomedical images.

Keywords: Active Contours, Characteristic function, Belief Function, Dempster Shafer rule.

1 Introduction

Active Contours (AC) models has proven to be very powerful segmentation tool in many computer vision and medical imaging applications [22,6]. Segmentation based AC models presents several challenges that are mainly related to image noise, poor contrast, weak or missing boundaries between imaged objects, inhomogeneities, etc. Exploiting high-level information about usual objects to ease the interpretation of low-level cues extracted from images, following the mechanism of visual attention, may be highly beneficial in the segmentation based AC. One way to overcome these difficulties is to exploit the prior knowledge in order

J. Blanc-Talon et al. (Eds.): ACIVS 2013, LNCS 8192, pp. 546–554, 2013.
© Springer International Publishing Switzerland 2013

to constrain the segmentation process. Due occlusion or texture this is often not appropriate to delineate object regions. Statistical knowledge [6,21] and additional information such as texture [6] can improved the segmentation based AC models for vector-valued image [5,24]. Another reason for failed segmentations is due local or global minimizer for AC models [4]. To overcomes these difficulties, the evidential framework appears to be a new way to improve segmentation based AC models for vector valued images [20,14,23]. The Dempster-Shafer (DS) framework [8] has been combined with either a simple thresholding [20], a clustering algorithm [15], a region merging algorithm [14] or with an AC algorithm [23]. In this paper we propose to use the evidential framework [8] to combine several information sources and incorporates them in the formulation of the AC models. The fusion of this information from different feature channels, e.g., color channels and texture offers an alternative to the Bayesian framework. Instead to fuse separated probability densities, the evidential framework allows both inaccuracy and uncertainty. This concept is represented as an interaction between Belief Functions (BFs) and represented as a distance in DS framework [8,7,9,2] which is particularly well suited to represent information from partial and unreliable knowledge. Many works address the problem of the interaction between belief functions [12]. Several approaches have been proposed for the definition of distances in DS framework. In [19] an extended Kullback-Liebler divergence for probability distributions has been proposed as an alternative distance. In [3], an other approach is used to calculate the distance between the focal sets using Euclidean distance. In [7], a Minkowski distance is performed between belief values. Two main aims may be identified regarding the use of distances between belief functions:

- optimization and estimation of the parameter rule
- conformity between sources of information

When using such BFs based distance within the formulation of AC based segmentation models, some formal properties are needed and others are not. Therefore, there is no distance which is preferred to others and the choice of such a distance is always guided by the specific application of the AC models. Then, the use of the BFs as an alternative to probability in segmentation process can be very helpful in reducing uncertainties and imprecisions using conjunctive combination of neighboring pixels. First, it allows us to reduce the noise and secondly, to highlight conflicting areas mainly present at the transition between regions where the contours occurs. In addition, BFs have the advantage to manipulate not only singletons but also disjunctions. This gives the ability to explicitly to represent both uncertainties and imprecisions. The disjunctive combination allows transferring both uncertain and imprecise information on disjunctions [8,2]. Then, the conjunctive combination is applied to reduce uncertainties due to noise while maintaining representation of imprecise information at the boundaries between areas on disjunctions. In this paper, we proposed to incorporate the BFs in the formulation of the AC models. In the next section, we briefly review the AC models based Vector-valued image segmentation in total variation framework, which is the essence for our segmentation framework. In section 3, we introduced our our improved AC based segmentation model incorporating BFs. We have applied our new improved model to some challenging biomedicale images and we have demonstrate the advantages of the proposed method. We conclude our work by comparing and addressing some limitations and future improvement of our approach.

2   Review of Globally Active Contours for Vector-Valued Image

The segmentation based AC for vector-valued images $\mathbf{I}$ consists in finding one or more regions Ω from $\mathbf{I}$. In Bayesian framework, we search for the domain Ω or the partition of an image $P(\Omega)$ that maximizing the a posteriori partition probability $p(P(\Omega)|\mathbf{I})$. The Maximum of $P(\Omega)$ can be given by minimizing the criterion as follows:

$$\partial\hat{\Omega} = \arg\min\left\{\underbrace{\log\left(\frac{1}{p(P(\Omega))}\right)}_{E_b(\partial\Omega)} + \lambda\underbrace{\log\left(\frac{1}{p(\mathbf{I}|P(\Omega))}\right)}_{E_{data}(\Omega,\mathbf{I})}\right\} \tag{1}$$

In equation (1), the first energy term corresponds to the geometric properties of $P(\Omega) = \{\Omega_{in}, \Omega_{out}\}$. Ω_{in} and Ω_{out} correspond respectively to inside and outside region to be extracted. The data-fidelity energy term $E_{data}(\Omega, \mathbf{I})$ allows the vector valued-image data $\mathbf{I} = \{I_1, ..., I_m\}$. The AC for vector-valued image can formulated in total variation framework [4] using characteristic function framework χ and Maximum-Likelihood [13] distance as follows:

$$E(\chi, \mathbf{I}) = \int_\Omega |\nabla\chi|\,d\mathbf{x}$$

$$+ \frac{1}{M}\sum_{j=1}^m \lambda_{in}^j \underbrace{\int_{\Omega_{in}} \log\left(\frac{1}{p_{in}^j}\right)\chi dx}_{E_{data}(\Omega_{in}, I_j)}$$

$$+ \frac{1}{M}\sum_{j=1}^m \lambda_{out}^j \underbrace{\int_{\Omega_{out}} \log\left(\frac{1}{p_{in}^j}\right)\chi dx}_{E_{data}(\Omega_{out}, I_j)} \tag{2}$$

Where $\mathbf{I}$ is vector-valued image and M the number of channels. We note by $p_{in/out}^j = p(I_j|\{\Omega_{in/out}\})$, $\lambda_{in/out}^{j=\{1,...,m\}}$ is the weighting parameters ensuring the trade-off between the inside/outside data-fidelity energy terms. Because of their independency, the foreground/background distribution $p_{in/out}^j$ can be estimated separately for each channel j using parametric [1] method or non parametric method [18]. In order to produce the foreground/background region $\Omega_{in/out}$ with two pdfs as disjoint as possible, the velocity of data-fidelity energy term in (2) is maximized by using the shape derivative tool [11]. Thus, the velocity $V_{in/out}^{j}$ can be written as:

$$V_{in/out}^{j} = \frac{1}{|\Omega_{in/out}|} \int_{\Omega_I} \log\left(\frac{1}{p_{in/out}^{j}}\right)\left(p_{in/out}^{j} - K\left(I_j - I\left(s\right)\right)\right) dI_j \qquad (3)$$

In characteristic framework, segmentation driven by AC can be expressed as:

$$\frac{\partial \chi}{\partial t} = \left(div\left(\frac{|\nabla\chi|}{|\nabla\chi|}\right) + \frac{1}{M}\left(\sum_{j=1}^{m}\lambda_j^{in}V_{in}^{j} - \sum_{j=1}^{m}\lambda_j^{out}V_{out}^{j}\right)\right) \qquad (4)$$

In the next section, we proposed to replace the sum for inisde/outisde region by only one inisde/outside velocity, fusing all channel information.

3 Globally Active Contours in Incorporating Both BFs and Statistical Knowledge

3.1 Dempster Shafer Rules

The evidential framework is provided through the definition of the plausibility (Pl) and belief (Bel) function [8,9], which are both derived from a mass function (m). For the frame of discernment $\Omega_{II} = \{\Omega_1, \Omega_2, ..., \Omega_n\}$, composed of n single mutually exclusive subsets Ω_i, the mass function is defined by $m : 2^{\Omega} \rightarrow [0,1]$.

$$m\left(\emptyset\right) = 0$$
$$\sum_{\Omega_i \subseteq \Omega} m\left(\Omega_i\right) = 1; \quad Bel\left(\Omega\right) = \sum_{\Omega_i \subseteq \Omega_{II}} m\left(\Omega_i\right) = 1 \qquad (5)$$
$$Pl\left(\Omega\right) = \sum_{\Omega_i \cap \Omega_{II} \neq \emptyset} m\left(\Omega_i\right)$$

The relation between mass function, Bel and Pel can be described as fellows:

$$m\left(\Omega_i\right) \leq Bel\left(\Omega_i\right) \leq p\left(\Omega_i\right) \leq Pl\left(\Omega_i\right) \qquad (6)$$

When $m\left(\Omega\right) > 0$, Ω is a so called focal element [14,8]. The independent masses m_m are defined within the same frame of discernment as:

$$m\left(\Omega_{i=\{1,...,n\}}\right) = m_1\left(\Omega_{i=\{1,...,n\}}\right) \otimes m_2\left(\Omega_{i=\{1,...,n\}}\right) ...$$
$$\otimes m_m\left(\Omega_{i=\{1,...,n\}}\right) \qquad (7)$$

The total belief assigned to a focal element Ω_i is equal to the belief strictly placed on the foreground region Ω_i. Then Belief Function (Bel) can expressed as:

$$Bel\left(\Omega_i\right) = m\left(\Omega_i\right) \qquad (8)$$

This relation can be very helpful in the formulation of our AC model.

3.2 Active Contours and Belief Function

Our proposed method uses the evidential framework to fuse the information issued from the multiple channels. Therefore, in Bayesian framework, partitioning probability can be expressed as:

$$p\left(P\left(\Omega\right)|\mathbf{I}\right) \propto p\left(\mathbf{I}|\,P\left(\Omega\right)\right)p\left(P\left(\Omega\right)\right) \tag{9}$$

Intuitively in the same manner in (2), the best $\partial\Omega$ can be obtained by maximizing the Maximum-Likelihood distance between $p\left(\Omega_{out}\right)$ the inside/outside region or minimizing the criterion:

$$\partial\hat{\Omega} = \arg\min \left\{ \begin{array}{c} \underbrace{\log\left(\dfrac{1}{p\left(P\left(\Omega\right)\right)}\right)}_{E_b(\partial\Omega)} \\[2ex] + \underbrace{\sum_{j=1}^{m} m_j\left(\Omega_{in}\right)\log\left(p_{in}^j\right)}_{E_{data}\left(\Omega_{in},\mathbf{I}\right)} \\[2ex] + \underbrace{\sum_{j=1}^{m} m_j\left(\Omega_{out}\right)\log\left(p_{out}^j\right)}_{E_{data}\left(\Omega_{out},\mathbf{I}\right)} \end{array} \right\} \tag{10}$$

Similairely as in [23], we used the definitions proposed by Appriou in [2] to define mass function for all image channels I_j as:

$$m_{j=\{1,\dots,m\}}\left(\Omega_{in/out}\right) = p_{in/out}^{j=\{1,\dots,m\}}$$
$$m_{j=\{1,\dots,m\}}\left(\Omega\right) = 1 - p_{in}^{j=\{1,\dots,m\}} + p_{out}^{j=\{1,\dots,m\}} \tag{11}$$
$$m_{j=\{1,\dots,m\}}\left(\emptyset\right) = 0$$

The pdfs p_{in}^j and p_{out}^j are estimated for all channels using Parzen kernel [18]. Our proposed method uses the total belief committed to foreground or back ground region. In the next section we proposed a fast version of our segmentation algorithm.

4 Fast Algorithm Based on Split Bregman

A fast and accurate minimization algorithm for TV problem is introduced in [4,10]. We propose to solve our segmentation in this new framework and we formulate the variational problem as:

$$\min_{\chi,d} \left(E\left(\chi,d\right)\right) = \int_\Omega |d\left(\mathbf{x}\right)| \, d\mathbf{x} + \int_\Omega V_{Belief}^{in} \chi\left(\mathbf{x}\right) d\mathbf{x}$$
$$- \int_\Omega V_{Belief}^{out} \chi\left(\mathbf{x}\right) d\mathbf{x} \tag{12}$$

The vectorial function d enforces $d = \nabla\chi$ using the efficient Bregman iteration approach [10] defined as:

$$
\begin{cases}
\left(\chi^{k+1}, d^{k+1}\right) = argmin \left\{ \begin{array}{c} \displaystyle\int_{\Omega} V_{Belief}^{in}\chi \\[2mm] - \displaystyle\int_{\Omega} V_{Belief}^{out}\chi \\[2mm] + \dfrac{\mu}{2} \displaystyle\int_{\Omega} \left| d - \nabla\chi - b^k \right|^2 \end{array} \right\} \\[12mm]
b^{k+1} = b^k + \nabla\chi^k - d^{k+1}
\end{cases}
\tag{13}
$$

The minimizing solution χ^{k+1} is characterized by the optimality condition:

$$
\mu\Delta\chi = V_{Belief}^{in} - V_{Belief}^{out} + \mu div\left(b^k - d^k\right), \chi \in [0,1]
\tag{14}
$$

Finally, the minimizing solution is given by soft-thresholding:

$$
d^{k+1} = sign(\nabla\chi^{k+1} + b^k)max\left(\left|\nabla\chi^{k+1} + b^k\right| - \mu^{-1}, 0\right)
\tag{15}
$$

Then, the final active contour is given by $\left\{ \mathbf{x} \in \Omega | \chi(\mathbf{x})^{final} \geq \frac{1}{2} \right\}$. The two iteration schemes are straightforward to implement. Finally, $V_{belief}^{in/out}$ are updated at each iteration using the belief function given in (11) and (8).

5   Results

We introduced AC model that integrates belief function as statistical region knowledge. To illustrate and demonstrates the accuracy of our segmentation method, we present some results of our method and compare them to segmentation done by the traditional AC model based vector value image and the model proposed in [23]. The images used in our study were taken from dataset in [17,16] with 5 cell types distributions: 1) Basophil, 2) Eosinophil, 3) Lymphocyte 4) Monocyte 5) Neutrophil. The five methods are evaluated on 371 color images. Traditional segmentation based AC for vector-valued and method in [23] are initialized by contour curve around the object to be segmented, our method is free initialization and the segmentation done by the three method are applied for all dataset challenging images. The accuracy of the segmentation done by our method and the method proposed in [23] is represented in term of F-measure coefficient.The proposed method give the best segmentation and the F-measure is better then the other methods (see Table.1).

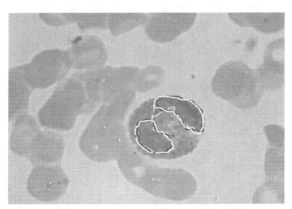

(a) Segmentation of Eosinophil cell

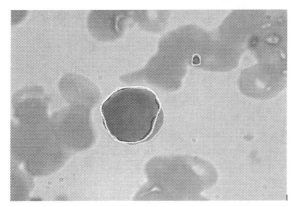

(b) Segmentation of Lymphocyte cell

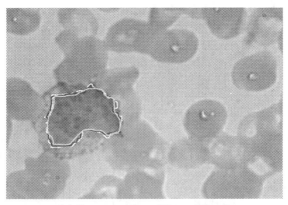

(c) Segmentation of Basophil cell

Fig. 1. Segmentation results of the images taken from the dataset in [17,16], In red color, the Segmentation done by our method. In yellow color, segmentation done by the method presented in [23], and in white color, the segmentation done by expert.

Table 1. Quantitative evaluation of the segmentation using F-measure

Images groups	Our method	Method in [23]
Basophil	0.71	0.65
Eosinophil	0.77	0.70
Lymphocyte	0.88	0.86
Monocyte d	0.71	0.68
Neutrophil	0.83	0.78

6 Conclusion

We have investigate the use of the evidential framework for AC model using DS theory. In this framework, we have investigated in particular the determining of mass function which represents a difficult task. The results have shown that proposed approach give the best segmentation for color and textured images. The experimental results show that the segmentation performance is improved by using the three information sources to represent the same image with respect to the use of on information. Indeed, there are some drawbacks of our proposed method. The proposed is very high time consuming for calculating the mass functions. Furthermore, the research of other optimal models to estimate the mass functions in the DS theory and the imprecision coming from different images channels are an important perspective issue of our work.

References

1. Allili, M.S., Ziou, D.: Object tracking in videos using adaptive mixture models and active contours. Neurocomputing 71(10-12), 2001–2011 (2008)
2. Appriou, A.: Generic approach of the uncertainty management in multisensor fusion processes. Revue Traitement du Signal 22(2), 307–319 (2005)
3. Blackman, S.S., Popoli, R.: Design and analysis of modern tracking systems. Artech House radar library. Artech House, Boston (1999)
4. Bresson, X., Esedoglu, S., Vandergheynst, P., Thiran, J.P., Osher, S.: Fast global minimization of the active contour/snake model. J. Math. Imaging Vis. 28(2), 151–167 (2007)
5. Chan, T.F., Sandberg, B.Y., Vese, L.A.: Active contours without edges for vector-valued images. Journal of Vis. Communi. and Image Repres. 11, 130–141 (2000)
6. Cremers, D., Rousson, M., Deriche, R.: A review of statistical approaches to level set segmentation: Integrating color, texture, motion and shape. Int. J. Comput. Vision 72(2), 195–215 (2007)
7. Cuzzolin, F.: A geometric approach to the theory of evidence. IEEE Trans. on Syst., Man, and Cyber., Part C 38(4), 522–534 (2008)
8. Dempster, A.P., Chiu, W.F.: Dempster-shafer models for object recognition and classification. Int. J. Intell. Syst. 21(3), 283–297 (2006)
9. Denoeux, T.: Maximum likelihood estimation from uncertain data in the belief function framework. IEEE Trans. Knowl. Data Eng. 25(1), 119–130 (2013)

10. Goldstein, T., Bresson, X., Osher, S.: Geometric applications of the split breg-man method: Segmentation and surface reconstruction. J. Sci. Comput. 45(1-3), 272–293 (2010)
11. Herbulot, A., Jehan-Besson, S., Duffner, S., Barlaud, M., Aubert, G.: Segmentation of vectorial image features using shape gradients and information measures. J. Math. Imaging Vis. 25(3), 365–386 (2006)
12. Jousselme, A.L., Maupin, P.: Distances in evidence theory: Comprehensive survey and generalizations. International Journal of Approximate Reasoning 53(2), 118–145 (2012)
13. Kim, J., Çetin, M., Willsky, A.S.: Nonparametric shape priors for active contour-based image segmentation. Signal Process 87(12), 3021–3044 (2007)
14. Lelandais, B., Gardin, I., Mouchard, L., Vera, P., Ruan, S.: Using belief function theory to deal with uncertainties and imprecisions in image processing. In: Denœux, T., Masson, M.-H. (eds.) Belief Functions: Theory & Appl. Advances in Intelligent Systems and Computing, vol. 164, pp. 197–204. Springer, Heidelberg (2012)
15. Masson, M.H., Denoeux, T.: Ecm: An evidential version of the fuzzy c. Pattern Recognition 41(4), 1384–1397 (2008)
16. Mohamed, M., Far, B.: An enhanced threshold based technique for white blood cells nuclei automatic segmentation. In: 2012 IEEE 14th International Conference on e-Health Networking, Applications and Services (Healthcom), pp. 202–207 (2012)
17. Mohamed, M., Far, B., Guaily, A.: An efficient technique for white blood cells nuclei automatic segmentation. In: 2012 IEEE International Conference on Systems, Man, and Cybernetics (SMC), pp. 220–225 (2012)
18. Parzen, E.: On estimation of a probability density function and mode. The Annals of Mathematical Statistics 33(3), 1065–1076 (1962)
19. Perry, W., Stephanou, H.: Belief function divergence as a classifier. In: Proceedings of the 1991 IEEE International Symposium on Intelligent Control, pp. 280–285 (1991)
20. Rombaut, M., Zhu, Y.M.: Study of dempster–shafer theory for image segmentation applications. Image and Vision Computing 20(1), 15–23 (2002)
21. Rousson, M., Paragios, N.: Prior knowledge, level set representations & visual grouping. Int. J. Comput. Vision 76(3), 231–243 (2008)
22. Sapiro, G.: Vector-valued active contours. In: Proc. CVPR 1996, p. 680. IEEE Computer Society, Washington, DC (1996)
23. Scheuermann, B., Rosenhahn, B.: Feature quarrels: The dempster-shafer evidence theory for image segmentation using a variational framework. In: Kimmel, R., Klette, R., Sugimoto, A. (eds.) ACCV 2010, Part II. LNCS, vol. 6493, pp. 426–439. Springer, Heidelberg (2011)
24. Tschumperle, D., Deriche, R.: Vector-valued image regularization with pdes: a common framework for different applications. IEEE Trans. Pattern Anal. Mach. Intell. 27(4), 506–517 (April)

Automatic Monitoring of Pig Activity Using Image Analysis

Mohammad Amin Kashiha[1], Claudia Bahr[1], Sanne Ott[2,3], Christel P.H. Moons[2],
Theo A. Niewold[3], Frank Tuyttens [2,4], and Daniel Berckmans[1]

[1] M3-BIORES - Measure, Model & Manage Bioresponses, Department of Biosystems, KU
Leuven, Kasteelpark Arenberg 30, B-3001 Leuven, Belgium
[2] Department of Animal Nutrition, Genetics, Production and Ethology, Ghent University,
Heidestraat 19, B-9820 Merelbeke, Belgium
[3] Division of Livestock-Nutrition-Quality, Department of Biosystems, KU Leuven,
Kasteelpark Arenberg 30, B-3001 Leuven, Belgium
[4] Institute for Agricultural and Fisheries Research (ILVO,), Animal Sciences Unit,
Scheldeweg 68, B-9090 Melle, Belgium
Amin.kashiha@biw.kuleuven.be

Abstract. The purpose of this study is to investigate the feasibility and validity
of an automated image processing method to detect the activity status of pigs.
Top-view video images were captured for forty piglets, housed ten per pen.
Each pen was monitored by a top-view CCD camera. The image analysis
protocol to automatically quantify activity consisted of several steps. First, in
order to localise the pigs, ellipse fitting algorithms were employed.
Subsequently, activity was calculated by subtracting image background and
comparing binarised images. To validate the results, they were compared to
labelled behavioural data ('active' versus 'inactive'). This is the first study to
show that activity status of pigs in a group can be determined using image
analysis with an accuracy of 89.8 %. Since activity status is known to be
associated with issues such as lameness, careful monitoring can give an
accurate indication of the health and welfare of pigs.

Keywords: Activity status, ellipse fitting, pig, eYeNamic, image analysis.

1 Introduction

Yearly, over 60 billion animals are slaughtered for food production [1]. This strong
demand for animal products forces producers to increase their capacity with fewer
available resources per animal since livestock are growing in numbers and to keep the
price low, fewer staff are hired to take care of them. To reconcile market forces with
animals' need for individual care, farmers might use automatic tools to monitor their
welfare and health.

In livestock science field, it is frequently necessary to measure animal behaviour in
a quantitative way. Specifically, monitoring activity in animals can serve different
purposes. It is an essential aspect of analysing different behaviours such as locomotor,

J. Blanc-Talon et al. (Eds.): ACIVS 2013, LNCS 8192, pp. 555–563, 2013.
© Springer International Publishing Switzerland 2013

agonistic behaviour and nest building or biological status of animals such as changes of body temperature [2]. Researchers have previously investigated different approaches to monitor activity and locomotion in animals, including image analysis. Electronic tags were a popular method in this field. Moore and Spahr [3] researched the accuracy and efficiency of oestrus detection using an electronic activity monitor tag in milking cows. More recently, accelerometers were used for activity monitoring. Cornou and Lundbye-Christensen [4] fitted sows (female pigs) with a neck collar containing an accelerometer to automatically classify activity types common among group-housed sows.

Many of these earlier studies require animals to be fitted with sensors or tags which raise biosecurity risks and pain [5]. Vision-based pig identification technology, however, is a non-intrusive technique that can be employed to assess activity in livestock. In one study, Lind *et al.* [6] introduced a system to automatically track pig locomotor behaviour. In another study, Cangar *et al.* [7] developed an automatic real-time monitoring technique to identify locomotion and posture of pregnant cows prior to calving.

To the authors' knowledge, there currently is no tool available that uses vision technology to automatically detect pigs' activity status in a group-housed environment. The objective of this study is to measure such a parameter through automated quantification of activity levels using continuous image analysis.

2   Materials and Methods

2.1   Animals and Housing

The experiments for this study were carried out at Agrivet research farm, Merelbeke, Belgium. Forty pigs, Rattlerow Seghers x Piétrain Plus, were selected after the battery period and randomly assigned (10 per pen) to four fully slatted and concrete floor pens *(2.25 m x 3.60 m)*. Pigs had a timer-controlled 12-hour light period from 07:00 h – 19:00 h.

2.2   Equipment and Data Collection

Since 1991 camera technology has been known as a non-disturbing method to monitor animals and provides a way to implement algorithms in research and field applications [8]. In the experiments of this work, cameras were installed in the rafters of the barn, in the location shown in figure 1 to capture top-view images. Using MPEG Recorder software from Noldus and black and white Panasonic WV-BP330 camera, images were recorded during 13 days for 12 hours per day. Images were captured between 07:00 and 19:00, resulting in 156 hours of video. Videos were recorded in MPEG-1 format, with a frame rate of 25 frames per second (down sampled to 1 fps for processing), frame width of 720 pixels, frame height of 576 pixels and data rate of 64 kbps. To provide light in the barn, six 36 watt, 120 cm Sylvania Luxline Plus white fluorescent tube lamps were installed at a height of 200 cm in locations shown in figure 1.

2.3   Development of the Automated Activity Quantification Protocol

The processing flowchart to monitor activity in a pen is shown in figure 2. First, to eliminate light effects, the histogram of the image was equalised using adaptive histogram equalization [9]. Second, each image was binarised to eliminate the background. The binarisation procedure was as follows: 1) the image was filtered using a 2-D Gaussian low-pass filter; 2) a global threshold was calculated using Otsu's method [10]; 3) The image was subsequently hard-thresholded; 4) To remove small objects such as slats edges from the image, a morphological closing operator using a disk-shaped structuring element with a size of 10 pixels [11] was performed on it.

Third, each image was segmented in order to find the location of the pigs. To segment the image, within each pen, the pigs' bodies were extracted as ellipses [12]. The procedure for fitting ellipses to the binary image is explained in the following sub-section.

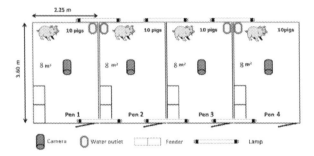

Fig. 1. Ground plan of the 4 pens in research barn in Agrivet, Merelbeke

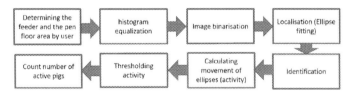

Fig. 2. Image processing flowchart to monitor activity in a pen

2.3.1   Ellipse Fitting

Since pigs in the image are similar to an ellipsoidal shape, to separate them, an ellipse fitting algorithm was implemented to approximate every pig. An ellipse is a conic that can be described by an implicit second-order polynomial:

$$F(x, y) = ax^2 + bxy + cy^2 + dx + ey + f = 0 \qquad (1)$$

with an ellipse-specific constraint:

$$b^2 - 4ac < 0 \qquad (2)$$

where a, b, c, d, e, f are coefficients of the ellipse and (x, y) are coordinates of sample points lying on it. The polynomial $F(x, y)$ is called the algebraic distance of a point (x, y) to the conic $F(x; y) = 0$. By introducing vectors

$$a = [a, b, c, d, e, f]^T \tag{3}$$
$$x = [x^2, xy, y^2, x, y, 1]$$

where T is the transpose operator.

Equation (1) can be rewritten to the vector as

$$F_a(x) = x.a = 0 \tag{4}$$

Fitting an ellipse to a general conic is to minimise the algebraic distance over the set of N data points in the least-square sense. To ensure an ellipse-specificity of the solution, because the vector a can be arbitrarily scaled, the following constraint equation can be considered instead of equation 2 [13]:

$$4ac - b^2 = 1 \tag{5}$$

This constraint could be expressed as $a^TCa = 1$, where constraint matrix C is of the size 6×6:

$$C = \begin{bmatrix} 0 & 0 & 2 & 0 & 0 & 0 \\ 0 & -1 & 0 & 0 & 0 & 0 \\ 2 & 0 & 0 & 0 & 0 & 0 \\ 0 & 0 & 0 & 0 & 0 & 0 \\ 0 & 0 & 0 & 0 & 0 & 0 \\ 0 & 0 & 0 & 0 & 0 & 0 \end{bmatrix} \tag{6}$$

The vector a could be calculated based on following equations:

$$Sa = \lambda Ca \tag{7}$$
$$a^T Ca = 1$$

Where S is the scatter matrix of the size 6×6, and λ is an eigen value for S:

$$S = D^T D \tag{8}$$

and the design matrix D of the size $N \times 6$ is

$$D = \begin{bmatrix} x_1^2 & x_1 y_1 & y_1^2 & x_1 & y_1 & 1 \\ & & & & & \\ x_i^2 & x_i y_i & y_i^2 & x_i & y_i & 1 \\ & & & & & \\ x_N^2 & x_N y_N & y_N^2 & x_N & y_N & 1 \end{bmatrix} \tag{9}$$

The ellipse-specific fitting problem can be solved by minimising constraint, $E = \|Da\|^2$ under the constraint equation 5. Introducing the Lagrange multiplier, it leads to the system equation 7, which is a generalized eigen vector system. The chosen eigenvector a_k (k is the eigrenvector number) corresponds to the minimal positive eigen value. The minimal value of $\|Da\|^2$ is then directly given by equation 10.

$$\|Da\|^2 = a^T D^T Da = a^T Sa = \lambda a^T Ca = \lambda \tag{10}$$

Then, the solution of the minimisation problem represents the best-fit ellipse for the given set of points. Every time, six edge sample points were randomly selected from the ordered edge points list for one ellipse fitting. The result of finding fitted ellipses is shown in figure 3b.

Thereafter, ellipse parameters such as "Orientation", "Major Axis Length", "Minor Axis Length" and "Centroid" for all objects in the image were calculated. figure 3a illustrates these parameters and figure 3b shows the ellipses fitted to the pigs' bodies. The next steps shown in figure 2 are explained in the following sections.

2.3.2   Identification

After localisation of the pigs using the ellipse fitting algorithm, they are needed to be identified to make tracking feasible. This was carried out using the method introduced in our previous work [14].

2.3.3   Image Activity

Image Activity (IA) is defined as amount of movement in pixels an object produces. Using ellipse models presented in the previous section, IA is mathematically explained as shown in the following equation and illustrated in figure 4.

$$IA = |Linear\ motion| + |angular\ motion| = |\overrightarrow{T}| + |\left(\measuredangle\overrightarrow{T}\right) * \frac{L}{2}| = T + \theta_T * \frac{L}{2} \quad (11)$$

Where IA is the Image Activity; in pixels, $\overrightarrow{T}$ is the movement vector (from ellipse E_1 to ellipse E_2); in pixels; T is the size of movement vector; in pixels; θ_T is the difference of orientation between ellipses E_1 and E_2; unit-less; L is average of size of the major axis of ellipses E_1 and E_2; in pixels; $\measuredangle$ is the angle operator;

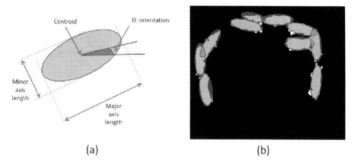

(a)   (b)

Fig. 3. a. Ellipse parameters; b. Ellipses fitted to pigs' body

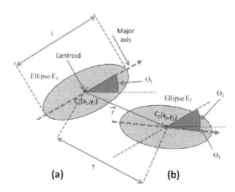

(a)   (b)

Fig. 4. Ellipse fitted to pig's image: (a) at time "t-1"; (b) at time "t"; T is the distance travelled

560   M.A. Kashiha et al.

2.3.4   Image Activity Status

IA was monitored over time and Image Activity Status (IAS) was determined based on the following parameter:

$$IAS = \frac{IA}{L} \tag{12}$$

Where IAS is the Image Activity Status; unit-less; IA is the Image Activity; in pixels; L is the average size of the major axis of ellipses E_1 and E_2 (figure 4); in pixels;

Next step was to decide based on IAS if a pig was active or inactive. Based on IAS parameter and an experimental threshold of 0.4, activity status was determined as active if IAS $\leq$ 0.4 or inactive if IAS > 0.4.

2.3.5   Manual Labelling

As a reference, manual "labelling" of recorded videos was done by an experienced ethologist. Human observations of pig behavioural activity were performed off-line using 2-min instantaneous scan-sampling in four 30-minute sessions on 6 selected days since labelling is a very time consuming work. Behaviour of each individual pig was labelled using the Observer XT 10.2 (Noldus, Wageningen, The Netherlands) software. Therefore 30 samples per pig per day were obtained. For each scan, all 10 individual pigs of one pen were scored either active or inactive. Active behaviour was defined as if pig was walking or running and/or performing other behavioural activity that includes physical movements of any body part. Otherwise, it was considered to be inactive. Finally, number of active pigs were summed to calculate how many pigs were scored as active in a pen. The rest of data that were not labelled were analysed by the introduced technique.

3   Results

3.1   Validation

In order to validate the automated image processing technique, image-detected activity statuses were compared with labelling results, as shown in table 1. In total, 14400 frames were analysed, which were recorded from four pens. Out of 5896 active statuses, 5297 were identified correctly, while 162 false positive identifications (2.75 %) and 599 false negative identifications (10.2 %) were recorded. This leads to an overall accuracy of 89.8 % for a stocking density of 1.23 pig/m^2.

3.2   Continuous Data Analysis

After validating the method all 13 days of the experiment data were analysed. There were in total 13 (days)* 12 (hours) * 3600 (seconds) * 10 (pigs) or 5.616 million (432k per day) samples per pen to analyse. Figure 5 shows average of active pigs per pen during the days of the experiment.

4   Discussion and Conclusion

In this study, an innovative approach using movement calculation of ellipses fitted to pigs' bodies was chosen to investigate the possibilities of automated activity status detection for fattening pigs using vision technology. It was shown that pig activity status detection is possible by localising individual pigs in the group by fitting ellipses onto their top-view body image and tracking those ellipses over time.

Among the previous methods used for pig activity monitoring, the eYeNamic tool was the most successful [15] and was taken as a reference to the introduced technique. This tool calculates the difference in image intensity between consecutive frames. From this difference image, the binary 'activity image' $I_a(x, y, t)$ is derived, containing the pixels for which the intensity change exceeded a certain threshold. A summation of the number of these pixels yields the total amount of activity at time t [15]. Since eYeNamic cannot determine number of active pigs, one development phase was launched to determine a threshold for number of pixels to decide how many pigs in a pen were active. In the validation phase, data presented in table 1 were also analysed with eYeNamic. Table 2 shows the results of this comparison. Upon these results IAS method reports 10.2% of error in detecting number of active pigs while eYeNamic categorizes activity status of pigs with an error of 39.2 %. In addition, false positives were 2.75% and 11.8% respectively. Thus, IAS method yields a higher accuracy in detecting activity status of pigs.

Table 1. Activity status in 4 pens, comparing labelling and automated image analysis;

Pen	Samples	Labelling Active status	Image analysis Active status- True positives	False positives
1	3600	1515	1432 (94.5 %)	48 (3.17 %)
2	3600	1343	1209 (90.0 %)	21 (1.56 %)
3	3600	1316	1131 (85.9 %)	61 (4.63 %)
4	3600	1722	1525 (88.6 %)	32 (1.86 %)
Total	14400	5896	5297 (89.8 %)	162 (2.75 %)

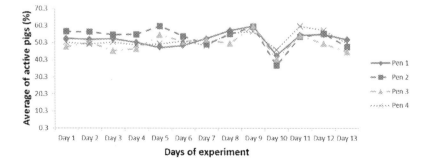

Fig. 5. Average of active pigs during 13 days of the experiment detected by IAS algorithm

Table 2. Comparison of labelling, IAS technique and eYeNamic tool in detecting number of active pigs in a pen

Pen	Samples	Labelling Active status (AS)	IAS	Image analysis Absolute error = |AS-IAS|	Image analysis By eYeNamic (eYe)	Absolute error = |AS-eYe|
1	3600	1515	1432	83 (5.5 %)	1042	473 (31.2 %)
2	3600	1343	1209	134 (10.0 %)	1851	508 (37.8%)
3	3600	1316	1131	185 (14.1 %)	891	425 (32.3 %)
4	3600	1722	1525	197 (11.4 %)	2640	918 (53.3 %)
Total	14400	5896	5297	599 (10.2 %)	6424	2324 (39.4 %)

The introduced technique was also robust against body shape variations in standing and lying position which made it quite suitable for the purpose of this study. It is worth mentioning that, due to variation in data, the occurrence of false positives in detection of activity is unavoidable. Nevertheless, our method could still detect active pigs in a light intensity range of 11.7 and 176.1 lux with an accuracy of 89.8 %.

However, there are still challenges to use the proposed technique in practical settings. A challenge would be to employ this technique in higher (practical) stocking density where segmentation is a neck. One way to address this problem is to combine activity status detection with activity calculation by comparing consecutive frames [15]. This will be investigated in future work.

Activity status monitoring can have many applications such as stressor response analysis. Moreover, since this technology is not dependant on type of the object it is monitoring, it can be applied to any moving, living organism such as humans, animals and cells. In conclusion, this activity status measuring protocol might contribute in future as a practical tool in livestock husbandry since health, welfare and performance are all variables that are related to activity status.

Acknowledgments. This project was funded by Agentschap voor Innovatie door Wetenschap en Technologie (IWT). (project number: 080530/LBO)

References

1. Prakash, A., Stigler, M.: FAO Statistical Yearbook: Food And Agriculture Organization of the United Nations (2012), http://faostat.fao.org/
2. Cornou, C., Lundbye-Christensen, S., Kristensen, A.: Modelling and monitoring sows' activity types in farrowing house using acceleration data. Comput. Electron. Agric. 76(2), 316–324 (2011)
3. Moore, A.S., Spahr, S.L.: Activity Monitoring and an Enzyme Immunoassay for Milk Progesterone to Aid in the Detection of Estrus. J. Dairy Sci. 74(11), 3857–3862 (1991)
4. Cornou, C., Lundbye-Christensen, S.: Classification of sows' activity types from acceleration patterns using univariate and multivariate models. Comput. Electron. Agric. 72(2), 53–60 (2010)

5. Hernandez-Jover, M., Schembri, N., Toribio, J., Holyoake, P.: Biosecurity risks associated with current identification practices of producers trading live pigs at livestock sales. Anim. 2(11), 1692–1699 (2008); PubMed PMID: WOS:000260907200017. English

6. Lind, N.M., Vinther, M., Hemmingsen, R.P., Hansen, A.K.: Validation of a digital video tracking system for recording pig locomotor behaviour. J. Neurosci. Methods 143(2), 123–132 (2005)

7. Cangar, Ö., Leroy, T., Guarino, M., Vranken, E., Fallon, R., Lenehan, J., et al.: Automatic real-time monitoring of locomotion and posture behaviour of pregnant cows prior to calving using online image analysis. Comput. Electron. Agric. 64(1), 53–60 (2008)

8. Van der Stuyft, E., Schofield, C.P., Randall, J.M., Wambacq, P., Goedseels, V.: Development and application of computer vision systems for use in livestock production. Comput. Electron. Agric. 6(3), 243–265 (1991)

9. Sherrier, R.H., Johnson, G.A.: Regionally Adaptive Histogram Equalization of the Chest. IEEE Trans. Med. Imaging. 6(1), 1–7 (1987)

10. Otsu, N.: A threshold selection method from gray-level histograms. IEEE Trans. Syst. Man. Cybern. 9(1), 62–66 (1979)

11. Gonzalez, R.C., Woods, R.E.: Digital Image Processing, p. 793. Addison-Wesley Longman Publishing Co., Inc. (2001)

12. Zhang, G., Jayas, D.S., White, N.D.G.: Separation of Touching Grain Kernels in an Image by Ellipse Fitting Algorithm. Biosyst. Eng. 92(2), 135–142 (2005)

13. Fitzgibbon, A., Pilu, M., Fisher, R.: Direct Least Square Fitting of Ellipses. IEEE Trans. Pattern Anal. Mach. Intell. 21(5), 476–480 (1999)

14. Kashiha, M., Bahr, C., Ott, S., Moons, C.P.H., Niewold, T.A., Ödberg, F.O., et al.: Automatic identification of marked pigs in a pen using image pattern recognition. Comput. Electron. Agric. 93, 111–120 (2013)

15. Leroy, T., Vranken, E., Van Brecht, A., Struelens, E., Sonck, B., Berckmans, D.: A computer vision method for on-line behavioral quantification of individually caged poultry. Transactions of the Asabe. 49(3), 795–802 (2006); PubMed PMID: WOS:000238860600023

IMM-Based Tracking and Latency Control with Off-the-Shelf IP PTZ Camera

Pierrick Paillet[1], Romaric Audigier[1], Frederic Lerasle[2,3],
and Quoc-Cuong Pham[1]

[1] CEA, LIST, LVIC, Point Courrier 173, F-91191 Gif-sur-Yvette, France
[2] CNRS, LAAS, 7 Avenue du Colonel Roche, F-31400 Toulouse, France
[3] Univ de Toulouse, UPS, LAAS, F-31400, Toulouse, France
pierrick.paillet@cea.fr

Abstract. Networked Pan-Tilt-Zoom cameras (PTZ) seem to replace
static ones in videosurveillance areas as they are easier to deploy, with
a larger field of view and can take high resolution pictures of targets
thanks to their zoom. However, current algorithms combining tracking
and camera control do not take into account order executing latency
and motion delays caused by off-the-shelf cameras. In this paper, we
suggest a new motion control strategy that manages inherent delays by
an Interacting Multiple Models prediction of the target motion and an
online evaluation of this prediction.

Keywords: Tracking, pan-tilt-zoom camera, PTZ, delay, prediction,
law of control, Interacting Multiple Models.

1 Introduction and State of the Art

Human tracking with fixed cameras is a well-known field of Computer Vision
and especially in video surveillance. Unlike fixed pattern usually displayed, PTZ
are able to pan and tilt around their center and take close-up shots of the target.
They are starting to replace fixed cameras in large areas, such as shopping centres
or stations. Networked commercial PTZ are easier to deploy and fewer devices are
needed to cover an identical videosurveillance area, thus reducing costs. However,
such off-the-shelf PTZ are black boxes, introducing more control delays unlike
prototypes used in laboratories.

A large amount of work have been done with one (or more) PTZ cooperating
with a fixed camera. Tracking is solved by assigning it to the fixed camera as
it does not suffer from PTZ delays and motion, then PTZ is driven by the
resulting tracking to another task, such as acquiring high resolution pictures of
the targets faces [16]. In [7], two PTZ play alternatively the fixed camera role
for more flexibility. However none of these approaches solved the mono-PTZ
tracking problem as a common field of view (FoV) is required to collaborate.

PTZ-only tracking imposes major constraints on the choice of tracking algorithms and needs a specific perception-decision-action (PDA) strategy to keep
the target into their FoV. First, unlike fixed cameras, PTZ are active mobile devices and can not rely on an off-line sequence to build a scene model. Panorama

J. Blanc-Talon et al. (Eds.): ACIVS 2013, LNCS 8192, pp. 564–575, 2013.

[5], visual landmarks [8] or optical flow [2,15] methods dynamically construct the model scene, but need features consistency between frames. On the contrary, Machine Learning detection algorithms [12] does not need hypothesis on PTZ motion or frame rate.

Secondly PDA strategy needs to manage important delays, due to motion actuators, network transmissions and irregular PTZ framerate (while moving, frames received are almost useless as no new command can be sent without delay). Human operator intuitive actions, such as driving the PTZ or zooming, must be anticipated to keep track of the target. State-of-the-art mono-PTZ methods [1,3] consists in assembling a PTZ prototype and modeling precisely all internal elements, such as motor-units, to build an ad-hoc law of control. However off-the-shelf PTZ is a black box as its internal elements are not accessible. An other approach mostly used in multi-PTZ tracking tries to balance motion delays by anticipating the position of the target with an additional prediction step. A constant motion model is mostly used, such as constant-velocity [10,15], Maximum-likelihood estimation [6] or Kalman filtering [16]. To our best knowledge, Varcheie et al. [15] are the only mono-PTZ tracking system managing PTZ delays in that way, but with a basic prediction. Moreover as no other camera can reliably track the target during PTZ motion in mono-PTZ tracking, prediction efficiency is crucial. However, all state-of-the-art predictions are accurate if target motion is nearly linear, but have troubles when non-linear yet common events appear, such that target turns back or avoids obstacles.

In this paper we present a visual servoing strategy applied on an off-the-shelf PTZ camera to track a person with a human detection process combined with a particle filter. Our PDA strategy manages motion delays with a camera motion model and an Interacting Multiple Model Kalman Filter (IMM KF) to improve prediction robustness to target behavior. Our approach also uses PTZ delays to reinforce prediction by online evaluation and maximize cost efficiency. Although applied with a particular tracking algorithm, our work is mainly focused on the PDA strategy and could be used with any IP PTZ and any tracking algorithm.

We briefly introduce in section 2 our PTZ person tracking algorithm. IMM KF is described in section 3. Off-line IMM KF evaluation on human trajectories then on-line experimental tracking results and relative comparison with [15] are shown in section 4. Finally section 5 concludes the paper.

2 Description of Our Architecture

2.1 Global Overview

In order to take into account PTZ delay and latency in our PDA strategy, we model our system as a four step loop, with associated delays :

- Image capture and transmission from PTZ to our system, with delay τ_1.
- Detection and tracking with our system, taking τ_2 seconds.

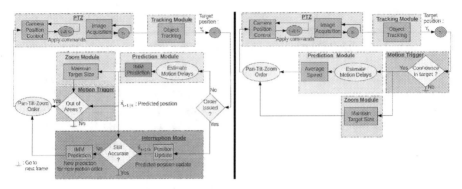

Fig. 1. Block diagram of our system architecture synoptic (left) versus [15] (right).
Cycle starts from the "Image acquisition" module. Improved elements are highlighted
in red

- A waiting step, also called latency, as motion order is transmitted to PTZ
  through network and from internal camera software to hardware. No motion
  is done during τ_3.
- An effective PTZ motion, taking τ_4 seconds to complete.

Delay τ_2 is the only one depending on our implementation, τ_3 and τ_4 are only
affected by the PTZ in use and the motion amplitude. τ_1 depends on network
traffic and in general $\tau_1 \ll \tau_2, \tau_3$ and τ_4. Delays are illustrated in figure 3. This
model is simple enough to suit all PTZ cameras, even if associated times could
differ. In our laboratory, we successfully used this model on several network PTZ
available (AXIS 233D and Q6034).

Depending on off-the-shelf PTZ software implementation, we noticed that internal camera information may be not correlated to real position when it moves.
This leads to use position servoing instead of speed control to command the PTZ
as it may cause tracking and 3D re-projection error when our system receives
blurred in-going frames instead of well located expected images. However, characteristic delays are easily evaluated by a global image motion detection, as no
motion is done during latency. Similar to [9,12], our AXIS 233D PTZ Camera[1]
shows a global motion delay $\tau_3 + \tau_4$ of 400 to 550 ms for a 20° motion. Latency
delay τ_3 seems to be independent of the amplitude motion, around 300 ms. Furthermore this model of PTZ continues to send unblurred images during latency,
allowing intermediate tracking iterations.

Figure 1 shows our block-diagram architecture and highlights differences with
Varcheie et al. approach [15], modules details are given in following sections 2.2-
2.4 and 3. For each image acquired at time t_k by the PTZ and sent through the
network, first a tracking module detects and extracts 3D target position. This
information is then updated by a prediction module to take into account the
known delays $\tau_1 + \tau_2$ and estimate time $\hat{\tau_3} + \hat{\tau_4}$ needed to center the PTZ to the
evaluated position. The predicted position at time $t_{k+1} = t_k + \tau_1 + \tau_2 + \hat{\tau_3} + \hat{\tau_4}$

---

[1] http://www.axis.com/fr/products/cam_233d/index.htm

is finally checked by the motion trigger and if conditions are met, then an order is given to center the PTZ on the predicted position.

If an order has already been issued but no PTZ motion detected, following static images are handled by the tracking module, then the interruption module is activated. This module tries to evaluate if the previously predicted position where the PTZ will be sent, is still accurate; if not then a new order is issued to recover the target.

2.2   Tracking Module

Our algorithm performs object tracking on the ground plane thanks to a geometric calibration [2] and a sampling-importance-resampling particle filter. 3D tracking increases target dynamic models precision and allows 3D scene information usage. Furthermore it is more adapted to collaborating with other networked devices. A gradient based machine learning detector leads the particles sampling on the ground plane. An ellipsoid with three parts, corresponding to the head, torso and legs of the target, is then plotted on every particle position and projected into the PTZ image plan. An appearance model is evaluated for each candidate part and compared to the target model, based on HSV color histograms and on SURF interest points to take into account the target shape. Finally, once the target is located in the image, each part of its model is updated by a boosting algorithm to be more robust to appearance change during tracking.

Allowed positions on the ground are discretized before evaluating the ellipsoid projection on a 2.5m by 2.5m grid around the image center projected on the ground (figure 2). As this projection depends only of camera pan-tilt-zoom parameters, it can be used as long as the PTZ remains still, improving particles evaluation speed for successive frames. Furthermore, as the final position is known when motion order is sent, grid projection is done on a parallelized thread during PTZ motion, without delaying the tracking process (figure 3).

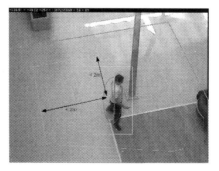

Fig. 2. Great green polygon plots the area where ellipsoid projection is evaluated, the blue one is the allowed area, target detection box is drawn in cyan and red ellipsoid corresponds to the target position.

2.3   Motion Trigger

The motion strategy objective is to keep target on the image center at each iteration. However this mainly means small motions, decreasing tracking algorithm performances as camera delays increase time between two images (cf section 4).

A common balance is done by untightening center condition, keeping the target *close to* the image center by defining a 2D *allowed* area around it where target motion does not trigger PTZ motion, limiting it to large motions.

We also need to keep our target inside the projection grid which corresponds to allowed positions. So if target 3D position comes too close to the grid edge, this also triggers a motion. Typically we choose an 0,5m offset, such that a target with a $1.5m/s$ speed will stay in the grid for two more iterations ($\approx 500ms$).

2.4   Zoom Control

Zoom provides a better target appearance but increases the risk of losing the target and is much slower than pan-tilt only motion. Here, our objective is to keep the target at a given size in picture but without slowing down tracking.

As it only depends on the PTZ, an off-line specific module evaluated maximum feasible zoom modification that would not delay the pan-tilt motion. Then during tracking, zoom amplitude such that the target size reaches the objective is limited to the pan-tilt motion used by motion order. It leads to reach the target objective size in few iterations but keeps our tracking system as fast as possible.

3   Prediction and Interruption Modules

3.1   Interacting Multiple Models Kalman Filter

Delays from 500ms to 1s may look small but, spread over two or more motions, could be sufficient to allow the target to come out of the camera FoV, especially with a zoom on the target.

As explained in the introduction, state-of-the-art prediction methods try to model human behavior with linear motion, but have troubles when this hypothesis is challenged. Common Kalman filter and extended versions are robust to noise but are restrained to only one dynamic model, chosen at the filter implementation. If the target motion differs too strongly from that model, the filter has to be updated and until the target recovers the expected dynamic, predictions have a poor quality.

To overcome this limitation, an Interacting Multiple Models Kalman Filter (IMM KF) is used in this system. Well known from filtering community [11,14], it has never been studied in monocular camera state-of-the-art algorithms. This filter is based on a probabilistic competition between multiple Kalman filters with different dynamics.

Each iteration is a five step cycle :

1. Models probabilities are updated according to an homogeneous finite-state Markov chain.
2. A mixed initial state is evaluated for each model according to models probabilities.
3. Each Kalman filter is run with this mixed initial state and updated with the new observation.
4. Measurement errors are used to update models probabilities according to the observation.
5. The final state is the sum of each model-conditioned final state, weighted by the probability that this model is in use during this iteration.

A more detailed algorithm can be found in [14].

One great IMM KF advantage is its ability to deal with different dynamics for a low cost efficiency, as just a few more Kalman filters run, possibly in a parallel architecture. An unexpected motion change can still not be predicted but can be understood quicker and following predictions will be more accurate.

3.2 IMM KF Implementation

IMM KF global architecture needs to be adapted to our specific system, namely the models in use, their number and the transition matrix modeling the finite-state Markov chain.

Models Design. Having too many models decreases the overall performance [14], in particular we noticed that too similar models decrease precision as no model is prevailing. We use five dynamics to model human behavior : a linear motion with a constant-velocity model and four nearly constant-turn models, with dynamic matrix F_{CV} and F_{CT} respectively. Denoting Δt our time-step, the state vector $X_k = (x_k, y_k, \dot{x}_k, \dot{y}_k)^T$, with (x_k, y_k) the target position on the ground plane and $(\dot{x}_k, \dot{y}_k)$ its speed, fourth order dynamic matrix would be :

$$F_{CV} = \begin{pmatrix} 1 & 0 & \Delta t & 0 \\ 0 & 1 & 0 & \Delta t \\ 0 & 0 & 1 & 0 \\ 0 & 0 & 0 & 1 \end{pmatrix}, F_{CT}(\omega) = \begin{pmatrix} 1 & 0 & \frac{sin(\omega \Delta t)}{\omega} & -\frac{1-cos(\omega \Delta t)}{\omega} \\ 0 & 1 & \frac{1-cos(\omega \Delta t)}{\omega} & \frac{sin(\omega \Delta t)}{\omega} \\ 0 & 0 & cos(\omega \Delta t) & -sin(\omega \Delta t) \\ 0 & 0 & sin(\omega \Delta t) & cos(\omega \Delta t) \end{pmatrix}$$

Rotational speeds ω are chosen such that, for $\Delta t = 200$ms, rotations correspond to quarter-turn and half-turn in each direction, i.e. $\omega = \pm 7.85^o/s, \pm 15.7^o/s$.
Here only linear Kalman models with the same dimension have been chosen, extensions exist [11,14] but require more computational complexity.

Markov Model. Almost no assumption is made as we seek for sudden motion change : The target has half chances to remain in the same dynamic, and half to change with equal probability of switching to any model. Denoting $\mathcal{M}$ the set of dynamic models and m_k^i the event that model $i \in \mathcal{M}$ is in use during the kth iteration, the transition probabilities will be, $\forall i \in \mathcal{M}, P(m_{k+1}^i | m_k^i) = 0.5$ and $\forall i, j \in \mathcal{M}, i \neq j, P(m_{k+1}^j | m_k^i) = 0.125$ in our case.

Prediction. The IMM KF is used in this system to provide a predicted position of the target at the next iteration. So the normal cycle is interrupted at the 3rd step and model-conditioned predicted position $\hat{X}^i_{k+1|k}$ are collected.

However, instead of using the same probabilistic sum that in the 5th step, only the most probable model is used as no observation could balance the predefined transition matrix bias introduced in the 1st step.

Denoting μ^i_k the probability the model $i \in \mathcal{M}$ is in use during the current iteration.

$$i^k_0 \leftarrow \text{argmax}_{i \in \mathcal{M}}(\mu^i_k)$$
$$\hat{X}_{k+1|k} = \hat{X}^{i^k_0}_{k+1|k}$$

3.3   Interruption Module

This module is our second innovation with IMM KF. Others state-of-the-art strategies do not evaluate the prediction accuracy once the motion order has been issued.

As explained in section 2.1 we take advantage of frames that the PTZ sends during latency, usually one or two images, before moving. First this reduces the gap between successive frames when ordering a motion, increasing feature consistancy and tracking robustness. Then this frames are used to evaluate if predicted position where the PTZ is being driven is still accurate.

For each intermediate frame, the system normally apply tracking step and a new prediction is then evaluated but at the same time t_{k+1} used to make the first prediction in order to update it. Made on a shorter period with new target observation, this new prediction is more reliable than the previous one. Figure 3 shows a complete motion and interruptions cycle.

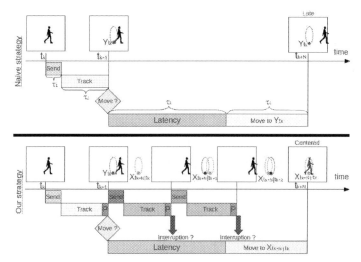

Fig. 3. A trivial PDA cycle synoptic (left) versus our strategy (right). Tracking result position is quoted with red ellipse, predicted position on which PTZ would be centered is in green and further predictions are in blue.

If the distance between the new prediction and the position where PTZ will be centered is too large or if the target will be going outside the PTZ FoV at the end of the motion, an emergency reaction is launched.

A third prediction is made, starting from the last interruption iteration but for a period of time corresponding to a normal PTZ motion. Then a new order is issued to drive the PTZ to this position. As a second latency period arises, the target may leave the FoV but it avoids leading the PTZ to a position where the target will most likely never be, increasing the system reactivity and decreases the risk of losing the target.

If used in a larger network, the distance between the two predictions could be used to evaluate how confident the system is about the position where the PTZ is being driven. Some other strategies may be used to reduce quicker the risk of losing the target, for instance driving a second PTZ on the area.

4   Experiments and Evaluations

In this section we first evaluate the prediction step apart from the rest of the algorithm. Then we apply the prediction to the global PDA strategy to evaluate its influence and compare its performances to a Varcheie [15] based method.

4.1   Prediction Method Validation

We validated our prediction step on a synthetic trajectory shown in figure 4, corresponding to a person moving at a $2m/s$ speed and twelve human trajectories coming from PETS 2009 Benchmark, S2.L1[2] with ground truth[3]. This second dataset contains four trajectories (n° 1-2-3-6 - 1537 frames) with unexpected motion changes, i.e. quarter-turn (QT) and half-turn (HT), while remaining trajectories (1337 frames) are almost linear. Details are given in table 1.

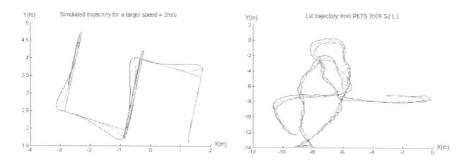

Fig. 4. Trajectories on the ground plane. Synthetic trajectory is left and 1[st]PETS 2009 trajectory is right. Ground truth is plotted in red, Kalman prediction in blue and IMM KF prediction in green.

---

[2] http://www.cvg.rdg.ac.uk/PETS2009/a.html#s2l1
[3] http://www.gris.informatik.tu-darmstadt.de/~aandriye/data.html

We compare prediction methods with the following metrics : the mean error between prediction and next position on the whole trajectory (WT), on the five following steps after quarter-turns (5-QT) and half-turns (5-HT), the maximal error on the five following steps after an event (Max) and the mean time needed to recover a prediction error close to the mean error after an event (Rec).

Table 1. Results for Kalman filter and IMM KF on different sets

Set	#frames	Timestep	#QT	#HT	Prediction	WT	5-QT	5-HT	Max	Rec
Simulation	189	400ms	4	3	Kalman	0.19m	0.37m	0.42m	0.62m	1.9s
					IMM KF	0.10m	0.19m	0.20m	0.45m	1.4s
PETS event	1537	570ms	15	6	Kalman	0.22m	0.44m	0.43m	0.92m	2.3s
					IMM KF	0.18m	0.24m	0.26m	0.65m	1.7s
PETS linear	1337	570ms	0	0	Kalman	0.19m				
					IMM KF	0.20m				

Results on table 1 show that Kalman filter and IMM KF perform well on linear motion as WT is low. Linear motion prediction is a good hypothesis most of time. However we note more errors on QT and HT, as illustrated in figure 4, Kalman filter reaction is much slower than IMM KF, from 400 to 500 ms, leading to greater prediction errors even if a good tracking position is given as input.

4.2   Data Acquisition and Metrics

No public dataset is available for testing a complete PTZ tracking system because of its dynamic nature. Instead we selected seven scenarii detailed in table 2 and played each five times for every strategy to reduce variance due to online evaluation and the Particle filter stochastic nature. First six scenarii include one specific motion event such as motion stop, QT and HT. Events may happen when target is on the allowed area center (on center) or near its limit (on limit). Last scenario tests our system over a trajectory illustrated in figure 6, adding more varied background, more complex lighting condition and target acceleration. We tried to keep the same experimental conditions for all sequences from a scenario. Trajectories have been marked on the ground and sequences have been made in a row with the same target. Once recorded, we extracted ground truths manually for performance evaluation.

Here we evaluate prediction step influence on the global strategy. We also compare in the 7th scenario those strategies to a third one based on [15], illustrated in figure 1, as it shares a similar PDA loop. Its prediction step is a speed average model and the motion trigger is based on target appearance score given by the tracking module. However we used our tracking module and appearance model instead of those proposed in [15]. As all three strategies compared use the same tracking module, we can evaluate here their impact on tracking results.

Fig. 5. System behavior as target turns back in scenario n°4. Red box is ground truth and blue one is our tracking results.

We use four metrics inspired by CLEARMOT [4] and Varcheie et al. [15] : *Precision* (P) represents tracking performance. *Centralization* (C) evaluates how close the target is to the image center. *Track fragmentation* (TF) indicates lack of continuity of tracking system and *Focusing* (F) evaluates the zoom control. Those metrics are denoted by :

$$P = \frac{\#TP}{NF}, \qquad C = \frac{\sum\limits_{i \in TP} D_i}{\#TP}, \qquad TF = \frac{\#T_{out}}{NF}, \qquad F = \frac{\sum\limits_{i \in TP} H_i}{\#TP}$$

TP denotes true positive frames set, i.e. frames where target bounding box and ground truth surface coverage is higher than 50%, $\#$ denotes the cardinality and NF is the total number of frames. D_i is the Euclidean distance between ground truth and image center, T_{out} is the number of frames where target is outside the FoV and H_i is the ratio between the size of the target and the image height.

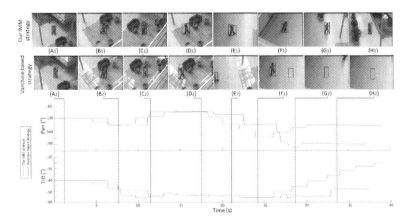

Fig. 6. 7[th]scenario. The red box is ground truth and the blue one our tracking results.

4.3   Events and Tracking Evaluation

As shown in table 2, IMM KF slightly improves tracking performance. In scenarii
3 to 6 the reaction time is a decisive element as target may go out of the FoV
before the system reacts to the event. Figure 5 illustrates a typical failure. In both
configurations (Figure 5.B and C) prediction drives camera too far as it does not
realize that target turns back. But this event is taken into account quicker with
IMM KF (Figure 5.D-1) and failure is avoided. Kalman filter moves again PTZ
(Figure 5.D-2), losing the target. Quarter turns also lead less often to failure
than half turn because motion amplitude is smaller, so the target may not leave
PTZ FoV before prediction assimilates the event.

Table 2. Results for Kalman filter and IMM KF over different scenarii

Sc.n°	Motion type	Duration	Prediction	P	C	TF	F	Fps	Failure
1	Stop on limit	9 s	Kalman	79 %	95 %	0 %	31 %	6.4	1 / 5
			IMM KF	**87 %**	97 %	0 %	32 %	6.5	0 / 5
2	Stop on center	8 s	Kalman	83 %	94 %	0 %	31 %	6.0	0 / 5
			IMM KF	84 %	96 %	0 %	31 %	**6.5**	0 / 5
3	QT on limit	10 s	Kalman	37 %	94 %	13 %	41 %	**7.1**	2 / 5
			IMM KF	**62 %**	94 %	1 %	42 %	6.4	**0 / 5**
4	QT on center	13 s	Kalman	68 %	94 %	7 %	27 %	6.8	2 / 5
			IMM KF	**83 %**	95 %	0 %	28 %	**7.0**	**0 / 5**
5	HT on limit	14 s	Kalman	58 %	94 %	10 %	31 %	6.0	3 / 5
			IMM KF	**77 %**	95 %	0 %	33 %	6.1	**0 / 5**
6	HT on center	14 s	Kalman	55 %	95 %	11 %	31 %	6.0	3 / 5
			IMM KF	**63 %**	95 %	4 %	32 %	6.1	1 / 5
7	QT,turn, stop,	42 s	Kalman	71 %	91 %	1 %	30 %	6.2	1 / 5
	HT, acceleration		IMM KF	**79 %**	92 %	0 %	29 %	**6.45**	**0 / 5**
			[15] strategy	61 %	85 %	7 %	30 %	5.4	2 / 5

Results from the 7th scenario show that our PDA strategy is also more reactive
and leads to better results than the one based on [15]. Their motion trigger leads
to small accumulated motions, decreasing framerate (Fps). For instance [15]
based strategy triggers many small motions as the target stops between figures
$6.C_2$ and $6.D_2$, while our stategy does not. Furthermore, camera view angle
and scene context may quickly change target appearance during the 7th scenario,
preventing motion trigger. This decreases performances (P) and (C) as well as
allows target to go out of the FoV as trigger condition is not met (figure $6.E_2$),
increasing fragmentation (TF) and finally leads to lose the target (figure $6.G_2$).

5   Conclusions and Perspectives

Our approach is focused on managing off-the-shelf IP PTZ camera delays for
person tracking. Our PDA strategy takes advantages of latency to improve the

tracking accuracy and it relies on two innovative features : an improved prediction step increasing reactivity to abrupt motion change through an IMM KF and an online evaluation of prediction errors during latency.

We first led experiments demonstrating that IMM KF is more efficient than usual Kalman filter and causes less failure in case of motion events. Then we showed the influence of prediction efficiency on a global PTZ tracking system to manage delays. Finally we demonstrated that our innovations improve robustness to context and motion change compared to state-of-the-art method [15] sharing similar architecture.

Further investigations will fall on increasing zoom control with model information from IMM KF. Then we will apply our monocular approach to collaborative PTZ network with partially common FoV.

References

1. Ahmed, J., Ali, A., Khan, A.: Stabilized active camera tracking system. Journal of Real-Time Image Processing (2012)
2. Badri, J.: Systeme de vision hybride: Modelisation et application au suivi haute resolution, Thèse de l'Université Blaise Pascal - Clermont-Ferrand II (2008)
3. Bellotto, N., Sommerlade, E., Benfold, B.: A distributed camera system for multi-resolution surveillance. ACM/IEEE ICDSC (2009)
4. Bernardin, K., Stiefelhagen, R.: Evaluating multiple object tracking performance: the CLEAR MOT metrics. J. Image Video Process (2008)
5. Biswas, A., Guha, P., Mukerjee, A., Venkatesh, K.S.: Intrusion Detection and Tracking with Pan-Tilt Cameras. IET ICVIE (2006)
6. Choi, H.C., Park, U., Jain, A.K., Lee, S.W.: Face Tracking and Recognition at a Distance: A coaxial & concentric PTZ Camera System. IEEE TCSVT (2011)
7. Everts, I., Sebe, N., Jones, G.: Cooperative Object Tracking with Multiple PTZ Cameras. In: 14th ICIAP (2007)
8. Kang, S., Paik, J., Koschan, A., Abidi, B., Abidi, M.: Real-time video tracking using PTZ cameras. In: IET ICQCAV (2003)
9. Kumar, P., Dick, A., Sheng, T.S.: Real Time Target Tracking with Pan Tilt Zoom Camera. In: DICTA (2009)
10. Liao, H.-C., Chen, W.Y.: Eagle Eye: A Dual PTZ Camera system for target tracking in a large open area. Information Technology and Control (2010)
11. Lopez, R., Danes, P., Royer, F.: Extending the IMM filter to Heterogeneous-Order state space models. In: 49th IEEE CDC (2010)
12. Mian, A.: Realtime face detection and tracking using a single Pan, Tilt, Zoom camera. In: 23rd IVCNZ (2008)
13. Qureshi, F.Z., Terzopoulos, D.: Planning ahead for PTZ camera assignment and handoff. In: Third ACM/IEEE ICDSC (2009)
14. Rong Li, X., Zhao, Z., Li, X.: General Model-Set Design Methods for Multiple-Model Approach. IEEE TAC (2005)
15. Varcheie, P.D.Z., Bilodeau, G.A.: Adaptive Fuzzy Particle Filter Tracker for a PTZ Camera in an IP Surveillance System. IEEE Transactions on Instrumentation and Measurement (2011)
16. Wheeler, W., Weiss, R.L., Tu, P.H.: Face Recognition at a distance system for surveillance applications. F- BTAS (2010)

Evaluation of Traffic Sign Recognition Methods Trained on Synthetically Generated Data

Boris Moiseev, Artem Konev, Alexander Chigorin, and Anton Konushin

Graphics and Media Lab, Lomonosov Moscow State University
aachigorin@graphics.cs.msu.ru

Abstract. Most of today's machine learning techniques requires large manually labeled data. This problem can be solved by using synthetic images. Our main contribution is to evaluate methods of traffic sign recognition trained on synthetically generated data and show that results are comparable with results of classifiers trained on real dataset. To get a representative synthetic dataset we model different sign image variations such as intra-class variability, imprecise localization, blur, lighting, and viewpoint changes. We also present a new method for traffic sign segmentation, based on a nearest neighbor search in the large set of synthetically generated samples, which improves current traffic sign recognition algorithms.

Keywords: synthetic data, traffic sign recognition, nearest neighbor search.

1 Introduction

Traffic-sign recognition has been a field of active research for decades due to its importance for many practical applications. Such methods can be used in advanced driver assistance systems (ADAS), road infrastructure management or in the construction of navigation maps.

Modern best-performing traffic sign recognition algorithms (see [1]) rely on machine learning techniques and require a large and representative training set. Due to the differences in signs appearance in various countries it is necessary to recollect a train dataset for each new region which requires a huge amount of manual work. A traffic sign is a rigid planar object and its inter-class variability is significantly lower than that of e.g. human, so the problem of data collection can be solved by using synthetic dataset. In this paper we evaluate several traffic sign recognition methods trained on synthetic images and show that such approach is effective for the recognition problem. We also present method for traffic signs segmentation based on the nearest neighbor search in the set of synthetically generated samples, which can significantly improve performance of evaluated methods.

2 Related Work

According to the classification in [2] there are two basic types of traffic sign recognition methods: similarity-based and feature-based.

J. Blanc-Talon et al. (Eds.): ACIVS 2013, LNCS 8192, pp. 576–583, 2013.

In similarity-based methods an input sign image is assigned to a class of the nearest prototype sample from the training set, according to some similarity metric. A hybrid of random forest and nearest neighbor classifiers with Euclidian distance metrics on HOG descriptors was proposed in [3]. Their nearest neighbor approach is quite similar to ours, but we achieve better results by using synthetic samples.

In feature-based methods a sample is represented by a feature descriptor, and a classifier is learned on these features to predict sample class. Maldonado-Bascon *et al.* [4] exploited the following classification scheme: a sign was assigned to one of the eleven groups, segmented from the background by means of a fixed mask, and raw pixels lying inside the sign mask were fed as a descriptor into SVM classifier. Two-stage classification scheme was also exploited in Timofte *et al.* [5]. At the first stage SVM classifier selects from six different traffic sign groups, then sign class is inferred inside the selected group by SVM classifier on raw pixels. Another type of the classifier frequently encountered in traffic signs recognition literature is an artificial neural network. In particular its variants called multilayer perceptron (MLP) and convolutional neural network (CNN) were combined in committee in [6]. MLP was trained on HOG features, whereas CNN - on randomly scaled, translated and rotated color images, preprocessed with contrast-limited adaptive histogram equalization (CLAHE) algorithm. Sermanet et al. [7] also used CNN with training on images converted to YUV color space with Y channel normalization.

The key aspect of our work is in generation of synthetic training data. It was successfully used in many applications, such as: human pose recognition [8], object 3D structure inferring [9], shape models learning [10], pedestrian detection [11][12][13], viewpoint-independent object detection [14], text recognition [15] and keypoints recognition [16].

There were also attempts to use synthetic images of traffic signs. Comparative evaluation of synthetic and real datasets for learning traffic sign detectors was presented in [17]. In that paper training detector on synthetic set showed significantly lower results than training on real data, but our results show that synthetic data could be successfully used for traffic sign classification. In [18] synthetically generated samples were also exploited but they are used for detector training too. In [19] synthetic dataset was used for training traffic sign classification method based on multi-layer neural network.

3   Synthetic Data Generation

We took widely available pictograms of traffic signs from Wikipedia[1] and applied series of transformations to them with intent to generate visually appealing synthetic images. Thorough evaluation for determining optimal parameters of transformations is not possible because the number of possible transformation parameters is huge. That is why we have conducted empirical experiments for identification of the most

---

[1] Data available at http://graphics.cs.msu.ru/files/research/ signs_recognition/pictograms.zip.

578   B. Moiseev et al.

important transformations for the tasks of traffic signs detection and recognition. That
led to the following algorithm for synthetic training set generation (see Fig. 1):

1. Sign mask segmentation from the pictogram. We assume that background is the
    biggest uniform outer segment on a pictogram.
2. Color scheme transformation from RBG to HSV.
3. Variation of value (V) and saturation (S) to model lighting variations.
4. Rotation of the pictogram and the sign mask around three axes by angles R_x, R_Y,
    R_Z.
5. Perspective transformation of the pictogram and the mask by moving top left
    and right corners by dx_{pl}, dy_{pl}, dx_{pr}, dy_{pr}.
6. Addition Gaussian blur with a standard deviation σ_B and motion blur with a
    filter of size l.
7. Addition of indentations dx_l, dx_r, dy_u, dy_d from four sides of a sign. This step
    is especially needed if recognizer is processing an output of detector that usually
    returns a lot of bounding boxes around the sign and non-maximal suppression
    does not give an exact bounding box.
8. Scaling to the number of sizes s_1, s_2, ... , s_n and back to the target size of a
    recognizer (in our case it equals 30x30 pixels). This step models the process of
    scaling up sign images that are smaller than a target size of the recognizer.
9. Addition of a random Gaussian noise with standard deviation σ_N to every pixel
    of an image. This step models the noise of a camera.
10. Addition of a background from real images according to the sign mask.

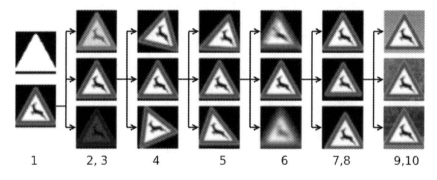

1   2, 3   4   5   6   7,8   9,10

Fig. 1. Visualization of synthetic images generation algorithm. Numbers at the bottom
correspond to steps of the algorithm. Images represent intermediate results after different steps.

All in all, there are 17 parameters of the algorithm that control resulting synthetic
set - V, S, R_x, R_Y, R_Z, σ_B, l, dx_l, dx_r, dy_u, dy_d, s, σ_N, dx_{pl}, dy_{pl}, dx_{pr}, dy_{pr}. They
can be sampled from any chosen distribution. In our experiments we sampled these
parameters from nodes of the uniform grid. Each pictogram underwent the same set of
pre-selected transformations. You can see examples of synthetic images in Fig. 2. Our
algorithm is in many ways similar to the method described in [17], but we also added
perspective transformation and motion blur.

4   Segmentation Algorithm Description

Ability to generate a large amount of training data drives us to the idea of using nearest neighbor approach for traffic sign recognition. Nearest neighbor search has one simple property – the more samples you generate, the better results you get. But if we suppose that we sample each of 17 parameter only three times, then we will get about 130 million synthetic samples only for one class. It makes impossible to use a k-nearest neighbor (kNN) classifier directly, so we propose a method, consisted of two stages: segmentation and classification. Various classifiers can be used as the second stage of our method; evaluation of these classifiers is described in part 5. Here we describe proposed segmentation algorithm.

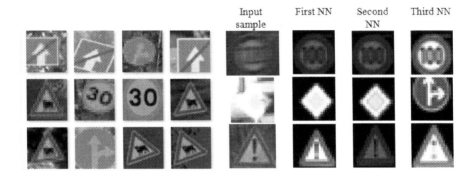

Fig. 2. Synthetic images example   **Fig. 3.** Examples of matching during segmentation

At the segmentation stage an input sign image is described by HOG descriptor and compared to the large number of synthetically generated images. The best match allows determining approximate sign transformations and background mask.

In the case of traffic signs recognition we approximately determine a sign mask on the image by searching among the wide range of sparsely sampled transformations. Then we crop sign from the image and remove background. This allows us to get rid of eight indentation parameters dx_l, dx_r, dy_u, dy_d, dx_{pl}, dy_{pl}, dx_{pr}, dy_{pr}. Note that synthetic dataset doesn't cover the space of all possible transformations densely enough for high-accuracy classification, but such covering is enough for precise image segmentation (see Fig. 3.).

5   Experiments and Results

In our experiments we evaluated following classifiers:

- Nearest neighbor (NN) classifier with Euclidian distance as a measure of similarity;
- Linear Discriminant Analysis (LDA);

- Linear Support Vector Machines (SVM);
- Convolutional Neural Network (CNN) with two convolutional layers (112 filters each, size of filter 5, stride 1, pooling of size 2) and two fully-connected layer (100 and 43 neurons).

The first three classifiers from this list are based on a HOG descriptor. In all experiments we used the same HOG parameters: cell size - 3x3, block size - 6x6, block stride – 3x3, number of bins – 9 with semicircle gradients. Parameters were selected using cross-validation.

Our NN classifier uses 0.3 seconds per sample, other classifiers are much faster. For CNN we used GPU-based implementation[2].

5.1   German Traffic Sign Recognition Benchmark (GTSRB) [1]

The dataset consists of more than 50000 German traffic sign images of 43 classes. The training and the test sets consist of 39209 and 12630 images respectively. Three best results were achieved by [6] – 99.46%, [7] – 98.31% and [3] – 96.14%. Interestingly, a human performed worse than the best performing method of [6] with accuracy of 98.84%.

5.2   Sweden Traffic Signs Dataset [20]

This dataset contains 20000 images with signs that correspond to 3488 physical instances. It consists of two annotated parts. Each part contains sign images sorted into four groups – "blurred", "occluded", "side road" and "visible". We evaluated our classifier on a "visible" subset of each part, excluding signs of class "OTHER" and "URDBL". Thus the first subset consisted of 1423 images and the second subset of 1373 images of 18 sign classes. This dataset was used in [21], but direct comparison of recognition accuracies is not possible, because they used this dataset for simultaneous evaluation of signs detector and recognizer.

5.3   Synthetic Dataset

For generation of synthetic dataset we used parameters shown in Table 1 (set #1). Parameters meanings explained in part 2. Perspective transformation parameters $dx_{pl}, dy_{pl}, dx_{pr}, dy_{pr}$ were taken randomly from the range -4:4. To model Sweden traffic signs we used other pictograms, but the same parameters.

Table 1. Synthetic set generation parameters for experiments with different classifiers

Set #	V [%]	S [%]	R_x	R_Y	R_Z	σ_B	l	dx_l [%]	dx_r [%]	dy_u [%]	dy_d [%]	Size [px]	σ_N
1	70	50	-20:20	-30:30	-6:6	2	8	-4:4	-4:4	-4:4	-4:4	30x30	1.5
2	70	50	-10:10	-10:10	-3:3	2	0	-2:2	-2:2	-2:2	-2:2	30x30	1.5
3	70	50	0	-30:30	-15:15	2	0	-10:30	-10:30	-10:30	-10:30	30x30	1.5

---

[2] See http://code.google.com/p/cuda-convnet/

5.4 Classifiers Comparison

Our training set was generated with parameters set #1 from Table 1 and consisted of more than 100 000 traffic sign images. Segmentation algorithm, described above, was trained by 650 000 images generated with set of parameters #3. For GTSRB dataset we obtained results, written in the first row in Table 2 (Training set #1). Training LDA and SVM classifiers on the real data gives significantly better results (see row Training set #2), that are comparable with results reported in [1]. We explain bad performance of these classifiers on synthetic data by their linear nature and that a simple linear model is insufficient for the classification of highly-varying images in a synthetic training set.

Table 2. Recognition results for different classifiers, trained on a synthetic and real data from GTSRB dataset

Training set #	Training set type	LDA[%]	Linear SVM [%]	k-NN [%]	CNN [%]
1	Acc. (synth. data)	43.6	79.01	93.15	97.87
2	Acc. (real data)	93.28	95.7	72.81	96.3
3	Acc. (synth. data after segmentation)	83.22	91	96.91	-

To confirm this hypothesis we tried to use these classifiers as the second stage of our segmentation and recognition method. The sign was accurately segmented from background on a previous stage, so the linear classifier deals with less complex data. For training we used less-varying training set (with parameters set #2 from Table 1). Using this scheme we obtained results written in the third row (Training set #3) in Table 2. It shows that decreasing variations in the training set can significantly increase accuracy of linear classifiers.

On the other hand the Nearest Neighbor (NN) classifier with a Euclidian distance metric, that was trained on the real data, described by HOG descriptor, gives 72.81% whereas the same classifier trained on synthetic data (generated with parameters for set #1 in Table 1) gives 93.15% of accuracy. This difference can be explained by the fact that synthetic training set covers the space of possible transformations more densely and uniformly.

Using NN classifier as the second stage of our segmentation and recognition method we obtained 95.3% on the official GTSRB test set. If we additionally use three color channels separately and weight HOG descriptor to increase the importance of internal sign regions then we obtain the best result 96.91%

The CNN classifier trained on synthetic samples (see column 6 in Table 2) shows better accuracy than trained on the real dataset due to the similar reason: deep neural network can be trained on a very complex data, so using a synthetic set gives better results.

For the evaluation on Sweden dataset we used the same parameters set as in the German dataset and obtained 97.47% on the first part, and 98.61% on the second part using k-NN classifier at the second stage of our method. We found two labeling errors in each of subsets, taking them into account our results would increase to 97.61% and 98.76% correspondingly. CNN showed comparable accuracy of 97.69% and 99.05%

6   Conclusion and Future Work

We evaluated several methods for traffic sign recognition trained on synthetic and real samples. Unlike the traffic sign detection problem, training on the synthetic data can improve recognition accuracy for some of classifiers which are complex enough to model highly-varying patterns. The best accuracy was obtained by using convolutional neural network trained on synthetic samples. Linear classifiers show better results if trained on real data. We also proposed traffic sign segmentation method specifically designed to be trained on a synthetic data that can significantly improve performance of existing classifiers.

The error analysis suggests that our synthetic samples generation algorithm could be improved – more complex modeling of lighting variation, occlusions and blur could be added. Some errors also show that several signs pictograms are not similar enough to their real-world counterparts therefore pictograms set could be expanded.

References

1. Stallkamp, J., Schlipsing, M., Salmen, J., Igel, C.: Man vs. Computer: Benchmarking Machine Learning Algorithms for Traffic Sign Recognition. Neural Networks (2012)
2. Paclik, P., Novovicova, J., Duin, R.: Building Road-SignClassifiers Using a Trainable Similarity Measure. IEEE Trans. Intell. Transp. Syst. 7(3), 309–321 (2006)
3. Zaklouta, F., Stanciulescu, B., Hamdoun, O.: Traffic sign classification using K-d trees and Random Forests. In: IEEE International Joint Conference on Neural Networks, San Jose, California, pp. 2151–2155 (2011)
4. Maldonado-Bascón, S., Lafuente-Arroyo, S., Gil-Jimenez, P., Gomez-Moreno, H., Lopez-Ferreras, F.: Road-Sign Detection and Recognition Based on Support Vector Machines. IEEE Trans. Intell. Transp. Syst. 8(2), 264–278 (2007)
5. Timofte, R., Zimmermann, K., Gool, L.V.: Multi-view traffic sign detection, recognition, and 3D localization. In: Workshop on Applications of Computer Vision, Snowbird, Utah, pp. 1–8 (2009)
6. Ciresan, D., Meier, U., Masci, J., Schmindhuber, J.: A Committee of Neural Networks for Traffic Sign Classification. In: IEEE International Joint Conference on Neural Networks, San Jose, California, pp. 1918–1921 (2011)
7. Sermanet, P., Lecun, Y.: Traffic Sign Recognition with Multi-Scale Convolutional Networks. In: International Joint Conference on Neural Networks, San Jose, California, pp. 2809–2813 (2011)
8. Shotton, J., Fitzgibbon, A., Cook, M., Sharp, T., Finocchio, M., Moore, R., Kipman, A., Blake, A.: Real-Time Human Pose Recognition in Parts from a Single Depth Image. In: Proceedings IEEE Computer Vision and Pattern Recognition, Colorado, USA, pp. 1297–1304 (2011)
9. Grauman, K., Shakhnarovichand, G., Darrell, T.: Inferring 3D structure with a statistical image-based shape model. In: Proceedings Ninth IEEE International Conference on Computer Vision, Nice, France, pp. 641–647 (2003)
10. Stark, M., Goesele, M., Schiele, B.: Back to the Future: Learning Shape Models from 3D CAD Data. In: Proceedingsof the British Machine Vision Conference, Aberystwyth, Wales, pp. 106.1–106.11 (2010)

11. Marin, J., Vazquez, D., Geronimo, D., Lopez, A.M.: Learning Appearance in Virtual Scenarios for Pedestrian Detection. In: Proceedings Computer Vision and Pattern Recognition, San Francisco, California, pp. 137–144 (2010)
12. Pishchulin, L., Thorm, T., Wojek, C., Andriluka, M., Thormahlen, T., Schiele, B.: Learning People Detection Models from Few Training Samples. In: Proceedings Computer Vision and Pattern Recognition, Colorado Springs, pp. 1–8 (2011)
13. Enzweiler, M., Gavrila, D.M.: A Mixed Generative-Discriminative Framework for Pedestrian Classification. In: Proceedings Computer Vision and Pattern Recognition, Anchorage, Alaska, USA (2008)
14. Liebelt, J., Schmid, C., Schertler, K.: Viewpoint-Independent Object Class Detection using 3D Feature Maps. In: Proceedings Computer Vision and Pattern Recognition, Anchorage, Alaska, USA (2008)
15. Wang, K., Babenko, B., Belongie, S.: End-to-End Scene Text Recognition. In: International Conference on Computer Vision, Barcelona, Spain (2011)
16. Ozuysal, M., Fua, P., Lepetit, V.: Fast Keypoint Recognition in Ten Lines of Code. In: IEEE Conference on Computer Vision and Pattern Recognition, Minneapolis, Minnesota, pp. 1–8 (2007)
17. Mogelmose, A., Trivedi, M., Mouslund, T.: Learning to Detect Traffic Signs: Comparative Evaluation of Synthetic and Real-world Datasets. In: 21st International Conference on Pattern Recognition, Tsukuba, Japan (2012)
18. Overett, G.M., Tychsen-Smith, L., Petersson, L., Andersson, L., Pettersson, N.: Creating Robust High-Throughput Traffic Sign Detectors Using Centre-Surround HOG Statistics. Machine Vision and Applications Special Issue Paper, 1–14 (December 2011)
19. Medici, P., Caraffi, C., Cardarelli, E., Porta, P.P., Ghisto, G.: Real Time Road Signs Classification. In: IEEE Conference on Vehicular Electronics and Safety, Columbus, OH, USA (2008)
20. Larsson, F.: Sweden traffic signs dataset,
    `http://www.cvl.isy.liu.se/research/traffic-signs-dataset`
21. Larsson, F., Felsberg, M.: Using Fourier Descriptors and Spatial Models for Traffic Sign Recognition. In: Proceedings of Scandinavian Conference on Image Analysis, Ystad, Sweden, pp. 238–249 (2011)

Robust Multi-camera People Tracking Using Maximum Likelihood Estimation

Nyan Bo Bo, Peter Van Hese, Sebastian Gruenwedel, Junzhi Guan,
Jorge Niño-Castañeda, Dirk Van Haerenborgh, Dimitri Van Cauwelaert,
Peter Veelaert, and Wilfried Philips

Image Processing and Interpretation/Vision Systems
Ghent University/iMinds
Ghent, Belgium
Nyan.BoBo@telin.ugent.be

Abstract. This paper presents a new method to track multiple persons reliably using a network of smart cameras. The task of tracking multiple persons is very challenging due to targets' non-rigid nature, occlusions and environmental changes. Our proposed method estimates the positions of persons in each smart camera using a maximum likelihood estimation and all estimates are merged in a fusion center to generate the final estimates. The performance of our proposed method is evaluated on indoor video sequences in which persons are often occluded by other persons and/or furniture. The results show that our method performs well with the total average tracking error as low as 10.2 cm. We also compared performance of our system to a state-of-the-art tracking system and find that our method outperforms in terms of both total average tracking error and total number of object loss.

Keywords: smart camera network, distributed computing, tracking, maximum likelihood estimation, data fusion.

1 Introduction

Nowadays, the availability of low cost digital cameras and fast computers makes more and more computer vision applications practical. Certain applications such as automatic surveillance, intelligent home, smart meeting room, human behavior analysis and elderly care demand a system capable of tracking multiple people reliably. Robust tracking of multiple persons is in fact a very challenging problem because the appearance of a person changes by body motion, pose and orientation changes with respect to the camera view, as well as the changes in the environment such as lighting. Furthermore, a person may be occluded by another person or objects in the scene. Occlusion often causes tracking loss and reduces tracking accuracy.

Many existing approaches track multiple persons using a single camera. In single camera tracking, some methods predict occlusion and handle it with reasoning and optimization techniques [10] while some try to track particular body

J. Blanc-Talon et al. (Eds.): ACIVS 2013, LNCS 8192, pp. 584–595, 2013.

parts, e.g. person's head, assuming that it is seldom occluded [1]. However, they become unreliable as soon as occlusion occurs. Another well-known approach is to use multiple overlapping cameras providing information from different view points to handle the problem of occlusion. The tracking accuracy is usually improved as well because the estimation of possible person's location is jointly made by estimates from different view points.

The tracker of Bredereck et al. [4] first detects persons using [5] and [6] in each camera view and then tracks their positions with a particle filter and greedy matching. The reported results show 216 identity switches in a video of 795 frames (approximately two minutes recording). By exploiting homography constraints, [9] and [11] combine information from multiple views to tackle the occlusion problem. The tracker of Yun et al. [11] uses a particle filter to track persons independently in each uncalibrated camera. Tracking results are then mapped between view points at each time instant to minimize the error on occluded view with another non-occluded view(s). To our knowledge, this system does not utilize estimates from all cameras to compute joint estimate.

Some multi-camera tracking systems [7,2] utilize the concept of probabilistic occupancy mapping to locate persons in each view and track/fuse using optimization techniques. Persons' trajectories are computed over batches of 100 frames in [7] and [2], i.e. four seconds delay for tracking in 25 fps video. The tracker of Gruenwedel et al. [8] estimates the persons' positions on each smart cameras locally with a Kalman filter and fusion center fused the estimates. In fusion center, the fused positions are tracked with a Bayesian filter. Although their tracker is able to track multiple persons in real-time, the reported average tracking error is relatively high to use for some applications in practice.

Our system uses a decentralized architecture as in [8]. Each smart camera estimates persons' positions, which are sent to a fusion center that makes joint estimates. Since, only positions are exchanged between the smart cameras and the fusion center, our system has a very low bandwidth requirement and is highly scalable. Similar to [11], we use a simple occlusion handling based on the assumption that a person is not occluded in at least one camera view. The evaluation results show that our method performs well in the sequences with frequent occlusions, achieving a total average tracking error as low as 10.2 cm with three object losses. Moreover, performance comparison reveals that our method outperforms the state-of-the-art tracking system in [8].

The detailed description of our proposed method is presented in Sect. 2. Thorough discussion on evaluation of our method, results and performance comparison to state-of-the-art tracking system is described in Sect. 3. Finally, this paper is concluded in Sect. 4.

2 Tracking System Architecture

Our proposed tracker system has a decentralized architecture, which consists of C intrinsically and extrinsically calibrated smart cameras and a data fusion center as illustrated in Fig. 1. Each smart camera c estimates the position of each

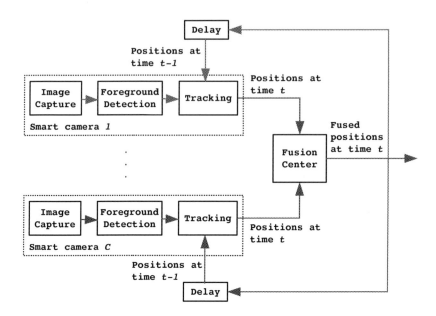

Fig. 1. Architecture of our proposed tracking system

person m within its viewing range at time t and sends all estimated positions to the data fusion center. Based on these estimated positions from all cameras, the fusion center computes the most likely positions of each person at t. The final estimated positions at t are fed back to the cameras with a single frame delay and are taking into account when estimating persons' positions at $t - 1$.

We define notation for a position on image coordinates as $\mathbf{r} = (i, j)^T$ and a position on ground plane in world coordinates as $\mathbf{s} = (x, y)^T$. Since cameras are calibrated, $\mathbf{s}$ can be project on to image plane $\mathbf{r} = P_c\mathbf{s}$, where P_c is a projection matrix of a smart camera c. The detailed description of each block of the proposed tracker are discussed in the following sections.

2.1   Local Tracking in a Smart Camera

On each smart camera, foreground objects are detected by finding the difference in texture between the captured image and the background image. Given the known location and models constructed at $t-1$, the tracker estimates the position at t by using maximum likelihood tracking method.

Foreground Detection. The purpose of foreground detection is to separate foreground objects, i.e. persons for our application, from other objects in the scene. We use a texture-based method that we have previously developed [3] because of its simplicity and robustness to illumination changes. It detects the foreground objects, by finding changes in texture between the frame of interest

I and a background image I_{bg}. The initial background image I_{bg} is simply the average of a number of frames captured when there is no foreground object presents in the scene. Then, in a sliding window $w(\mathbf{r})$ which center is at $\mathbf{r}$, correlation $\rho(\mathbf{r})$ of pixels of I within $w(\mathbf{r})$ and the corresponding pixels of I_{bg} is calculated:

$$\rho(\mathbf{r}) = \frac{\sum_{\mathbf{r'} \in w(\mathbf{r})} I(\mathbf{r'})I_{bg}(\mathbf{r'})}{\sqrt{\sum_{\mathbf{r'} \in w(\mathbf{r})} I(\mathbf{r'})^2 \sum_{\mathbf{r'} \in w(\mathbf{r})} I_{bg}(\mathbf{r'})^2}}. \tag{1}$$

A pixel at $\mathbf{r}$ is considered foreground (1) if $\rho < \rho_{min}$ or background (0) otherwise.

$$F(\mathbf{r}) = \begin{cases} 1 & \text{if } \rho(\mathbf{r}) < \rho_{min} \\ 0 & \text{otherwise} \end{cases} \tag{2}$$

An example input frame I, background image I_{bg} and output foreground image F is shown in Fig. 2. When there is no/few texture present on a person and a background, there will be false negatives. However, a boundary between a person and a background usually create enough texture to obtain true positive detections for reliably tracking. Sometimes, persons may bring in new objects such as chairs or may relocate existing objects in the scene and these appear as foreground objects in F, which is not desirable. We would like those objects to incorporate slowly into I_{bg}. So, the background image I_{bg} is updated as follows:

$$I_{bg} = (1 - \alpha)I_{bg} + \alpha I, \tag{3}$$

where α is the learning factor. The higher α value indicates higher weight on current I incorporating into I_{bg}. We experimentally found that a sliding window size of 10×10 pixels^2 with $\rho_{min} = 0.99$ and $\alpha = 0.001$ gives the best system performance.

Maximum Likelihood Tracking. As mentioned before, all smart cameras receive joint estimates of each person m in world coordinates at $t - 1$, denoted as $\mathbf{s}_{t-1}^m$, from the fusion center. Each smart camera c projects $\mathbf{s}_{t-1}^m$ into its image coordinates $\mathbf{r}_{t-1}^m = P_c \mathbf{s}_{t-1}^m$, where P_c is a projection matrix of the smart camera c. The task of each smart camera is to estimate the persons' positions at t, denoted as $\mathbf{r}_t^m$.

In our system, we model a person as a cuboid with fixed height (e.g. 180 cm, which is the average height of adult person) in world coordinates at position $\mathbf{s}$. This cuboid can be projected into image coordinates with projective geometry as $\Omega(\mathbf{r})$. The projected region of the cuboid at the last known position $\mathbf{r}_{t-1}^m$ is denoted as $\Omega(\mathbf{r}_{t-1}^m)$. An example of $\Omega(\mathbf{r}_{t-1}^m)$ is shown in Fig. 3 (a) for person 1 ($\Omega(\mathbf{r}_{t-1}^1)$) and (b) for person 2 ($\Omega(\mathbf{r}_{t-1}^2)$).

We assume higher frame rate ($fps \geq 15$) so that a person can not move very far from $\mathbf{r}_{t-1}^m$ and the shape of the foreground pixels of a person does not change much from frame to frame. This assumption is mostly valid in practice. Therefore, $\mathbf{r}_t^m$ can be estimated by finding a position in current foreground image

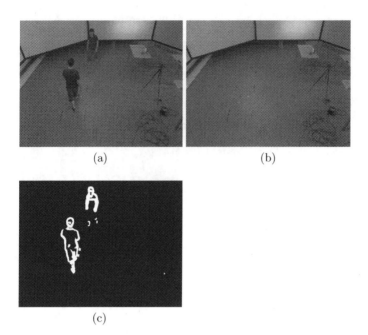

(a)   (b)

(c)

Fig. 2. An example of (a) input frame I, (b) background image I_{bg}, (c) detected foreground F (foreground pixels in white).

F_t, where the pixels within $\Omega(\mathbf{r}_{t-1}^m)$ in the foreground image of previous frame F_{t-1} match the best. We statistically model foreground pixels of m as:

$$p_{fg}^m(\mathbf{r} - \mathbf{r}_{t-1}^m) = \begin{cases} 1 - \epsilon & \text{for } F_{t-1}(\mathbf{r}) = 1 \text{ and } \mathbf{r} \in \Omega(\mathbf{r}_{t-1}^m) \\ \epsilon & \text{for } F_{t-1}(\mathbf{r}) = 0 \text{ and } \mathbf{r} \in \Omega(\mathbf{r}_{t-1}^m) \\ 0 & \text{for } \mathbf{r} \notin \Omega \end{cases} \tag{4}$$

where ϵ is a small constant (0.001 for our tracker). An example of a foreground model p_{fg}^m is shown in Fig. 3 (b) and (c). We also define $q_{fg}^m(\mathbf{r}) = 1 - p_{fg}^m(\mathbf{r})$.

The foreground pixels outside of $\Omega(\mathbf{r}_{t-1}^m)$ of person m are due to the presence of other persons or other changes in the scene, such as displacement of furniture. These pixels are considered as background/noise pixels for m. Suppose we hypothesize that a person m is at the position $\mathbf{r}_t^m$. If many background/noise pixels are observed within $\Omega(\mathbf{r}_t^m)$, it is less likely that m is at hypothesized position $\mathbf{r}_t^m$. The probabilistic model for background pixels p_{bg}^m for a person m is defined as:

$$p_{bg}^m(\mathbf{r}) = \begin{cases} 1 - \epsilon & \text{for } F_{t-1}(\mathbf{r}) = 1 \text{ and } \mathbf{r} \notin \Omega(\mathbf{r}_{t-1}^m) \\ \epsilon & \text{for } F_{t-1}(\mathbf{r}) = 0 \text{ or } \mathbf{r} \in \Omega(\mathbf{r}_{t-1}^m) \end{cases} \tag{5}$$

Figure 3 (e) and (f) illustrate an example p_{bg}^m for person 1 and 2 respectively. As short hand notation $q_{bg}^m(\mathbf{r})$ is defined as $1 - p_{bg}^m(\mathbf{r})$.

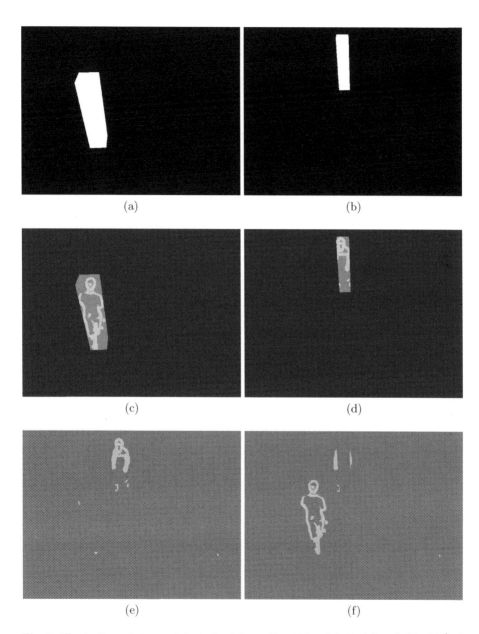

Fig. 3. Illustration of the models derived from F_{t-1} (Fig. 2 (b)); (a) and (b) $\Omega(\mathbf{r}_{t-1}^1)$ and $\Omega(\mathbf{r}_{t-1}^2)$ (white pixels represent projected cuboid), (c) and (d) foreground models p_{fg}^1 and p_{fg}^2 (light gray represents $1 - \epsilon$ and dark gray represents ϵ), (e) and (f) background/noise models p_{bg}^1 and p_{bg}^2 (black represent pixels with value 0).

For simplicity, we fix the shape and size Ω to be the same as $\Omega(\mathbf{r}_{t-1}^m)$ for all positions in the image. Thus, we can just translate Ω to a position $\mathbf{r}_t^m$ as $\Omega(\mathbf{r}_t^m) = \mathbf{r}_t^m + \Omega$. Assuming that value of all pixels are independent, we can compute the likelihood that a person m is at $\mathbf{r}_t^m$ in F_t using defined models p_{fg}^m and p_{bg}^m:

$$l(\mathbf{r}_t^m) = \prod_{\mathbf{r} \notin \mathbf{r}_t^m + \Omega} p_{bg}^m(\mathbf{r})^{F_t(\mathbf{r})} q_{bg}^m(\mathbf{r})^{1-F_t(\mathbf{r})}$$
$$\prod_{\mathbf{r} \in \mathbf{r}_t^m + \Omega} p_{fg}^m(\mathbf{r} - \mathbf{r}_t^m)^{F_t(\mathbf{r})} q_{fg}^m(\mathbf{r} - \mathbf{r}_t^m)^{1-F_t(\mathbf{r})}. \tag{6}$$

After several steps of derivation from (6), log likelihood can be written as a convolution form:

$$\log l(\mathbf{r}_t^m) = F_t * h(\mathbf{r}_t^m) - i * f(\mathbf{r}_t^m), \tag{7}$$

with

$$f(\mathbf{r}) = (\log p_{bg}(\mathbf{r}) - \log q_{bg}(\mathbf{r}))F_t(\mathbf{r}) + \log q_{bg}(\mathbf{r}), \tag{8}$$

$$h(\mathbf{r}) = \begin{cases} \log p_{fg}(\mathbf{r}) - \log q_{fg}(\mathbf{r}) & \text{for } \mathbf{r} \in \Omega \\ 0 & \text{elsewhere} \end{cases} \tag{9}$$

and

$$i(\mathbf{r}) = \begin{cases} 1 & \text{for } \mathbf{r} \in \Omega \\ 0 & \text{elsewhere} \end{cases} \tag{10}$$

The value of $\log l(\mathbf{r}_t^m)$ is maximum when $\mathbf{r}_t^m$ is very closed to true position of a person m. The maximum a posteriori estimate of the position of a person is given by

$$\hat{\mathbf{r}}_t^m = \arg\max_{\mathbf{r}_t^m}(\log P(\mathbf{r}_t^m) + \log l(\mathbf{r}_t^m)), \tag{11}$$

with $P(\mathbf{r}_t^m)$, the prior on the person's position. We simply set the prior to be uniform over the whole image.

Occlusion Handling. There can be more than one person in the scene. If this is the case, they can occlude one another or be occluded by other objects in the scene. In the case of occlusion(s), we assume that a person occluded in one view can still be tracked in at least one of the other views in the camera network. With this assumption, we ignore the occluded person(s) and send the positions of non-occluded person(s) to the fusion center. Furthermore, when occlusion occurs in a view of a smart camera, the occluded person is excluded from local tracking of that camera. Since all cameras receive final fused positions of all tracked persons, the tracking of occluded person in a particular view can be resumed once the occlusion is over.

2.2 Data Fusion

Each smart camera in our system locally estimates the positions of all tracked persons and sends estimated positions to the fusion center. Let us denote an unknown position of a person in world coordinates as $\mathbf{s}_t^m$ and the estimated positions sent by a set of $C \neq \emptyset$ smart cameras as $\hat{\mathbf{r}}_t^{m,1}, \hat{\mathbf{r}}_t^{m,2}, \cdots, \hat{\mathbf{r}}_t^{m,C}$. The fusion center estimates $\mathbf{s}_t^m$ as:

$$\mathbf{s}_t^m = \arg\min_{\mathbf{s}} d(\mathbf{s})$$
$$= \arg\min_{\mathbf{s}} (\sum_{c=1}^{C} \| P_c \mathbf{s} - \hat{\mathbf{r}}_t^{m,c} \|^2) \qquad (12)$$

where P_c is the projection matrix that projects a position in world coordinates to image coordinates of smart camera c. The cost function $d(\mathbf{s})$ in (12) computes the squared sum of distances between projections of $\mathbf{s}$ in image coordinates and local estimates of each camera. This cost function takes into account that same error magnitude in estimation made at different positions in the image coordinates may reproject into world coordinates with different error magnitudes.

3 Performance Evaluation

3.1 Test Data Set

The performance of our method is evaluated on the multi-camera video data set used by Gruenwedel et al. in [8]. This video data contains three sequences that are captured in a room of 8.8×9.2 m^2 using five cameras with overlapping views (four side-views and one top-view). All cameras are both intrinsically and extrinsically calibrated. Videos are captured at 20 fps with the resolution of 780×580 pixels^2. Ground plane positions of each person are manually annotated every 20 frames and used as ground truth for evaluation.

3.2 Evaluation Metrics

We use two objective performance measures, which are also used in [8]: total average tracking error (TATE) and total number of object loss (TNOL) (same performance measures as in [8]). The total average tracking error is an average of the Euclidean distances between positions estimated by the tracker and the corresponding ground truth positions. Tracking of a particular person is lost when the Euclidean distance between estimated position and ground truth position is more than 100 cm. For both measures, lower values indicate better performance.

3.3 Results and Discussion

Sequence 1. This sequence contains four persons entering, walking around (often occluding one another) and leaving the room. This sequence is captured using only four side-view cameras in aforementioned room setup with no furniture, and lasts about one and a half minutes. The lack of a top-view camera makes handling of occlusions more difficult. Despite this, our method still gives a relatively low TATE of 14.3 cm and loses track of persons six times. Most of the object losses are due to occlusion(s) in all views.

Sequence 2. It contains only two persons doing similar actions as in the first sequence, but it is captured by all five cameras. There is no furniture in the scene and the sequence is almost two minutes long. Although a top-view camera is available in this sequence, the tracking in this sequence is difficult because two persons come very close to each other and then suddenly switch places several times. This is the main reason for the three tracking losses. The TATE is 10.2 cm.

An example of the estimated positions in each camera view and fused results in world coordinates is shown in Fig. 4. The two persons are very close to each other in all views and occlude one another in camera 1, 2 and 3. Despite of occlusion in three camera views, fusion center still makes joint estimates with relatively high accuracy. The Euclidean distance from fused position of person 1 (red) and person 2 (green) to corresponding ground truth positions, 18.1 cm and 3.7 cm respectively.

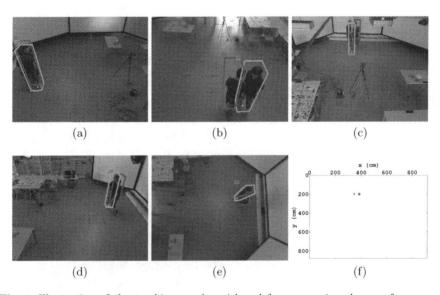

Fig. 4. Illustration of the tracking results with red for person 1 and green for person 2 (frame 780 of sequence 2). (a)–(e) camera views in which dots near the projected cuboids positions of each person ($\hat{\mathbf{r}}_t^1$ and $\hat{\mathbf{r}}_t^2$) estimated by the smart cameras, (f) fused positions on ground plane (in a room of 8.8×9.2 m^2). Two person occlude one another in (a), (b) and (d).

Sequence 3. This sequence is a meeting scenario (with table and chairs in the scene) captured by all five cameras for almost three minutes. In the video, three persons come into the room, one after another, shake hands, sit down, change seat, give a presentation and leave the room near the end of the sequence. The TATE of our method goes up to 16.9 cm because lower body parts of the persons are often occluded by furniture so that foreground detection failed to detect lower body parts of the persons. Although TATE is a bit higher compared to other sequences, the TNOL is only two.

Figure 5 shows the estimates for the frame number 1840, in which person 1 and 3 are sitting while person 2 is walking. The lower body parts of both seated persons are occluded by a table and chairs. However the Euclidean distances between fused estimates and corresponding ground truth positions are small: 11.5 cm for person 1 and 28.6 cm for person 3. This shows that our method can track a seated persons well. In this particular frame, the accuracy of fused estimate of person 2's positions (walking person) is very high, since the Euclidean distance from its ground truth position is only 8.7 cm.

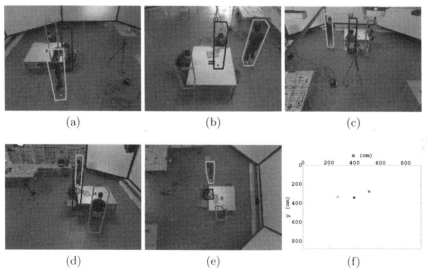

(a)   (b)   (c)

(d)   (e)   (f)

Fig. 5. Illustration of the tracking results with red for person 1, green for person 2 and blue for person 3 (frame 1840 of sequence 3). (a)–(e) camera views in which dots near the projected cuboids are positions of each person ($\hat{\mathbf{r}}_t^1$, $\hat{\mathbf{r}}_t^2$ and $\hat{\mathbf{r}}_t^3$) estimated by the smart cameras, (f) fused positions on ground plane (in a room of 8.8×9.2 m²). Although lower body parts of two seated persons (person 1 and 3) are occluded by the table, our method can still make accurate estimates.

Performance Comparison. Our method outperforms the tracker of Gruenwedel et al. reported in [8], in both TATE (shown in Fig. 6 (a)) and TNOL (shown in Fig. 6 (b)). Both plots clearly show that when there is no top-view camera available, the performance of the tracker by Gruenwedel et at. drops significantly,

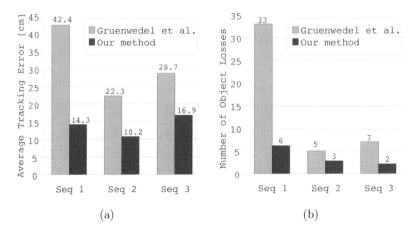

Fig. 6. Performance comparison with tracker of Gruenwedel et al.; (a) total average tracking error (TATE) and (b) total number of object loss (TNOL). Both graphs show that our method outperforms.

whereas the performance of our method is quite stable for all sequences. The TNOL of the two methods is almost the same in the sequence with two persons, showing that the case of two persons getting very close and then suddenly switch places is difficult for both methods and both usually lose track of the persons.

Our method does not rely on any motion model whereas system in [8] uses a Kalman filter with a constant velocity motion model. When a walking person accelerates or decelerates suddenly, the local estimates of the smart cameras in [8] become inaccurate, which leads to poor system performance. For each smart camera, the estimation of a position of a person who is closer to the camera usually has higher accuracy than a person who is further away. Our fusion method takes this into account to make more accurate joint estimates from the positions estimated by all smart cameras.

4   Conclusion

We presented a novel method to track multiple persons using a network of smart cameras with decentralized architecture. Our method achieves total average tracking error (TATE) of 14.3, 10.2 and 16.9 cm on three test sequences. The total number of object loss (TNOL) is six, three and two respectively. The evaluation results indicates that our method performs well in sequences containing frequent occlusions, even without a top-view camera. This favors using the tracker in real life applications such as automatic surveillance since video from top-views cameras are not often available. Our method outperforms the tracker of Gruenwedel et al. in both TATE and TNOL.

The performance of our method can be further improved by choosing more appropriate models, for instance, use ellipsoid, which better describes the shape of a human body than cuboid. Most object losses of our method are due to occlusions in all views. Occlusion even occurs in the top-view camera because of its wide-angle lens. At the moment, occlusion is handled assuming that a person is not occluded in at least one view. However, the TNOL can be reduced by more efficient and complex occlusion detection and handling. For example, keep tracking the non-occluded body parts of the occluded instead of ignoring the person completely when occlusion occurs. In future work, we will evaluate the performance of our method on public data sets and compare its performance to more state-of-the-art tracking methods.

References

1. Ali, I., Dailey, M.N.: Multiple human tracking in high-density crowds. Image and Vision Computing 30(12), 966–977 (2012)
2. Berclaz, J., Fleuret, F., Turetken, E., Fua, P.: Multiple object tracking using k-shortest paths optimization. IEEE Trans. on Pattern Analysis and Machine Intelligence 33(9), 1806–1819 (2011)
3. Bo Bo, N., Gruenwedel, S., Van Hese, P., Niño Castañeda, J., Van Haerenborgh, D., Van Cauwelaert, D., Veelaert, P., Philips, W.: Phd forum: Illumination-robust foreground detection for multi-camera occupancy mapping. In: Proceedings of the Sixth International Conference on Distributed Smart Cameras, ICDSC (2012)
4. Bredereck, M., Jiang, X., Korner, M., Denzler, J.: Data association for multi-object tracking-by-detection in multi-camera networks. In: The 2012 Sixth International Conference on Distributed Smart Cameras, ICDSC (2012)
5. Dalal, N., Triggs, B.: Histograms of oriented gradients for human detection. In: IEEE Computer Society Conference on Computer Vision and Pattern Recognition, vol. 1, pp. 886–893 (2005)
6. Felzenszwalb, P., Girshick, R., McAllester, D., Ramanan, D.: Object detection with discriminatively trained part-based models. IEEE Transactions on Pattern Analysis and Machine Intelligence 32(9), 1627–1645 (2010)
7. Fleuret, F., Berclaz, J., Lengagne, R., Fua, P.: Multicamera people tracking with a probabilistic occupancy map. IEEE Trans. on Pattern Analysis and Machine Intelligence 30, 267–282 (2008)
8. Gruenwedel, S., Jelača, V., Niño-Castañeda, J., Hese, P.V., Cauwelaert, D.V., Veelaert, P., Philips, W.: Decentralized tracking of humans using a camera network. In: Proceedings of SPIE, Intelligent Robots and Computer Vision XXIX: Algorithms and Techniques, vol. 8301. SPIE (2012)
9. Khan, S.M., Shah, M.: Tracking multiple occluding people by localizing on multiple scene planes. IEEE Trans. on Pattern Analysis and Machine Intelligence 31, 505–519 (2009)
10. Papadakis, N., Bugeau, A.: Tracking with occlusions via graph cuts. IEEE Transactions on Pattern Analysis and Machine Intelligence 33(1), 144–157 (2011)
11. Yun, Y., Gu, I.H., Aghajan, H.: Maximum-likelihood object tracking from multiview video by combining homography and epipolar constraints. In: The 2012 Sixth International Conference on Distributed Smart Cameras, ICDSC (2012)

A Perception-Based Interpretation of the Kernel-Based Object Tracking

Vittoria Bruni[1] and Domenico Vitulano[2]

[1] Dept. of SBAI, University of Rome La Sapienza
via A. Scarpa, 16 00161 Rome - Italy
`vittoria.bruni@sbai.uniroma1.it`
[2] Istituto per le Applicazioni del Calcolo "M. Picone" — C.N.R.,
via dei Taurini 19, 00185 Rome, Italy
`d.vitulano@iac.cnr.it`

Abstract. This paper investigates the advantages of using simple rules of human perception in object tracking. Specifically, human visual perception (HVP) will be used in the definition of both target features and the similarity metric to be used for detecting the target in subsequent frames. Luminance and contrast will play a crucial role in the definition of target features, whereas recent advances in the relations between some classical concepts of information theory and the way human eye codes image information will be used in the definition of the similarity metric. The use of HVP rules in a well known object tracking algorithm, allows us to increase its efficacy in following the target and to considerably reduce the computational cost of the whole tracking process. Some tests also show the stability and the robustness of a perception-based object tracking algorithm also in the presence of other moving elements or target occlusion for few subsequent frames.

1 Introduction

The recent diffusion of both inexpensive video cameras and high-powered computers gave target tracking a fundamental role in Computer Vision based real-time applications [1]. The objective of target tracking is to estimate the trajectory of an object as it moves around a scene from a sequence of images acquired by a video-camera. Despite the advances of research in this field, the problem is very difficult due to the complexity of object motion, non rigid nature or complex geometry of the targets, partial or full occlusion of the object, changes in scene illumination, presence of noise or loss of information, real-time processing, etc. (see [1]-[2]-[3] for a complete survey).

In this paper we are interested in evaluating the impact of the use of HVP concepts in object tracking with respect to the quality of tracking and its computational effort. In fact, as the literature of the last decade shows, HVP gave new ways of solving some image and video processing problems, such as digital restoration, quality assessment, image/object representation, thanks to the change of perspective in information processing problems: from the actual information (functional perspective) to the perceived information (human/visual

J. Blanc-Talon et al. (Eds.): ACIVS 2013, LNCS 8192, pp. 596–607, 2013.

perspective). In this perspective, classical information theory concepts have been revised in agreement with the way human eye encodes what it sees [4]. An interesting example is image quality assessment, where image similarities are measured as the amount of the mutual information between two images [5], or through the normalized information distance (NID) [6], or using the Jensen-Shannon divergence (JSD) [7]. In this work we are interested in exploiting these concepts for better characterizing target appearance and improving its tracking in subsequent frames, without requiring additional computational effort. Specifically, the aim is not to propose a new tracker but just to give a way to improve existing ones thanks to a 'visual interpretation' of the tracking problem. As a matter of facts, there are several papers in the literature that use visual attention to characterize the target, see, for example, [12,13]. They are mainly based on the computation of image saliency maps or fixations points. However, they may require many operations that often involve multiscale/orientation transform and/or PCA based processing to reduce the number of feature points. In this paper, we want to introduce visual attention in tracking by using simple operations that do not drastically change the basic tracker. To this aim, among the large number of existing trackers, a very popular and widely investigated (see, for example, [9]-[11]) object tracking algorithm, the Kernel based Object Tracking (KbOT) [8], has been considered. It is simple, modular and quite effective and then it is particularly suitable for our task. KbOT represents target through its weighted color histogram and tracks it in subsequent frames using the mean shift algorithm combined with the Bhattacharyya coefficient to measure the distance between histograms. As a results, KbOT gives a natural partition of the tracking process in steps that mainly depend on human perception: characterization of the target with a weighted histogram, and use of a proper similarity metric for detecting the target in subsequent frames. Accounting for some recent neurological studies [14,15], in this paper target features are defined in a space that depends more on image luminance and contrast, while the similarity measure depends on JSD, that is an effective tool for measuring the information shared by two quantities, in agreement with human perception [16,17,7]). The use of these two ingredients allows KbOT to achieve a more faithful tracking, to be more stable and robust to the presence of other moving targets or temporary target occlusion. It also guarantees a considerable reduction of the computing time, making it more suitable for real time applications.

The remainder of the paper is the following. Section II briefly describes the original KbOT algortihm. Section III gives the details regarding the embedding of HVP in KbOT. Section IV evaluates its computational cost while Section V shows some results, giving guidelines for future work.

2   Kernel-based Object Tracking

Kernel-based object tracking (KbOT) in [8] consists of the following iterative procedure:

1. Compute the weighted color histogram (target feature)

$$q_u = c \sum_{i=1}^{n} k(\|\mathbf{x}_i\|^2)\delta(b(\mathbf{x}_i) - u)$$

of the reference target in the reference frame. u is the color bin, m is the number of bins, $\mathbf{x}$ indicates pixels location in the target region, b maps $\mathbf{x}$ into the corresponding bin in the quantized feature space, δ stands for the delta function, n is the number of target pixels, c is a normalization constant and k is an isotropic kernel that gives more importance to the central pixels in the target region;

2. Compute the histogram $p_u(\mathbf{y}_0)$ of the candidate target and evaluate the quantity $\rho[p(\mathbf{y}_0, q)]$.

$$p_u(\mathbf{y}) = c_h \sum_{i=1}^{n_h} k\left(\left\|\frac{\mathbf{y} - \mathbf{x}_i}{h}\right\|^2\right)\delta(b(\mathbf{x}_i) - u), \tag{1}$$

is the *candidate target* feature, c_h is the normalization constant, $\mathbf{y}$ is the center of the target in the current frame, n_h is the number of target pixels and h is a scaling parameter that sets the bandwidth accounting for the morphological changes of the target [8]. $\rho[p(\mathbf{y}), q] = \sum_{u=1}^{m} \sqrt{p_u(\mathbf{y})q_u}$ is the Bhattacharyya coefficient that defines the similarity metric that is minimized by the mean shift algorithm [8];

3. Set the weights $w_i = \sum_{u=1}^{m} \sqrt{\frac{q_u}{p_u(\mathbf{y}_0)}}\delta[b(\mathbf{x}_i) - u]$;

4. Find the candidate target $\mathbf{y}_1 = \frac{\sum_{i=1}^{n} \mathbf{x}_i w_i}{\sum_{i=1}^{n} w_i}$ via the mean shift algorithm [8] using a linear kernel k;

5. Compute the new histogram $p_u(\mathbf{y}_1)$ of the candidate target and evaluate $\rho[p(\mathbf{y}_1, q)]$;

6. While $\rho[p(\mathbf{y}_1, q)] < \rho[p(\mathbf{y}_0, q)]$, set $\mathbf{y}_1 = \frac{1}{2}(\mathbf{y}_1 + \mathbf{y}_0)$ and evaluate $\rho[p(\mathbf{y}_1, q)]$;

7. If $\|\mathbf{y}_1 - \mathbf{y}_0\| < \epsilon$ then Stop; otherwise go to Step 2.

3   The Proposed Model

In this section HVP is used for *i)* defining a feature space as the combination of image luminance and visual contrast; *ii)* introducing a kernel that fits fovea; *iii)* defining a metric that well correlates with HVP and easy to compute. These choices automatically reduce tracking computational cost, as it will be clearer later.

3.1   Perception-Based Feature Space

Several studies [14],[15],[18]-[21] have shown that local *luminance* and *contrast* well characterize natural images. Moreover, just very few points, namely *fixation points*, of a scene are able to attract human attention in the early vision.

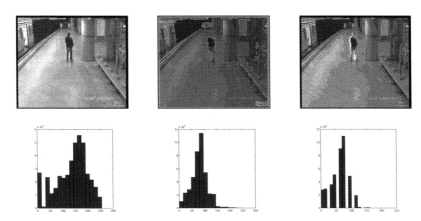

Fig. 1. One frame of the test sequence *Subway*. Quantized luminance L_l (*topleft*), S_l, as in eq. (2), without (*topmiddle*) and with $C_{T,l}$ (*topright*), their histograms (*bottom*).

Fixation points also are foveated since human attention decreases as one moves away from them. Specifically, fixation points are those points showing independence between local luminance mean and contrast; and, the farther these points the more uncorrelated their luminance values as well as their contrasts. On the other hand, the amplitude of the spectra of natural images may be sufficient to understand retinal function; in particular, there is a close relationship between the distributions of Michelson contrasts in natural images and the contrast response functions of neurons. It turns out that luminance and contrast are quite informative visual quantities and they are two of the most representative quantities to which the retina is more sensitive. That is why, as in [22], we use the histogram of the feature space as target feature but the feature space, S_l, now depends on both the local luminance L_l and the contrast C_l of the target region. The former usually contains about 90% of the whole image information; the latter characterizes more the visual appearance of the target with respect to its background. Specifically, by denoting with

$$C_M(L(\Omega)) = \frac{max_\Omega L(\Omega) - min_\Omega L(\Omega)}{max_\Omega L(\Omega) + min_\Omega L(\Omega)}$$

the Michelson contrast [23] of a region Ω with luminance $L(\Omega)$, C_l is defined as the ratio between the Michelson contrasts of the target O and its background B, that is $C_l(O) = \frac{C_M(O)}{C_M(B)}$.

Hence, for the $l-$th frame of the analysed sequence, the feature space is defined as the combination of the three different independent sources L_l, C_l and $C_{T,l}$, i.e.

$$S_l(\mathbf{x}_i) = L_l(\mathbf{x}_i) + (1 - \lambda(\mathbf{x}_i))C_l(\mathbf{x}_i) + \lambda(\mathbf{x}_i)C_{T,l}(\mathbf{x}_i) \tag{2}$$

Fig. 2. Three subsequent frames of *Subway*. Target detection using the quantized luminance (*left*) and S_l (*right*) as feature space.

where $\mathbf{x}_i$ is a point of the target region, L_l is the corresponding luminance, C_l its visual contrast, while

$$C_{T,l}(\mathbf{x}_i) = \frac{|L_l(\mathbf{x}_i) - L_{l-1}(\mathbf{x}_i)|}{L_l(\mathbf{x}_i) + L_{l-1}(\mathbf{x}_i)}$$

is the visual contrast computed inter-frames and $\lambda(\mathbf{x}_i)$ is a binary parameter that indicates if motion is detected at $\mathbf{x}_i$. $C_{T,l}$ takes into account the instinctive sensitiveness of HVP to moving objects so that moving target points can have a high discrimination power in tracking (see Fig. 1). L_l and C_l are independent quantities in the vision process; motion is able to capture human attention independently of the object under study. Visual contrast then gives a more distinctive appearance to the target, making tracking more robust and stable (see Fig. 2).

16 bins have been used for the luminance L_l, that is normalized to half the range of gray levels (i.e., 128), and 4 bins for the contrast, that is also normalized to a range of width 128. It is not necessary to assign more bins to the contrast, since the aim is to emphasize few target points that catch human attention at first sight.

3.2   Perception-Based Kernel

HVP is a space-variant system: spatial resolution (human attention) is higher at fixation (foveation) point and decreases rapidly with increasing eccentricity. The decreasing law of attention, as in [21], can model the kernel in KbOT, i.e.,

$$k(\mathbf{x}) = e^{-\mathbf{x} r_e(\mathbf{x})} \tag{3}$$

where $r_e(\mathbf{x}) = 1/tan(\|\mathbf{x} - \mathbf{x}_0\|_2/(Nv))$ is the retinal eccentricity, v the viewing distance and N the image size.

3.3   Perception-Based Similarity Metric

Some recent research works applied concepts of Information Theory to HVP by modeling vision as a coding process, where the receiver (decoder) is human eye [5,6,15]. The Normalized Information Distance

$$NID(s,t) = \frac{max\{K(s|t), K(t|s)\}}{max\{K(s), K(t)\}}. \tag{4}$$

measures the shortest program whose output is the string s if the input is t and viceversa [24]. It depends on Kolmogorov complexity $K(\cdot)$ [25], i.e. the length of the shortest program that gives $(\cdot)$, and minimizes any admissible distance between s and t [24]. Despite its incomputability, NID captures the essential features of an object, independently of its nature even if K is approximated by a coding algorithm [26]. As a matter of fact, a straightforward approximation of NID can be obtained in agreement with the two following results: *i)* the expected value of the Kolmogorov complexity of a string with recursive probability distribution equals its Shannon entropy up to a constant term [24,27]; *ii)* H approaches K for long strings generated by stationary ergodic sources. Therefore, eq. (4) can be rewritten as

$$NID(p,q) = \frac{max\{H(p|q), H(q|p)\}}{M_H} = 1 - \frac{I(p,q)}{M_H}, \tag{5}$$

where p and q are the pdfs of s and t, $I(p,q)$ is their mutual information and $M_H = max\{H(p), H(q)\}$. It is worth observing that, due to the independence of luminance and contrast of fixation points, the assumption $K \approx H$ is not unfeasible in S_l. Unfortunately, $I(p,q)$ requires the knowledge of the joint entropy $H(p,q)$ and the *mean-shift* used in KbOT is not straightforward for NID, due to the dependence of NID on max function. That is why it cannot be straighforwardly embedded in KbOT algorithm.

The papers [7,16] proved that Jensen Shannon divergence (JSD) well correlates with HVS since it has a close relationship with Michelson contrast that, in turn, is related to neurons contrast response functions [20]. Moreover, both JSD and NID depend on the Shannon entropy and

$$JSD(p,q) = \frac{D_{KL}(p,r) + D_{KL}(q,r)}{2} = H(r) - \frac{H(p) + H(q)}{2} =$$

$$= H(r) - \frac{1}{2}H(p,q) - \frac{(1 - NID(p,q))}{2}M_H. \tag{6}$$

where $r = \frac{p+q}{2}$, $D_{KL}(p,q)$ is the Kullbach-Leibler divergence [25] between p and q and $H(p,q) + I(p,q) = H(p) + H(q)$. Hence, JSD depends on NID and it is bounded by quantities that still depend on NID. More precisely, since NID minimizes any admissible distance function [24], we have $log(2)NID(p,q) \leq JSD(p,q)$. On the other hand, by setting $m_H = min\{H(p), H(q)\}$ and omitting the dependence on p and q, we can prove the following proposition:

Proposition: Let p and q the p.d.fs of two RV, then

$$JSD \leq log(2) - \sum_u \frac{p_u q_u}{p_u + q_u} + \frac{m_H - M_H}{2} + NID\frac{M_H}{2} \tag{7}$$

Proof: Since $H(p,q) \geq M_H$ and

$$H(r) \leq log(2) + \frac{H(p) + H(q)}{2} - \sum_u \frac{p_u q_u}{p_u + q_u},$$

from eq. (6) we have

$$JSD(p,q) \leq H(r) - M_H + \frac{NID(p,q)}{2}M_H, \qquad \text{that is,}$$

$$JSD \leq log2 + \frac{m_H - M_H(1 - NID)}{2} - \sum_u \frac{p_u q_u}{p_u + q_u} \qquad \bullet$$

In addition, JSD can also be simply embedded in the mean-shift algorithm [8]. In fact, following the formal procedure given in [8], JSD can be locally approximated by its first order Taylor expansion, i.e.,

$$JSD(p(\mathbf{y}),q) \approx JSD(p(\mathbf{y_0}),q) + \frac{\partial JSD}{\partial p}\|_{\mathbf{y}=\mathbf{y_0}}(p(\mathbf{y}) - p(\mathbf{y_0})) =$$

$$= \frac{1}{2}JSD(p(\mathbf{y_0}),q) + \frac{1}{2}\sum_{i=1}^{n_h} w_i k\left(\|\frac{\mathbf{y} - \mathbf{x_i}}{h}\|^2\right)$$

where the weights $w_i = \sum_u log\frac{2p_u(\mathbf{y_0})}{p_u(\mathbf{y_0})+q_u}\delta(b(\mathbf{x} - u))$, while p and q respectively are the target histograms in the current and reference frames of the analysed sequence.

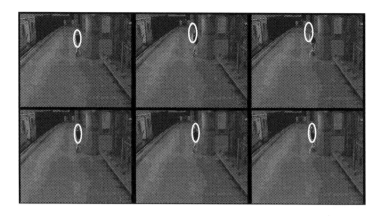

Fig. 3. Object tracking using one iteration of *mean-shift* with Bhattacharyya distance (*top*) and JSD (*bottom*) as similarity metric

4 Computational Cost

An interesting aspect of the use of luminance/contrast feature space is that it also reduces the computational load of the tracking process. In fact, KbOT [8] requires $nlog_2(m) + 2n_hlog_2(m) + 2mn + 4n + 12n_h + 5mn_h + 4m - 3 + (2m + n_h)c_s$ operations (*ops*), that include additions, multiplications, divisions and comparisons. Specifically:

1. $nlog_2(m) + 2mn + 4n$ are required for the computation of q_u, where $nlog_2(m)$ are comparisons;
2. $n_hlog_2(m) + 2mn_h + 4n_h$ are required for the computation of p_u and $(2m - 1 + mc_s)$ *ops* for ρ, where c_s are the *ops* for the computation of the square root;
3. $(m + 1 + c_s)n_h$ are for the weights w_i;
4. $3n_h - 1$ are for $\mathbf{y}_1$;
5. $n_hlog_2(m) + 2mn_h + 4n_h + 2m - 1 + mc_s$ are for $p_u(\mathbf{y}_1)$ and $\rho[p(\mathbf{y}_1, q)]$.

On the contrary, the computational cost of the proposed modified KbOT is

$$nlog_2\sqrt[3]{m} + 2n_hlog_2\sqrt[3]{m} + 2\sqrt[3]{m}n + 8n + 20n_h + 5\sqrt[3]{m}n_h + 4\sqrt[3]{m} - 3 + (2\sqrt[3]{m} + n_h)c_s.$$

It is the same required by th original KbOT except for the fact that m is replaced by $\sqrt[3]{m}$ and the computation of S_l has been included. The latter requires $4n$ *ops* in Steps 1 and $4n_h$ *ops* in Steps 4 and 5.

5 Experimental Results

The proposed algorithm has been tested on various video sequences with assigned reference target. It has been compared only with the original KbOT [8] since

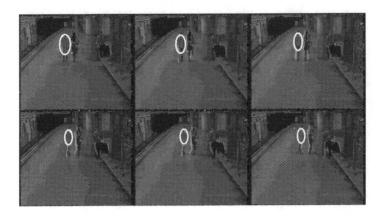

Fig. 4. Six frames of *Subway*. The target (the leftmost girl) is tracked in the presence of other moving objects.

Fig. 5. Six frames of *Subway*. Tracking results using the original KbOT algorithm.

the paper aims at improving tracking capabilities of KbOT by making it more dependent on human perception. The proposed perception-based feature space has highly discriminating properties and allows us to faithfully track the target. In fact, as Fig. 2, 4 and 5 show, the ellipse better centers the target in subsequent frames in the modified KbOT. This is due to the fact that visual contrast gives the target a more distinctive appearance that allows to better discriminate it from the surrounding information. In addition, the mean shift algorithm remains stable by using weights that depend on the Jensen Shannon divergence, making tracking more precise, as Fig. 2 still shows. In fact, the sole luminance is more unstable as it is more sensitive to lighting changes as well as errors due to quantization. JSD also allows the mean-shift algorithm to converge faster than the Bhattacharyya distance. As it can be observed in Fig. 3, using just one iteration of the mean-shift algorithm, JSD seems to better capture the distinctive

Fig. 6. Three frames of *Subway*. The target is tracked when it is partially occluded by the pillar and it reappears after total occlusion.

Fig. 7. The ellipse is enlarged (*left*) in frames of *Subway* where target disappears till motion is detected and target is re-captured (*right*)

features of the target: it immediately gives the best location of the candidate target in subsequent frames. Accordingly, for frames containing more than one moving object, as in Fig. 4, the value of JSD well discriminates the right target to follow.

The proposed tracker is robust even in case of complete (temporary) occlusion, as shown in Fig. 6, where the guy is hidden by the column for some frames. In fact, if the target disappears from the scene and no motion is detected from measurements, the target is searched for into growing regions in subsequent frames till moving areas are detected, i.e. enlarging the fovea region as shown in Fig. 7.

Most of the computational effort of KbOT is required by color histograms. The reduced dimension of S_l allows us a considerable saving of the computing time. For example, for $n \sim n_h \sim m$ and $c_s = 16$, the computational gain G of the proposed method is

$$G = \frac{3m log_2(m) + 7m^2 + 68m - 3}{m log_2(m) + 7\sqrt[3]{m}m + 36\sqrt[3]{m} + 44m - 3},$$

that is $G \sim 171$ for $\sqrt[3]{m} = 16$, as in [8]. In terms of computing time, the proposed tracker is three time faster than the original KbOT, using a PC equipped with an Intel Core i7 Processor, 2.80GHz CPU and 6GB RAM.

Presented results are encouraging: they represent an improvement of tracking performance of KbOT thanks to the use of simple rules that guide human attention; in addition, they are achieved using simple and inexpensive operations. Future research will be oriented to give a perceptual interpretation to other

existing trackers in order to assess to what extent a deeper dependence on perception rules is able to improve their performance, in terms of both faithfulness
of tracking and reduced computational effort. Furthermore, the research will be
also devoted to generalize the proposed model to more complicated contexts by
embedding more information coming from the mechanisms that regulate human
vision. In particular, the case with more than one moving and crossing objects
will be investigated more in depth.

Acknowledgements. The authors would like to thank Prof. Zhou Wang (University of Waterloo, Canada) for his helpful suggestions and for providing them
useful references.

References

1. Yilmaz, A., Javed, O., Shah, M.: Object tracking: a survey. ACM Computing
   Surveys 38(4) (December 2006)
2. Yang, H., Shao, L., Zheng, F., Wang, L., Song, Z.: Recent advances and trends in
   visual tracking: A review. Neurocomputing 74, 3823–3831 (2011)
3. Wu, Y., Lim, J., Yang, M.H.: Online Object Tracking: A Benchmark. In: Proc. of
   CVPR 2013 (2013)
4. Bruni, V., Vitulano, D., Wang, Z.: Special issue on human vision and information
   theory. Signal, Image and Video Processing 7(3), 389–390 (2013)
5. Sheikh, H.R., Bovik, A.C.: Image information and visual quality. IEEE Trans. on
   Image Processing 15(2), 430–444 (2006)
6. Nikvand, N., Wang, Z.: Image Distortion Analysis Based on Normalized Perceptual
   Information Distance. In: Wang, Z., Bruni, V., Vitulano, D. (eds.) Signal Image
   and Video Processing, Special Issue on Human Vision and Information Theory,
   vol. 7(3), pp. 403–410 (May 2013)
7. Bruni, V., Rossi, E., Vitulano, D.: Jensen-Shannon divergence for visual quality
   assessment. In: Wang, Z., Bruni, V., Vitulano, D. (eds.) Signal Image and Video
   Processing, Special Issue on Human Vision and Information Theory, vol. 7(3), pp.
   411–421 (May 2013)
8. Comaniciu, D., Ramesh, V., Meer, P.: Kernel-based object tracking. IEEE Trans.
   on Pattern Analysis and Machine Inteligence 25(2), 564–577 (2003)
9. Shen, L., Huang, X., Yan, Y., Bai, S.: An improved mean-shift tracking algorithm
   with spatial-color feature and new similarity measure. In: Proc. of Int. Conf. on
   Multimedia Tech., ICMT (2011)
10. Hu, J., Juan, C., Wang, J.: A spatial-color mean-shift object tracking algorithm
    with scale and orientation estimation. Pattern Recognition Letters 29(16), 2165–
    2173 (2008)
11. He, S., Yang, Q., Lau, R.W.H., Wang, J., Yang, M.H.: Visual Tracking via Locality
    Sensitive Histograms. In: Proc. of CVPR 2013 (2013)
12. Siagian, C., Itti, L.: Rapid Biologically-Inspired Scene Classification Using Features
    Shared with Visual Attention. IEEE Trans. on Pattern Analysis and Machine In-
    teligence 25(4), 861–873 (2009)
13. Dodge, S.F., Karam, L.J.: Attentive Gesture Recognition. In: Proc. of ICIP 2012
    (2012)

14. Frazor, R., Geisler, W.: Local luminance and contrast in natural images. Vision Research 46, 1585–1598 (2006)
15. Raj, R., Geisler, W.S., Frazor, R.A., Bovik, A.C.: Contrast statistics for foveated visual systems: fixation selection by minimizing contrast entropy. J. of Optical Soc. Am. A 22(10) (October 2005)
16. Bruni, V., Rossi, E., Vitulano, D.: On the Equivalence Between Jensen-Shannon Divergence and Michelson Contrast. IEEE Trans. on Information Theory 58(7), 4278–4288 (2012)
17. Ijiri, Y., Lao, S., Han, T.X., Murase, H.: Human re-identification through distance metric learning based on Jensen-Shannon kernel. In: Proc. of VISAPP, pp. 603–612. SciTePress (February 2012)
18. Arnow, T., Bovik, A.: Foveated visual search for corners. IEEE Trans. Image Processing 16(3), 813–823 (2007)
19. Bruni, V., Ramponi, G., Vitulano, D.: Image Quality Assessment through a Subset of the Image Data. In: Proc. of IEEE ISPA 2011 (2011)
20. Simoncelli, E., Olshausen, B.: Natural image statistics and neural representation. Ann. Rev. Neuro. 24, 1193–1216 (2011)
21. Wang, Z., Lu, L., Bovik, A.C.: Foveation Scalable Video Coding with Automatic Fixation Selection. IEEE Trans. on Image Processing 12(2) (February 2003)
22. Bruni, V., Rossi, E., Vitulano, D.: Perceptual object tracking. In: IEEE Workshop BIOMS (September 2012)
23. Winkler, S.: Digital Video Quality-Vision Models and Metrics. J. Wiley and Sons (2005)
24. Li, M., Chen, X., Li, X., Ma, B., Vitanyi, P.: The similarity metric. IEEE Trans. on Information Theory 50(12), 3250–3264 (2004)
25. Cover, T., Thomas, J.: Elements of information Theory. Wiley (1991)
26. Cilibrasi, R., Vitanyi, P.M.B.: Clustering by compression. IEEE Trans. on Information Theory 51(4), 1523–1545 (2005)
27. Cover, T., Gacs, P., Gray, M.: Kolmogorov's contributions to information theory and algorithmic complexity. Ann. Probab. 17, 840–865 (1989)

Efficient Detection and Tracking of Road Signs Based on Vehicle Motion and Stereo Vision

Chang-Won Choi, Sung-In Choi, and Soon-Yong Park

School of Computer Science and Engineering
Kyungpook National University, Daegu, Republic of Korea
choi408@vision.knu.ac.kr, ellim5th@naver.com, sypark@knu.ac.kr

Abstract. The road signs provide important information about road and traffic to drivers for safety driving. These signs include not only common traffic signs but also the information about unexpected obstacles and road constructions. Accurate detection and identification of road signs is one of the research topics in vehicle vision area. In this paper we propose a stereo vision technique to automatically detect and track road signs in a video sequence which is acquired from a stereo vision camera mounted on a vehicle. First, color information is used to initially detect the candidates of road signs. Second, the Support Vector Machine (SVM) is used to select true signs from the candidates. Once a road sign is detected in a video frame, it is tacked from the next frame until disappeared. The 2-D position of the detected sign on the next frame is predicted by the motion of the vehicle. Here, the vehicle motion means the 3-D Euclidean motion acquired by using a stereo matching method. Finally, the predicted 2-D position of the sign is corrected by the template matching of a scaled sign template in the near regions of the predicted position. Experimental results show that the proposed method can detect and track road signs successfully. Error comparisons with two different detection and tracking methods are shown.

Keywords: stereo, traffic sign, detection, tracking, motion.

1 Introduction

With the emergence of the vehicle vision many smart technologies such as forward and backward obstacle detection, navigation systems, and unmanned vehicle driving have many research attention. Despite the development of automobile technologies, still the driver's negligence causes many accidents on the road. The road signs are very simple but give very important information about the road condition and dangerous situation to the drivers and pedestrians to avoid accidents. If the technology can be used to automatically detect and recognize road signs we can avoid most of these accidents caused by the negligence of the drivers. In this research we introduce an automatic road sign detection and tracking technique to provide safety information to vehicle driver.

Many researches have been studied to detect and recognize road signs in various road and environment conditions. Some of them have used color information to detect

J. Blanc-Talon et al. (Eds.): ACIVS 2013, LNCS 8192, pp. 608–619, 2013.
© Springer International Publishing Switzerland 2013

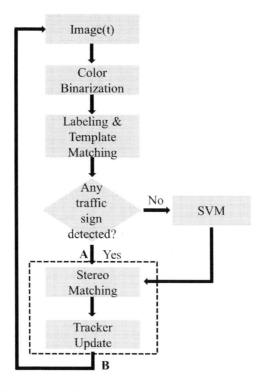

Fig. 1. A block diagram of the proposed algorithm

the road signs or machine learning techniques to recognize the signs [1][2][3]. However, when some obstacles occlude the road signs or color information is not clear with the weather changes, it is difficult to detect the road signs correctly. Some methods have used the edges and color features to detect the traffic signs based on neural networks [4]. In order to track the road signs, they assumed that the speed of the vehicle and the physical sizes of the road signs are known. Then the road signs in the next frame are detected using this information. Some investigations have been introduced to make use of the transformation matrix between the camera coordinate system and the object coordinate system to find the 2D-3D point correspondences for detecting traffic signs [5][6]. In recent researches, various methods have been used together for detecting and recognizing the road signs more accurately and robustly. In [7], color information, cross-correlation function, and PCA (Principal Component Analysis) are used to detect the road signs and a binary tree is used to recognize them.

In this paper, we propose a road sign detection and tracking technique using the 3D information from a stereo vision camera mounted on a moving vehicle. Color information and the SVM (Support Vector Machine) are used to detect road signs. The 3-D position of a detected sign is provided by the depth map calculated by the stereo vision camera. Then the 3-D position information is projected to the image space of the next from to track the sign. By applying this sign tracking algorithm based on the information found in the previous frame, the proposed method is more robust to the environmental changes. As the first step of the proposed sign detection and tracking technique, we classify color objects in a video frame using a look-up table in HSI color space. Then we run labeling and canny edge extraction algorithms to find the candidates of traffic sign objects. After founding candidates, we perform a template matching to filler out some erroneous traffic signs from these candidates and detect true signs sing SVM [8]. Once a road sign is detected, its 3-D position is obtained from the depth map of the current frame as mentioned above. Then the 3-D position is projected to the 2-D image plane of the next frame to predict the road sign. The predicted road sign is refined by a template matching of the sign. When doing the template matching, the template of the sign in the previous frame is scaled according to the actual 3-D size of the sign. This scaled template increases the tracking performance. The tracking algorithm runs iteratively until the sign disappear from the sequence.

2   Road Signs Detection and Tracking

Road sign detection from an image sequence is the first step of the proposed technique which is followed by road sign tracking. A stereo camera is mounted on a moving vehicle to acquire the image sequences. Fig. 1 shows the overall processes of the proposed tracking technique. First, in every video frame, RGB color model is converted to HSI color model and the hue component is converted to a binary image by a threshold value [8]. Second, initial sign candidates are obtained by labeling and matching with sign templates of triangle, circle and rectangle, and etc. Third, using the learning data of SVM, we decide correct signs from the candidates. At the same time, the 3-D positions of detected signs are computed from the depth map of the current frame, which is obtained by the SGBM (Semi Global Block Matching) stereo matching method. Fourth, the 3-D positions of the signs are projected to the image plane of the next frame using the PPM (Perspective Projection Matrix) of the stereo camera. The sin tracking algorithm in the next frame will be described later in another section.

2.1   Image Threshold Using Color Information

To detect road signs in a video frame, we use the color information of the road signs. In general, the color of road sign composed of red, blue, yellow, and white. To extract the candidates of sign, first we convert every image frame to HIS color image. In order to detect road objects such as temporary construction signs and general traffic signs, the hue image is converted to a binary image using Equation 1 which divides color value as achromatic and chromatic values. The reason we use Equation 1 is that most road signs is chromatic. In Equation 1, the range of R,G and B is 0 to 255. If f is greater than 1, it is regarded as the chromatic and the remainder is filtered out considering it as achromatic. The total range of hue value is $0° \sim 360°$, and we use hue value of $330° \sim 360°$ and $0° \sim 40°$.

$$f = \frac{|R - G| + |G - B| + |B - R|}{60} \tag{1}$$

2.2   Labeling and Template Matching

A group of sign candidates is decided in the binarized video frame through the labeling process. When there is a binary image, the labeling process is to give identification to each object group. Therefore, different groups of objects have different labels. Also, If the two road signs is connected, we must divide these. We can distinguish the two road signs using canny edge extraction algorithms. To decide whether a given labeled object is a road sign or not, we match them with the standard shape of road signs, circles, triangles, inverted triangles and etc. After the image of candidate is scaled same with the template image size, the template matching method measures brightness difference between the template and candidates. Table 1 shows the number and type of the template matching stages.

Table 1. Number and type of traffic sign templates

Form of templates	Number of templates
Triangle	12
Inverted triangle	12
Circle	6
Rectangle	6
Rhombus	4

2.3   Traffic Sign Detection Using SVM

In this stage we decide whether a labeled object is a traffic sign or not through previous learning data. The SVM is a method to classify observations with the two categories basically. When a sign object is tested, it is recognized as positive and negative. In this paper, sign images are actually small and environment images are set as training data. Then the traffic signs are set positive, the environment elements are set negative. When the data is trained, feature elements are values of brightness, data size is 80×80, the number of positive images is 500, and the number of negative images is 2000.

2.4   Stereo Matching

Stereo matching is performed to determine the 3-D motion of the vehicle and the 3-D coordinates (x,y,z) of a detected traffic sign. After performing the calibration of our stereo camera by Zhang's calibration method [9], we obtain the Perspective Projection Matrix (PPM) of the stereo cameras. PPM consists of camera focal length, image scale and origin of the difference between image plane and pixel plane. By setting the two dimensional coordinates(x,y) of sign objects in the left and right image planes as the input, we compute the three-dimensional coordinates of the objects. In this paper, we extract the sign objects from the left image and set the ROI(Region Of Interest) based on the information. We generate a 3-D depth map from the stereo image by using SGBM[10], which is a common matching method. The motion between consecutive video frames is computed based on the depth map. And the 3-D coordinates of the matched signs are obtained by using the depth map also.

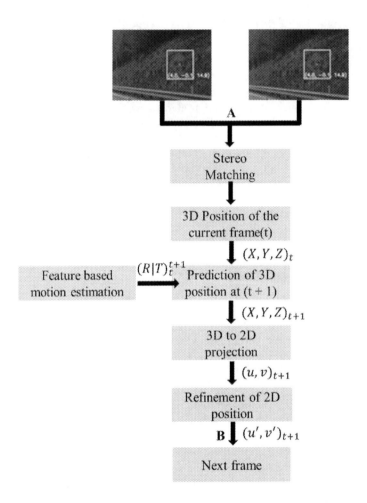

Fig. 2. The tracking algorithm, based on motion and stereo vision

2.5   Traffic Sign Tracking

There are two major reasons that sign tracking is needed. First, in the current frame, if we cannot find the signs which is found in the previous frame due to the changes in the image color or the sign is blocked by an obstacle we can use the tracking method to find it. Second, if the current signs are the same as the signs in the previous frame, we can improve the execution speed of the detection step by skipping the SVM operation that takes time. Fig. 2 shows the overall process of the proposed tracking method.

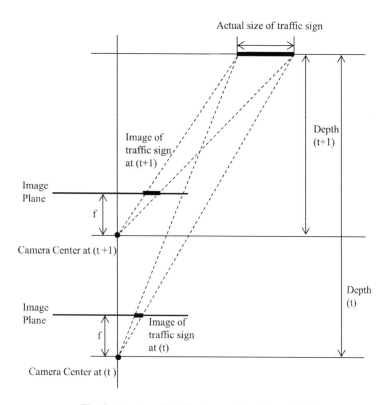

Fig. 3. The size of traffic signs at time (t) and (t+1)

Suppose the time of the current frame is t and the next frame is $t+1$. The camera motion information is calculated in the form of transformation matrix between the frame t and $t+1$[11]. In [11], after three-dimensional information of road sign is calculated based on the depth map, Random Sample Consensus (RANSAC) algorithm is performed. Then, the initial motion vector is calculated. Later, the motion vector is refined by using a non-linear model. For more information, see [11]. And at frame t, we estimate the three-dimensional coordinates of the signs at frame $t+1$ using the three-dimensional coordinates of the signs and the transformation matrix at frame t. We calculate the two-dimensional pixel coordinates in the $t+1$ frame from operation between three-dimensional value that obtained by transformation matrix operation and inverse PPM of the camera information.

2.6   Tracking Refinement

The sign position obtained by the motion of the vehicle is not accurate due to the motion estimation error. Thus, based on object information in the pixel coordinates of predicted signs at $t+1$ frame, we calculate accurate pixel coordinates of the sign by template matching. Template matching is done after setting the ROI in the $t+1$ frame using the normalized correlation coefficient map. In order to perform correct template matching, we need exact image size of road signs. If we don't know the image size of the signs, template matching gives erroneous results. To know the exact image size, we calculate the size using geometric relations between t and $t+1$ frames. Fig. 3 shows how to calculate the size of the road signs. Here, f is focal length. First, we have to calculate the actual size of the signs. The actual size of the signs is calculated using Equation 2. In Equation 2, D is depth between the camera and a detected sign, W is the width of the sign in the world coordinate, and w is the width of the sign in the pixel coordinate. Also in Equation 3, H is the height of the sign in the world coordinate and h is the height of the sign in the pixel coordinate. Once we calculate the actual size of the sign in t frame, we can calculate the size of the sign in $t+1$ frame. Calculation of the size is applied to width and height. Finally, we perform template matching in the $t+1$ frame with the calculated size of the signs.

Actual tracking process is managed by a structure object in the C++ programming language. One structure object stands for one road sign. We manage the structure object during our tracking algorithm. When the tracking algorithm finds a road sign, frame number, image size of the sign, pixel position, ROI, and type of the sign are stored in the structure object. And, the information of the same sign tracked in the next frame is updated also. The sign information in the structure object is maintained until the sign disappears.

$$W = \frac{D \times w}{f} \tag{2}$$

$$H = \frac{D \times h}{f} \tag{3}$$

3   Experiment

To obtain experimental video sequences, we use a Bumblebee XB3 stereo camera with 800×600 resolutions at 30 frames rate. Fig. 4 shows the algorithm flow of a road scene. Fig. 5 shows sign detection results with and without tracking method. The left image is t frame, and the right image is t+1 frame. With tracking method, more signs are detected in the consecutive frames. Quantitative performance comparisons of the proposed method are done with two other methods. In the color segmentation with SVM method, tracking algorithm is not performed. In other words, only the sign detection algorithm is performed. The third method is tracking only method. When applying only template matching, the vehicle motion information and the predicted image size of the sign are not used. Cumulative number of missing signs is shown in Fig. 6. In this figure, x-axis represents frame number and y-axis represents the cumulative number of missing signs. Using color and SVM, average processing speed is six frames per second and about 45% of road signs in the test video frames are not detected. In case of using the third method, average performance speed is about eight frames per second and the missing rate of the sign is about 30%.

Fig. 4. The Image step of function

Fig. 5. Result of the tracking algorithm, (a) without tracking algorithm, (b) with tracking algorithm

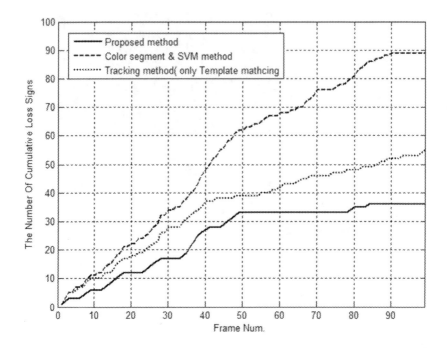

Fig. 6. Number of cumulative missing signs

Table 2. Experiment results table of Color segment & SVM

	Data set 1	Date set 2	Data Set 3	Data Set 4
Number of full signs	192	57	35	108
Number of detected signs	109	30	18	58
Success rate	55.1%	52.6%	51.4%	53.7%

Table 3. Experiment results table of Tracking method (only template matching)

	Data set 1	Date set 2	Data Set 3	Data Set 4
Number of full signs	192	57	35	108
Number of detected signs	138	40	25	74
Success rate	71.8%	70.1%	71.4%	68.5%

Table 4. Experiment results table of the proposed method

	Data set 1	Date set 2	Data Set 3	Data Set 4
Number of full signs	192	57	35	108
Number of detected signs	162	48	31	90
Success rate	84.4%	84.2%	88.6%	83.3%

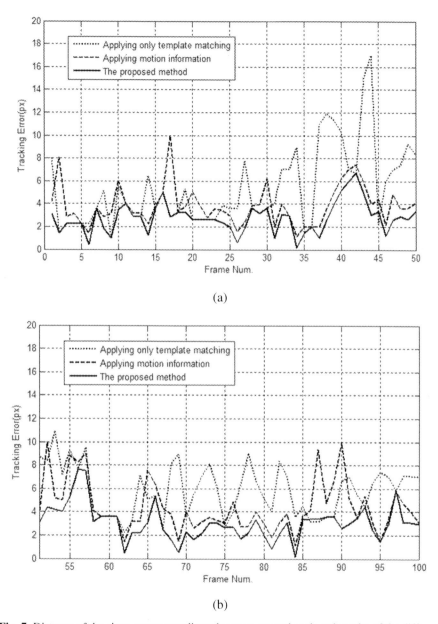

(a)

(b)

Fig. 7. Distance of the signs center coordinate between ground truth and results of the different methods

Contrast to above mentioned methods, the proposed algorithm runs eight frames per second in average and the missing rate of the signs is about 15%. The graph shown in Fig. 6 shows that higher detection rate of the sign is achieved by using the proposed methods. However, if we use only the template matching, the system will not be able to adapt to the changes of the sign size in each frame while the vehicle is moving. The camera motion information can be used to track the signs more accurately. In the evaluation we check the detection of the signs in each frame. If there is a sign closer than 80m from the vehicle, but it is not detected by the algorithm, we consider it as a missing sign. Main reasons of missed sign are bad color information of the sign and occlusion by obstacles. Table 2, 3 and 4 gives the number of total signs available in the data set, number of successful detections and its percentage using the same three methods respectively. Each data set is different road video with different kind of signs in daytime.

Fig. 7 shows the error of tracking algorithm measured by the distance between the tracked location and the ground truth of the sign center. Prior to the experiment, we find the center coordinate of the signs on each frame manually and make the ground truth. In the figure x-axis represents the frame number and y-axis represents the distance between ground truths and results in pixels. Three different lines represent the three methods and two graphs shows the results for two different data sets.

Motion information method calculates the center coordinate of the signs by multiplying the three-dimensional coordinate of the signs on the previous frame with the camera motion matrix. This method does not use the template matching. Results in Fig. 7 shows that when the signs are closer, the error will be higher when we use only the template matching because it is not considered the changes of the sign size on the frame. The average error is 6.073 pixels for the method which uses only the template matching, 4.410 pixels for the method which uses only the motion information and 3.126 pixels for the proposed method.

4   Conclusion

With the experimental results we find that our proposed method has advantages in road sign detection and processing speed. Once a road sign is detected in a video frame, its 3-D position is calculated by using stereo matching. And the 2-D position of the sign in the next frame is calculated by the motion of the vehicle computed by the stereo vision method. Since we can measure the size of the sign using the 3-D information of the sign, accurate 2-D size of the sign is calculated. This gives better template matching and accurate sign detection. Although we apply a new tracking method for road sign detection, still there is a problem due to color variation among the video sequences. Currently there are about 15% signs are not detected due to color segmentation error, SVM recognition error and so on. In the future, we will continue to increase the detection rate.

Acknowledgment. This research was supported by the MSIP(Ministry of Science, ICT & Future Planning), Korea, under the C-ITRC(Convergence Information Technology Research Center) support program (NIPA-2013-H0401-13-1005) supervised by the NIPA(National IT Industry Promotion Agency) and the Industrial Strategic technology development program, Development of Driver-View based in-Vehicle AR Display System Technology Development(10040927), funded by the Ministry of Knowledge Economy (MKE, Korea).

References

1. Ruta, A., Li, Y., Liu, X.: Detection, Tracking and Recognition of Traffic Signs from Video Input. In: 11th International IEEE Conference on Intelligent Transportation Systems, ITSC 2008, October 12-15, pp. 55–60 (2008)
2. de la Escalera, A., Armingol, J.M., Pastor, J.M., Rodriguez, F.J.: Visual sign information extraction and identification by deformable models for intelligent vehicles. IEEE Transactions on Intelligent Transportation Systems 5(2), 57–68 (2004)
3. de la Escalera, A., Moreno, L.E., Salichs, M.A., Armingol, J.M.: Road traffic sign detection and classification. IEEE Transactions on Industrial Electronics 44(6), 848–859 (1997)
4. Fang, C.-Y., Chen, S.-W., Fuh, C.-S.: Road-sign detection and tracking. IEEE Transactions on Vehicular Technology 52(5), 1329–1341 (2003)
5. Ruta, A., Li, Y., Uxbridge, M., Porikli, F., Watanabe, S., Kage, H., Sumi, K., Amagasaki, J.: A New Approach for In-Vehicle Camera Traffic Sign Detection and Recognition. In: Proc. IAPR Conference on Machine Vision Applications, Japan, (2009)
6. Timofte, R., Prisacariu, V., Van Gool, L., Reid, I.: Combining TrafficSign Detection with 3D Tracking Towards Better Driver Assistance. Emerging Topics in Computer Vision and Its Applications (2011)
7. Uchida, T., Hanaizumi, H.: An automated method for understanding road traffic signs in a video scene captured by a mobile camera. In: 2012 IEEE International Conference on Industrial Technology (ICIT), March 19-21, pp. 108–111 (2012)
8. Maldonado-Bascon, S., Lafuente-Arroyo, S., Gil-Jimenez, P., Gomez-Moreno, H., Lopez-Ferreras, F.: Road-Sign Detection and Recognition Based on Support Vector Machines. IEEE Transactions on Intelligent Transportation Systems 8(2), 264–278 (2007)
9. Zhang, Z.: Camera calibration with one-dimensional objects. In: Heyden, A., Sparr, G., Nielsen, M., Johansen, P. (eds.) ECCV 2002, Part IV. LNCS, vol. 2353, pp. 161–174. Springer, Heidelberg (2002)
10. Dröppelmann, S., et al.: Stereo Vision using the OpenCV library (2010)
11. Choi, S.-I., Zhang, L., Park, S.-Y.: Stereo Vision Based Motion Adjustment of 2D Laser Scan Matching. In: Image and Vision Computing New Zealand, IVCNZ 2011 (November 2011)

Incremental Principal Component Analysis-Based Sparse Representation for Face Pose Classification

Yuyao Zhang[1], Y. Benhamza[2], Khalid Idrissi[1], and Christophe Garcia[1]

[1] University de Lyon, CNRS
INSA-Lyon, LIRIS, UMR CNRS 5205, F-69621, France
[2] Laboratoire LARATIC, INTTIC Oran Algrie
{Yuyao.Zhang,khalid.Idrissi,Christophe.garcia}@insa-lyon.fr,
ybenhamza@ito.dz

Abstract. This paper proposes an Adaptive Sparse Representation pose Classification (ASRC) algorithm to deal with face pose estimation in occlusion, bad illumination and low-resolution cases. The proposed approach classifies different poses, the appearance of face images from the same pose being modelled by an online eigenspace which is built via Incremental Principal Component Analysis. Then the combination of the eigenspaces of all pose classes are used as an over-complete dictionary for sparse representation and classification. However, the big amount of training images may lead to build an extremely large dictionary which will decelerate the classification procedure. To avoid this situation, we devise a conditional update method that updates the training eigenspace only with the misclassified face images. Experimental results show that the proposed method is very robust when the illumination condition changes very dynamically and image resolutions are quite poor.

Keywords: Sparse Representation, Pose Classification, Incremental Principal Component Analysis.

1 Introduction

Human face pose estimation from 2D images is a hot research topic, with lots of applications in expression and face recognition [1], driver monitoring [2] or human-computer interaction [3]. The challenges to overcome are due to the large variability of the images, like facial expressions, illuminations and image resolutions. There exists a large amount of solutions for face pose estimation. A review of related works can be found in [4]. *Active Appearance Models (AAMs)* rely on learning the primary modes of variation in shape and appearance to predict the face pose [5]. The main limitation of AAMs is that facial features are required to be precisely located which is hard to achieve when the image resolution is low. *Regression based methods* estimate the pose by learning a linear or non-linear function between the image and continuous angles using for instance Support Vector Regressions (SVR)[6]. Generally, such methods suffer from irregularly

J. Blanc-Talon et al. (Eds.): ACIVS 2013, LNCS 8192, pp. 620–631, 2013.

distributed data and noise which exist in either training or test data. *Manifold embedding techniques* produce a low dimensional representation of the original facial features in supervised or unsupervised fashion and then use template, classification or regression methods to compute the angle in a supervised manner. For instance, Li *et al.* search for a set of localized linear manifolds to approximate the global head pose manifold [7]. Proposed by Balasubramanian *et al.* in [8], the Biased Manifold Embedding (BME) framework relies on using the pose angle information of the face images to compute a biased neighbourhood of each point in the feature space. For learning the non-linear mapping, they use a Generalized Regression Neural Network (GRNN), and a linear multi-variant regression is finally applied on the low-dimensional space to obtain the pose angle.

Most recent methods aim at estimating finer estimation of continuous 3D head pose. Hybrid combinations of manifold embedding methods and regression methods are reliable solutions for continuously fine head pose prediction. In [9], Huang proposes to build generative local linear subspace models for dealing with the problem of non-uniform sampling of the training set. The method is proved to be robust to noise and able to estimate continuous pose. In [10], Ji presents a convex sparse regression for removing noise and outliers from data and learning the regression between image features and pose angles. This approach is proved not to be prone to outliers, but the training sets rely on medium to high resolution images captured under normal illumination conditions that actually guarantee the quality of the images. In [11], Sarfraz and Hellwich present a discriminative method which is based on a Pose Similarity Feature Space (PSFS) to simplify the multi-class problem into a two-class problem. Then the classification is realised with an improved AdaBoost Classifier. The estimation system is evaluated on the CMU PIE database to verify the robustness to illumination and expression variations.

The real world face pose estimation is a more complicated problem. Low-resolution and occlusions are two of the major challenges. There are existing methods for pose estimation in low-resolution images that treat the problem as a multiclass discrete pose classification problem. In [12], Benfold and Reid propose to segment a colour based skin-hair regions from the background of a low-resolution video frame in order to classify head pose by using Hidden Markov Model. This approach critically relies upon good segmentation of regions of interest from the video sequences. Orozco et al. [13] propose an approach to construct feature vectors using similarity distance maps by indexing each pixel of a head image to the mean appearance template at different poses via KL divergence. Then, the distance maps are applied to train a multi-class Support Vector Machine for pose classification. In [14], Sarfraz and Hellwich present a discriminative method which is based on a Pose Similarity Feature Space (PSFS) to simplify the multi-class problem into a two-class problem. Then the classification is realised with an improved AdaBoost Clas-sifier. The estimation system is evaluated on the CMU PIE database to verify the robustness to illumination and expression variations.

In this paper, we propose an efficient online sparse representation method which is designed to take account of the strong appearance variability in a large facial image database. The method updates the appearance basis vectors with the current face image via Incremental Principal Component Analysis. To avoid high computing cost, we devise a conditional update method that renews the training basis vectors only with the misclassified face images. The proposed conditional update of the training basis vectors stabilizes classification accuracy and improves the classification performance especially when the illumination conditions change very dynamically or the image resolution is low.

2   The Proposed Method

2.1   Incremental Principal Component Analysis

The incremental subspace learning algorithm is proposed in [15]. Let us consider a set of d-dimensional vectorized training images $I = \{I_1, I_2, \cdots, I_n\}$, where d is the dimension of each vectorized image. Classically, the initial eigenspace of the training images can be obtained by solving the singular value decomposition (SVD) of the covariance matrix:

$$C = \frac{1}{n} \sum_{i=1}^{n} (I_i - \overline{I})(I_i - \overline{I})^T \tag{1}$$

Where $\overline{I} = \frac{1}{n} \sum_{i=1}^{n} I_i$ is the mean image of image set I. The initial K eigenvalues $\{\lambda_1, \lambda_2, \cdots, \lambda_K\}$ lie on the diagonal of matrix $\Lambda \in R^{K \times K}$, and the corresponding eigenvectors are represented in matrix $U = \{u_1, u_2, \cdots, u_K\} \in R^{d \times K}$. This initial eigenspace defines an orthogonal linear transformation that projects the training images into a new coordinate system. The Incremental PCA learning is then built based on the initial eigenspace. When a new training image I_{n+1} is considered, the incremental procedure updates the mean image and the eigenvectors as described in [15]. The mean image is updated as:

$$\overline{I}' = \frac{1}{n+1}(n\overline{I} + I_{n+1}) \tag{2}$$

Using the current eigenvectors U as the basis set, the new image I_{n+1} can be reconstructed, but with a loss represented by the residual vector v, computed as:

$$v = (U\alpha_{n+1} + \overline{I}) - I_{n+1} \tag{3}$$

where $\alpha_{n+1} = U^T(I_{n+1} - \overline{I})$. The vector v is then normalized:

$$\hat{v} = \frac{v}{\|v\|_2} \tag{4}$$

The updated eigenspace U' is acquired by a rotation, R, of the current eigenspace plus the residual vector:

$$U' = [U \ \hat{v}] R \tag{5}$$

The rotation matrix R and updated eigenvalues Λ' can be obtained by solving the SVD of D matrix:

$$DR = R\Lambda' \tag{6}$$

where we compose $D \in R^{(K+1)\times(K+1)}$ as:

$$D = \frac{n}{n+1}\begin{bmatrix} \Lambda & 0 \\ 0^T & 0 \end{bmatrix} + \frac{n}{(n+1)^2}\begin{bmatrix} \alpha_{n+1}\alpha_{n+1}^T & \beta\alpha_{n+1} \\ \beta\alpha_{n+1}^T & \beta^2 \end{bmatrix} \tag{7}$$

where $\beta = \hat{v}_{n+1}^T(I_{n+1} - \bar{I})$.

The solution to Equation 6 yields the new eigenvalues directly, and the new eigenvectors are then computed from Equation 6. The details of the whole procedure can be found in [15]. With this Incremental PCA algorithm, the new training image I_{n+1} is taken into account by the basis eigenspace as a new type of variation.

2.2 Classification Based on Sparse Representation

In this section, we make use of the Sparse Representation (refered as SR) method presented in [16] to generate a robust pose classification algorithm. Let us consider a classification problem with M distinct categories, then we build M eigenspaces $A_m = \begin{bmatrix} \bar{I}_m & U_m \end{bmatrix}, m = 1, 2, \cdots, M$, on each category by Incremental PCA learning mentioned in section 2.1, where $\bar{I}_m$ is the normalized mean image and U_m are the eigenvectors of the mth pose class in the training samples. We suppose that the target can be classified with the arranged vector matrix A, where A is a combined eigenspace of M pose categories:

$$A = [A_1, A_2, \cdots, A_M] \tag{8}$$

With dictionary A, any new test image $y \in R^{d\times 1}$ can be approximately represented by a linear span of the training eigenspace associated with its class m:

$$y = A_m a_m \tag{9}$$

where $a_m = [1, a_m^1, a_m^2, \cdots, a_m^k]$ is the reconstruction coefficient vector in the mth sub-eigenspace.

Practically, the test image y could be partially corrupted or occluded. In this case, the above model in (9) should be rewritten as:

$$y = \begin{bmatrix} A & E \end{bmatrix}\begin{bmatrix} a \\ b \end{bmatrix} = Aa + Eb \tag{10}$$

where $a = [0, \cdots, 0, a_m, 0, \cdots, 0]$ is the sparse coefficient vector whose elements are zero except those contained in a_m, and $E = [\Omega, -\Omega] \in R^{d\times 2d}$ represents the additive trivial basis set for occluded or corrupted targets, where $\Omega \in R^{d\times d}$ is the identity matrix, and b is the coefficient vector on E. The optimal coefficients $\begin{bmatrix} a \\ b \end{bmatrix}$ are obtained by solving the following objective function:

$$l_0 = \min_{a,b} \|a\|_0 + \|b\|_0 , \quad subject \quad to \quad y = Aa + Eb \tag{11}$$

where $\|x\|_0$ counts the number of nonzero elements in x. In case of our pose estimation, the size of the over-complete basis being larger than the dimention of images, Equation 11 is typically underdetermined, so that the solution is not unique. Recent development in the emerging theory of sparse representation and compressive sensing [17] reveals that if the solution $\begin{bmatrix} a_0 \\ b_0 \end{bmatrix}$ is sparse enough, the solution of the l_0-minimization problem (11) is equal to the solution to the following l_1-minimization problem:

$$l_1 = \min_{a,b} \|a\|_1 + \|b\|_1 , \quad subject \quad to \quad y = Aa + Eb \tag{12}$$

This problem can be solved in polynomial time by standard linear programming method. A test sample y from one of the classes in the training set is represented with the solution $\begin{bmatrix} a_1 \\ b_1 \end{bmatrix}$ and the over-complete basis set $\begin{bmatrix} A\ E \end{bmatrix}$. Ideally, the nonzero elements will all be associated with the columns of A from a single pose class m, and we can easily assign the test sample y to that class. But because of the noise in the data, there could be small nonzero elements associated with multiple object classes. In this case, we compute a reconstruction residual RE_m for each single pose class and then classify y to the class corresponding to the minimal reconstruction error.

$$\min_m RE_m = \|y - (Aa_1^m + Eb_1)\|_2 \tag{13}$$

where a_1^m represents to the elements from coefficient vector a_1 which is associated with the mth class.

2.3   A Framework of Incremental Principal Component Analysis-Based Sparse Representation Classification

In this section, we explain in details the framework of the Adaptive Sparse Representation pose Classification (ASRC). The essential idea of this framework is to build an online face pose dictionary with the current training face image via Incremental Principal Component Analysis. However, the amount of the training images is large, and there exists a lot of redundancy variations and noise which may affect the final classification results. To overcome this situation, we devise a conditional update method that updates the training appearance basis eigenspace only with the misclassified face images. Algorithm 1 summarizes the complete classification scheme.

In order to provide a suitable training set for Incremental PCA, for each class m, the training samples are divided into two subsets. The first one contains a small number, n_m, of face images, and it is modelled via PCA as an initial eigenspace, and the second one is used for Incremental PCA learning. The combination of the eigenspaces of all pose classes are used for Sparse Representation

Algorithm 1. Framework of the Adaptive Sparse Representation pose Classification (ASRC)

1:Input: a matrix of training images $I = \left\{ I^1, I^2, \cdots, I^M \right\}$ from M classes, where $I^m \in R^{d \times n_m}$ represents the image set of the class m where d is the dimension of each image (in vector form), while n_m is the number of images in the class m) .

2:Apply standard PCA on each image set to obtain the initial eigenspaces $A_m = \left[\bar{I}_m \, U_m \right] (m = 1, 2, \cdots, M)$.

3:Solve the l_1-minimization problem in Equation 12 for the sparse representation $\begin{bmatrix} a_1 \\ b_1 \end{bmatrix}$ of a new image from the second training subset.

4:Label the new training image with the class m for which the reconstruction residual of the new training image is minimal in Equation 13.

5:Judge if the new image is labelled with the correct class?

Yes $\rightarrow$ return to **step 3**;

No $\rightarrow$ continue to **step 6**.

6:Update the online eigenspace of the class to which the new training image belongs to via Incremental PCA as in subsection 2.1.

7:Return to **step 3**.

Classification as an over-complete dictionary. Afterwards, new training samples are added into the basis eigenspace by applying Incremental Principal Component Analysis in case of the Sparse Representation Classifier made a mistake. Therefore the dictionary of SR is updated with every misclassification. The incorporation of incorrectly classified pose makes our classifier more adaptive.

The proposed conditional update of the training basis dictionary stabilizes classification accuracy and improves the classification performance especially when the image resolution is very low or the illumination condition changes dynamically.

3   Experiments

In this section, we first evaluate the method on the LIRIS Low-resolution Pose database to demonstrate the robustness of the proposed ASRC algorithm for low resolution images and to compare it with several classic classifiers. Second, we evaluate its robustness versus pose and illumination variations on the CMU PIE [18] database.

3.1   Performance on Low-Resolution Face Images

For testing the proposed algorithm with low-resolution images, we build a large database of 248,025 face images sorted in five categories that we called the LIRIS

Low-resolution Pose database (referred to as the LLP database). We extracted face images, from the internet and face databases using the online face detector face.com (http://face.com). With their out-of-plane angle deviations and some manual selections/corrections, face images were cropped and classified into five pose categories (64770 Frontal faces, 30469 Left profile faces, 39993 Right profile faces, 56396 Quarter left faces, 56396 Quarter right faces). The face images were all resized to 36 × 36 pixels. Some examples of the cropped faces of the LLP database are shown in Figure 1.

frontal view

quarter views
(left and right)

profile views
(left and right)

Fig. 1. Some examples of the face images from the LIRIS Low-resolution Pose database

To choose the best face image size for classification in the following experiments, we downsampled the original image from 36 × 36 pixels to 30 × 30, 24 × 24, 18 × 18 and 9 × 9 pixels. The average classification rates for the different face image resolutions are shown in Table 1, where the two best classification rates of 91.03% and 91.78% are obtained respectively for the resolution of 18 × 18 and 24 × 24. This result show that the proposed framework is very efficient on a very challenging database and therefore, in the following experiments, we subsample the original images to the resolution 24 × 24.

Table 1. Classification rate for different image resolutions

	9 × 9	18 × 18	24 × 24	30 × 30	36 × 36
Class Rate	81.88%	91.03%	91.78%	88.46%	82.41%

In this second experiment, we tested the sensitivity of the face pose estimation versus the number of samples in the training set. The initial eigenspace for incremental PCA is built on 50 randomly selected images from each pose class. Then we add varying numbers of training samples to update the eigenspace, until the number of training samples reach 100, 500, 1000, 1500, 2000, 3000, 6000 (per class) respectively. To achieve a reliable result, we repeat the training procedure 10 times, then apply the framework on the same test set which included 8000 test samples for each single pose class. All the training sets are constructed from a random selection of the entire LLP database. Both training and test sets are based on face images of resolution 24 × 24. The results of the experiments are illustrated in Figure 2 (a) and Table 2. Figure 2 (a) shows the average classification rate for each pose class. The average global classification rate for all classes is also presented. One can notice that the highest classification rate is obtained for 1000 training samples per class. Table 2 shows the mean accuracy and variance on various sizes of training set for 10 experiments. The highest classification rate of 91.03%±1.42% is obtained for 1000 training samples per class. After this peak, with the number of training samples increasing, the classification rate remains stable. Table 3 shows the confusion matrix, where the classification rate is obtained for each pose category. One can notice that the classification confusions are low and generally between close categories (i.e. L and QL, R and QR).

Table 2. Variance and average classification rate on variable sizes of the training set (experiments are repeated 10 times)

	Initial	100	500	1000	3000	6000
AVG Rate	75.40%	80.60%	87.87%	92.89%	91.13%	91.67%
Variance	6.17	6.04	1.47	1.42	1.32	0.26

Table 3. Confusion matrix of face pose classification on the LLP database

Class	L	QL	F	QR	R
L	92.66%	6.68 %	0.66%		
QL	3.86%	91.55%	4.59%		
F	0.81%	1.2%	95.65%	1.9%	0.36%
QR			4.03 %	89.74%	6.24%
R			0.16%	8.83%	91.00%

We compare the ASRC framework with the standard PCA based eigenspace SRC in Figure 2 (b). It is clear that, thanks to the online eigenspace, Incremental PCA outperforms PCA when the number of training samples is over 500.

We finally compare the proposed framework with three classical algorithms, which are K-Nearest Neighbour (KNN), and Support Vector Machine (SVM), with linear and non-linear kernels. For fair comparison, we use the same training and test sets as well as the same feature space for each experiment. As shown in Figure 2 (c), the proposed algorithm outperformed the KNN (K=1, K=100) and SVM classifiers (with linear and polynomial kernels) in these low-resolution and high-noise conditions, for all sizes of the training set.

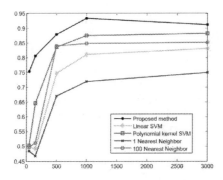

(a) Average classification performance for varying numbers of
training samples for 5 pose categories, on the LLP database

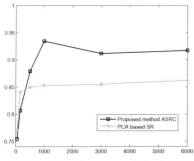

(b) Classification rate of the ASRC
algorithm compared with PCA
based SR classification algorithm

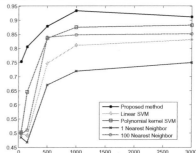

(c) Classification rate of the ASRC
algorithm compared with SVM and
K-Nearest Neighbour classification

Fig. 2. Experimental results

3.2   Performance on Face Pose with Illumination Variations

To evaluate the robustness of the proposed method to illumination variations, we
apply the algorithm to the CMU Pose Illumination and Expression database. The
CMU PIE dataset contains 68 facial images of 70 different people across 13 poses,
under 43 different illumination conditions, and with 4 different expressions. The
pose ground truth was obtained with a 13 cameras array, each positioned to
provide a special relative pose angle. The chosen subset consists of 12,600 images
of 68 people (9 different poses as shown in the top row of Figure 3, and 20 variable
illumination conditions of each pose illustrated in the second and third rows of
Figure 3). For Algorithm ASRC, in training procedure, we use images from 30
people (180 samples per person) of varying illuminated pose views. The faces
are first located by the Viola-Jones face detector [19]. The face region is then
down sampled to a 24×24 patch. The initial eigenspace for incremental PCA
is built from 360 images (including 9 pose and 20 illumination conditions) of 2
people, and the images of the other 28 people in the training set are then added

Table 4. Confusion matrix of face pose classification on the CMU PIE database (in percentage) for the 9 different poses

Class	1	2	3	4	5	6	7	8	9
1	93.7%	5.7%	0.6%						
2		97.2%	2.8%						
3		0.8%	97.5%	1.7%					
4				94.9%	5.1%				
5				0.9%	98.2%	0.9%			
6						95.0%	4.2%	0.8%	
7						0.6%	95.8%	3.6%	
8						0.08%	4.2%	93.2%	2.5%
9							1.9%	5.9%	92.2%

Table 5. Comparison of the classification rates between the PSFS algorithm and the ASRC algorithm on the CMU PIE database (in percentage) for the 9 different poses

Class	1	2	3	4	5	6	7	8	9	AVG
PSFS	96.8%	78.4%	65.0%	79.5%	96.8%	93.8%	53.4%	90.0%	92.5%	84.1%
ASRC	97.2%	96.0%	97.1%	94.6%	98.3%	96.2%	97.0%	95.7%	96.8%	96.5%

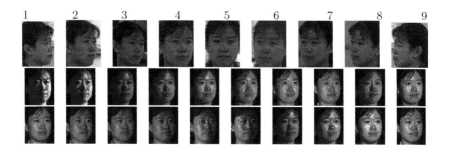

Fig. 3. Top row: 9 different face pose images under the same illumination condition. Botton two rows: 20 different illumination conditions.

into the basis eigenspace by applying Incremental PCA. The confusion matrix of the classification results for the 9 different poses is shown in Table 4.

Comparison with Other Classification Methods. We compare the proposed method with one state-of-the-art classification method [11], which is based on a Pose Similarity Feature Space (referred as PSFS), and classify different poses via an AdaBoost classifier combined with statistical procedure. The evaluation of this paper is also performed on the CMU PIE database, including illumination variations in each pose class. For fair comparison, we build training and test data sets as done in [11]. There are 15 people included in the training set, 4 illumination variations corresponding to flashes 01, 04, 13 and 14, and expression variations are neutral, smiling and blinking. The other images from 53 people are used for test. Table 5 compares the classification rates between our algorithm and the algorithm in [11], showing its superiority and its stability for all illumination conditions.

4   Conclusion

In this paper, we have presented a very robust face pose estimator using the Adaptive Sparse Representation pose Classification (ASRC) algorithm. We propose to combine Incremental Principal Component Analysis and Sparse Representation to improve pose classification and to make it more robust to illumination variations and low resolution images. First, a small amount of images from the same pose are modelled via PCA as an initial eigenspace. The combination of multiple eigenspaces of every pose class is used for Sparse Representation Classification as an over-complete dictionary. Afterwards, new training samples are added into the basis eigenspace by applying Incremental Principal Component Analysis in case of the Sparse Representation Classifier made a mistake. Therefore the dictionary of SR is updated with every misclassification. The incorporation of incorrectly classified pose makes our classifier more adaptive. The Sparse Representation Classifier is robust to appearance changes such as those caused by varying illumination, occlusions and resolutions. Experimental results show that the combination of the two methods improves the performance in terms of classification accuracy. In view of the classification results obtained on the LLP database, the proposed algorithm appears particularly robust to deal with low-resolution images, and the experiments on the CMU PIE database demonstrate a large tolerance to variations in expression and illumination.

References

1. Huang, T., Tu, J., Xiong, Y.: Calibrating head pose estimation in vidoes for meeting room event analysis. In: IEEE International Conference on Image Processing (ICIP), pp. 3193–3196 (2006)
2. Murphy-Chutorian, E., Trivedi, M.: Head pose estimation for driver assistance systems: A robust algorithm and experimental evaluation. Intelligent Transportation Systems, 709–714 (2007)
3. Ohayon, S., Rivlin, E.: Robust 3d head tracking using camera pose estimation. In: International Conference Pattern Recognation (ICPR), pp. 1063–1066 (2006)
4. Murphy-Chutorian, E., Trivedi, M.M.: Head pose estimation in computer vision: A survey. IEEE Transactions on Pattern Analysis and Machine Intelligence 31(4), 607–626 (2009)
5. Matthews, I., Baker, S.: Active appearance models revisited. International Journal of Computer Vision 60(2), 135–164 (2004)
6. Moon, H., Miller, M.L.: Estimating facial pose from a sparse representation. In: International Conference on Image Processing (ICIP), pp. 75–78 (2004)
7. Yuan, J., Li, Z., Fu, Y., Huang, T.: Query driven localized linear discriminant models for head pose estimation. In: ICME, pp. 1810–1813 (2007)
8. Jieping, Y., Balasubramanian, V., Panchanathan, S.: Biased manifold embedding: A framework for person-independent head pose estimation. In: Proc. CVPR, pp. 1–7 (2007)
9. De la Torre, F., Huang, D., Storer, M., Bischof, H.: Supervised local subspace learning for continuous head pose estimation. In: IEEE Conference on Computer Vision and Pattern Recognition (CVPR), pp. 2921–2928 (2011)

10. Su, F., Su, Z., Ji, H., Liu, R., Tian, Y.: Robust head pose estimation via convex regularized sparse regression. In: IEEE International Conference on Image Processing (ICIP), pp. 3617–3620 (2011)
11. Saquib Sarfraz, M., Hellwich, O.: Head pose estimation in face recognition across pose scenarios. In: VISAPP, pp. 235–242 (2008)
12. Benfold, B., Reid, I.: Colour invariant head pose classification in low resolution video. In: Procedings of the British Machine Vision Conference, BMVC (2008)
13. Xiang, T., Orozco, J., Gong, S.: Head pose classification in crowded scenes. In: Procedings of the British Machine Vision Conference (BMVC 2009), pp. 120.1–120.11 (2009)
14. Sarfraz, M.S., Hellwich, O.: Head pose estimation in face recognition across pose scenarios. In: VISAPP (1) 2008, pp. 235–242 (2008)
15. Hall, P.M., Marshall, D., Martin, R.R.: Incremental eigenanalysis for classification. In: British Machine Vision Conference, pp. 286–295 (1998)
16. Arvind Ganesh, S., Sastry, S., Wright, J., Yang, A.Y., Ma, Y.: Robust face recognition via sparse representation. IEEE Transactions on Pattern Analysis and Machine Intelligence (PAMI) 31(2), 210–227
17. Donoho, D.: For most large underdetermined systems of linear equations: the minimal l1-norm solution is also the sparsest solution. Comm. on Pure and Applied Math. 59(6), 797–829 (2006)
18. Baker, S., Sim, T., Bsat, M.: The cum pose illumination and expression database. IEEE Trans. Pattern Analysis and Machine Intelligence 25(12), 1615–1618 (2003)
19. Viola, P., Jones, M.: Robust real-time object detection. International Journal of Computer Vision (2001)

Person Detection with a Computation Time Weighted AdaBoost

Alhayat Ali Mekonnen, Frédéric Lerasle, and Ariane Herbulot

CNRS, LAAS, 7 Avenue du Colonel Roche, F-31400 Toulouse, France
Univ de Toulouse, UPS, LAAS, F-31400 Toulouse, France
{alhayat-ali.mekonnen,frederic.lerasle,ariane.herbulot}@laas.fr

Abstract. In this paper, a boosted cascade person detection framework with heterogeneous pool of features is presented. The boosted cascade construction and feature selection is carried out using a modified AdaBoost that takes computation time of features into consideration. The final detector achieves a low Miss Rate of 0.06 at 10^{-3} False Positive Per Window on the INRIA public dataset while achieving an average speed up of $1.8\times$ on the classical variant.

Keywords: Person Detection, AdaBoost, Feature Selection.

1 Introduction

Person detection is one of the prominent problems considered in Computer Vision. It has a vast pool of applications spanning surveillance systems, human-robot interaction, biometric data acquisition, and pedestrian protection systems in the automotive industry, to name a few. At the same time, it is a very challenging task owing to the physical variation of persons, variable appearances, occlusion, background clutter, and many more. Designing a detection system that is capable of overcoming these challenges while fulfilling real time detection requirements of many applications is still an open problem [3].

Depending on the type of sensor(s) utilized, different approaches could be employed for person detection. In this work, we focus only on monocular images which could be from a classical camera either fixed or mounted on a moving vehicle (no static camera assumption). We present a person detection system that makes use of heterogeneous pool of features–five of the most commonly used features: Haar like features [14], Edge Orientation Histograms (EOH) [4], Local Binary Patterns (LBP) [17], Histogram of Oriented Gradients (HOG) [1]–with a boosted cascade detector configuration [14]. Contrary to classical approaches which only take detection performance into consideration, our boosted cascade detector is constructed taking detection performance and feature computation time into consideration simultaneously. Our implementation shows very promising detection performance on the INRIA public dataset [1] with only a 6% Miss Rate at 10^{-3} FPPW while on average taking $1.8\times$ less time than that of a similar detector constructed without computation time consideration.

1.1 Related Works

The problem of person detection has been studied for more than a decade by researchers. Through these times, a large number of different approaches have been proposed; it is

J. Blanc-Talon et al. (Eds.): ACIVS 2013, LNCS 8192, pp. 632–644, 2013.

practically impossible to mention all due to space constraints. We will restrict this section by highlighting works on monocular images that employ heterogeneous features in a sliding window candidate generation scheme (see recent survey papers [3,5] for a broader review).

The interesting pioneering works on person detection were first reported using Haar like features [11,15]. Since then, person detection has improved a lot. The work of Dalal and Triggs [1] which introduced and used HOG features was next in line to set the bar high. To date, HOG is the most discriminant feature, and in fact, a majority of detectors proposed hence-after make use of HOG or its variant one way or another [3]. Most of the works that have improved over [1] combine HOG with multiple other features (e.g. with LBP [17], with edgelets and covariance descriptors [18]), *i.e.*, they consider heterogeneous features.

Different features try to capture different facets of a given image: edge distribution, intensity differences, appearance variations, *etc.* Using heterogeneous features, thus, helps acquire complementary information that could be useful to handle challenging detection tasks. This has clearly been demonstrated in the literature. To mention a few: Walk et al. [16] considered HOG, Histogram Of Flow, and CSS features and carried out different experiments by combining them combinatorially. The best results were reported when considering a feature set made up by concatenating the three sets. Schwartz et al. [13] presented a detection system composed of HOG, color frequency features, and co-occurrence features, asserting similar conclusions. The same goes to Hussain and Triggs [7] whom considered feature sets made up of HOG, LBP, and Local Ternary Patterns (LTP).

The main issue to consider with heterogeneous features is how to combine them. The trivial approach is to concatenate all features to make a very high dimensional vector and use SVM as a classifier [16]. The downside with this is the high computation time required to extract the complex features and to apply the SVM weights on each candidate window which inevitably leads to low frame rates. Applying a dimensional reduction scheme [7,13] might help performance and speed up training period, but, it still suffers during detection because of the data projection involved. In addition, different features could possibly be best dealt with different classifiers–they could for example lie in linear or non-linear spaces which may require different classification techniques [18].

A second approach is to gather all heterogeneous features in one big pool and learn an ensemble classifier using a boosting technique. Employing an attentional cascade configuration [14] is natural with this as it speeds up detection drastically. This has the added advantage that different classifier types well suited to a specific feature could be used as weak learners in the boosting framework. Representative works include the works of Dollár et al. [2], which used heterogeneous integral channel features in a boosting framework, and Geronimo et al. [4], which combined EOH and Haar like features via AdaBoost. At each iteration of the boosting learning cycle, the feature which reflects the best detection performance on the training set, measured by the weighted classification error, is added to the ensemble. Evidently, this tends to favor complex features amongst different candidates irrespective of the associate computation time. The preferred way would be to weigh detection performance against computation time and privilege features that make a compromise between the two. In this vein, Jourdheuil et al. [8] proposed to add a multiplicative factor to penalize the criterion to minimize in AdaBoost with a normalized computation time corresponding to each feature. This way features are selected only if their combined detection performance and normalized computation time are better (have the minimum value) than the other candidates. The authors used this to detect persons in a stereo camera using features extracted from depth maps and images. Their implementation led to a detector with an acceptable detection performance and reduced computation time. Inspired by this, we use a similar formalization to learn a cascaded person detector on heterogeneous features extracted from monocular images. This work differs from [8] in three main aspects: First, it is intended for monocular images and hence employs five commonly used heterogeneous features that have never been considered all together. Second, unlike [8] which use a single node, it uses a cascaded configuration to allow early rejection for improved detection speed. Third, evaluations and results are presented on the INRIA public dataset [1]. These points conglomerated make the gist of the contribution this paper tries to make.

This paper begins by highlighting the different heterogeneous pool of features properly categorized in section 2. In section 3, it describes the classifier learning algorithm with emphasis on computation time consideration. Finally, experimental results are detailed in section 4 finishing off with concluding remarks in section 5.

2   Heterogeneous Pool of Features

The heterogeneous pool of features considered are a mix of both scalar and multi-dimensional features. Five different families of features are used. Scalar features: Haar like and Edge Orientation Histogram features; multi-dimensional features: Color Self Similarity, Local Binary Patterns, and Histogram of Oriented Gradients. Each feature family is extracted within a given fixed size image candidate window of 64x128 pixels. To generate the overcomplete set of features, the position and scale (width and height) of the region the features are computed is exhaustively varied within the candidate window. The computation time of each feature is determined irrespective of any implementation optimization that can be done during detection, e.g. use of caches to buffer some features. This helps establish an upper bound on it. For each feature considered, the computation time is made up of two components. A part associated with image pre-processing (including rudimentary feature preparation) that is mostly shared by features of the same family, and a second part pertaining to the feature extraction and necessary computation during detection (e.g., multi-dimensional feature projection). For a feature indexed by j, these are represented as $\tau_{p,j}$ and $\tau_{e,j}$ consecutively; the combined computation time of that feature becomes $\tau_j = \tau_{p,j} + \tau_{e,j}$. These values are determined by averaging over $1,000$ times repeated computation iterations.

2.1   Scalar Features

Haar Like Features. Haar like features represent a fast and simple way to compute region differences. These features have been extensively used for face, person, and various object detections, e.g. [4, 9, 11, 14]. For a given feature, the response is obtained by subtracting the sum of pixels spanned by the black region from the sum of pixels spanned by the white region. In this work, we have used the extended Haar like features from Viola and Jones [14] and Lienhart and Maydt [9], which contains upright and tilted filters of various configurations as shown in fig. 1. In our implementation, a horizontal and vertical stride of 2 pixels is used to generate the overcomplete set, $\mathcal{F}_{haar}$. As these features furnish scalar feature values, a decision tree is used as a weak classifier. Computationally, these features are very cheap to extract. The pre-processing stage

Fig. 1. Set of extended Haar like features used

for this family of features corresponds to the integral image computation. The feature extraction is carried out efficiently with a few additions and subtractions on the integral image; feature evaluation (prediction) during detection is done via a table lookup operation (using a table expanded from the decision tree).

Edge Orientation Histogram (EOH). EOH is another feature set that has been used for person detection [4]. These features represent ratios of gradients computed from edge orientations histograms. Within a given overlaid region, first gradients are computed. Then, a gradient histogram is built by quantizing the gradient orientations. Finally, the ratios of each histogram bin with one another makes up individual features. The overcomplete EOH feature pool set, denoted $\mathcal{F}_{EOH}$, is constructed by extracting feature values for all possible combinations of overlaid region location and size within the candidate window.In this work, gradient orientation quantization levels of 4 (shown to give best results in [4]) and horizontal and vertical strides of 4 pixels are used. Owing to the scalar feature values, decision trees are used as a weak classifier.

The pre-processing step, here, corresponds to the gradient computation (this is also shared by HOG features). The feature extraction relates to the gradient histogram construction and bin ratio computation. Similar to Haar like features, the feature evaluation during detection is merely a memory lookup operation.

2.2 Multi-dimentional Features

Color Self Similarity (CSS). CSS features, proposed by Walk et al. [16], encode color similarities in different sub-regions. To compute the features, first the image window is subdivided into non-overlapping blocks of 8x8 pixels. Then within each block, a 3x3x3 color histogram in HSV space is built with interpolation. Then, similarities are computed by intersecting individual histograms. In [16], all histogram intersections values are used to define one feature vector. But, here, we define the intersection of one histogram block with the rest of the blocks as a single feature. With an 8x8 block size and 64x128 candidate window, there are 128 different blocks. The intersection of one block with the rest gives 127 scalar values (excluding intersection with itself). These

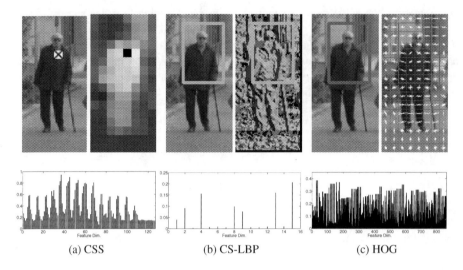

    (a) CSS   (b) CS-LBP   (c) HOG

Fig. 2. Sample extracted multi-dimensional features

scalar values all together make the feature vector computed for the block location. This is repeated for each block resulting in 128 different features, the CSS feature pool set ($\mathcal{F}_{CSS}$), of 127 dimensions each. Fig. 2a shows an exemplar feature computed at the crossed block position. The figure at the bottom is an unrolled representation of the feature shown at the top right; observe how neighboring blocks are similar. These features are few in number and multi-dimensional, hence, SVM is used as a weak classifier.

The complete set of features extracted from this family rely on a histogram computed once for each block. If one feature is extracted, extracting another feature involves using the same histogram with changed reference block for the histogram intersection. Keeping this in mind, the pre-processing stage encompasses the histogram computation. The rest of the computation time is consumed by the extraction (histogram intersection) and the multiplication by the SVM hyperplane during detection.

Local Binary Pattern (LBP). Local Binary Patterns were initially proposed as a texture characterization features [10]. Since then, they have been used in many applications–primarily facial analysis, e.g. [19], and person detection, e.g. [17]. To date, many variants of LBP have been proposed. In this work, we adhere to Center-Symmetric Local Binary Pattern (CS-LBP) as feature because of the short histograms it furnishes and its demonstrated good performance on person datasets [6]. In our implementation, CS-LBP is computed over a 3x3 pixel region (best results reported in [6]) by comparing the opposite pixels and adding a modulated term accordingly (see [6] for detail). This gives a scalar value less than 16 which is assigned to the center pixel. This is done for all the pixels in the candidate window, top right image in fig. 2b (values are scaled to aid visibility). Finally, the actual feature is constructed by constructing a CS-LBP histogram over a given overlaid region. Fig. 2b bottom shows an exemplar histogram obtained from the overlaid rectangular region shown on top. Similarly, by varying the position and scale of the overlaid region exhaustively within the candidate window gives the LBP feature pool, denoted $\mathcal{F}_{CLBP}$. The histograms have 16 bins corresponding to CS-LBP quantization levels. Since the feature vectors are no more scalar, Fisher's Linear Discriminant Analysis (LDA) with decision tree is used as a weak classifier. Fisher LDA is preferred over SVM because of its comparatively short training duration. Given the large number of features in this feature pool family (table 1), employing SVM would lead to an overwhelming training period.

The pre-processing stage for this feature family corresponds to the raw CS-LBP feature computation. The rest is made up of histogram construction (extraction phase), and LDA projection during detection.

Histogram of Oriented Gradients (HOG). HOG features are extracted first by computing the gradient, then by constructing a histogram weighted by the gradient in an atomic region called a cell. Histograms of neighboring cells are grouped into a single block, cross-normalized and concatenated to give a feature vector per block. The final extracted feature within a given detection window is the concatenation of the vectors from each feature block (details in [1]). In this work, we use the original HOG features as proposed by Dalal and Triggs [1] with a cell size of 8x8 pixels, a feature block size of 2x2 cells and an 8 pixel horizontal and vertical stride. For a given overlaid region, the feature vector corresponds to a concatenation of all block features within it. The overcomplete set, $\mathcal{F}_{HOG}$, is then generated by varying the location and scale of the overlaid region. Fig. 2c demonstrates a sample feature computed in this manner. Computation time wise, the gradient computation falls in the pre-processing step and the rest in the extraction part.

Table 1. Feature pool summary with minimum and maximum feature computation time in each feature family. Time is reported as a multiple of the cheapest feature computation time of 0.0535 μs.

Feature Type	No of features	τ_{min}		τ_{max}		Weak Classifier
		$(t_p)_{min}$	$(t_e)_{min}$	$(t_p)_{max}$	$(t_e)_{max}$	
Haar like	672,406	0.6	0.4	1.88	1.6	Decision Tree
EOH	712,960	2.72	2.11	315.65	2.1	Decision Tree
LBP	59,520	1.24	14.26	111.6	282.04	LDA + Decision Tree
CSS	128	560.75	457.19	560.75	457.19	SVM
HOG	3,360	10.59	479.12	315.75	51103.8	SVM

Table 1 summarizes the characteristics of the heterogeneous pool of features considered. The total number of features in each family, the minimum and maximum feature computation time (both pre-processing, t_p, and extraction, t_e)–scaled with 0.0535 μs[1] which corresponds to the combined computation time of cheapest feature, a two boxed horizontal Haar feature–along with the weak classifier used are listed. Finally, the complete feature pool is determined by merging all heterogeneous feature pool sets, i.e. $\mathcal{F} = \{\mathcal{F}_{Haar}, \mathcal{F}_{EOH}, \mathcal{F}_{CLBP}, \mathcal{F}_{CSS}, \mathcal{F}_{HOG}\}$. The computation time of each individual feature is denoted as τ_j, where $j \in \{1, 2, ..., |\mathcal{F}|\}$. Each feature is also associated with a weak learner h_j that maps each instance of the training set to a discrete label, $h_j : X \rightarrow \{-1, +1\}$.

---

[1] Computed on a core i7 machine running at 2.4 Ghz

3   Classifier Learning Algorithm

3.1   Feature Computation Time

Equation 1 shows the smoothed normalized computation time, $\tilde{\tau}_j$, for each feature which will be used within AdaBoost. $\beta \in [0, 1]$ is an exponential smoothing coefficient. $\tau_{max,i}$ denotes the maximum computation time registered within each distinct feature pool family, *i.e.*, $i \in \{Haar, EOH, CLBP, CSS, HOG\}$.

$$\tilde{\tau}_j = \frac{\tau_j^{\beta}}{\sum\limits_{i} \tau_{max,i}^{\beta}} \tag{1}$$

The computation time associated with each feature, $\tau_j = \tau_{p,j} + \tau_{e,j}$, is not constant (consequentially $\tilde{\tau}_j$ changes too). The exact value evolves during the classifier learning stage. It changes in two cases. The first is when a feature that has already been selected is considered in future cascade nodes, and the second is when a feature from the same family gets selected. In the prior case, the computation time of the selected feature is replaced by a constant time, τ_0, in future references which accounts for only memory access. In the latter case, the computation time for all of the features in the same family gets affected, specifically, the time associated with the pre-processing stage, $\tau_{p,j}$, is set to zero for all the features in that family. This is logical and is done to favor features of the same family. For example, if a Haar feature is selected, it will better to consider another Haar feature so the integral image computation can be done once for the area spanned by the two features, rather than considering another feature from a different family which will require a different pre-processing step. This way the computation time of the features within the same family will be levied significantly speeding up detection. Accordingly, the normalized computation time of all affected features is updated. The computation time, $\mathcal{T}_k$, of a trained cascade node k is determined straightforward by adding the computation time of each selected component features (associated weak learners), *i.e.*, $\mathcal{T}_k = \sum\limits_{t=1}^{T} \tau_t$. Here, an index t is used to signify reference of a selected feature and T represents the total number of features in this cascade node.

3.2   Modified Discrete AdaBoost

Given the complete heterogeneous feature pool, $\mathcal{F}$, and associated computation time, $\{\tau_j\}_{\{j=1,2,...,|\mathcal{F}|\}}$, a modified version of Viola and Jones Discrete AdaBoost [14] is used to learn a strong classifier for each node of the cascade. As discussed in section 2, each feature is associated with a unique weak learner, h_j, that maps the given training set X to a discrete label, *i.e.*, $h_j : X \rightarrow \{-1, +1\}$ [2]. The original Discrete AdaBoost algorithm constructs a strong classifier by iteratively selecting the best weak classifier, h_t, based on the error distribution on the training set, ϵ_j, weights it, with α_t, and adds it to the ensemble. Each subsequent addition tries to correct the errors made by previously added

---

[2] Because of this we can use a weak learner and a feature interchangeably.

Algorithm 1. Modified Discrete AdaBoost

Given: A set of labeled examples $\{(x_m, y_m)\}\{m = 1, ..., (n_+ + n_-)\}$ where $x_m \in X$, $y_m \in Y = \{-1, +1\}$

Extract Features: $\mathcal{F} = \{\mathcal{F}_{Haar}, \mathcal{F}_{EOH}, \mathcal{F}_{CLBP}, \mathcal{F}_{CSS}, \mathcal{F}_{HOG}\}$

Initialize: $D_1(m) = \dfrac{1}{(n_+ + n_-)}$ \\distribution over training samples

For $t = 1, ..., T$

- Select 3000 features randomly, $\mathcal{F}^* \subset \mathcal{F}$
- Find the best weak learner $h_t : X \rightarrow \{-1, +1\}$

  - **Compute** $\tilde{\tau}_j = \dfrac{\tau_j^\beta}{\sum\limits_i \tau_{max,i}^\beta}$

  - $h_t = \underset{h_j \in \mathcal{F}^*}{\arg\min}\ \tilde{\tau}_j * \epsilon_j$ where $\epsilon_j = \sum\limits_{m=1}^{n_+ + n_-} D_t(m)[y_m \neq h_j(x_m)]$
- **Update the computation time of the selected feature τ_j to τ_0**
- **Update the computation time of the features in the same family as the selected feature by setting their pre-processing time to 0, i.e., $\tau_j \leftarrow \tau_{e,j}$**
- $\alpha_t = \dfrac{1}{2}\ln\dfrac{1 - \epsilon_t}{\epsilon_t}$
- $D_{t+1}(m) = \dfrac{D_t(m)\exp(-\alpha_t y_m h_t(x_m))}{Z_t}$ \\$Z_t$ is a normalization factor used to make D_{t+1}

  a distribution

Strong classifier: $H(x) = \mathrm{sign}(\sum\limits_{t=1}^{T} \alpha_t h_t(x))$ **Computation time of cascade node:** $\mathcal{T} = \sum\limits_{t=1}^{T} \tau_t$

---

weak classifiers. The modification here is to select the best weak classifier that minimizes the error weighted with a normalized computation time of the features, equation 2. This modification enables AdaBoost to select the feature (weak learner) that offers the best compromise between computation time and detection error. This is detailed in algorithm 1 (main modifications on the classical one are shown in bold typeface).

$$h_t = \underset{h_j \in \mathcal{F}}{\arg\min}\ \tilde{\tau}_j * \epsilon_j \tag{2}$$

Given the vast number of features involved, looping through each feature set at each iteration of AdaBoost is infeasible. Hence, as is commonly done, e.g. in [18,20], at each AdaBoost iteration 3000 features are randomly sampled, proportional to the number of features from each family, to build the strong per node classifier incrementally. 3000 is well way above the suggested number of trials, ≈ 299, required to obtain amongst the best 0.05 estimates of random variables with a probability of 0.99 [12](pp. 180). Once, the required detection performance, specified a priori via a Node Miss Rate (NMR) and Node False Positive Rate (NFPR), is achieved on a separate validation set, the feature addition stops and the node is retrained using both the training and validation set up until the previously validated number of features have been added (see [14] for details). The final ensemble obtained is the strong classifier for this node and construction proceeds to the next node.

3.3 Cascade Construction

The cascade detector construction is inspired by the works of Viola and Jones [14]. The detection performance requirement of each cascade node are specified by two parameters, the NMR and NFPR. Given a total of N_+ and N_- cropped positive and negative training windows respectively (bear in mind $N_- \gg N_+$), the construction begins by randomly selecting a subset of negative windows, n_-, and using all positive training windows, $n_+ = N_+$. This is divided into a training and validation set, in our case 60% and 40% respectively. Following, the modified AdaBoost is used to learn the strong classifier for this node using the heterogeneous features set.

This learning is monitored via the validation set; at each boosting iteration the zero threshold is lowered to see if the strong classifier meets the NMR and NFPR criteria. When that is achieved, the AdaBoost is retrained using the whole training and validation set to the point determined during validation. This completes the construction of the first node. Henceforth, all N_- are tested with the trained node and all those that get misclassified (harder examples) are used in consecutive stages of the cascade. The process continues until such a point where the number of negative windows is less than the positive windows, in which case the construction terminates furnishing the whole detector cascade. The MR and FPR of the entire cascade are products of the nodes NMR and NFPR consecutively.

4   Experiments and Results

4.1   Evaluation Metrics

To evaluate the detection performance, Detection Error Tradeoff (DET) curves with Miss Rate versus False Positive Per Window (FPPW) on a log-log scale are used [1]. To determine these values the True Positives, False Positives, True Negatives, and False Negatives of the test set are determined via a per-window approach [3]. The per-window approach relies on cropped labeled positive and negative train and test set. The training is performed using these cropped images and the test likewise (please refer [3] for details).

4.2   Dataset

Experiments are carried out using the public INRIA person detection dataset [1]. The training set for this dataset consists of 2,416 cropped positive instances and 1,218 images free of persons (out of which many negative train cropped windows are generated). The test set contains 1,132 positive instances and 453 person free images for testing purposes. This is the most widely used dataset for person detector validation and comparative performance analysis. For constructing the cascade the complete positive instances and randomly sampled, at different scales and locations, 2.55×10^6 negative cropped instances from the training set are used. During cascade construction, the number of negative windows per each node, n_-, has been kept equal to the positive windows n_+, *i.e.*, 2,416. For testing, the $1,132$ positive instances and uniformly sampled 2×10^6 cropped windows from the test set are used.

4.3   Results

Validation: In our framework the parameters that need to be specified are per node NMR and NFPR and the depth of the decision tree to use. Since we want the cascade to detect all possible positive instances, a 0.0 NMR is used for each node. The NFPR on the other hand affects the number of cascade nodes built. Higher values result in more number of nodes to exhaust the training set. As a compromise, NFPR of 0.5 is used so each node is required to discard at least 50% of the incoming candidate windows.

The best depth of the decision trees for Haar like features, EOH, and LBP features is determined empirically using a 1 fold cross validation. A decision tree depths of 2, 3, and 3 are used for Haar like features, EOH features, and LBP features respectively. The weak classifiers learned using these depths offer a better trade off between detection performance and overfitting on the validation set. Computing Fisher LDA weights, for LBP features, per each node makes the classifier overfit on the training set with deteriorated performance on the validation set. Hence, the LDA weights for LBP computed at the first node are used throughout the cascade by learning only new decision trees.

Similarly, the exact value of β, the computation time smoothing exponential factor, to use in the modified AdaBoost is determined empirically through a validation step. The modified AdaBoost is used to learn a single nodal cascade using different β values on a subset of the training set. Then the classification errors on a validation set and the conglomerated computation time of the trained node is determined to select the best value that offers a good trade-off. Fig. 3 shows the validation result plots for different values of β. Clearly, higher β reduces smoothing, in effect, features with low computation time dominate improving speed but with poor detection performance. Lower values favor complex features. As a compromise, a β value of 0.2 is used to train the final cascade classifier.

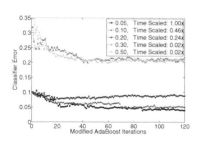
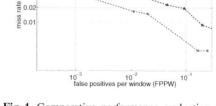

Fig. 3. β parameter tuning in the modified algorithm

Fig. 4. Comparative performance evaluation of the cascade detector on the INRIA dataset

Table 2. Proportion of features in the final cascaded detector

	Haar like	EOH	LBP	CSS	HOG	Average Time Improvement
Classical AdaBoost	25.36%	53.79%	10.16%	4.00%	6.67%	1.0x
Modified AdaBoost	86.72%	0.00%	9.14%	2.40%	3.90%	1.8x

Test results: A complete boosted cascade detector is learned using the framework presented, *i.e.*, with a modified computation time weighted AdaBoost, using the combined training and validation dataset (referred as modified AdaBoost hereafter). As a benchmark, a second complete cascade detector is also learned using the classical Discrete AdaBoost (referred as classical AdaBoost hereafter). The modified AdaBoost cascade has ten nodes with a combined total of 821 features. The minimum and maximum number of features per node are 6 in the first and 350 on the 7th node, respectively. The proportion of selected features from each family is shown in table 2. The most used features are Haar like features, 86.72%, and the least are CSS features, 2.40%. Compared to the classical cascade, there is smaller number of the complex multi-dimensional features. No EOH features are selected. This is because, Haar like and EOH features exhibit comparable detection performance but Haar like features have less computation time thus are privileged. The selected features for the first node of the cascade are shown in fig. 5. For HOG and LBP, the illustrations show the support region of the selected features. The four selected Haar like features are also shown in fig. 5c and 5d. Indeed, four out of six selected features are from the computationally cheapest feature category.

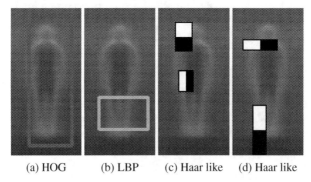

(a) HOG   (b) LBP   (c) Haar like   (d) Haar like

Fig. 5. The features selected and used in the first node of the cascade superimposed on an average human gradient image

The performance of this modified detector on the test set is depicted as an MR vs FPPW plot in fig. 4. It achieves a 0.06 MR at 10^{-3} FPPW. This is a 2% loss compared to the detection performance achieved by the classical AdaBoost at the same FPPW. But, this reduction results on an average 1.8× accelerated speed. The final detector misses only 97 persons out of the total 1132 tested instances. A majority of these mistakes correspond to persons with non-upright/non-conventional poses. Some of the detection mistakes are shown in fig. 6 for both positive and negative samples.[3]

---
[3] Sample detections are not shown here due to space constraints. Please visit homepages.laas.fr/aamekonn/acivs/ for illustration.

(a)	(b)	(c)	(d)	(e)	(f)	(g)	(h)

Fig. 6. Sample misclassified positive (a to d) and negative (e to h) instances

5   Conclusion

In conclusion, in this work, a computation time weighted AdaBoost has been presented to learn a cascaded person detector using heterogeneous pool of features. The final detector achieves 1.8× average speed up compared to a classical AdaBoost based cascade with only a 2% detection performance loss at 10^{-3} FPPW. At this point, it is capable of detecting persons with a very low Miss Rate of 6% as demonstrated on the INRIA public dataset.

Currently, investigations are on the way to use this detector in a tracking-by-detection framework in the context of Robotic navigation in crowds.

Acknowledgment. This work was supported by a grant from the French National Research Agency under grant number ANR-12-CORD-0003.

References

1. Dalal, N., Triggs, B.: Histograms of oriented gradients for human detection. In: Proc. CVPR, pp. 886–893 (2005)
2. Dollar, P., Tu, Z., Perona, P., Belongie, S.: Integral channel features. In: Proc. BMVC, pp. 1–11 (2009)
3. Dollar, P., Wojek, C., Schiele, B., Perona, P.: Pedestrian detection: An evaluation of the state of the art. IEEE T-PAMI 34(4), 743–761 (2012)
4. Gerónimo, D., López, A., Ponsa, D., Sappa, A.D.: Haar wavelets and edge orientation histograms for on–board pedestrian detection. In: Martí, J., Benedí, J.M., Mendonça, A.M., Serrat, J. (eds.) IbPRIA 2007. LNCS, vol. 4477, pp. 418–425. Springer, Heidelberg (2007)
5. Geronimo, D., Lopez, A., Sappa, A., Graf, T.: Survey of pedestrian detection for advanced driver assistance systems. IEEE T-PAMI 32(7), 1239–1258 (2010)
6. Heikkil, M., Pietikinen, M., Schmid, C.: Description of interest regions with local binary patterns. Pattern Recognition 42(3), 425–436 (2009)
7. Hussain, S., Triggs, B.: Feature sets and dimensionality reduction for visual object detection. In: Proc. BMVC, pp. 1–10 (2010)
8. Jourdheuil, L., Allezard, N., Chateau, T., Chesnais, T.: Heterogeneous adaboost with real-time constraints - application to the detection of pedestrians by stereovision. In: Proc. VIS-APP, pp. 539–546 (2012)
9. Lienhart, R., Maydt, J.: An extended set of haar-like features for rapid object detection. In: Proc. ICIP, pp. 900–903 (2002)

10. Ojala, T., Pietikinen, M., Harwood, D.: A comparative study of texture measures with classification based on featured distributions. Pattern Recognition 29(1), 51–59 (1996)
11. Papageorgiou, C., Poggio, T.: A trainable system for object detection. IJCV 38(1), 15–33 (2000)
12. Scholkopf, B., Smola, A.J.: Learning with Kernels: Support Vector Machines, Regularization, Optimization, and Beyond. MIT Press, Cambridge (2001)
13. Schwartz, W.R., Kembhavi, A., Harwood, D., Davis, L.S.: Human detection using partial least squares analysis. In: Proc. ICCV, pp. 24–31 (2009)
14. Viola, P.A., Jones, M.J.: Robust real-time face detection. IJCV 57(2), 137–154 (2004)
15. Viola, P.A., Jones, M.J., Snow, D.: Detecting pedestrians using patterns of motion and appearance. In: Proc. ICCV, pp. 734–741 (2003)
16. Walk, S., Majer, N., Schindler, K., Schiele, B.: New features and insights for pedestrian detection. In: Proc. CVPR, pp. 1030–1037 (2010)
17. Wang, X., Han, T., Yan, S.: An HOG-LBP human detector with partial occlusion handling. In: Proc. ICCV, pp. 32–39 (2009)
18. Wu, B., Nevatia, R.: Optimizing discrimination-efficiency tradeoff in integrating heterogeneous local features for object detection. In: Proc. CVPR, pp. 1–8 (2008)
19. Zhao, G., Pietikainen, M.: Dynamic texture recognition using local binary patterns with an application to facial expressions. IEEE T-PAMI 29(6), 915–928 (2007)
20. Zhu, Q., Yeh, M.C., Cheng, K.T., Avidan, S.: Fast human detection using a cascade of histograms of oriented gradients. In: Proc. CVPR, pp. 1491–1498 (2006)

Perspective Multiscale Detection of Vehicles for Real-Time Forward Collision Avoidance Systems

Juan Diego Ortega[1], Marcos Nieto[1], Andoni Cortes[1], and Julian Florez[2]

[1] Vicomtech-IK4, Paseo Mikeletegi 57, San Sebastian, Spain
{jdortega,mnieto,acortes}@vicomtech.org
[2] Tecnun, University of Navarra, Paseo Manuel Lardizabal 13, San Sebastian, Spain
florez@tecnun.es

Abstract. This paper presents a single camera vehicle detection technique for forward collision warning systems suitable to be integrated in embedded platforms. It combines the robustness of detectors based on classification methods with an innovative perspective multi-scale procedure to scan the images that dramatically reduces the computational cost associated with robust detectors. In our experiments we compare different implementation classifiers in search for a trade-off between the real-time constraint of embedded platforms and the high detection rates required by safety applications.

Keywords: Intelligent Transportation Systems, Object Detection, Machine Learning, Pattern Recognition.

1 Introduction

Problems concerning traffic mobility, safety, and energy consumption have become more serious during the past decades as the number of vehicles in the roads has increased. Particularly, a large emphasis has been given to develop Advanced Driver Assistance Systems (ADAS) incorporated to vehicles to try to help the driver reduce his workload while driving, preventing accidents and its associated societal and economical impact. Services like Lane Departure Warning, Blind Spot Detection and Forward Collision Warning had grown mature, just to mention a few, mainly due to the research in computer vision and the reduced costs of cameras and embedded processors.

Considering the challenges of extracting information about the environment of the vehicle with video processing techniques, vehicle detection is one of the more complex, mainly because of i) the varying appearance of objects of the same class, ii) the process of image acquisition (variable illumination, rotations, translations, scales, distortions, etc.), iii) the moving background induced by the motion of the vehicle, and iv) the real-time requirement of most applications.

Many approaches in the field of Forward Collision Warning Systems combine radar and vision (using supervised machine learning) technologies for detecting vehicles [3]. However, radar-based systems only work relatively well with metallic and reflectant objects and are very expensive. This makes vision-based a very

J. Blanc-Talon et al. (Eds.): ACIVS 2013, LNCS 8192, pp. 645–656, 2013.

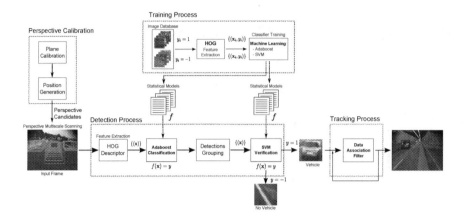

Fig. 1. Proposed approach of the system

interesting alternative due to its cost-effectiveness and ability to detect any object without relying on the object material's properties. Nevertheless, an existing drawback in vision-based approaches is the limited computational capabilities of embedded processors and the computationally demanding nature of vision systems.

The trend in vision-based systems applied to object detection is to use detection-by-classification approaches, combined with an exhaustive scanning of the whole image at different scales, looking for possible locations of the object. Such multiscale approaches are not practical for embedded platforms due to the elevated computational cost and the application real-time requirements. Hypothesis generation (HG) algorithms [2] are, therefore, normally used as a previous step to the hypothesis verification (HV) which usually involve using statistical classifiers. HG usually rely on simple techniques such as color segmentation, edge detection, symmetry and shadows, etc [12]. However, these are likely to be less robust than detection-by-classification and can throw a large number of undesirable false positives and false negatives, which within safety systems is not acceptable.

In this paper we propose to combine the use of detection-by-classification methods with calibration information of the scene to find a trade-off between the robustness of these detectors with the real-time requirements of vehicle detection in embedded platforms. We propose to exploit the known perspective of the scene, which can be computed with a calibration stage, to generate a perspective multi-scale scan grid of the image. Such perspective-based grid dramatically enhance the HG stage which is much more efficient focusing on positions in the image likely containing vehicles and decreasing the computational cost associated to traditional detection-by-classification.

The detection stage was carried out using a linear Adaboost classifier trained with Histograms of Oriented Gradient (HOG) [5] of the training images. It is common to combine HOG descriptors with linear Support Vector Machine (SVM) classifiers. Nonetheless, in this paper we show that it is possible to get similar results with Adaboost-HOG classifiers with lower classification time.

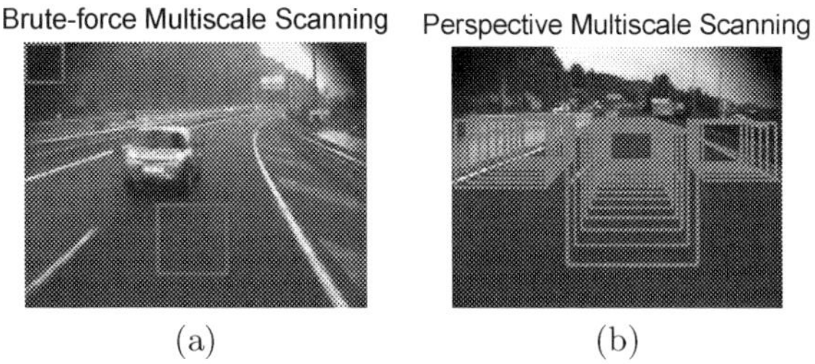

Brute-force Multiscale Scanning   Perspective Multiscale Scanning

(a)   (b)

Fig. 2. Posible scanning aproaches: (a) Brute-force and (b) Perspective multi-scale (please note that we have used a very reduced amount of rectangles in this figure for a better understanding; the actual configuration of the grid is governed by two parameters defining the distances between 3D parallelepipeds)

An analysis of the training and testing errors of these statistical classifiers is shown in order to validate our results.

The detection of vehicles in our system consists in an initial phase of classification of perspective-related positions using an Adaboost classifier trained with HOG features. A posterior grouping of the detection is carried out to reduce the number of candidates which are finally verified using an SVM classifier, also trained with HOG features.

The proposed detection strategy in this paper can be easily used in combination with tracking strategies for applications like robust real-time forward collision avoidance systems. Our experiments hold our decisions and show that this is actually a good way to proceed, compared to other options or combination of methods. To understand the framework proposed, the entire system is depicted in figure 1. Besides, we show detailed performance numbers of our system in real conditions, using a hand labeled ground truth reference.

2   Perspective Analysis of the Scene

The calibration of the camera and the computation of its relative pose with respect to the ground plane offers valuable information for the detection of vehicles in images. In this work we propose to formalize the exploitation of the perspective of the scene by means of computing the projection matrix and defining a multi-scale detection approach according to it.

Figure 2 illustrates the proposed approach: (a) the simplest way to proceed once a detector has been trained is to run a multi-scale scanning of the image evaluating each image patch with the classifier in order to determine the presence of objects in the image, we have called this method *brute-force multiscale*; (b) when the projection matrix is known, we can determine a grid of positions in the 3D world in front of the camera where vehicles might appear, and project them into the image. The main difference between these alternatives is that the perspective analysis of the scene focuses significantly the effort of the classifier resulting in a much more efficient scan of the image.

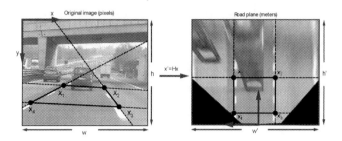

Fig. 3. Points correspondences between the image plane and road plane

2.1   Ground Plane Calibration

The calibration of the scene required to apply the proposed perspective multi-scale approach can be obtained in a two-steps process: (i) obtain the intrinsic parameters K of the camera using well known calibration methods [8]; (ii) determine the relative rotation R and translation $\mathbf{t}$ between the camera coordinate system, and a coordinate system on the ground plane (we assume the ground plane to be planar since it is a common practice by many authors [9]). For simplicity in terms of computational cost, the above extrinsic parameters are computed offline and keep constant.

The second step can be done in a variety of ways, although we propose to use a homography between the image and the ground plane. The world or road coordinate system can be selected such that the road plane is defined by $Z = 0$. In such situation, the projection of a point $\mathbf{X} = (X, Y, Z, 1)^{\top}$ into a image point $\mathbf{x}$ yields:

$$\mathbf{x} = K(R|\mathbf{t})\mathbf{X} = K(\mathbf{r}_1\ \mathbf{r}_2\ \mathbf{r}_3\ \mathbf{t})\left(X\ Y\ 0\ 1\right)^{\top} \tag{1}$$

and therefore $\mathbf{x} = K(\mathbf{r}_1\ \mathbf{r}_2\ \mathbf{t})\left(X\ Y\ 1\right)^{\top}$, which is a 3×3 homography between the image and world plane points: $H = K(\mathbf{r}_1\ \mathbf{r}_2\ \mathbf{t})$.

If we calibrate the homography matrix, we have $K^{-1}H = (\mathbf{p}_1\ \mathbf{p}_2\ \mathbf{p}_3)$.

This way, once we have computed and calibrated the homography we can extract the rotation and traslation from the columns of the resulting matrix. Note that since these are homogeneous matrices it is necessary to normalize the columns of the matrix in order to get the vectors: $\mathbf{r}_1 = \frac{\mathbf{p}_1}{\|\mathbf{p}_1\|}$, $\mathbf{r}_3 = \frac{\mathbf{p}_2}{\|\mathbf{p}_2\|}$ and $\mathbf{r}_2 = \mathbf{r}_1 \times \mathbf{r}_3$.

The homography H can be computed using a variety of methods, although the simplest one is to use the Direct Linear Transform (DLT [8]) which computes the homography from four point correspondences. Figure 3 illustrates the concept of point correspondences between the image plane, and the world plane (e.g. a road plane in this example).

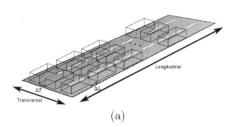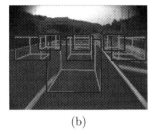

(a)   (b)

Fig. 4. (a) Grid of 3D vehicle positions: ΔT is the distance between positions in the transversal axis; and ΔL the distance in the longitudinal axis. These values can be defined to have overlaping parallelepipeds. (b) Parallepipeds projections in the image plane (light blue) and bounding boxes (dark blue). For seek of clarity only a few intances are drawn.

2.2 Vehicle Position Generation

Once knowing the camera calibration matrix K and the extrinsic parameters, the projection matrix can be constructed as $P = K[R|\mathbf{t}]$. It can be used to project 3D points into the image. Therefore, we can model a vehicle as a parallelepiped and create a grid of interest positions on the ground plane. The grid can be defined with two parameters, ΔL and ΔT, as the longitudinal and transversal distances between positions in the grid respectively in the directions of the plane. Figure 4 (a) depicts the composition of the grid.

The projection of a parallelepiped in an image is a convex polygon whose bounding box can be easily computed and used to determine the region of the image that will be evaluated with the classifier. Figure 4 (b) shows the set of projections of the grid into an image and the corresponding bounding boxes.

This parameterization makes the system very flexible and adaptable to the computational resources available. The higher values of ΔL and ΔT the lower processing cost of the algorithm, although at the cost of having more sparse detections.

3   Detection Stage

Supervised learning is commonly employed in detection-by-classification tasks in computer vision. The goal of supervised learning is to learn the function $y = f(\mathbf{x})$, where $\mathbf{x}$ is an unseen input feature vector and y is the output variable. In classification problems the output variable is the label to which the input feature vector belongs to (in our case, "vehicle" or "non-vehicle").

Discriminative learning methods have been used in the majority of works referred to object and vehicle detection [10]. Within this kind of methods, variations of SVM and Adaboost algorithms stand out in the literature[2]. The main idea underlying the training of classifiers is to find a model which could map the input feature vector to a set of output labels. The training stage involves the application of supervised training algorithms to a set of feature vectors extracted from the image database. This database must have positive images (e.g. "vehicles") and negative images (e.g. "non-vehicles"). In this work we have used a public available database of rear-view vehicle images (GTI-UPM vehicle database [1]), which consists of 3425 positive and 3900 negative images. The result of the training is a statistical model used in the detection stage. Both Adaboost and SVM implementations of the training algorithms have been evaluated.

An important decision in pattern recognition and machine learning is the set of image features with which the images will be represented. This is, feature extraction process is carried out before classifier training. Different combinations of classfiers and feature decriptors have been reported in the literature such as Haar-like features and a cascade of boosted classifiers [13], Gabor Filters and SVM [11] or HOG and SVM [5]. In this paper we propose a combination of Adaboost and SVM classifiers trained with HOG descriptors due to its outstanding capabilities to visually describe objects.

3.1   HOG Feature Vector

The HOG method [5] consists on evaluating well-normalized local histograms of image gradient orientations in a dense grid. The basic idea is that local object appearance and shape can often be characterized by the distribution of local intensity gradients or edge directions, even without precise knowledge of the corresponding gradient or edge position. It captures edge or gradient structure that is very characteristic of local shape, upholding invariance to geometric and photometric transformations, except for object orientation. Therefore, it makes this method an interesting alternative to use in our task of vehicle detection.

In our system, four configurations of HOG decriptors were tested in combination with the learning algorithms. These configurations result in different feature decriptors which vary in length depending on the parameters chosen to compute the HOG. The proposed configurations are presented in table 1.

Table 1. HOG descriptor configurations used for training vehicle classifiers

	HOG-1	HOG-2	HOG-3	HOG-4
Image size (pixels)	64 × 64	64 × 64	32 × 32	32 × 32
Cell size (pixels)	8	8	4	4
Block size (pixels)	16	16	8	8
Num. of bins, β	9	18	9	18
Block stride (pixels)	8	8	4	4
Descriptor length	1764	3528	1764	3528

Note that the image size used for computing the descriptors restricts the minimum size of an object to be detectable. Therefore, this restriction could determine the HOG configuration to use in a practical problem.

3.2 Adaboost Classifiers

Binary classifiers are obtained using the Dicrete Adaboost algorithm described in [7]. Adaboost, which stands for *Adaptive Boosting* produces an additive classifier which is a linear combination of several weighted weak classifiers. We denote the set of N training points as $(\mathbf{x}_1, y_1), \ldots, (\mathbf{x}_N, y_N)$, where each $\mathbf{x}_i$ is an $n-dimensional$ input vector such that $\mathbf{x}_i \in \mathbb{R}^n, i = 1, \ldots, N$ and $y_i \in \{-1, +1\}$, indicates the class to which the point $\mathbf{x}_i$ belongs.

The goal of Adaboost learning algorithm is to estimate a function:

$$f : \mathbf{x}_i \in \mathbb{R}^n \mapsto y_i \in \{-1, +1\} \tag{2}$$

Moreover, it can be interpreted as a procedure for iteratively fitting an additive model using a set of basic functions or weak learners, h_t, repeatedly over a series of rounds $t = 1, \ldots, T$, [6]. The final model is a linear combination of the weak learners weighted by a set of values, α_t, $t = 1, \ldots, T$. The final strong model, thus, has the form:

$$f(\mathbf{x}) = \sum_{t=1}^{T} \alpha_t h_t(\mathbf{x}), \tag{3}$$

Hence, the decision function is given by equation (4):

$$f(\mathbf{x}) = \text{sign} \left(\sum_{t=1}^{T} \alpha_t h_t(\mathbf{x}) \right) \tag{4}$$

For our application, decision trees were selected as weak learners since they are the most popular weak classifiers used in boosting schemes. Additionally, their simplicity makes the training of Adaboost classifiers an easy and quick task.

3.3 SVM Classifiers

The SVM algorithm [4] finds the hyperplane defined in (5) which best separates the training examples by maximizing the distance between the closest elements of the two classes and the hyperplane. This distance is called margin.

$$(\mathbf{w} \cdot \mathbf{x}) + b = 0, \quad \mathbf{w} \in \mathbb{R}^N, b \in \mathbb{R} \tag{5}$$

where $\cdot$ is the dot product and $\mathbf{w}$ is a normal vector to the hyperplane and b is the classification threshold of the model. Thus, the decision function yields:

$$f(\mathbf{x}) = sign\,(\mathbf{w} \cdot \mathbf{x} + b) \tag{6}$$

To simplify the training, linear SVM were used in conjuction with the four configurations of HOG decriptors of table 1. SVM parameters where chosen taking the recommendation of Dalal and Triggs [5]; where a soft linear SVM was used for training their classifiers. However, a trial and error study was done to

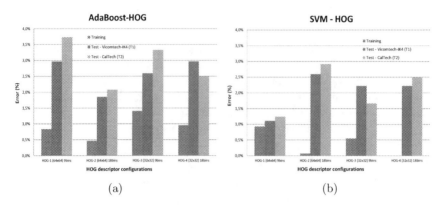

Fig. 5. Training and testing errors: (a) Adaboost-HOG, (b) SVM-HOG classifiers

tune the parameters so that a better performance is obtained for our application. As stated in the decription of our system, SVM classifiers are used to verify the hypothesis generated by the Adaboost classifier. In this way, computation time will be reduced.

3.4   Classifiers Training and Testing

The vehicle detection strategy proposed in this paper establishes the use of Adaboost as a first stage and a SVM classification as a verification stage. Both classifiers were trained using HOG features. The GTI-UPM vehicle database was used for training, although we have tested our classifiers with two additional testing databases, denoted as "Vicomtech-IK4 (T1)" and "Caltech (T2)". The former contains 155 positive and 115 negative images, which were obtained from video sequences in roads in San Sebastian. The latter is a public available image database of vehicles [14] and consists of 126 positive and 115 negative high-resolution images.

Results of the training and testing errors for Adaboost and SVM are shown in figure 5. For our study, these errors were defined as the proportion of missclassified images over the total number of images in the database. To calculate the errors, the image sets undergo a classification process. The results of the classification are then compared with the labeled data, resulting in an error rate. The final error comprises the resultant misclassification rate. For training error the image database was the one used for training while for testing error the databases used where completely unkown by the classsifier.

The global training error gives some notions of how well the learning algorithm could separate the feature space used for training. Regarding the global testing error, the process is analogous but using a totally unseen set of images. In this matter, the global testing error comprises the generalization capacity of the statistical classifier. Notice that, in most of the cases, SVM classifiers achieved lower testing errors than Adaboost. However, SVM requiere much more time

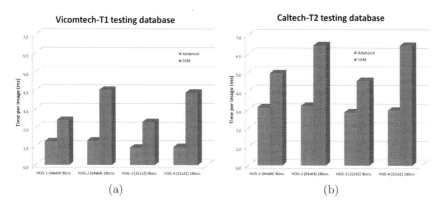

Fig. 6. Execution times between Adaboost and SVM classifiers for: (a) Vicomtech-T1 and (b) Caltech-T2 databases

for training the classifiers, namely, an average of 62% more time is needed for training an SVM. The difference in training time is likely to be due to the intrinsic properties of each of the learning algorithms used for learning. Adaboosts splits the data to generate the best decision trees while SVM solves a quadratic programming optimization problem [4].

The difference in behaviour was also evidenced in execution time. Time for processing each image in the database was also computed and compared. The improvement in time using Adaboost classification ranges between 30% to 70% when comparing the time for classifying an image with SVM (times per image are depicted in figure 6).

Thus, our detection strategy uses an Adaboost classifier to classify the candidate position retrieved by the perspective multiscale calibration. Then, a grouping process is carried out in order to reduce the number of hypothesis to be verified in the next stage. The latter will group in one candidate hypothesis all those bounding boxes which overlap each other. Finally, these candidates are verified using a SVM classifier.

4   System Test and Discussion

The proposed algorithm has been tested using image sequences of highways captured under different ilumination and weather conditions so that robustness could be verified. Additionally, a sample two minutes ground truth video containing several challenging situations (entering and exiting a tunnel, heterogeneous pavement color, casted shadows, overtaking maneouvres, etc) was annotated and has been used to extract values of true positives (TP) and false positives (FP) by applying a bounding box overlapping criterion.

For the sake of completeness we have applied a simple tracking algorithm which joins detections in time attending to their coherency in position and appearance, and uses a Kalman Filter to predict the position of given tracks in the absence of detections (which tends to happen using detection-by-classification).

The objective of this section is to compare our system with the default brute-force multiscale detection strategy normally used with classifiers. This method consists on scanning the entire image at different positions and scales. In each position an SVM classifier is executed, which imply the extraction of the HOG features. Three parameters define the total number of evaluating windows in the brute-force multiscale method: the scale at which the searching window changes in size, s, the number of levels each window is resized, $nLevels$, and the stride at which the window moves across the image frame. For this comparison, we fixed the scale and window stride to 1.05 for the former and the cell size for the latter. In this way, only the $nLevels$ is involved.

On the other hand, our method is dependant of the number of longitudinal and transversal level used for creating the perspective grid. Different configurations of perspective multiscale and brute-force multiscale were tested for comparison and compared in terms of execution time and values of TP and FP.

The feature descriptor vector used for testing was the HOG-3. This is, the minimum window size is 32×32 pixels and hence, the minimimum vehicle size detectable. We have chosen this feature descriptor because our video size, 320×240 pixels, has vehicle instances which are very small. Depending on the frame resolution it is possible to use a different configuration of HOG descriptor, achieving similar results.

In table 2 are presented the results from applying **perspective multiscale** and **brute-force multiscale** to our ground truth video. Tests were done in an IntelÂŎ CoreâĎć i5-3330 CPU 3.00 GHz, 8.00 GB RAM.

Table 2. Results of Perspective Multiscale and Brute-force multiscale

Perspective Multiscale						Brute-force Multiscale				
# Hypotheses	ΔL	ΔT	T(ms)	TP	FP	# Hypotheses	$nLevels$	T(ms)	TP	FP
10	3000	1000	2.3	153	155	3869	1	11.2	95	263
18	3000	600	3.8	214	204	7613	2	11.4	114	492
20	1500	1000	4.5	236	189	11357	3	11.7	137	661
29	1000	1000	4.4	207	201	35746	10	30.6	264	844
34	3000	333	4.9	308	391	51156	15	32.7	332	878
37	1500	600	5.2	300	318	64287	20	33.9	320	1275
54	1000	600	6.3	279	329	74941	25	34.6	288	1513
70	1500	333	8.2	368	455	82787	30	36.8	283	1262
104	1000	333	10.4	352	512	87630	35	40.7	284	1238

As expected, the execution time of the brute-force multiscale increases considerably as the number of levels increase. The raise in the number of evaluation windows produce an increase in the value of TP; however more FP are also encountered. Moreover, tests had proven that brute-force multiscale could not process the video at real-time when the number of scales is greater than 10.

Fig. 7. Examples of detections in real videos

On the other hand, our method is able to process the image in much less processing time without reduction in detection performance. Brute-force multiscale generates more false positives as the number of levels increases. The advantange of using the knowledge of the perspective scene allows our classifiers to focus in regions where vehicles are more likely to appear. Then, no time is wasted scanning absurd hypothesis (very large and very small vehicles) or out the relevant regions of the image.

The use of Adaboost as a first classification stage provides the best performance. Adaboost was trained using decision threes as weak learners, which are very fast structures to be accesed. Hence, the classification time is very low comparing to SVM. The combination of Adaboost and SVM makes the algorithm robust and fast. SVM reduces the ammount of false positives that were generated by Adaboost classification without increasing significantly the computational cost of the algorithm.

Some results of the detection system are illustrated in figure 7. As can be observed, very different vehicles, in terms of size, colour or aspect-ratio are successfully detected, highly accurately delimiting their contour.

As a reference, we have shown the feasibility of our approach for embedded platforms implementing an instance of the algorithm in an ARM processor. The computing limitation of an ARM device are well-known, hence a fast and reliable system is required. Tests were carried out using the perspective multiscale in an ARM® dual-core Cortex™-A9 MPCore™ / 800 MHz, 512 MB DDR3 using 10 longitudinal positions and 3 transverse positions (i.e. 20 hypothesis positions). An approximate procesing time of 40ms (25fps) was obtained.

5   Conclusions

We have presented an efficient way of detecting vehicles in videos using the knowledge of the perspective of the scene in combination with machine learning classifiers. This approach has reduced processing times by detecting vehicles in two stages. First, a fast yet robust Adaboost-HOG classifier is applied on regions of the image defined by a perspective-based scan process, which allows to focus the attention in the regions where vehicle appearance is most likely neglecting uninteresting or absurd hypotheses. Then, an intermediate grouping phase is done to reduce the number of detections. Finally, an SVM classifier validates the hypotheses. The proposed detector can be combined with any kind of tracking system. In this work, a simple tracking system is proposed which will be extended in future publications. Our perspective multiscale system has proved to achieve better execution times than using a regular brute-force multiscale, getting reductions in time of more than 50%. The results show that our approach is suitable to be integrated in embedded platforms achieved a trafe-off between robustness and accuracy, while keeping real-time operation.

Acknowledgements. This work has been partially supported by the program ETORGAI 2011-2013 of the Basque Government under project IEB11.

References

1. Arróspide, J.: GTI vehicle database (2012), http://www.gti.ssr.upm.es/data/
2. Arróspide, J.: Vision-based vehicle detection and tracking with a mobile camera using a statistical framework. Ph.D. thesis, Universidad Politécnica de Madrid (2012)
3. Bertozzi, M., Bombini, L., Cerri, P., Medici, P., Antonello, P.C., Miglietta, M.: Obstacle detection and classification fusing radar and vision. In: Intelligent Vehicles Symposium, pp. 608–613. IEEE (2008)
4. Cortes, C., Vapnik, V.: Support-vector networks. Machine Learning 20(3), 273–297 (1995)
5. Dalal, N., Triggs, B.: Histograms of oriented gradients for human detection. In: Proc. Computer Vision and Pattern Recognition, vol. 1, pp. 886–893. IEEE (2005)
6. Freund, Y., Schapire, R.E.: A decision-theoretic generalization of on-line learning and an application to boosting. In: Vitányi, P.M.B. (ed.) EuroCOLT 1995. LNCS, vol. 904, pp. 23–37. Springer, Heidelberg (1995)
7. Friedman, J., Hastie, T., Tibshirani, R.: Additive logistic regression: A statistical view of boosting. The Annals of Statistics 28(2), 237–407 (2000)
8. Hartley, R.I., Zisserman, A.: Multiple view geometry in computer vision. Cambridge University Press (2004)
9. Kim, Z.: Robust lane detection and tracking in challenging scenarios. IEEE Transactions on Intelligent Transportation Systems 9(1), 16–26 (2008)
10. Papageorgiou, C., Poggio, T.: A trainable system for object detection. International Journal of Computer Vision 38(1), 15–33 (2000)
11. Sun, Z., Bebis, G., Miller, R.: Improving the performance of on-road vehicle detection by combining gabor and wavelet features. In: Proc. Int. Conf. on Intelligent Transportation Systems, pp. 130–135. IEEE (2002)
12. Sun, Z., Bebis, G., Miller, R.: On-road vehicle detection using optical sensors: A review. In: Proc. International Conference on Intelligent Transportation Systems, pp. 585–590. IEEE (2004)
13. Viola, P., Jones, M.: Rapid object detection using a boosted cascade of simple features. In: Proc. Computer Society Conf. on Computer Vision and Pattern Recognition, vol. 1, pp. 511–518. IEEE (2001)
14. Weber, M.: Caltech rear view car image database (1999), http://www.vision.caltech.edu/html-files/archive.html

Learning and Propagation of Dominant Colors for Fast Video Segmentation

Cédric Verleysen and Christophe De Vleeschouwer

Université catholique de Louvain, ICTEAM institute,
Place du Levant 2, B-1348 Louvain-La-Neuve, Belgique
cedric.verleysen@uclouvain.be

Abstract. Color segmentation is an essential problem in image processing. While most of the recent works focus on the segmentation of individual images, we propose to use the temporal color redundancy to segment arbitrary videos. In an initial phase, a k-medoids clustering is applied on histogram peaks observed on few frames to learn the dominant colors composing the recorded scene. In a second phase, these dominant colors are used as reference colors to speed up a color-based segmentation process and, are updated on-the-fly when the scene changes. Our evaluation first shows that the proprieties of k-medoids clustering make it well suited to learn the dominant colors. Then, the efficiency and the effectiveness of the proposed method are demonstrated and compared to standard segmentation benchmarks. This assessment reveals that our approach is more than 250 times faster than the conventional mean-shift segmentation, while preserving the segmentation accuracy.

Keywords: Segmentation, clustering, color learning, k-medoids, box-cox transform.

1 Introduction

Video segmentation has always been a major topic in computer vision and multimedia. Indeed, partitioning the frames of a video into non-overlapping areas with different semantical contents has tremendous applications in data compression, tracking, augmented reality, activity or object recognition, video annotation and video retrieval. Although all these applications are very different from each other, the developed segmentation methods can be categorized into two classes.

The first class of segmentation algorithms aims at partitioning each frame of an arbitrary video, that could represent static scenes, into a complete set of non-overlapping regions. In this case, despite the strong temporal redundancy of video frames, most of the proposed methods still segment the frames individually. For example, in [9], a frame-by-frame process ($2D$) first smoothes the images using a variant of anisotropic diffusion and then merge the neighboring color pixels according to their color similarity. In [19] and [5], a frame-to-frame framework ($2D + t$) is used to associate independent segmentations of $2D$ frames and refine the segmented regions. Because image segmentation methods are often quite costly both in memory resources and in computational power [13],

J. Blanc-Talon et al. (Eds.): ACIVS 2013, LNCS 8192, pp. 657–668, 2013.
© Springer International Publishing Switzerland 2013

such approaches are unsuitable for real-time applications. Spatio-temporal segmentation methods (segmenting directly the $3D$ volume of the video) have also been recently investigated [15]. Specifically, due to its good performances on various type of images/videos, mean-shift segmentation [7] has gained considerable attention these last years. However, because of its slow convergence [6], this algorithm is also not adapted to real-time applications.

The second class of methods aims at segmenting a specific moving object in a video sequence. In this case, it is possible to take advantage of the motion analysis to segment the object. For example, Ellis and Zografos [10] use a semi-supervised appearance learning method coupled with a motion segmentation algorithm to perform on-the-fly segmentation. However, because the segmented region is determined using motion features, their fast segmentation method is restricted to moving objects, as it is the case in [17] and [16].

In this paper, we combine the strengths of both classes by proposing a color segmentation algorithm that autonomously learns the dominant colors of the recorded scene, and both propagates forward and updates this weak prior to speed-up the segmentation. More precisely, on a few frames at the beginning of the video sequence, the dominant colors composing the scene are recursively determined using a k-medoids algorithm applied on the principal mode of the images color histograms. On the next frames, these dominant colors are used as reference colors to segment the frames into regions of approximatively uniform color. The approach is especially relevant when dealing with video sequences whose color distribution does not significantly change over time. In that case, the initial training phase just needs to be run once on few frames at the beginning of the sequence, to define the dominant colors for the whole sequence. This case typically happens both when the camera viewpoint does not significantly change over time, like in surveillance contexts capturing scenes with still cameras, and when capturing a scene with low variance color distribution, as it happens in sport scenes for example. To make our method valid for arbitrary sequences, we however propose a simple approach to update the set of dominant colors when required. By restarting the learning process when a certain percentage of the pixels are not represented by the list of learnt dominant colors, we avoid regular manual corrections of the propagated segmentation cues, as done in [2] and [20]. Moreover, as it is shown in Section 3.1, because the dominant colors are determined by k-medoids clustering, the learnt colors are actually present in the image. This enable to create artistic stylizations (e.g. cartoons and paintings) without manual rectification of the colors, as opposed to [25].

This paper is organized as follows. The proposed algorithm is first described in Section 2. Section 3.1 shows that the better robustness of a k-medoids clustering makes it more adapted for the learning of dominant colors than the usual k-means clustering. Finally, in Section 3.2, we highlight the key advantage of our approach by showing that the computation time of the proposed color segmentation is significantly smaller than the one of conventional segmentation methods working without color prior, such as the mean-shift algorithm, while preserving the segmentation effectiveness.

2   Color Segmentation with Autonomous Learning of Dominant Colors

This section introduces the main contribution of our work, which consists in exploiting dominant color priors to segment the video stream in a spectaculary efficient, whilst effective, manner. As illustrated in Algorithm 1, the proposed approach relies on three complementary phases: the learning of dominant colors, the fast color segmentation and the update of the learnt dominant colors. Each phase is individually detailed in the rest of this section.

Algorithm 1 . Fast color segmentation algorithm

Input: *videoStream*, N (amount of frames to learn a dominant color),
            T_1 (thresholds the color dissimilarity) and T_2 (triggers the state change)
Output: $\{segFrame_i\}$ (the segmented frames of *videoStream*)

Initialize: $i \leftarrow 1$; $n \leftarrow 1$; *isLearning* $\leftarrow true$; *isStable* $\leftarrow false$; $D_c \leftarrow [\ ]$; $D_{\text{tmp}} \leftarrow [\ ]$;

Procedure:
while NOT(end of *videoStream*) **do**
    $I \leftarrow getFrame(videoStream, i)$;
    $segFrame_i \leftarrow [\ ]$;
    if *isLearning* OR NOT(*isStable*) **then**
        $mask \leftarrow \{\mathbf{x} \mid (d(I, \mathbf{x}, D_c) > T_1)\}$;
        $D_{\text{tmp}} \leftarrow \text{concatenate}\big(D_{\text{tmp}}, \underset{b \in \mathbf{bins}}{\text{argmax}}\ hist3D(I(mask))\big)$;
        $n \leftarrow n + 1$;
        if $n > N$ **then**   } Learning phase
            $D_c \leftarrow \text{concatenate}\big(D_c, \text{kmedoids}(D_{\text{tmp}}, k = 1)\big)$;
            $D_{\text{tmp}} \leftarrow [\ ]$; $n \leftarrow 1$; *isLearning* $\leftarrow false$;
        end if
    end if
    if NOT(*isLearning*) **then**
        ∘ Replace each pixel $\mathbf{x}$ of I with its closest (minimum   } Running phase
          $d(I, \mathbf{x}, D_c)$) dominant color of D_c and store in $segFrame_i$;
        ∘ Compute percentage p of pixels $\mathbf{x}$ with $d(I, \mathbf{x}, D_c) > T_1$;
        if $p > T_2$ **then**
            if *isStable* **then**
                ∘ Remove from D_c the dominant color with the
                  largest mean dissimilarity $d(I, \mathbf{x}, D_c)$;
                isStable $\leftarrow false$;   } Update phase
            end if
            isLearning $\leftarrow true$;
        else
            isStable $\leftarrow true$;
        end if
    end if
    $i \leftarrow i + 1$;
end while

2.1 Learning Phase: Determination of the Dominant Colors

The learning phase recursively determines the dominant colors based on sets of N consecutive frames. Each set is used to learn a new dominant color[1], by taking into account only the pixels that are not similar with the previous learnt dominant colors. More precisely, let D_c denote the list of the first c dominant colors identified on c previous sets of N consecutive frames. The recursive learning process starts with an empty set D_0 of identified dominant colors. A pixel of coordinate $\mathbf{x} \in \mathbb{R}^2$ of a frame I (where $I \in \mathbb{R}^{m \times n \times d}$ is the image, m is the height of the image, n is its width and d is its number of channels) of the $(c+1)^{\text{th}}$ set is said to be active if its distance to all colors in D_c is larger than a threshold T_1. The distance between a color pixel $I(\mathbf{x})$ and a reference color $C \in \mathbb{R}^d$ is computed using a variant of the robust contrast adaptive color dissimilarity proposed in [4]:

$$d(I, \mathbf{x}, C) = 1 - \exp \left(\frac{-\|I(\mathbf{x}) - C\|^2}{2\langle \|I - C\|^2 \rangle} \right)$$

where $\|I(\mathbf{x}) - C\|$ is the $\mathcal{L}_2$ norm of the RGB color difference and $\langle . \rangle$ is the expectation operator. To learn the jth dominant color, the color that appears the most frequently among the active pixels of each frame of the jth set is computed. Because this value corresponds to the highest peak in the color d-dimensional histogram of the active pixels, we name it the first histogram mode. By assuming that the color distribution of the recorded scene does not significantly change over the N consecutive frames of the jth set, the vectorial center of these N accumulated first histogram modes gives a reliable representation of the jth dominant color. In Section 3.1, two different definitions of vectorial centers, namely centroid and medoid, and their associated computation methods (k-means clustering and k-medoids clustering), will be compared. As it will be seen, because of its robustness to noisy data, medoid is chosen to define the dominant color from a set of N first histogram modes. Also, because the authors of [23] have shown that k-medoids clustering process runs faster than k-means (complexity of $\mathcal{O}(ikl)$, where i is the total number of iterations, k is the total number of clusters, and l is the total number of data points) under normal distribution of the data points, we first pre-process the N first histogram modes in order to make them more normal distribution-like. Practically, this is done by stabilizing their variance with a box-cox transform [3]. For a vector $[x_1 \ldots x_P]$ of strictly positive entries ($x_p > 0$, $\forall\, p \in [1; P]$), the box-cox transform determines a parameter $\lambda \in \mathbb{R}$ such as to maximize the correlation of the transformed data distribution with a normal distribution plot. The following transformation is then applied:

$$x_p^{(\lambda)} = \begin{cases} \frac{x_p^\lambda - 1}{\lambda} & \text{if } \lambda \neq 0 \\ \log(x_p) & \text{if } \lambda = 0 \end{cases}$$

---

[1] Instead of learning multiple dominant colors per set, we propose to reduce N.

Although the box-cox transform preserves the similarity of the orderings of the data, the imperfect symmetry of the transformed distribution could produce a small bias in the medoid estimation. However, in practice, as observed in [11], this bias has only a negligible impact on the final solution, while enabling an important speed-up. Finally, the learning process stops if the percentage of pixels that are correctly approximated by one of the learnt dominant colors reaches a threshold T_2, *i.e.* when the percentage of active pixels drops below T_2.

2.2   Running Phase: Fast Color Segmentation

Once the dominant colors have been determined, they are used as color priors in a segmentation process. First, based on the robust color distance presented previously, all the pixels of a new frame are compared with all the learnt dominant colors. For a given pixel, only the smallest distance and the index of the associate dominant color are stored. After, despite the use of a robust metric for labelization, it could happen that some pixels are not labelled consistently, *i.e.* their label does not correspond to the label of the surrounding pixels that belong to the same region. It mainly appears when the sensor used to record the scene is noise sensitive or when the video is highly compressed, leading to wrong local colors or noisy frames. For this reason, we propose to filter the result of the labelization process by a median filter (size 3×3). In this way, the frames are segmented into regions of uniform color and connected pixels.

2.3   Update Phase: Renewing of the List of Dominant Colors

In the two last sections, a color prior has been learnt and propagated temporally. However, in both static and dynamic camera setups, the color distribution generally changes over time. For this reason, we propose to extend the list of learnt dominant colors by learning several new dominant colors from batch of N consecutive frames when the percentage of active pixels overshoot T_2. In order to avoid a discontinuous segmentation of the frames, these N frames are also segmented using D_c. Also, to limit the expansion of the list of learnt dominant colors, we delete the least representative dominant color from D_c, *i.e.* the one with the highest mean color dissimilarity $d(I, \mathbf{x}, C)$, before adding a newly learnt dominant color. Finally, the switch from the update phase to the running phase is done when the percentage of active pixels drops below T_2.

3   Experimental Validation

In this section, we first show the necessity of determining each dominant color in a robust way. This is done by comparing the results of two different validations. The first validation learns a dominant color by representing the set of accumulated first histogram modes by its centroid (computed via k-means clustering), while the second one represents the set by its medoid[2] (computed via

---

[2] A medoid can be seen as a generalization of a median value when the dimension of the data space is higher than 1.

k-medoids clustering). This comparison support the well-known robustness of k-medoids over k-means clustering [23], which makes it more adapted to learn the dominant colors. After, the efficiency and the effectiveness of the proposed segmentation method are evaluated on three different datasets.

3.1   Comparison between k-means and k-medoids Learning

K-means [21] and k-medoids [23] are both partitions-based clustering methods. They aim at dividing a database into groups, such that the samples that belong to the same group are similar and those belonging to different groups are dissimilar. More precisely, a partitioning method generates k clusters from a given set of n data objects. Because image/video segmentation is defined as partitioning n pixels into separated regions, such methods are thus perfectly adapted to the segmentation problem. However, while k-means clustering has been deeply investigated in segmentation [24,18], k-medoids tends to be rarely used.

K-medoids and k-means differ in the way of representing a cluster. While k-means represents a cluster by the average value (called centroid) of its associated data, k-medoids takes the most centrally located data (called medoid) of the cluster to represent it. The fact that the k-medoids method defines a cluster by its most representative point has two major consequences:

- K-medoids clustering is robust to outliers and noisy data, as opposed to k-means clustering [23]. Indeed, while a mean is highly sensitive to extreme values, a medoid is perfectly suited to derive a representative tendency from its central sample, even in skewed distributions.
- By definition, a medoid belongs to the data space. In contrast, if the space is not convex, a centroid (average) may lie outside the space. This might end up in the definition of a reference "dominant" color that is close to several colors of the scene, without actually matching any of those colors.

These two fundamental differences between k-means and k-medoids are illustrated in Figure 1.

The first row represents different frames taken from a video. The second row represents the first histogram mode for each frame, as defined in Section 2.1. The third row illustrates the dominant color computed by the 1-means clustering (left) and 1-medoids clustering (right), based on the set of first histogram modes extracted from the frames. Because this video focuses on a panda, we expect the first dominant color to be either black or white.

As a first observation, the first histogram mode detected on the third frame corresponds to the bright color of the wall. It can thus be considered as an outlier in the set of first histogram modes, where the black color of the panda is preponderant. The grey dominant color learnt by k-means clustering (third row of Fig. 1) shows that this outlier highly attracts the centroid in the k-means clustering, while it does not influence the medoid of the k-medoids clustering. The learning of dominant colors based on k-means clustering is thus strongly biased by noisy data, while a learning based on k-medoids clustering is robust.

Frames

Color of the first histogram mode

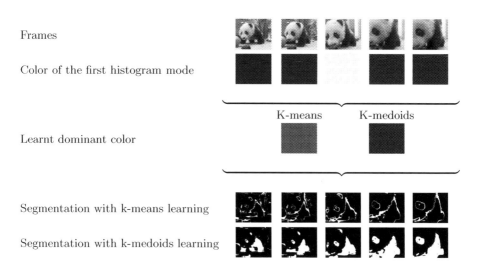

K-means   K-medoids

Learnt dominant color

Segmentation with k-means learning

Segmentation with k-medoids learning

Fig. 1. The dominant color (3rd row) determined on the first histogram modes (2nd row) of a video (1st row) shows that a learning based on k-medoids clustering (5th row) is more robust to noisy data than one based on k-means (4th row)

As a second observation, the dominant color learnt by k-means clustering (grey) does not represent a color of the panda. Any segmentation algorithm that tries to segment the panda based on this learnt dominant color will thus fail, as illustrated in the fourth row of Fig. 1. At the opposite, the last row of Fig. 1 shows that k-medoids clustering is well adapted to recursively learn the reference colors used in a color-based segmentation. Those two observations led us to prefer k-medoids over k-means clustering. In the proposed method, k-medoids clustering is thus applied to determinate a dominant color from N first histogram modes. To still decrease the sensitivity to noisy data in the determination of a dominant color, the medoid is defined by minimizing the sum of the L_1 dissimilarities to the data, instead of the common euclidian distance.

3.2 Performances

The efficiency and the effectiveness of the proposed segmentation method are evaluated on three different datasets. On the one hand, as the ground-truths are not available for the first dataset, we visually compare our results with others. On the other hand, the ground-truth of the second dataset is used to objectively measure the efficiency of the proposed algorithm. Finally, the last dataset validates the effectiveness of the proposed update phase.

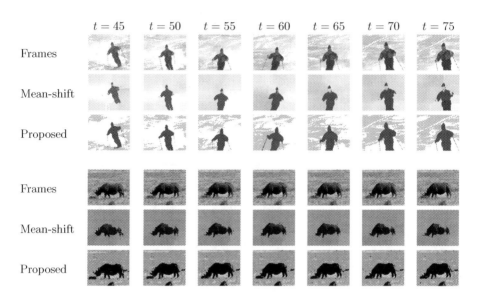

Fig. 2. For a dense segmentation ($T_1 = 0.35$ and $T_2 = 1$ in our method; $h_s = 50$ and $h_r = 30$ for the mean-shift segmentation), a learning of the dominant colors on $N = 15$ frames gives similar segmentation results, while segmenting more than 250 times faster

Fig. 3. For an over-segmentation ($T_1 = 0.2$ and $T_2 = 1$ in our method; $h_s = 50$ and $h_r = 10$ for the mean-shift segmentation), a learning of the dominant colors on $N = 5$ frames gives similar segmentation results, while segmenting more than 250 times faster

Frames

Fukuchi
et al [12]

Proposed

Fig. 4. Our method achieves similar effectiveness than [12], while using only a weak prior in the segmentation process ($N = 3$, $T_1 = 0.65$ and $T_2 = 1$)

The first dataset, proposed by [12], is composed of several video clips representing natural scenes and is used to give a qualitative comparison between our video segmentation method and the conventional mean-shift algorithm [8]. Figure 2 (Figure 3) illustrates the results of both algorithms when the color range parameters (h_r in the mean-shift algorithm and T_1 in our method) are high (low), in such a way to segment the video into a very small (high) amount of regions. First of all, as shown on these figures, the proposed method preserves the segmentation effectiveness. After, the computational complexity (in terms of running time of a Matlab implementation on a 3GHz Intel I7 CPU, 8Gb RAM machine) of both methods has been evaluated on all the video sequences of this dataset. This assessment shows that while the mean-shift algorithm segments at approximatively 0.026 fps, our algorithm is more than 250 times faster (7.24 fps).

In Figure 4, we propose a similar qualitative comparison between our method and the one proposed in [12] (from which this first dataset has been provided). By extracting the regions corresponding to the dominant color of the fox, we can see that our method achieves similar effectiveness, while using only a weak prior in the segmentation process.

The second evaluation is used to go one step beyond the general validations proposed in video segmentation, by giving a complementary quantitative assessment. To the best of the authors' knowledge, no segmentation ground-truth exists for the entire frames of a video. However, elaborated benchmarks and ground-truths are available for individual image segmentation. For this reason, we evaluate the accuracy of the proposed video segmentation method on videos constituted of a repetition of these test images. This validation is thus complementary to the first one: after having shown that the learning and segmentation of our method are effective, we objectively assess their efficiency. We follow the segmentation evaluation methodology proposed by [1], by computing the

Table 1. Our method outperforms conventional algorithms

Algorithms	F-measure
Proposed method	**0.94 ± 0.107**
Alpert et al. (CVPR'07) [1]	0.86 ± 0.012
Galun et al. (ICCV'03) [14]	0.83 ± 0.016
Shi and Malik (PAMI'00) [22]	0.72 ± 0.018
Comaniciu and Meer (PAMI'02) [8]	0.57 ± 0.023

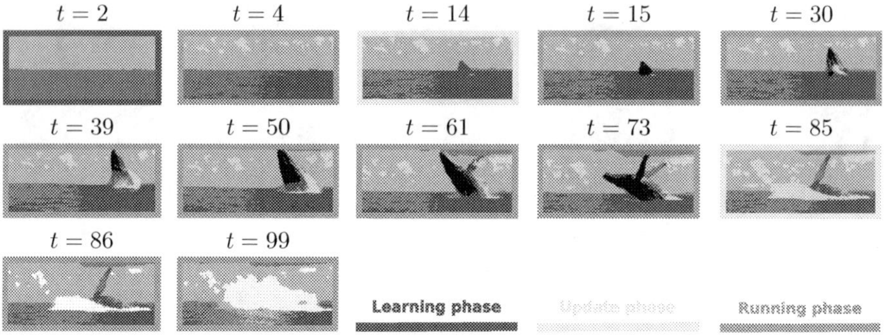

Fig. 5. The list of dominant colors is updated on-the-fly when the colors of the scene change (segmentation obtained with $N = 1$, $T_1 = 0.2$ and $T_2 = 1$)

F-measure (harmonic mean of precision and recall [1]) on segmentation results obtained on various complex images and multiple corresponding ground-truths. In Table 1, the F-measure of our method is compared with several standard methods and shows that our method outperforms them.

As a last validation, we proof the effectiveness of the update of the dominant colors. Figure 5 illustrates a video of another dataset, proposed by [15]. As a first observation, only few frames are dedicated to learn and update the list of dominant colors. More precisely, in this arbitrary video, less than 8% of the frames are used either for the learning or for the update phase, explaining the high computing speed of our algorithm. As a last observation, the effectiveness of the update phase is demonstrated at $t = 14$ and $t = 85$. Indeed, because of the apparition of the whale at $t = 14$, the list of dominant colors is automatically updated by detecting and adding its dark color. Also, at $t = 85$, when the whale falls back in the sea, the list of dominant colors is anew updated, because of the apparition of the light color representing the scum.

4   Conclusion

In this article, a computationally efficient video segmentation method has been presented. The proposed approach learns, on few frames at the beginning of the video sequences, the dominant colors representing the recorded scene. We have shown that k-medoids clustering is more adapted than k-means clustering to recursively and robustly determine these dominant colors. This color prior is then used to speed-up a fast on-the-fly color-based segmentation of the next frames of the video sequence. To deal with videos in which the color distribution of the scene changes over time, we have proposed and validated an approach to update the list of learnt dominant colors. Finally, the efficiency and the effectiveness of the proposed method have been demonstrated on three standard segmentation benchmarks. This assessment shows that our approach is more than 250 times faster than the conventional mean-shift segmentation, while overcoming the segmentation performances of some state-of-the-art methods.

References

1. Alpert, S., Galun, M., Basri, R., Brandt, A.: Image segmentation by probabilistic bottom-up aggregation and cue integration. In: Proc. of IEEE CVPR 2007, pp. 1–8 (June 2007)
2. Bai, X., Wang, J., Simons, D., Sapiro, G.: Video snapcut: robust video object cutout using localized classifiers. ACM SIGGRAPH 28(3), 70 (2009)
3. Box, G., Cox, D.: An analysis of transformations. Journal of the Royal Statistical Society. Series B (Methodological), 211–252 (1964)
4. Boykov, Y., Funka-Lea, G.: Graph cuts and efficient N-D image segmentation. IJCV 70(2), 109–131 (2006)
5. Brendel, W., Todorovic, S.: Video object segmentation by tracking regions. In: Proc. of IEEE ICCV 2009, pp. 833–840 (2009)
6. Carreira, M.: Gaussian mean-shift is an EM algorithm. IEEE PAMI 29(5), 767–776 (2007)
7. Cheng, Y.: Mean shift, mode seeking, and clustering. IEEE PAMI 17(8), 790–799 (1995)
8. Comaniciu, D., Meer, P.: Mean shift: A robust approach toward feature space analysis. IEEE PAMI 24(5), 603–619 (2002)
9. Dorea, C., de Queiroz, R.: Depth map reconstruction using color-based region merging. In: Proc. of IEEE ICIP 2011, pp. 1977–1980 (2011)
10. Ellis, L., Zografos, V.: Online learning for fast segmentation of moving objects. In: Lee, K.M., Matsushita, Y., Rehg, J.M., Hu, Z. (eds.) ACCV 2012, Part II. LNCS, vol. 7725, pp. 52–65. Springer, Heidelberg (2013)
11. Fitzmaurice, G.M., Lipsitz, S.R., Parzen, M.: Approximate median regression via the box-cox transformation. The American Statistician 61(3), 233–238 (2007)
12. Fukuchi, K., Miyazato, K., Kimura, A., Takagi, S., Yamato, J.: Saliency-based video segmentation with graph cuts and sequentially updated priors. In: Proc. of IEEE ICME 2009, pp. 638–641 (2009)
13. Fulkerson, B., Soatto, S.: Really quick shift: Image segmentation on a GPU. In: Kutulakos, K.N. (ed.) ECCV 2010 Workshops, Part II. LNCS, vol. 6554, pp. 350–358. Springer, Heidelberg (2012)
14. Galun, M., Sharon, E., Basri, R., Brandt, A.: Texture segmentation by multiscale aggregation of filter responses and shape elements. In: Proc. of IEEE CVPR 2003, pp. 716–723 (2003)
15. Grundmann, M., Kwatra, V., Han, M., Essa, I.: Efficient hierarchical graph based video segmentation. In: IEEE Conference on Computer Vision and Pattern Recognition, CVPR (2010)

16. Huang, Y., Liu, Q., Metaxas, D.: Video object segmentation by hypergraph cut. In: Proc. of IEEE CVPR 2009, pp. 1738–1745 (2009)
17. Li, Y., Sun, J., Shum, H.: Video object cut and paste. ACM SIGGRAPH 24(3), 595–600 (2005)
18. Mignotte, M.: A de-texturing and spatially constrained k-means approach for image segmentation. Pattern Recognition Letters 32(2), 359–367 (2011)
19. Moscheni, F., Bhattacharjee, S., Kunt, M.: Spatio-temporal segmentation based on region merging. IEEE PAMI 20(9), 897–915 (1998)
20. Price, B., Morse, B., Cohen, S.: Livecut: Learning-based interactive video segmentation by evaluation of multiple propagated cues. In: Proc. of IEEE ICCV 2009, pp. 779–786 (2009)
21. Seber, G.: Multivariate observations. Wiley (1984)
22. Shi, J., Malik, J.: Normalized cuts and image segmentation. IEEE PAMI 22(8), 888–905 (2000)
23. Velmurugan, T., Santhanam, T.: Computational complexity between k-means and k-medoids clustering algorithms for normal and uniform distributions of data points. Journal of Computer Science 6(3), 363–368 (2010)
24. Verleysen, C., De Vleeschouwer, C.: Recognition of sport players' numbers using fast color segmentation. In: Proc. of the SPIE-IS&T Electronic Imaging (SPIE 2012), vol. 8305 (2012)
25. Wang, T., Guillemaut, J., Collomosse, J.: Multi-label propagation for coherent video segmentation and artistic stylization. In: Proc. of IEEE ICIP 2010, pp. 3005–3008 (2010)

A Key-Pose Similarity Algorithm
for Motion Data Retrieval

Jan Sedmidubsky, Jakub Valcik, and Pavel Zezula

Masaryk University, Botanicka 68a, 602 00 Brno, Czech Republic
{xsedmid,xvalcik,zezula}@fi.muni.cz

Abstract. Analysis of human motion data is an important task in many research fields such as sports, medicine, security, and computer animation. In order to fully exploit motion databases for further processing, effective and efficient retrieval methods are needed. However, such task is difficult primarily due to complex spatio-temporal variances of individual human motions and the rapidly increasing volume of motion data. In this paper, we propose a universal content-based subsequence retrieval algorithm for indexing and searching motion data. The algorithm is able to examine database motions and locate all their sub-motions that are similar to a query motion example. We illustrate the algorithm usability by indexing motion features in form of joint-angle rotations extracted from a real-life 68-minute human motion database. We analyse the algorithm time complexity and evaluate retrieval effectiveness by comparing the search results against user-defined ground truth. The algorithm is also incorporated in an online web application facilitating query definition and visualization of search results.

1 Introduction

The development of motion capturing technologies (e.g., Microsoft Kinect) has caused an explosion in the usage of human motion data in different fields. For example, motion data are analyzed in sports to compare performance aspects of athletes, in security research to identify special-interest persons, in health care to determine the success of rehabilitative treatments, and in computer animation to synthesize realistic motions. In particular, production of high-quality computer games and animations requires an expensive and time-consuming synthesis of movements performed by specialized actors. To make animation and game production more efficient, there is a rising need to reuse the recorded motions in a database. One way is to manually or automatically annotate the database motions by textual descriptions [9,11,14]. Although it is very efficient in text retrieval, textual descriptions cannot always sufficiently express desired motions and limit users to search for only certain classes of movements. To overcome this limitation, content-based search techniques are used to retrieve motions that are similar to an arbitrary query motion example.

Content-based search techniques can be further divided to *sequence*-based and *subsequence*-based approaches. The sequence-based approaches [3,17,18] use a

J. Blanc-Talon et al. (Eds.): ACIVS 2013, LNCS 8192, pp. 669–681, 2013.

global similarity measure to compare entire motions against a query, and thus can not be meaningfully employed for matching motions of significantly different lengths. For example, a 5-minute dance motion can not be considered as globally similar to a 2-second pirouette motion. On the other hand, the 5-minute dance motion can contain several instances of pirouette *sub-motions* that are already meaningfully similar to the 2-second pirouette motion. To locate all such sub-motions, subsequence-based approaches are used. In this paper, we focus on the subsequence-based concept which constitutes a much harder task since up to 2^K possible sub-motions can exist in the motion of length K frames.

The crucial challenge of content-based sub-motion retrieval is to achieve high search *efficiency* (performance) and *effectiveness* (accuracy). The effectiveness is influenced by the choice of (1) the kind of motion features (e.g., distance-based [2] and relational [12]) extracted from the motion data and (2) a similarity function comparing the features of two (sub-)motions in space and time dimension. The appropriate choice of the motion features and the similarity function usually depends on the needs of the specific application. To achieve high search efficiency, the motion data have to be preprocessed offline. Considering the motion data as multidimensional time series, efficient preprocessing and subsequence retrieval techniques for general time series can be utilized [6]. Although there are quite a lot of existing papers on sub-motion retrieval, most of them primarily focus either on search effectiveness, or efficiency, disregarding their trade-off.

The early content-based approaches [2,7] indexed the motion data to efficiently obtain a set of sub-motion candidates that can be similar to a query. The obtained candidates were ranked by the Dynamic Time Warping (DTW) technique. However, DTW is not scalable for large candidate sets due to its quadratic time complexity. To reduce time complexity to linear, several systems have been developed to speed up similarity search [5,8,15]. However, all these approaches did not evaluate search accuracy by considering both recall and precision.

Search accuracy was already evaluated by Demuth et al. [4]. They used 39 relational features [12] capturing semantically meaningful boolean relations between specific joints. Although they achieved 96 % recall and 50 % precision for five different sport activities (jump, cartwheel, elbow-to-knee, jumping jack, punch) on the HDM05 dataset [10], each query had to be manually tuned in order to select a subset of features describing important aspects of the given query activity. To suppress the dependence on manual feature selection, Baak et al. [1] utilized the idea of motion templates built on top of the relational features and proposed an efficient keyframe-based algorithm to speed up the retrieval process. Nevertheless, the selection of keyframes is not fully automatic, so the user has to manually add or remove suitable keyframes to avoid false negatives.

The main contribution of this paper is the proposal of a universal content-based retrieval algorithm capable of identifying similar sub-motions with spatial and temporal variances. The algorithm can index and search for any kind of numerical (i.e., distance-based) motion features. Indexing numerical features constitutes a much harder task than indexing relational features by inverted files, which is the principle used in related approaches [1,4,11]. We demonstrate the

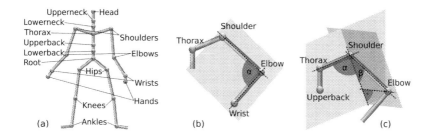

Fig. 1. (a) Skeletal kinematic chain model consisting of rigid bones that are flexibly connected by joints (circular markers with joint names). (b) Computation of the single elbow angle α. (c) Computation of two angles α, β of the shoulder joint.

algorithm search power by indexing motion features in form of joint-angle rotations, introduced in Section 2. We present the algorithm principles in Section 3 and evaluate its retrieval effectiveness and efficiency in Section 4.

2   Pose Feature Extraction

Motion data can be seen as a sequence of frames that consist of 3D coordinates describing positions of specific joints of a human skeleton at a given time. We process the 3D joint coordinates to extract motion features in form of *joint-angle rotations*. A joint-angle rotation constitutes a discrete time series expressing how the angle related to the specific joint changes in time. Individual angles are computed independently of the observer view plane – they are computed in planes defined relatively to the examined joint and relevant joints in its surrounding.

We adopt the skeletal model in Figure 1a to extract joint-angle rotations of 18 important joints that significantly influence the human motion. In particular, we process each frame to extract (1) a single angle α for 8 joints (left and right wrist, left and right elbow, left and right knee, and left and right ankle) moving in one plane and (2) two angles α, β for 10 joints (left and right shoulder, head, upperneck, lowerneck, thorax, upperback, lowerback, and left and right hip) that move in two planes (see Figure 1b,c). In total, 28 angles are computed in each frame. Then we can define a motion D of length K frames as a sequence $D = (P_1^D, P_2^D, \dots, P_K^D)$ of *poses* $P_i^D (i \in [1, K])$, where each pose P_i^D constitutes a 28-dimensional vector of specific joint angles captured in the i-th frame.

3   Sub-Motion Retrieval

The objective of the proposed subsequence retrieval algorithm is to identify in a given database all *sub-motions* (segments) that are similar to a query motion. Remark that a relevant sub-motion can be situated at any position within its parent database motion. For better clarity, we assume that the database consists only of a single database motion (such motion is perceived as a long sequence of arbitrary movements performed by an actor) – in case of more database motions, they are searched separately and the query results are finally merged.

The retrieval algorithm principally works as follows. Firstly, it determines *query key poses* and efficiently retrieves poses within the database motion which are similar to any query key pose. Secondly, poses in the surroundings of each pose retrieved in the previous step are carefully examined to determine a single sub-motion candidate by locating its *candidate key poses*. Similarity between a sub-motion candidate and the query motion is computed on the basis of closeness between their key poses. Finally, the set of identified candidates is processed to retain only the most similar and non-overlapping motions. Before presenting our retrieval algorithm in Section 3.3, we introduce notations and basic search principles in Section 3.1 and describe a preprocessing stage that indexes the poses of the database motion for higher efficiency in Section 3.2.

3.1   Retrieval Concept

Let $D = (P_1^D, \ldots, P_K^D)$ and $Q = (P_1^Q, \ldots, P_M^Q)$ be sequences of extracted poses $(M \ll K)$ representing a *database motion* and *query motion*, respectively. The retrieval principle is based on locating segments of continuous database-motion poses that are similar to query-motion poses. Similarity (closeness) between the *query pose* $P_i^Q (i \in [1, M])$ and *database pose* $P_j^D (j \in [1, K])$ is defined as the Manhattan distance function *sim*:

$$sim(P_i^Q, P_j^D) = \sum_{k=1}^{28} \left(\left| P_i^Q[k] - P_j^D[k] \right| \right), \tag{1}$$

where $P_i^Q[k]$ and $P_j^D[k]$ stand for the k-th joint angle extracted in the i-th query and j-th database motion frame, respectively. The value of this distance-based measure expresses a spatial variance between two poses.

To reduce dimensionality of the query $Q = (P_1^Q, \ldots, P_M^Q)$, we only consider selected poses, called the *query key poses*. Such key poses are simply selected as each δ-th pose. The fixed parameter $\delta \in \mathbb{N}$ determines the spacing between two neighboring key poses from which the total number N of the query key poses is derived as $N = \lfloor \frac{M}{\delta} \rfloor$. Formally, a sequence $q_1, q_2, \ldots, q_N$ of indices determines the query key poses $P_{q_1}^Q, P_{q_2}^Q, \ldots, P_{q_N}^Q$, where $q_i, i \in [1, N]$, is defined as:

$$q_i = (i - 1) \cdot \delta + 1. \tag{2}$$

A continuous sequence of database poses $(P_s^D, \ldots, P_t^D), 1 \le s < t \le K$, represents a sub-motion *candidate* of the query result if there exists a sequence $r_1, r_2, \ldots, r_N$ of increasing indices $s = r_1 < r_2 < \ldots < r_N = t$ determining *candidate key poses* $P_{r_1}^D, P_{r_2}^D, \ldots, P_{r_N}^D$ that are more or less similar to the query key poses in corresponding order. The index r_1 and r_N determines the first and last pose of the identified sub-motion candidate. The distance between two neighboring candidate key poses is not fixed to δ frames (as in case of query key poses) but is kept in a tolerated time bound to enable a temporal variance of the identified candidate. Inspired by [1], such variance is controlled by the *stiffness* parameter $\sigma \in (0,1]$. This parameter allows the candidate to have the length in interval $[M \cdot \sigma, M \cdot \frac{1}{\sigma}]$, where M denotes the query length (the setting $\sigma = 0.5$ expresses that sub-motion candidates can be maximally two times shorter or longer with respect to the query length). The candidate key poses must fulfill the following three conditions:

$$\exists root \in [1, N] : sim(P^Q_{q_{root}}, P^D_{r_{root}}) \leq \tau \tag{3}$$

$$\forall i \in [1, N-1] : \delta \cdot \sigma \leq r_{i+1} - r_i \leq \delta \cdot \frac{1}{\sigma} \tag{4}$$

$$\forall i \in [1, N] : sim(P^Q_{q_i}, P^D_{r_i}) \leq sim(P^Q_{q_i}, P^D_j), \tag{5}$$
$$j \in \begin{cases} [r_i - \delta, r_i + \delta] & i = root \\ \left[r_{i+1} - \delta \cdot \frac{1}{\sigma}, r_{i+1} - \delta \cdot \sigma\right] & i < root \\ \left[r_{i-1} + \delta \cdot \sigma, r_{i-1} + \delta \cdot \frac{1}{\sigma}\right] & i > root. \end{cases}$$

Condition (3) implies the existence of *root pose* $P^D_{r_{root}}$, which is the database pose similar to some query key pose. Two poses are considered as similar if their similarity distance is not higher than the fixed threshold τ. Condition (4) ensures that two neighboring candidate key poses $P^D_{r_i}$ and $P^D_{r_{i+1}}$ ($i \in [1, N-1]$) are within the tolerated time bound. Condition (5) states that the i-th candidate key pose is the most similar pose to the i-th query key pose in the tolerated bound.

The identified sub-motion candidate represented by the candidate key poses $P^D_{r_1}, P^D_{r_2}, \ldots, P^D_{r_N}$ is considered as *similar* to the query Q – represented by the query key poses $P^Q_{q_1}, P^Q_{q_2}, \ldots, P^Q_{q_N}$ – if the following equation holds:

$$\frac{1}{N} \cdot \sum_{i=1}^{N} sim(P^Q_{q_i}, P^D_{r_i}) \leq \tau. \tag{6}$$

This similarity measure completely ignores movements performed between consecutive key poses to increase spatial variances of identified candidates. It is the reason we do not use sophisticated similarity measures such as DTW. Moreover, our approach scales linearly in contrast to quadratic DTW.

3.2 Indexing

We index the poses of the database motion D by the $sim()$ function to efficiently retrieve the set of database poses that are similar to a query pose. There are a lot of metric-based and vector-space-based index structures that can be utilized for this purpose. We chose the *Metric-Index* (M-Index) [13] that supports execution of precise as well as approximate range and k-nearest-neighbor queries. In particular, we use the *range query* $RQ(P^Q_{q_i}, \tau) = \{P^D_j \mid sim(P^Q_{q_i}, P^D_j) \leq \tau, j \in [1, K]\}$ to retrieve database poses that are similar to the i-th query key pose up to the threshold τ. We have experimentally observed that M-Index needed to access roughly 6% of indexed 28-dimensional poses to answer a single range query on average. In the future, we plan to utilize approximate queries to be able to efficiently index even larger database motions.

3.3   Key-Pose Retrieval Algorithm

The key-pose retrieval algorithm looks for all query-similar sub-motion candidates. A single candidate is identified for each database pose, called the root pose $P^D_{r_{root}}$ in Equation 3, that is similar to some of N query key poses. The root pose then corresponds to a given candidate key pose and the rest $N-1$ candidate key poses are simply located by scanning the neighboring poses of the root pose. Similarity between the identified candidate and query motion is then computed on the basis of Equation 6. The retrieved candidates are finally ranked by their similarity and less-similar and overlapping ones are ignored. The whole process is described in the following three paragraphs in detail.

Retrieval of Root Poses. This phase constitutes search for all parts within the database motion $D = (P^D_1, \ldots, P^D_K)$ that have a potential to be similar to the query $Q = (P^Q_1, \ldots, P^Q_M)$. Firstly, the query key poses $P^Q_{q_1}, \ldots, P^Q_{q_N}$ are identified according to Equation 2. Secondly, for each identified query key pose $P^Q_{q_{root}}$ ($root \in [1,N]$), we efficiently retrieve the set of similar database poses by evaluating the M-Index range query $RQ(P^Q_{q_{root}}, \tau)$. Thirdly, for each retrieved pose $P^D_j \in RQ(P^Q_{q_{root}}, \tau)$, we construct a pair $\langle P^D_j, root \rangle$ to only keep the association between the retrieved pose and $root$-th query key pose. The constructed pairs of all N range queries are then unionized into the single *root pose set* R, i.e., $R = \bigcup^N_{root=1} \left(\bigcup_{P^D_j \in RQ(P^Q_{q_{root}}, \tau)} \langle P^D_j, root \rangle \right)$. Finally, we remove each such pair from R for which a more similar pose exists within $2 \cdot \delta$ frames. The reason is that if a given pose is similar to some query key pose, neighboring poses of the given pose are also similar, so we keep only the most similar one. The poses of the remaining pairs in the set R are called the *root poses*.

Identification of Candidate Key Poses. This phase identifies a single sub-motion candidate for each pair $\langle P^D_j, root \rangle \in R$ by locating the candidate key poses $P^D_{r_1}, P^D_{r_2}, \ldots, P^D_{r_N}$. Figure 2 schematically illustrates this process. In general, the candidate key poses are located in the following three steps:

1. The pose $P^D_{r_{root}}$ is taken as the input root pose P^D_j, i.e., $r_{root} = j$;
2. Candidate key poses $P^D_{r_1}, P^D_{r_2}, \ldots, P^D_{r_{root-1}}$ are sequentially identified in reverse order from $P^D_{r_{root-1}}$ to $P^D_{r_1}$. To identify the key pose $P^D_{r_i}$ ($i \in [1, root-1]$), the tolerated time bound $\left[r_{i+1} - \delta \cdot \frac{1}{\sigma}, r_{i+1} - \delta \cdot \sigma \right]$ is sequentially scanned to find the most similar pose to the query key pose $P^Q_{q_i}$. Such the most similar pose then corresponds to the searched pose $P^D_{r_i}$;

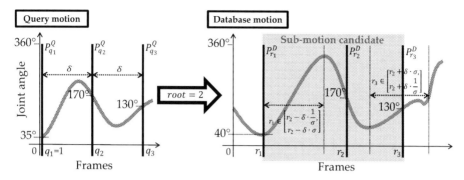

Fig. 2. Schematic process of identification of candidate key poses $P^D_{r_1}, P^D_{r_2}, P^D_{r_3}$ to the fixed query key poses $P^Q_{q_1}, P^Q_{q_2}, P^Q_{q_3}$ (for better clarity, only a single joint-angle rotation is shown, instead of illustrating all 28 dimensions). Firstly, the input root pose corresponds to pose $P^D_{r_2}(root = 2)$. Secondly, the $P^D_{r_1}$ pose is identified as the most similar to $P^Q_{q_1}$ within $[r_2 - \delta \cdot \frac{1}{\sigma}, r_2 - \delta \cdot \sigma]$. Thirdly, the $P^D_{r_3}$ pose is identified as the most similar to $P^Q_{q_3}$ within $[r_2 + \delta \cdot \sigma, r_2 + \delta \cdot \frac{1}{\sigma}]$.

3. The remaining candidate key poses $P^D_{r_{root+1}}, P^D_{r_{root+2}}, \ldots, P^D_{r_N}$ are computed in order from $P^D_{r_{root+1}}$ to $P^D_{r_N}$. The key pose $P^D_{r_i}(i \in [root+1, N])$ is identified as the most similar pose to the query key pose $P^Q_{q_i}$ within the tolerated time bound $[r_{i-1} + \delta \cdot \sigma, r_{i-1} + \delta \cdot \frac{1}{\sigma}]$.

The candidate key poses $P^D_{r_1}, P^D_{r_2}, \ldots, P^D_{r_N}$, with respect to the input root pose P^D_j, represent a single sub-motion candidate $(P^D_s, \ldots, P^D_t)$ which starts at the s-th pose ($s = r_1$) and ends at the t-th pose ($t = r_N$) of the database motion D.

Ranking of Sub-motion Candidates. The last phase of the algorithm ranks sub-motion candidates identified in the previous phase in order to retain only the most similar and non-overlapping ones. Each candidate is checked on the basis of Equation 6 whether it is similar to the query, or not. The dissimilar candidates are not considered for further processing. The remaining candidates are sorted in ascending order according to their similarity distance and being sequentially added to the *result set RS*, which is initially empty. If a candidate, which is being added to RS, overlaps with any more-similar candidate already present in this set, it is not added. We consider two candidates $(P^D_s, \ldots, P^D_t)$ and $(P^D_{s'}, \ldots, P^D_{t'})$ as overlapping if and only if $max(s, s') < min(t, t')$. After processing all the candidates, RS constitutes the result set of non-overlapping query-similar sub-motions.

The pseudo-code of the retrieval algorithm is described in Algorithm 1. The algorithm evaluates a query Q on a database motion D by executing function SEARCH$(Q, D, \delta, \tau, \sigma)$, where δ, τ, σ are the fixed parameters. In particular, line 7 utilizes M-Index to search for root poses similar to the query key pose $P^Q_{q_{root}}$. At line 11 the pairs of such root poses whose similarity is lower than of the pose dis-

Algorithm 1. Key-pose sub-motion retrieval algorithm.

1: **function** SEARCH$(Q, D, \delta, \tau, \sigma)$ $\triangleright$ $Q = (P_1^Q, \ldots, P_M^Q)$, $D = (P_1^D, \ldots, P_K^D)$
2:    $N \leftarrow \lfloor \frac{M}{\delta} \rfloor$ $\triangleright$ Number of query key poses
3:    $R \leftarrow \emptyset$ $\triangleright$ Set of pairs $\langle P_j^D, root \rangle$ of poses P_j^D similar to $P_{q_{root}}^Q$ ($root \in [1, N]$)
4:    $RS \leftarrow \emptyset$ $\triangleright$ Result set of query-similar sub-motions
5:    **for** $root \leftarrow 1$ **to** N **do**
6:      $q_{root} \leftarrow (root - 1) \cdot \delta + 1$ $\triangleright$ Index of $root$-th query key pose
7:      **for all** $P_j^D \in RQ(P_{q_{root}}^Q, \tau)$ **do** $\triangleright$ Poses P_j^D similar to $P_{q_{root}}^Q$ (M-Index)
8:        $R \leftarrow R \cup \langle P_j^D, root \rangle$
9:      **end for**
10:   **end for**
11:   consolidate R $\triangleright$ Removes pairs of less-similar poses up to $2 \cdot \delta$ frames
12:   **for all** $\langle P_j^D, root \rangle \in R$ **do**
13:      $r \leftarrow array[1..N]$ $\triangleright$ Array of candidate key pose indexes
14:      $r[root] \leftarrow j$ $\triangleright$ Index of $root$-th candidate key pose
15:      **for** $i \leftarrow root - 1$ **downto** 1 **do**
16:        $r[i] \leftarrow$ GETMOSTSIMILARPOSEINDEX$(P_{q_i}^Q, D, r[i+1] - \delta \cdot \frac{1}{\sigma}, r[i+1] - \delta \cdot \sigma)$
17:      **end for**
18:      **for** $i \leftarrow root + 1$ **to** N **do**
19:        $r[i] \leftarrow$ GETMOSTSIMILARPOSEINDEX$(P_{q_i}^Q, D, r[i-1] + \delta \cdot \sigma, r[i-1] + \delta \cdot \frac{1}{\sigma})$
20:      **end for**
21:      **if** $\frac{1}{N} \cdot \sum_{i=1}^{N} sim(P_{q_i}^Q, P_{r[i]}^D) \leq \tau$ **then** $\triangleright$ Checks sub-motion similarity
22:        $RS \leftarrow RS \cup (P_{r[1]}^D, P_{r[1]+1}^D, \ldots, P_{r[N]}^D)$
23:      **end if**
24:   **end for**
25:   consolidate RS $\triangleright$ Removes less-similar overlapping sub-motions
26:   **return** RS
27: **end function**

tant up to $2 \cdot \delta$ frames are removed. Line 14, lines 15–17, and lines 18–20 show the three steps of identification of candidate key poses for each retrieved root pose. The pseudo-code of the GETMOSTSIMILARPOSEINDEX$(P_{q_i}^Q, D, fromInd, toInd)$ function is not presented since it only sequentially scans the database poses $(P_{fromInd}^D, \ldots, P_{toInd}^D)$ and returns the index of the most similar pose to the input pose $P_{q_i}^Q$.

The algorithm was also incorporated into an online web application facilitating query definition and visualization of search results [16]. The web application is available at http://mufin.fi.muni.cz/motion-retrieval/.

4   Experimental Evaluation

We evaluated effectiveness and efficiency of the proposed subsequence retrieval algorithm by indexing motion features in form of joint-angle rotations. To evaluate search effectiveness, we adopted a similar technique like the authors of [11] by comparing retrieved results of our algorithm against user-defined ground truth. Efficiency was evaluated by analyzing algorithm time complexity and presenting the actual number of similarity comparisons needed to answer particular queries. The first part of this section introduces a used motion capture database together with predefined ground truth. The second and third part presents the description of experimental evaluation of effectiveness and efficiency.

4.1   Database

We utilized a motion capture database HDM05 [10] to extract motion features in form of joint-angle rotations (Section 2) from 102 motions of total length of 68 minutes (491,847 frames). Individual motions contain various types of movements performed by five actors according to a given scenario. These motions were manually annotated by the authors of [11] to obtain *user-defined ground truth*. This ground truth categorizes sub-motions within the database motions into 15 motion classes: *neutral pose*, *T-pose* (standing subject with spread arms), *move*, *turn*, *sit or lie down*, *stand up*, *hop on one leg*, *jump*, *kick*, *punch*, *rotate arms*, *throw*, *grab deposit*, *cartwheel*, and *exercise*. In total, 1,476 sub-motions were manually annotated within the 102 database motions.

4.2   Effectiveness Evaluation

To evaluate effectiveness of our algorithm, we constructed a specialized batch of queries for each of the 102 database motions and each of the 15 ground-truth motion classes (in total, $102 \cdot 15$ batches were constructed). In particular, for a single database motion D and a given motion class p, we constructed the batch of queries consisting of sub-motions of class p which were manually annotated in all database motions except the examined motion D. All such queries were evaluated by the proposed algorithm on the given database motion D and the retrieved sub-motions were finally unionized on the level of individual frames. As a result, we obtained a set of unionized continuous sub-motions for each motion class p and each database motion D.

The search effectiveness was evaluated by the *precision* ($\mathcal{P}$) and *recall* ($\mathcal{R}$) metrics computed for each of the 102 database motions. Both the metrics were computed on the basis of the frame-level comparison between the retrieved unionized sub-motions and ground-truth sub-motions with respect to a given motion class p and database motion D. The metrics were then averaged separately for each database motion over all 15 motion classes. To report effectiveness of our approach globally, we averaged the precision and recall metrics over all 102 database motions. Moreover, we also measured a harmonic mean of $\mathcal{P}$ and $\mathcal{R}$ by standard performance $\mathcal{F}$-measure:

$$\mathcal{F}(D) = 2 \cdot \frac{\mathcal{P}(D) \cdot \mathcal{R}(D)}{\mathcal{P}(D) + \mathcal{R}(D)}.$$

We fixed the parameters δ and σ ($\delta = 10$, $\sigma = 0.5$) of the retrieval algorithm and measured the precision, recall, and $\mathcal{F}$-measure for a different setting of parameter τ, which determines the threshold of pose similarity (see Section 3.1). The setting $\delta = 10$ of the distance (in frames) between neighboring query key poses expresses an enough time interval of roughly 80 ms (motion sampling frequency is 120 Hz) in which a subject can not dramatically change their movement

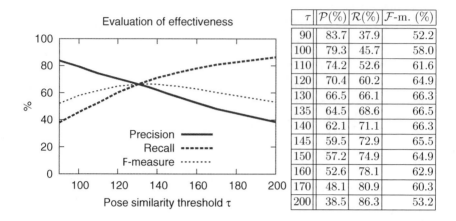

Fig. 3. Evaluation of recall, precision, and $\mathcal{F}$-measure on the basis of the frame-level comparison by changing the pose similarity threshold parameter τ

style. The setting $\sigma = 0.5$ of the stiffness parameter allows the algorithm to retrieve only sub-motions whose length is maximally two times shorter or longer with respect to the query motion length. The results are depicted in Figure 3 (in form of figure and table) for a changing value of the pose similarity threshold parameter τ. We can notice that the setting of τ influences the trade-off between precision and recall. By lowering the value of parameter τ to 90, the 84 % precision, 38 % recall, and 52 % $\mathcal{F}$-measure was achieved. Such setting suits for search engines that usually prefer the most precise and highest relevant top-ten results with a possible loss of remaining less relevant results. This variability allows us to customize the algorithm for the needs of the specific application and specific distance-based motion features.

To the best of our knowledge, there is no existing retrieval approach that evaluates the recall and precision metrics against available ground truth on the HDM05 dataset. We can only compare our results against a specialized motion annotation technique [11]. This technique achieved the 49 % precison and 80 % recall without using *keyframes*, which corresponds to our results with the setting $\tau = 170$. When using *keyframes*, the precision further increased to 70 %. Even this specialized annotation-based technique achieved slightly better results, it does not support content-based sub-motion retrieval and requires a number of positive as well as negative example motions to determine key-frames.

4.3   Efficiency Evaluation

We analyze theoretical time complexity of the retrieval algorithm and then present the actual computational costs in terms of number of similarity comparisons needed to answer particular queries. Let $Q = (P_1^Q, \ldots, P_M^Q)$ be a query of $N = \lfloor \frac{M}{\delta} \rfloor$ key poses which is being evaluated on database motion

$D = (P_1^D, \ldots, P_K^D)$ of K poses. Theoretical time complexity is expressed by the number of calls of similarity-distance function $sim()$ with respect to N and K. This function is called in Algorithm 1 at line 21 and at lines $7, 16$ and 19 where the actual calls are hidden in the M-Index range query evaluation and the GETMOSTSIMILARPOSEINDEX$(P_{q_i}^Q, D, fromInd, toInd)$ function. We can ignore N evaluations at line 21 because they have been already computed in the GETMOSTSIMILARPOSEINDEX() function and thus can be easily remembered.

The evaluation of M-Index range query $RQ(P_{q_{root}}^Q, \tau)$, $root \in [1, N]$, requires K calls of the $sim()$ function in the worst case, so complexity of line 7 is $O(K)$. Nevertheless, our experimental results confirmed that the M-Index structure needed to access only about 6% of indexed poses on average. Focusing on a single retrieved root pose $P_j^D \in RQ(P_{q_{root}}^Q, \tau)$, the $sim()$ function is called at lines 16 and 19 between each query key pose (except the root pose) and each pose within the tolerated interval, whose length is always fixed to $\delta \cdot \frac{1}{\sigma} - \delta \cdot \sigma$. It means that $(N - 1) \cdot (\delta \cdot \frac{1}{\sigma} - \delta \cdot \sigma)$ calls are performed for each root pose P_j^D.

To sum up, $O\left(N \cdot K + |R| \cdot (N - 1) \cdot (\delta \cdot \frac{1}{\sigma} - \delta \cdot \sigma)\right)$ of similarity evaluations are performed, where $|R|$ denotes the total number of all root poses identified (see Section 3.3). By considering the worst case $|R| = \frac{K}{2 \cdot \delta}$, the algorithm complexity degrades to $O(N \cdot K + \frac{K}{2 \cdot \delta} \cdot (N - 1) \cdot (\delta \cdot \frac{1}{\sigma} - \delta \cdot \sigma)) = O(N \cdot K)$. However, we experimentally evaluated that complexity approached the level of K similarity comparisons in a real-world scenario in which the queries had a meaningful length. For this reason, we evaluated all $1,476$ ground-truth queries (disregarding their motion class) whose average length corresponded to $M = 285$ poses. To evaluate a single ground-truth query on the whole database of $K = 491,847$ poses (the total number of poses of the 102 database motions), the algorithm required $432,352$ similarity comparisons on average. This experiment needed even a smaller number of similarity-distance evaluations compared to the total number of poses of all database motions. In particular, M-Index required $13,310$ similarity comparisons on average to evaluate a single key-pose range query. The total number of root poses obtained from the results of N range queries corresponded roughly to 147, i.e., $|R| = 147$. The experiment utilized M-Index with 100 random pivots (i.e., 100 randomly chosen poses from random database motions) and was evaluated with the following setting of parameters: $\delta = 10$, $\sigma = 0.5, \tau = 120$.

Although theoretical time complexity of the algorithm is $O(N \cdot K)$, the experimental evaluation demonstrated that complexity is linear to the database-motion length in the real-world scenario with a reasonable length of queries.

5 Conclusions

We propose a universal subsequence retrieval algorithm that examines database motions and identifies all their sub-motions that are similar to a query motion example. The algorithm does not require any initial learning phase and any explicit knowledge of queries nor database motions. Moreover, it can cope with time and space deformations of movements and can index any kind of distance-based motion features. The algorithm capability is demonstrated by indexing motion features in form of joint-angle rotations. By using this kind of features, we achieve high effectiveness in terms of similar values of recall, precision, and $\mathcal{F}$-measure as the specialized motion-annotation technique [11]. Efficiency of the algorithm is theoretically analyzed and also demonstrated by evaluating real-world queries that require a linear number of similarity comparisons with respect to the length of database motions. In the future, we would like to further improve algorithm efficiency so that its theoretical time complexity does not depend on the number of parallel query key poses.

Acknowledgements. This research was supported by the Czech Science Foundation (GAČR) project No. P103/12/G084.

References

1. Baak, A., Müeller, M., Seidel, H.-P.: An Efficient Algorithm for Keyframe-based Motion Retrieval in the Presence of Temporal Deformations. In: 1st Int. Conf. on Multimedia Information Retrieval (MIR 2008), pp. 451–458. ACM Press (2008)
2. Chiu, C.-Y., Chao, S.-P., Wu, M.-Y., Yang, S.-N., Lin, H.-C.: Content-Based Retrieval for Human Motion Data. Journal of Visual Communication and Image Representation 15(3), 446–466 (2004)
3. Choensawat, W., Choi, W., Hachimura, K.: Similarity Retrieval of Motion Capture Data Based on Derivative Features. Journal of Advanced Computational Intelligence and Intelligent Informatics 16(1), 13–23 (2012)
4. Demuth, B., Röder, T., Müller, M., Eberhardt, B.: An Information Retrieval System for Motion Capture Data. In: Lalmas, M., MacFarlane, A., Rüger, S.M., Tombros, A., Tsikrika, T., Yavlinsky, A. (eds.) ECIR 2006. LNCS, vol. 3936, pp. 373–384. Springer, Heidelberg (2006)
5. Deng, Z., Gu, Q., Li, Q.: Perceptually Consistent Example-based Human Motion Retrieval. In: Symposium on Interactive 3D Graphics and Games (I3D 2009), pp. 191–198. ACM (2009)
6. Esling, P., Agon, C.: Time-Series Data Mining. ACM Computing Surveys 45(1), 1–12 (2012)
7. Forbes, K., Fiume, E.: An Efficient Search Algorithm for Motion Data Using Weighted PCA. In: SIGGRAPH/Eurographics Symposium on Computer Animation (SCA 2005), pp. 67–76. ACM (2005)
8. Huang, T., Liu, H., Ding, G.: Motion Retrieval Based on Kinetic Features in Large Motion Database. In: 14th International Conference on Multimodal Interaction (ICMI 2012), pp. 209–216. ACM Press (2012)
9. Lan, R., Sun, H., Zhu, M.: Text-Like Motion Representation for Human Motion Retrieval. In: Yang, J., Fang, F., Sun, C. (eds.) IScIDE 2012. LNCS, vol. 7751, pp. 72–81. Springer, Heidelberg (2013)
10. Müller, M., Röder, T., Clausen, M., Eberhardt, B., Krüger, B., Weber, A.: Documentation Mocap Database HDM05. Tech. Rep. CG-2007-2 (2007)
11. Müller, M., Baak, A., Seidel, H.-P.: Efficient and Robust Annotation of Motion Capture Data. In: ACM SIGGRAPH/Eurographics Symposium on Computer Animation (SCA 2009), p. 10. ACM Press (2009)
12. Müller, M., Röder, T., Clausen, M.: Efficient Content-based Retrieval of Motion Capture Data. In: SIGGRAPH 2005, pp. 677–685. ACM Press (2005)

13. Novak, D., Batko, M., Zezula, P.: Metric Index: An Efficient and Scalable Solution for Precise and Approximate Similarity Search. Inf. Sys. 36(4), 721–733 (2011)
14. Park, J.P., Lee, K.H., Lee, J.: Finding Syntactic Structures from Human Motion Data. Computer Graphics 30(8), 2183–2193 (2011)
15. Ren, C., Lei, X., Zhang, G.: Motion Data Retrieval from Very Large Motion Databases. In: Int. Conf. on Virtual Reality and Visualization (ICVRV 2011), pp. 70–77 (2011)
16. Sedmidubsky, J., Valcik, J.: Retrieving Similar Movements in Motion Capture Data. In: Brisaboa, N., Pedreira, O., Zezula, P. (eds.) SISAP 2013. LNCS, vol. 8199, pp. 325–330. Springer, Heidelberg (2013)
17. Wang, P., Lau, R.W.H., Zhang, M., Wang, J., Song, H., Pan, Z.: A Real-time Database Architecture for Motion Capture Data. In: 19th International Conference on Multimedia (MM 2011), pp. 1337–1340. ACM (2011)
18. Wu, S., Wang, Z., Xia, S.: Indexing and Retrieval of Human Motion Data by a Hierarchical Tree. In: 16th Symposium on Virtual Reality Software and Technology (VRST 2009), pp. 207–214. ACM Press (2009)

Training with Corrupted Labels to Reinforce a Probably Correct Teamsport Player Detector*

Pascaline Parisot, Berk Sevilmiş, and Christophe De Vleeschouwer

Université Catholique de Louvain, ICTEAM-ELEN,
Place du Levant, 2, 1348 Louvain-La-Neuve, Belgique
pascaline.parisot@uclouvain.be

Abstract. While the analysis of foreground silhouettes has become a key component of modern approach to multi-view people detection, it remains subject to errors when dealing with a single viewpoint. Besides, several works have demonstrated the benefit of exploiting classifiers to detect objects or people in images, based on local texture statistics. In this paper, we train a classifier to differentiate false and true positives among the detections computed based on a foreground mask analysis. This is done in a sport analysis context where people deformations are important, which makes it important to adapt the classifier to the case at hand, so as to take the teamsport color and the background appearance into account. To circumvent the manual annotation burden incurred by the repetition of the training for each event, we propose to train the classifier based on the foreground detector decisions. Hence, since the detector is not perfect, we face a training set whose labels might be corrupted. We investigate a set of classifier design strategies, and demonstrate the effectiveness of the approach to reliably detect sport players with a single view.

Keywords: detection, random ferns, corrupted label.

1   Introduction

Detecting people in images is an important question for many computer vision applications including surveillance, automotive safety, or sportmen behavior monitoring. It has motivated a long history of research efforts [8], which have recently converged into two main trends.

On the one hand, background subtraction approaches have gained in popularity since they have been considered in a multi-view framework. In each view, those approaches build on a background model to compute a mask that is supposed to detect the moving foreground objects in the view. The foreground silhouettes computed in each view of a calibrated multi-camera set-up are then merged to mitigate the problems caused by occlusions and illumination changes when inferring people location from a single view. Several strategies have been

---

* Part of this work has been funded by the Belgian NSF, and the walloon region project SPORTIC.

J. Blanc-Talon et al. (Eds.): ACIVS 2013, LNCS 8192, pp. 682–694, 2013.

considered to fuse the masks from multiple views [13,10,1,6]. They generally rely on the definition of a ground occupancy probability map, which exploits the verticality of people silhouettes to estimate the likelihood that a particular ground plane position is occupied or not by someone. All of these approaches build on the multiplicity and diversity of viewpoints, and their performances significantly degrade when a single viewpoint is available.

On the other hand, efforts have been carried out to detect people or objects of interest based on their visual appearance. Modern approaches make an extensive use of training samples, to learn how the object is defined in terms of topologically organized components [9,2] and/or in terms of texture statistics [15,4]. The pioneering work of Viola and Jones [19] illustrates the success of those approaches to detect objects in images. It relies on boosting strategies to select and combine a large number of weak binary tests to decide whether the content of a (sub-)image corresponds to the object-of-interest or not. Since the tests are defined in terms of the average luminance observed on small patches defined by their size and location in the image, their statistics intrinsically capture the spatial topological organization of the image textures. Several recent works have been inspired by the same intuition to detect people. Representative examples are the work in [7] and in [20], which analyze the content of an image in terms of a multiplicity of pixel features -like color, gradient, or motion. Those methods appear to be efficient in detecting people, as long as a sufficiently large and representative database is available to train the classifier. The collection of those training samples is however performed manually in most previous works, which prevents to adapt the detector to the appearance specificities encountered in the particular case at hand. Such adaptation capability is especially relevant in a teamsport analysis context, since the background and all the players of each team are characterized by a specific shirt.

Our paper takes advantage of the two trends presented above. It aims at improving the foreground silhouette detector (referred as foreground detector in the following), by using an appearance-based classifier to differentiate false and true positives among the foreground silhouette detections. The main idea of our paper, and its main contribution from a system design point-of-view, consists in training the classifier based on the probably correct decisions taken by the foreground detector. Because it exploits color and gradient visual features, the appearance-based classifier offers a complementary information compared to the one provided by the foreground detector, thereby making the overall detection more reliable. This idea is in-line with co-training approaches [3]. The similarities and differences between our proposal and co-training approaches will be discussed in Section 3. More importantly, because our approach defines the training samples of the classifier based on the foreground detector decisions, no manual annotation is required to generate the training set, which makes it possible to retrain and adapt the classifier to the case at hand.

In addition to the original integration of two families of people detection algorithms, our paper also brings significant contributions related to the design of the classifier itself. Indeed, primarily, our paper introduces an original people detection method that relies on an ensemble of random sets of binary tests to characterize the texture describing the visual appearance of the target. The binary tests consist of comparison of pixel values within a block. Specifically, we extend the approaches in [15] and [17] to the description of large image patterns (see Section 4.2). Our experimental results demonstrate that the use of simple binary tests on raw pixel color or gradients of image blocks is more effective in characterizing sport player patterns than the integral image features recommended in [7] for pedestrians.

As a second contribution related to the design of appearance-based classifiers, our paper shows that, in the particular case of large deformations of the objects of interest as encountered in a sport context, ensembles of random classifiers outperform the boosted classification methods, traditionally adopted for pedestrian detection [7]. Ensembles of random classifiers have gained popularity in recent years, mainly because they reduce the risk of overfitting and offer good generalization properties in case of training samples scarcity [12]. Our work reveals that those random classifiers are also more robust to labels corruption than AdaBoost solutions.

The rest of the paper is organized as follows. Section 2 presents the overview of our system. Section 3 discusses the similarities and differences between the co-training framework and our approach. Section 4 then defines our proposed classifier. It is supposed to differentiate human player patterns from arbitrary background patterns, and consists of an ensemble of random ferns, each fern characterizing a block of the image in terms of the stochastic distribution of its visual features. Section 5 validates our approach.

2   System Overview: Training with Corrupted Labels

The proposed detection scheme is depicted in Figure 1.

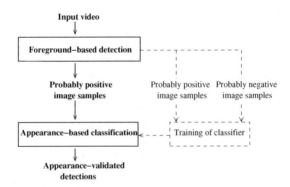

Fig. 1. Solid lines depict the proposed people detection scheme. The foreground-based detections are validated or rejected based on their appearance. Dashed lines depict the training phase. The appearance-based classifier is trained with image samples that are labelled with a good rate of success by the foreground detector.

People/player image samples are continuously detected with a high detection rate and a reasonable false alarms rate, based on the foreground mask approach described in [6]. The resulting probably positive samples are then processed by a classifier, which further investigates the visual features of each foreground detected object to decide whether it corresponds to a human/player or not. Optionally, the foreground detected samples can feed the training of the classifier. Specifically, two classes of training samples are defined based on the ground occupancy map computed in [6]. The first class of training samples corresponds to the probably positive samples. Those samples are defined by cropping a rectangular sub-image in the camera view, around the backprojection of a probably occupied ground position. The training samples of the second class correspond to probably negative samples, which are randomly cropped around backprojected ground positions that are considered to be unoccupied by the detector. Examples of image samples from both classes are presented in Figure 2.

(a)   (b)

Fig. 2. Examples of samples labelled as probably positive (a) or probably negative (b) by the foreground detector

We observe a significant variability among the samples of each class, which makes the learning of a classifier challenging, and motivates the careful investigation carried out in Section 5. Regarding the people/no-people decision expected from the classifier, those samples are subject to label corruption. This is because those labels are defined based on the error-prone decisions of the foreground detector. As a consequence, the appearance-based classifier should be designed so that its learning is robust to label corruption. In the next section, we motivate the need of online training and position our work with regard to the co-training framework, which shares similarities with our approach, whilst being different.

3   Specificities of Our Applicative Context vs. Related Work

To motivate both the need for online training, and the development of an original solution to this problem, it is worth presenting the specificities of our application context.

In short, we are interested in the detection of teamsport players to control the autonomous production of images to render a sport game action [5]. In other words, the information about players positions is used to select the view point to adopt to render the action, typically by cropping within a fixed view. Hence, we are not interested in the accurate segmentation of each individual, but we are eager to determine whether a given foreground activity either results from (one or several) players, or is caused by some other reason like, for example, dynamic advertisement panels or spot lightings. As another consequence of our application context, our system has to deal with severe deformations of the object-of-interest (players are running, jumping, falling down, connecting to each others, etc). Hence, to be effective, it can not only rely on the characterization of the standard appearance of a standing human, like it is done for pedestrian detection for example, but it has to exploit as much of the *a priori* information that is available about the appearance of the object (e.g. players'jerseys have a known color) and of the scene (sport hall, known background advertisements). Since this *a priori* information changes from one game to another, the classifier has to be trained online, so as to adapt to the game at hand.

Besides motivating the online training, the wide range of deformations encountered by our application also prevents the use of most of the solutions that have been proposed in the past to learn online, without manual labelling of the training samples. Specifically, in the late nineties, Blum and Mitchell [3] have introduced the co-training framework to reduce the amount of labelled samples required to train a classifier. Their purpose was to exploit unlabelled samples to jointly reinforce two complementary classifiers, i.e. that look at the data from different points of view, using independent features. In a straightforward implementation of their framework, the two classifiers are initially trained based on a small set of manually labelled samples, and are then jointly improved by increasing the training set of one classifier based on the *reliable* labels assigned by the other classifier [14]. In more recent works, motion detection has been considered to initialize the learning process, so that manual labelling is not required anymore [18,16]. In both kinds of approaches, however, a key issue lies in the selection of *reliably labelled* samples. To identify those reliable samples, earlier works make the explicit or implicit assumption that the appearances of the objects-of-interest are sufficiently similar to be accurately described by some fixed discriminative (appearance) model. They then propose to learn such discriminative model from the dominant statistics observed among the positively labelled samples of each classifier, either in terms of PCA [18] or simply in terms of motion blobs aspect ratio [16]. In our sport analysis context, however, the assumption about the existence of a stable appearance model does not hold anymore. Players are very active, and their silhouettes change a lot depending on the action at hand (see variability in Fig. 2-(a)). Bottom line, we can not rely on some simplistic appearance model to select reliable samples among the ones detected based on motion analysis. For this reason, we have to deal with erroneous labels during the training. We show in the rest of the paper that ensembles of random classifiers better support such errors in labelling than AdaBoost solutions.

4   Classification of Human Patterns Based on Weak Binary Tests Combination

Many recent works have demonstrated the advantages of combining (weak) binary tests to solve image classification problems [15,4,19,7,17]. We follow this paradigm. Section 4.1 defines the binary tests either in terms of pixel values or integral images comparisons. Section 4.2 presents two approaches to combine the binary tests. The first one follows the well-known AdaBoost method [11], as used in [19,7]. The second one adopts a more recent Semi-Naive Bayesian formulation, and classifies samples based on the joint probability distributions associated to random ferns, i.e. to small sets of randomly selected binary tests [17]. In contrast to previous usages of ferns, which have focused on the description of small texture patches around keypoints, our paper proposes to exploit ferns to classify entire and semantically meaningful image patterns.

4.1   Definition of Binary Tests

In our work, the tests are carried out on so-called image channels, defined in [7] as the R, G, and B components, the gradient magnitude GM, and the magnitude of oriented gradients $OG_j, 0 \leq j \leq 5$.

For a given channel, a binary test is then defined to compare either the intensities of two pixel locations, or the integrals of pixel intensities over two rectangular supports. Comparisons of pixel intensities are performed within a small block, e.g. limited to 16×16 pixels, because they aim at describing local textures through the combination of many local comparisons of pixel intensities. In contrast, integral supports are defined on the entire image since those integral values are supposed to capture discriminating behavior of the image signal on some spatial area. The first kind of test follows the approaches in [15] and [17], while the second one follows [19] and [7].

In a more formal way, a binary test b_i is defined by (i) the test image channel $I_i \in \{R, G, B, GM, \{OG_k\}_{0 \leq k \leq 5}\}$, (ii) the test type $t_i \in \{pixel, integral\}$, and (iii) a pair of pixel locations $(m_{i,1}, m_{i,2})$ (defined in a 16x16 block) or a rectangular support $(r_{i,1}, r_{i,2})$ (defined over the entire image). Letting $w_{i,1}$ and $w_{i,2}$ denote two intermediate values defined as follows:

$$\forall j \in \{1,2\}, \quad w_{i,j} = \begin{cases} I_i(m_{i,j}), & \text{if } t_i = pixel \\ \frac{1}{|r_{i,j}|} \sum_{m \in r_{i,j}} I_i(m), & \text{if } t_i = integral \end{cases} \tag{1}$$

where $|r_{i,j}|$ is the number of pixels in the rectangle, we simply write:

$$b_i = \begin{cases} 1, & \text{if } w_{i,1} > w_{i,2} \\ 0, & \text{otherwise} \end{cases}. \tag{2}$$

4.2   Combination of Binary Tests

Two approaches are considered to combine the weak binary classifiers.

The first one follows the AdaBoost algorithm [11]. It will be used as a baseline reference since its effectiveness and efficiency in solving object detection problems in images have already been extensively demonstrated [19,7].

The second combination approach is an original contribution of our paper. As told above, it is inspired by a number of earlier works dealing with image texture classification [15] and keypoint identification [17]. It differs from those previous works by the fact that it is designed to describe the semantically meaningful pattern corresponding to the projection of an object or a human-being. Therefore, the binary tests are selected over the entire image support, and have to be defined in terms of their relative position compared to the image support. This is simply done by normalizing the image sizes, typically to 128×64 pixels in our work. To explain the other specificities of our approach compared to [17], it is worth reminding the principle underlying the classification with ensemble of random sets of binary tests, also named random ferns (RF) classification.

Let D denote the random variable that represents the class of an image sample. In our problem, $D = 1$ if the sample corresponds to a player, and $D = 0$ otherwise. Given a set of N binary tests $b_i, i = 1, ..., N$, the sample class MAP estimate $\hat{d}$ is defined by:

$$\hat{d} = \underset{d \in \{0,1\}}{\operatorname{argmax}} P(D = d|b_1, ..., b_N). \tag{3}$$

Bayes' formula yields:

$$\hat{d} = \underset{d \in \{0,1\}}{\operatorname{argmax}} P(b_1, ..., b_N|D = d), \tag{4}$$

if we admit a uniform prior $P(D)$.

Learning and maintaining the joint probability in Equation (4) is not feasible for large N since it would require to compute and store 2^N entries for each class. A naive approximation would assume independence between binary tests, which would reduce the number of entries per class to N. However, such representation completely ignores the correlation between the tests. The semi-naive bayesian approach proposed in [17] accounts for dependencies between tests while keeping the problem tractable, by grouping the N binary tests into M sets of size $S = N/M$. These groups are named ferns, and the joint conditional probability is approximated by:

$$P(b_1, ..., b_N|D = d) = \prod_{k=1}^{M} P(F_k|D = d), \tag{5}$$

where F_k denotes the kth fern.

The training phase estimates the class conditional probability distribution of each fern independently, and is detailed in [17]. Compared to AdaBoost, random ferns have the advantage to support incremental training. This is especially interesting in our teamsport analysis context, since it allows to initialize the process with default ferns distributions (e.g. averaged on several games), and to progressively update the distributions along the game, as new samples are collected.

Now that the random ferns classification principles have been reminded, we explain how our approach differs from earlier works in terms of tests assignment to ferns. This subtle change is required to characterize large image patterns, and not just small texture patches as in [17]. In [17], to split the N tests into ferns of S tests, they use a random permutation function with range $1...N$. This is motivated by the fact that all tests have *a priori* the same chance to be (in)dependent. In our case, this assumption reasonably holds for integral image tests, since their supports cover large fractions of the image, which gives all pairs of tests a similar chance to be (in)dependent. In contrast, the assumption does not hold anymore for the tests dealing with pixel intensities. Those tests are local by definition, since they compare the intensities of two locations that are close to each other. Hence, two tests dealing with the same image area are more likely to depend on each other than two tests dealing with far apart pixels. Since dependencies are only handled within a fern, it becomes relevant to assign to each fern a set of tests that correspond to the same spatial area. In final, when using pixels intensities comparisons, our proposed approach can be summarized as follows. The image support is split into a grid of non-overlapping blocks of 16×16 pixels, and all tests of a given fern are defined based on a pair of pixels that are selected within the same block.

5   Experimental Validation

This section considers a typical real life basket-ball player detection scenario. The training sets are defined automatically, as explained in Section 2. The set of probably positive samples detected by the foreground detector [6] is referred to as the detector set in the following, while the set of probably negative samples is named random set. In addition, a reference ground truth label has been assigned manually to each detector sample, so as to split the detector set into a positive and a negative set. The positive set includes the valid detections, while the negative set contains the false detections, resulting from a foreground detector error.

In our experiments, we train the classifiers based on detector and random training sets, and measure how well those classifiers discriminate between positive and negative test sets.

The detector sets considered in our experiments are derived from a game that happened in the Spiroudome sporthall (http://www.spiroudome.com), on a period of time during which 2723 positive samples have been manually annotated. Several detector (and random) sets have been defined on the same period of time. Each detector set is composed of 1000 samples randomly picked among the foreground detected samples, but is affected by a different rate n of false detections, ranging from $n = 2\%$ to $n = 10\%$, as a function of the foreground detector operating point. In addition, an Oracle defines uncorrupted detector sets ($n = 0\%$), based on the manual groundtruth. Five pairs of detector and random sets have been picked up randomly at each corruption rate, so as to repeat the experiments and compute average and standard deviation performance metrics.

The test set is defined by 1000 manually labelled samples (900 positive samples, and 100 negative ones), extracted in a different period of time of the same Spiroudome game.

For all those sets, each image sample is characterized by 10 image channels, and the classifiers parameters are set as follows. There are 5 tests per fern, and 200 ferns per 16x16 image block. For each fern, the common channel of the 5 tests is randomly selected among the 10 image channels. Hence, there are 32000 tests for a normalized image of size 128x64. The same number of tests is considered for AdaBoost classifiers.

In the first experiment, we compare different kinds of binary tests. Therefore, we train the random ferns classifier on uncorrupted labels, and consider three kinds of binary tests: pixel comparisons within a block, pixel comparisons within the whole image and integral image comparisons within the whole image. Figure 3-(a) plots the obtained ROC curves, that is the detection rate on the positive set versus the detection rate on the negative set (which corresponds to the false alarm rate on the detector set). The number of binary tests are the same in the three cases. We observe that significantly better performances are obtained with tests comparing two pixels in a block. Tests comparing integral images or pixels on the whole image are not able to discriminate player activity patterns from background activity. In the following, we only consider comparison of pixels within a block.

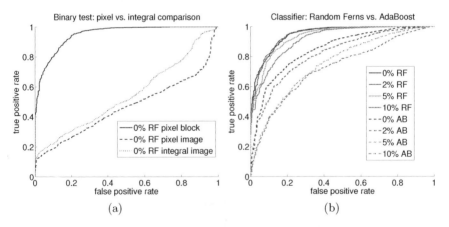

Fig. 3. (a) Receiver Operating Characteristic (ROC) curves resulting from the random ferns (RF) classifier trained on uncorrupted labelled samples (0%) for three kinds of binary test: "pixel block", i.e. pixel comparison within a block, "pixel image", i.e. pixel comparison within the whole image and "integral image", i.e. integral comparison within the whole image. Binary test based on the comparison of pixels within a block outperforms the two other kinds of binary test ; (b) ROC curves resulting from training sets with uncorrupted labels (0%) and corrupted labels (rate of 2, 5 and 10%), for both kind of classifiers: random ferns (RF) and AdaBoost (AB). Random ferns classifier outperforms AdaBoost ones and is less sensitive to uncorrupted labels.

In the second experiment, we analyze the impact of the label corruption rate when training AdaBoost and random ferns classifiers. Figure 3-(b) plots the ROC curves for both kinds of classifiers, and for different corruption rates. It reveals that our proposed random ferns approach outperforms the AdaBoost classifier, and is more robust to label corruption than AdaBoost (see the decrease of "area under curve" in Table 1). Additional experiments that are not reported here have shown that increasing the number of weak classifiers in the case of AdaBoost has no significant impact on the obtained performances.

Table 1. Area under curve measured in Fig. 3-(b) (mean ± standard deviation)

	Uncorrupted labels (0%)	Corrupted labels		
		2%	5%	10%
Random Ferns	0.949 ± 0.006	0.947 ± 0.009	0.934 ± 0.007	0.915 ± 0.006
AdaBoost	0.848 ± 0.042	0.822 ± 0.035	0.757 ± 0.047	0.730 ± 0.040

In the third experiment, we investigate how online training improves performances compared to offline training. We train the random ferns classifier on different training sets. The first training set is based on the Spiroudome game with different rates of corrupted labels. The second training set is based on the Apidis dataset (http://www.apidis.org/Dataset) with uncorrupted labels. Finally, the last training set is composed by a mixture of samples from the Spiroudome and Apidis datasets: 500 positive samples from the Apidis dataset, 500 probably positive samples from the Spiroudome dataset (with 10% of corrupted labels) and 1000 probably negative samples from the Spiroudome dataset. The obtained ROC curves are plotted in Figure 4-(a). The best curves are obtained from the Spiroudome training set with small corruption rates ($\leq$ 5%), or from a mixed training set when the corruption rate increases. We also observe that keeping the false alarm rate below 5% (which is reasonable to avoid video production inconsistencies) results in a selection rate lower than 40% for offline training, but higher than 60% with mixed online training.

As a last experiment, we have measured the impact of our proposed system on the operating points of a single-view player detector integrating the foreground detector and the random ferns classifier. For this purpose, we have defined manually a detection ground truth over 280 regularly spaced frames, in an interval of 4min40s of a Spiroudome basketball game. This ground truth information consists of the bounding boxes of the players and referees in the frame view coordinate system. We have then compared this ground truth to the detections computed by the foreground detector in [6], and to the subsets of those detections that are considered to be positive by the classifier trained with the 10% corrupted training set in the second experiment (see Fig. 3-(b)). For this comparison, we consider that two objects cannot be matched if the overlapping of the detected bounding boxes on the frame is smaller than 50%. Figure 4-(b) presents, in solid line, the ROC curve of [6], i.e. using the foreground detector only. The dotted, dashed-dotted and dashed lines correspond to the ROC curves

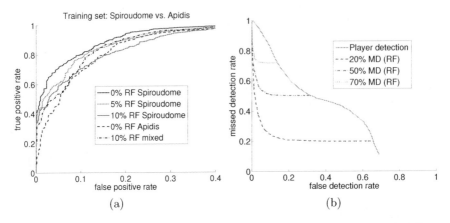

Fig. 4. (a) ROC curves for three kinds of training sets: Spiroudome set with different rates of label corruption, Apidis set and mixture of them. We conclude that online training helps even in case of corrupted labels ; (b) Improvement of ROC curve resulting from our proposed random ferns (RF) classifier, trained on corrupted labels: The solid green line depicts the initial foreground detector ROC. Dotted, dot-dashed, and dashed lines plot the ROC curves obtained after classification of the samples detected by the foreground detector, respectively working with 70%, 50% or 20% of missed detections (MD).

obtained when using the random ferns classifier to sort the foreground detections into false and true positives. Each of these 3 curves is derived from a particular foreground detector operating point, respectively corresponding to 20%, 50% and 70% of missed detections. We conclude from Figure 4-(b) that the classifier significantly improves the operating trades-off compared to the ones obtained based on foreground detection only, which definitely demonstrates the relevance of the scheme proposed in Fig. 1.

6 Conclusion

As a first and primary contribution, the paper has proposed an original framework to reinforce a (visual object) detector. The framework assumes that a reasonably correct detector is available, but that it fails to use some available (visual) features that are actually discriminating with respect to the detection task. Based on those assumptions, our framework proposes to train a classifier to discriminate between detected samples, which are probably positive regarding the detection goal, and randomly selected samples, which are probably negative. Our experimental results demonstrate that the resulting classifier offers good generalization properties and captures the essence of the knowledge needed to differentiate false and true positives among the samples detected by the initial foreground detector, thereby shifting the receiver operating characteristics of the reinforced detector towards smaller false alarm rates for a given detection rate.

As a second contribution, our paper has shown that an ensemble of random classifiers achieves better performances than conventional boosted solutions for large intra class variability, and when the labels of the training samples are corrupted. Regarding the definition of the binary tests that are combined through boosting or random strategies, it appears that the comparisons of neighbouring pixel values offer better performances than comparison of pixels or integral images on the whole image.

References

1. Alahi, A., Jacques, L., Boursier, Y., Vandergheynst, P.: Sparsity driven people localization with a heterogeneous network of cameras. Jour. of MIV 41(1-2), 39–58 (2011)
2. Amit, Y., Geman, D.: Shape quantization and recognition with randomized trees. Neural Computation 9(12), 1545–1588 (1997)
3. Blum, A., Mitchell, T.: Combining labeled and unlabeled data with co-training. In: Proc. of COLT, pp. 92–100 (1998)
4. Bosch, A., Zisserman, A., Munoz, X.: Image classification using random forests and ferns. In: Proc. of ICCV (2007)
5. Chen, F., Delannay, D., De Vleeschouwer, C.: An autonomous framework to produce and distribute personalized team-sport video summaries: a basket-ball case study. IEEE Trans. on Multimedia 13(6), 1381–1394 (2011)
6. Delannay, D., Danhier, N., De Vleeschouwer, C.: Detection and recognition of sports (wo)men from multiple views. In: Proc. of ACM/IEEE ICDSC (2009)
7. Dollar, P., Tu, Z., Perona, P., Belongie, S.: Integral channel features. In: Proc. of BMVC (2009)
8. Dollar, P., Wojek, C., Schiele, B., Perona, P.: Pedestrian detection: a benchmark. In: Proc. of IEEE CVPR (2009)
9. Felzenszwalb, P., Girshick, R.B., McAllester, D., Ramanan, D.: Object detection with discriminatively trained part-based models. IEEE Trans. on PAMI 32(9), 1627–1645 (2010)
10. Fleuret, F., Berclaz, J., Lengagne, R., Fua, P.: Multi-camera people tracking with a probabilistic occupancy map. IEEE Trans. on PAMI 30(2), 267–282 (2008)
11. Freund, Y., Schapire, R.E.: A decision-theoretic generalization of on-line learning and an application to boosting. Jour. of CSS 55(1), 119–139 (1997)
12. Geurts, P., Ernst, D., Wehenkel, L.: Extremely Randomized Trees. Machine Learning 36(1), 3–42 (2006)
13. Khan, S.M., Shah, M.: A multiview approach to tracking people in crowded scenes using a planar homography constraint. In: Leonardis, A., Bischof, H., Pinz, A. (eds.) ECCV 2006. LNCS, vol. 3954, pp. 133–146. Springer, Heidelberg (2006)
14. Levin, A., Viola, P., Freund, Y.: Unsupervised improvement of visual detectors using co-training. In: ICCV, pp. 626–633 (2003)
15. Marée, R., Geurts, P., Piater, J., Wehenkel, L.: Random subwindows for robust image classification. In: Proc. of IEEE CVPR, pp. 34–40 (2005)
16. Nair, V., Clark, J.J.: An unsupervised, online learning framework for moving object detection. In: Proc. of IEEE CVPR, vol. 2, pp. 317–324 (2004)

17. Ozuysal, M., Calonder, M., Lepetit, V., Fua, P.: Fast keypoint recognition using random ferns. IEEE Trans. on PAMI 32(3), 448–461 (2010)
18. Roth, P., Grabner, H., Skočaj, D., Bischof, H., Leonardis, A.: Conservative visual learning for object detection with minimal hand labeling effort. In: Kropatsch, W.G., Sablatnig, R., Hanbury, A. (eds.) DAGM 2005. LNCS, vol. 3663, pp. 293–300. Springer, Heidelberg (2005)
19. Viola, P., Jones, M.: Robust real-time object detection. In: Proc. of the Int. Workshop on SCTV (2001)
20. Xing, J., Ai, H., Liu, L., Lao, S.: Multiple player tracking in sports video: A dual-mode two-way bayesian inference approach with progressive observation modeling. IEEE Trans. on Image Processing 20(6), 1652–1667 (2011)

Spherical Center-Surround for Video Saliency Detection Using Sparse Sampling

Hamed Rezazadegan Tavakoli, Esa Rahtu, and Janne Heikkilä

Center for Machine Vision Research, University of Oulu, Finland
{hamed.rezazadegan,esa.rahtu,janne.heikkila}@ee.oulu.fi
http://www.cse.oulu.fi/CMV

Abstract. This paper presents a technique for detection of eminent (salient) regions in an image sequence. The method is inspired by the biological studies on human visual attention systems and is grounded on the famous center-surround theory. It hypothesis that an item (center) is dissimilar to its surrounding. A spherical representation is proposed to estimate amount of salience. It enables the method to integrate computation of temporal and spatial contrast features. Efficient computation of the proposed representation is made possible by sparse sampling the surround which result in an efficient spatiotemporal comparison. The method is evaluated against a recent benchmark methods and is shown to outperform all of them.

1 Introduction

The low cost localisation of eminent information (i.e. *region of interest*) in images can help to the efficiency of a wide range of image and computer vision related applications (e.g. object recognition, detection and segmentation, image/video indexing, creating thumbnails, video retargeting and frame rate conversion, compression and coding). Such a process becomes more crucial when considering the vast amount of information that an image sequence contains. At the first glance, proposing a general solution that can handle many scenarios seems difficult. But, it is doable by studying the attention mechanism of the human visual system. Such a study can help detection of the target of interest relying on almost no prior knowledge. For instance consider compressing an image sequence (e.g. video) that contains some objects, a human observer will likely focus on them – no matter what the objects are – and will expect compression preserves their quality.

Motivated by the necessity of a general solution to the region of interest localisation in videos (i.e. image sequence), this paper presents a spatiotemporal saliency detection method. Providing a video, the proposed method estimates a map of eminent regions (*saliency map*) for each frame on a scene-driven (i.e. bottom-up) basis by assessing the pop-out quality of each pixel between its surrounding neighbours in a spatiotemporal volume. Scene-driven methods rely on the preliminary features of the image and have no prior assumption about the task/content.

J. Blanc-Talon et al. (Eds.): ACIVS 2013, LNCS 8192, pp. 695–704, 2013.
© Springer International Publishing Switzerland 2013

1.1   Saliency in Video

In general, the term "salience" can be used to reference a wide range of concepts and can refer to address any target of interest (*e.g.* object of interest in object detection, different motion in motion anomaly detection, foreground in background subtraction and etc). To be more precise, salience of item is the state by which the item stands out and saliency detection is supposed to be an attentional mechanism that helps organisms to focus their perceptual and cognitive resources on the seminal sensory data. Thus, we specifically focus on methods and techniques that try to model human visual attention and apply it in computer vision. They are widely recognised as saliency detection techniques/models.

Saliency detection are widely studied for still images (e.g. [1,2,10,19]). The first mode of video reported by Borji *et al.* [1,2] is [7]. In essence, it is an extension of [8] which is developed for still images. The extension adds foveation mechanism, motion and flicker[1] features to support video. A famous model of attention formulates spatiotemporal saliency as surprise [9]. It exploits the difference between posterior and prior beliefs to define surprise in a Bayesian framework. The idea of surprise is somewhat similar to the traditional background subtraction algorithms(e.g. [5,13,23]) since it defines saliency in terms of change in knowledge. However, the main difference is that it is model free and relies on no predefined/learnt background model.

Bruce and Tsotsos [3] introduced an information theoretic framework by estimating the likelihood of content whiten a central patch and its surround. To this end, they extract response of independent component analysis (ICA) basis functions from each local neighbourhood. Afterwards, they apply a density estimation to compute response distributions and estimate likelihood of each central patch response to its surround. Shannon's measure of self-information is used to translate the likelihood into saliency map. Another information theoretic method uses Difference-of-Gaussian (DoG) filters [21] to compute self-information and log-likelihood. Seo and Milanfar [17] define saliency in terms of self-resemblance of local regression kernels (i.e. local descriptors). They consider a central cube and its surrounding volume while estimating salience probability using Parzen density estimator.

Contrary to the above methods, Mancas *et al.* [12] rely only on temporal features. They extract optical flow features and try to spot rare motions to determine saliency. To compute rarity, they quantise the motion vector into 20 Bins (considering 4 possible direction and 5 possible speed) and make a histogram out of all the motion vectors to determine the dominant motion and spot the vectors that are different. Their recent study [16] shows that such an approach outperforms the state-of-the-art.

Although motion is a significant feature considering videos, they are not the only features that affect the human visual system. This suggests proposal of salience descriptors that utilise different features more effectively. Instead, the proposed model relies on sparsely sampled pixels' contrast values in spatiotemporal domain

---

[1] A temporal change detector.

which implicitly learns motion salience as well as colour and contrast salience. It will be shown that the proposed technique outperforms the motion feature.

To sum-up, the contribution of this paper lies on 1) proposal of spherical representation of center-surround for video salience analysis, 2) application of non-parametric salience measuring using sparsely sampled features for video salience analysis and 3) simple and efficient spatiotemporal salience processing.

2 Method

2.1 Spatiotemporal Center-Surround

The proposed model is defined on the basis of center-surround dissimilarity hypothesis. It is founded on the theories of visual information processing in early stages of human vision and is shown to have decision-theoretic optimality [6]. In case of still images, an image patch is usually divided into a central region and its surrounding. This theory hypothesises that the central region contains the item of interest. Video saliency techniques either get advantage of the same representation on a frame by frame basis (*e.g.* [14]) or use it in a cubic style (*e.g.* [11]).

Defining each pixel as a triple of (x, y, t), this paper introduces a spherical representation of center-surround. The spherical representation is an extension to the circular representation [15] in spatial domain. It enables implicit consideration of motion features. Figure 1 depicts different center-surround strategies. As shown the proposed representation considers temporal surround which enables study of temporal differences. The rest of this paper explains how to estimate salience from such a spherical representation.

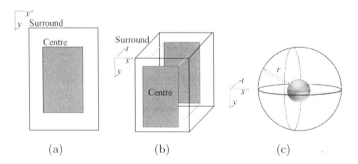

(a)   (b)   (c)

Fig. 1. Different center-surround representations, (a) still image, (b) cubic video representation, (c) proposed spherical representation.

2.2 Estimating Salience

Let's assume $V(\mathbf{x})$ is a video where $\mathbf{x} = (x, y, t)$ represents the space-time coordinates and $H_{\mathbf{x}}$ is a binary random variable defining saliency of $\mathbf{x}$. In spherical representation, the center-surround hypothesis states $\mathbf{x}$ is salient and $H_{\mathbf{x}} = 1 \iff \mathbf{x} \in \mathcal{C}$ where $\mathcal{C}$ is the central sphere and $H_{\mathbf{x}} = 0$ otherwise. In essence, salience estimation depends on the approximation of $p(H_\mathbf{x} = 1|V(\mathbf{x}), \mathbf{x})$, written as $p(1|V(\mathbf{x}), \mathbf{x})$ for short. Knowing that the salience is related to the feature and the position [18]; Bayes' theorem can be applied to write

$$p\,(1|V(\mathbf{x}), \mathbf{x}) = p(1|\mathbf{x})p(V(\mathbf{x})|1, \mathbf{x})/p(V(\mathbf{x})|\mathbf{x}). \tag{1}$$

The denominator can be further expanded to $p(V(\mathbf{x})|\mathbf{x}) = p(V(\mathbf{x})|1, \mathbf{x})p(1|\mathbf{x}) + p(V(\mathbf{x})|0, \mathbf{x})p(0|\mathbf{x})$. Estimation of (1) requires estimate of $p(V(\mathbf{x})|H_\mathbf{x}, \mathbf{x})$ (i.e. $p(V(\mathbf{x})|1, \mathbf{x})$ and $p(V(\mathbf{x})|0, \mathbf{x})$). To this end, applying non-parametric kernel density estimation to $p(V(\mathbf{x})|H_\mathbf{x}, \mathbf{x})$ suggests that

$$p(V(\mathbf{x})|H_\mathbf{x}, \mathbf{x}) = m^{-1} \sum_{i=1}^{m} \mathcal{G}(V(\mathbf{x}) - V(\mathbf{x}_i)), \tag{2}$$

where m is the total number of samples, $\mathbf{x}_i$ is the i_{th} sample and $\mathcal{G}(.) = (\sqrt{2\pi}\sigma_C)^{-1} \exp(||.||/2\sigma_C)$ is the Gaussian kernel.

Estimation of $p(V(\mathbf{x})|H_\mathbf{x}, \mathbf{x})$ is performed under two assumptions of 1) central sphere $\mathcal{C}$ contains one pixel, 2) the surround $\mathcal{S}$ consists of sufficient small number of pixels which are scattered at distance r from the central sphere. Figure 2 depicts such a scenario which is an approximate to the original spherical representation. Having a singleton kernel (i.e. a kernel consisting of one pixel), estimation of $p(V(\mathbf{x})|1, \mathbf{x})$ for $\mathbf{x}$ belonging to center boils down to the constant value of $(\sqrt{2\pi}\sigma_C)^{-1}$ where σ_C is the standard deviation of the Gaussian kernel[2]. Thus,

$$p_{n,r}\,(H_\mathbf{x} = 1|V(\mathbf{x}), \mathbf{x}) = \left(\frac{1}{\sqrt{2\pi}\sigma_C} + \frac{p(0|\mathbf{x})}{np(1|\mathbf{x})} \sum_{i=1}^{n} \mathcal{G}(V(\mathbf{x}) - V(\mathbf{x}_{i,r})) \right)^{-1}, \tag{3}$$

where n is the number of samples in the surround $\mathcal{S}$ that are at distance r from the center and x_i is the i_{th} sample belonging to surround. Eventually, the final saliency is defined as

$$S(\mathbf{x}) = \mathcal{N} \left(\left(\mathcal{G}_\sigma * \sum_{n,r} p_{n,r}\,(H_\mathbf{x} = 1|V(\mathbf{x}), \mathbf{x}) \right)^{\alpha} \right), \tag{4}$$

where $\mathcal{N}$ is a function that normalizes values to $[0,1]$, $\mathcal{G}_\sigma$ is a Gaussian smoothing kernel of standard deviation σ, $*$ is the symbolic convolution and α is an attenuation control parameter.

3   Experiments

To assess the presented model, we ran it using the following parameters, $n = 48$, $r = [13, 25, 38]$, $\sigma = 0.05$, $\sigma_C = 1$. To compute $P(1|\mathbf{x})$, average of fixation

---

[2] $\mathcal{G}(V(\mathbf{x}) - V(\mathbf{x})) = (\sqrt{2\pi}\sigma_C)^{-1} \exp(||V(\mathbf{x}) - V(\mathbf{x})||/2\sigma_C) = (\sqrt{2\pi}\sigma_C)^{-1}.$

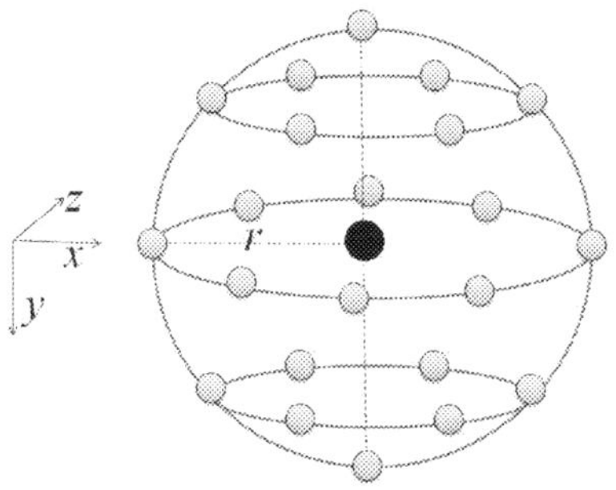

Fig. 2. Sparse sampling to simplify the spherical representation, the black circle denotes the central pixel of the singleton center and gray circles are the n samples from the surround uniformly scattered at distance r from the center

data of human observers over still images provided by [20] under assumption of temporal independence was used. Later, $p(0|\mathbf{x}) = 1 - p(1|\mathbf{x})$. Each video frame was normalised to 128×171 and converted to CIE-Lab colour space because of the similarity of its design to human vision system.

The dataset of evaluation is ASCMN provided by [16]. It is proposed to provide a standard benchmark for saliency evaluation. The main advantage of this dataset is that it contains anomalous motion which attracts attention. It consists of 24 videos each belonging to one of the 5 class categories of abnormal (containing abnormal motion), surveillance (surveillance video), crowd (people mass motion), moving (contains moving cameras) and noise (noise motion with sudden salient item appearance). The ground-truth contains eye movement of 13 observers.

The benchmark of ASCMN consists of comparison of a baseline method based on two consecutive frame absolute difference proposed by [16], method of Culibrk *et.al.* [4] which is based on background modelling, SUNDAy [21] which is an extension of [22] to dynamic analysis of scenes, Seo [17] and Mancas [12]. This paper uses the same saliency models as a comparison reference to assess the proposed method.

The ASCMN evaluation scheme requires preprocessing of the saliency maps using morphological operators to avoid effect of lag or advancement of human gaze as well as providing a fair relative comparison of methods. The parameters are selected for each method to maximise evaluation metrics. The aptness metrics include the area under the receiver operating characteristic curve (AUC). The AUC is computed by comparing the human fixation density maps to the estimated saliency map. The procedure involves initially measuring Receiver Operating Characteristic (ROC) curve estimating true positive and false positive rates of saliency map compared to the fixation density map over a moving threshold value and computing the area under the curve of the obtained ROC.

3.1   Results

Figure 4 provides the proposed model's saliency map and the corresponding video frame for qualitative observation. The saliency map is superimposed on the original frame providing a heat map to represent more salient places in red.

The proposed method is initially analysed in each image category. Figure 3 depicts the results on individual categories. There are 5 categories in total, the first is abnormal which consists of 5 videos containing some moving items having different speed or direction compared to the main stream. Close observation shows that the proposed method is the top method with AUC of 75% followed by pure motion based method of Mancas which scores 74%. Nature of videos in this category and the fact of Mancas's rely on motion features suggests that the proposed method captures the motion features effectively. The second category is surveillance videos which consist of 4 streams of classical surveillance application that are noise free and have static background. The proposed model is still the best.

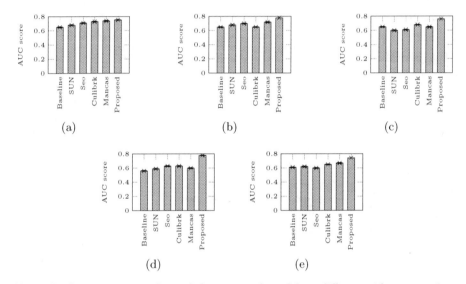

Fig. 3. Performance comparison of the proposed model on different video categories, a) abnormal, b) surveillance, c) crowd, d) moving and e) noise. The proposed model has the best value as depicted.

Study of the 5 Crowd videos –they contain dense or sparse mass of people– reveals us that the proposed model is still the best having AUC of 76%. The next category contains 4 sequences with moving camera (moving). In these sequences Seo with AUC of 63% ranks second after the proposed model which scores 77%. The nature of videos suggest that a good method shall be able to handle spatial information well which holds for the method of Seo. Consequently, the same claim holds for the proposed model. The last category of videos (*i.e.* noise) contains videos of items with sudden salient motion and Mancas method with score of 67% follows the proposed model which scores 74%.

Fig. 4. Visualised saliency maps of the proposed model for qualitative observation. Each frame and its corresponding saliency map are depicted. The saliency map is projected on the saliency map to make a heat map.

The above study reveals us that the proposed method outperforms all the methods with a large margin in all the categories. Table 1 summarizes the overall performance of different saliency detection models. As depicted the proposed method has the best performance compared to the rest of the techniques and is 11% ahead of the best of reported methods on the ASCMN.

Table 1. Performance comparison of different methods in terms of Area Under the Curve (AUC) reported at 95% confidence interval. The table contains the average AUC over all the video sequences.

	Baseline	SUN	Seo	Culibrk	Mancas	Proposed
AUC	$62.6 \pm 6.1e^{-3}$	$63 \pm 9.2e^{-3}$	$65 \pm 6.7e^{-3}$	$66.8 \pm 6e^{-3}$	$67.9 \pm 6.3e^{-3}$	$75.8 \pm 9e^{-4}$

Although the proposed model is comparably simple, it has outstanding performance. In the sparse representation which is the underlying model of computation for the proposed framework, one pixel is compared to several pixels which are scattered around it at distance r. Each video frame that intersects with the hypothetical sphere contributes to the surround of central pixel. Thus, the current video frame provides spatial comparison and the pixels of other frames that belong to the surround are grounds for temporal comparison. The proposed model does a spatiotemporal dissimilarity comparison which was shown a powerfull means of salience computation by the experiments.

4   Conclusion

In this paper, a method of saliency detection for videos was presented. The introduced model is based on the biologically plausible center-surround hypothesis. It proposed use of a spherical representation of center-surround for videos. To compute the salience the method assumes a singleton center (*i.e.* center contains one pixel) and a sufficiently small number of surrounding pixels that are uniformly scattered around the central pixel. This facilitates spatiotemporal comparison of pixels dissimilarity.

The method was prototyped and ran on a benchmark database. The results showed that the proposed model efficiently incorporates motion and colour contrast features to estimate saliency. Comparison with several methods reveals us that the proposed method powerfully estimates salience and exceeds the performance of the state-of-the-art.

References

1. Borji, A., Itti, L.: State-of-the-art in visual attention modeling. IEEE Trans. Pattern Anal. Mach. Intell. 35(1), 185–207 (2012)
2. Borji, A., Sihite, D.N., Itti, L.: Quantitative analysis of human-model agreement in visual saliency modeling: A comparative study. IEEE Trans. Image Process. 22(1), 55–69 (2013)

3. Bruce, N.D.B., Tsotsos, J.K.: Saliency, attention, and visual search: An information theoretic approach. J. Vis. 9(3) (2009)
4. Ćulibrk, D., Mirković, M., Zlokolica, V., Pokric, M., Crnojević, V., Kukolj, D.: Salient motion features for video quality assessment. IEEE Trans. Image Process. 20(4), 948–958 (2011)
5. Elgammal, A., Harwood, D., Davis, L.: Non-parametric model for background subtraction. In: Vernon, D. (ed.) ECCV 2000. LNCS, vol. 1843, pp. 751–767. Springer, Heidelberg (2000)
6. Gao, D., Mahadevan, V., Vasconcelos, N.: On the plausibility of the discriminant center-surround hypothesis for visual saliency. J. Vis. 8(7) (2008)
7. Itti, L., Dhavale, N.: Realistic avatar eye and head animation using a neurobiological model of visual attention. In: Proc. SPIE, pp. 64–78. SPIE Press (2003)
8. Itti, L., Koch, C., Niebur, E.: A model of saliency-based visual attention for rapid scene analysis. IEEE Trans. Pattern Anal. Mach. Intell. 20(11), 1254–1259 (1998)
9. Itti, L., Baldi, P.: Bayesian surprise attracts human attention. Vision Res. 49(10), 1295–1306 (2009)
10. Judd, T., Durand, F., Torralba, A.: A benchmark of computational models of saliency to predict human fixations. Tech. Rep. MIT-CSAIL-TR-2012-001, Massachusetts institute of technology (2012)
11. Mahadevan, V., Vasconcelos, N.: Spatiotemporal saliency in dynamic scenes. IEEE Trans. Pattern Anal. Mach. Intell. 32(1), 171–177 (2010)
12. Mancas, M., Riche, N., Leroy, J., Gosselin, B.: Abnormal motion selection in crowds using bottom-up saliency. In: 18th IEEE International Conference on Image Processing, pp. 229–232 (2011)
13. Monnet, A., Mittal, A., Paragios, N., Ramesh, V.: Background modeling and subtraction of dynamic scenes. In: Proc. 9th IEEE International Conference on Computer Vision, vol. 2, pp. 1305–1312 (October 2003)
14. Rahtu, E., Kannala, J., Salo, M., Heikkilä, J.: Segmenting salient objects from images and videos. In: Daniilidis, K., Maragos, P., Paragios, N. (eds.) ECCV 2010, Part V. LNCS, vol. 6315, pp. 366–379. Springer, Heidelberg (2010)
15. Rezazadegan Tavakoli, H., Rahtu, E., Heikkilä, J.: Fast and efficient saliency detection using sparse sampling and kernel density estimation. In: Heyden, A., Kahl, F. (eds.) SCIA 2011. LNCS, vol. 6688, pp. 666–675. Springer, Heidelberg (2011)
16. Riche, N., Mancas, M., Culibrk, D., Crnojevic, V., Gosselin, B., Dutoit, T.: Dynamic saliency models and human attention: A comparative study on videos. In: Lee, K.M., Matsushita, Y., Rehg, J.M., Hu, Z. (eds.) ACCV 2012, Part III. LNCS, vol. 7726, pp. 586–598. Springer, Heidelberg (2013)
17. Seo, H.J., Milanfar, P.: Static and space-time visual saliency detection by self-resemblance. J. Vis. 9(12), 1–27 (2009)
18. Tatler, B.: The central fixation bias in scene viewing: selecting an optimal viewing position independently of motor bases and image feature distributions. J. Vis. 14(7), 4, 1-17 (2007)
19. Toet, A.: Computational versus psychophysical bottom-up image saliency: A comparative evaluation study. IEEE Trans. Pattern Anal. Mach. Intell. 33(11), 2131–2146 (2011)
20. Tsotsos, J.K., Bruce, N.D.B.: Saliency based on information maximization. In: Weiss, Y., Schölkopf, B., Platt, J. (eds.) Advances in Neural Information Processing Systems 18, pp. 155–162. MIT Press (2006)

21. Zhang, L., Tong, M.H., Cottrell, G.W.: Sunday: Saliency using natural statistics for dynamic analysis of scenes. In: Thirty-First Annual Cognitive Science Society Conference (2009)
22. Zhang, L., Tong, M.H., Marks, T.K., Shan, H., Cottrell, G.W.: Sun: A bayesian framework for saliency using natural statistics. J. Vis. 8(7) (2008)
23. Zivkovic, Z., van der Heijden, F.: Efficient adaptive density estimation per image pixel for the task of background subtraction. Pattern Recogn. Lett. 27(7), 773–780 (2006)

Semantic Concept Detection Using Dense Codeword Motion

Claudiu Tănase and Bernard Mérialdo

EURECOM
Campus SophiaTech
450 Route des Chappes
06410 Biot France

Abstract. When detecting semantic concepts in video, much of the existing research in content-based classification uses keyframe information only. Particularly the combination between local features such as SIFT and the Bag of Words model is very popular with TRECVID participants. The few existing motion and spatiotemporal descriptors are computationally heavy and become impractical when applied on large datasets such as TRECVID. In this paper, we propose a way to efficiently combine positional motion obtained from optic flow in the keyframe with information given by the Dense SIFT Bag of Words feature. The features we propose work by spatially binning motion vectors belonging to the same codeword into separate histograms describing movement direction (left, right, vertical, zero, etc.). Classifiers are mapped using the homogeneous kernel map techinque for approximating the $\chi 2$ kernel and then trained efficiently using linear SVM. By using a simple linear fusion technique we can improve the Mean Average Precision of the Bag of Words DSIFT classifier on the TRECVID 2010 Semantic Indexing benchmark from 0.0924 to 0.0972, which is confirmed to be a statistically significant increase based on standardized TRECVID randomization tests.

Keywords: content based video retrieval, semantic indexing, TRECVID, spatio-temporal features, motion feature.

1 Introduction

With the ever increasing accessibility of devices capable of recording video and the popularity of video hosting websites, large collections of user submitted videos are becoming the focus of important research in content-based multimedia retrieval and classification. The core problem of automatically categorizing a new video based on its content has proven to be considerably harder than the image counterpart. The goal of our research is to simply be able to tell whether a predefined semantic concept such as "car" or "running" is present or not in a video.

Most of the state on the art in video concept detection works almost exclusively with image features by extracting a relevant keyframe from the video. A very successful combination, found in almost every submission to the Semantic

J. Blanc-Talon et al. (Eds.): ACIVS 2013, LNCS 8192, pp. 705–713, 2013.

Indexing challenge of TRECVID[10], is the SIFT descriptor and Bag of Words model.[9] We believe that the perceived motion of each of the SIFT patterns is useful in recognition. In this work we are upgrading the BoW representation of the Dense SIFT descriptor with motion information extracted locally from the corresponding keypoint positions in the frame. Our feature is based on the idea that because SIFT patches successfully describe object patterns, the objects' motion in the scene is in some measure captured by the motion of the SIFT codewords[14]. The strength of our method is in the fact that it can reuse the information stored in the DSIFT Bag of Words feature vectors, thus greatly reducing feature extraction time. Classification takes in average around one second for a feature matrix of 119685 vectors of dimensionality 2500.

In this paper we propose a new set of content description features, derived from DSIFT, that take into account the motion of the SIFT patches. Using a simple binning technique, we create 3 features named ZN, ZHV and ZLRUD that capture not only the codeword information stored in DSIFT histograms but also the quantity and direction of movement of the SIFT patch. The addition of our features to an existing concept detection system based on DSIFT features comes with the relatively low cost of extracting sparse optic flow from one keyframe per video shot. By using the well-known homogeneous kernel map[13] method we can efficiently approximate the non-linear $\chi 2$ kernel and train linear SVMs in a fraction of the non-linear SVM computation time. By using a linear score combination, we combine DSIFT with our Z features and obtain an increase in Mean Average Precision (MAP) of about 5%. By applying an official TRECVID tool that compares submission runs based on randomization testing, we are able to confirm that the aforementioned improvement is statistically significant.

2   Related Work

One particular web video collection has been the subject of considerable research in recent years. In the TRECVID[10] Semantic Indexing task, a benchmark of annotated videos is used for detecting a large set of predefined concepts. The traditional concept detection in video, as shown by works published in TRECVID workshops, uses keyframe techniques. One keyframe is selected from the shot in question and all subsequent processing deals with the keyframe as sole representative of the shot, much like a CBIR system. Compared to the few existing spatio-temporal content descriptors[8,1], this approach is hugely more efficient in time and memory. The disadvantage is that obviously all the motion and sequence information is lost.

Of these keyframe methods, the Bag of Words (BoW) technique has been prevailing in TRECVID for many years. Although newer methods like Fisher vectors [6] and super-vectors [17] supersede BoW, it remains widely used in the community. In the BoW model a set of local visual features is extracted from the image. As a result of K-means clustering of a pool of features, a codebook a.k.a. visual dictionary is created. Each centroid obtained in the clustering represents a codeword or visual word. According to the precomputed codebook each extracted feature is assigned to its nearest element in the codebook. The final feature is a histogram of occurrences of each codeword. In the vast majority of situations, this technique uses SIFT[9] as the visual feature, whether using the original interest point detection or by dense sampling[12]. Recent work seems to suggest that in this context the dense extraction seems to slightly outperform interest point methods[4,7,16].

There are several local features called spatio-temporal descriptors that describe image sequences, most notably used in the action recognition community. One notable example is Laptev's Spatio-Temporal Interest Point descriptor[8] (STIP), which detects 3D interest points using a 3D extension of the Harris operator and describes them using histograms of oriented gradients and histograms of flow (HOGHOF). Wang's dense trajectories descriptor[15] extracts and tracks features throughout the entire video volume. Chen's MoSIFT[1] is an extension of SIFT that adds in a similar feature where the gradient is replaced by optic flow. Since all these methods analyze a 3D volume instead of a 2D image, the computational complexity is much higher than the standard keyframe approaches, to the point that implementing a spatio-temporal technique on TRECVID might prove too computationally heavy for some systems. By comparison, our feature computes the optic flow on a single keyframe in the video. The extraction of DSIFT, codebook assignment and motion feature construction take in average 8.27 seconds for any TRECVID video, while any of the 3 descriptors mentioned earlier take in average well beyond 30 seconds to compute, depending on video length.

Our approach shares some similarity with part of the work of Wang et. al.[14] in that codeword motion is considered. Two important aspects differ. Firstly, the input features come from dense sampling in our work and from keypoint detections in [14]. Features computed at keypoints will extract information from salient zones in the image and will ignore uniform or weakly-textured zones. They concentrate on details so that they are better suitable at object recognition rather than detection. Dense sampling ensures that every pixel in an image is covered by at least one patch, which makes it less likely to miss an object. This leads to the background forming an important element. Also, in dense sampling more features are selected and variability is higher. In short, keypoints are better for precision, dense is better for recall. The second difference is in the way motionless patches are processed. In [14] an orientation histogram is built using projections that cumulate in each bin. Patches with small amounts of motion contribute little to the resulting orientation histogram. Our features contain a Z (zero) bin, which stores the number of patches with little or no motion, which means that the information on static codewords is not lost.

3   Extracting Codeword Motion

Dense SIFT works by extracting features from evenly spaced keypoints. In our version we use a grid of size 8 pixels. The densely extracted SIFT features are quantized and assigned to one of the $k = 500$ codewords. The value of k has been

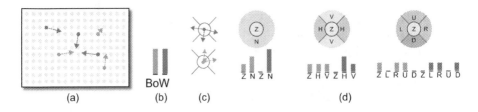

Fig. 1. Overview of feature construction: (a) DSIFT patches assigned to codewords (green and red) are extracted along with their oprtic flow. (b) Bag of Words histogram is built by counting the occurrences of each codeword. (c) Motion vectors are grouped by codeword. (d) Histograms are being constructed for every bin and every codeword by counting the number of flow vectors in each bin.

empirically chosen as a good compromise between performance and computation speed. In the normal DSIFT, keypoint locations are ignored and only the total count of codeword occurrences are taken into consideration. However we keep for each keypoint position x, y the index of the codeword c.

In order to extract motion, we first access the keyframe in the video file. We then advance by a small time interval and extract a second frame corresponding to slightly later time in order to have sufficient difference. The motion between these frames is subjected to a mostly uniform background camera movement that can be compensated for. We use a camera stabilization function similar to the one in [5]. This method does dominant motion compensation by estimating a homography with RANSAC over detected feature correspondences. This homography is then used to produce a synthetic motion vector field modeling the camera movement which is used as an initial estimate for the full-frame optic flow using Farneback's method[3]. The displacement between the synthetic background motion field and the actual motion field can then be used as an estimation of foreground objects, since motion in background areas is compensated for. Having computed the motion compensated flow, we can now sample it at the keypoint positions x, y. Thus, for every keypoint i we now have its coordinates x_i, y_i, a codeword value c_i and the optic flow f_i^x, f_i^y.

4   Spatial Codeword Motion Histograms

We now group our features by codeword. For each codeword c, we quantize the flow coordinates f_i^x, f_i^y according to the spatial histograms in figure 1. The bin corresponding to the region where the (f_i^x, f_i^y) point falls is incremented. The zero (Z) bin will capture features with zero or small motion. The value of the Z bin radius θ has been chosen as the median of all the optic flow velocities in the collection in order to ensure the balance between the number of features falling inside and outside of Z (which is the non-zero bin N). Since there is an intuitive conceptual distinction between horizontal and vertical movement, we separate our space in 2 corresponding bins. Horizontal and vertical bins H and

V take advantage of origin symmetry, are spatially discontinuous and quantize feature orientation. Left, right, up and down bins L, R, U and D separate motion direction (bearing). The 3 features we are studying in this paper are:

1. ZN which describes *whether the codeword moves or not*
2. ZHV which discriminates between codewords moving horizontally and vertically, thus contains information on *orientation*, and
3. ZLRUD which discriminates codewords moving left, right, up and down, therefore encodes the *direction*

Since there are several spatial bins for each codeword, the final feature size will have size $2 \times K$ for the ZN variant, $3 \times K$ for ZHV and $5 \times K$ for ZLRUD. Since Z features are decompositions of the DSIFT features, the relation between these bins is given by the following formula:

$$DSIFT = Z + N = Z + H + V = Z + L + R + U + D \qquad (1)$$

The baseline DSIFT BoW approach works by directly counting codeword occurrences, which makes it equivalent to a single bin covering all the space. All resulting histograms are normalized using the L1 norm.

5   Classification and Fusion

The experimental setup closely follows the TRECVID 2010 Semantic Indexing evaluation. We are evaluating 50 concepts, with sparse training annotations available on a development set containing 119,685 sequences, and applied on a test set of 146,788 sequences. We also use the MAP (Mean Average Precision) as performance measure. In order to benefit from the superior classification power of non-linear kernels, we employ kernel approximation techniques described in[13]. In practice, the $\chi 2$ kernel seems to perform very well when using Bag of Words features. We map our features using the homogeneous kernel map of order $N = 3$, implemented in the Scikit-learn library[11] which yields a new feature dimensionality of $7\times$ the original one. The new feature vectors can be used to train a linear SVM, which will approximate the non-linear $\chi 2$ SVM classifier. For that we use the Liblinear[2] implementation found in Scikit-learn by training on half of the development set (59,842 sequences) and cross-validating on the other half in order to optimize the C parameter of the SVM. After finding the optimal value of C, we train another linear SVM with this value of C on the entire development set and test on the testing set. The classifier confidence values found in the validation set are kept for later use in the linear fusion. We apply this procedure for DSIFT, ZN, ZHV and ZLRUD features. As it is routinely done in TRECVID, this process is done using training annotations from one of the 50 concepts at a time. Using the SVM confidence values and the ground truth on the testing set we compute the Average Precision for each concept. The run is finally evaluated by averaging these average precisions (MAP).

Classification scores from the different features are then combined using late fusion. This is done by finding the linear combination of score weights that maximize the MAP on the validation set and reapply these weights on the testing set confidence values. Since the computation of weighted sums and of the MAP are almost instantaneous, a grid search on the weight values is possible. We experiment with the fusion of the baseline DSIFT, ZN, ZHV and ZLRUD, as described in the next section. Each weight is tested in 0.1 increments.

We use the TRECVID randomization testing[10] to estimate the statistical significance of the increase in MAP. Each test implements a partial randomization test of the hypothesis that two search runs, whose effectiveness is measured by MAP, are significantly different - against the null hypothesis that the differences are due to chance. We use this approach to pairwise compare DSIFT, ZN, ZHV, ZLRUD and the fusion result.

6   Experimental Results

Table 1 shows the MAP for the classifier DSIFT, ZN, ZHV and ZLRUD. Although more information is contained within the Z features than in DSIFT, their overall MAP is lower. The reason is that the 4 features have different dimensionalities (DSIFT=500, ZN=1000, ZHV=1500, ZLRUD=2500) and are trained with the same classification technique. A more robust comparison would have been for instance DSIFT with a codebook of size $k = 2500$ compared to the present ZLRUD feature, but such a comparison would require calculating DSIFT features and Bag of Words for both k=500 and k=2500, which would defeat the purpose of this work.

Table 1. Mean average precision of the 4 features and fusion

	DSIFT	ZN	ZHV	ZLRUD	fusion
dim	500	1,000	1,500	2,500	n/a
MAP	0.0924	0.0853	0.0809	0.0723	0.0972

Figure 2 shows the weight of each feature in fusion and can be interpreted as an indication of what type of movement is the most informative for classifying the concept, e.g. if the DSIFT component has a high weight, then the concept is more easily classified based only on static visual information. High ZN weight means that the presence or absence of movement is a good cue for detecting the concept. ZHV has high weight if the direction of movement is important and ZLRUD is high when both direction and orientation of movement are relevant.

The TRECVID randomized test for statistical significance have confirmed that for a significance level of 0.05 the fusion run statistically outperforms all of the features. The conclusion of said test is that the improvement of the MAP from 0.0924 to 0.0972 is in fact a statistically significant improvement and not due to chance.

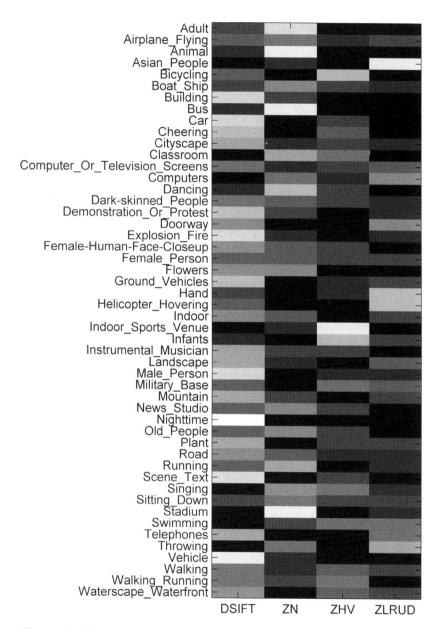

Fig. 2. Weight contributions of each feature in the optimal best performing concept classifier. Values are grayscale, white is one, black is zero.

7   Conclusions

In this paper we have presented a new feature that builds on the DSIFT Bag of Words classifier by incorporating local motion information. The proposed features are constructed using optic flow information at the DSIFT patch positions and the corresponding codewords. Using minimal computation, 3 spatial histogram features ZN, ZHV and ZLRUD are constructed from existing DSIFT feature codeword data and optic flow information and are mapped using the homogeneous kernel maps and classified using linear SVM. The strength of the method is that it relies on the widely available DSIFT bag of words feature data, and requires minimal feature extraction, namely optic flow at a keyframe level, and that linear classification is extremely fast, thanks to the homogeneous kernel map. Linear descriptor fusion show that the new features can improve the performance of the retrieval system by a statistically significant 5% without requiring any of the more computationally complex spatio-temporal techniques.

References

1. Chen, M., Hauptmann, A.: Mosift: Recognizing human actions in surveillance videos (2009)
2. Fan, R.E., Chang, K.W., Hsieh, C.J., Wang, X.R., Lin, C.J.: Liblinear: A library for large linear classification. The Journal of Machine Learning Research 9, 1871–1874 (2008)
3. Farnebäck, G.: Two-frame motion estimation based on polynomial expansion. In: Bigun, J., Gustavsson, T. (eds.) SCIA 2003. LNCS, vol. 2749, pp. 363–370. Springer, Heidelberg (2003)
4. Gorisse, D., Precioso, F.: IRIM at TRECVID 2010: Semantic Indexing and Instance Search. In: TREC Online Proceedings, Gaithersburg, United States. gDR ISIS (November 2010)
5. Ikizler-Cinbis, N., Sclaroff, S.: Object, scene and actions: Combining multiple features for human action recognition. In: Daniilidis, K., Maragos, P., Paragios, N. (eds.) ECCV 2010, Part I. LNCS, vol. 6311, pp. 494–507. Springer, Heidelberg (2010)
6. Jégou, H., Perronnin, F., Douze, M., Sánchez, J., Pérez, P., Schmid, C.: Aggregating local image descriptors into compact codes. IEEE Transactions on Pattern Analysis and Machine Intelligence (2011), http://hal.inria.fr/inria-00633013
7. Jurie, F., Triggs, B.: Creating efficient codebooks for visual recognition. In: Tenth IEEE International Conference on Computer Vision, ICCV 2005, vol. 1, pp. 604–610. IEEE (2005)
8. Laptev, I., Lindeberg, T.: Space-time interest points. In: Proceedings of the Ninth IEEE International Conference on Computer Vision 2003, vol. 1, pp. 432–439 (October 2003)
9. Lowe, D.: Object recognition from local scale-invariant features. In: The Proceedings of the Seventh IEEE International Conference on Computer Vision 1999, vol. 2, pp. 1150–1157. IEEE (1999)
10. Over, P., Awad, G., Fiscus, J., Antonishek, B., Michel, M., Smeaton, A., Kraaij, W., Quénot, G., et al.: An overview of the goals, tasks, data, evaluation mechanisms and metrics. In: TRECVID 2011-TREC Video Retrieval Evaluation Online (2011)

11. Pedregosa, F., Varoquaux, G., Gramfort, A., Michel, V., Thirion, B., Grisel, O., Blondel, M., Prettenhofer, P., Weiss, R., Dubourg, V., et al.: Scikit-learn: Machine learning in python. The Journal of Machine Learning Research 12, 2825–2830 (2011)
12. Vedaldi, A., Fulkerson, B.: VLFeat: An open and portable library of computer vision algorithms (2008)
13. Vedaldi, A., Zisserman, A.: Efficient additive kernels via explicit feature maps. In: 2010 IEEE Conference on Computer Vision and Pattern Recognition (CVPR), pp. 3539–3546. IEEE ((2010)
14. Wang, F., Jiang, Y.G., Ngo, C.W.: Video event detection using motion relativity and visual relatedness. In: Proceedings of the 16th ACM International Conference on Multimedia, pp. 239–248. ACM (2008)
15. Wang, H., Klaser, A., Schmid, C., Liu, C.: Action recognition by dense trajectories. In: 2011 IEEE Conference on Computer Vision and Pattern Recognition (CVPR), pp. 3169–3176. IEEE (2011)
16. Wang, H., Ullah, M., Klaser, A., Laptev, I., Schmid, C., et al.: Evaluation of local spatio-temporal features for action recognition. In: BMVC 2009-British Machine Vision Conference (2009)
17. Zhou, X., Yu, K., Zhang, T., Huang, T.S.: Image classification using super-vector coding of local image descriptors. In: Daniilidis, K., Maragos, P., Paragios, N. (eds.) ECCV 2010, Part V. LNCS, vol. 6315, pp. 141–154. Springer, Heidelberg (2010)

Author Index

Abdelfattah, Riadh   49
Al-Hamadi, Ayoub   150, 162, 192, 342
Alimi, Adel M.   310
Anavatti, Sreenatha G.   60
Assoum, Ammar   182
Astola, Jaakko   402
Audigier, Romaric   564

Bahr, Claudia   555
Balazs, Peter   80
Banerjee, Biplab   274
Barina, David   91
Battisti, Federica   402
Behrens, Stephanie   192
Ben Abdallah, Wajih   49
Bendicks, Christian   342
Benhamza, Y.   620
Berckmans, Daniel   555
Bo Bo, Nyan   584
Bourennane, Salah   460
Boussahla, Miloud   546
Bruni, Vittoria   596
Bruno, Alessandro   250

Calnegru, Florina-Cristina   102
Cappabianco, Fábio   203
Carli, Marco   402
Casola, Valentina   414
Castejon, Emiliano Ferreira   504
Chehdi, Kacem   402
Chigorin, Alexander   576
Chmelar, Petr   378
Choi, Chang-Won   608
Choi, Sung-In   608
Cichowski, Janusz   13
Condorovici, Razvan George   262
Corlay, Patrick   1
Cortes, Andoni   645
Coudoux, François-Xavier   1
Cretu, Ana-Maria   389
Curtis, Phillip   389
Czyżewski, Andrzej   13

Daubney, Ben   138
Deknudt, Christophe   1

de la Cruz, Jesús M.   37
De Neyer, Quentin   366
Deng, Jingjing   138
Derraz, Foued   546
De Vleeschouwer, Christophe   366, 657, 682
Devy, Michel   126, 354
de With, Peter H.N.   492
Do, Luat   492
Dornaika, Fadi   182

Egiazarian, Karen   402
El Traboulsi, Youssof   182
Esposito, Mariana   414

Falcão, Alexandre   203
Fang, Hui   138
Flammini, Francesco   414
Florea, Corneliu   262
Florez, Julian   645
Fonseca, Leila Maria Garcia   504
Freye, Christian   342
Froml, Vojtech   378
Fularz, Michał   321
Fusek, Radovan   538

Galčík, František   330
Garcia, Christophe   620
Gargalík, Radoslav   330
Gaura, Jan   480
Gazalet, Marc   1
Ghanem, Khadoudja   172
Gharbi, Mohamed   1
Gomez, Emmanuel   516
Grant, Phil W.   138
Greco, Luca   250
Gressin, Adrien   450
Gruenwedel, Sebastian   584
Guan, Junzhi   584
Guerrero, José M.   37
Guijarro, María   37

Halder, Kalyan Kumar   60
Handrich, Sebastian   150
Hanêne, Ben-Abdallah   114

Hannuksela, Jari   215
Hayes, Monson H.   25
Hazar, Mliki   114
Heikkilä, Janne   695
Herbulot, Ariane   632

Idrissi, Khalid   620
Ieremeiev, Oleg   402

Jackway, Paul   438
Jiao, Licheng   298
Jin, Lina   402
Jolivet, Isabelle   516

Kashiha, Mohammad Amin   555
Kasiński, Andrzej   321
Konev, Artem   576
Konushin, Anton   576
Körting, Thales Sehn   504
Kostek, Bożena   13
Kraft, Marek   321
Krylov, Vladimir A.   227
Krzeszowski, Tomasz   426
Kuo, C.-C. Jay   402
Kwolek, Bogdan   426

La Cascia, Marco   250
Laurent, Hélène   516
Lee, Seungwon   25
Lefebvre, Olivier   126
Lerasle, Frédéric   126, 632
Lerasle, Frederic   564
Levada, Alexandre   203
Li, Songnan   470
Lilienblum, Erik   342
Lin, Tao   460
Liu, Ming   298
Luckner, Marcin   526
Luengo, Lydie   516
Lukin, Vladimir   402

Malik, Aamir Saeed   68
Mallet, Clément   450
Marchant, Ross   438
Marot, Julien   460
Mas, Stéphane   126
Masse, Jean-Thomas   126
Mazzocca, Nicola   414
Mekonnen, Alhayat Ali   632
Mérialdo, Bernard   705

Meriaudeau, Fabrice   68
Mertens, Luc   286
Mishra, Pradeep Kumar   274
Mohamed, Hammami   114
Mohan, Buddhiraju Krishna   274
Moiseev, Boris   576
Monin, André   126
Montalvo, Martín   37
Moons, Christel P.H.   555
Mozdřeň, Karel   538

Nakamura, Rodrigo   203
Nelson, James D.B.   227
Nemeth, Jozsef   80
Ngan, King Ngi   470
Niese, Robert   192
Nieto, Marcos   645
Niewold, Theo A.   555
Niño-Castañeda, Jorge   584
Nowicki, Michał   321

Ortega, Juan Diego   645
Osaku, Daniel   203
Ott, Sanne   555

Paik, Joonki   25
Paillet, Pierrick   564
Pajares, Gonzalo   37
Papa, João   203
Paparoditis, Nicolas   450
Parisot, Pascaline   682
Park, Soon-Yong   608
Payeur, Pierre   389
Penne, Rudi   286
Pesek, Martin   378
Peyrodie, Laurent   546
Pham, Quoc-Cuong   564
Philips, Wilfried   584
Ponomarenko, Nikolay   402
Pragliola, Concetta   414

Rahtu, Esa   695
Rashid Ahmad, Omer   162
Redweik, Eicke   192
Rezazadegan Tavakoli, Hamed   695
Ribbens, Bart   286
Romeo, Juan   37
Rymut, Boguslaw   426

Saad, Naufal   68
Salih, Yasir   68
Sallem, Nizar K.   354

Sanberg, Willem P.   492
Schmidt, Adam   321
Sedmidubsky, Jan   669
Sevilmiş, Berk   682
Shi, Ran   470
Sidibé, Désiré   68
Śluzek, Andrzej   238
Sojka, Eduard   480, 538
Sroka, Adrian   526
Šurkala, Milan   538

Tahtali, Murat   60
Tănase, Claudiu   705
Treuillet, Sylvie   516
Tuyttens, Frank   555

Valcik, Jakub   669
Van Cauwelaert, Dimitri   584
Van Haerenborgh, Dirk   584
Van Hese, Peter   584
Varjo, Sami   215

Varma, Surender   274
Veelaert, Peter   584
Verleysen, Cédric   657
Vertan, Constantin   262
Vincent, Nicole   450
Vitulano, Domenico   596
Volf, Tomas   378
Vozel, Benoit   402

Walha, Ahlem   310
Wali, Ali   310
Walter, Nicolas   68
Wu, Yan   298

Xie, Xianghua   138

Zemcik, Pavel   91
Zendulka, Jaroslav   378
Zezula, Pavel   669
Zhang, Qiang   298
Zhang, Yuyao   620